Roman Realities

Finley Hooper

Wayne State University

ROMAN

REALITIES

Wayne State University Press   Detroit, 1979

Library of Congress Cataloging in Publication Data

Hooper, Finley Allison, 1922–
   Roman realities.

   Bibliography: p.
   Includes index.
   1. Rome—History. I. Title.
DG209.H69   945'.632   78-15237
ISBN 0-8143-1593-3
ISBN 0-8143-1594-1 pbk.

Waynebook 43

Grateful acknowledgment is made to Diether Haenicke, Provost and Vice President, Wayne State University, for his assistance in publishing this book.

Permissions

Acknowledgment is made for permission to quote from sources protected by copyright:

To Harvard University Press for quotations from volumes in the Loeb Classical Library: *The Surviving Books of the History of Ammianus Marcellinus,* 3 vols., translated by John C. Rolfe, 1963–64; Livy, *From the Founding of the City,* 14 vols., translated by various hands, 1919; Pliny, *Letters and Panegyricus,* 2 vols., translated by Betty Radice, 1969; and Sallust, *The War with Catiline* and *The War with Jugurtha,* translated by John C. Rolfe, 1931.

To Hart-Davis, MacGibbon/Granada Publishing Ltd., for quotations from *The Poetry of Catullus,* translated by C. H. Sisson, 1966.

To Penguin Books Ltd., for a quotation from Juvenal, Satire VII, *The Sixteen Satires,* translated by Peter Green (Penguin Classics), copyright © by Peter Green, 1967, 1974.

To E.P. Dutton & Co., Inc., and J. M. Dent & Sons Ltd. for quotations from *Caesar's War Commentaries,* translated by John Warrington, Everyman's Library, 1958; from Cicero, *The Offices, Essays, and Letters,* translated by Thomas Cockman and W. Melmoth, Everyman's Library, 1909; and to E. P. Dutton & Co., Inc., and George Allen & Unwin Ltd. for quotations from *Catullus: The Complete Poems for the American Reader,* translated by Reney Myers and Robert J. Ormsby, copyright © 1970 by Reney Myers and Robert J. Ormsby.

To Robert Graves, for quotations from *The Eunuch,* in *The Comedies of Terence,* translated by Laurence Echard, edited by Robert Graves, Chicago: Aldine Press, 1962; and from Suetonius, *The Twelve Caesars,* translated by Robert Graves, Baltimore: Penguin Books, 1957. Reprinted by arrangement with A.P. Watt & Son, London.

To Donald R. Dudley, for quotations from *The Annals of Tacitus,* translated by Donald R. Dudley, copyright © 1966 by Donald R. Dudley. Reprinted by arrangement with The New American Library, Inc., New York, New York.

To Columbia University Press, for quotations from *Roman Civilization,* 2 vols., edited by Naphtali Lewis and Meyer Reinhold, 1951.

To the University of Michigan Press for quotation of poems 43, 69, and 70 in *Gaius Valerius Catullus: The Complete Poetry,* translated by Frank O. Copley, 1957.

To Indiana University Press for quotations from Polybius, *The Histories,* 2 vols., translated by Evelyn S. Shuckburgh, 1966; and from Martial, *Selected Epigrams,* translated by Rolfe Humphries, 1963.

To my sister
Marion L. Hooper
1919–1978

Contents

Illustrations, Maps, and Charts

Maps

Charts

Preface

Rome is a city of monuments. If there is a place for one more, it might be a memorial to the many generations of senators who accepted the yoke of time-honored virtue as part of their duty. Rome owes its greatness, in large measure, to them. I heard about the self-sacrifice and quiet dignity of these men from the late Arthur E. R. Boak, long-time professor of ancient history in the University of Michigan, who was something of a noble Old Roman himself. I shall always be indebted to him for what he taught me. I remember, too, the encouragement I have received from my friends who are now retired from the Kelsey Museum in Ann Arbor: Elinor M. Husselman, Enoch E. Peterson, and Louise A. Shier.

The recent helpfulness and guidance of Bernard M. Goldman, director of the Wayne State University Press; Richard R. Kinney, associate director; and Barbara C. Woodward, chief editor, have made the publication of *Roman Realities* possible, and I am most grateful to them. I wish to thank Professor Wayne Andrews, Wayne State University; Professor Arthur W. Forbes, University of Michigan; William H. Peck, curator of ancient art, and F. Warren Peters, librarian, Detroit Institute of Arts, for the

11

photographs they have given me the privilege of using. I also
want to thank John G. Printz of the Purdy Library for his frequent
kind assistance.

Finally, I must express my gratitude to my former student
and friend William D. Darby for his generous help and to my
colleague Goldwin Smith for being a patient listener, a wise coun-
selor, and for his ineluctable cheerfulness along the way.

Textual Note

The citations given in parentheses in the text are to the works of the authors mentioned, as listed in "Works Cited," Bibliography.

Introduction

From ancient fables and modern films about Rome the stalwart heroes and mad emperors are best remembered. Who will forget that Julius Caesar was murdered on the Ides of March? But the stories and events, pleasant or grim, do not in themselves teach the lessons to be learned in a thousand years of Roman history; rather, they are embedded in the experience of a people who fought as much among themselves as they did with enemies abroad. At the outset, there was a struggle over civil rights, a conflict between an entrenched minority of wellborn, well-to-do families and the great majority of citizens who were by custom excluded from public office. The rhetoric, politics, and occasional violence which erupted sound familiar. It was the slow process of compromise by worried politicians and the extraordinary patience of common men which eventually brought a solution. A stable constitution, in which the interests of all were protected, evolved in time for Rome's wars with Carthage. When they began, the enemy had the military advantage. That Rome emerged victorious was in large part due to the earlier resolutions of domestic problems. Carthage, on the other hand, was weakened precisely because those at home were not united in a common cause.

15

So it was that others looked to the Romans for guidance in law and administration of orderly and stable government. How then did it happen that later, during a century of violence, the very constitution which had served Rome so well in peace and war was brought to ruin? Power and wealth were the fruits of victory, but it mattered more how the shares of success were distributed. The building of a mighty empire abroad was at the same time at home the cause of bitter class rivalries and finally civil war.

To those interested in causes which carry the banner of social justice, the Roman experience offers valuable advice about what can go wrong with progressive programs. In this instance, ever present irrational factors played a special role. Fears about how much some would lose in order that others could gain, suspicions about the real motives of the reformers and their followers, the hesitation of those who worried about the side effects of major changes, the precipitous haste of self-righteous men who would make everything right in a hurry—all these were present during a major crisis of the Roman Republic when the Gracchi brothers sought to do so much good and died so young in the process. The three most famous Romans of the century to follow, Pompey, Cicero, and Caesar, were all murdered—victims of an age of violence which saw one bloody sequel after another.

It happened with the Romans, as it has with others since, that a people who failed to rule themselves became the willing subjects of a man with an army to enforce law and order. The first Roman Emperor, Augustus, disguised his power with a façade of constitutionalism; yet the truth was known if not voiced. In the Senate, renowned for its debates, there was soon less to talk about, and some thought it safer to be silent.

As the years passed, whether witnessing the horror of a Caligula or the majesty of Marcus Aurelius, the government of Rome became a naked despotism stripped of any pretense about honoring the will of the Senate or the people. So it was finally rulers like Constantine who, despite all the power at their disposal, were yet baffled by problems of inflation, ruinous taxes on the middle class, and not enough money for defense.

In the meantime, the state failed in its effort to suppress a radical religious sect which kept growing despite frequent persecutions. The Christians defied the emperors by refusing to worship the very gods who were believed to be the protectors of the state. Worse, they actually said such gods did not exist. The story of the struggles of the Christians and their eventual success—a success which brought them problems too—is interwoven with the history of the Roman Empire. When the last emperor in the West was gone, a pope took his place. But the pope was not the recognized leader of all Christians; in ancient times there already appeared the problem of unity which still hampers the mission of Christianity.

These are some of the highlights in an extraordinary story. Anyone concerned about present problems will profit from reading about how the Romans went about solving theirs—with the added advantage of knowing how it all turned out.

I

In the Beginning:
An Old Story and a Few Facts

Today, it is perhaps only visitors to Rome who hesitate amid the hustle and bustle of the Piazza Venezia to look at the balcony of the fifteenth-century palace where Benito Mussolini once stood in glory, speaking to the crowds in the square below. They might also reflect on the ignominious end of that "sawdust Caesar." A short distance away, a statue of the real Caesar stands close to the Roman Forum, where he often spoke to the people in the first century before Christ. With the aid of a map, persistent tourists look for the place nearby where Julius Caesar was assassinated. What they find are modern tenements where once stood a theatre built by Caesar's rival Pompey. It was in the entrance hall, where the Senate occasionally met, that Caesar was stabbed twenty-three times and collapsed to die with a bloody toga as his shroud.

Some of the conspirators who killed Caesar felt the act was justified because they feared he wanted to make himself a king. Others joined in because they said he was already a tyrant. Among the senators who held daggers was Marcus Junius Brutus (*ca.* 85–42 B.C.), a distant descendant of Lucius Junius Brutus, who five centuries earlier had helped to drive out the last king of

early Rome, also denounced as a tyrant.* The story of the Roman
Republic falls between these two dramatic events—the expulsion
of Tarquinius Superbus in 509 B.C. and the murder of Julius
Caesar in 44 B.C. To be exact, the Republic lasted for another
seventeen years, until 27 B.C., when Caesar's heir, his grandnephew Octavian, became the first emperor and was given the
title "Augustus." But, with either date, we have a period of
roughly five hundred years during which a people who owned
small farms, ate porridge, and raised sheep came to rule the western world.

The early chapters will describe the habits and decisions
which gave the Romans an advantage over their enemies. Succeeding chapters will review the problems of success and how the
victorious Romans began to fight among themselves—a struggle
which led to the collapse of the Republic. Could men in later
times profit from their experience of what went right and what
went wrong? The historian Titus Livius, or Livy, as we call him,
certainly thought so when he took on the task of telling the whole
story.

Those who stress the importance of the old-time virtues in
Roman society have Livy as their guide. He strongly favored the
ways of the past and pointed to the later disrespect for tradition as
one of the reasons the Republic failed. Livy witnessed the last
years of the Republic, lived through the forty-year rule of the first
emperor, Augustus, and died in A.D. 17 during the reign of the
second emperor, Tiberius. Although a native of Patavium (modern Padua), he spent most of his life in Rome, albeit it was like
him to go home to die. If he had wanted his writings to say
anything about himself, it would have been that he was respectable and industrious. His history about "the foremost people of
the world" was a long one, 142 books, entitled *Ab Urbe Condita—
From the Founding of the City.* The last events he recorded occurred
in 9 B.C. The work as a whole was a gigantic mural with a
personal touch added here and there. Livy thought that musicians
drank too much and the Greeks talked too much. Any solid citizen from Patavium would have agreed.

---

*Marcus was his praenomen, or what we would call his given name; Junius was
his nomen, the name of his *gens,* or clan, an affiliation by blood of a number of
families; and Brutus was his cognomen, or surname, the name of his particular
family. Thus, the full name of the better known Julius Caesar, mentioned below,
would be Gaius Julius Caesar.

Educated Romans were generally skeptical about the legends that described the founding of their city. But Livy felt that if any people deserved these heroic tales the Romans did—the Old Romans anyway, the generations of men who had built the city and brought it to greatness. There was less to be said for his contemporaries. In fact, one reason for reading about the past, he said, was to take men's minds off the present. He reminded his readers "how, with the gradual relaxation of discipline, morals first gave way, as it were, then sank lower and lower, and finally began the downward plunge which has brought us to the present time, when we can endure neither our vices nor their cure" (I. Preface. 9).

Livy had some faults, if not vices, of his own. He could tell a story twice without realizing that he was repeating a different version of the same event. At times he was careless about his facts; yet he was conscientious enough to express doubts about the sources he was using and not to follow them blindly. For instance, he doubted the unusually high number of casualties which earlier writers cited for Rome's enemies. A report that the neighboring Volscians lost 13,470 men in a single battle in 462 B.C. seemed highly suspect to him. In other instances, he was puzzled that some writers mentioned an event while others did not. He reported the discrepancy to his readers and left it at that.

Occasionally, it is not possible to be certain of a site, particularly a battlefield, which Livy mentioned, because many of the towns he referred to have completely disappeared and some of the battles may never have occurred. Certain stories Livy repeated were probably fictions invented, or perhaps borrowed from Greek history, by earlier writers who used them when they had no other sources to depend on. There were other problems. Livy was not sure which officials were in charge of a war the Romans waged in 322 B.C., and he pointed out that the record was confused for various reasons: "It is not easy to choose between the accounts or the authorities. The records have been vitiated, I think, by funeral eulogies and by lying inscriptions under portraits, every family endeavoring mendaciously to appropriate victories and magistracies to itself—a practice which has certainly wrought confusion in the achievements of individuals and in the public memorials of events. Nor is there extant any writer contemporary with that period, on which authority we may safely take our stand" (VIII. 40. 3–5).

Given such a frank appraisal of the material he was using, it is ironic that Livy's work is now the only source for certain periods of the Republic. Yet he would not have been so troubled by the shortcomings of his history as some modern critics are. His primary goal was to show that when the Romans remained true to their ancestral traditions they succeeded and when they abandoned them, they failed. That message could survive a few facts gone astray.

With a characteristic Roman preference for the practical, Livy was more interested in the right result. It follows that he believed the Romans triumphed not only because of who they were but because of who they thought they were. In other words, he felt it was necessary for a people to retain a positive image of themselves. That in turn meant confidence and the capacity for bold action. The same might be said for an individual whose chance for success could depend to some extent on how highly he rated himself and, perhaps, by the degree to which he was motivated either by religious beliefs or historical ideals. They could be beneficial precisely because he believed in them. Whether they were true or not was another matter.

The American philosopher William James (1842–1910) wrote in his *Pragmatism,* "If there be any life that it is really better that we should lead, and if there be any idea which, if believed in, would help us to lead that life, then it would be really *better for us* to believe in that idea, *unless, indeed, belief in it incidentally clashed with other greater vital benefits*" (*Pragmatism,* p. 78). Livy would have agreed with James and would also have insisted that the history of the Roman Republic proved him right. Certainly the way he told the story it did. But his history was not mere polemic; it was pleasant to read. Livy's manner was reminiscent of the Greek storyteller Herodotus. They both knew how to hold a reader's interest even if Livy's tales are at times burdened by his moralizing. To him, Rome's history was a dramatic panorama with tragic overtones. From it men might learn of the wonders wrought by good Romans born and bred and of the wickedness perpetrated by those who neglected their duty. It was a history of heroes who saved the city and of scoundrels who nearly destroyed it. Everybody else was more or less part of the scenery.

Livy's story of the founding of Rome has much flavor but lacks the facts of the detailed, if unavoidably prosaic, monographs written by archaeologists who report on a different kind of evidence. Excavations allow modern researchers to begin a lengthy story of man in Italy long before there were any Romans. As elsewhere in Europe, skeletal remains of primordial hunters of the Old Stone Age (Palaeolithic) speak for ungainly creatures roaming Italy possibly half a million years ago. The far more numerous New Stone Age (Neolithic) sites indicate how the nomadic life of hunters gave way to the more settled existence of farmers living in villages. Implements and weapons, although somewhat refined, were still of stone, but the surplus food being produced allowed for other occupations. Woven cloth, clay pots, and boats show major advances. The subsequent use of copper, bronze, and iron in turn gave a new dimension to the industry and warfare of prehistoric Italy. Since metals and their use were known earlier in such places as Cyprus and Crete and in the Danubian region, it has been easy to suggest that they signaled the many changes wrought in this land by invaders.

By 1000 B.C., many northern tribes had travelled through the Alps or by way of the Adriatic coast, headed for the warm climate and rich lands of the south. Among them were the Latins, who settled in that region of the Tiber River we know as Latium. Some of these migrants chose to build their huts where the river was most easily fordable. But they may not have been the first people to find a refuge from the swamps on those now famous surrounding hills. The evidence is meagre, but there was probably a settlement in this locality around 1500 B.C., or maybe earlier. Whoever the settlers may have been, they had departed long before the Latins arrived. For those who want an archaeological birthplace and date, the evidence of huts still to be seen on the Palatine and long dated to the ninth century B.C., or more recently to the eighth century, can be considered the earliest remains of a settlement which would one day be in the center of Rome.

Although modern archaeologists who study crude artifacts know more about the origins of Rome than Livy did, his version is still of vital importance. He was a gentleman scholar sitting in a comfortable study, using only the oral and written traditions of his ancestors. But he wrote of what the Romans believed about themselves and that had a crucial impact on how they behaved and what they accomplished. For that reason, Livy thought it all worth repeating. He began with a familiar legend.

In the Beginning

The ancestors of the Romans once lived in fabled Troy, and after its destruction the stalwart Aeneas led a band of hardy refugees to Italy. In Vergil's *Aeneid,* a stirring epic about Rome's destiny, Aeneas was shipwrecked at Carthage and stayed long enough to love and leave Queen Dido and so root future trouble in a misadventure of the past. Livy omitted that story and brought him directly to Italy, where at a place near the coast about nineteen miles south of Rome he founded the city of Lavinium (whose antiquity archaeologists have confirmed). Eventually, as this place grew and prospered, Aeneas' son Ascanius led settlers to found a second city, Alba Longa, where events happened which led to the founding of Rome.

There was a long succession of kings before Proca came to the throne at Alba Longa. He had two sons, Amulius and Numitor—a veritable Cain and Abel. When the elder, Numitor, succeeded his father, he was overthrown by his brother, who also killed Numitor's male descendants and hoped to deny motherhood to a daughter, Rhea Silvia, by promoting her to be one of the Vestal Virgins, guardians of the perpetual fire of the hearth goddess Vesta. Nor was Rhea Silvia taken by any man but by Mars (a god of agriculture in the beginning and only later of war). Mars, she said, had fathered her twins, Romulus and Remus. A divine ancestry for these sons of destiny was to be expected in ancient myths. That was all right with Livy, except that he could not help wondering if Rhea Silvia made up the story about Mars to hide a less-redeeming incident. No matter, Livy was anxious to concede that the founding of Rome was not by mere accident: "But the Fates were resolved, as I suppose, upon the founding of this great City, and the beginning of the mightiest of empires next after that of Heaven" (I. 4. 1–2).

There would be several fortuitous happenings. After their mother was confined to prison by Amulius, the baby boys were placed in a basket and put in the river where they were expected to drown. But the waters receded, and they were soon rescued and mothered by a wolf whose role in Roman history has been dramatized by a famous sculpture. Livy asked if the wolf tale could have been a corruption of a more believable story. The man who discovered the babies had a wife named Larentia, who because of her careless morals was called a "she-wolf" (*lupa,* prostitute) by her neighbors. Was that how Romulus and Remus came to have a wolf for a mother?

When the boys were grown they killed Amulius and restored their grandfather Numitor to the throne. Now, Livy said, they wanted to have their own city, a new city in the place where they had been saved. Yet, in their moment of triumph and, ironically, with many successful adventures behind them, they quarreled as to which of them would have preeminence. When Romulus killed Remus, the city was his, and Livy said it was named after him. It seems more likely that the legend followed the event and that Romulus was named after Rome.

By Livy's day, several dates had been suggested for the founding of the city. One of Livy's contempories, the antiquarian Varro (116–27 B.C.), decided on 753 B.C., and that date still stands, at least officially. The anniversary of the founding is celebrated on April 21, and children in Rome readily agree, for they have a holiday from school.

The Monarchy in Rome

According to tradition, Romulus was the first of the seven kings of Rome. Livy gave their names, the dates of their reigns, and recorded their principal acts. This information from earlier writers was all he knew. The founder of the city was naturally credited with establishing its oldest institutions. Livy says that after Romulus made the Palatine his citadel, he gave the Roman people the laws by which they should live. These would be obeyed because he so commanded. His authority was glorified by striking symbols. In public he was accompanied by twelve lictors who cleared the way for him. These attendants bore the *fasces,* a bundle of rods to signify the king's power to scourge a man, and among them an axe which meant that in more serious cases the condemned could be beheaded. The king's toga was trimmed with purple, and on state occasions he sat in a special curule chair—a seat with arms like a campstool and with curved legs.

The monarch received advice from a council of elders, the Senate, Rome's oldest deliberative body. Again, Livy ascribed its origin to Romulus who, he said, made the first appointment of one hundred *patres,* fathers. It was Romulus too who was said to have given the Roman people their first political division into thirty *curiae,* or brotherhoods, ten for each of three tribes: the Tities, Ramnes, and Luceres. Similar to the Greek tribes, divided into phratries, these associations of families held common religious rites and voted together in the earliest known Roman assembly, called the *comitia curiata*. This folk gathering gave the king a place to rally the people to war. It was not really a formal legislative or elective body. Presumably the Curiate Assembly was dominated by the same families whose elders sat in the Senate. To ascribe these fundamental institutions to Romulus provided an orderly account of events for which later historians had no contemporary records.

Romulus' name and reputation were also available for explaining anything else lost in obscurity. For instance, in later times, many Romans said their ancestors were Sabines, a people whose language was akin to Latin. A convenient legend, with Romulus in the foreground, explained this. The story of course had more color than a modern archaeological report which surmises that although the Sabine homeland was northeast of Latium there were some Sabine settlements in the region of the seven hills, but says no more than that. The Romans at least could talk about their great hero who did all things well. Romulus was an exceptional warrior. He was also, like Odysseus, a wily operator. The most famous of his legendary exploits concerned the disgruntled neighboring Sabines who, by modern standards at least, had a fair cause for complaint. The male settlers of Rome had built a city and given it everything except a future. For that women were needed. Romulus first sought peaceful alliances calling for intermarriage with nearby peoples, but without success. The neighbors might prefer to see this fledgling city have a brief career. The king then devised a plan which led to the famous incident known as the "Rape of the Sabine Women"—a tale which added a note of rough virility to Rome's past. Surrounding peoples were invited to a festival, and the unsuspecting Sabines came with their families. All was pleasant until, suddenly, their young daughters were gathered in by the Romans like so many prizes at a fair. The Sabines were outraged and called upon the gods for help, since a festival in the gods' honor had been interrupted by foul play.

Impetuous, and unprepared, neighbors were moved to act before the Sabines did and were quickly scattered by the Romans, an event which prompted Livy to make the earth-bound observation that "anger without strength" is of little use. Later, when the Sabines attacked in reprisal, a battle raged back and forth between the hills of Rome. Before either side could claim a victory, the Sabine daughters, now wed to Romans, intervened and brought peace between their fathers and husbands—a scene commemo-

1. *Separation of Fathers and Husbands by the Sabine Women,* by Jacques
Louis David. The Louvre. Photograph courtesy of the Musées Natio-
naux, Paris.

rated in a famous painting by the founder of the French classical
school, Jacques Louis David (1748–1825).

The reputed events of Romulus' reign could give rise to
many colorful paintings. In the end there was a spectacular departure. Romulus was standing in the Campus Martius when "suddenly a storm came up, with loud claps of thunder, and enveloped
him in a cloud so thick as to hide him from the sight of the
assembly; and from that moment Romulus was no more on
earth" (I. 16. 1–2). He was proclaimed "a god and a god's son,
the King and Father of the Roman City" (I. 16. 3). No one would
do so well again until Julius Caesar.

According to one tale, Romulus descended from the sky and
spoke to a man named Proculus Julius, saying, "Go and declare to
the Romans the will of Heaven that my Rome shall be the capital
of the world; so let them cherish the art of war, and let them
know and teach their children that no human strength can resist
Roman arms" (I. 16. 7). Like so many other people, when the

Romans got around to writing their history they found that the will of heaven had been with them early on.

Six Other Kings

Tradition said that the Senate elected the pious Numa Pompilius as the second king of Rome. The origins of many religious rites and priestly colleges (boards of officials who performed the necessary ceremonies) were traced to his reign. Romulus had given the Romans laws and a strong city. Numa gave them a fear of the gods. He was also credited with inventing a lunar calendar which, with some adjustments, agreed precisely with the sun every twenty years.

After the relatively peaceful reign of Numa, who it was said ruled forty-three years, a youthful warrior, Tullus Hostilius, was elected king. He led the Romans in a long and ultimately successful struggle with the nearby Albans. If there is any truth in the stories surrounding that conflict, it was in the report that the war began with charges about cattle rustlers on both sides. Very likely that was a major cause of trouble in the seventh century B.C. when the Romans were still living a largely pastoral life.

Livy's account of a series of wars with various neighboring peoples sounds contrived, but there were undoubtedly a number of skirmishes fought over relatively minor matters such as would concern small towns. Yet another "war" with the Sabines was provoked by the seizure this time of Romans at a fair and counterclaims by the Sabines that certain of their people were being held by the Romans. A single battle decided the matter in Rome's favor.

Tradition holds that Tullus, after a thirty-two year reign, was killed in a fire caused by lightning striking his house. That was probably a common enough occurrence, but too common for a king. So, it was said that Jupiter cast his thunderbolt in anger because of the careless fashion in which the king had conducted religious rites. Nothing of the sort was likely to happen to the next ruler, Ancus Marcius, a grandson on his mother's side of Numa Pompilius, who was eager to uphold his family's reputation for religious scrupulousness. It was believed that during his reign the famous wooden bridge, the Pons Sublicius, was built across the Tiber. Presumably, it was after this bridge that the chief priest in Rome, the *pontifex* (bridge-maker) *maximus,* took his name.

The Romans believed that the three kings following Ancus were "foreigners." The Etruscans, who lived in the area we call Tuscany, north of the Tiber, figured prominently in the development of Italy. They built the first major centers of culture and industry, perhaps as early as the ninth century B.C. Modern excavations of Etruscan cities and particularly their tombs have revealed the kind of furniture they used, how they dressed, and what they liked to do with their time. The tomb paintings give a vivid impression of a people who worked hard and played hard. They were not given to contemplation, but were always busy, even if only fishing. What the Etruscans taught the Romans was generally both practical and realistic. The talented minds among these down-to-earth people were busy devising means of making cities more liveable and fields and mines more productive. If later Romans found Greek philosophical speculations little to their taste and even unsettling to their fixed habits, they could perhaps thank the Etruscans for having inspired them to build better roads and bridges.

Still, the Etruscans have long been called a mysterious people. One of the mysteries is where they came from. They probably arrived in Italy in the late ninth or early eighth century B.C., but ancient authors were not agreed about their native land. The Greek historian Herodotus said it was western Asia Minor, and he was probably right. There were striking similarities to the ways of that region in the types of tombs the Etruscans built, the style of their ships, and their divination practices; that is, their use of omens or other means of determining the will of the gods or what the future would be. It was presumably by their superior weapons and tactics, akin to those of the advanced civilizations of the East, that they became the overlords of their neighbors.

In the late seventh or early sixth century B.C., a group of Etruscan chieftains and their followers moved south and took over key sites in Latium and Campania. They also built new settlements. Capua, the most heralded among them, would one day rival the coastal city of Cumae, settled earlier by the Greeks, which managed to resist the Etruscans and so to set a limit to their expansion. In the north, nothing stopped them short of the Alps. They crossed the Apennines late in the sixth century and founded Felsina. Farther north, Parma and Mantua were among their new settlements. On the east coast of Italy, Ravenna, prominent in the later Roman Empire, was founded, and the Etruscan town of Adria gave a name to the Adriatic Sea.

Italy and Sicily

Etruscan advances in the north, however, were accompanied by eviction in the south. Toward the end of the sixth century, the Latins began to rid themselves of their Etruscan rulers, who may well have been their own undoing in cities like Rome, which they had occupied. Over the years they improved the standard of living of the same people who would one day drive them out. Their advanced techniques in mining and agriculture and their widespread trade connections, from Carthage to Phoenicia, meant growth and a greater prosperity. The richness and variety of imported goods were largely paid for by their export of iron and bronze products, including strong helmets and reliable pails.

But the Etruscans left as their legacy to Rome much besides craftsmanship and hardware. The trappings of office, including the *fasces* and the purple-trimmed toga, by which Roman magistrates would later distinguish themselves, were, as Livy said, borrowed from the Etruscans. The mural-sized frescoes in the tombs which wealthy Etruscans built on a grand scale are brilliantly painted scenes which mirror a life of banqueting, flute playing, wrestling, and dancing. A famous mural in the so-called Tomb of Chariots shows an enthusiastic crowd of men and women watching athletes race on foot and in chariots, as well as others performing acrobatic stunts. Other paintings show the harsher sport of gladiators out to maim and kill. Whatever the origin of that pastime, whether from contests over the kingship or from human sacrifice, it was a sad inheritance for Rome.

Excavations of their cities have shown that the Etruscans were careful planners. Paved streets were laid out on a simple grid plan and supplied with excellent drains. Towering over all else were temples, for heaven was much on the Etruscans' minds. They had very old and well-respected means of determining whether the gods were pleased or angry. As might be expected, the conquered Romans added the Etruscan divination apparatus to their own. Of particular use was a kind of liver "palmistry"—the reading of lines on the livers of sacrificial animals—an age-old device of the Near East. Times changed but not religious practices. The Romans always felt that these neighbors had some special gift in such matters. What was old was best. That assumption proved embarrassing during Rome's later troubles with the Etruscans when genuine soothsayers became a wartime shortage.

Seen in its proper context, the arrival and departure of the Etruscans in Latium was only one episode in the larger story of

2. Etruscan embossed pail, bronze, 750–650 B.C. Courtesy of the Metropolitan Museum of Art. Gift of J. Pierpont Morgan, 1917.

the expansion and decline of an Etruscan "empire." By comparison, Livy's account of the Etruscan kingship sounds almost entirely fanciful. Rather than having Rome fall under the dominion of the Etruscans in the late seventh of early sixth century B.C., as happened to cities much farther to the south, he had the city "conquered," as it were, by one man. Lucius Tarquinius Priscus, called Tarquinius the Elder, was presumably a refugee from the Etruscan city of Tarquinii who had come to Rome and prospered while at the same time ingratiating himself with the king Ancus, enough so to become a guardian of Ancus' children and to have them conveniently absent from the city when the king died. He then had himself elected. The traditional date for that event given by Varro was 616 B.C. After further wars with the Sabines and various Latin peoples, he was said to have begun notable public works, including sewers. For the moment, Livy had hold of a fact. One way or another those improvements were certainly attributable to the Etruscans who, at the time, were far advanced in engineering over the Romans.

Tarquinius was killed in a plot managed by the two sons of the former king Ancus. They were, however, unable to prevent Tarquinius' son-in-law, Servius Tullius, from coming to power.

Presumably he too was an Etruscan, although he had a Latin name. The succession was not easily managed, and Servius was fortunate that a renewal of hostilities with neighboring cities helped to ease the strain. By his leadership, he presumably earned the kingship, and his statesmanship confirmed it.

The beginning of the census at Rome was attributed to Servius. The people, divided into classes according to wealth, would thereafter serve in the army according to the kinds of equipment they could afford. In the first class, for instance, were men carrying both a spear and a sword. In the fifth class were the stone-throwers, who did at least have slings. Horn-blowers were in an extra category along with other service personnel who did not fight.

Servius was well respected except within his own family. His principal rival was his son-in-law Lucius Tarquinius, who was either the son or grandson of Tarquinius the Elder. Livy accepted the decision of most ancient historians that Lucius was the son and then recounted how the kingship was brought to an end because of his foul deeds. He and his brother were both married to daughters of the king, but Lucius and his sister-in-law Tullia were more alike in nature, and, after two sudden deaths in the family, became wedded partners in future crimes. Tullia was Livy's Lady Macbeth with ambition to spare. "It was the woman who took the lead in all the mischief." Although it was Tarquinius and his henchmen who actually killed Servius, Tullia was said to have run her carriage over her dead father's body, and so earned a well-deserved reputation.

Whereas Servius Tullius had had a long reign of forty-four years, the tenure of Lucius Tarquinius, called Superbus, and so "Tarquin the Proud," was by all signs destined to be much shorter. He was not a king at all but a tyrant, ruling by terror and killing his enemies, even prominent men in the Senate. He gave all the orders, consulting neither the Senate nor the people. In the continuing border wars, Lucius kept the Romans ahead but in un-Roman fashion, for he used deceit to do it. Livy told a story about him which had an obvious parallel in Herodotus. Lucius sent his youngest son, Sextus, to pose as a deserter in the town of Gabii. Sextus played his part well, even leading the Gabini in raids against Rome, and was soon accepted as their foremost general. Later, Sextus sent a messenger to find out what his father wanted him to do. Livy said Lucius, possibly suspicious of the messenger, did not speak to him but, as they were walking, "struck off the heads of the tallest poppies with his stick." The messenger was baffled, but not Sextus, who proceeded by one means or another to get rid of all the prominent men in Gabii, and finally succeeded in delivering the town to his father without a fight. In Herodotus, a new ruler had received from an older, more experienced tyrant the same kind of message (V. 92). The story appears to be an example of the way the Romans enlivened their own literature by selecting passages from earlier Greek writers.

Although Sextus had proved his worth to his father, in the end he was his father's worst liability. The downfall of the monarchy resulted from an outrageous act by the king's son. Sextus was attracted by the beauty and modesty of Lucretia, the wife of his cousin Tarquinius Collatinus, and was determined to have his way with her even if by force. While her husband was away, Sextus arrived unexpectedly and was received as a guest. In the night he went to Lucretia's bedroom and assaulted her. She would have died rather than give in to him except that he threatened her with something worse. If she did not submit, he would kill both her and his slave and leave them naked side by side so that it would appear she had been slain in a compromising situation. Now she gave in. Later, after telling her father and his friend Lucius Junius Brutus what had happened, she stabbed herself fatally. A noble mind had put a tainted body to death. In Livy's day her sacrifice must have seemed an act of moral fanaticism, but he wanted to emphasize the scrupulousness of the early Romans, and Lucretia was his star.

Holding the bloody knife aloft, Brutus pronounced a death sentence on the royal family and delivered a fiery speech to the Romans, who had many other grievances besides this "shameful defilement of Lucretia." Tarquin the Proud and his sons were driven into exile. Even so, the fear of old Tarquinius remained until his death in 495 B.C., which Livy said was an occasion for joyful celebration in Rome.

Legends make exciting news. The abduction of Helen had brought the downfall of Troy, whence the ancestors of the Romans had come. Now the rape of Lucretia marked the end of the Roman monarchy. That was the story and Livy repeated it. Very likely, as mentioned above, what really happened was that the Etruscans were driven out during the rebellion of a number of cities in the area. The traditional date for the end of the monarchy was 509 B.C. If the city was founded in 753 B.C., the reigns of the seven kings covered a span of 244 years. The result is a chronology with four rulers serving thirty-eight years or more and even the shortest reign calculated at twenty-four years. Such an unusual record has only served to further undermine confidence in the received history of the period. At the very least, however, the news that there were once kings, and the last one a brutal tyrant, does ring true. Otherwise, why would the Romans have always expressed such fear of having another one?

Consuls and Heroes

With the expulsion of the last Etruscan king, the dignity of the Senate was restored and the voices of the "fathers" who dominated the Curiate Assembly were again heard in the land. Still, an executive office was needed to replace the defunct monarchy. It must be assumed that within the powerful families a decision was made, by one means or another, to give extraordinary powers to two men who were elected to replace the former king. They would one day be called consuls; whether that was their original title is not certain. That two men were chosen instead of one was not unusual. Earlier, at Athens, the powers of the last king were distributed among three officials called archons. The device was an obvious hedge against tyranny. In Rome, either consul could veto the acts of the other. And, unlike archons in Athens, who had different duties, both Roman consuls possessed the highest military and civil authority in the state. In short, they held jointly the position which is given today to the president of the United States. Why the decision was made in Rome to transfer the king's power intact to two consuls rather than to separate their duties is not known. Suffice it to say it proved fortunate. Governments wherein military and civil power are divided often suffer from an unsettling internal rivalry; in fact, one of Rome's future enemies, Carthage, was at a disadvantage for that very reason.

Usually, the consuls came to a gentlemen's agreement about how to share their duties. For instance, in military matters, they would customarily draw lots to see which one would head a campaign. Occasionally, the senators would suggest that one or the other was better suited for an assignment. Or, one consul might recognize his colleague as being superior and so play the role of a silent partner while retaining equal status in the eyes of the public.

In day-to-day affairs, the consuls did not try to consult each other about every detail. They alternated in taking charge of state business, and lictors carrying the insignia of the office accompanied whichever consul was at the moment giving the orders. There could be an appeal to the people from a consul's command within the city but not when he headed an army in the field. Then his word was final. That was what it meant to have *imperium*.

If the Romans were satisfied with a strong executive, they were at the same time wary of any lengthy stay in office. A consul was elected for one year at a time; and while in the early years outstanding men were frequently reelected, later in the Republic a mandatory ten-year interval between terms was decided upon to thwart "unbridled ambition." That such a safeguard was not needed in the early centuries, and that it did not work during the declining days of the Republic, says something again about the much heralded virtues of the Old Romans—which brings us back to Livy. His account of the early years at Rome gave full credit for noble deeds to stalwart heroes—men of self-sacrifice, courage, and dedication. Lucius Junius Brutus headed the list.

Brutus was elected as one of the two consuls who inherited the former king's authority. The story that he shared the consular power with the ill-fated Lucretia's husband, Tarquinius Collatinus, is considered to be a later fabrication. According to tradition, Brutus and his colleague, Publius Valerius, called Publicola, "friend of the people," were honest and fair-minded men, happy to have brought an end to capricious one-man rule. Fair-mindedness meant an end to privilege too. For that reason, the new day looked less promising to young scions of the old regime than it did to the man in the Roman street. Livy described the age-old distinction between a personal style of government and one ruled by law: "A king was a man, from whom one could obtain a boon, whether it were just or unjust; there was room for countenance and favour; a king could be angry, could forgive, could distinguish between friend and enemy. The law was a thing without ears, inexorable, more salutary and serviceable to the pauper than to the great man; it knew no relaxation or indulgence, if one exceeded bounds" (II. 3. 3–4).

The two sons of Brutus were soon caught up in a plot to restore the monarchy. As consul it was Brutus' duty to put them to death along with the others. And he did just that, yet surely with wonderment about his sons' behavior in view of his own noble endeavors and success. When Brutus died during a new war with the Etruscans, he was given a grand funeral and genuinely mourned, especially by the women. They remembered Lucretia.

Livy's second hero was Horatius Cocles. In 508 the Romans were attacked by Lars Porsenna, the powerful king of the Etruscan city of Clusium, who was sympathetic to the Tarquinii and their efforts to restore the monarchy at Rome. According to a much celebrated story, it was Horatius standing on a bridge who saved the day. Across the Tiber, the Janiculum Hill had been captured by the forces from Clusium. Nearby, a wooden bridge offered access to the city. Horatius, on duty when the enemy attacked, displayed a stoutheartedness unmatched by his companions. He kept them from running away by promising to hold off the enemy while they destroyed the bridge behind him. At first, two soldiers stood by, but even these he sent to the rear and the Etruscans found themselves looking at a single warrior who stared back, and with only one eye at that. His effort lasted long enough; and, according to Livy, Horatius jumped into the river when the bridge collapsed and managed to get ashore. A different tradition said he was killed in the battle. Either way, such self-sacrifice seemed hardly to be believed in Livy's day. Yet even in his own time, Horatius was admired because his bravery was exceptional. There were enough such men, however, to allow Livy to quote another young hero in the same year who said "both to do and to endure valiantly is the Roman way" (II. 12. 10).

II

The Old Romans:
The Struggle with Themselves

Tales about the brave and dutiful deeds of Old Romans in the early Republic were, to be sure, inspiring. But other stories better picture the day-to-day problems of the city. Livy offers a melodramatic account of an unsavory but politically significant affair. At the center of the story was Appius Claudius, a consul, who, in contrast to Brutus, was as wicked an Old Roman as there could be. He pursued with much passion and little patience a beautiful girl who would have nothing to do with him and was, in fact, already engaged to a young man with a promising career. Nothing deterred Appius Claudius. One of his lackeys seized the girl in the street and loudly announced that she had been born to one of his slave women and so rightly belonged in his house. A crowd gathered and a struggle ensued. Whereupon the lackey confidently said he was willing to take the matter before a magistrate who, to be sure, was Appius Claudius himself. Livy was not certain what arguments Appius used in handing down his decision that Verginia was indeed the slave of his client, but he said the verdict was received with dumbfounded silence.

Appius had prepared for trouble and had sufficient force on

hand to insure that his orders be obeyed. Now Verginia's father, seeing that resistance was impossible, feigned respect for Appius and asked permission to speak to his daughter before she was taken away. This granted, he took her aside and, in the sight of a horrified crowd, stabbed her to the heart. Knife in hand, he managed to make his escape from the city with the help of friends. Meanwhile, such a commotion ensued in the Forum that only a call for the Senate to meet quieted things down. Later, Appius was brought to trial, but he killed himself before it was over. The Senate had been forced to take strong action because the crisis had threatened the stability of the state. What made the matter so serious was that Appius Claudius belonged to the patrician class and the ill-fated Verginia, according to Livy's account, was the daughter of a lowly plebeian.

Nobody knows how or why it came about that the Roman people were divided into two groups. The patricians were a small caste of families who intermarried with one another and enjoyed the service of a large body of clients who were obliged to them for a livelihood, and hence all other matters. The plebeians, including the clients, made up about nine-tenths of the population. As they were encouraged by their lowly circumstances to feel inferior, they generally felt they were. This is how matters stood when legend gave way to history.

Some historians have suggested that the patricians were descendants of earlier conquerors in the area or that there was a racial distinction between the two groups. A more likely conclusion is that over many generations the talented and acquisitive few managed to win superiority over the less energetic and complaisant many. In time, the separation was sanctified by a tradition forbidding intermarriage. Presumably, patricians and plebeians had nothing in common. Events would change that. The patricians did all the fighting in the earliest years and, only later, after Rome's border wars became more intense under the king Servius Tullius, did the plebeians begin to share this duty. Whether at that time the patricians knew it or not, the willingness of the plebeians to serve as soldiers was the beginning of a bargain.

Under the Tarquins there was little chance for the patricians to be heard, let alone the plebeians. During the Republic, the situation was different. The patricians (who alone served in the magistracies and the priesthoods) became worried about the safety of the state should the plebeians refuse to fight. Nor would the plebeians for long risk their lives without receiving in return some fundamental political rights. Although concessions would always have benefited the plebeians, they were not granted until the time arrived when to do so was good for everybody. Nor were concessions made without a struggle, albeit with surprisingly little violence, given the emotions involved.

Interestingly enough, it was at this same time, the fifth century B.C., that a much heralded popular democracy was in its heyday at Athens. There too the commoners had won a greater voice because so many of them were rowers in an expanded fleet which was vital to Athenian defense. Ancient history thus offers two examples of demands for more rights being directly related to military service, and this news leaves no room for surprise if in modern democracies the same has been true.

The popular view that the early Romans were always attentive to duty and obedient to their magistrates is not realistic. On occasion they refused to fight and at other times gave the day to the enemy by abandoning a consul in the field. Disobedience to the magistrates was caused by domestic problems, particularly quarrels over debt slavery and land. These disputes, carried to camp, became a great embarrassment to Roman commanders who, as Livy said, were at times "in danger from two armies at the same time."

Debt slavery was the major cause of trouble. The poor borrowed from the rich, using their own bodies as surety, and in default the creditor claimed his collateral. A man who was forced to work off a debt was soon in a state worse than that which had prompted his indebtedness in the first place.

Since the early Romans were primarily farmers, the problem of unequal land holdings was complicated by the self-righteousness of those who succeeded because they worked hard and the genuine need of those who failed, if even by their own lack of effort. As time passed, the problem grew worse. Some of the land in question belonged to the state—the so-called public lands plus acreage confiscated from defeated neighbors. Apparently, the wealthy patricians often succeeded in using this land which did not belong to them, making the already existing inequities worse. Throughout the fifth century, the plebeians pressed for an agrarian law to expel the patricians from public lands. On the other side, the patricians claimed that plebeians had been offered their share of conquered territory, but that some of them had refused it

because they wanted a farm closer to Rome. Little was gained
from the charges hurled in both directions.

Livy probably exaggerated the importance of the land question in the early centuries of Rome, reading into that period a
crucial problem of later times. But whether Livy's account was
factually true or not, the overall story revealed an old dilemma in
human affairs. From the beginning, the plebeians saw little hope
for improvement so long as the government was controlled by
patricians who discounted trouble in the streets as merely instigated
by rabble-rousers. Seize a few, it was said, and the whole business
would quiet down. Not all of the patricians thought that way. One
of the early consuls, Publius Servilius, elected for 495 B.C., had
argued that there must be concessions to alleviate grievances or
there would be worse trouble in the future. The hard line of the
obstinate patricians was condemned for producing more hatred.
On the other hand, Servilius' soft approach was criticized for inviting further demands. As usual, evidence supported both positions.

Servilius, as might also be expected, suffered all the penalties
inflicted on a moderate. The plebeian soldiers wanted him to free
veterans from their debts altogether, and that he was reluctant to
do. But his firm stand on the issue did not make him popular with
the powerful senators. They still thought his general attitude was
too generous toward the plebeians, who on the other hand did not
think he was generous enough. Livy was reflective. Moderation in
the midst of a crisis was unpopular, "owing to party spirit and
consideration for private interests, things which have always been
hurtful to public deliberation and always will be" (II. 30. 2).

The plebeians decided to help themselves. If they saw a man
being seized for debt they used force to free him. When the violence got out of hand, the city was faced with an emergency
which even the consuls could not handle. A special authority was
needed, and fortunately one was at hand. From the beginning,
problems were bound to arise from the dual consulship, if only
that two men could not always agree. But especially at times of
acute crisis when quick decisions were needed, a single hand at the
helm seemed more advisable. So, it had become customary in
such instances to appoint a dictator, who was allowed six months
and no more to solve the problem and step down. The nomina-
tion of the right man for the job was made by a consul whenever
the Senate deemed such a concentration of power to be necessary.
The dictator made his own appointment of a right-hand man

called Master of the Horse. It was some time around the end of
the sixth century B.C. (Livy was not sure of the date) that this
arrangement was first used. In the future, a dictator was appointed
not only to restore order during acute political disturbances but
also during crucial military operations, when he could be more
effective than consuls elected, perhaps more for reasons of prestige
than for ability, from the best families. Although the title of dictator was held by regular magistrates in certain Italian towns, at
Rome it was a designation of power which was obviously intended to be used only rarely. The citizenry, especially the plebeians, saw the dictator as a necessary evil. His power without appeal
was absolute, and that frightened them, even though he quieted
the city. It was not until 300 B.C. that a law was passed providing
for appeal from a dictator's ruling. Even so, the dictator's authority remained a solemn check on lawless uprisings within the city.
In the light of this fact, the plebeians very early adopted a nonvio-
lent form of protest, one which proved extraordinarily successful.

Tribunes of the Plebs

At some time during the first half of the fifth century B.C., the
plebeians appear to have set up camp on the Aventine Hill and
refused to participate in the usual activities of the city. In other
words, they went on strike. Whether this event occurred as early
as 494 or as late as 471 is not known for certain because the
sources, including Livy, give variant accounts of the event. But,
the date aside, this unusual move apparently resulted in a crucial
concession by the patricians, who realized that the plebeians were
needed for the protection of the city from hostile neighbors. They
did not challenge a decision of the plebeians to elect certain of
their leaders as tribunes of the plebs (*tribuni plebis*), who, although
not to be accepted officially as magistrates, were nevertheless to
have broad powers. It is again not certain how many of these
tribunes were chosen at the outset; but later, when records were
more reliable, ten of them were elected annually by the plebeians,
whose rights they swore to protect. The plebeians in turn promised to protect the tribunes. Their persons were to be inviolable,
and anyone who ignored their veto or sought to harm them had
the majority of the citizens to answer to. No longer were plebeians to be at the mercy of patrician officials in seeking redress of
grievances. The tribunes were always to remain in the city and to

be available to the plebeians. Theoretically, they could veto each other's actions but, in practice, they worked together to challenge the magistrates. Their protective power was apparently limitless.

The plebeians had been given a great boon, and they were grateful. But the concessions only evoked extreme bitterness from many patricians. They were alarmed by what they saw happening. A consul might order a man to be taken into custody and, as soon as one of his lictors made a move to do so, a plebeian tribune would use his veto power to countermand the order. At times, a showdown was avoided because the consuls refused to become involved at the street level for fear that amidst a disorder they might suffer humiliation.

Roman officials valued their *dignitas* highly. And it was well that they did, for with it they earned respect, and that was part of a greater design. The magistrates respected the gods, the fathers respected the magistrates, and the sons respected the fathers. Realistically, this was not always true on a day-to-day basis, as the above example shows, but the early Romans believed that it ought to be true. Only later, Livy said, when the belief was abandoned, did things really go wrong.

In the meantime, the patricians and plebeians continued to tolerate each other, albeit generation after generation were at odds over the same old problems, accompanied, as usual, by self-righteousness on both sides. It was often charged that the plebeian tribunes were not really interested in reform but sought only to advance their own power. One consul claimed that the tribunes were given to loud complaints because they would "rather lead an evil cause than none" (III. 68. 11–12). Even when the patricians were trying their best to make compromises to ensure domestic peace, the tribunes would suspect a conspiracy. Why should the tribunes want peace when they prospered amid dissension? Their critics gave them little rest: "your power was obtained for the purpose of assisting individuals, not for the destruction of us all," and, "you were elected tribunes of the plebeians, not enemies of the Senate" (III. 9. 11–12). Time and time again the patricians voiced their impatience with the seemingly endless plebeian demands. No sooner was one demand satisfied than another was offered. "In Heaven's name what would you have? . . . What end will there be to our dissensions? Will a time ever come when we can have a united City?" (III. 67. 7, 10).

On the other side, the tribunes claimed that the patricians

only made concessions because of the need for plebeian soldiers. Even then, they might break their promise after the danger had passed. Furthermore, the leaders of the Senate were accused of inventing wars in order to send young plebeians off on wartime duty for fear they would become active at home in seeking reform.

The two classes did not even share the same heroes. In the long list of glorious Old Romans, Coriolanus and Cincinnatus stand tall, but in their own day that was a minority opinion. Both were known for bravery on the battlefield and reactionary politics everywhere else.

In the year 493 B.C. fame first came to a youthful aristocrat named Gnaeus Marcius, whom Livy described as having an "active mind and ready hand." He was later given the surname Coriolanus because of his undaunted courage during the Roman siege of Corioli. Military prowess notwithstanding, the plebeians disliked his biting criticism of their tribunes. He also presumably denounced the need to import grain and sell it at low prices to the plebeians who, by going out on strike the year before, had left the fields uncultivated and so created a famine. While he remained a hero to the patricians, his unpopularity with the plebeians and his disgust with their increasing power prompted him to go into exile. Neighboring Volscians welcomed him and enjoyed his harangues against the Romans. Eventually, he led them in a triumphal march through the surrounding countryside and camped before Rome itself. Dissension in the city increased the threat, for "the plebs preferred anything to war." Coriolanus insisted that land taken from the Volsci be returned to them and refused to barter with either Roman envoys or priests. Finally his mother, his wife, and his two small boys turned him away from the city. His elderly mother Veturia's strong words had a telling effect: "Is it this to which long life and an unhappy old age have brought me, that I should behold you an exile and then an enemy? Could you bring yourself to ravage this country, which gave you birth and reared you? . . . had I not been a mother, Rome would not now be besieged! Had I no son I should have died a free woman, in a free land!" (II. 40. 6–8). Coriolanus withdrew.

Livy did not know how or when Coriolanus died, but he repeated the saying attributed to Coriolanus that "exile was a far more wretched thing when one was old" (II. 40. 11). Shakespeare's play added the final word, "yet he shall have a noble memory" (Act V, sc vi, 153).

Lucius Quinctius Cincinnatus, forever a prime example of the Roman sense of duty, was another "minority" hero. In 458 B.C., when the consuls seemed unable to check the Sabines, he was summoned to serve as dictator. Officials found him with a plow, working his land. Wiping the dirt from his hands, he assumed the highest office of the state and was given an enthusiastic welcome by the patricians of the city. The plebeians managed to be restrained. (Cincinnatus was known to oppose the changes they were seeking.) And if, as the story goes, he resigned his dictatorship and returned to his plow after sixteen days, the plebeians were glad for their own reasons.

Such stories very likely reflect the dissension in Rome, but it would be unrealistic to think that the tribunes of the plebs always behaved according to strict class lines. While they were primarily interested in the welfare of the plebeians, they did at times, in 461 B.C. for instance, use their veto to protect a patrician from being ill-treated. And it happened more than once that a patrician who was being abused by his own class officials sought the protection of a fair-minded tribune. The tradition does not suggest that a tribune could be bribed for his services at this early date, but toward the end of the Republic, amid widespread corruption, it was not difficult to find one with a price.

At times, arguments between the consuls gave the plebeians a chance to advance. In 431 B.C., the consuls were so stubbornly opposed to each other that the government came to a standstill. The plebeian tribunes intervened and ordered the consuls to follow the advice of the Senate or face arrest. It was an unprecedented show of tribunitial power.

Over the years, compromise and common sense prevailed enough to see the city through a painful period of growth. Despite extremists on both sides, patricians and plebeians occasionally joined together in a common outburst of civic pride or exuberant celebration of a crucial victory. They also suffered together. The frequent epidemics striking the city and surrounding countryside affected all classes alike. In the early centuries, before the Punic wars, the standard of living of the wealthiest Romans was not very different from that of the poorest. Life was rudimentary, as on the early American frontier. The wealthy did not own villas a pleasant distance from the miseries of the city, as they would in later times. Livy wrote concerning 453–452 B.C. that men were no better off than animals in a year when the fields were barren and the city was ravaged by disease. Neither wealth nor class was a safeguard. A consul died that year, he says, and so did four of the tribunes.

The Law of the Twelve Tables

As soon as the plebeians found their voice at Rome, they began to ask that the laws of the city be written down and made available to all citizens. The legitimacy of this complaint made it one of the earliest to be satisfied. It was the second major concession by the patricians after the appointment of the tribunes. Now the plebeians would know exactly what the law said, even if the administration of justice remained a patrician prerogative.

In 451 B.C., a board of ten men, the decemvirs, were substituted temporarily for the two consuls. In addition to governing the city, they were charged with providing a codification of the law. By the time they were finished in 449, a series of twelve bronze tablets, or tables as they are called, had been placed in the Forum. These were a summation of traditional laws and included very little that was new, but at least the rights and responsibilities of all citizens were now embraced in precise language. As with all early law codes, certain provisions were primitive in their harshness and others, presumably of a later date, more sophisticated.

The Law of the Twelve Tables offers the best evidence about life in early Rome. Unfortunately, much of this basic law of the city has been lost since the time of Cicero, who said that Roman schoolboys in the first century B.C. were required to know the Twelve Tables by heart. Other legislation, of course, covered the needs of the intervening centuries.

When the laws were first written down, Rome was an agricultural community. There were frequent references to land and crops, but no mention of coinage. Without it commerce could not have been much advanced. "Persons shall mend roadways. If they do not keep them laid with stone, a person may drive his beasts where he wishes." "Should a tree on a neighbor's farm be bent crooked by a wind and lean over your farm, action may be taken for removal of that tree."

In Table VIII, the ancient "eye for an eye" clause appeared, but the actual statement, "let there be retaliation in kind," was qualified by the reservation that a settlement could be made if the plaintiff was agreeable. The same table made a distinction in penalties between theft by night or by day, armed or unarmed, and whether the crime was committed by an adult or "a person under the age of puberty." It made a difference whether buildings or crops had been burned intentionally or by accident. In the latter case, if the guilty party was too poor to replace the loss, he was assessed a lesser fine. The punishment for being caught stealing at night, or with the use of a weapon by day, was death.

The head of a household was responsible for the minor children or slaves under his control. Table XII stated: "Arising from delicts (offenses against the law) committed by children and slaves of a household establishment . . . actions for damages are appointed whereby the father or master could be allowed either to undergo 'assessment for damages,' or hand over the delinquent for punishment." Boys under puberty were likely to be flogged. Slaves were hurled from the Tarpeian Rock. In all early agricultural societies, property was sacred and stealing was akin to murder.

The death penalty was pronounced for perjury, for bribes taken by a judge, or for connivance with the enemy. Moreover, in a characteristically Roman pronouncement, it was stated that: "If any person has sung or composed against another person a song such as [causes] slander or insult to another, he shall be clubbed to death."

Although capital punishment was often mentioned, it may have been applied only rarely. Early in their history, the Romans showed a preference for letting a man go into voluntary exile rather than killing him. In the fifth century this choice was recognized as equal to "a legal sentence." An exile was not expected back; to add to his ignominy, his house might be pulled down. An entire clan could do penance for the disgrace of one of its members by refusing to give his name to any descendant.

Certain provisions in the laws revealed the Roman attitude on family matters. Table IV stated: "Quickly kill . . . a dreadfully deformed child." "If a father thrice surrender a son for sale, the son shall be free from the father." "A child born ten months after the father's death will not be admitted into a legal inheritance." Table VI provided for a marriage in which a woman need not be subject to the authority of her husband if she was "absent three nights in succession every year." Given that circumstance, she remained legally a member of a household headed by her father, uncle, or brother. A woman was never on her own.

The law on interest stated: "No person shall practice usury at a rate more than one twelfth (8.33 percent)," but that was enough to make loans (in kind) a very profitable business and, as mentioned above, the abuses which followed caught the poorest element in a familiar squeeze.

Table X set the pattern for future legislation aimed at curbing extravagant living by outlawing costly or showy funerals. "Anointing by slaves is abolished, and every kind of drinking bout. Let there be no costly sprinkling . . . no long garlands . . . no incense boxes. . . . But him whose teeth shall have been fastened together with gold, if a person shall bury or burn him along with that gold, it shall be with impunity."

Table XI simply stated that "Intermarriage shall not take place between plebeians and patricians" (Lewis and Reinhold, Vol. I, pp. 102–9).

The Early Assemblies

The Roman constitution was not a written document like the Constitution of the United States, which the people can look at if they want to. It was rather a collection of laws and unwritten traditions which developed over the years, as in the British system. When new institutions were added, the Romans tended to hold onto the old ones even though for practical purposes they had been displaced. For instance, in the fifth century B.C., the elective and legislative functions of the old Curiate Assembly were taken over by a new assembly based on the army. The Centuriate Assembly (*comitia centuriata*) was composed of "centuries" of fighting men assigned according to an assessment of their worth, which included the amount and kind of combat gear they could afford. The older body composed of the thirty *curiae,* or brotherhoods, belonging to the three original tribes (these were political divisions), continued to meet for perfunctory purposes. In fact, it met at least symbolically as late as the first century B.C., when a special corps of thirty lictors, who had traditionally summoned the people to these meetings, alone represented the thirty *curiae* in a ceremonial confirmation of magistrates. By this time there was no reason to continue the formality except that it provided a sense of continuity with the earliest times.

One of the original functions of the Curiate Assembly was

to confer the *imperium* on new consuls. This it continued to do even after losing its other powers. The ceremony was a solemn one, for the consuls, who also headed the army, were being given the power of life or death over all those who served under them. As noted earlier, only inside the city itself, where the army was not allowed to asemble, could there be any appeal from a consul's orders. Here is a typical example of Roman practicality. Where the *imperium* was useful it was provided, but where absolute power was not necessary it was denied.

The new Centuriate Assembly reflected in Rome the shift away from the importance of family status based on birth. Whereas the old Curiate Assembly had been dominated by the patricians and their clients, the Centuriate Assembly was organized so as to give the weight of opinion to those who had money, no matter what their family name or connections.

The shift from an emphasis on birth, which cannot be changed, to an emphasis on wealth, which can, was a step in the direction of democracy, but not a very big one, for the majority of citizens possessed neither noble birth nor money. The organization of the Centuriate Assembly was rigged in favor of the wealthy. They were assigned more centuries than the poor and of course had fewer persons in each century. (A century did not mean a hundred men, as it had in the past; and some of the centuries, especially of the seniors, men over forty-six, were very small in comparison to others.) The cavalrymen (*equites*),* the wealthiest men who could afford a horse, and the other well-to-do members of the army had ninety-eight centuries among them out of a total of 193. If they agreed in voting on a proposed law, the decision was made before most of the citizens had been heard from.

For a long time, the independence of the Centuriate Assembly was restricted by the authority of the Senate which, until 339 B.C., held a veto power over its decisions. The Publilian Law of that year ended this arrangement and, thereafter, the Centuriate Assembly had the final word. But this assembly had certain disadvantages. Meetings had to be held outside the city because, as mentioned earlier, it was unlawful for the army to come together inside Rome. Furthermore, the Centuriate Assembly could only be called by magistrates having the *imperium*.

---

*In the later Republic, this term is used to denote businessmen.

Compromise

Neither of the early assemblies at Rome provided an outlet for pent-up plebeian frustration. The repeal of the law prohibiting intermarriage was one of the two demands which the plebeians made in 445 B.C., even as their die-hard enemies had predicted they would, once they had begun to win concessions. The prohibition was degrading to the plebians as men and insulting to them as citizens. They did not necessarily want to marry into patrician families, and the patricians could always by their own choice prevent them from doing so. The law itself was what offended them, for it legalized their inferiority.

The patricians responded with remarks about "the debasement of their blood" and asked, "For what else was the object of promiscuous marriages, if not that plebeians and patricians might mingle together almost like beasts?" (IV. 2. 6). Even so, the call for intermarriage was not considered as dangerous as the other proposal that plebeians be allowed to stand for the consulship. Rather than think of the best leaders the plebeians had produced, the patricians were horrified to think that rabble-rousing types with more lung power than intelligence would become eligible for the highest office in the state. Nothing could be worse than a tribune like Gaius Canuleius becoming consul. He rallied the plebeians with strong language: "Have you any conception of the contempt in which you are held? They would take from you, were it possible, a part of this daylight. That you breathe, that you speak, that you have the shape of men, fills them with resentment" (IV. 3. 8–9). To him it was particularly galling that the patricians were now so exclusive, since many of them were descendants of once alien Sabine and Alban families. Was not the state built by admitting talented outsiders rather than relying on men with inherited reputations?

The picture of two classes completely opposed to each other is inaccurate, however. The Senate itself was divided about the demands the plebeians were making. Some senators met secretly to map strategy, but others stuck to a moderate path and looked for a compromise. One was finally found. It was agreed that both patricians and plebeians would be eligible for election as military tribunes. These officers would have the same power as consuls but would not be given the name. The military tribunes were a different group altogether from the tribunes of the plebs, who were primarily the protectors of the commoners' rights. The sources do not give a cogent explanation why, in certain years down to 367 B.C., there were consuls chosen only from among the patricians and, in other years, military tribunes from both classes. In fact, the record is not always clear which were elected for a given year. It does appear, however, that certain men served repeatedly. In 386, according to Livy, Quintus Servilius Fidenas, a patrician, held the office of military tribune for the sixth time.

Whatever the details of this arrangement, it would appear that giving the title of consul to a plebeian bothered the patricians more than letting him have the power under another name. Given the peculiarities of human nature and the Roman attachment to traditional forms, such an attitude may be understood, if not appreciated. In other words, military tribunes represented a halfway measure which gave the plebeians hope and the patricians time to prepare themselves for the election of a plebeian consul, which finally did occur in 367 B.C. The old tradition prohibiting a plebeian consulship was thus technically upheld for nearly eighty years, although for all intents and purposes it had been breached. Each side could live with the compromise.

While the election of military tribunes apparently eased plebeian demands for the consulship, it created another problem. Choosing several military tribunes—the number varied—increased the chance of disagreement at the highest level in a military campaign. During an attack on Veian territory in 426 B.C., Livy said that the Roman army became "confused" when an order to attack was given at the same time as a call for retreat. The ensuing disgraceful defeat resulted in an early demand for a dictator by the Senate.

The military tribunes represented the entire state, whereas the tribunes of the plebs were political leaders of a single class. At first, the plebeians seemed curiously reluctant to pick members of their own class over patricians. The earliest military tribunes were all patricians. The plebeians were accused by their leaders of having a low opinion of their own people. By "their besotted admiration of the men they hated, they kept themselves in perpetual servitude." Further, "No plebeian would despise himself when plebeians should cease to be despised" (IV. 35. 5–6, 9). The plebeian tribunes were particularly incensed to see the ridicule heaped on plebeian candidates and to have it followed by their ignominious defeat. How could plebeians prove themselves worthy of office if they were not allowed to try? The tribunes made the familiar call for pride among the plebeians. Still, there persisted a perennial respect for "name" candidates, men of the patrician class whose fathers and grandfathers had been consuls. In the election of 420 B.C., all the military tribunes chosen were again patricians, as were the four quaestors, although they too could have been selected from either class.

The quaestorship was the lowest magisterial office and probably the oldest. It may have been that the kings appointed quaestors. The early consuls used them as treasurers in the city and quartermasters in the field. The quaestors also had charge of public records and could initiate proceedings against tax dodgers. In other words, they inquired into a man's business. Hence, our term *inquisitor*. In the beginning there were only two quaestors, but in 421 B.C., when the plebeians were first eligible, the number was increased to four. During the latter years of the Republic, it would grow to twenty, and, finally Julius Caesar added twenty more.

There were two men running for the four quaestorships in 420 B.C. who were expected to win. But both the son of one plebeian tribune and the brother of another were defeated. "What in the world, they asked, was the meaning of this? Had neither their own services nor the wrongs which the patricians had inflicted, nor even the pleasure of exercising a right—since what had before been unlawful was now permitted—availed to elect a single quaestor from the plebs, let alone a military tribune?" (IV. 44. 4–5). It was enough to make them think that fraud had been used to elect the patricians. The charge was freely made. But their own statements were not entirely honest, either. In the early years of the Republic, conscientiousness about duty and respect for office undoubtedly provided the Romans, as a rule, with excellent administrators. The controversy between the two classes was real, but for a long time past the majority of the patricians had given responsible and honest service to the state and the plebeians knew it.

According to Livy, a single event rather than words prompted the plebeians to start voting for their own people. In 409 B.C., they were angry that a consular election was held instead of one for military tribunes. Their reaction was to elect plebeians to the quaestorship for the first time. Of the four elected only one was a patrician.

By the end of the fifth century, the plebeians had become used to the idea of electing their own people to office; and, according to Livy, in 400 B.C. Publius Licinius Calvus, a man of mature years, was the first plebeian chosen as a military tribune. Livy adds that Licinius was surprised by the peacefulness with which he took office. Apparently his own mild behavior defused some of the patrician resentment. The point Livy wants to make concerning this event is essentially correct, but his facts may not be. Modern commentators suggest that there may have been a plebeian elected to this office as early as 444 and another in 422, but certainly it was at this time a rare event. Thus, as Livy shows, in the election for 399 an amazing reversal did take place. Only one patrician was elected as a military tribune; all the rest were plebeians.

Whether consuls or military tribunes were elected, they were too busy with seemingly endless wars to handle all their domestic duties. In 443 B.C., the office of censor had been created to provide for the taking of a long overdue census. The assessment of the worth of each citizen marked his class for fighting in the army and voting in the Centuriate Assembly. In addition, the two censors supervised the letting of public contracts for roads and the like. Eventually, they assumed the role of censors as we use the term. It was up to them to expel a man from the Senate if he was found guilty of "un-Roman" behavior. At first the censors, because of the need for continuity, were given a five-year term; but within a decade the old fear of concentration of power caused a reduction of the time to eighteen months. It became customary for the censors to be chosen from among the ex-consuls. In other words, they were senior statesmen.

A Patrician for the Plebeians

Although certain patricians may have recognized from time to time the need for reform, and demanded it, not until 385 B.C. did a patrician, Marcus Manlius Capitolinus, actually become a spokesman for the plebeian cause. Livy describes him as a proud man, "through a defect of nature, impetuous and passionate," who was angry not to have stood higher in patrician ranks and so looked to the plebeians for support. The patricians, of course, labled him a demagogue. Livy agreed. Manlius, he said, was unfair to his own class and valued his popularity with the plebs more than he did his honor. For all that, his defection was a serious blow to the patrician hierarchy.

Manlius went to the rescue of a plebeian centurion, an excellent soldier, who was under arrest for debt. After paying what the man owed in order to free him, he used the occasion to condemn the ruthlessness of the money-lenders and the support given to them by the patrician class. A fine soldier who risked his life to save the city had nearly been ruined by a vicious debt system. He had paid out enough money to repay several times over the original amount he borrowed because most of his expense went for interest and very little was applied to the principal.

Manlius, his ambition aside, had good intentions, but such a man may go too far. He made wild charges against the Senate, which he could not substantiate. According to Livy, a dictator, Aulus Cornelius Cossus (others say it was Camillus, the hero of Veii), ostensibly appointed because of a war with the Volsci, called him to account. To Manlius that meant the dictator was also suspect. Manlius accused him of conspiring with the Senate to trump up a war which would be useful at the moment for the patricians. He had a reason to be cynical about patrician motives. After he was arrested and imprisoned, he learned something about the plebeians. Not one of them raised a hand in his defense. The age-old respect for authority was too much a part of the Roman mentality. Livy said, "There was none that could endure to behold or hear this shame; but there were certain rules of conduct which the citizens, deeply submissive to regular authority, had made inviolable; nor did either the tribunes of the plebs or the plebs themselves dare to lift their eyes or open their mouths against the power of the dictator" (VI. 16. 3-4).

Yet there were visible signs of plebeian sympathy for Manlius. They let their hair and beards grow as a symbol of mourning. Downcast looks, however, were not going to help him. He had, in a sense, been betrayed by silence. Later, when the dictator stepped down after his triumph, the people felt a little less restrained. The Senate's conciliatory decision to free Manlius was misread by his followers as weakness. There was open talk of rebellion. "How long, pray," Manlius asked the plebeians, "will you remain ignorant of your own strength, which nature has willed that even brutes shall know? At least count up your numbers and the numbers of your adversaries. . . . Make but a show of war, and you shall have peace. Let them see you ready to

resist and they will give you your rights of their own accord"
(VI. 18. 5, 7).

Manlius had still another lesson to learn. His call to arms
was not supported by the plebeian tribunes. They had for too
long watched him usurping leadership they felt to be theirs. Now
they turned the plebeians against him with an old and reliable
accusation. Manlius wanted to make himself a king, they said, and
for such "treason" he deserved to be punished. He was arrested a
second time and tried, but sentenced to death only by a small
council of the people hastily summoned by the tribunes for that
purpose. The tribunes hurled him from the Tarpeian Rock on the
Capitoline, where he had recently taken an heroic stand in defense
of the city against the Gauls. So it was, as Livy commented, that
he had first won fame and was later executed in the same place.
An epidemic which followed soon afterwards was thought by
many to be evidence of the gods' displeasure about Manlius'
death.

367 B.C., A Year for the Plebeians

Gaius Licinius and Lucius Sextius, who served ten consecutive
terms as plebeian tribunes, were the men most instrumental in
winning plebeian demands. It was time, they said, for the plebeians to share in the consulship and so possess the *imperium,* the
highest power in the state. They insisted that the practice of electing military tribunes be abandoned and, henceforth, only consuls
be chosen. Furthermore, according to tradition, they insisted that
one of the two consuls must be a plebeian, that otherwise there
would be no true progress. But in this instance, the tradition
appears to have been faulty. Afterwards, two patricians were
often chosen; and that would have been unlikely, had a law forbidden it.

In addition, the tribunes wanted debts to be settled as follows: interest already paid would be subtracted from the principal
and the remainder cleared up in three further payments. As for the
land issue, they would limit the amount of public land held by an
individual to five hundred *iugera* (one iugerum equalled about
three-fifths of an acre) and so give the poor a chance to increase
their acreage. Sextius and Licinius swore to use their veto to block
the election of military tribunes until their demands were met, and
their obstinacy led to what Livy described as desperate struggles.

Familiar accusations were made by both sides. The tribunes claimed that individual patricians held as much land as any three hundred plebeians. The harsh debt laws were making every patrician house a jail.

The patricians used their strongest ammunition against the plebeian tribunes, claiming that insistence on a package of laws would not allow for the separation of good measures from bad. Sextius and Licinius were scored for their insolence, with the epithets "our perpetual tribunes" and "Tarquin tribunes." Patricians predicted that if the present landowners were forced to part with their holdings vast deserts would result because the poor could not properly develop new tracts. The debt law, they said, would destroy the system of credit altogether. These attacks on the tribunes and their proposals did not eclipse the central issue concerning the election of a plebeian consul. Here the tribunes had the best argument. They noted that there had been no drastic alteration in the fortunes of the state since the election of the first plebeian to a military tribuneship. In fact, whereas in the past patrician officials had been removed for poor performance, no plebeian serving as a military tribune had been forcibly ousted. The tribunes might also have pointed out that for a plebeian to break into the power structure he had to be a man of impeccable reputation and high ability, whereas patricians of only average worth or worse found election possible because they belonged to the right families.

The momentum of events was on the side of the tribunes. In 368 B.C., threats to the state from without and within had brought Marcus Furius Camillus to another dictatorship. His appointment of a plebeian as his Master of the Horse was a sign of hope. In addition, Sextius and Licinius were able to obtain a law giving to the plebeians half of the ten seats on the board handling the state rituals.

In 367 B.C., Lucius Sextius became the first plebeian elected to the consulship. When the Senate threatened not to recognize the election, the plebeians declared they would again secede; but Camillus saved the day with a bargain—at least that is what the tradition said, according to Livy. The plebeians would be allowed to have their consul, but another patrician magistracy would be created. Two praetors overseeing the courts of the city would further relieve the busy consuls of some of their duties. It was a concession to help ease patrician anxieties while they were getting used to the idea of plebeians sharing the highest office.

Old resentments died hard. In 362 B.C., legions serving under a plebeian consul were severely beaten and the consul was killed. Obviously, such a thing could have happened to either a patrician or a plebeian, but that argument was no match for irrational feelings. Patrician diehards saw the event as a justification for their position. Since the law allowing a plebeian consul had been won by tribunes who did not have the guidance of the auspices, it was bound to have bad results.

More time was needed to allay bad feelings. When the first plebeian praetor was elected in 337 B.C., a patrician consul who opposed the election and threatened to void it did not receive much support from the Senate. Slowly, very slowly, nearly everybody began to accept the idea that plebeians were to have equal rights with patricians.

Earlier, in the momentous year 367 B.C., the growth of Rome was reflected in the doubling of the number of magistrates known as aediles. Originally, the office had been created at the same time as the plebeian tribuneship with two aediles chosen by the plebeians. They were assistants to the plebeian tribunes and in this capacity looked after paper work—a kind of secretaryship. Later, they came to have supervision of public buildings, markets, and games, as well as the water supply; hence their duties were important to the city as a whole. They also kept an eye open for anybody disturbing the peace. The early Romans generally policed themselves; an aedile presumably laid a hand only on those who neglected their duty. Now, in 367 B.C., four of them were needed to handle Rome's problems, which were increasing along with the population. The two new officers were given the special honor which went with curule chairs and, at first, only patricians were eligible, but, in keeping with the times, plebeians were admitted the following year.

The five hundred *iugera* limit which Sextius and Licinius had asked for was adopted in 367 B.C. Prosecutions during the year 298 showed that until that time at least the prohibition was being strictly enforced. Still, during the fourth century B.C., adjusting to change went hand in hand with quarreling about new proposals.

Reform—Slow but Steady

A major plank in the plebeian reform program was one calling for a lower rate of interest. A law in 357 B.C. set a limit on the amount to be charged, but how it was to be calculated is not clear from Livy's description. The modern estimates of 8⅓ percent or 10 percent seem to be the most reasonable. In any event, in 347, the rate was said to be cut in half and "debts were made payable, one-fourth down and the remainder in three annual installments." The plebeians were not entirely satisfied.

It was not until about 325 B.C. (the sources disagree on the date) that the practice of imprisonment for debt was finally abandoned. Thereafter, a man's property could be seized to satisfy a debt, but not his body. The reform was probably long overdue and a result of persistent complaints about the abuse of prisoners. Livy cited a particular case as having brought the matter to a head. A personable young man had surrendered himself to a well known money-lender so that his father could remain free. He did not consider it part of the bargain that he should submit to the man's desires, and he was severely beaten for his stubbornness. When he managed to escape, his scars were a vivid testimony to a foul business. According to Livy, the Senate reacted quickly to the public outrage and urged that the law be changed. It was. Those held in bonds were set free.

By this time the plebeians had made several other gains. The first plebeian dictator, Gaius Marcius Rutulus, was appointed in 356 B.C. to meet the challenge of the Etruscans, now finally united. When he appointed a plebeian Master of the Horse, this sweep of the top emergency powers made the patricians bristle. Even though Marcius was successful in ending the danger, it was only by the people's vote, and not with the Senate's consent, that he was awarded a triumph—the customary parade with banners flying of a victorious general, who rode in a chariot through the streets of Rome with his army and musicians accompanying him. Presumably he paid for it himself.

The worst fears of the aristocracy proved groundless when in the ensuing election both consuls chosen were patricians, one of them for a third time. Yet, in the following year, 354 B.C., many of the plebeians protested by refusing to vote. The old feelings persisted in the years ahead as patricians or plebeians revelled in the success of one of "their" consuls. In 348, Popilius marked his victory over the Gauls with a great celebration in which every plebeian could feel personally elated.

In 351 B.C., Marcius, having served as the first plebeian dictator, was the best man the plebeians could have nominated to

be the first plebeian censor. There was the expected patrician outcry, but Marcius won and another patrician wall was breached.

There is often a reference in Roman history to a "new man,"
novus homo. It means a man who had become the first in his family
to sit in a curule chair as a result of being elected to the consulship, praetorship, or curule aedileship. Whether he was sitting
down or not, he could still be recognized. A curule magistrate
wore a white toga trimmed in purple.

By 337 B.C., when the praetorship was opened to them, plebeians were eligible for every position in the *cursus honorum*, the
honorable course of offices from quaestor to consul. A young man
would begin his career with ten years of military service and then
stand for the quaestorship at twenty-eight, to be followed presumably by an aedileship, praetorship, and finally the much coveted
office of consul. It was a measure of the conservatism of Roman
society that experience and age were characteristic of a public career. Those at the top could veto the acts not only of a colleague but
also of magistrates below them. They had served on the lower
rungs of the ladder, knew the duties, and could sympathize with
the problems of these officers. It was a government of careerists—
men with the same general background, the same education and
experience. They understood one another, and they knew how to
talk to one another without having to abuse their veto power.

Only very gradually did men of low birth acquire prominence. Generally, only the wealthier plebeians could afford to
serve in the magistracy. The "new nobility" was, in effect, a circle
of family and friends—a circle which, practically speaking, was
closed to those without independent income. Still, a man's ancestry was not forgotten. Gnaeus Flavius was the son of a freed slave.
He was also a man of talent. His election to a curule aedileship,
however, seemed a special affront to certain of the well-born, and
some of them showed it by refusing to wear their ornaments of
gold as though to say that all things had been debased. Furthermore, when Flavius went to call on a man who was sick, young
nobles seated at the bedside refused to stand when he entered. He
at least had a curule chair to sit on.

Would the Gods be Alarmed?

In 300 B.C., two tribunes who were also brothers, Quintus and
Gnaeus Ogulnius, led an attack on the last bastion of patrician

strength. Religion was a great protector of tradition. Now it was
proposed to pack the priestly colleges. The boards of the augurs,
who announced whether the signs of the sky were favorable to
any public action, and the pontiffs, who performed the major
ceremonials of the state, were to have new plebeian appointments.
Patrician indignation was expected and on time. The patricians
asserted that the gods would be more alarmed than they were.
Surely there would be terrible consequences if this law was
passed! But now the bluster was almost perfunctory. Once the
plebeians had been admitted to the higher magistracies their admittance to the priesthoods could only be a matter of time. An
advocate of the law said of one plebeian dignitary: "If men shall
read with equanimity, in the inscription that accompanies his portrait, of consulship, censorship, and triumph, will their eyes be
unable to endure the brightness, if you add to these the augurate
or pontificate?" (X. 7. 11–12). It was also pointed out that all
traditions had once been innovations. The plebeians were added to
the priesthoods, and after two centuries they became eligible at
last for any and all offices in the state.

The Third Assembly

By the early third century B.C., the Centuriate Assembly had lost
its legislative functions to the more "popular" Tribal Assembly
(*comitia tributa*), which had been formed some time during the
fourth century. In addition, although the Centuriate Assembly
continued to elect the higher magistrates—consuls, praetors, and
censors—the Tribal Assembly elected the quaestors, aediles, curule aediles, and tribunes of the plebs.

Earlier, at a time when the plebeians were almost frozen out
of the government, they had an assembly of their own called a
concilium, which constituted only part of the citizenry, as distinct
from the *comitia,* which, in theory, included everybody. The *concilium plebis* offered resolutions which were not originally binding
on the state but did represent the opinion, or plebiscite, of a
majority of the citizens. From some time late in the fourth century, these plebiscites were given the force of law with the approval of the Senate.

It is not certain how to relate the informal *concilium* to the
Tribal Assembly, an assembly which, by 241 B.C., was formed
from thirty-five geographical tribes (voting districts). The old Cur-

iate Assembly, though political in character, had arisen out of the religious and blood ties of the three tribes composing it. The patricians were excluded from the *concilium,* and may have simply stayed away from the Tribal Assembly, where the vote was taken on the basis of number rather than birth or wealth. They, of course, would have been outvoted. Whether the *concilium* merged with the Tribal Assembly, became the Tribal Assembly, or was always maintained separate from it is somewhat academic, since the same people controlled both.

The capstone of the Roman constitution was a law passed in 287 B.C., under the dictator Hortensius, which made the decisions of the Tribal Assembly binding on the entire state with or without the Senate's concurrence. Henceforth, the Tribal Assembly was the primary legislative body of Rome. It could be called and presided over either by a magistrate with *imperium* or by a tribune.

The Tribal Assembly was the most democratic of the assemblies, for it gave power to a majority of the citizens. Yet it was not a hotbed of agitation for reform. Most of the members of the tribes lived on small farms and their politics reflected the conservatism of their lives.

Dissension among the Romans was what their enemies hoped for. It was, Livy said, "the only poison" which could have ruined them. During the long political struggles in Rome, outside events usually meant, at least, a temporary accommodation at home. The fledgling Republic was not destroyed within a generation as might have been expected, but survived to win the world. Livy attributed that to a happy coincidence. Concessions were made by the patricians because they had prudence, he said. Prudence was given time because the plebeians were patient (II. 44. 9).

III
The Old Romans:
The Conquest of Italy

The English poet Edward Fitzgerald once remarked that he did not "care much for the Greeks and their piddling quarrels; one must go to Rome for wars." Livy would have agreed. But he tired of writing about them. Once, he paused to wonder where all the manpower could have come from, especially in view of such frequent losses. His conclusion was that the countryside was probably more densely populated than in his own day, when the fields were kept under cultivation only by the employment of a large number of slaves.

Livy could not avoid a wearisome repetitiousness in his early books. Year in and year out the Romans were at war with one or another of the same neighboring peoples because of real or imagined provocation—or mostly, it would seem, as a matter of habit. They often had to get ready to defend themselves in a hurry. Smoke rising from farmhouses set afire might be the first warning of trouble. Soon there were families hurrying into the city and bringing details of an attack.

In the young Republic, help was easily enlisted from the other Latin towns who had the same language and cultural tradition as well as the same enemies. To the north were the Etruscans, who had recently been expelled from Latium. To the east, in the valleys of the Apennine Mountains, were the Sabines and Aequi, whose desire to expand toward both the Mediterranean and Adriatic coasts made them aggressive. They were among the numerous peoples, including the Samnites, who lived in the central and southern Apennine region and are known collectively as the Umbro-Sabellians. Also in this group were the Volsci, who had managed to colonize part of the southern coastal area of Latium and resisted any attempt to dislodge them. More closely related to the Latins were the Hernici, who lived on the eastern border of Latium. They usually allied themselves to Rome, although, as events show, more out of fear than friendship.

The Latins, including the Romans, and the Umbro-Sabellians, and other tribes not so neatly classified, were Italic, as distinct from the Etruscans in the north or the Greeks along the southern coastline. Rome fought bitterly with the other Italic peoples for over two centuries and in the process became stronger. Her ultimate success by 265 B.C. meant the conquest of Italy.

There was no design in it. Rome, given a strategic central position in the peninsula, simply kept making friends and defeating enemies so as to build an ever expanding sphere of influence. There were so many setbacks overcome along the way that the Romans felt entitled, after the fact, to speak of destiny.

The Romans were not the best of neighbors. In 495, Livy says they caught the Volscians off guard and forced them to hand over three hundred children as hostages. That prompted the Volscians to make better preparations for the next round, and they began by forming a secret alliance with the Hernici. Some of the Roman campaigns were "preventive." Neighbors might be suddenly attacked to keep them from joining more distant enemies who were on the way.

Livy describes Rome's relations with certain cities as "neither peace nor war, . . . but something very like freebooting." Speaking of the Veientes, he says: "In the face of the Roman legions they would retreat into their city; when they perceived the legions to be withdrawn they would make raids upon the fields, evading war by a semblance of peace, and peace in turn by war. Hence it was impossible either to let the whole matter go or to end it" (II. 48. 5–6). By the last quarter of the fifth century, Livy says, the Romans looked toward war with the Aequi "as to an annual occurrence."

The early historical tradition retold in Livy is often discounted because it was taken from writers who presumably embellished their material with stories designed to put the past in the best light. The history of Rome's early battles is not based on eyewitness accounts, and it has even been suspected that some of them were made up. Yet Livy's writings are not simply patriotic lore. Rome's strengths and weaknesses are recorded and the Romans are by no means always seen at their best.

Over and over we read of generals who had to work hard to arouse their soldiers and get them up for a battle. At times spirit surely made the difference. On one occasion the enemy was driven off by the sight of the Romans, whose flashing eyes displayed their anger. At other times, a consul had to trick his men to get them to stand fast. Once, when a general saw his soldiers faltering, he shouted to them that the enemy was fleeing at the other end of the line. It was not true, but Livy says that the Romans attacked and because they thought they were winning, they did. The Romans were by no means invincible and sometimes used clever tricks just to get by. In 359–358 B.C., a dictator found his army outmatched and faked a show of strength by mounting a thousand men on mules and putting them among a hundred regular horsemen. Soon the enemy was surprised by what appeared to be a mighty Roman cavalry. On another occasion an auxiliary unit dragged branches on the ground and stirred up enough dust to scare the enemy into believing that far greater numbers were arriving than they expected.

By the time of the Samnite Wars in the late fourth century, the Romans usually used four legions in a campaign. Each legion consisted of five thousand soldiers and three hundred horsemen. A formation was planned to give the enemy the impression that they were always facing fresh troops. The *hastati* formed the first line of defense, and if necessary they slowly merged with a second group, the *principes,* according to a pre-arranged pattern. If the pressure was still too much, this line backed up and joined the *triarii* where a third and final stand was taken. "To have come to the *triarii*" was an old saying for bad news.

It is refreshing to find in the pages of Livy's history Roman soldiers who are occasionally boisterous men and not just statistics. In 410 B.C., a consul entering the city in full military regalia was jeered by soldiers standing along the way. They shouted crude slogans and made his arrival an embarrassment. According to Livy, the rudeness of the soldiers "was virtually an established custom." Apparently Roman footsoldiers, on their own at home, could be obnoxious and often were.

The Roman reputation for tight discipline has been and should be stressed by historians. But it should also be mentioned that excessively cruel treatment was deeply resented by the average soldier. Livy records an incident during the Samnite wars which was included in only some of his sources. He seemed to feel it said something about the Romans which was very probably true, whether the story was or not. Rigid discipline in the Roman army was for everybody, top to bottom. The common soldier knew that every tenth man in a unit which faltered was liable to be killed, guilt or innocence aside, as a means of instilling fear and stiffening backbones. High-ranking officers were more likely to be executed for disobeying an order. During a campaign in the late fourth century B.C., a dictator was temporarily absent. His Master of the Horse, Quintus Flavius, saw a good chance to attack the enemy. Contrary to orders, he did so and won a stunning victory. The dictator was not impressed. He could think of nothing except that his orders had been disobeyed. In the past, officers had been killed for a similar breach of discipline, regardless of the outcome of their actions. This time, when the dictator demanded the death penalty, there was widespread opposition. He blamed it on the changing times. The complaint that young men were being pampered and so were not as obedient as their fathers had been was as perennial in ancient times as in our own.

Discipline by the book sometimes made no sense. Not long after Flavius' disregard of orders, a number of men foraging for food were caught in a trap by the enemy. They died because a junior officer hesitated to act without specific orders from his superior. It is reasonable to believe that the friends of those who were killed called the lieutenant stupid.

Roman commanders, of course, varied in their degree of sternness even as they would in other qualities. Livy tells the story that in 319 B.C., the consul Papirius Cursor was annoyed with one of his subordinates for failing to get his men into a battle on time. As he was passing the man's tent he called out to a lictor to bring an axe. The officer stood transfixed, fearing the worst. Papirius, however, merely ordered the lictor to remove a troublesome root in the pathway. The officer was told he would have to pay a fine for his negligence; he could have been killed on the spot. Livy said he was already half dead of fright.

Livy records the many sides of war. A man could be killed for private reasons. There was a story about a soldier who was outspoken in his criticism of certain generals and was subsequently sent on a special mission. Those who went with him had been instructed to murder him and make it appear that he had died in an ambush. Later, men sent out to bury him guessed what had really happened. The news sent a chill through the army.

It should never be forgotten that in the long series of wars by which the Romans won their way to power they had considerable help from non-Romans. The point is not stressed by the earliest Roman writers whom Livy used. Still, it can be said that, by the mid-fifth century, Rome was fighting battles in which perhaps as many as two-thirds of her soldiers were being supplied by her sometime allies such as the Latins and the Hernici. It was true too that these neighbors, aware they were not full partners, occasionally sided with the enemy.

The Etruscans Again

Throughout the fifth century B.C., Rome's battles with the Etruscans were fought generally on a larger scale than were the periodic skirmishes with her other neighbors. An Etruscan outpost at Fidenae, six miles north of Rome on the Tiber, was a source of trouble. It had fallen under the control of nearby Veii about the time when the threat to Latium by the Etruscan leader Porsenna was thrown off. The Romans suffered a severe reverse trying to take the place about 480 B.C. and did not succeed in driving the Etruscans out until the latter part of the century. According to Livy, this well-fortified, well-stocked town was taken by means of a tunnel. Keeping the enemy busy fighting elsewhere, the Romans dug through a hill and then up into the citadel, which they captured. The rest of Fidenae fell by default.

It was not until 405 B.C. that the Romans felt equal to an attack on Veii, one of the major cities of Etruria. The military tribunes who began the siege were encouraged by the indecision of the other Etruscan cities whether to interfere or not. The detailed story which Livy tells about the ten-year siege of Veii is probably a tapestry woven from tales told by earlier writers to

3. Bronze helmet, Etruscan or Roman, third or second century B.C. Courtesy of the Detroit Institute of Arts.

give this great victory the same status as the ten-year battle for Troy. Marcus Furius Camillus was the hero of the story. He had been chosen dictator to get the job done. Discipline had broken down and soldiers were even running away. Livy says Camillus' stern measures taught "his men that the enemy was not the worst thing they had to fear."

Camillus was at the height of his popularity during the unprecedented four days which the Senate voted should be given over to thanksgiving to the gods. Yet earlier, at Veii, it was said that he slipped as he was about to offer a prayer, and this was taken as an omen that he too would fall. His popularity with the people was indeed short-lived. Generals are often very conservative. Camillus' outspoken condemnation of the undisciplined citizenry at Rome was reminiscent of those other heroes, Coriolanus and Cincinnatus, and politically disastrous for him. He was particularly upset because the plebeians had recently turned against two of their own tribunes who had used their veto powers in ways which were generally unpopular. If each of the tribunes was not allowed to act independently in using the veto, then why have this check at all? Camillus felt they had acted responsibly, but his stout defense of them cost him dearly. Ironically, he was hurried into exile about the time when the Romans needed him most. They were about to inherit a problem which the weakened Etruscan cities could no longer handle: how to contain the restless and dangerous Gauls who lived in the north of Italy.

The Gauls

In 391 B.C., it was a measure of Rome's new importance that the Etruscan city of Clusium turned to her for help against the Gauls rather than to their fellow Etruscans, who were busy guarding their own lands. The Gauls had been roving the region between the Alps and the Apennines for two hundred years. Some of them had settled on lands taken from the Etruscans, and presumably all of them enjoyed the wine which later writers suggested attracted them in the first place. From time to time, of course, new tribes crossed the Alps and, finding the nearby land occupied, roamed southward. It was the Senones, Livy says, who attacked Clusium. Whether their initial success prompted other tribes to join them is not certain.

The Clusini were "allies and friends" of the Roman people who sent an unusual family commission, made up of the three sons of Marcus Fabius Ambustus, to ask the Gauls why they thought themselves entitled to other people's land. They replied first that the Clusini had more land than they needed and second "that all things belonged to the brave." That kind of talk and impetuosity on both sides led to a skirmish. Forgetful of their proper role, the three young Roman envoys joined in the contest and one of them, Quintus Fabius, killed a Gallic chieftain.

The incensed Gauls now sent their own ambassadors to Rome to demand that the three Fabii be turned over to them "in satisfaction for their violation of the law of nations" (V. 36. 8–9). That is what Livy says, although it seems a little early to be talking about international law. The Senate was inclined to agree with the Gauls but nevertheless turned the request over to the people, whose mood was just the opposite. Instead of giving up the Fabii, the people elected them to consular tribunates, an action that undercut the position of the older Gallic leaders who favored negotiation with Rome rather than war. As soon as the Gauls heard what had happened, they started to march. The Romans were caught off guard by the fast movement of events and only managed to intercept the Gauls eleven miles from the capital, where the river Allia flows into the Tiber. Of the Gauls, Livy says, "Their wild songs and discordant shouts filled all the air with a hideous noise" (V. 37. 8). The Gauls won a quick and decisive battle. Their leader, Brennus, had shrewdly directed his attack against the Roman reserves rather than the main army, which was shortly to be overwhelmed by his hordes of followers. Although the Romans might have been expected by temperament and training to behave with their traditional valor, the battle at the Allia was a rout. Many officers and men, unnerved by Gallic might, thought only of getting to Veii instead of Rome, as if knowing in their hearts that their city could not now be saved. Hundreds who ran from the battlefield without even trying to defend themselves were killed trying to escape. Those who had forgotten to remove their heavy armor drowned in the Tiber. But Livy says the majority of the soldiers made it safely to Veii. The rest ran so fast to the citadel at Rome that they did not even bother to close the gates of the city. Maybe they would have failed anyway, with so many people fleeing for refuge in the countryside and neighboring towns. The pursuing Gauls were suspicious to find the gates unguarded and spent a cautious night outside the walls. At dawn, they entered the largely unprotected city. Only the citadel was armed.

The Gauls heard no other voices except their own as they passed through the streets. It was as though they were about to loot a graveyard in which the corpses were still breathing. Sitting just inside open doorways were some of the most distinguished elders of the city, wearing ceremonial robes and seated on curule chairs, which revealed them to have been past holders of the highest magistracies, former dictators, Masters of the Horse, consuls, and censors. These men, too old to fight or share the crowded quarters of the citadel, passively awaited their fate. The story says that one of them struck a Gaul who teasingly stroked his beard. Thus began the slaughter. Looting and burning followed. The city was destroyed and with it every man, woman, or child found outside the citadel. To those few who now stood alone against the barbarian army, Livy offered an eloquent testimony: "Yet, oppressed as they were, or rather overwhelmed by so many misfortunes, nothing could alter their resolve: though they should see everything laid low in flames and ruins, they would stoutly defend the hill they held, however small and naked, which was all that Liberty had left" (V. 42. 7).

It took only one disastrous uphill attack on the Roman position to convince the Gauls that they had no chance of dislodging the Romans on higher ground by any frontal daylight attack. It would take fewer soldiers to camp around the hill and keep food from reaching the beleaguered defenders. The rest of the Gallic army was free to attack surrounding towns. At the same time the Roman soldiers who had fled to Veii recovered their courage and made plans to send some relief to the city. The force at Veii was constantly increased by stragglers and by soldiers from Latium who offered to serve.

Camillus, the exiled hero at Ardea, had already led a force which took a Gallic camp by surprise. He was the natural choice to lead an army to recover the city. But time was needed to get ready, and it was doubtful that the men slowly starving in the citadel could hold out for long. Among the animals as yet uneaten were the geese sacred to Juno. According to the old story they saved everybody after all. The Gauls attempted a nighttime climb, one by one, up the side of the hill. They were quiet enough to escape detection by the guards or dogs, but the geese heard them and set up a terrific commotion. Marcus Manlius, an ex-consul, was able to reach the precipice in time to knock the first Gaul back on top of the others. The citadel was saved, and dramatically so, but time was running out. The enemy was scarcely faring any better. They were short of supplies, and being on low ground were caught in the burned-out city amid the ashes and dust which the winds whirled around them. With both sides looking for an escape, terms were easily arranged. The tribune Quintus Sulpicius offered the Gallic leader Brennus a thousand pounds of gold if he would withdraw. Livy wryly refers to the ransom as "the price of a people" who would soon rule the world. Some humiliation was added, however. When the tribune accused Brennus of using false weights, the chieftain threw his sword into the balance with the blunt statement, "Woe to the conquered!"

The melodrama which Livy unfolds continued with the arrival of Camillus, who had been named dictator. He insisted that the tribune had no business negotiating with Brennus and pronounced the proceedings void. Livy says the Gauls began to fight recklessly and were immediately set back. It appeared that the gods were again on the Roman side. A second battle was fought eight miles from the city where the Gauls regrouped themselves. Here the Romans, inspired by Camillus, drove them off with a vengeance. It would be a long eight centuries before the "barbarians" would take the city again.

After having saved Rome from the Gauls, Camillus had to save the city from the Romans themselves, especially from the plebeians, who wanted to abandon the site and start over at Veii. To Camillus this was tantamount to abandoning the gods. His speech to the people with the Senate in attendance is a fair statement of what religion meant. The gods, in return for obedience to their will and the respect of proper rituals, gave men rewards. He said, in part: "Consider these past few years in order, with their successes and reverses; you will find that all things turned out well when we obeyed the gods, and ill when we spurned them" (V. 51. 5–6). Comparing the present Romans to their ancestors, he urged them not to abandon the temples of the gods: "Our ancestors, refugees and herdsmen, at a time when there was nothing in this region but forests and marshes, built quickly a new City; and are we loath, though Capitol and Citadel are untouched and the temples of the gods are standing, to rebuild what has been destroyed by fire?" (V. 53. 9). The people were willing but in a hurry. The city which resulted was no credit to the Roman reputation for orderliness.

Religion without Love

Religion is a subject which comes up often in Roman history. Yet to say the Romans were a deeply religious people might be misleading. Their religion was not a heartfelt experience in which they thanked a loving god with promises of charity toward their fellow man. They were "religious" in carrying out ceremonies with solemn preciseness; the emphasis was on piety. *Pietas* meant not only dutifulness toward the gods, but also a demonstrative respect for parents and other relatives. In addition, it included a warmth of feeling toward the state which nowadays might be reserved for a church.

Roman rituals, including sacrificial offerings, were to show recognition of the power which the gods wielded. The gods knew the future and controlled all things. Gifts to them were usually made in advance. But a general might also burn captured weapons in gratitude for a victory.

There were skeptics among the Romans as there were among the Greeks. Some men, even without the aid of precision instruments, concluded that the universe operated as a mechanism with set laws. But given the anxieties of life and the mysteries of nature, only a few men were willing to speculate. The rest worshipped a variety of man-like gods whose power they saw revealed in wind and lightning.

Among ancient peoples, the Jews alone gave their allegiance to a single god, one who asked for a different kind of worship. In Amos, the Lord said: "I hate, I despise your feast days, and I will not smell in your solemn assemblies. Though ye offer me burnt offerings and your meat offerings, I will not accept them: neither will I regard the peace offerings of your fat beasts. Take thou away from me the noise of thy songs; for I will not hear the melody of thy viols. But let judgment run down as waters, and righteousness as a mighty stream" (5: 21–24). Primitive Christianity took root in the same message. Worship was to be with the heart and not the hands. One day, conversion to Christianity would mean a radical change for the Romans. Traditionally, they had not viewed religion as a regenerative power working within themselves to change their lives spiritually. They wanted to do whatever was necessary to gain divine help in practical and worldly matters.

The Romans felt their relations with the gods to be contractual. It was typical for the dictator in 431 to promise the gods that he would sponsor a festival of games in their honor if he was successful against the enemy. "You do this for me and I will do that for you" is a common but very human form of prayer. But it is not the same as the prayer which says "Thy will be done."

The Romans were in touch with the gods on a day-to-day basis. The consuls were expected to "take the auspices" by searching the sky for signs before conducting any business. Especially important were messages which came from birds. An outcry from one of them rendered the proceedings ineffective. Otherwise, the direction of their flight was observed; the manner in which eagles and vultures flew was considered significant. An inspection of the entrails of sacrificial animals gave further clues to the will of the gods. When decisions of more than ordinary importance were to be made, as on a day of battle, there were special techniques for learning what the chances for success might be. A Roman general kept a chicken coop on hand. If the keeper threw the chickens grain and they only pecked at it, the answer was negative. If they ate excitedly, it was a sign to go ahead. It is not surprising that those who watched the chickens were at times impatient with the answers. On the eve of a battle in 293, the Roman soldiers were eager for action, and the keeper of the chickens caught the fever. He declared that the auspices were favorable even though the chickens had refused the grain. Later, rumors about this false report reached the consul's nephew, who after his own investigation dutifully reported to his uncle what had happened. "The young man," said Livy, in an oblique reference to his own time, "had been born before the learning that makes light of the gods" (X. 40. 10). But the consul, as eager for the battle as the rest of his army, said he would proceed as planned. The man who had lied was to be left to the gods with an assist from the consul, who put him in the front lines. He was killed almost immediately. His death was considered a sign of the gods' concurrence and hence their favor in that the general had so quickly punished his sacrilegious aide. The Romans pressed on to victory.

As would be true of any people, some Romans, although not skeptics, were still less susceptible to irrational fears than were the majority. But Livy remarked that at a time of extreme stress even the leaders became superstitious. Obviously, they were not usually excited by every report of a strange sign. Nor perhaps were average citizens, unless the times were so bad as to make everybody jittery or unless several omens confirmed one another. Many persons saw portents; but if they saw them alone, they might have a hard time convincing others, then as now.

Roman religion had many superstitious aspects, but it would be wrong to think of a whole people being equally affected. A passage in Livy is particularly significant. During the years 430–427 B.C., the city and its environs were again struck by an epidemic, an ill wind which meant good times for the numerous charlatans who lived off the fears of their fellow citizens, enough so for foreign cure-peddlers to find a profitable market in the city. Livy said the better educated Romans were appalled at this spectacle, and the aediles were soon busy putting a stop to the "business." Sacrifices were to be made only to the traditional gods and to be performed in the standard way.

But maybe the charlatans were not the only ones taking advantage. At times, the tribunes charged that patrician officials made use of alleged occurrences to manipulate the fears of the average citizen and hold up public business in the process. The year 461 B.C. was tense as the plebeians pressed for new concessions. It was also a big year for unaccountable events. Livy gave a report of strange happenings, as he frequently did, without offering any personal opinion about them. "This year the heavens were seen to blaze, and the earth was shaken with a prodigious quake. That a cow had spoken—a thing which had found no credence the year before—was now believed. Among other portents there was even a rain of flesh, which is said to have been intercepted by vast numbers of birds flying round in the midst of it; what fell to the ground lay scattered about for several days, but without making any stench" (III. 10. 6–7). Patrician officials saw these portents as warnings of an external danger to the state; the tribunes saw the whole business as internal politics. So said Livy, but at that time such trickery was unlikely. In later times, the auspices were actually manipulated by skeptical politicians.

Today, most people expect public officials to take emergency economic measures or to initiate defense programs or maybe just to pass flood control legislation. In ancient times, when there was trouble, the first priority was to get things right with the gods. There were various actions the priests and magistrates could take, depending on the degree of the catastrophe. Usually, the sacrifice of a few animals would do. If the consul's spear was taken by the enemy, expiation would be offered to Mars by the sacrifice of three animals: a pig, a sheep, and an ox. For greater trouble, a special sacrifice of numerous sheep or oxen might be made to show the anxiety of the worshippers and their desire to please.

At Rome, serious trouble called for special action. To learn what it might be, a commission consulted the Sibylline books, a collection of oracles valued above all others. It was believed that Tarquin the Proud had obtained these writings of ancient origin from the renowned Sibyl of Cumae, a priestess of Apollo, and, according to legend, a shrewd one to bargain with. When the king at first refused to buy the nine books because of the price, the priestess is said to have burned six of them and then sold him the remaining three for what she had asked for the complete set. The tradition says Tarquin deposited his costly purchase in the temple of Jupiter on the Capitoline and appointed two patricians, the *duumviri,* to be their guardians. The books did not tell the future, but they were believed to reveal the course of action needed to mitigate the effects of a dire event. For instance, in 433–432 B.C., the *duumviri* interpreted the books to mean that a new temple to

4. Jupiter Capitolinus. Courtesy of the Metropolitan Museum of Art. Gift of Henry G. Marquand, 1897.

Apollo must be built for the sake of allaying an epidemic. But the promise to Apollo did not abate the severity of the plague.

On certain grave occasions a *lectisternium* was ordered by those who consulted the Sibylline books. The rite consisted of setting up a table and couches holding images of the gods reclining and being served with an elaborate feast. The grandeur of the city ceremony was recreated on a lesser scale in individual homes, even as commemorative Christmas tableaux have both a public and private level. Today, the *lectisternium* may sound childlike in its naiveté. Yet it is human for men to feel it necessary to do something in the face of anxiety about the unknown.

Two passages in Livy which suggest a more sophisticated attitude about the gods give balance to the usual view of Roman religion. The Romans believed not only that the gods could hurl thunderbolts and stir up the seas, but that they worked indirectly through men. In 384 B.C., when the ex-war hero Manlius was at odds with his fellow patricians, he called on the plebeians whom he had championed to save him from being killed. He said, "You do well to express abhorrence. The gods *will* forbid such a thing; but they will never come down from heaven on my account; they must give you the inspiration to forbid it, as they gave me, in war and in peace, the inspiration to defend you from the barbarity of your foes and the arrogance of your fellow citizens" (VI. 18. 9–10). Another passage about divine justice follows the same pattern: "The gods themselves never laid hands upon the guilty; it was enough if they armed with an opportunity for vengeance those who had been wronged" (V. 11. 16).

Livy's own view of religion was that of an educated man who had not wandered off into speculation, on guard about the foolishness that often crept in but at the same time an orthodox believer. For instance, speaking of 312 B.C., he accepted a report that a prominent family died out within a year because it had taught certain rituals to slaves. That event, Livy said, should make men think twice about overturning the religious customs of the past.

The state employed several boards of priests or priestesses, each with special duties and various degrees of prestige. The usual description of the Vestal Virgins gives the impression of six statues standing in a row. The young women chosen were undoubtedly selected for their serious demeanor, in keeping with the sanctity of their role. Individuality was not appreciated, and one young Vestal who happened to have a sense of humor was soon in trouble. In 420 B.C., a girl named Postumia was found innocent of the charge of "unchastity," but the *pontifex maximus* gave her fair warning to stop making clever remarks and start dressing more conservatively. Others were less fortunate. In 337 B.C., a Vestal Virgin was buried alive for having broken her vow of chastity. Her own slaves testified against her and the high priests were prepared to believe them. They had observed the daring way in which this particular Vestal Virgin had been dressing.

A New Enemy

In 345 B.C., the Romans were drawn into a series of protracted wars with tribes known collectively as the Samnites, who inhab-

5. Samnite warrior. The Louvre. Photograph courtesy of Maurice Chuzeville.

ited the central Apennine mountains. E.T. Salmon's book *Samnium and the Samnites,* a cautious modern scrutiny of the ancient sources on these wars, says of the Samnites: "They were numerous enough and spirited enough to refuse to submit tamely to Rome, and the military and political opposition that they put up against her was of the toughest. It is a commonplace that they, and they alone, were the really redoubtable rivals of Rome for the hegemony of peninsular Italy, and they came within measurable distance of winning it" (p. 1).

Many of the people living in the plains south of Latium, particularly Campania, were themselves descendants of Samnite pioneers who had come in search of land. These settlers mingled with the earlier population and shared in the growing prosperity of the plains. In time, relatively large cities became centers of a civilized life much advanced over the rough and rudimentary towns of the mountains. The settled conditions of the plains meant barriers to the herdsmen of the hills, who during the winter were wont to bring their flocks to the surrounding grassy areas. In brief, farmers and ranchers fought over fences. Furthermore, the people of the plains discouraged further Samnite migrations lest their own area become overcrowded. As a rule, ancient writers like Livy said little about the underlying geographic or economic problems. Livy simply wrote that the Samnites attacked their near neighbors, the Sidicini, because they felt they could defeat them. The Sidicini appealed to the Campanians for help, but soon found that their allies had grown soft with luxury and were no match for the hardy Samnites.

Before long, Capua, the foremost city of Campania, found itself besieged and appealed to the Romans for aid. The question which the Campanian envoys put to the Senate explains how the Samnite wars got started. "Should Capua and all Campania augment Rome's power, or that of Samnium?" The collapse of Campanian resistance had created a vacuum. Presumably, the Romans did not originally intend to dominate this region, but their decision to intervene set in motion a series of contingent events which amounted to the same thing. First, ambassadors were sent to the Samnites to warn them to leave the Campanians alone. The Romans had had friendly relations, even alliances, with the Samnites. In the past, interests had not conflicted. Now they did. Roman envoys were rudely treated; an order was given in their presence for an attack on Campania. The Roman people had been insulted. The Senate sent *fetiales,* priestly officials who lent sanctity to Roman negotiations. They gave the Samnites a chance to change their minds. When the Samnites refused, the *fetiales* declared war in the formal and solemn Roman way. So began the First Samnite War, 343–341 B.C. As Salmon observes (pp. 195–200), Livy's account of the war was undoubtedly based on material more inspired by patriotism than dedicated to accuracy; but this need not mean, as it has been speculated, that there was no war at all.

Livy's remark that the war was fought by the Romans with only varying success is a telling understatement. The Romans were soon to admit that the Samnites were the toughest fighters they had ever faced. Early success in Campania was offset by reverses in Samnium, where haste and unfamiliarity with the country meant unexpected traps. Livy records the heroism of certain Romans and the rewards heaped on them. In 341 B.C., the Samnites, anxious to be done with the tenacious Romans, asked for peace and a renewal of the old treaty of friendship. After blaming the Samnites for all that had happened and being assured that Campania was safe, the Senate agreed. The Sidicini, who had never directly sought Roman help, were left unprotected and were attacked again as soon as the Romans went home. That was how the former war had started. Now the Latins and Campanians, emboldened by Rome's relative success against the Samnites, began their own forays into Samnium. Soon, the Romans were hearing complaints from the Samnites, who asked them to control their allies. This was embarrassing. Rome's relations with the Latins had deteriorated seriously.

A Final Reckoning

If the Romans thought that trouble could be forestalled by inviting Latin leaders to Rome to discuss their differences, they were in for a surprise. The Latins had been flexing their muscles of late, and now made threatening noises. They demanded total equality with the Romans, including the sharing of the consulship and the Senate. The Latin position was the same as the one taken by the plebeians at Rome in the previous century. They said if their manpower was needed, they expected to have a voice about where and how it was used.

One of the consuls, Titus Manlius, was shocked, or at least appeared to be. He recalled the battle at Lake Regillus, a much celebrated event of 496 B.C. in which, according to Roman tradition, the gods Castor and Pollux had led the Romans to victory over their near neighbors. Was it forgotten, he asked, how fair the Romans had been then? That was not the point. The Latins thought they could win. Thus began the Latin War, 340–338 B.C.

The final test of strength was bound to be bitter. Weapons, style of fighting, and discipline were much alike on both sides. In the end, outstanding leadership by the Roman consuls made the difference. Even the death of one of them in the first major battle served the Roman cause by firing his soldiers with renewed spirit.

The Samnites had hesitated to send help to Rome and only showed up after the battle was over. On the other side, the Lavinians exhausted themselves discussing whether they should go to the aid of the Latins or not. They were finally on their way, when news reached them that the Latins had lost a battle. As they turned around, one of their leaders made the apt remark that "they would have to pay a large price to the Romans for that little march" (VIII. 2. 4).

After a second major victory in the same year, 340 B.C., the Romans began confiscating land from both the Latins and any Campanians who had helped them. New farms were to be made available to the Roman plebeians. The Latins, angry and humiliated, fought on two more years. In 338, several of their towns lost hope and surrendered. The rest were attacked and forced to give in. When the war was over, the Romans did not dictate blanket terms but treated each place separately according to the intensity of the local feelings toward Rome. In the long run the Romans were well served by the common sense with which they treated former enemies. They gained not by fear alone but by forgiveness; an enemy was beaten and then given fair treatment. Added to respect was gratitude. In later times, the Romans had to depend on these former enemies, and their loyalty proved the wisdom of Rome's policy. The argument against a harsh peace was well stated in the Senate. The Romans could not expect the defeated to become faithful friends if they were treated as though they were slaves.

As a result of the Latin War, the Lanuvini, Aricini, Nomentani and Pedani were given full Roman citizenship. The Veliterni, who already possessed citizenship and had betrayed their fellow citizens, had their walls torn down and colonists put on some of their lands. At Antium, citizenship was granted, but warships were confiscated. A Roman colony was established there as a safeguard. The Tiburtines and Praenestini both lost land because of their part in the Latin cause, not to mention that at an earlier time they had sided with the Gauls. The other Latin towns were kept divided by a prohibition against trading, intermarriage, or political dealings. The Campanians were given citizenship but without the right to vote. Full Roman citizenship was given only to those whom the Romans trusted the most. The rest were promised rewards for good behavior and punishments for making trouble. That was the pattern for the future.

The Samnites Again

A new war with the Samnites loomed. In 330 B.C., two Volscian cities, long-time enemies of Rome, felt sufficiently threatened by the Samnites to ask for Roman protection. There could be no better proof of Rome's dominant role in central Italy. The Samnites kept quiet because they were not ready for another war. Further incidents in the next few years made one inevitable, particularly since Rome was having troubles with the Greek cities which had fallen within her orbit. Neapolis (modern Naples) mistreated some Roman citizens living nearby and made matters worse by a rude answer to Rome's protest. This bluster did not surprise Livy, who with an obvious Roman bias suggested that the Greeks as a people were "more valiant in words than in deeds." If the Greeks needed help it was readily available. After the Romans had declared war against Neapolis, the Samnites sent four thousand soldiers into the city. These local clashes belonged to the larger question of whether Samnites or Romans would dominate the peninsula. That was the issue in the Second Samnite War, 327–304 B.C.

The city of Neapolis was besieged by a Roman army led by the consul Quintus Publilius Philo, who became the first magistrate to hold his powers beyond the end of his term. With the city about to fall it seemed impractical to relieve him of his duty. He was hence given the title of proconsul for the duration of the campaign by a special act of the assembly. In the future, the proconsulship would enable a man of experience to be used on special assignments. It also kept down the number of new magistrates required. The use of proconsuls was obviously favored by the office-holding families, whether patrician or plebeian, since expansion of the magistracy would in the long run bring in new men to share the power.

No sooner did Neapolis surrender than the Romans were at odds with Tarentum (modern Taranto), the major Greek city on the southern coast of Italy. That the Lucanians and Apulians had been quick to join the Roman side only made the Tarentines more defiant, for they felt themselves surrounded. All of southern Italy seemed in danger of being overwhelmed. Who could know that Rome was shortly to suffer one of the greatest disasters of her history? The Caudine Forks was a never-to-be-forgotten place of humiliation and infamy. The truce with the Samnites in 323 B.C. was shaky, and the war was resumed in 322. In 321, the Romans heard that one of their allies, the city of Luceria, was being besieged in Apulia and that the Lucerini were on the verge of surrender. The Samnites had spread this false report themselves, and it brought the desired result. The consuls, in great haste to save

6. Temple of Poseidon, Paestum, Italy, *ca*. 450 B.C. Courtesy of the Italian Government Travel Office, Chicago.

the region, chose the worst possible route. Because the road along the Adriatic seemed too long, they hurried toward a place well known to the Samnites. The Caudine Forks was a defile surrounded by mountains, with a narrow wooded passageway at either end. Once the Roman army was on the road through the defile, they were trapped. The footsoldiers on the campaign never ceased talking about the almost incredible neglect of the officers who had failed to scout the exit. They found it blocked, as was the entrance by the time they realized what had happened.

A Samnite elder cautioned against treating the encircled Romans harshly, for he correctly forecast that such treatment would never convert them to friends, but only move them to revenge. It was that kind of practicality by which the Romans were building their powerful confederation in Italy. But one wise old Samnite was not a Senate, and the Romans were intentionally humiliated. They were ordered to pass unarmed under a yoke and then to retreat from Samnite territory. Of course they could have refused and died, but how would that have helped Rome? The consuls said nothing. One of the ex-consuls (327 B.C.) present, Lucius Cornelius Lentulus, reminded the soldiers that by submitting they would at least save an army of experienced men. To resist would be the loss of everything. The Romans had

7. Temple of Ceres, Paestum, Italy, *ca*. 525 B.C. Courtesy of the Italian Government Travel Office, Chicago.

8. Temple of Ceres (another view), Paestum, Italy. Courtesy of the Italian Government Travel Office, Chicago.

given gold to the Gauls to save their city. This time it would be pride.

The rank and file were angry and confused. They felt their consuls had been utterly irresponsible. Yet, though they cursed them they still looked away when their generals were denied the company of lictors and sent half-naked under the yoke. Their officers followed according to rank and then the legionaries.

The Romans marched home in sullen silence past the eyes of those they had once conquered. To some onlookers they seemed crushed, defeated without even a chance to fight. Others sensed that downcast eyes reflected determination. They were not thinking of those who saw them go by but only of revenge. When the legions arrived in Rome, the terms which had been made with the Samnites were immediately repudiated and the officers who had agreed to them were according to custom turned over to the enemy. In the Roman mind that put the clock back. The Samnites could punish those who had given them a false peace without the consent of the people. The war went on.

In 320 and 319 B.C., the Romans won a series of bloody engagements and, fired by their rage, destroyed even property they might have seized. Finally, they reached the Samnite stronghold of Luceria. Here they had their revenge. It was the Samnites' turn to pass under the yoke. The Romans recovered their standards lost at the Caudine Forks, along with their weapons. Livy recorded this restoration of power as being one of the most momentous events in Roman history and was anxious to believe the old stories about the commander of all the Samnite forces being sent under the yoke to avenge the treatment of the Roman consuls.

The Roman successes in 319 B.C. led to a two-year truce with many of the Samnite cities. All were not involved, however, and the war continued to drag on for several more years, although it was now apparent that the Romans would prevail. They knew it themselves and began to build for the future.

Making Friends from Enemies

One day the Roman Empire would be tied together by a network of excellent roads. The first main artery, the Appian Way, was begun in 312 B.C. under the auspices of the irascible old censor Appius Claudius. His name still lives because the Appian Way is still in use. Originally, the road was built from Rome to Capua. Later, it went to Beneventum and eventually to the port city of Brundisium (modern Brindisi). It was the prime means by which the Romans could control the region. In years to come, legions would move swiftly to the south and embark at Brundisium for duty overseas.

An aqueduct to bring fresh water to Rome was another of Appius Claudius' projects; it helped to make him the best remembered of all the men by the same name who appear in the pages of Roman history. His contemporaries were divided in their opinion of him for two reasons. He ruthlessly purged the Senate, and he tried to hold on to the censorship past the eighteen-month limit. His unpopularity in certain quarters gave currency to the claim that his later blindness was a judgment by the gods.

As the fourth century was drawing to a close, the Romans strengthened their hold on the Italian peninsula in different ways. They continued to win the last battles with those who resisted them, additional colonies gave them a presence in new areas, and their institutions began to have an impact on the diverse peoples now allied to them. As early as 318 B.C. the Romans were giving their allies laws as well as protection. For all of Rome's own domestic turmoil, conflicts elsewhere were often worse. Others envied the relative stability which the Romans had achieved through established laws strictly enforced. When a town asked for assistance, the Romans would send a commission to draw up a code of laws suitable for local needs and even to administer it while the townspeople gained the experience of living according to the Roman style. In 318, Capua asked that Roman officials be sent to help with her affairs. Another fifty years would pass before Rome would control Italy, but obviously a great capital was in the making.

In 311 B.C., one consul, Quintus Aemilius Barbula, was busy with a serious threat resulting from a widespread uprising by the Etruscans. The other consul, Gaius Junius Bubulcus, led the annual Samnite campaign. The Romans won major victories against both these enemies, albeit with heavy losses. In 312 B.C., the major Etruscan cities sought peace and were given a thirty-year truce. That enabled the Romans to concentrate on their war with the Samnites, which seemed to be winding down gradually. By 304, the Samnites said they were again ready for peace, but they were not the only people whom the Romans had known to talk about peace while getting ready for war. The way to be sure of their intentions was to insist on "inspection"—an old-new solution which modern nuclear powers discuss. The Romans sent an army under the consul, Publius Sempronius, to sweep through Samnite country with an eye on any suspicious signs. The consul reported to the Senate that he was satisfied the Samnites were telling the truth. The old treaty of friendship (354 B.C.) was renewed.

At the same time, old truces were being broken. Trouble erupted with the Etruscans in 309 B.C. and again in 302. After defeating them the second time, the Romans granted only a short truce so they could test the Etruscan mood for more lasting arrangements. In 298, they were challenged anew by the Samnites. By this time these old enemies had occupied land belonging to Rome's allies and when told to leave had answered with a familiar defiance. So began the Third Samnite War (298–290 B.C.)

Within two years the Samnites succeeded in gathering together a greater coalition than Rome had ever faced. It was a last-ditch effort. The Etruscans, Umbrians, and Gauls (who Livy says were hired) joined together with a Samnite army in northern Italy. The Romans were already heavily engaged in the south because the Samnites had again attacked in Campania. The threat in the north created near panic in Rome. Even the city itself was now thought to be in danger. The Senate ordered the courts to be closed—a sure sign of the gravity of the situation. News from the consul, Lucius Volumnius, about a victory over the Samnites in Campania brought a measure of relief, but Rome did not feel safe until after the crucial battle at Sentinum in 295 B.C. Fortunately for the Romans, they did not have to face all four enemies at once. The Etruscans and Umbrians were diverted to protect their own territories. At Sentinum, the Romans managed to overwhelm the Gauls and Samnites, with whom they were almost evenly matched. Livy did not believe all the patriotic stories told about the battle, and, in his opinion, earlier writers had greatly overestimated the numbers involved on both sides. Still, the result was momentous.

The battle of Sentinum had decided the future of Italy. At least that is apparent now if not at the time. Then it seemed that no matter how many victories the Romans won, they continued to have trouble in both Etruria and Samnium. The successes of 295 B.C. by no means brought the compliance they sought. This was disheartening, for Roman losses in the wars with the Samnites were especially severe, so much so that Livy writes they could scarcely rejoice about a victory which meant the loss of 7,800 men in two days. In 293, news of a victory against the Samnites arrived about the same time as did a message telling of new uprisings in Etruria. The Romans were lucky in that most of the time they were only seriously threatened in one place or the other. But while they were putting out one fire, news of their trouble inspired another.

This sporadic warfare continued to 280 B.C., when the Romans were faced with a new major challenge headed by a dynamic leader. The Greek seaport of Tarentum, located on the instep of the Italian "boot," was determined to remain independent of Rome and if possible to maintain her own sphere of influence in southern Italy. Her fleet, the largest in Italy, patrolled the coastal waters, and on land her armies had fought a series of wars with hostile Italian neighbors. When Thurii, a Greek city which formerly sought Tarentum's protection, turned to Rome instead, in 282, it was a signal for others to follow. The Tarentines had sooner or later to take a stand against Rome or become isolated.

As they had in the past, the Tarentines again looked to Greece for a commander to mastermind their war effort. Pyrrhus, the king of Epirus (*ca.* 318–272 B.C.), accepted their invitation because it was an uncommon opportunity for himself. Someone once compared Pyrrhus to a good dice player who never made much out of the game. In his lifetime he knew many successes but they never added up to anything impressive. His gains in one direction were generally dissipated while he was on some new adventure. Contemporaries ranked him highly as a leader of men and a general but they were put off by his restlessness and his ambition for fighting as an end in itself. Everybody called him an adventurer—an erratic one. The Romans were lucky that he was.

It was Pyrrhus, not Hannibal, who brought the first elephants to Italy. The Roman soldiers were thrown into a panic to see these enormous "tanks" lurching toward them. Their horses were disturbed by the scent. But it was not by surprise alone that Pyrrhus won the battle of Heraclea in 280 B.C. He was a skilled tactician and greatly enjoyed the art of war. On the other hand, his army suffered severe casualties without actually destroying the Roman capacity to fight again. Later at Ausculum, about eighty-seven miles northeast of Rome, he announced after a similar experience that another such victory would be his undoing. But his "Pyrrhic victories" were not his only trouble. The Roman allies remained loyal and refused to consider any of his overtures. Consequently, he would have welcomed a settlement with Rome, and there were those in the Senate who would have given it to him. However, tradition has an aged and blind Appius Claudius being carried into the Senate to protest any accommodation with this foreign king, who was probably dreaming of an empire of his own in southern Italy and Sicily. His emotional appeal, joined as it was with a promise of assistance from powerful Carthage, ended the negotiations.

Pyrrhus' prospects suddenly looked better in Sicily, where the Greek cities urgently needed his leadership in holding off a new threat from the Carthaginians, who controlled the western half of the island. Although Pyrrhus was successful in helping the Greeks, he was too successful for his own good. His presence and ambitions now became another kind of burden. The Greeks decided to make their own terms with the enemy. Pyrrhus therefore went back to Italy where he fought and lost his last battle with the Romans at Beneventum in 275 B.C. He then returned to Greece, where three years later he died in a curious way during a battle at Argos. An old woman standing on the top of a house saw Pyrrhus challenging her son and hurled a tile which so stunned the famous warrior as to leave him helpless against an enemy officer, who cut his head off. In that same year, 272, Tarentum surrendered to Rome and became an ally with a watchful Roman garrison present to insure her loyalty.

Minor troubles remained here and there in Italy, but by 265 B.C. these mopping up operations were over. All the peoples of Italy who did not already have full Roman citizenship or at least certain privileges of citizens were gathered into a confederation. Some of the allies were allowed to intermarry with the Romans and to trade and hold property in Rome with the full protection of her laws. All of the allies were required to have the "same friends and enemies" as the Romans and in time of war to supply ships or offer trained soldiers for her service.

The success of this arrangement, as mentioned earlier, was due largely to common sense. The Roman Senate did not arrive at the separate treaties by the book but sent commissioners to investigate local problems in order to achieve an agreement convenient to both parties. The respect for local autonomy in most matters where such independence seemed desirable gave the Romans a well deserved reputation for combining firm authority with sensible dealings. In later years of the third century B.C., the Roman Republic would go through its darkest days. That the Romans had recently converted enemies into good friends was one reason they survived.

IV

Rome Against Carthage

The story of how the Romans began to build their empire was written by a Greek who came to Rome as a hostage. In 167 B.C., the Romans felt it necessary to hold captive a thousand sons of the Achaean League to insure the peaceful behavior of their fathers and fellow citizens. Polybius (*ca.* 200–*ca.* 117 B.C.), an Achaean in his early thirties, was well educated and already known as a writer. Scipio Aemilianus, who was prominent in Roman politics and an admirer of all things Greek, had met Polybius in Greece and found him to be excellent company. Exchanging books and discussing them led to a lifelong friendship. Scipio introduced Polybius to the best circles in Rome and even took him along as a companion on his campaigns overseas. As the years passed, Polybius, a most congenial hostage, became convinced that the Romans were a people peculiarly gifted in the art of government. They could discipline others because they had learned to discipline themselves. One purpose in writing his history was to show "by what means, and under what kind of polity, almost the whole inhabited world was conquered and brought under the dominion of the single city of Rome, and that too within a period of not quite fifty-three years" (I. 1). That it was fortunate would be seen from his discussion of Roman institutions.

As an historian, Polybius said he intended to be impartial. "Holding ourselves, therefore, entirely aloof from the actors, we must as historians make statements and pronounce judgment in accordance with the actions themselves" (I. 14). His disinterestedness obviously did not extend to other writers. He made frequent criticisms of earlier historians, particularly Timaeus (*ca.* 345–250 B.C.), whom he accused of carelessness and a failure to make sound judgments about the credibility of his witnesses. In fact, Timaeus was not even capable of properly reporting what he saw for himself. Polybius called him "a carping, false and impudent writer; . . . unphilosophical, and, in short, utterly uninstructed" (XII. 25). His comment had a certain impudence of its own; but judging Polybius by his works, he was certainly entitled to sit in judgment on Timaeus. His history of Rome for the years 220 to 146 B.C., with introductory material going back to 264, was carefully written, although unfortunately much of it survives only in fragments. Polybius was cautious about his sources and anxious to be fair. In his opinion, history was practical because it was instructive of human behavior: "The knowledge gained from the study of true history is the best of all educations for practical life. For it is history, and history alone, which, without involving us in actual danger, will mature our judgment and prepare us to take right views, whatever may be the crisis or the posture of affairs" (I. 35). For this reason Polybius insisted on the plain truth. Chiding other historians for their ignorance of geography, he occasionally gave out misinformation of his own, however, as in his inaccurate description of the Rhone Valley. He also shows bias here and there; for instance, he did not like the Aetolians or the Boeotians. Yet, all in all, he is a trustworthy guide to the tumultuous years of Roman empire-building.

The First Punic War

The Romans fought their first war outside of Italy over a city in Sicily. Messana (modern Messina), along with the already friendly Rhegium on the mainland, dominated the straits between Sicily and the toe of the Italian peninsula. The Romans knew the significance of Messana but could not know that their arrival in this city would mark the beginning of an era of conquest by which the whole Mediterranean region would be brought under their control. The Romans did not intervene at Messana necessarily because they wanted to rule the city, but to prevent others from doing so, particularly the Carthaginians, a seafaring people whose home city was situated in what is now Tunisia, that area of the North African coast closest to Sicily. They were of Phoenician stock; from the Latin form of their name, *Poeni,* we have the name of the Punic Wars.

Carthage was built by colonists from Tyre. The actual founding of the city probably occurred later than the traditional date of 814 B.C., sometime during the early eighth century. True to its Phoenician heritage, the city sent out its own seafaring tradesmen to establish commercial settlements whereby goods became widely exchanged in the western Mediterranean. A special source of wealth was the transport of metals, including tin and gold. In the sixth century B.C., by the time the Persians had taken over the eastern Mediterranean coastal area, including the Phoenician homeland, Carthage had begun to build an empire of her own. Her preponderant role as a commercial power was evident in contacts with Rome. There has been much discussion about three treaties between these two cities, one presumably dating from shortly after the founding of the Republic, the second to around 348 B.C., and the third aimed at Pyrrhus in 279 B.C. The very existence of the first treaty and the date of the second have been contested. It would appear, however, that since Carthage did enter into agreements with both Etruscan and Greek cities about matters of mutual interest, Rome would have been included sooner or later. The earliest treaties show that the Romans had no sizeable overseas trade to protect, and the clauses excluding them from competing with Carthaginian merchants in certain areas like Spain were obviously no hardship. In return, the Carthaginians were expected to refrain from establishing colonies in Italy.

The Greek cities of southern Italy and Sicily were the major competitors of Carthage in international markets. Not until after Rome had extended her protection over the Italian peninsula did she become involved in the age-old concern for the control of certain waterways, the Straits of Messana being a case in point. Carthage, the major naval power of the western Mediterranean, was bound to be touchy about seaways. Her empire in its heyday included not only the coastal areas of North Africa and southern Spain but also the islands of Sardinia and Corsica, and the western half of Sicily. It even extended to trading stations on the Atlantic coast beyond Gibraltar.

Political power in Carthage was held by an oligarchy of wealthy businessmen who took responsibility for the prosperity of the city and the security of its interests abroad. As the Latin poet Ennius put it they "peddled" their wars, which is to say that mercenaries were hired by Carthage from all parts of the Mediterranean world and especially from neighboring peoples, the Libyans and Numidians in particular. They served, however, under Carthaginian commanders who were professional soldiers. A son was trained by his father, as Hamilcar had raised Hannibal in the famous Barca family. This professionalism gave the Carthaginians an advantage over the Romans, who instead of relying on skilled generals put their armies in the hands of annual consuls, who were inevitably of uneven quality. On the other hand, the suspicions and rivalries between the civilian rulers at Carthage and the experienced generals who conducted their wars was a serious weakness. One of the reasons Carthage lost the Punic wars was that she did not have the kind of "constitutional" stability which the Romans possessed after 287 B.C. Interestingly enough, when later on, in the first century B.C., the Romans created special commands for favored generals, they suffered the same kind of rivalry and the instability which went with it.

Before the First Punic War (264–241 B.C.) began, the city of Messana had fallen under the domination of a group of mercenaries, the Mamertines, who had come from Campania and taken Messana by treachery. Once in control, they needed assistance in protecting the city from the Carthaginians and Syracusans and asked the Romans to extend their protective shield to include the straits and Messana. The request set off a vigorous debate at Rome. The average Roman citizen had misgivings about dealing with the cutthroats who ruled Messana. Roman officials were more concerned that, like it or not, Rome's interests extended to sea, for she now controlled the longest coastline in the Mediterranean. Magna Graecia included all the Greek cities of southern Italy, the chief commercial competitors of the Carthaginians. Their problems had become Rome's problems. If Carthage managed to conquer Messana and Syracuse she would control Sicily— a convenient base from which to attack Italy. Prevention was the strongest argument for intervention. Senators who thought so talked of financial gain for civilians and soldiers alike, which helped to arouse some support, since the recent struggles with the Italic tribes, and the war with Tarentum, concluded in 272, had been costly. Still, the Senate was skeptical about the project and divided enough to defer judgment. The decision was left up to the people, and in this instance it was probably made by the Centuriate Assembly. With mixed motives and little enthusiasm, Rome sent an expeditionary force in 264 B.C., under the consul Appius Claudius (not to be confused with the famous censor of a generation earlier). He first drove off the Carthaginian and Syracusan forces besieging Messana and then attacked Syracuse. Roman standards were in Sicily to stay. The real enemy of course was Carthage.

In the protracted war over Sicily, a severe test of strength, the Romans proved their mettle. Polybius says, "It would not be easy to mention any war that lasted longer than this one; nor one in which the preparations made were on a larger scale, or the efforts made more sustained, or the actual engagements more numerous, or the reverses sustained on either side more signal" (I. 13). At the outset, several Sicilian cities decided to take their chances with the Romans. Hostility toward the Carthaginians was the usual result of years of occupation. Hiero, the king of Syracuse, also decided to submit to the Romans and signed a treaty of friendship with them.

The Carthaginians, alarmed by the suddenness with which Sicily seemed to be slipping away, assembled Ligurian, Celtic, and Iberian mercenaries at Agrigentum, their base of operations near the southern coast of Sicily. Additional fighters were hired from North Africa. The Romans reacted by besieging Agrigentum, and after five months the fifty thousand men shut up in the city began to feel the strain. Their commander appealed to the home government for a relief force. It arrived, equipped with elephants. The Romans, weakened by an epidemic in their camp, still managed to win the set battle which followed. Although they carelessly permitted the troops inside the city to slip away the same night, the city was taken and there was cause for rejoicing. Everything so far in Sicily had gone the Romans' way. Yet, nothing had been decided, nor were the Romans even in command. The Carthaginians had the advantage so long as they controlled the sea.

The Romans had never had a navy, but would need one if they were going to push the Carthaginians out of Sicily. A major-

ity of the Senate were now determined to build Roman sea
power, and that meant starting from the water's edge. Polybius
says: "There could be no more signal proof of the courage, or
rather the extraordinary audacity of the Roman enterprise." They
also had some luck. A Carthaginian ship grounded in the Straits
of Messana fell into Roman hands and became the model for their
shipbuilders. Even before the first ship was launched, the Romans
were busy with simulated exercises on the land by which they
practiced rowing. It would take more time to produce experienced commanders. In 260 B.C., the consul Gnaeus Cornelius
Scipio was trapped in the port of Lipara and lost seventeen ships
the first time at sea. But Roman ingenuity soon produced better
news. A device was developed, consisting essentially of a plank
which could be dropped by a pulley and secured with a spike onto
the deck of the enemy ship. By means of this "bridge," the Romans, who did their best fighting hand to hand, could continue to
do so. Polybius says that in an engagement off the coast near
Mylae in 260, the Carthaginians were caught by surprise, being
forced to fight as though they were on land instead of the sea. The
resulting confusion cost them many lives and fifty ships. The
other consul, Gaius Duilius, who had commanded the Roman
fleet, was given many honors in Rome, including the first naval
triumph, for this first major victory.

For the next three years the two fleets traded blows the way
boxers do in preliminary flurries. Another major test came in 256
B.C. near Ecnomus. Again the Roman technique of grappling and
boarding the Carthaginian ships won the day. The Romans then
landed in North Africa on Cape Bon, and after a siege took Aspis,
located there. They soon captured other cities, including Tunis,
from which an assault could be launched on Carthage. There was
much to encourage the consul Regulus. Carthage was overcrowded and short of food, as families from the surrounding area
poured in to escape not only the Romans but the Numidians, who
now chose to ravage the country on their own behalf. Regulus
wanted to use these advantages to win a great victory before he
could be relieved by the next consul. He obviously wanted a
victory more than peace. His harsh terms to the Carthaginians
ruled out the latter. But no sooner had they turned down his offer
than their prospects began to improve. From Sparta came a soldier of fortune, Xanthippus, who was bold enough to tell the
Carthaginians that they could win by replacing their mediocre

generals with one good one. They chose him and he kept his word. By a particularly sagacious disposition of elephants, he soundly defeated the Romans and amidst the rout captured Regulus. The story of a stunning upset gave Polybius a chance to lecture his reader:

> This event conveys many useful lessons to a thoughtful observer. Above all, the disaster of Regulus gives the clearest possible warning that no one should feel too confident of the favors of fortune, especially in the hour of success. . . . For it was one man, one brain, that defeated the numbers which were believed to be invincible and able to accomplish anything; and restored to confidence a whole city that was unmistakably and utterly ruined, and the spirits of its army which had sunk to the lowest depths of despair. I record these things in the hope of benefiting my readers. There are two roads to reformation for mankind—one through misfortunes of their own, the other through those of others: the former is the most unmistakable, the latter the less painful. (I. 35)

Their victory in 255 B.C., including the capture of Regulus, gave the Carthaginians a rare chance for rejoicing. On the Roman side, if the story later retold by Cicero and the poet Horace is true, Regulus proved to be a man of remarkable self-sacrifice. According to the tradition, he promised his captors that he would return from Rome if the Senate refused to release certain young Carthaginian officers captured by the Romans. But when Regulus reached the Senate floor, he advised against letting these skilled fighters go in exchange for himself who was "already bowed with age." Despite the pleas of his wife and children and friends he kept his oath to the enemy and returned to Carthage to face a cruel death. The act earned him a place in the annals of Roman courage, although some commentators have been unwilling to believe that any man's oath could ever have been that sacred. It has also been suggested that the story may have been invented to excuse the torture of the Carthaginian prisoners in Rome. Moreover, it is argued, he may only have been sent to Rome by the Carthaginians to try to negotiate a peace.

In the meantime, at Rome, there was a crash program for outfitting a new fleet in order to rescue those who had escaped capture and remained on Libyan soil. This effort also ended in disaster. The men were rescued at Aspis, but off the coast of Sicily, near Camarina, the fleet was struck by a fierce storm. Only eighty ships survived out of 364. The Roman commanders were at fault because they had ignored warnings about sailing along the southern Sicilian shore during the early summer. Polybius sometimes attributes events to fortune but never if they could be blamed on the failings of men.

A victory over the enemy, elephants and all, near Panormus (modern Palermo), on the northern shore of Sicily, in 251 B.C., gave the Romans a new confidence, and in 250, two hundred ships were sent to join their land forces in the siege of Lilybaeum (modern Marsala), on the west coast of the island, a stronghold from which the Romans could again launch a campaign in Libya. This was to be one of the crucial engagements of the war, and it was a long one. The wooden siege towers built by the Romans, easy targets for the flaming torches hurled by the Carthaginians, were at one point destroyed. Yet the Romans persisted and were still there when the war ended in their favor in 241.

In 247 B.C., Hamilcar Barca, the father of the famous Hannibal, was given command of the Carthaginian fleet, and in the next three years he conducted intermittent raids on the Italian coastline. Between times he challenged the Romans at their various strongpoints in Sicily. But both sides were feeling the strain of a protracted war. Nevertheless, at Rome, the civic leaders were willing to contribute the funds for two hundred quinqueremes, ships having five rowers on each oar. The Carthaginians had not expected their enemy to have either the desire or the wherewithal for yet another fleet. These ships were to win the war.

A Carthaginian fleet sailed to Sicily weighted down with supplies for their forces at Eryx (modern Erice). Their commander was anxious to unload his freight before engaging the Romans, but he was not given the chance. His fleet was caught by less burdened Roman ships. The Carthaginians lost fifty of their own; another seventy were captured. Their forces in Sicily were now without supplies. It was time for a hard decision and the rulers at Carthage let Hamilcar make it. He asked the Romans for terms. In essence, they required the Carthaginians to leave Sicily, return all prisoners, and pay a large indemnity. With this agreed, the Romans and Carthaginians became "friends."

What lesson does Polybius draw from this long war with its enormous loss of ships and men? "It was *not* by mere chance or without knowing what they were doing that the Romans struck their bold stroke for universal supremacy and dominion, and justified their boldness by its success. No: it was the natural result of discipline gained in the stern school of difficulty and danger" (I. 63). The Carthaginians knew "the stern school of difficulty and danger" better than the Romans did. Not only had they lost the war but in its aftermath they faced a protracted struggle with their mercenaries. The Numidians and Libyans took arms against them for what profit they could find.

In ordinary circumstances the Carthaginians considered it an advantage that their mercenaries came from a variety of tribes speaking different languages. Such soldiers did not freely mingle or communicate with one another, and the danger of their uniting against their employer was minimal. But when Carthage defaulted on their pay and her leaders even tried to talk them into accepting less than they were due, they suddenly found a common voice. And says Polybius: "Armies in such a state are not usually content with mere human wickedness; they end by assuming the ferocity of wild beasts and the vindictiveness of insanity" (I. 67).

The efforts of the Carthaginian leaders to appease the rebels only raised the price for peace. The intensity of feeling accounted for the worst wartime atrocities on both sides which Polybius had ever heard of. His sympathies, however, were clearly with Carthage, which finally triumphed over the rebels after three years and four months. The leaders of the mercenaries were tortured to death and their Libyan allies subdued.

The Roman position during the Mercenary War was one favorable to Carthage, in accordance with their treaty of friendship. In particular, they did not at this time take advantage of the revolt by mercenaries in Sardinia, and they allowed the movement of supplies to Carthage while refusing this favor to her opponents.

The widespread support which the mercenaries had received from Carthage's neighbors was not surprising in view of the harshness with which they had been treated when the Carthaginians had the upper hand. The Romans knew better. Over the years they had behaved with exceptional fairness toward their former enemies in Italy and so built a confederation of neighbors who with few exceptions remained loyal in a time of crisis. This support was helpful in the First Punic War and may have been the deciding factor in the second one.

No sooner had the Carthaginians put down their rebellious mercenaries than they had cause for renewed ill-feeling toward Rome. Their hopes of regaining power in Sardinia were thwarted by Rome's decision to include this island in her circle of defensive bases, along with Sicily, which would guard the Tyrrhenian Sea. Although the Carthaginians objected vehemently, they were in no position to go to war and, in fact, had to pay the Romans an indemnity for suggesting that they were even thinking about it. We view the wars from the Roman side; even so, the Romans do not always look good. Polybius was sharply critical of the Roman grab of Sardinia and says he could see no grounds for it; quite frankly, that he could find no excuse for it.

Having lost Sicily and Sardinia, and having barely survived the mercenary uprising, the Carthaginians were due for better news. It came from Spain, where Hamilcar won back with hard fighting the territories which had recently slipped away. Hannibal was nine when he went with his father to Spain in 238 B.C., and was eighteen when Hamilcar was killed in battle. Though trained to lead, Hannibal did not yet have the years to succeed his father. In the meantime, the command went to his brother-in-law Hasdrubal.

Carthaginian operations in Spain were directed from a well-fortified city appropriately called New Carthage. The Spanish mines and manpower were sources of renewed hope. The Romans were aware of the Carthaginian success in Spain but at the moment were preoccupied with problems closer to home. As at Messana, they were concerned with the sea lanes around the Italian peninsula; hence, Hasdrubal had a more or less free hand in Spain, but with limits. A treaty was arranged with him which made the Iberus River (modern Ebro) in Spain the border of his ambitions. For a time that was where matters stood.

The Illyrian Problem

The Illyrians, who lived on the Balkan side of the Adriatic, were pirates, born and raised. Their uneasy neighbors could not remember when they had been anything else. Attacks on foreign fleets and lands were intensified after Queen Teuta took the throne when her husband died in 231 B.C. What was going on had been known in Rome for a long time but only now, with Rome's new sense of authority, did the Senate send envoys to talk to the queen. In a sharp exchange of words, she refused to give them the assurances they demanded. En route home, one of the emissaries was killed. Polybius accepts the story that he was assassinated by the queen's orders. The Romans certainly thought so, and soon launched a war in which they were well supplied with allies. Polybius remarked that it was not just some people who disliked the Illyrians, it was everybody. The approach of the Romans prompted several tribes in Illyricum to give in without a fight. In 228, Queen Teuta asked for terms. To the delight of all concerned, including the Aetolian and Achaean leagues, her domain was substantially reduced, and she was forced to limit the range of her ships and to keep unarmed those travelling any distance. The Greeks wholeheartedly welcomed Roman intervention because it served their local interests. Soon athletes from Rome were invited to compete in the Isthmian games near Corinth. Relations between the Romans and the Greeks thus began on a happy note. The First Illyrian War had been a victory for both.

The Gallic Problem

In 228 B.C., the Romans were concerned not only with the Illyrians but also with sporadic Gallic uprisings closer to home. The Gauls had been a problem to the Romans for centuries. According to Polybius, "brutal drunkenness and intemperate feeding" were among the traditions passed down from generation to generation among these people of northern Italy. In any event their traditional way of life had nothing to do with stability. They never built a Rome, much less an Athens. Polybius says they did not even construct permanent buildings; their tribal life was unrefined by schools or theaters. The fathers knew only farming and fighting, which they taught their sons. The Romans had started out that way themselves and well remembered their rugged forefathers, who knew the simpler life which the Gauls still led.

Periodically, these northerners would begin to roam southward. In 299 B.C., when themselves threatened by other tribes from beyond the Alps, they redirected their enemies, and even joined them, in a successful campaign against the Romans. But squabbling among the various Gallic groups, some of which prospered more than others, kept them from consolidating their power. They also were impulsive fighters known to be best at the beginning of a battle, but easily discouraged by small setbacks. Nevertheless, the Gauls remained among the roughest opponents the Romans faced in their early years. Later, Roman success permitted Polybius to conclude that these strenuous struggles had been helpful after all. Although often defeated, the Romans had gained a rigorous schooling in warfare, which prepared them for their subsequent wars with Pyrrhus and for the First Punic War. During that time, a period of about forty-five years, the Gauls and Romans remained at peace. But as Rome's prestige and power mounted rapidly, many Gauls became convinced that the Romans intended to drive them off their land and perhaps even exterminate them. And the Romans always feared another Gallic uprising. Mutual suspicion led to renewed warfare in Italy.

In 225 B.C., the Gauls attacked on a greater scale than ever before, and Polybius says there was panic in Rome, for it was remembered that the Gauls had once taken the city. The Romans were terror-stricken and so were their allies, who hastened from all parts of Italy to help them. A praetor's army was defeated near Clusium, but afterwards the Gauls were caught between two consular armies, one under Lucius Aemilius Papus, whose legions had been stationed at Ariminum, and the other under Gaius Atilius Regulus, freshly arrived with his forces from Sardinia. The Gauls fought with the intensity which sometimes makes the inferior role seem to be an advantage. The consul Atilius died in "reckless bravery," but his men were generally more cautious amid a raging seesaw battle. Widespread recklessness among the Gauls eventually defeated them. Some, wanting to be unimpeded by clothing, rushed into battle naked—a strange sight and an easy target for Roman spears. When the warriors leading the attack were routed, panic erupted among the ranks. Eventually, the Gauls were driven off, with one of their kings captured and the other a suicide. For the next three years consular armies invaded the north and ended the threat from this quarter by thoroughly humiliating the Gauls.

The Second Punic War

During his eight-year tenure in Spain Hasdrubal made more friends for the Carthaginians than they had ever had in Sicily. He had also kept his word to the Romans. When he was killed at his home in 221 B.C. because of some personal matter, Hannibal became the commander of the Carthaginian forces in Spain. Hannibal was the single most dangerous foe the Romans ever had. The Second Punic War is often called the Hannibalic War, for good reason. When he came to power there was probably no way to avoid another conflict. Hannibal started it, and, for all that he accomplished, he should have won it.

When writing about the Second Punic War, Polybius borrows facts from the historian Fabius Pictor, who had been a senator at the time. Polybius cared less for Fabius' military theories. Fabius had insisted that the war was brought on by the exploits of Hasdrubal, who actually lacked the support of his home government. Polybius called this explanation superficial, contending that the roots of a new war went deeper. He argued that Hamilcar had never accepted the defeat in Sicily as final and would have resumed the war immediately, had it not been for the mutiny of the mercenaries. As Polybius saw the situation, the Roman seizure of Sardinia increased Hamilcar's desire for revenge, and his plan for developing Spain began with another war in mind. He would not live to fight it, but according to an old story his hatred of Rome was firmly implanted in his son. Years later, Hannibal supposedly told how his father had one day led him to an altar and there had him swear eternal enmity to Rome. Perhaps he renewed the oath when he took over the command from Hasdrubal. His first encounter with Roman ambassadors suggests that. They warned him against making any moves against Saguntum, the one city in Spain below the Iberus River which had resisted Carthaginian domination. Rome's close relationship had begun with Saguntum "several years before the time of Hannibal," when the Saguntines chose the Romans rather than the Carthaginians to arbitrate a local dispute. If the Romans felt it necessary to land in Spain, Saguntum would be the best place. Hannibal angrily accused both the Romans and Saguntines of recent misdeeds and left no room for compromise. Each side was in an ugly, suspicious mood and could have started a war anywhere. Saguntum was available. Hannibal's quick strike against the city was a foretaste of the future: when he moved, he moved fast. Forced to wait out an eight-month siege, he managed to overcome all difficulties and take the city along with its wealth. Some of this he distributed at home and some in his camp to bolster morale on both fronts. He would use the rest for the greater campaign ahead.

In the same year, 219 B.C., the Romans were again struggling with the Illyrian problem. Their old friend Demetrius, who ruled Pharos, an island in the Adriatic off the southwest coast of what is now Yugoslavia, was serving himself instead of Rome and being encouraged by the Macedonians, who had an interest of their own in the Adriatic seacoast. The arrival of an army under the consul Lucius Aemilius Paullus began a brief and victorious campaign, which has been called the Second Illyrian War (220–

219 B.C.) After Queen Teuta, Demetrius was the second victim of Roman power in the Balkans. It would be a long roll call before the Romans finished building their empire.

The fall of Saguntum gave the Romans little time for rejoicing over their success in Illyria. Envoys were sent to Carthage to demand that Hannibal be turned over for punishment. The answer was abrupt. Rome had no business in Saguntum, since this city had not been counted as an ally on either side in the last treaty the Romans had concluded with Carthage.

Polybius held that it was understandable for the Carthaginians to seek revenge for the Roman seizure of Sardinia, but that they were wrong in seizing Saguntum. Considerations of right and wrong did not delay Hannibal's plans for an attack on Italy. He alloted sufficient forces for the defense of the homeland and for Spain, where his brother Hasdrubal (with the same name as his late brother-in-law) would be in charge during his absence. Word arrived that the Gauls in northern Italy, smarting from their recent defeat by the Romans, were ready to aid him. They would guide the Carthaginians along the best routes into northern Italy and help them with their supplies. While Hannibal was on his way, some of the Gauls attacked the Roman colonists who had settled in their territory.

By the spring of 218 B.C. all was ready. Hannibal's army, travelling light, crossed the Iberus River and moved rapidly toward the Rhone. The Romans were on the move too. One consul, Publius Cornelius Scipio, left for Massilia (modern Marseilles) with sixty ships; the other consul, Tiberius Sempronius Longus, with a much larger armada, headed for North Africa to attack Carthage. Upon landing at Massilia, Publius was surprised to find Hannibal already in the vicinity. He was even more surprised to learn a little later that the Carthaginian army had crossed the Rhone and was heading for the Alps.

Unfriendly natives on the eastern bank of the Rhone posed a minor problem for Hannibal; his major problem was getting thirty-seven elephants to cross the river against their will. He accomplished it by tying rafts together and securing them at the water's edge by ropes tied to trees on the shore. Then he covered the area with earth to the level of the land, forming an artificial promontory jutting into the river. Larger rafts covered with earth were attached loosely at the farthest point in the water. Two female elephants were used to entice their male companions onto the rafts. The outermost floats were then cut loose and pulled across the river by boats. In several trips most of the elephants made it, but a few became agitated enough to fall off. These saved themselves by rearing their trunks above the water. Their short-nosed mahouts were not so fortunate.

Polybius knew the pass in the Alps used by Hannibal, for he boasts of having followed it himself and of having talked with older men who had first-hand information about Hannibal's famous venture. Yet the pass is not actually identified, for presumably readers of his time did not need to be told. One thing is certain: the trip was extremely hazardous. The Celts who guided the Carthaginians could not save them from hostile tribes along the way, much less from the weather. Short of food and bitterly cold, the army could only keep going or die. Those who made it survived a gruelling fifteen-day ordeal—with the occasional help of Hannibal's good judgment. Polybius mentions only one of Hannibal's famous morale sessions, held at a time when his first view of Italy ahead gave him something to talk about. But men whose stomachs were aching with hunger and whose feet were either sinking in snow or sliding on ice were better served by tight lips and a grim countenance. Nor could Hannibal have looked less grim as he daily watched pack animals plunge over precipices, carrying his sorely needed supplies with them.

Passing through the Alps, Hannibal faced his most danger-ous challenge from the Allobroges, a tribe living in an area which is now in southeast France. On the rocky and narrow passage Hannibal could not count on his cavalry. When wounded, the Carthaginian horses panicked and created havoc in the line of march. Hannibal learned that the Allobroges held their positions only by day and returned to nearby towns at night. He began a series of nighttime operations against them, which proved suc-cessful. But dangerous miles remained ahead, and Hannibal knew that even those Gauls who pretended to be friends might make surprise attacks by raining stones from above onto the slow-mov-ing line below. The only defense he could manage was to keep his best soldiers at the end of the line and save an otherwise impossi-ble situation by a counterattack. The snow, ice, and landslides were even more deadly enemies. Hannibal reached Italy with only 20,000 footsoldiers, 6,000 horsemen, and fewer horses. He had lost about half the men he started out with and an even greater percentage of his animals.

When Hannibal reached the Po Valley, he learned that not all of the natives welcomed him by any means, and much to his amazement the consul Publius Scipio confronted him with an army at the Po. The news that Hannibal was marching through the Alps had caused the consul Scipio to change his plans in a hurry. His brother Gnaeus took charge of the forces which would challenge the Carthaginians in Spain while the consul quickly returned to Italy. According to Polybius, Scipio was equally surprised that Hannibal had passed through the Alps as well as he did. The other consul, Tiberius Sempronius, was quickly recalled from Sicily to meet the unexpected threat. Neither consul had any idea what they were really facing. November, 218 B.C., saw the beginning of one of the darkest periods in Roman history.

We use the term *Carthaginian,* but we really mean a collection of diverse peoples whom Hannibal welded into an amazing fighting force. His capacity to lead men of different customs and languages was one of his strongest points. There was also a good practical reason for the spirit and endurance of Hannibal's soldiers, now in the enemy country a long way from safety. They had to win to survive, and Hannibal never let them forget it. Success itself remained the best morale builder, and the Carthaginian momentum was built up through a series of victories.

At the Ticinus River, Hannibal's cavalry outmatched the Romans. Scipio, wounded and frightened by Carthaginian superiority, went on the defensive. It was only one engagement, and a small one at that, but the Celts serving in the Roman camp, alarmed for fear of being on the wrong side, staged a sneak nighttime attack on their hosts and fled to Hannibal's side, bringing some Roman heads to facilitate their welcome.

Tiberius Sempronius soon arrived with his army from Sicily, joining Scipio at his camp near the Trebia River. Both consuls had lost their earlier confidence that Hannibal could be easily defeated. There were murmurings of doubt at Rome. Hannibal was not an impulsive Celtic chieftain who might be expected to rush excitedly into battle. He chose his moves carefully and would quickly retreat, even sacrificing many soldiers, if he saw his chances for victory diminishing. With the Celts rallying to his side he was anxious for action, but patient enough to make elaborate plans. He wanted to be sure that it would be the Roman consuls who made the mistakes and could hardly have hoped for the cooperation they unintentionally gave him.

A disadvantage of the short consular term was the eagerness of certain consuls to score a great victory before their year was up. Hannibal found their eagerness useful. At the Trebia, he selected the site for an ambush. There were no trees in the area to arouse suspicion, only brush along the banks of a stream where a small group of elite warriors could hide with weapons, helmets, and shields beside them. Very early one morning, a contingent of cavalry made a feint toward the Roman camp and then retreated, enticing the Romans to chase them. Tiberius took the bait, and his men were soon testing their legs against the biting cold of a December day. Missing their breakfast was an unexpected nuisance, which Hannibal had carefully scheduled. Wading across the Trebia with icy water nearly to their shoulders left them shivering for the march against the enemy. Once engaged, the Roman cavalry faltered, leaving the flanks of the army exposed. No sooner was this danger evident than Hannibal's hidden soldiers burst forth to attack the rear of the Roman line. Only the strong core of Tiberius' army had any hope of escaping alive from this disaster. By pressing straight ahead they swept aside the Celts now surging toward them and succeeded in reaching the refuge of nearby Placentia. They had only succeeded in killing more Celts than Carthaginians.

Hannibal's North African and Spanish contingents found the weather worse than the enemy. A driving sleet storm kept them from pursuing the Romans, and the continued cold felled many of those who had survived the rigors of the recent battle. Many horses were lost, and of the elephants only one survived. In spite of these problems, Hannibal's army faced the new year with exuberant morale. The Romans looked to the spring when two new consuls, Gnaeus Servilius and Gaius Flaminius, could offer renewed hope.

Meanwhile in Spain, Gnaeus Cornelius Scipio, brother of the consul Publius Scipio, had seen both victory and defeat. His campaign against inland strongholds north of the Iberus River was a great success, and he took some valuable prisoners. But his men stationed with the fleet were overconfident about his protection for them. Hasdrubal's lightning raid against the careless forces settled around Emporium showed that he as well as Hannibal could profit by the Romans' mistakes.

In the spring of 217 B.C., Gaius Flaminius and his army were stationed at Arretium, with the other consular army standing guard at Ariminum. Astride the two main roads into Etruria, they were sure to catch the Carthaginians. The alternate route south of the Arno led through heavy marshes. Hannibal kept his army sloshing through those marshes for four days. As usual, the Celts had the worst of it, for the North Africans and Spaniards led the way, churning up the mud in the process. Only by putting his brother Mago at the end of the line did Hannibal keep his wet, tired, and unhappy allies moving ahead. While crossing the marshes, Hannibal rode the only elephant he had left, but in his high and dry position he suffered more than his men, with no relief from the burning pain of an inflamed eye. It went untreated, and he eventually lost the sight of that eye.

Once in Etruria, Hannibal based his strategy on what was known about the consul Flaminius, a magistrate who had come to power because it was his turn rather than for any skill he possessed as a general. By combining their highest civil and military offices the Romans ran that risk. Flaminius might be expected to act impetuously, seeking some proof of talent he lacked. As often happened, fear of having to share a victory with his colleague was also a weakness, or so it was reported (being a plebeian did not help him with the hostile writers of the nobility). As Polybius observed, Hannibal was well aware that the soft spots of an enemy were not always to be found in its army but in the minds of its leaders. Flaminius did exactly what Hannibal wanted him to do. When word arrived that the Carthaginians were marching in the direction of Rome, burning everything in sight, he set his army on the road with such haste that Hannibal was given the sole decision about where the battle would be. His choice gave him one of the most conclusive victories of all time. On the night of June 21, he posted contingents of his army in the hills near Lake Trasimenus, ten miles west of modern Perugia. Early in the morning, the mists which rose near the lake provided unusually good cover, so good that Flaminius marched his army into a nearly escape-proof trap.

The Romans had blamed their earlier losses, in part, on the inexperience of their new recruits, who had never seen the Carthaginians in battle before. At Lake Trasimenus, they still did not see the enemy because of the fog. The attack from all sides created confusion, and only those Romans in the lead who pressed straight on across a hill managed to get away. Even they were later captured. Many of their comrades were driven into the lake and drowned by the weight of their armor or were killed by their pursuers. Flaminius died in the thick of the battle. Polybius and Livy give different accounts of what took place, but agree on the result. It is for a humiliating defeat that Flaminius is usually remembered rather than for his completion of the Via Flaminia from Rome to Ariminum when he was censor in 220 B.C.

Nearby, where Hannibal buried his dead, there are today both English and German cemeteries. In the vicinity of this same lake, a major battle was fought in World War II, June 28 to July 3, 1944. It was in 1961 that a young Italian archaeologist, Giancarlo Susini, discovered, by means of an aerial survey, the cemetery where the Romans had been buried after their terrible defeat in the late third century B.C.

At Rome, officials had excused the earlier losses in the north, attempting to gloss over bad news with new plans. But this disaster was too close to home. A tight-lipped praetor announced to the Tribal Assembly: "We have been beaten in a great battle." The people were comforted by knowing where to look for guidance. By habit they turned to the Senate. Earlier, the senators had been advised that a substantial force which the other consul Gnaeus Servilius had sent to help Flaminius had been intercepted and defeated by the Carthaginians. The senators now realized that they could no longer afford the luxury of taking chances with the type of men who were elected to the consulship. As in times past, a man of exceptional ability with the power of a dictator was needed. Quintus Fabius Maximus was chosen, and Marcus Minucius was his Master of the Horse. The remaining consul, Gnaeus Servilius, now gave up his command, and Fabius took charge of the Romans and all their allies under arms.

In the meantime, Hannibal made a rare mistake. He allowed his exuberant soldiers to roam about the countryside, knocking down anybody who stood in their way and taking whatever they wanted. This was the wrong move if he hoped to win the hearts of the Italians, who now had a good reason for staying loyal to Rome. As yet not one city in Italy had voluntarily submitted to him.

Fabius' plan of action was to have none. The previous two pairs of consuls had rushed into battle with Hannibal and had been badly beaten. Fabius would not fight at all. He recognized the superiority of the enemy under battle conditions and was content that Hannibal could be beaten another way. The Romans had an ample supply of food and a great reservoir of manpower. Hanni-

bal was in a hostile land, shy of both. Later the poet Ennius (239–
ca. 169 B.C.) wrote that Fabius "saved the state by patience."
"Fabius the delayer" he was called. (In modern times, it is from
him we have the term "Fabian," used to describe a kind of piece-
meal socialism.)

Fabius was content to follow Hannibal and to kill enemy
stragglers or those daring enough to approach the vicinity of his
camp. Before long this was not enough to satisfy the hopes at
home. Even his Master of the Horse, Minucius, was critical of
Fabius' unwillingness to engage Hannibal. The grumbling was
bound to grow, especially so when Hannibal invaded the rich
Campanian plains where Capua was the chief city. By reaching
for the wealth of this area Hannibal hoped to attract a battle. The
closest Fabius came to action was to set up an ambush in a pass
which the Carthaginians had used before and might use again. It
was a perfect place for a trap. Hannibal thought so too, and left
the plain by a narrow gorge. He first diverted the Romans from
their position by having oxen driven in a different direction with
lighted sticks attached to their horns, giving the appearance at
night of an army on the move.

Fabius did not appease his critics by his handling of this
matter. When he went to Rome to appease the gods with new
sacrifices the more aggressive Minucius was left in charge. Minucius had some success in attacking isolated parties of Carthaginians gathering grain for their winter stores. Unfortunately, the
result of these minor skirmishes only made the capital unduly
optimistic. Minucius was given equal status as a dictator alongside
Fabius. This was asking for trouble, for Fabius had not changed
his mind about strategy and took half the army into a separate
camp. Hannibal was watching. He very soon drew the impetuous
Minucius into a battle for which he had laid elaborate plans by
hiding groups of soldiers in the area around a contested hill. Minucius lost some of his best men in the engagement and would
have suffered more if Fabius had not rushed to his rescue. After
that episode, Fabius resumed full command, but the war was not
to be his. With the election of consuls for 216 he was required to
give up his office.

The election of new consuls each year offered the hope of
wiser management or at least better luck. When Lucius Aemilius
Paullus and Gaius Terentius Varro took office in 216, the Senate
was willing to finance the greatest force the Romans had ever

mustered. In fact, they doubled the stakes by authorizing eight legions instead of the usual four; these contained five thousand foot soldiers (instead of four thousand) and three hundred horsemen (instead of two hundred), with a correspondingly higher ratio of allies attached to each legion. There was to be an all-out effort. The Senate especially looked to Aemilius, who had conducted the Illyrian War so well. He told the legionaries all they needed was a vigorous spirit to win. He was wrong.

Of all the battles in the Punic wars the name of Cannae has been best remembered. In addition to the present consuls, the consuls of the previous year led the additional legions. Moreover, they now had under arms men experienced in fighting with the Carthaginians. The people of Rome solicited the help of the gods in every way possible. Polybius said, "The city was one scene of vows, sacrifices, supplicatory processions, and prayers" (III. 112). Against all of this was Hannibal's wily decision about where and how a battle should be fought. Aemilius was more experienced and more cautious than his colleague, Gaius Terentius, but they took full command on alternate days. Aemilius knew it was dangerous to fight Hannibal in the open country where the Carthaginian strength in cavalry would be crucial. Terentius was more impressed by the fact that there was no place for Hannibal to hide men in this flat country. There he stood ready with his whole army in full view. It was reasonable for the Romans to believe that this time they had him. Terentius ordered the army into battle on the second of August, 216 B.C.

Hannibal had a different trap set this time, and it only became apparent during the battle itself. He arranged his various contingents in what Polybius calls a crescent—heavy in the middle and thin toward the ends. It might be thought that such an arrangement would be curved away from the Romans, in a concave fashion so as to draw them immediately into a circle. But Hannibal had it curved the other way, toward their line, in convex style, so that the main forces made contact first. When a weak contingent of Celts at the front of the crescent gave way, the Romans began to press toward this weak spot. When they broke into the crescent the various Roman units were consolidated in a core. The outer pincers of the Carthaginian line were then able to encircle this mass precisely according to Hannibal's plan because of his cavalry's superiority. Seventy thousand Roman foot-soldiers, outnumbering the Carthaginians by two to one, were encircled and

annihilated. Aemilius died along with two consuls of the previous
year. Only Terentius and some horsemen on the left of the Roman line managed to get away. A reserve force of ten thousand
which Aemilius had kept nearby was captured.

The battle of Cannae allowed Hannibal to believe that he
had won the war. A few Italian and Greek cities, ready to agree,
joined him. It was Rome's darkest hour, but the Romans were a
people too blindly stubborn to know when they were finished.
They stood with their backs to the wall—hanging on for the sake
of hanging on. A beleaguered people sometimes wins that way.

Some Carthaginian leaders also thought the Romans might
win out. As mentioned earlier, Carthage's military commanders
never had unanimous support at home. Even after the great victory at Cannae, Hannibal was attacked in the Carthaginian Senate
as a man who was deceiving his own people about their ultimate
chances. He had sent his brother Mago to report on his recent
triumph and at the same time to ask for more money and supplies
which he urgently needed. Hanno, an old enemy of Hannibal's
family, with bitter memories about the First Punic War, mocked
Hannibal with some disturbing questions in the Carthaginian Senate: " 'I have slain armies of the enemy. Send me soldiers!' What
else would you ask for if you had been defeated? 'I have captured
two camps of the enemy,' full of booty and supplies, of course.
'Give me grain and money!' What else would you beg if you had
been despoiled, if you had lost your camp?" (XXIII. 12. 13–15).
Hanno said, moreover, that there had been no hint of Roman
surrender or even that the Romans intended to make any overtures for peace. He argued that now, if indeed the Carthaginians
had the upper hand, they should offer the Romans reasonable
terms and end a costly war as best they could before their luck
gave out, as it had in the previous war. But his words fell on deaf
ears, for the jubilant Carthaginian senators overwhelmingly favored sending Hannibal more reinforcements and supplies.
Another fourteen years would pass before Hanno was proven to
have had the best judgment after Cannae. Although never as famous as Hannibal, he has gone into the history books as Hanno
the Great.

In 216 B.C., one measure of Roman resistance was the Senate's refusal to ransom the captives Hannibal held. They did not
want to pay him ransom money, nor did they want to give the
impression to their own men or to their allies that surrendering

quickly meant an easy passage home. If Hannibal had figured to win with the Romans paying him into the bargain, he was disappointed. Now if he failed to take the city of Rome itself he might not win at all.

Of all the cities which surrendered to Hannibal, Capua was the severest loss to the Romans. Other allies were bound to follow the example of this wealthy city, which dominated one of the most fertile regions of Italy. By 213, the Romans had succeeded in preventing these Campanians from planting any crops and in the following year began a full-scale siege of Capua. There was trouble too in Sicily, for the Syracusans saw a chance to obtain at least half of the island by dividing it with the Carthaginians. A more serious threat and one with more far reaching consequences resulted from an alliance between Hannibal and Philip V, king of Macedon. Even so, with the capital threatened and the allies wavering, the Romans continued the war on three other fronts. A sizeable force was still stationed in Spain and a fleet stood near Greece, waiting for Philip to make a move. During 215–214, Syracuse was put under siege. The Romans hoped to save the Syracusans from the folly of their leaders. In command of the land forces was the propraetor Appius Claudius, and in charge of the naval forces was Marcus Claudius Marcellus. Neither general anticipated a difficult time, nor did they know what was in store for them. Syracuse's secret weapon was the physicist Archimedes, one of the ancient world's most inventive minds.

Roman ships moving in to attack the walls and towers of the city could not elude the spray of missiles thrown by Archimedes' catapults, which were built to aim at different distances and were as deadly as modern-day mortar fire. Any ships that managed to get through the barrage were targets for arrows and darts shot through small holes in the city's walls. Any ship near the walls might find itself upended by a grappling device worked by a crane. The Roman attack by sea was completely frustrated, and the land assault had no better result. Stones rained down on the siege machines which the Romans tried to move toward the walls. Syracuse had nothing to fear except a blockade which would cut off her food supplies. Since all else had failed, the Romans set up a blockade. They knew it would take time before supplies in the city ran low (it took eight months), but a blockade required fewer soldiers. Some of the Roman forces were diverted to service elsewhere.

Syracuse fell in the autumn of 212, brought down not only

by the shortage of food but by the plentifulness of wine. The
Roman commander Marcus Marcellus heard from a deserter that
the Syracusans were having a festival and unwisely drinking on
empty stomachs. Attacking at night, Marcellus' men scaled the
walls unnoticed, found the guards too drunk to comprehend what
was happening, and had no trouble in reaching a gate to admit the
entire Roman army. Archimedes did not survive. There are conflicting stories about the death of this genius, whether he was
killed for disobeying the order of a Roman soldier or because the
conquerors thought he was carrying some gold.

Syracuse was the first major city of the world which the
Romans had seized and was the first they systematically robbed of
its wealth. Polybius saw an excuse. Perhaps the best way, he said,
to keep others in check is to take their wealth and leave them
nothing with which to fight. But was that necessarily a good
policy? How does the conqueror avoid ruining himself with what
he wins? The Romans not only took the money of this ancient
city but carried off statues and paintings and personal property.
Polybius, writing at a later day, looked back and saw the plunder
as "wrong then, and wrong now." About the Romans he wrote,
"While leading lives of the greatest simplicity themselves, as far as
possible removed from the luxury and extravagance which these
things imply, they yet conquered the men who had always possessed them in the greatest abundance and of the finest quality.
Could there have been a greater mistake than theirs? Surely it
would be an incontestable error for a people to abandon the habits
of the conquerors and adopt those of the conquered; and at the
same time involve itself in that jealousy which is the most dangerous concomitant of excessive prosperity." Instead, he said, the
Romans should have "raised . . . [their] reputation . . . not with
the pictures and statues, but with dignity of character and greatness of soul" (IX. 10). That was hindsight. The Rome he knew
was moving dangerously close to being ruined by its success.

While the Romans were taking Syracuse, Hannibal was plotting some means of capturing the citadel of the great port city of
Tarentum (modern Taranto) in southern Italy. He had had no
success during the summer of 213 in his attempt to wrest the city
from the Romans. In 212, he received help from inside the city.
Tarentine hostages being held at Rome had been caught trying to
escape, and the harsh treatment they received caused a sharp reaction at home. Hannibal was let in at a gate where young conspira-

tors had on signal killed the guards. As the Carthaginians poured into the town they took up the cry that the Tarentines had nothing to fear and should remain in their houses. The plotters had acquired Roman bugles beforehand and now blew a call to arms which brought the leaderless and confused Romans scurrying into the streets to almost certain death at the hands of the Carthaginians and Celts who awaited them. Some managed to escape to the citadel, including the Roman commander, who, though aroused from a drunken stupor, ran to safety. The citadel, which stood guard over the entrance to the harbor, looked more secure than it was. Hannibal decided to haul the ships in the harbor through the town on wheels to the sea on the south side. This done, he blockaded the citadel from the open sea, prevented the Romans from receiving supplies, and starved them out. The Tarentines had worried about Hannibal's capacity to protect them. Now they could believe in it.

In 211, Hannibal tried to break through the Roman siege of Capua, but the result was a stand-off. He could neither reach the city nor draw out the Romans from their entrenched position where they were safe from his cavalry, which had cost them so much in open battles. Although the Carthaginians could roam the countryside at will, they could not accomplish much. In fact, since the Romans had previously ravaged the nearby region, there was a shortage of hay for the Carthaginian horses. Hannibal had to move, and he decided on a thrust toward Rome which might succeed in drawing their forces away from Capua. But Quintus Fulvius and Appius Claudius, the two former consuls in charge of the siege, had been ordered to stand fast; and to Hannibal's amazement, in spite of his threat to Rome, that is exactly what they did.

Hannibal camped only about thirty miles from Rome—the closest he had ever approached it. In the city, men busied themselves with the defenses and women took up the supplication of the gods, "sweeping the pavements of the temples with their hair." What Hannibal saw were two consular armies massed before the city under the leadership of Gnaeus Fulvius and Publius Sulpicius. Rather than attack, he scorched the countryside. Then, with a heavy load of booty, he retreated. Since the Carthaginian siege of the Roman position at Capua had also been given up, both cities were now safe. As Hannibal withdrew, the Romans attacked, and at first wreaked some damage on his retreating army; but a few days later the Carthaginians took a stand, and the

Romans were beaten back. Hannibal then moved quickly southward and almost caught Rhegium unawares. His constant moving
about was a measure of his frustration.

Polybius had praise for both sides in the war. Hannibal was
admired for what he had attempted. His efforts at Capua, Rome,
and Rhegium were daring if not successful and nobody could fault
his energy. As for the Romans, they had remained indomitable
both at home and at the siege of Capua: "they remained unshaken
and firm in their purpose" (IX. 9). Polybius had advice for future
leaders. Judging from the past, he said that "in an adventurous
and hazardous policy it often turns out that audacity [is] the truest
safety and the finest sagacity" (IX. 9).

Up to this point it was Hannibal against the Romans, one
man against a people. In 210, the Romans found they had a great
leader of their own—a man who could defeat Hannibal at least
once—the one time that would be necessary. If ever Polybius'
enthusiasm might be said to have had the best of him, it must be
in the case of Publius Scipio, later called Africanus. He hailed
Scipio as a man unmatched in ability and sharply rebuked previous writers who attributed his rise as much to luck as to anything
else. Polybius insisted that Scipio was a man of extraordinary
intelligence and sterling character. He called him "god-like and
god-beloved." Such uncompromising adulation possibly helped
to make Scipio less well known in history than men like Alexander and Caesar. These men come alive as fascinating personalities, with their talents and faults plain to see. Scipio rarely escaped
from the mold of the Old Roman Hero. He was often pictured as
being above the temptations of ordinary men. It was said that he
was "fond of the society of women," but when some of his
young aides presented him with the prettiest girl during the capture of New Carthage, he could not accept her lest he be dis-
tracted from his responsibilities. Scipio was always sober, always
on duty. Otherwise, his success was attributed to foresight and
good judgment. But he had something else, too. He managed to
convince his soldiers that he was the recipient of divine dispensa-
tions which gave his plans a special advantage. For soldiers who
were careful about the gods, even when not in danger, this news
added a "greater courage and cheerfulness." Scipio's own bravery
was attributed to a heroic and unquenchable inner spirit. He first
encountered the Carthaginians in 218 B.C., while serving under
his father near the Padus River (modern Po). When the elder

Scipio was wounded and surrounded, his eighteen-year-old-son rushed to the rescue and shamed those who held back until they witnessed his unreserved daring.

Young Scipio showed another kind of boldness when he twice announced that he had had dreams in which he was elected aedile. Although his older brother was due to be elected as one of the young patricians eligible for the office, Publius wanted to stand with him. He put on the white toga of a candidate (*candidus* means shining white), joined his brother in the Forum, and was elected. Polybius said it did not matter if the dreams were fictitious because Scipio was "kind, open-handed, and courteous."

In 210, Scipio was in charge of the Roman forces in Spain. Earlier, both his father and uncle, campaigning together, had been defeated and killed by the Carthaginians, aided by Spanish natives who chose to betray the Romans. That these untrustworthy ex-allies were now on the other side could be counted as an advantage. In addition, the Carthaginian commanders were at odds with each other. Given these circumstances, Scipio decided to attack New Carthage, the central supply depot for three enemy armies stationed at widely varying spots in Spain. It had an excellent harbor. Scipio studied his intelligence reports and carefully laid plans for an assault on the city by land and sea. He then told his army that he had had a dream in which Poseidon told him how to proceed and even promised to be there to give proof of his support.

Poseidon helped those who helped themselves. Scipio had three men carrying large shields to protect him from the enemy as he rallied his troops along the wall. When the mid-afternoon assault lost momentum, he called for a retreat, but he meant no relief for the city. In the late afternoon, the water receded from the lagoon on a side of the wall where the defenders were expecting the least action. Here Scipio planned his breakthrough. And he succeeded with hardly a blow struck. The weary Carthaginians were caught off guard and the city was taken suddenly. Scipio told his men to slaughter every man and beast in their path. Here as elsewhere the Romans practiced terrorist tactics. Polybius says that butchered dogs were part of a gory scene which gave warning to others of the Romans' impatience with resistance.

Preparations for the clash between Scipio and Hannibal's brother Hasdrubal (the same name as his deceased brother-in-law) began in the early months of 208. Scipio made a surprise attack on

Hasdrubal at Castulo in southern Spain. He wanted to fight him alone before either Mago or another Hasdrubal, who is called "the son of Gesco," could arrive with his army. Practically speaking, the battle was over before the Carthaginians managed to form their lines. Hasdrubal fled toward the Pyrenees, headed for Gaul. The Iberians now hailed Scipio as "king" but he modestly insisted that "general" would do. He was merely a servant of Rome; the old traditions still held. Polybius could not resist speaking again of Scipio's "greatness of soul."

During the following spring, in 207 B.C., Hasdrubal led an army of reinforcements through the Alps into Italy by a route which Polybius describes as easier and shorter than the one Hannibal had taken. The soldiers he brought were sorely needed, and whether Hannibal would get them or not was of decisive importance. At this point the Romans had an extraordinary piece of good luck. A message which Hasdrubal had sent to his brother was intercepted. It gave his position and plans. The consul, Gaius Claudius Nero, hurried to join his colleague, Marcus Livius Salinator, at Sena Gallica on the Adriatic coast, and together they attacked near the Metaurus River.

The battle seesawed back and forth, and so did Hasdrubal's elephants, which showed no partisanship in trying to escape the javelins flying overhead. A sharp maneuver by which the consul Claudius shifted his forces from the right wing to the Carthaginian rear decided the battle. Although Hasdrubal knew his cause was lost, he kept on fighting, and died with his men, perhaps knowing that Hannibal's chances were dying with him. Polybius speaks well of Hasdrubal. Both in Spain and in Italy he did his best to help his brother. But he failed. Rome was swept up in ecstatic celebrations. The tide had turned at last.

The news from Spain also continued to be good. In 206, near Ilipa, a town in Baetica, southern Spain, Scipio's army repelled an attack by Mago and then engaged the main Carthaginian forces under Hasdrubal, son of Gesco. Hannibal was not the only general who could plan surprises. Scipio abandoned the old order by which his forces lined up for battle. He also set a new time. Attacking at dawn, he caught the Carthaginians unprepared and forced them to fight on empty stomachs. That was a crucial factor by midday, and only a violent rain storm saved the Carthaginians from a total rout. The victory was sufficient to make Scipio feel that the Romans could now safely carry the war to the Carthaginian homeland in North Africa, no longer having to worry about a hostile Spain at their back. But Scipio's optimism was short-lived, for he soon received a shocking setback.

Somehow it seems out of order to talk about mutiny in a Roman army. We think of the legions as made up of hardy, well-disciplined men, forever on the march at the command of their superiors. Scipio was himself perplexed to find a full-scale revolt on his hands in the fall of 206. The soldiers had not been paid recently. Instead of bringing their complaints to Scipio they allowed a few outspoken ringleaders to encourage them to mutiny. It seems ironic that the mutiny occurred at a time in the war when Roman fortunes never looked better. But, according to Polybius, maybe it was not so ironic. An earlier experience of his own as a cavalry officer and a diplomat motivated him to write: "To decide on the right method of resisting intestine factions, revolutions, and disturbances is difficult, and requires great tact and extreme acuteness; and moreover, the observation of one maxim suitable in my opinion to all armies, states, and bodies alike, which is this: never in such cases to allow any lengthened idleness or repose, and least of all at a time of success and when provisions are abundant" (XI. 25).

The handling of the mutiny offered concrete evidence of Scipio's abilities. He knew how to manage men. First, he called the army together and pointed out the shamefulness of their acting like mercenaries when they were in fact the defenders of their own homes and families. He gave them further reason to feel ashamed by telling them they would be promptly paid—nor had it been his fault in the first place. He then pardoned them. There was always the excuse that they had been duped: "a crowd is ever easily misled and easily induced to any error" (XI. 29).

Scipio needed a confident army; hence the blame was shifted to the thirty-five ringleaders, who would take the whole punishment. Earlier, they had been led to believe that Scipio would negotiate with them and by this deception were seized and held until he put them to death before the eyes of their recent followers. With the unpleasantness of the mutiny thus over, Scipio and his army could forgive and forget old wrongs, real or imagined. The guilt belonged to the thirty-five dead men.

Another problem needed settling before Scipio could leave Spain. The native tribes seemed to remain loyal only to foreign commanders who were losing. When the Carthaginians were dominant the Iberians switched over to the Romans. After Scipio's position became secure they turned against him. Late in the year 206, he hurried northward and defeated the Iberian chieftain Andobales, whose open rebellion might have encouraged others had not the Romans at once soundly defeated him. Scipio had told his soldiers that they would fight alone without any native allies, to prove that Romans needed only to rely upon themselves to win.

In 206, having settled his troops at Tarraco for the winter, Scipio returned to Rome to plan the invasion of North Africa. He was elected consul for 205 B.C. and during that year set up headquarters in Sicily. Laelius was sent as his advance man to North Africa. Scipio arrived in the spring of 204 after his *imperium* had been extended. The next year, according to Livy, he was given an open-ended assignment of *imperium* for the duration of the war. The regular consuls, Gnaeus Servilius Caepio and his colleague Gaius Servilius Geminus, were in charge of operations in Italy.

The brunt of Scipio's attack in 204 struck Utica. While this city was still under siege in 203, Scipio turned his attention to the camps of both the Carthaginians and their Numidian allies. He had established contact with Syphax, the Numidian king, whom he knew to be anxious for peace, and arranged that emissaries sent to negotiate with Syphax be allowed to bring servants with them. Disguised in this fashion were several of Scipio's sharp-eyed agents, who could return with the information he wanted about the enemy camp. He already knew he was going to burn it down because the Numidians only used reeds and thatch for building their winter huts.

By appearing busy with his siege of Utica and at the same time sincere in his intentions for peace, Scipio managed to lull both the Numidian camp and the Carthaginian camp under Hasdrubal, son of Gesco, into an ideal state of unpreparedness. One night, Gaius Laelius and half the army were sent with great speed to hurl fire into the Numidian camp. Sleeping soldiers awoke to a raging nightmare. Many were trampled to death trying to escape and probably died thinking that the fire was accidental. Those who managed to outrun the flames soon knew the truth. They were cut down by Laelius' soldiers, who were posted in all directions. Some of the ten thousand horsemen and fifty thousand soldiers managed to flee. Syphax escaped, too.

The fire was seen in the nearby Carthaginian camp. Hasdru-

bal and his soldiers had only started to wonder what had happened when they were attacked. While the Carthaginian huts were
of wood rather than reeds, they too were soon engulfed in flames.
Polybius describes the panic-stricken Carthaginians fleeing the fire
without their weapons or even their clothes and being slain by the
Romans who surrounded the camp. He then offered unreserved
praise for his hero: "It is . . . impossible for the imagination to
exaggerate the dreadful scene, so completely did it surpass in horror everything hitherto recorded. Of all the brilliant achievements
of Scipio this appears to me to have been the most brilliant and
the most daring. . ." (XIV. 5).

There would soon be a repeat performance. The Carthaginians mustered their forces, and with Syphax and a remnant of his
army at their side they challenged Scipio in a place called the Great
Plains. This battle on the 24th of June, 203, was another singular
victory for Scipio, especially since Italian horsemen now bested
the renowned Numidian cavalry. Syphax fled all the way back to
his homeland where he was later captured by Laelius and taken to
Rome in chains. He died there.

Hasdrubal returned to an unhappy Carthage where every
day brought more bad news. Unlike the Roman confederation in
Italy which held firm for so long, many of the communities near
Carthage quickly opened their gates to the Romans. Forcing the
rest to submit was only a matter of time. Badly divided about
what to do, the Carthaginians began to do everything at once. An
attack on the Romans besieging Utica was planned, preparations
were begun to defend Carthage if necessary, and Hannibal was
ordered back from Italy. The Carthaginian leaders also considered
what terms they might reasonably accept to end the war.

To get ready for the defense of Carthage was a wise idea.
Scipio soon brought his army within sight of the city, but he left
again as soon as he heard that the enemy was sending a relief force
to Utica. He was master on land, but the Carthaginian fleet was
better prepared at sea. The result was a standoff which led to an
armistice—a prelude to peace. What happened next spoiled the
chance of ending hostilities. The Carthaginians saw an opportunity to capture some Roman supply ships and did so in direct
violation of the armistice agreement. At Carthage, Roman emissaries delivered harsh words concerning the betrayal. Their indignation seemed to rule out the possibility of a polite answer and, in
fact, they were sent away without one. The Carthaginians even
hatched a plot to kill them as they made their way back to the

Roman camp. It did not succeed, but tension heightened because of it.

By this time Hannibal had returned. His arrival gave the Carthaginians an unusual sense of hope, for he was a living legend returning to his homeland after an absence of thirty-five years. The Carthaginians were confident that with his leadership they could still win the last battle. Maybe Hannibal was not so sure. He requested a conference with Scipio. He had obviously been impressed by the string of victories which Scipio had won in Spain and North Africa and desired to meet him to see if there actually needed to be another battle. The two men, accompanied by bodyguards, rode out from their respective camps and alone with their interpreters spoke frankly to each other. Hannibal, who had once threatened Rome, now sought to save Carthage. Gone was the childhood pledge of eternal enmity. His "honorable" terms would recognize Roman control of Sicily, Sardinia, and Spain, but Carthage would be left secure in her local domain. Scipio reminded Hannibal that such an arrangement including other concessions had previously been agreed upon in the armistice, which had been promptly broken by the Carthaginians. Scipio demanded an unconditional surrender; otherwise there would have to be a decisive battle. As Hannibal refused to submit, it was fought the following day.

The battle made famous the name of Zama, southwest of Carthage. Polybius called the contest one of history's most crucial events. For human interest alone there was the memory of Hannibal's victory over Scipio's father at the Trebia River. Now he was challenged by the son. Two of the greatest generals of ancient times faced each other for the first and last time. The stakes were high indeed: "For it was not merely of Libya or Europe that the victors in this battle were destined to become masters, but of all other parts of the world known to history,—a destiny which had not to wait long for its fulfillment" (XV. 9).

It was Rome versus Carthage and Hannibal versus Scipio; but, for all that, there were contingents of Numidian cavalrymen on both sides, and the conflict between them may have been the deciding factor. They had already engaged when Hannibal ordered more than eighty elephants against the Roman line. The noise of the trumpets caused some of the elephants to become confused and they turned against his Numidian horsemen, forcing them to scatter. The Numidian riders on the Roman side pursued them. At the same time, at the other end of the line, the Roman cavalry routed the Carthaginians. The main battle itself was an even match, with the losses heavy on both sides, yet each remaining hopeful of victory. Then the Roman cavalry and their Numidian allies returned from their pursuit and attacked the rear of the Carthaginian position. It was all over for Hannibal. He managed to get away and ride to Hadrumetum (modern Sousse), southeast of Carthage. He had finally lost a set battle. Was it because, as Polybius says, "there are times when chance thwarts the plans of the brave" or had he simply at last met his match? Partisans on both sides fight the battle of Zama to the present day. Scipio in victory was magnanimous. He made no attempt to humiliate Hannibal who was, in fact, allowed to take a prominent role in the affairs of postwar Carthage.

The Romans considered their terms to be generous, and Hannibal agreed that they might easily have been worse. An indemnity was imposed and hostages taken as usual; in addition the Romans demanded the surrender of every elephant Carthage had left and all except ten of her warships. The clause which deserves the most attention is the one in which Rome prohibited the Carthaginians from going to war against any state outside Libya (the ancient Greek name for North Africa, except Egypt) and permitted them to declare war inside Libya with Rome's consent only. That particular restriction had the effect of putting Carthage at the mercy of her neighbors. It was bound to cause trouble. For the time being, however, she was at the mercy of Rome and the retention of her territory without a permanent occupation by the Romans was, at Hannibal's urging, accepted as a blessing.

Publius Scipio's triumphant return to Rome was one of those momentous events often recalled in later years. The festivals and games went on for days as the Roman citizenry combined their exuberant victory celebration with the relief of a narrow escape.

Ironically, one of the greatest figures in Roman history is a Carthaginian. It is not easy to say how honest the Romans were about Hannibal and that included the nurses who warned their young charges, "Be good or Hannibal will get you." There were bound to be different reports about his reputation precisely because he was a complex and controversial figure—behaving differently on different occasions and giving different impressions to those who knew him. It was always claimed that he was cruel, whether because of his strict discipline or because he drove his men mercilessly during tough going. Polybius thinks some of his aides may have been harder than he was and that his reputation gathered in all the horrible stories. Polybius' summation of Hannibal was that "the prevailing notion about him, . . . at Carthage was that he was greedy of money, at Rome that he was cruel" (IX. 26). As for the charge that Hannibal would employ any means for getting money, Polybius simply says that most Carthaginians would do the same thing.

Stories about Hannibal show him to have been thoughtful and shrewd. His success in judging what his enemy would do in a given situation was not just a result of guesswork. A careful observer, he knew that the tradition-bound Romans would be more than likely to behave in the future as they had in the past. On the other hand, he found the Celts who had joined his camp to be unpredictable, and he worried that they might one day try to kill him. He kept several wigs and changes of clothing at hand to disguise himself, and sometimes even fooled his own aides. Maybe he enjoyed that. But if there was a lighter side to this tough soldier it is largely left out of historical accounts.

One story, often repeated, although not everybody believes it, suggests a sardonic sense of humor. One day, long after the battle of Zama, Hannibal met Scipio and they talked about old times. Scipio asked him whom he considered to be the greatest generals of all time. Hannibal placed Alexander first, Pyrrhus of Epirus second, and himself third. Scipio laughed and asked him where he would have ranked himself if Scipio had not beaten him at Zama. Hannibal replied that he would then have given himself first place (Livy, XXXV. 14. 5–12; Appian, XI. 10; Plutarch, pp. 464–65). There was no joking about the fact that he considered himself superior to Scipio. As they walked together, they approached a narrow place where one would have to go ahead of the other. Unhesitatingly, Hannibal took the lead and Scipio graciously followed. The proud Carthaginian had lost the war to become one of history's magnificent failures. For once the "godlike" Scipio looked very human by falling in behind.

The Case for the Romans

As mentioned earlier, Polybius stated that the purpose of his history was to show how Rome came to be the dominant power in the Mediterranean. He felt that Rome's success was particularly due to the stability of her government. All wars are not won on the battlefield. Rome was strong on the home front, where her enemies were often weakest. Yet why should a constitution which gave the Romans an advantage in building their empire break down after they had won? There is no avoiding that question in the chapters ahead. Polybius described the constitution in its heyday. At least he told how it should have functioned. Theory was one thing; practice, given the human factor, was another.

In theory, the Romans had a balanced constitution. The Greek philosophers, Aristotle in particular, had observed that whether a government was by one man (monarchy), a few (aristocracy) or many (democracy) there was inevitably a tendency toward an abuse of power. A monarchy might degenerate into a tyranny, an aristocracy into an oligarchy, and democracy into mob rule, unless, as Aristotle pointed out, there was a proper check on the ruling faction, be it one man, a small clique, or the majority of the people. What Polybius found so attractive about the Roman system was the combination of monarchic, aristocratic, and democratic features. He saw the first represented by the consuls, the second by the Senate, and the third by the assemblies.

The consuls of course had enormous power. They were at one and the same time the chief military and civil authorities of the state. Only the tribunes who were committed to protect the rights of the plebeians were outside the immediate jurisdiction of the consuls. The consuls conducted the meetings of the Senate and the popular assemblies and it was their duty to see that the decrees of the Senate and laws of the people were carried out. Solely responsible for the defense of the state, they decided the number of soldiers needed from the allies and the appointment of the military tribunes. They had the authority to put any man to death for insubordination when the army was in the field. There was no limit on what they could spend. Obviously election to the office implied an enormous amount of trust.

Polybius saw the chief power of the Senate to be in its management of all money matters, except what the consuls chose to spend for the purposes they deemed fit. Questions about public works, including costs, were decided by the senators. They also had charge of Rome's foreign relations. Envoys from other lands did not work through a foreign office or department of state but brought their business before the Senate and received their answers there. Committees of senators would be sent overseas for various reasons, whether to look over the site for a new colony or arbitrate some question between neighbors. In addition, the Senate acted as a grand jury in order to investigate criminal matters of public concern, as for instance cases of conspiracy.

The assemblies passed the laws and elected the officials. There could be no declaration of war without a vote by the citizenry. Aside from a consul's prerogative while in the field, the people alone had the power to put a man to death.

The division of powers among the magistrates, the Senate, and the people left each of them dependent on the others. When a consul was on duty overseas he counted on the Senate to keep him furnished with men and supplies. The Senate decided if he should continue in his post as a proconsul for another year or be replaced by a newly elected consul. When he did come home he might be rewarded by a triumph, a lesser ovation, or nothing at all. The Senate would decide that too. An assembly would hear a report of his expenditures and decide if anything was amiss. The "Scipionic Trials" were a famous case, although the details are much in question. Lucius Cornelius Scipio was called to account for a sum of five hundred talents which he had collected in tribute money from the Seleucid king Antiochus III (an event to be discussed in Chapter V). Whether his famous brother, Scipio Africanus, who had recently served with him in the East, was also charged is not certain. There is no doubt, however, that the pride of the mighty Africanus was injured; and it was with indignation, which the accuser Cato the Elder could understand, that Africanus publicly tore up the record sheets in question. Nevertheless, the matter did not end until three years later when a tribune's veto put a stop to what was essentially a quarrel between personal rivals. Actually, the most significant consequence of this investigation was that it ended the public career of Africanus, who died soon after, having withdrawn from Rome in a bitter frame of mind.

While the Senate, because of its prestige and continuity, had the greatest influence on a long term day-to-day basis, it still could be frustrated by the veto power of the tribunes, who were sensitive about the interests of their plebeian supporters. The people themselves were dependent on the experience and leadership of the Senate. Until the second century B.C., senators exclusively had been chosen to sit on juries. Obviously, in this capacity they were expected to display a strong sense of honor. In fact, the whole system could not have worked had there not been a general inclination for all parties to do what was best for the general welfare. Consider the power of the tribunes. Each of ten men had the power to bring the business of the state to a standstill. The Senate could not even be called into session if one of them interposed his veto. In the early centuries of the Republic such power was rarely abused, for the tribunes behaved responsibly and like the consuls and the senators played the game of politics in the Old Roman way during the time when the Romans were united in a common struggle against their enemies in Italy and abroad. After they had won the world, the trouble began.

If Polybius had been pressed to name the one decisive factor by which the Romans eventually defeated Carthage, he would have named their spirit. The enemy's mercenaries might be more experienced and more skillful, but they lost out to the obstinacy of the Roman heart. The Romans would do anything to win, partly out of the pride which had been instilled in them from their earliest days. Family funerals were solemn events likely to impress a young boy, especially if he was the son of a man who had distinguished himself in the service of the state. The bier of such a man would be carried into the Forum and his record read in public. Later, a death mask of the deceased would be placed alongside those of his ancestors so that together they could bear witness to the living of an illustrious past. These masks would be worn at funerals by men dressed in togas appropriately designating whether the ancestor had been a consul or a censor.

The young Roman of the ruling class was given his place in the world. He grew up in a household filled with the memories which tied him to a continuing tradition. Pride was a stern master. He was expected to protect the family name and to be equal to its honors. One day his mask would be carried in a funeral procession and he too would be remembered. Who would not want that? And how better to obtain it than by some singular act of self-sacrifice? Horatius at the bridge was *the* Roman. He was too busy doing his duty to wonder why one of the others did not come and take his place.

In the extraordinary rise of Rome, it was the Romans themselves who made the difference. They followed a strict morality and did not wink at bribery as a means of obtaining office. The Carthaginians and Greeks, according to Polybius, were so far corrupted that being honest or dishonest no longer held any meaning. Where that had happened to others, he said, it was because of a decline in religious faith. Not so the Romans, he said, in a famous passage:

> The most important difference for the better which the Roman commonwealth appears to me to display is in their religious beliefs. For I conceive that what in other nations is looked upon as a reproach, I

mean a scrupulous fear of the gods, is the very thing which keeps the Roman commonwealth together. To such an extraordinary height is this carried among them, both in private and public business, that nothing could exceed it. Many people might think this unaccountable; but in my opinion their object is to use it as a check upon the common people. If it were possible to form a state wholly of philosophers, such a custom would perhaps be unnecessary. But seeing that every multitude is fickle, and full of lawless desires, unreasoning anger, and violent passion, the only resource is to keep them in check by mysterious terrors and scenic effects of this sort. Wherefore, to my mind, the ancients were not acting without purpose or at random, when they brought in among the vulgar those opinions about the gods, and the belief in the punishments in Hades: much rather do I think that men nowadays are acting rashly and foolishly in rejecting them. This is the reason why, apart from anything else, Greek statesmen, if entrusted with a single talent, though protected by ten checking-clerks, as many seals, and twice as many witnesses, yet cannot be induced to keep faith; whereas among the Romans, in their magistracies and embassies, men have the handling of a great amount of money, and yet from pure respect to their oath keep their faith intact. And, again, in other nations it is a rare thing to find a man who keeps his hands out of the public purse, and is entirely pure in such matters: but among the Romans it is a rare thing to detect a man in the act of committing such a crime. (VI. 56)

Polybius did not see religion as an opiate by which men were lulled into acceptance of hard masters who exploited them. Rather, he believed that religion was useful insofar as it held Roman society together by providing the rules which kept men, especially common men who lacked the discipline of philosophy, from preying upon each other.

On their past record, Polybius believed that the Romans deserved to rule the world. He was not so sure of the future. Possibly, events toward the end of his life gave him a forewarning, recorded in this prophetic observation:

When a commonwealth, after warding off many great dangers, has arrived at a high pitch of prosperity and undisputed power, it is evident that, by the lengthened continuance of great wealth within it, the manner of life of its citizens will become more extravagant; and that the rivalry for office, and in other spheres of activity, will become fiercer than it ought to be. And as this state of things goes on more and more, the desire of office and the shame of losing reputation, as well as the ostentation and extravagance of living, will prove the beginning of a deterioration. (VI. 57)

V

The Macedonian Wars

The victory over Carthage in the Second Punic War made Rome the most powerful state in the Mediterranean world. Her importance could soon be measured by the number of foreign emissaries waiting their turn to address the Senate, even as today prime ministers and kings arrive with an obvious frequency in Washington. Polybius says the years 184 to 180 B.C. saw a record count of envoys from Greek states arriving to ask for Roman advice and support, usually against one another. Not all of the states sending delegations to Rome agreed with her policies, nor would they have wanted to seek her aid under other circumstances; but Rome now had the authority to enforce decisions. Legions stood ready to sail from Brundisium to wherever the peace was threatened. With that in mind it was always to be hoped by smaller powers that Rome's decisions would be fair. In earlier days, the Senate might have been embarrassed or perhaps angry to see the grovelling manner in which even kings now presented their cases. "Hail, ye gods my preservers!" one is said to have shouted. Now, the senators were willing to reward such obvious tactics by which the "mean" and "unmanly" debased themselves.

As might be expected, the relative warmth or chilliness with which a foreign dignitary or commission was received offered a clue to the Senate's feelings. In the early years of the second century, nobody was welcomed with greater pomp or entertained more lavishly than King Eumenes of Pergamum, a valuable ally in the Greek world. During the Third Macedonian War, however, when Eumenes began to resent the ubiquitousness of Roman power and to plot secretly against it, the Senate passed a special resolution forbidding foreign kings from visiting Rome. Eumenes heard the news when he reached Brundisium on his way to Rome. He must have had a thoughtful trip home. Earlier, when he had been in better favor, the Senate had found it difficult to arbitrate his disputes with Rhodes, which at the time was also a staunch friend of Rome. Each side accused the other of deceit and self-interest, and the Senate had the problem of finding some tactful way to avoid offending either one. Delegating a commission to investigate matters at first hand had the advantage of providing a cooling-off period. The final result was usually predictable: between friends, the Romans had a habit of splitting the difference.

The number of commissions sent to Greece and Asia Minor by the Senate was proportionate to the number of foreign envoys coming to Rome to ask for help against their local enemies. Investigations were needed if conflicting reports and claims were to be sorted out. To a certain extent, Roman foreign policy began to rest in the hands of three or more commissioners because the Senate often gave such men wide latitude for decisions to be made on the spot. Unfortunately, they were not always the kind of men the Romans could be proud of. Then as now, politics might produce curious choices. A commission sent to Bithynia caught the eye of Marcus Porcius Cato, called Cato the Elder (234–149 B.C.), a prominent conservative and stern guardian of public morality, who was easily moved to make comments. The aging Bithynian king, Prusias II, was in danger of losing his throne to his son Nicomedes, who was said to be conniving with his father's enemies. Nicomedes claimed his father was no longer able to defend the kingdom. All parties awaited the arrival of the investigative commission sent from Rome. Cato wondered if it would ever get there. One man, he said, was lame from gout and could hardly walk, a second had been severely wounded by a roof tile which had fallen on his head, and the third was described as the stupidest man in Rome. What is such a commission to accomplish, Cato asked, if it has "neither feet, head, nor intelligence?" (Polybius, XXXVII. 6).

Cato was equally concerned, but for a quite different reason, about envoys sent to Rome from Greece. In 155 B.C., the Athenians sent three men to ask the Senate to revoke a fine they were required to pay resulting from the arbitration of a recent dispute with nearby Oropus in Boeotia. It was a delegation of philosophers—Carneades the Academic, Diogenes the Stoic, and Critolaus the Peripatetic. While waiting their turn to address the Senate they gave lectures which attracted youthful audiences—and Cato's scorn. Greek philosophy was full of questions, in contrast to the solid answers provided by Roman tradition. Indeed, Carneades argued alternately and most persuasively on both sides of any given question. Cato urged his fellow senators to give the philosophers a quick hearing and send them on their way.

The Senate had various means of coercion when dealing with the separate states in Greece. A major power was the Achaean League, dating from 280 B.C., which had originally consisted of four towns of ancient Achaea, a region along the Peloponnesian coast of the Gulf of Corinth. Later, non-Achaeans joined and eventually the league dominated most of the Peloponnesus. The term *Achaean* was thus given a broader meaning. When the league let it be known that it would no longer refer border disputes or like questions to Rome but would look after its own interests, the senators sent out word that they were no longer concerned about what happened to the Achaeans, as if to invite neighboring states to take advantage of the situation. As time passed, this touchiness at Rome became increasingly apparent. The Senate reacted in a testy and petty fashion when any foreign dispute, even one of no immediate concern to Rome, was not immediately brought to its attention for deliberation and a decision. Pride and prosperity were now mixed with destiny and duty. As men of different speech and dress came hurrying to the city, Rome began to look like the capital of the world. In a century it would be.

Greece

At the outset, the Senate was reluctant to use force to back up its advice about affairs in Greece. Circumstances brought a reversal of this policy. The senators became aware that certain Greek politicians with little else to recommend them had come to power because of outspoken opposition to Roman interference. Once in power they blocked the implementation of Roman directives. All too often Rome did nothing to see that her policies were carried out. As a result, Greek leaders who had depended on Rome's support were left disappointed, if not in jeopardy, and the general citizenry lost confidence in the word of the Senate. When the Senate reversed its policy, it was apparent that there were pitfalls along the opposite road. Subservient Greek politicians openly voiced their friendship to Rome, using force against local "patriots" who resisted. Whether they personally agreed with the Senate or not, they accepted its policies blindly in order to stay in power. Then Polybius says, "the Senate had an abundance of flatterers, but a great scarcity of genuine friends" (II.24.12).

Philopoemen (*ca.* 253–183 B.C.), one of the greatest soldier-statesmen the Achaeans ever had, was willing to accept direction from the Senate except when he felt it to be out of line with Achaean law or with the terms of the Achaean alliance with Rome. Then he would ask to have the matter negotiated. By Philopoemen's day the Roman involvement in the Balkan Peninsula was already an old story. First there had been the Illyrian Wars, and late in the third century came trouble with Philip V, the king of Macedon.

Over a period of nearly seventy years, from late in the third century to the middle of the second century, the Romans fought four Macedonian wars. From their standpoint, they had acted in self-defense and to protect the small states of the Aegean world from their predatory neighbor, Philip V. The first war (215 to 205 B.C.) began when Philip entered into an alliance with Hannibal after the Roman disaster at Cannae. At the time it looked to him like a good risk. His primary interest was to make Macedon a power in the Adriatic region where Rome had earlier established herself after the trouble with Queen Teuta and the Illyrians. Philip's maneuvering was more of a worry to the Romans than a blessing to the Carthaginians. By 205, with Hannibal's chances fading, there was reason for an accommodation. The terms of the peace treaty gave the Macedonians a foothold on the Adriatic—a concession which the Romans were reluctant to make. They would not forget that Philip had taken advantage of their difficulties.

In 201, ambassadors from Rhodes and Pergamum came to Rome to ask for help against Philip. These two trading powers complained of an increasing number of attacks on their ships. In the background was a warning to the Senate that Rome too was in danger. Philip's connivance with the Seleucid king, Antiochus III, if allowed to go unchecked, could ultimately pose a threat to Italy. Antiochus III now ruled the kingdom his ancestor Seleucus I had carved from the Empire of Alexander the Great. Centered in Syria, it claimed all of the eastern territories of Alexander, even to India. Whether or not there was a formal alliance between Philip and Antiochus is not positively known, although one was generally assumed. In any event, Philip and Antiochus were partners in spirit, and the suspicions they aroused called for preventive action. Philip never had a shortage of pretexts; a quarrel with Athens would do. The Romans warned Philip that they were prepared to guarantee Athenian independence. He ignored them. The leaders at Rome who favored action were thus handed an insult they could use to win support. They needed something. In 200 B.C., the Roman people were war-weary. The long struggle with Hannibal had ended only a year earlier and they could muster little enthusiasm for further conflict.

The shades of opinion in Rome about increasing entanglements overseas, particularly in Greece, can be summed up this way. There were always isolationists, who feared that local problems would be neglected or that the Romans would be used by others, particularly in pulling Greek chestnuts out of the fire. Especially vocal were old-line moralists, who worried that the Roman style of life would become contaminated by foreign contacts. These men looked askance at the Greek heritage (as we call it), observing that loose attitudes about many things, including sexual practices, were infiltrating Roman life, along with strange philosophies. To a stolid Old Roman the past with its time-honored values mattered more than Roman hegemony in the Mediterranean. Since some outspoken isolationists were members of the Fabian gens, this side of the question was associated with the Fabian faction. A Claudian faction favored expansion of Roman interests overseas as a matter of destiny. Past victories were a prelude to greater triumphs to come. The Romans should use their power to check the aggression of others. Who else could prevent the Illyrian pirates from interrupting peaceful trade in the Adriatic? What was to be done about the possible connivance of Philip V and Antiochus III against Rome? The Claudians were realists. Rome had won control of Italy and the western Mediterranean. She must use her new position to serve her own interests and those of her allies. The Claudian view was a popular one.

Others favored selective intervention. With that familiar idealism which intellectuals affect, they disavowed any real self-interest. Like the Byrons and Shelleys of modern times, the philhellenes at Rome were sentimental about the Greeks—their faults notwithstanding. At the other extreme, some who favored selective intervention were exploiters who hoped to build a greater military reputation along the way.

The conflict of views in the Senate resulted in constant wrangling over foreign policy. Adding to the confusion was the problem of determining which of the delegations from the various Greek cities might be telling the truth. Obviously, at the beginning, the Romans had no definite policy toward Greece—certainly not one of military conquest. Only after much talk, unnecessary trouble, and considerable misunderstanding were the Greek states finally incorporated into Roman provinces. Earlier, those who favored intervention insisted that putting Philip in his place immediately would save Rome from worse trouble later. In July, 200 B.C., the Centuriate Assembly voted, with considerable reluctance, to declare war. Then the wrong man was chosen to command the expeditionary forces which launched the Second Macedonian War (200–196 B.C.). Publius Sulpicius Galba is a revealing example of the worst type of Roman leadership. His record as proconsul in Illyria was stained with wanton thefts by which he enriched himself at the expense of the natives. Nor was his skill as a commander worth even a slight amount of corruption. He was at his best where he could overwhelm the opposition with sheer power—strategy was hardly needed. The Greeks whom he was supposed to be helping hated him, as did his own soldiers. The war was not popular in the first place and Galba's heavy-handedness made it worse. In the winter of 199, his army mutinied.

If Galba was one of the worst of the Roman leaders, Titus Quinctius Flamininus (*ca.* 227–*ca.* 174 B.C.) was one of the best, not that he lacked shortcomings, but because of his excellent intentions. He was among the philhellenes at Rome—a lover of all things Greek, who wrote and spoke the language. His service in Greece was a mission to save the land from outside oppressors. The same policy, he thought, would best serve Roman interests in the area.

Flamininus' career began during the war with Hannibal, and

from the outset he looked promising. If he coveted praise and fame, it was for the right reasons. Plutarch (*ca.* A.D. 50–120), who wrote *The Lives of the Noble Grecians and Romans,* thinks he was a dedicated man, albeit not very humble about it. Flamininus boldly stood for the consulship without having passed through all the lower offices which others felt bound by tradition to hold in turn. This risk paid off, and he was elected to the highest office before he was even thirty. The climax of his career was the command against the Macedonians, and that came at a correspondingly early age. Nobody could have been better suited to win the loyalty of the Greeks, who were so openly hostile to Galba.

Flamininus' first encounter with the enemy was in Epirus. He forced Philip's army to flee and then gave the residents of the area a rare show of discipline as his victorious soldiers moved through the countryside without injury to any man or his property. The Aetolians had already allied themselves with Rome. Now the Achaeans joined in, along with several Greek towns. Flamininus was the liberator they had been waiting for.

It is wrong to view the Romans as militarists in single-minded pursuit of victory. During this unpopular war there were repeated efforts to reach a peaceful settlement, but a political accommodation was obviously difficult so long as neither side felt it had to give in. Moreover, not all the allies on Rome's side had the same goals.

During the winter of 198–197 B.C., a conference was held at Nicaea in Locris to see if all parties concerned, King Attalus I of Pergamum, the Rhodians, the Achaeans, the Aetolians, the Romans, and Philip could agree on a settlement for ending the war. Philip asked the other representatives to submit their demands in writing so he could think about them and chided Flamininus for having such a large party, whereas he had come alone. According to Polybius, Flamininus was quick to reply: "Of course you are alone, Philip: for you have killed all the friends likely to give you the best advice!" (II.18.7).

When the conference reached an impasse, it was decided that all parties should send delegations to Rome to discuss their individual demands before the Senate. Philip did not admit to all charges against him, but said he was willing to accept what the Senate should decide. Flamininus doubted Philip's intentions but was willing to go along with the idea; he always wanted to be generous and hoped for the best. Besides it was winter, a bad time for fighting.

The Senate was informed of events and proposals by three personal representatives from Flamininus, seven envoys from the Aetolians, one from the Achaeans, one from King Attalus and two from Athens. The Greek envoys told the Senate that so long as Philip controlled Chalcis, Corinth, and Demetrias it did not matter what he promised, for these places by his own estimation were the "fetters of Greece," the key to domination of the whole land. The Greeks then begged the Senate to continue the war against him until he gave them up—adding that he had already been defeated in two major engagements. After the Greek pleas, Philip's envoys barely got in the door. When asked about Chalcis, Corinth, and Demetrias, they replied that they were not empowered to discuss those places. Upon hearing this, the Senate sent instructions to Flamininus to pursue the war at his own discretion.

The battle which decided the Second Macedonian War (200–196 B.C.) in Rome's favor was fought in Thessaly in June, 197, at a place called Cynoscephalae, so named after nearby hills. The terrain was rough and Philip had his doubts about fighting, but Flamininus had offered battle and the king was caught up in the eagerness of his soldiers for a fight. The massive block of the Macedonian phalanx was a powerful force when it held together. Flamininus saw the right wing of the enemy sweep forward and realized that his best chance would be on the other side where the line broke because of the ground. Once the Macedonians in heavy armor became detached from their "block" they were easily overpowered. When the Romans broke through on the left it was possible to swing around and catch Philip's high-powered right wing in the rear. Philip was finished.

The Roman victory at Cynoscephalae was marred by a serious rift with the Aetolians when Flamininus agreed to give Philip terms which did not altogether destroy him. The Aetolians' aim was to depose Philip for all his past deeds and in fact to build their own power at his expense. Having fought hard, they expected some profit. Flamininus, who sometimes sounds like a Roman version of Woodrow Wilson, sought a just peace which would consider the fair interests of all. The Greeks were due to have some second thoughts about him. For the moment, however, he was a hero to most of them, even though the Aetolians spread the word that he was too soft where Philip was concerned. Flamininus was intent on the freedom of all the Greek states and did not intend to remove the threat from Philip only to create a new

threat from the ambitious Aetolians. When Flamininus agreed to
enter into discussions with Philip, the Aetolians suspected he had
been bribed. Polybius says they were simply attributing to the
Romans habits well known among themselves.

Flamininus had not lost sight of Rome's best interests. He
was aware that the Seleucid king Antiochus the Great (*ca.* 242–187
B.C.) may well have been planning a counterthrust against Rome.
By coming to terms with Philip, Rome would escape the danger
of being caught on two fronts. Plutarch said Flamininus "at once
disappointed Antiochus of his first hopes and Philip of his last" (p.
456). When Flamininus called a parley at Tempe in 197 B.C. to
discuss the terms to be given Philip, the Aetolians insisted that
there would be no peace or freedom for Greece unless Philip was
forced to give up his throne. They wanted revenge. Flamininus
clearly did not. His practical argument for leaving a moderate
amount of power in Philip's hands was that Macedon had long
served as a buffer between the Greeks and their dangerous neighbors, the Thracians and the Gauls. He allowed Philip to keep his
kingdom so long as he kept out of Greece—and that meant with-
drawing all of his so-called diplomatic agents. Flamininus also
ordered Philip to pay an indemnity and to reduce his fleet to a
nominal size. Furthermore, Philip's younger son, Demetrius, with
some of his friends were to be sent to Rome as hostages. The
Aetolians were not given the cities Philip held, which they coveted. This turned them totally sour on the Romans, whose help
they had originally solicited.

The Senate sent ten commissioners to Greece to make arrangements for the peace. Flamininus pleaded with them to remove all Roman forces from Greece, but the commissioners felt
that the danger from Antiochus was serious enough to require
them to hold on to Demetrias, Chalcis, and the Corinthian citadel
Acrocorinthus. The Aetolians scoffed at this solution, claiming
that the Romans now controlled the "fetters of Greece," but the
overwhelming majority of the Greeks were grateful for all the
Romans had done for them and viewed their three garrisons as
defensive.

The dramatic announcement of the Roman plans came at
the Isthmian Games in July, 196. Peace having made travel possible, people came from all parts of Greece and so a great assembly heard the proclamation: "The Senate of Rome and Titus
Quinctius, proconsul and imperator, having conquered King

Philip and the Macedonians in war declare the following peoples free, without garrison, or tribute, in full enjoyment of the laws of their respective countries: namely Corinthians, Phocians, Locrians, Euboeans, Achaeans of Phiotis, Magnesians, Thessalians, and Perrhaebians" (Polybius, XVIII. 46). Plutarch left no doubt about the roar of approval from the listening crowd. The noise "was heard as far as the sea" and crows flying overhead "fell down dead" (pp. 156–157).

Never had the Greeks fared so well at the hands of foreigners. The Romans of their own free will had come to liberate them from their oppressors and now were leaving them to their own resources. It was, Plutarch said, more than they had ever won by their own efforts. Amid the celebrations, the Greeks did not stop to consider that Flamininus was a Roman of a special breed, whose love for Greek culture was not necessarily shared by some of his hard-headed colleagues at home. Flamininus and his friends have been described as having engaged in sentimental politics. The phrase suggests some naiveté. To the Romans, liberty circumscribed by order meant peace. Plutarch said Flamininus, visiting Greek cities, "exhorted them to the practice of obedience to law, of constant justice, and unity, and friendship one towards another" (p. 458). To the Greeks, however, liberty meant full latitude for pursuing their own ends—that usually led to trouble. The difference in the two positions would one day become evident to the Romans, but not yet.

Flamininus considered the liberation of Greece to be the capstone of his career. Throughout the Aegean world there was new respect for Roman liberality as well as power. The weak everywhere could take heart. The Romans would protect them. At Rome, Flamininus' triumphal procession in 194 was hailed with a special warmth. He brought home twelve hundred fellow citizens who had been captured by the Carthaginians and sold into slavery in Greece.

The representatives of the Senate dispatched to oversee the settlement in Greece sent a warning to Antiochus: he was to leave the autonomous cities in Asia (in Asia Minor) alone and to give up any which had previously belonged to Philip or Ptolemy. He was also told not to set foot in Europe. Antiochus was understandably provoked about the Roman interest in Asia Minor, and asked the ambassadors how the Senate would feel if he began interfering in the affairs of Italy. Earlier, when he had entered Europe to take control of cities in the Chersonesus Thracica (modern Gallipoli Peninsula) and Thrace, he felt he had a perfect right to do so. History was on his side, for Alexander's general Lysimachus had received these places as his share of the empire and lost them in a war with Antiochus' ancestor Seleucus. Why should they remain in the hands of Philip or Ptolemy? Antiochus merely intended to recover what belonged to him, and it was no concern of Rome. If the Romans had decided to become the policemen of the eastern Mediterranean, Antiochus wanted them to know that they were not welcome.

Antiochus brought his army from Syria across the Hellespont in 192 and was soon welcomed to Greece by the Aetolians, who felt Roman insistence on the status quo to be oppressive. Before the year was over, Antiochus had taken Chalcis, where he spent the winter happily celebrating his marriage to a local young girl of high birth. He was fifty, and a man who Polybius says drank too much.

In 191, the Romans declared war on Antiochus. It was short. Ostensibly, Antiochus had come to "liberate" the Greeks from the Romans. Only a few cities were willing to pretend that he was needed, and the Roman consul Manius Acilius soundly defeated him at Thermopylae before any others could make up their minds. It was almost three centuries earlier at Thermopylae that a band of Spartans, clawing and biting, had died to a man, being caught in a trap by the Persians. This time, Livy, quoting a lost section of Polybius, says only five hundred of 10,000 of Antiochus' soldiers escaped. We might wonder about this, but it was undoubtedly a decisive victory for the Romans, and among them was Marcus Porcius Cato (234–149 B.C.), who seven years later became the best known censor in Rome's history. Antiochus was forced to retreat all the way to Ephesus in Asia Minor. The embarrassed Aetolians were left to shift for themselves. Now they were at the mercy of Philip, who had eagerly joined the Romans in this war and was allowed by the consul to take some profit. Although Flamininus was now assisting the consul and was disturbed to see how Philip was behaving, he could do little about it. He was kept busy protecting those Greek cities which had displeased Acilius from receiving the full brunt of the consul's anger. The Greeks continued to reward Flamininus by erecting monuments in his honor. He was a man who had a forgiving nature and the Greeks had much need of forgiveness.

In 190, Philip sent envoys to the Senate to proclaim his steadfast support of Rome and to remind the senators how he had served them during the recent trouble with Antiochus. They rewarded him by sending his son Demetrius home and further promised to cut his indemnity if he remained loyal.

The consuls in 190 were Lucius Cornelius Scipio and Gaius Laelius. When Lucius went to Greece in the spring of that year, his famous brother Publius Scipio Africanus went along as his legate. They entered into negotiations with the Aetolians and eventually granted them a six-month truce, during which their envoys could seek to work out an agreement with the Senate. A treaty which called for an indemnity and hostages was ratified in 189 B.C. Key passages placed the Aetolian League inside the Roman circle of friends:

> The people of the Aetolians shall in good faith maintain the empire and majesty of the people of Rome.
>
> They shall not allow hostile forces to pass through their territory or cities against the Romans, their allies or friends, nor grant them any supplies from the public fund.
>
> They shall have the same enemies as the people of Rome; and if the Roman people go to war with any, the Aetolian people shall do so also (Polybius XXI. 32).

In 190, the more pressing problem was Antiochus, who after his severe defeat in Greece hoped to prevent the Romans from crossing into Asia Minor by controlling the sea. Again, he was disappointed. In the first engagement of his fleet with the Romans in 190 B.C., he lost forty-two ships off the coast of Asia Minor near Teos. After this setback, Antiochus sought a negotiated peace, but was not willing to make the necessary concessions to achieve it. Hostilities continued, and a decisive battle was fought in the fall of 190 at Magnesia ad Sipylum, south of Ephesus in Asia Minor. Antiochus' defeat there forced him to accept the very terms he had rejected the previous year. Antiochus had to quit Europe and the region in Asia Minor west of the Taurus Mountains. An indemnity and hostages were required. Included was a demand that Hannibal be given up. Political troubles in Carthage had prompted him to flee to Antioch. He now fled again; later, when trapped in Bithynia, he committed suicide to avoid being handed over to the Romans.

Problems in Greece

Although the Romans withdrew their forces from Greece a second time in 188, they continued to consider themselves the protectors of the peace. Unfortunately, however, the Senate was no more attuned to the underlying problems of the Greek states than Flamininus had been. As usual, border squabbles and other local quarrels combined with human perversity to account for a certain amount of trouble.

The major problem in Greece was a matter of simple economics. There was never enough land to support the number of people trying to live on it. From ancient times until the present day large numbers of Greeks have left their homeland in order to survive. Those remaining have seen over and over again the truth of Aristotle's prophecy that instability is to be expected in a commonwealth when a sizeable middle class is lacking. This was certainly true at the time the Romans arrived in Greece, for then as now the opulence of a few shipbuilders, traders, and large landowners offered an unseemly contrast to the prevalent poverty in the land. Earlier, in the third century, the slogans of popular movements called for a redistribution of land and a cancellation of debts. The wealthy were wont to dismiss the leaders of these uprisings as demagogues, and some of them were, but not men like Agis and Cleomenes. These two Spartan kings were sincerely concerned about the dire needs of most of the people. Both failed and were killed—victims of insidious political intrigues which like entangling vines darkened Greece and strangled men of good intentions. There was a numbing sense of frustration throughout the land. Not even the bitter quarrels between the various states could alleviate class warfare, for one faction or another within a city would often side with the enemy against its own citizens.

The social ills of Greece have been made evident by some unsettling statistics. Polybius says that Greek families of the second century were raising only one or two children. While they could not control the numbers who were born, they could limit the number who lived by the age-old expedient of infanticide. W.W. Tarn, in his *Hellenistic Civilization* (rev. ed. with G.T. Griffith, Meridian paperback, p. 101), does not question that this practice was widely used. Citing details from one thousand families from about 228 to 220 B.C., he notes that in seventy-nine families there were one hundred and eighteen sons but only twenty-eight daughters. Obviously the prospect for female babies was grim, especially so in families conscious of future dowry commitments or, if not that, life-long support for a daughter. Young men made their own expenses as mercenaries abroad, or by emigrating to foreign lands in search of employment, as in fact they are still doing. Polybius seems to speak primarily of families of some means who chose to limit their families in order to hold on to their financial status. It may be imagined that among the poor there was little choice if they were to eat at all.

While most Greeks were forced to live frugally, a fortunate few were enjoying costly imports from the east. Fine furniture, richly woven cloths, perfumes, and tapestries meant a new opulence in the life of bankers, manufacturers, and government officials. Traders who carried goods to the west were especially prosperous; they were major employers of the laborers who loaded the goods criss-crossing through Greek ports to other lands. But the prosperity was not deep. Great fortunes were reflected in the numbers of slaves certain men owned, the dowries they gave with their daughters, and their collections of vases and statuary, which the Romans would in time carry home. Then as now, the average man might look with awe at the wealth of a great shipowner, but given the chance he might also be a revolutionary. He had nothing to win by supporting the status quo and a chance to gain with a change. The Roman insistence on peace came to mean solid support for the ruling classes and no hope for the depressed. At Rome, foreign policy was determined by the Senate, and the senators were for the most part landowners. That very many of them would consciously support agitation for land redistribution in Greece is not to be imagined. On the other hand, any foreign power wanting to cause trouble for the Romans in Greece would do exactly that.

So many complaints were carried to Rome by envoys of King Eumenes, the Thessalians, and others against Philip in 185, that the Senate sent a commission to investigate. As the ambassadors sent by Philip had naturally denied the allegations, the Senate decided a fact-finding mission was imperative.

Philip remained cautious about offending Rome outright, and to counteract continuing reports about his hostility he sent his son Demetrius to smooth things over. Demetrius had made so many friends at Rome during his earlier stay as a hostage that he was the ideal person to keep the Romans off guard about his father's real sentiments. Demetrius' popularity with the Senate was not lost on his father or his elder brother Perseus at home. They could easily assume that the fortunes of Macedon were being maintained by Demetrius alone and further that the Senate was already planning to have him succeed his father in Macedon. At the moment, Demetrius might be elated by the good will shown toward him by the Senate but, ironically, it later cost him his life.

Perseus and the Third Macedonian War (171–167 B.C.)

Perseus, being Philip's elder son, expected to succeed his father and was worried that Demetrius, being favored by the Romans, might supplant him as heir to the throne. According to Livy, he used a forged letter, which had presumably been signed by Flamininus, to convince Philip that Demetrius had betrayed him in Rome. Philip then consented to his son being put to death, and with some strong-arming and a little poison it was done in 181.

Before Philip died in 179, he learned the truth about Perseus' plot against Demetrius, too late to do anything about it. Even though he would have preferred to have Antigonus, a distant relative, succeed him, it was Perseus who came to the throne. His crimes aside, he at least looked like a king. He was of a royal stature and affected a proper degree of austerity. His father had lived up to the family traits as a roistering drinker and lecher, but Perseus was a man of moderation in almost everything except ambition.

Perseus reaffirmed his father's alliance with Rome and then began to work against it. There was no evidence, of course, which the Romans could put a finger on. Perseus simply began to show an unusual liberality toward the underprivileged in Macedonia and even toward outcasts. Political exiles and men who had fled from their debts were allowed to return, and in some instances could reclaim their previously forfeited property. Since Perseus had announcements posted at Delphi and elsewhere of his generous new policy, the Greeks who sought reform and a better life were soon aware that he was sympathetic to their cause. By the same token, the ruling classes in Greece, protected by the Roman doctrine of the status quo, a kind of "drachma diplomacy," began to wonder about Perseus as they had so often wondered about his father. His marriage to Laodice, the daughter of Seleucus IV, was not an unlikely match; yet this alliance with Antioch brought back memories of his late father's reputed intrigues with Antiochus III.

By 173, the Senate was sufficiently concerned to send a representative to talk to the Aetolian and Achaean leagues, an envoy to Thessaly to see what was happening to Perseus' near neighbors, and a five-man commission to Macedon itself. What they learned agreed with the warnings King Eumenes delivered to the Senate in person in 172. Specifically, he said that Perseus was undermining the position of Rome everywhere by working against those who supported the Roman peace. Under the guise of local intrigues some of Rome's best friends were being executed or exiled. Eumenes charged that Perseus was recruiting a new army among the rugged Thracians and that his supporters occupied high places in Boeotia, Thessaly, Perrhaebia, and among the Aetolians.

The boldness of Perseus' agents in Greece was made obvious by what happened to Eumenes on his way home from Rome. As was the custom with dignitaries, he stopped at Delphi to pay his respects to the oracle. While there, he narrowly escaped being crushed by large rocks which suddenly came rolling down the mountain side. He was badly injured but later recovered. While everybody else was talking about this obvious attempt at assassination, the Romans decided to act. Perseus was accused of aggression against certain neighboring tribes which had entered into alliances with Rome. With this pretext, the Romans forced him into a war, ready or not. All considered, Perseus managed to do fairly well against the odds for about four years. The early engagements of the Third Macedonian War were not important, but in the summer of 171 Perseus managed to turn back the consul, Publius Licinius, and, after doing so, sought to negotiate on the basis of an insignificant victory. It was of course the wrong time to ask the inexorable Romans for anything. Polybius takes the opportunity to comment on Roman policy: "This is a peculiarity of the Romans, which they have inherited from their ancestors, and are continually displaying,—to show themselves most peremptory and imperious in the presence of defeat, and most moderate when successful: a very noble peculiarity, as everyone will acknowledge; but whether it be feasible under certain circumstances may be doubted" (XXVII. 8).

During the war, Perseus carried on a busy campaign of

propaganda in Greece. In his favor was the unmistakable secret satisfaction many Greeks had in seeing somebody challenge mighty Rome, and, for the time being anyway, get away with it. Most of them had suffered more at the hands of the Macedonians than they had from the Romans, but Perseus won the sympathy that comes to an underdog. He was of course anxious to have the Greeks accept him as their liberator, but he was unwilling to pay them for the honor. Polybius said that if he had agreed to spend some money on certain politicians and had given gifts to a few cities he could have caught the Romans on all sides with a people openly hostile to them. As it was, they were happy to see him do well, but took no chances of their own.

As the war dragged on, Romans grumbled about it. The reaction of the military was predictable. Lucius Aemilius Paullus, before leaving for Macedonia, issued a blunt evaluation of public opinion which a professional soldier might still find useful. Concerning his fellow citizens, he said:

> Their one idea, expressed at parties or conversations in the street, was, that they should manage the war in Macedonia while remaining quietly at home in Rome, sometimes by criticizing what the generals were doing, at others what they were leaving undone. From this the public interests never got any good, and often a great deal of harm. The generals themselves were at times greatly hampered by this ill-timed loquacity. For as it is the invariable nature of slander to spread rapidly and stop at nothing, the people got thoroughly infected by this idle talk, and the generals were consequently rendered contemptible in the eyes of the enemy. (XXIX. 1)

L. Aemilius Paullus, consul for 168, had ended Perseus' power by midsummer, with the help of two courageous lieutenants, one of them his eldest son. Perseus had established himself in an excellent position on the river Enipeus in Macedonia, but was caught off-guard by a daring Roman unit which crossed through mountains and came up behind him. He then moved his forces toward Pydna, and it was near this place that the decisive battle was fought. Some believed a recent eclipse of the moon foretold the downfall of the king, and what happened confirmed their belief. Perseus was forced to flee for his life. The Romans caught up with him on the island of Samothrace. After the humiliating experience of walking as a prisoner in Paullus' triumphal procession, he was given the royal privilege of living quietly at Alba Pompeia, in northwest Italy, in the manner of an exiled king waiting out the rest of his years. So passed from the scene, in undramatic fashion, the last of the Macedonian successors to Alexander the Great. The kingdom of Macedon, a remnant of Alexander's empire, had come to an end. The Romans who had once boasted of their support for monarchies had found one they could not tolerate. They would find others. A variety of alliances would be transformed into a single empire. The presence of Rome was daily becoming more visible. While Perseus was fighting at Pydna, pedestals were being erected at Delphi to support statues of himself. After the war, Paullus ordered them finished and substituted his own majesty for that of the retired king. Everywhere in Greece those who had remained loyal to Rome did the talking; her enemies were quiet.

Roman Domination

By order of the Senate, Macedon was divided into four republics, each with its own assembly and magistrates. Pella was retained as a capital of one district. Thessalonica, Amphipolis, and Pelagonia were the seats for the other governments. Each would have its own laws and pay its own tribute to Rome. A citizen of one republic was forbidden to marry a woman or own property in any of the others. This settlement was valid only on paper. The Macedonians had been accustomed to strong personal rule, and they neither took well to their new "democracy" nor to the unnatural division of the land which the Romans had imposed. Within four years the Senate was sending a commission to investigate the problems which their supposed solution had created. Actually, they had only given the Macedonians something else to fight for—unity. Within twenty years the monarchists had found a leader in Andriscus, who claimed to be a son of Perseus. Very little is known about this man who Polybius says seems to have "fallen out of the sky." He may actually have been the son of a weaver, but many people wanted to believe his claims and that insured him at least a temporary success. The Romans knew that Perseus' real son had died in Italy two years after the king, but they were fighting not so much a mere adventurer as a dream of unity. The first force sent to capture Andriscus failed because it was too small, but in 148 a larger army defeated him. These two minor campaigns were called the Fourth Macedonian War (149–148 B.C.). Andriscus was not accorded the privilege of a royal imprisonment. He was executed in Rome. With a wearying half century of experience behind them, the Romans now combined Macedonia, Thessaly, and Epirus into a single unit and annexed the region as a province. The military governor was to keep an eye on Dalmatia and also Illyria, which after the Third Illyrian War had been divided into three republics.

After the Third Macedonian War the Roman Senate began to exhibit a growing impatience toward smaller powers which Rome suspected of not being wholly loyal. This was part of the shift from cooperation toward domination.

During the war with Perseus, which few could doubt Rome would win, two of her old friends began to waver. Rhodes and Pergamum had energetically sought Roman help to save them from the Macedonians and the Seleucids. Now who was left to save them from Rome? Both of these small powers were split internally between factions. One favored support for Rome no matter what the cost; the other was anxious to preserve its independence. At Rhodes, leaders wary of Rome were looking around for friends in the Aegean region with whom they might organize a league to resist Roman encroachment. Earlier, at Pergamum, King Eumenes himself had entered into secret negotiations with Perseus. For five hundred talents he was willing to defect from the Romans and for fifteen hundred to bring about a negotiated settlement. That these two old enemies could trust each other about anything was hard to imagine, and that Eumenes would succeed in losing Rome's trust was a foregone conclusion. Polybius calls the scheme absurd. It was a good example of what the Romans were having to put up with even from their allies, amid the befuddled politics of the Greek world.

Before long it was apparent that the Romans had nothing good to say for Eumenes but were fulsome in their praise for his brother Attalus, whom they obviously preferred on the throne of Pergamum—the sooner the better. But after the war, the Gauls were again a menace, and the brothers, divided about Rome, were united in face of a more immediate danger. Eumenes remained in power until his death in 160 or 159 B.C., when Attalus II succeeded him and Rome and Pergamum became once more the firmest of friends.

After the war with Perseus, the Romans showed their displeasure with the insincere Rhodians by practically ruining them as the dominant naval power in the Aegean. First, Rome stripped them of possessions on the mainland, Caria and Lycia, which had been awarded to them in 189 B.C. for their cooperation against Antiochus III. A worse blow was Rome's decision to give Delos to a friendly Athens and to make this island trading center a free port. As a result, the prosperity of Rhodes was seriously undermined and she could no longer afford so powerful a fleet as in years past. But Rome's revenge boomeranged. For years, the Rhodians had successfully checked pirates and slave hunters in the Aegean. By removing this sea arm the Romans invited a return of bold outlaws in the area, which later proved a threat to their own interests. Rome's treatment of Rhodes was shortsighted. There was more of that kind of thinking than there used to be.

As Polybius saw it, the misfortune of Perseus was a distinct bit of luck for the Ptolemies. There had been a series of wars between the Ptolemies and various Seleucid rulers over the coastal lands of the eastern Mediterranean, including Palestine. One of the settlements along the way had provided for the marriage of Ptolemy V to a daughter of Antiochus III. At the time of the Third Macedonian War their son, Ptolemy VI, called Philometer, was engaged in new hostilities with his uncle, Antiochus IV. They signed another agreement in the summer of 169, but soon internal trouble in Egypt gave Antiochus the prospect of conquering the land for himself. A power struggle between Ptolemy VI and his brother Ptolemy VIII weakened the country to the point where Antiochus felt safe in claiming the crown for himself. In the spring of 168 he did so at Memphis and then marched toward Alexandria to take over. He was met a few miles from the city by a delegation from Rome headed by Gaius Popillius Laenas.

The Roman Senate, informed about what was happening, had sent a decree to be delivered to Antiochus, which in effect ordered him out of Egypt. Popillius carried out his mission with a stern manner and a stony face. He would not even shake hands with Antiochus until he was assured that the king would obey Rome's orders. When Antiochus said he would like some time to think about the decree, Popillius used a vine stick to draw a circle around the place where the king was standing. He instructed him to answer before he moved. The "circle of Popillius" was an arrogant show of Roman power and an insult to the king. Yet Antiochus IV knew he would have no help from Perseus, and without that his chances were slight. He gave Popillius his promise to obey the Senate and promptly led his army back to Syria. It was a humiliating experience.

When Antiochus IV Epiphanes died in 164, the Senate intervened in Syria to safeguard the throne for his young child, and, by insisting on this succession, gave comfort to the nobility, who here as elsewhere benefited from Rome's predilection for the status quo. Antiochus had himself been an erratic ruler. It was said that shortly before his death he had attacked the temple of Artemis in Elymais in order to rob its treasury. In any event that story helped to explain the report that he was insane. It was said that the gods often inflicted such retribution for crimes against their sanctuaries.

Polybius insisted that history could only be written properly by those who had a firsthand knowledge of events, not an unexpected opinion from a man who was a close friend of many leaders in Rome. In 167, after the defeat of Perseus, the Romans captured the king's archives, which contained letters showing that he had had secret support from high ranking Achaean officials. As mentioned earlier, one thousand of their fellow citizens, including Polybius, were taken to Rome as hostages, to prevent further political action by this group. Polybius soon had a high regard for some of the Romans, but not for all. He considered Scipio Aemilianus, called Scipio the Younger, to be truly worthy of his famous grandfather (by adoption), the great Africanus, known as Scipio the Elder. Yet Polybius had to admit that it was easy for a man of fine qualities to appear exemplary at Rome. Aemilianus looked especially good because so many of his contemporaries looked so bad. Polybius said, "Some had wasted their energies on favorite youths; others on mistresses; and a great many on banquets enlivened with poetry and wine, and all the extravagant expenditure which they entailed, having quickly caught during the war with Perseus the dissoluteness of Greek manners in this respect. . . . And to such monstrous lengths had this debauchery gone among the young men, that many of them had given a talent for a young favorite" (XXXII. 11). By comparison, Polybius stressed Aemilianus' goodness and purity in being generous to his natural mother, who had been divorced by his father and had thereafter lost her place in society.

Early in his life Aemilianus showed the courage, vigor, and intellect which Polybius later praised as the ideal qualities of a man. When Aemilianus was about seventeen, he fought under his father at Pydna. After the Third Macedonian War, Polybius

writes that Aemilianus was given charge of a large hunting area in
Macedon preserved by the kings and having all manner of game.
He "devoted his whole time to this business, as long as the army
remained in Macedonia. . . . Having then ample opportunity for
following this kind of pursuit, and being in the very prime of his
youth and naturally disposed to it, the taste for hunting which he
acquired became permanent" (XXXII. 15). Later, he became better known as a patron of the arts. His house was a gathering place
for the Scipionic Circle, a group of fellow intellectuals who joined
him in his patronage of the playwright Terence and the philosopher Panaetius. But according to Polybius, he never lost his
"popular reputation for manly courage." By comparison, Polybius found his fellow Greek politicians sadly wanting. If any of
them succeeded it was by luck. Aemilianus owed his success to his
sterling character. This was a favorite theme with Polybius.

Further Trouble in Greece

In 151, Polybius asked his friend Aemilianus to talk to the powerful Cato about the possibility of sending the Achaean hostages
back to Greece. They had been in Rome for sixteen years, and the
older ones in particular longed to go home. With strong opposition expressed in the Senate, the debate dragged on until Cato
tipped the balance. "As though we had nothing else to do," he
said, "we sit here the whole day debating whether some old
Greek dotards should be buried by Italian or Achaean under-
takers!" (XXX. 6).

Those who opposed the move eventually had the last word.
Soon after the restoration of the hostages, further trouble arose
with Achaea. In the fall of 150, Sparta wanted to have the Senate
arbitrate its dispute with the Achaean League. To forestall this
action the league passed a law forbidding the appeals of individual
states and reserving the right to the league alone. This led to
fighting in both 149 and 148, but nothing was resolved before the
arrival in 147 of commissioners sent from the Senate. Rome had
decided to detach Sparta, Corinth, Argos, Heraclea near Aete, and
Orchomenus in Arcadia from the league, "as not being united by
blood, and only being subsequent additions."

When the Corinthians heard what the Romans decreed they
vented their anger on the Spartans living in the city, and even the
Roman envoys who tried to reason with them barely got away

with their lives. The Senate sent a new commission with a sharply worded warning to the Achaeans. Anger at Rome was mixed with disappointment, for the Senate had always considered the Achaean League to be the most stable government in Greece. The current unpleasantness was much regretted. Unfortunately, some leaders of the Achaean League preferred to ignore the Roman expressions of good will and, on the contrary, hoped to gain from the fact that the Romans were at the moment hotly engaged in both Spain and North Africa. Critolaus was especially outspoken against the Romans and travelled from town to town stirring up trouble against them. Popular support for the anti-Roman party was easily arranged; Critolaus won the multitude of poor to his side when he called for an easing of all laws and restrictions on debtors.

During the winter 147–146 B.C., Quintus Caecilius Metellus, who was in Macedonia, sent legates to talk to the Corinthians, but again they were rudely treated and, in fact, not heard at all because of the uproar in the assembly. Critolaus whipped the crowd to fury with a familiar tactic, shouting that the real enemies were not the Romans or Spartans but rather those men among themselves who called for conciliation. Moderate opinion was thus silenced, and Critolaus soon triumphed completely by having a law passed, contrary to the Achaean constitution, giving the next elected commander full control of the war against Sparta. Such "drivelling folly," as Polybius called it, could only lead to a stern reaction from Rome.

In the spring of 146 B.C., Critolaus went all the way and persuaded the Achaean League to declare war against the Romans. The Thebans joined in because of resentment over a recent fine levied on them by the Romans as a result of a local dispute. The consul Mummius was sent with an adequate force to deal with the Achaeans, but Metellus, who was in Macedonia, came south and defeated Critolaus' army before Mummius arrived. It is not certain whether Critolaus drowned while trying to escape or committed suicide.

The Achaeans had only succeeded in bringing the full brunt of Roman wrath upon the Greeks. Polybius writes of the universal despair: "The whole country seemed to be under an evil spell; everywhere people were throwing themselves down wells or over precipices; and so dreadful was the state of things, that as the proverb has it 'even an enemy would have pitied' the disaster of Greece" (XXXIX. 9).

When Mummius arrived Metellus retired to Macedonia. The Achaeans had some success in their initial encounter with Mummius' army, but they were crushed shortly afterwards. Corinth was taken and burned. Polybius described the senseless destruction: "The soldiers cared nothing for the works of art and the consecrated statues. I saw with my own eyes pictures thrown on the ground and soldiers playing dice on them" (XXXIX. 13). The ruins of the ancient city may be visited today. Modern Corinth stands nearby.

The Romans dissolved the Achaean League and forbade any leagues in Greece. Henceforth all Greek cities were to be independent and subject to censure by the governor of Macedonia. What had happened to Corinth was a warning to all. The soft approach of Flamininus and the Scipios had vanished. The Roman Senate now took a harsh position. It was made plain that wherever the power of the Romans extended they would have peace one way or the other.

The Third Punic War (149–146 B.C.)

Wise men never cease advising great powers to be patient, for in reality those in authority are likely to be short-tempered. While the frustration of the Romans mounted in Greece, they were also moving toward a final settlement with Carthage. Only the desperate courage of the Carthaginians made it any contest at all. Neighboring Numidia had continued to stir up trouble; and, when Carthage retaliated without Rome's consent, the treaty which ended the Second Punic War was violated. Reports that Carthage was secretly rearming reached Rome and helped to raise the fever for a war which the ageing Cato and his friends had long advocated. Carthage had made substantial gains in her overseas trade—a sinister comeback in the eyes of Roman investors. But those who watched Cato display plump Carthaginian figs in the Senate may also have joined him in coveting the rich soil of their old enemy's domain. Cato's campaign was relentless. No matter what subject he might be speaking on or what question he might be answering he always finished the same way: *Ceterum censeo delendam esse Carthaginem.* "Furthermore, in my opinion, Carthage must be destroyed."

A commission sent to North Africa in 154 was given a rude reception, and when Cato arrived with another commission in 151

the time for compromise had passed. The Senate sent an ultima-
tum ordering the Carthaginians to disband their army and navy or
face the consequences. In 150, before any envoys arrived from
Carthage, the war was voted and preparations begun. Faced with
the worst and already smarting from the defection of Utica to the
Romans, the Carthaginians declared themselves at the mercy of
Rome. It was unconditional surrender without a sword raised.
From their past experience with the Romans they thought they
could expect reasonably fair treatment. At first it seemed confirmed, because under the formalities of their surrender they gave
up all they possessed to the Romans and the Senate handed it back
to them by granting them "freedom and the enjoyment of their
laws; and moreover, all their territory and the possession of their
own property, public or private" (XXXVI. 4). But there was a
catch to this. It was contingent on the Carthaginians' giving up
three hundred hostages and accepting whatever other orders the
consuls might give them. Other orders? This was where the
trouble came. First, the consuls demanded that the Carthaginians
surrender all their weapons. When this was carried out, the Romans saw that the city had indeed been building up its arms
supply for some time. Then the consuls issued an order which for
a thriving trading center amounted to suicide. The Carthaginians
were told to move their city inland more than ten miles from the
sea. They preferred to fight. Some Italians were unfortunate
enough to be in the city when the Roman order arrived; they
became the first casualties in the desperate, hopeless struggle
which is called the Third Punic War (149–146 B.C.). Although the
Carthaginians had given up an enormous store of weapons, they
were still ready to make a stand. The city's strength was akin to
that of a dying man fighting for life.

By the fall of 147, the Romans had won control of the
countryside around Carthage and the city stood alone. In the
spring of 146, its agony was a slow torture. Street by street the
defenders fought desperately to delay the Romans, but the harbor
area was lost, followed by the market region, and finally the
citadel was taken by storm.

Hasdrubal, who had led the city's defense, evoked the greatest disgust not only on the part of his fellow Carthaginians but
from the Romans too, when, after so long proudly proclaiming
that "the day would never come in which the sun would see Hasdrubal alive and his native city in flames," he nevertheless at the

end threw himself before Scipio and begged for his own life. Even his wife turned from him, and rather than beg for mercy hurled herself and her children from the citadel into the fires below.

Polybius was with Scipio Aemilianus at Carthage, and he tells us that his friend wept when he saw the city burning. How many other proud capitals had fallen and how many more would be destroyed in the future ? Polybius listened as Scipio quoted from Homer the lines about Troy's fall:

> The day shall be when holy Troy shall fall
> and Priam lord of spears, and Priam's folk.

What would Cato have thought to see a Roman commander not jubilant but sad in witnessing the destruction of an enemy city? Obviously, Scipio had been captured by the tragic view of life prevalent in Greek literature. It was not just Carthage fallen and Rome enthroned that he saw but an event in a never ending cycle of triumph and defeat in which the past was a prophecy of the future.

VI

The Problems of Success:
The Gracchi Brothers

In the mid-second century B.C. the ranking member of the Senate was an ex-consul and ex-censor named Appius Claudius Pulcher. Appius Claudius is a familiar name in the annals of Rome. An Appius Claudius appears on the list of consuls in every century of the Republic. Best known among them was the famous censor of the late fourth century B.C. who gave his name to the Appian Way. Although these men belonged to different families in the Claudian gens, they had a common ancestry and a common pride. A son should have a distinguished career, a daughter a good marriage.

One day, Appius Claudius Pulcher hurried home with exciting news. When he called to his wife that he had arranged for a husband for their daughter, she asked, "Why so suddenly, unless you have chosen Tiberius Gracchus?" It was Tiberius—a young man with a sterling reputation and a distinguished ancestry—all a Roman mother could hope for. He had been born in the very year that his father was consul (for the second time) and he had the same name, Tiberius Sempronius Gracchus. Plutarch hails the elder Tiberius as an outstanding soldier and a man of unblemished character. Splendid as the praise may be, the best remembered event of his life was his marriage to Cornelia, the daughter of Scipio Africanus, the man who defeated Hannibal. Cornelia was considerably younger than her husband and lived long after him to raise their two sons, whose combined careers mark a climactic time in the history of the Republic.

The elder son was the Tiberius Gracchus (163–133 B.C.) whose demeanor and prospects had delighted Appius Claudius and his wife. It was easy to predict a brilliant career for this youth. None could have predicted that it would be so brief. Tiberius, reformer and champion of the discontented, was assassinated at thirty. Within a decade, his younger brother, Gaius (153–121 B.C.), took his place as the hero of the poor. He was killed in an election riot at the age of thirty-two. These were the Gracchi brothers, Cornelia's "jewels." They belonged to that generation which had to meet the crisis of domestic problems created by Roman success abroad.

Too many men had gained too little or nothing at all from the wars of conquest. Some of them had even lost their farms while fighting overseas. At the same time public officials, traders, bankers, and those with money to invest were enjoying a better life than even the wealthiest Romans of bygone days. Their prosperity was particularly galling to veteran foot-soldiers now unemployed. Another kind of complaint came from Rome's Italian allies, who were asking for Roman citizenship, or at least the franchise, as a reward for their loyalty and service. Tiberius and Gaius Gracchus said that these and other injustices had to be corrected or the Republic would be doomed. In their view, short-sighted and selfish men sitting in the Senate were bent on blocking any and all reforms. The Gracchi were determined to prevent this—so determined that the means they used to save the state were, in part, the cause of its destruction.

Tiberius Gracchus

Tiberius, older than Gaius by nine years, preceded him in the public eye. During the siege of Carthage, while serving under the command of his sister's husband, Scipio the Younger, Tiberius won the enviable reputation of being "the first over the wall." Later, in Spain, under the command of a less able general, other qualities endeared him to his fellow soldiers.

In 137 B.C., a Roman army in north central Spain was

caught in an unexpected trap by the Numantines, skillful fighters who had time and again defeated the consul, Gaius Mancinus. With his forces at their mercy, the Numantines refused even to speak to him; they insisted on negotiating with Tiberius Gracchus. He was respected as his father had been, for the elder Tiberius had beaten the Numantines a long time before and treated them fairly. He had always kept his word. So it would be again. Tiberius arranged for an honorable peace which allowed for the safe withdrawal of 20,000 Romans. All property which the Numantines had seized was conceded to them, including Tiberius' account books. He was serving as a quaestor under Mancinus, and it bothered him to think that in the absence of proper records his rivals at home might question his handling of the army's funds. In a day or two, after the Romans had begun their withdrawal, he risked returning to the Numantine camp to ask for the return of his ledgers. It proved to be no risk at all. The Numantines treated him as an honored guest, giving him what he came for and offering him whatever else he wanted from the captured booty. A man so well treated by the enemy might scarcely escape suspicion at home, yet the same courage, courtesy, and modesty which won the respect of the Numantines guaranteed Tiberius' popularity with his fellow citizens. Their support and that of his fellow soldiers, plus the influence of Scipio, protected Tiberius from the punishment which befell the disgraced consul. According to the treatment usually meted out to officers who had asked for terms from an enemy, Mancinus was bound in chains and delivered to the Numantines. The Roman people had cast him out. Tiberius was spared; his fate was to be decided by events at home.

While travelling to and from Spain, Tiberius was an eyewitness to disturbing conditions which the poor could have told him about long before. The small landholders working a few acres and trying to maintain an independent livelihood were fast disappearing. The land which had once supported many families was becoming the property of the few.

In the light of human history, it does not require the inspiration of a Marxist to admit that those who have the most capital are in a strong position to enrich themselves at the expense of those who have the least. In Italy, after the Second Punic War, special circumstances gave the well-to-do an unusual advantage. They alone possessed the necessary wealth with which to develop two types of land which became available as a direct result of

Hannibal's invasion. The Romans expropriated territory from those Italian cities which had guessed wrong and surrendered to the Carthaginians. Most of this land was transferred to loyalists in the vicinity, either sold to private owners or distributed among the poor, who were expected to pay a small rent on a lease basis. Part of the confiscated land was given to Roman colonists. Much larger tracts of land had been left ravaged and depopulated by Hannibal's armies. The government did not reassign this property systematically; it simply allowed owners in the vicinity to extend their cultivation to include as much land as they were willing to redevelop. It was expected that they would pay for the privilege by giving the government an annual share of grain, fruit, or animals. The plan was intended to promote the welfare of Italian farmers in general, but the few who could afford to claim the most acreage never seemed to balk at increasing the size of their holdings. Efforts to win compliance to an earlier law which limited the amount of public land a man could lease (500 *iugera* = 330 acres) were not altogether successful. Land, like money, can be held under various names. Those who wanted to acquire more could obtain it from the smallholders, who found it easier to sell out than to compete. In some remote valley, a long distance from Rome, a threat from a powerful neighbor might also promote a sale. As the years passed, the large estate-owners grew bolder. Gradually, they ceased to make any distinction between private property and holdings which were theoretically public land. Payments in kind fell in arrears and in a generation or two were forgotten altogether.

The little man was more inclined to talk about the greed of his neighbors than the hard dictates of geography. Yet the latter was probably the more implacable foe. The import of large quantities of grain paid as tributes by the newly won provinces overseas, particularly Sicily and Sardinia, seriously hurt the Italian market. The small farmer was helpless. Only those with large capital could conveniently switch over to growing olives, producing wine, or raising cattle. The soil and the climate of Italy favor the orchard and the vine rather than grain. Much of the land is well suited to ranching. So it was the "nature of things" rather than man's will which called for the import of grain and the export of products better suited to Italy.

The added circumstances that recent wars were fought overseas and required long campaigns away from home made matters

worse for the small landowner. The ordinary soldier was on duty
in Africa or in Greece for perhaps a year or more and his family
was hard pressed to manage in his absence. The soldier in the rank
and file of armies winning the world was at the same time in
danger of losing all that he owned back home.

In modern America, the rise of large-scale capital farming
(with its expensive machinery) and the decline of a "country
store" society have taken place at a faster pace. Yet in the twentieth century the indigent farmer may find a job in industry. The
ancient world never knew an industrial development remotely
akin to what we have now. The unemployed of that time had
either to be restored to the land or to obtain food by way of
government subsidies. If not, they would starve.

In Tiberius' day, the unemployed and the landless who
flocked to Rome included many embittered veterans. The Senate,
however, was dominated by wealthy landowners who were inclined to feel comfortable with the status quo. So were prospering
business interests. The landless needed a man to speak for them
who was bound to be heard. Tiberius Gracchus took up their
cause and he spoke bluntly. The common soldiers of Rome, he
said, "were styled the masters of the world, but in the meantime
had not one foot of ground which they could call their own"
(Plutarch, p. 999). Tiberius called the restless poor in the city a
threat to political stability. For the safety of all, then, it was urgent that as many families as possible be restored to the land. For
those who did not think in terms of "justice" there was yet
another argument. From ages past, hard-working farmers with a
modest acreage had been the mainstay of both the Roman army
and the allied contingents which the Romans needed so badly.
According to Appian, Tiberius would have agreed that the decline
of this class was putting the welfare of Rome in jeopardy.

Tiberius saw something else in his travels. Gangs of slaves
labored in the fields of the latifundia, large estates of plantation
size. The employment of these slaves, captured in the recent wars,
posed a double danger. The importation of foreign workers, some
of them highly skilled, not only crippled the free labor market, it
added the fear of widespread slave revolts. In Tiberius' day there
was cause for alarm. Sicily had already been through a gruesome
uprising. Sixty years later that particular nightmare was to become real for the Romans.

Tiberius was only one of the ten tribunes elected to serve in

133 B.C. Yet he was the one, destined from birth as it were, who would play a leading role in the unusual events of that year. His illustrious ancestry was a commitment which his mother would not let him forget. Cornelia, an ambitious woman, knowledgeable about Roman politics, and with the best connections in Rome, chided her sons because she was still known only as the daughter of Scipio Africanus. She wanted to win a wider fame as the mother of the Gracchi.

When her sons were young, Cornelia employed one of the leading teachers of the day as their tutor. He was Blossius, a devout Stoic and one of the first missionaries of the "gospel of reason" in Rome. The influence he may have had on the Gracchi is usually cited as an example of the impact of Greek thought on Roman events.

Stoic doctrine stressed the idea that a good and wise man keeps his mind in tune with the divine intelligence which governs the universe. A man's life should be set, steady and determined, by strict obedience to reason. The emphasis was on adherence to principle without concern for the petty vicissitudes which beset men of less resolve. To the Stoic, what is right according to reason was equivalent to the "divinely ordained." The hand of Providence must not be stayed. As in all times, men impelled by such a sentiment were not inclined to compromise. Perhaps it is only a coincidence, but the Gracchi brothers in their politics displayed a typically Stoic steadfastness—or stubbornness, depending on how you look at it. It was necessary to be firm, they felt, because their position was so right.

Stoicism is a philosophy adaptable to different purposes. Zeno (335–263 B.C.), the reputed founder of this philosophy, had a strong sense of duty to himself. He was not a man interested in social problems. Rather, he was concerned with how best one man might maintain his own serenity amid the strife and disorder engulfing others. At Rome, Stoicism took a different turn. Blossius and other Stoic teachers, of whom Panaetius was the most prominent, tempered the self-centeredness of Greek Stoicism by emphasizing public duty in accordance with the Roman preoccupation with family and community. A particular aspect of Stoicism took on a special meaning. This was the notion of a brotherhood of all men, based on the concept that each man along with every other possesses a spark of the divine reason which is infused throughout the universe. At Rome, the Stoic sense of right was tied to a sense of duty toward one's fellow man. The overtone of religiosity is obvious. Stoicism asked men to be kinder than they seemed to be and gave them reason as a guide. This philosophical system, devised by men, was a way of life. It did not offer its adherents the revealed word of an omnipotent Father; nevertheless, the standards of behavior in Stoicism were in a general way much like those of Judaism, Christianity, and Islam.

Tiberius Gracchus was never called a philosopher. His enemies often accused him of wanting to be a king. The oppressive rule of the last Etruscan king, whose expulsion made the birth of the Republic possible, had not been forgotten. Since that time any popular figure with an unusual amount of influence could expect to be criticized for seeking to subvert the constitution. Especially suspect would be a man like Tiberius who insisted that property must be taken from the well-to-do and distributed amongst the poor. To talk about Tiberius' ambition was an obvious excuse for not talking about the need for reform. Reform was all that Tiberius talked about, and he was supported by a circle of intellectuals who encouraged his growing sense of self-righteousness. Plutarch names Diophanes, a rhetorician from Mitylene, and Blossius, his old mentor, a philosopher from Cumae, as two men who helped to build the fire of Tiberius' idealism. These men had ideas about how to remake society but little capacity for practical management. Tiberius did have advisers, however, who were noted for their political experience and sagacity—his father-in-law for one, the much respected Appius Claudius, and the consul Publius Mucius Scaevola, himself a lawyer. These men supported him because they were concerned about the future of the Roman army. Their outlook was very different from that of the intellectuals; yet they felt strongly that land reform was necessary to the security of the state. They did not see the question as merely a matter of rich against poor.

Still, in the background was the clamor of the crowd and Tiberius heard that message too. Plutarch writes that "it is also most certain that the people themselves chiefly excited his zeal and determination in the prosecution of it, by setting up writings upon the porches (*stoas*), walls and monuments, calling upon him to reinstate the poor citizens in their former possessions" (p. 998).

Tiberius knew the size of this vote. There is no reason to doubt that he could be sincere in purpose and also somewhat opportunistic. Appian calls him "an illustrious man, eager for glory"

(III. 1.9). And he was not without rivals. A certain Spurius Postumius who was of about the same age had won a large following with his eloquence. By the time Tiberius returned from Spain, Postumius appeared to be ahead in the race for public honor and Tiberius needed a popular issue with which to overtake him. Land reform had proven too touchy for others. It would not for him. Opportunism? Why not, in a city which throve on politics?

The land bill which Tiberius offered was mild, even conciliatory. The limit of 500 *iugera* on the amount of public land to be owned by an individual was retained. Tiberius added an allowance of 250 *iugera* for each of two sons with the total for a given family not to exceed 1,000 *iugera* (660 acres). The land had theoretically belonged to the state and so was now to be considered a gift to be held free and clear. This would be reimbursement for any improvements which had been made on excess acreage reclaimed by the state. Tiberius hoped thus to soften the measure and give an appearance of sympathy for those who would suffer a loss. The landowners did not so regard it. A family which had cultivated fruitful vineyards for a generation or two saw no reason why it should hand them over to strangers. If a man had paid a squatter for his piece of public land, and if this property was now claimed for redistribution, he lost everything. Appian's history includes a long list of grievances. There were family burials on some of the land. Other portions had been reserved for dowries. What about land which had been given as collateral for a loan? Would the state reclaim that too? The diehards who opposed any redistribution were infuriated by the patronizing tone of Tiberius' offer. On the other hand, Tiberius' attempt at compromise strengthened the resolve of his followers. If radical steps became necessary, they could now be blamed on the intransigence of selfish men who stubbornly opposed a just solution. Under the circumstances, hope for an accommodation grew dim.

What Tiberius wanted to do and how he went about it can be discussed together, but in the long run it was his methods which had the greatest impact on the future of the Republic. At the time, men were sharply divided in their opinions about what was happening. Some saw only the goodness of Tiberius' intentions. Others hated him for selfish reasons or feared him because of the threat he posed to constitutional government. Unfortunately, Tiberius himself had become an issue and that in turn would lead to much harm.

Tiberius ignored customary procedure and took his land reform bill directly to the people without giving the Senate a chance to debate it. The haste with which he acted was considered unseemly by those with fixed ideas about how a Roman should behave. Not only was the tempo of the event "unRoman," it also meant a break with tradition. Tradition was the iron in the constitution.

There was one constitutional check which Tiberius could not avoid. Any one of the other nine tribunes could veto his bill. In the past, the sympathies and goals of the tribunes had been generally the same and they had usually acted in concert. On this occasion, however, it was not only a matter of what should be done, but, as some men insisted, whether the legislation was actually worth the ill-feeling and disruption which it would cost. Behind all the talk was an issue of fundamental importance. Would the Senate continue to give overall direction to the government, as had been the case since the Second Punic War, or would a popular tribune with public support, in effect, take over the affairs of the state?

Many senators insisted that their opposition to Tiberius was not because of his land reform proposals. They claimed to be sincerely worried about Tiberius' ambitions. It is not fair to think that all of them were lying. Those who called on the tribune Marcus Octavius to oppose Tiberius were probably sincere in their motives. At first, Octavius was reluctant to interfere. We are not sure why he finally did so. Plutarch says that he was an honorable man who was moved to block the bill by an appeal to his sense of duty. Maybe so, but, at the time, Tiberius' partisans were quick to scent a bribe. Even Tiberius seems to have felt that because Octavius was a large landowner there must necessarily be a personal interest involved. He offered to buy any land which Octavius stood to lose. This strategy did not work. Octavius continued to stand squarely in Tiberius' path. The interposition of his veto was perfectly legal, perfectly constitutional. It should have been the final word. That it was not gives the year 133 B.C. a somber significance in the history of the Roman Republic.

The fever of opinion and the sharp division of interests prevented a general acceptance of the decision which the constitution allowed Octavius to make. There were threats and counterthreats. Rumors that the wealthiest landlords would procure the murder of Tiberius helped to increase the tension.

Two members of the Senate whom Tiberius trusted persuaded him to give that body a chance to settle the matter, but it was a futile exercise. Most senators were satisfied to see Tiberius frustrated. Their position was not statesmanlike. It may not even have been moral, but it was legal. Tiberius would have to make the next move. His only choice was to call for the removal of Octavius from office. To do so meant a second break with tradition. It was nothing less than an attack on the "checks and balances" principle built into the Roman constitution.

Tiberius decided to put his particular brand of truth above the constitution. Tradition must not be used by those who would block needed reforms. He was aware of the seriousness of his action and, outwardly at least, he gave the appearance of a man anxious to avoid it if at all possible. His friends saw him as a conscientious leader who was being forced into radical action by enemies of the people. Tiberius called for a vote of confidence, offering to resign if the citizenry did not support him. If they did, then Octavius should submit to the same question. Tiberius had the Tribal Assembly on his side and he knew it. His proposal was rigged. Octavius shrewdly observed that the constitution did not require either tribune to be deposed. Tiberius proceeded anyway. According to Plutarch, he publicly pleaded with Octavius to yield; and even after the voting had begun, "he embraced and kissed him before all the Assembly, begging with all the earnestness imaginable, that he would neither suffer himself to incur the dishonour, nor him to be reputed the author and promoter of so odious a measure" (p. 1001). Still the deed was done.

Appian's account of the event is low keyed. He says that after Octavius was removed from office he "slunk away unobserved" (III. 1. 12). Plutarch gives an altogether different account of the sequel and turns the scene into a grim foreshadowing of the events to follow. Tiberius' own men physically evicted Octavius from the Assembly, setting off a riot. When Octavius' servants and friends sought to protect him from a few of Tiberius' fanatic adherents, one of them was blinded. If Plutarch has his story straight, Tiberius was shocked and troubled by the violence; yet he was determined to have his way.

With Octavius out of the way, the land reform bill was passed, including a provision for a commission of three men to put the law into effect. Contrary to precedent which excluded interested parties from such positions, Tiberius placed himself, his brother Gaius, and his father-in-law Appius Claudius on the board. At the same time he gave Octavius' tribuneship to an underling, Mucius. To his enemies, these moves were a sign of willful arrogance, but Tiberius thought them logical. There was no point in removing Octavius if his replacement was unfriendly or the board of commissioners uncooperative. Tiberius was taking advantage of his popularity to carry out his responsibilities as he saw them. There was little the Senate could do except to retaliate by the petty denial of customary conveniences and allowances. That would not stop Tiberius. He had broken three precedents and would break another if need be.

How to obtain the necessary financing for the new program was a major problem. Tiberius was lucky. Attalus III, the wealthy monarch of Pergamum, had recently died, leaving his land and all its wealth to Rome. The Senate should have decided how this property was to be used, but again Tiberius interposed the will of the people. He promoted a law which diverted the treasury of Attalus into a fund for supplying the stock and seed necessary to put poor farmers back on their feet. His interference with the Senate's customary prerogative in matters of finance and foreign policy was interpreted by his enemies as another step toward the day he would declare himself a king. Those who wanted to believe this had every reason to do so.

Tiberius was aware that even among his own supporters there were many who felt uneasy about his methods. He was, in fact, enough concerned to offer an interesting, if somewhat predictable, justification for his actions, especially for the removal of Octavius. The deposed tribune, he said, was himself to blame for what had happened. The Senate was the bulwark of the better classes and the tribunes were the sworn protectors of plebeian interests. Tiberius argued that it was Octavius himself who had broken this trust by turning against the best interests of the people and serving the will of the moneyed aristocracy. Accordingly, Octavius had ceased to be a tribune when he decided to oppose the land reform bill. The people merely formalized his removal by casting their votes against him. Since Octavius had been elected by the vote of the Assembly, why should he not be dismissed by the same process? Indeed there were precedents for removing those who violated the authority entrusted to them. Had not the last Etruscan king been forcibly removed? Was it not customary to bury alive a Vestal Virgin who had been found guilty of dishonor? Tiberius argued that the tribuneship was a public trust and, by citing precedent, sought to save himself from the charge that he had recklessly abandoned the past. He wanted his followers to believe that although extraordinary circumstances might force him to bypass precedent in favor of the truth, he was as much concerned with tradition as the next man. Even his decision to stand for reelection was based on a precedent, although Tiberius had to go back more than a century to find it.

Tiberius' decision to hold onto his office for another year was more than his enemies could bear. Earlier, Tiberius had urged the people to care for his wife and children if anything should happen to him. At that time he may only have been playing for the sympathy of the crowd. Since then much had happened. Now his fears grew serious and his days were spent in terror. Volunteers stood guard near his house at night.

Ancient writers embellished their accounts of Tiberius' agony by recording the various omens which seemed so sinister. He stumbled as he left his house the morning of the election. Later, as he went to speak to the people, a squawking raven caused a stone to fall at his feet. If Tiberius was disturbed, his companion Blossius was not; with philosophical calm he told Tiberius to ignore a "silly bird." Unfortunately, on this occasion, the bird's forecast was accurate. When Tiberius arrived on the Capitoline Hill, demonstrations broke out both for and against his presence. Tribunes who opposed Tiberius' election helped to prevent any balloting. Amid the jostling of the crowd a senator friendly to Tiberius reached his side with a grim warning. His enemies in the Senate were at that very moment dispatching their friends and servants to attack him. Tiberius had broken several precedents; now those on the other side would break one. They would kill him.

He had insisted that his cause was too noble, too just, too right ever to be turned back. His enemies used the same language in support of their own cause. The leader of the opposition was Publius Scipio Nasica, the *pontifex maximus,* who was also a large landholder due to suffer a sizeable loss in the curtailment of holdings. Nasica claimed that he acted only for duty and honor. Tiberius had said that Octavius must be removed to save the state. Now Nasica, and other men of strong will, insisted that Tiberius too must be removed. Their meaning was clear. He was too popular to be deposed except by force.

Those who were near Tiberius in the crowd relayed the news of the impending clash to others. Appian says that Tiberius gave a prearranged signal for a pitched battle. Plutarch's account is different. He shows us an unprepared Tiberius caught up in the swirl of events and says that the tribune merely raised a hand to his head to indicate that he was in danger. According to this version, when a report of his gesture reached the Senate, it was interpreted to mean that Tiberius was asking for a crown. Despite the earlier report that many senators were already determined to take action, this news was said to have been the real cause for the violence which followed. Yet why would Tiberius choose a mob scene as the appropriate occasion to announce his plans? The presiding consul may well have considered this. He refused to be pressured into any rash action, yet his efforts to quiet the Senate were to no avail. Nasica, with shouts about the "safety of the state" and "defense of the laws," was followed from the chamber by several prominent leaders of the city. Accompanied by clients and servants armed with clubs they snatched up crude weapons, even pieces of broken chairs, as they rushed toward the place where Tiberius stood with his friends. Amid the ensuing confusion Tiberius was caught trying to escape. His toga was torn from his body and he was beaten to death in a hail of blows. More than three hundred of his followers were slain with him. Nor was passion appeased by death alone. Gaius Gracchus was not allowed to recover his brother's body. It was hurled into the Tiber along with the others. The massacre of the first day set a gruesome pattern for the following days, when the friends and sympathizers of Tiberius were caught and slain as they tried to flee the city.

Could this calamity have been avoided? In the past, civil strife had been forestalled by concessions. In 133 B.C., stubbornness on one side and the demand for immediate action on the other created an explosive atmosphere. Tiberius talked of justice more than of order, his opponents of order more than of justice. In this way, violence seemed foreordained. The murder of Tiberius was the first overt political murder in Roman history. It was the "monstrous deed" from which the Republic never recovered. The assassination of Julius Caesar, nearly a century later, is a better known event in history, but it came near the end of a century of violence. The blows which struck down Tiberius mark the beginning.

The Roman Republic was not a democracy, yet its intricate system of checks and balances, as in a democracy, was intended to prevent undue haste in matters of legislation, no matter how righteous the reasons for action. Such a system seems to favor the status quo. It even appears, at times, to protect those who cloak themselves in legality and use the status quo for selfish reasons. From time to time, there appears a man like Tiberius Gracchus who will insist that his cause is above history or experience and too noble to bear opposition with patience. That an honest and courageous man who seeks to succor those in need may also open the door to irrational lawlessness is one of the lessons of the Gracchan crisis. As Appian says of Tiberius: "He lost his life in consequence of a most excellent design too violently pursued" (III. 1. 17).

Once the holocaust subsided the Senate could afford to be generous. In view of the temper of the populace it was a wise move, especially since the anger of the commoners was mixed with guilt. Many supporters of Tiberius had fled the scene of his murder in terror or cowardly over-respect for the great men of the day. They would need someone to blame. The chief target of their scorn was Nasica, who was singled out as the principal instigator of what had happened. The Senate eased him out of public life by assigning him to duties in the East, where after a brief time he died.

In the hope of quieting things down, the recent land law was allowed to take effect as planned. Nor did the senators in the future interfere with the election to the land commission of men sympathetic to reform, such as Fulvius Flaccus and Papirius Carbo. It was difficult to determine which land was public and so liable to confiscation. Some families had lost track of the dividing line between their original holdings and the adjoining land they had been cultivating for so long a time. Instances where property had changed hands created additional problems. Existing records were sometimes old and often unreliable. As a result, the redistribution program bogged down in a morass of testy lawsuits. The problem was further complicated by the loud protests of large Italian landholders who were non-citizens and felt themselves unfairly treated. They had had nothing to say about the original legislation, and now they were subject to the rulings of a commission not likely to give them a sympathetic hearing. One prominent Roman friendly to their cause was

Scipio Aemilianus, who brought the complaints of the Italians to the Senate's attention. There was nothing underhanded about this. Though his marriage to Sempronia, sister of the Gracchi, was not a happy one, Scipio had been close to them and had never opposed land reform in principle. What he wanted was to be fair to all sides. That was part of his reputation, but his highmindedness did not impress the poor, who accused him of catering to the landed interests. Thereafter he was often interrupted by noisy demonstrations when he tried to speak. One morning he was found dead in bed. Whether or not he was murdered we do not know. The body was unmarked, but Appian says there were rumors that he had been suffocated. It was also possible that because of his sudden loss of popularity he committed suicide. At the time few men seem to have cared. The man who had destroyed Carthage was not even given customary funeral honors.

In 125, when Marcus Fulvius Flaccus became consul, he represented those who wanted a compromise solution for settling the land problem with the Italian allies. Fulvius favored giving them the franchise. By making them partners with the Romans they would be more likely to give up the needed land without further delay. The Senate, however, remained opposed to expanding the voter registration, and the Italians continued to find ways of stalling the partitioning of their property.

Fulvius discovered, as had other magistrates before him, that urgent business overseas could provide a breather from perplexing problems at home. The Senate was usually ready with distant assignments for officials who talked about major policy changes, especially for those who talked about them seriously. The departure of Fulvius for Gaul was a letdown for the allies. Frustration flared into revolt at Fregellae, a Latin colony located in the Liris valley. The Romans reacted sharply. The town was wiped out and its people forced to settle elsewhere. Such was the punishment meted out to an ally which had shared in the destruction of Carthage and Corinth. Cruel retaliation had become the final solution overseas, but farsighted Romans were agreed that this policy would not work in Italy. To rule abroad, Rome must have the willing support of her neighbors at home. An accommodation was imperative. That this point was not obvious to more members of the Senate is simply another instance of senatorial intransigence of which there are examples to spare.

Gaius Gracchus

In the immediate aftermath of his brother's assassination, Gaius, then in his early twenties, shunned domestic politics and turned to soldiering. Tiberius had launched his career by winning a reputation in the army, and, as the years passed, reports of Gaius' physical courage served to remind the people of Rome how much he resembled his popular brother. Members of the senatorial faction were alarmed and alerted by this.

Elected as quaestor, Gaius was assigned in 126 B.C. to the staff of the consul Orestes, who commanded an army in Sardinia. Just as Tiberius had done in Spain, Gaius clearly outclassed the man he was serving. It was a hard winter in Sardinia, yet the Senate had refused to allow the consul to requisition needed clothing from the local citizens. Gaius, by eloquent pleas, won from them what was needed without coercion. Micipsa, the king of Numidia, dispatched grain to Sardinia, saying that the shipment was sent out of admiration for Gaius. Certain senators who were convinced that young Gaius was promoting himself in the manner of his brother received this news rather testily. Angered by the Senate's attitude, Gaius resigned his post as quaestor and returned to Rome. This abrupt action was typical of the impetuousness for which he was noted.

Gaius did not have Tiberius' mild manner. Plutarch remarks that the two brothers looked somewhat alike and then goes on to say that although "there was a strong general likeness in their common love of fortitude and temperance, in their liberality, their eloquence, and their greatness of mind, yet in their actions and administrations of public affairs, a considerable variation showed itself" (p. 994). Particularly was this true in their public speaking. Tiberius was soft-spoken and often sought sympathy from his audiences. Gaius' delivery was bombastic, at times even shrill. He was extraordinarily blunt, and opponents had good reason to fear his caustic tongue. On one public occasion, Gaius turned on a man with known effeminate traits who had slighted Gaius' widowed mother. How could he be so insulting, Gaius asked, when it was well known that Cornelia had refrained from relations with men longer than he had?

Of the two brothers, Gaius was the crowd-pleaser. As might be expected, his showmanship left him open to the charge of demagoguery. But who could say whether he was less sincere than Tiberius? Plutarch offers a sympathetic view. He says of Gaius: "It is certain that he was borne rather by a sort of necessity than by any purpose of his own into public business" (p. 1008).

Among the ancients, it was taken for granted that a man's destiny could be foretold. Plutarch's great men have no ordinary dreams. He borrows from Cicero the story that Gaius had a dream in which his brother came to him and said, "There is no escape; one life and one death is appointed for us both, to spend the one and to meet the other in the service of the people" (p. 1008).

Gaius' abrupt return from Sardinia disturbed even his admirers. Yet he was entirely within his rights, for he had already served longer than the required term. Also, he lost no chance to stress the fact that he had not come home laden with treasure, as was common with other officers who had seen duty overseas. He sounded like a man running for office and he was. Gaius was seeking a tribuneship, and that was probably the real reason he had returned to Rome. He was energetic, ambitious, courageous, and a member of the right family.

Gaius found numerous occasions on which to remind the people of what had happened to his brother. All of the old wounds were reopened. The treachery and selfishness of the senators, said he, made them enemies of the people. Gaius was the people's champion, but he was not yet their first choice; in the election of tribunes for 123 B.C., he ran fourth among the ten chosen. He was kept from the coveted first place by voters who feared a return to the troubles of a decade earlier if he should arouse the Tribal Assembly as his brother had done. To such men, the laws which Gaius proposed, once elected, gave no comfort. His program included the full range of sensitive issues which others had avoided for the sake of peace in the city. As might be expected, the redistribution of public lands was at the top of the list. But Gaius went beyond the land issue in his effort to give the majority of Roman citizens a new deal. Remembering the problem in Sardinia about clothing, he asked that the average soldier in the future be clothed at the expense of the state. At home, he wanted a lower price for grain, although it was already being supplied to the poor at less than the market rate. His foes might well hope to settle for that, since Gaius also talked about giving the grain away, a suggestion more radical than anything Tiberius had ever made.

The courts were a touchy issue. Judges were chosen only from the senatorial class. Gaius insisted that wealthy men who were not senators be included too. They were to be chosen from among the equestrians (*equites*), no longer meaning simply "cavalrymen," as in the fifth century. In Gaius' time the equestrians were men whose wealth and education gave them a social status almost the same as that of the nobility, but who were primarily interested in business rather than politics—except insofar as politics affected their business. Gaius' reform, to be sure, would leave the conduct of the courts still in the hands of moneyed men, but it would break up the monopoly of a single faction. Moreover, equestrian members of a panel might be willing to take a closer look at the conduct of a senator than had been true in the past. On three recent occasions, senators had been acquitted of taking bribes by a jury of their colleagues, even though the evidence was overwhelmingly against them. Most senators were embarrassed by these scandals and did not oppose the measure which Gaius took to the Tribal Assembly for approval; they were of course aware that Gaius' bill would win him valuable allies among the equestrians; still they felt that something had to be done to correct abuses. Yet, as Appian points out, there was no moral gain in the long run. The new men who gained control of the courts proved to be as corruptible as the senators. Eventually, the equestrians even went so far as to refuse to hear cases involving bribery. That was certainly the way to avoid any unfavorable publicity.

Gaius called for full citizenship for the allies of Latin extraction, who of course lived closest to Rome, and renewed an appeal for admission to the franchise of other Italians throughout the peninsula. The latter would not have full citizenship, which included the right of judicial appeal, but they would be able to vote for the reform legislation which Gaius was advocating. Giving the Italians the franchise would be, to be sure, a step in the direction of full citizenship. This was an explosive issue which differed from all the others in one significant respect—it gave no direct benefit to the Roman citizens. On the contrary, in the name of justice it asked the commoners of Rome to share with others the benefits they had won. The allies had long been fighting on Rome's side and now expected their reward. For the average Roman this was asking too much. He did not object to a popular tribune using the term *justice* to win concessions from the ruling classes in his own behalf. He was less interested in the idealism which asked what he could give to those less advantaged than himself. Gaius was courting disaster by pressing the issue of the franchise. His risk was analagous to that of a modern-day craft union leader who insists that apprenticeships be offered to all comers. He might soon have competition from other men who could outbid him in what he could offer his supporters and at the same time would refrain from taking an idealistic posture about justice. In Rome, the men who decided to outbid Gaius were members of the Senate. On the franchise issue, at least, the people and the Senate were in accord. The senators opposed any move to expand the citizenship because it would greatly increase the number of voters to be canvassed. Worse, it would mean new competition for the highest offices at Rome, which had long remained in the hands of a relatively few families. If the senators could manage to block the extension of the franchise, they could serve not only their own interest but also cater to the people.

The Senate, aware of the hold Gaius had on the minds of the commoners, turned to one of his fellow tribunes to carry their own case to the people. Marcus Livius Drusus, a member of one of Rome's leading families, was well qualified to be a spokesman for popular causes. Since a tribune was not required to state why he was vetoing a bill, Drusus' veto of the franchise measure was assumed by the people to be on their behalf. Gaius was only one of a series of reform leaders to be frustrated by such an unusual partnership. Moderates feared a calamitous war if something was not done for the Italians, and some thirty years after Gaius' proposal was blocked such a war did come.

Gaius had many irons in the fire. He directed the construction of new storehouses in which to store grain for the needy. His famous road-building program kept large numbers of men at work. All those who benefited, including wealthy contractors, hailed him as a man of energy and purpose who actually did something about current problems, and he was easily reelected tribune for the succeeding year, 122 B.C. This did not make him any more acceptable to the Senate.

Gaius proceeded in an orderly way to promote overseas colonies as a means of reducing the number of unemployed, but his proposal of two new colonies was swamped by Drusus' suggestion that there be twelve. Drusus reminded the people that the Senate favored what he proposed, and by comparison with his fulsome generosity Gaius sounded cautious indeed. For one thing, Gaius expected the poor who received a grant of public lands to pay at least token rent as a guarantee of responsibility. Livius Drusus, with the Senate's connivance, offered the more popular alternative—excusing the recipients from any payment at all. By this grandiose gesture, Gaius' enemies sought to undercut his position, which was, after all, based on practical principles and considerations.

Gaius, like his brother before him, seemed always to have a hand in the project he proposed; Livius on the other hand remained aloof from the actual planning or execution of any programs—a policy which gave him more time to criticize the efforts of others and particularly to plot the undoing of Gaius. He was aided in this endeavor by some fortuitous circumstances. Although the proposal to resettle Carthage, destroyed in 146 B.C., was made by another tribune, it fell to Gaius to carry it out. The new colony, named Junonia, was not particularly popular. Many people had misgivings, for they were superstitious about the place. Reports of ill omens, including the claim that wolves had carried off the boundary stakes, did not help matters any. In this unrewarding task, Gaius suffered a political setback at home. While he increased the number who could participate in the colony beyond original estimates, he also expanded the quota for the Italians. He made no effort to cater to the selfish interests of the Roman citizenry. He even appeared to be generous at their expense. The subject of Italian citizenship kept coming up. Fulvius, one of Gaius' associates, became a whipping boy for Livius Drusus, who accused him of encouraging agitation among the allies. Fulvius may have been scholarly, as Cicero described him, but he was easily provoked, and his intemperate replies to Drusus hurt the cause which he and Gaius represented.

The risk and heartbreak of politics are well illustrated in Gaius' career. When he returned from North Africa to mend his fences with the people, his efforts evoked more trouble. Some of his fellow tribunes accused him of promoting himself at their expense, and his failure to be elected tribune for a third time was perhaps due to their outcry against him. There were also rumors of fraud in the election.

Even Gaius' enemies recognized his ability, grudging though their praise might be. He was an excellent administrator. He kept a firm hand on all programs which he organized. The men he appointed personally to the courts or as his own assistants were a credit to the government. Above all, he was himself a model of energy and fairness. Still, he remained a controversial figure, feared as much for his good qualities as for the bad. Nothing could shake the conviction of some men that he was a conniver, eager to succeed as a king where his brother had failed.

Out of office, Gaius realized that his "constructive" program—all that he had worked for—was in jeopardy. One of the new consuls, Lucius Opimius, was an avowed enemy who intended to have Gaius' laws revoked and to halt the projects already begun. Junonia was a prime target. The challenge by Opimius provoked Gaius to take rash action. Perhaps that is what the consul had hoped for.

Supported by men like Fulvius, the former consul who had served as a tribune with him in 122, Gaius resolved to muster what force he could against Opimius. It was a bad risk. Gaius did not even have the wholehearted support of his own followers. His program had offended the Senate, as we have seen, and, in addition, on some issues he failed to carry his fellow tribunes or the mass of the voters with him. It was unfortunate that the first act of violence was inflicted by his own partisans. Some of Gaius' most dedicated followers felt that their leader and they themselves had been insulted by the haughty behavior and language of an attendant of one of the consuls. The man was struck down and killed in a sudden outburst of anger. There would have been further rioting and more bloodshed in the Forum that day, had it not begun to rain.

Many senators sought to dramatize the lawlessness of the times by making much ado about this murder of a consul's aide. More honored in death than he had been in life, this hired plebeian suddenly was presented as a martyr to the senatorial cause. The partisanship of the Senate was an affront to those who remembered the death of Tiberius and his supporters, and how his body had been thrown unceremoniously into the Tiber. Now, in 121 B.C., after a single assistant official had been slain, the Senate granted the consul Opimius emergency powers to use all means necessary against those considered to be enemies of the public order. The *senatus consultum ultimum* was a resolution tantamount to a license for revenge. The grim hours which followed were reminiscent of those before the assassination of Tiberius. At night, Gaius' house was under guard. By day, an air of foreboding surrounded him as he stood in thought before his father's statue. Gaius' forefathers were honored men who had sat among their peers in the Senate and were respected for their service to the state and in the cause of empire. Gaius might well reflect on how he and his brother, who had grappled with the ills which the empire had created, were accorded a far less glorious destiny.

A scene in the *Iliad* between Hector and Andromache establishes the motif of the anxious wife bidding farewell to a husband in danger. Plutarch offers a similar scene as Gaius leaves to address the people on the morning of the day he was killed. His wife, Licinia, wants to hold him back: "You go now to expose your person to the murderers of Tiberius, unarmed indeed, and rightly so, choosing rather to suffer the worst of injuries than to do the least yourself. But even your very death at this time will not be serviceable to the public good. Faction prevails; power and arms are now the only measures of justice" (pp. 1016–17).

Fulvius and many of Gaius' closest associates had spent the previous night drinking and encouraging one another with loud boasting. When daylight came, they were routed by the senatorial forces. In a series of incidents, three thousand were killed, including Fulvius. The consul Opimius offered a pardon to all who would submit peaceably to the government; his gesture broke the back of the resistance. Gaius fled from the city accompanied by a single servant, unaided by any of the commoners whose troubles he had made his own. They now looked to their own safety and welfare.

Gaius was trapped at last in a grove where he had hoped to hide. Of his death, two accounts survive. Generally it is thought that his servant, in mercy, killed him and then turned the dagger on himself. The other story says they were both captured and then slain. Gaius' head was severed from his body and given to Opimius. His corpse was thrown into the Tiber. Plutarch concludes his life of Gaius with a tribute to Cornelia, whose pride in her sons showed itself in the dignity with which she accepted their sacrifice.

The story of the Gracchan period at Rome has the quality of a morality tale—the insufferable rich on the one side and the long-suffering poor on the other. Reality is less exact. If the Gracchan dream of a small plot of land for every able-bodied farmer did not come true, it was not entirely the fault of those opposed to reform. Many among the poor saw no reason why they should work from dawn to dusk in order to subsist, when they could live in the city on cheap grain and be entertained besides. Soon after the death of Gaius Gracchus, the law prohibiting the indigent from reselling their land grants was repealed. Many of those familiar with life in the city voluntarily sold out and went back to Rome. Others were encouraged to do so by wealthy neighbors who used pressure tactics to obtain more acreage. Later, the public land still in the hands of private owners was declared to be theirs for a small rent, which would be used as welfare payments for the landless poor. In time that too was dropped. By 118 B.C., the Gracchan program intended to relieve the poor and build up a large class of self-sufficient landholders was completely undone. It was a noble experiment in which the best and the worst of human intentions were evident.

The failure of the Gracchi gave warning that the problems of Rome would not be solved quietly. The machinery of the constitution had become jammed. A complicated system of checks and balances was only workable if self-interest was sacrificed to tradition and if honor was valued more than material gain. The reformers had attacked long-standing traditions because they were determined to have their way. Were they justified? Had the ruling classes already undermined the customs of the past in a more subtle fashion? How long had they been giving anything more than lip service to the old values of honesty and steadfastness in their conduct of the government? Who had begun the exploitation in the provinces?

Corruption in high places was part of what had gone wrong. The example was set at the top. If men of old and honorable families with the best education and the highest offices were scrambling for what they could win, why should any man refuse a share of the spoils? In much that has been written about the Gracchan era the ruling classes have been blamed for the decay of honesty and fair dealing. Yet, as the wise Solon of Athens once observed, the rich are not inherently any more greedy or corruptible than their poorer fellow citizens. At Rome, their powerful positions, overseas commands, and inside information had simply given them the first chance.

VII
The Politics of Violence:
Marius and Sulla

The use of violence against the Gracchi brothers had been a disillusioning, sorry, but successful business. The major landowners and their powerful allies in the Senate could insist that they had kept two ambitious young men from wrecking the constitution. As the years passed, it became apparent that they had accomplished the very opposite. More men than ever before became convinced that traditional procedures, sanctified as constitutional, hindered rather than helped to reform. Muscle was needed. Where better to get it than from a victorious general with loyal veterans at his side—especially one who was looking for votes in Rome? In the last years of the second century, the people discovered Gaius Marius (ca. 157–86 B.C.). They soon learned that he was a better general than he was a politician, but from the beginning at least he shared the same enemies with them. Complaints against the aristocracy were intensified because of the incompetence and corruption evident in an agonizing war in North Africa.

The story was retold in detail by the first-century historian Sallust (ca. 86–ca.. 35 B.C.), who was born about the time that Marius died. Although Sallust had a strong bias of his own against the nobility (*nobiles*), an almost closed circle of powerful patrician and plebeian families, he read the past with enough perspective to know that the decline in public morality was not a scandal of a single group. He voices a familiar theme—the Republic was a victim of its own success:

> Before the destruction of Carthage, the people and Senate of Rome together governed the Republic peacefully and with moderation. There was no strife among the citizens either for glory or for power; fear of the enemy preserved the good morals of the state. But when the minds of the people were relieved of that dread, wantonness and arrogance naturally arose, vices which are fostered by prosperity. Thus the peace for which they had longed in time of adversity, after they had gained it proved to be more cruel and bitter than adversity itself. For the nobles began to abuse their position and the people their liberty, and every man for himself robbed, pillaged, and plundered. Thus the community was split into two parties, and between these the state was torn to pieces. (XLI. 2–5)

In the two monographs which account for his fame, *The War with Jugurtha* and *The War with Catiline,* Sallust mentions here and there the excesses of the crowd. Most of the time, however, he constructs a towering indictment against the nobility. Their crimes seemed worse because they had betrayed their responsibility, but the bitterness with which Sallust attacks the ruling families suggests some private malice. He had been removed from the Senate in 50 B.C. because of complaints which may have been a cover-up for political censorship. As a friend and confidant of Julius Caesar, he later regained a place in the government, but he never fully recovered his reputation. In any event, his exposé of the nobility offered a convenient apology for Caesar, who could one day feel justified in sweeping a hoary establishment aside. Yet a careful reading of Sallust's works offers evidence of more than mere spite toward the Senate and gratitude toward Caesar. It is not unreasonable to say that as an older and wiser man he wrote about the past, with some remorse to be sure, primarily to record certain lessons which he considered worth remembering.

The War with Jugurtha tells of Rome's efforts in the late second century to establish stability in Numidia, a country which bordered the coastal province of Africa on the west and south. Sallust also describes the beginning of Marius' career and some of the events which launched his meteoric rise in Roman politics.

The Numidia story is a tabloid tale of intrigue, murder,

and betrayal with an uncommon scoundrel, Jugurtha, at the center of things. Regardless of expense and effort, the Romans seemed incapable of bringing this wily prince to account. Lurid details enliven what for Sallust is essentially a morality tale. Spoiled men of "inherited" wealth are responsible for Rome's failure. The man who finally succeeds is a "new man," Marius, who has his faults, to be sure, but also possesses ability and wants to be rewarded for it.

As it often happens when a large power involves itself in the internal affairs of a small state, the Romans drifted into far more trouble than they had bargained for. Numidia had been a good friend in the past. During the Second Punic War, the Numidian king, Masinissa, had been particularly helpful, and when the Romans enlarged their own domain they saw to it that his was extended too. Later, Masinissa's son, Micipsa, never missed an opportunity to display his allegiance; he was the king who sent badly needed grain to Gaius Gracchus in Sardinia. During the last years of Micipsa's reign his troubles began. He had two sons, Adherbal and Hiempsal. After his brother Mastanabal died, he also brought up Mastanabal's son, Jugurtha, whose mother was a concubine.

Jugurtha's inferior birth gave him an unequal status with Micipsa's legitimate heirs. In all other respects he was apparently their superior. If there was a king among the three it was surely this personable youth, handsome and strong, with an appealing manner, looking and acting the hero's part. His agile mind and courage made him a conqueror of men and lions. He had in fact more than enough of everything, including ambition. At first, Micipsa was proud of Jugurtha, who was older than his own sons, but as time passed he began to worry about the future. His young charge grew more and more popular with the Numidians and therefore less so with Micipsa. When he left for Spain to serve with the Romans at the head of a cavalry unit, Micipsa was happy to see him go. Nor would Micipsa have been grief-stricken had he not returned. As it happened, Jugurtha came home with more than honor. His contact with the Romans had shown him how easy it was to bribe their officers, even those of the highest rank. Not all of them were corruptible, but Jugurtha had seen enough to convince him that in any dealings with the Romans, money would be the equal of intellect or courage.

After Jugurtha returned from Spain, he was formally

adopted by Micipsa, despite the king's misgivings. Micipsa hoped for the best and advised his three heirs that unity made a small power stronger than a great state beset with dissension. While the king lived, the enmity among the brothers was glossed over. When he died, in 118 B.C., his advice was quickly forgotten. For a time there was talk about dividing the kingdom, but suddenly it was clear that such talk was mere camouflage. Willing henchmen murdered Hiempsal and brought his head to Jugurtha, whose quick action greatly improved his chances for success. The best soldiers rushed to his side. Adherbal hurried to Rome in fright and anger. Jugurtha sent money. His agents were instructed to distribute gifts to prominent Romans whom Jugurtha knew to be susceptible to bribes. They were also to look for other officials who might be willing to help his cause.

Adherbal reminded the Senate of the long-time loyalty of his father and grandfather and told how Jugurtha had betrayed the family which had given him more than his due. He spoke of Jugurtha's "intolerable audacity, wickedness and arrogance" evident in the purge of all those loyal to Adherbal after the murder of Hiempsal. Adherbal called the Senate's attention to the money Jugurtha was spending in Rome to finance a lobby for himself. Would they let this blatant usurper deceive them?

The Numidians who spoke for Jugurtha explained that Hiempsal had been killed because of his cruelty and charged that Adherbal himself had caused the trouble after his father's death. Most of the senators preferred this version of events. Eventually, a commission was appointed to settle the matter by alloting separate territories to Jugurtha and Adherbal. Lucius Opimius, who as consul had suppressed Gaius Gracchus and his followers, was named to head the group. He and his fellow commissioners awarded Jugurtha the western half of Numidia. This would not for long be enough for a man who found the Romans so easy to handle. In 112, Jugurtha invaded Adherbal's territory, the more prosperous eastern section, and spread terror throughout the land. Although Adherbal knew the odds were against him, he felt obliged to take up the challenge. He soon found himself besieged in his capital, Cirta, which had the one advantage that many Italians, especially grain brokers, lived in the city. Their fate, if not his own, might arouse the Senate to action. The Senate did send a message to Jugurtha ordering him to withdraw, but he pleaded innocent to all charges and begged for time to send mes-

sengers to Rome with his side of the story. In the meantime he
sought by any means possible to take Cirta and silence his enemy.

The Italians trapped in Cirta trusted Jugurtha to have some
sense of justice. They insisted that Adherbal surrender the city, for
they supposed that Jugurtha would at least spare their lives out of
respect for Rome. Jugurtha knew more about Roman politics than
they did. Some senators would find excuses for him, no matter
what his crimes. When Cirta fell into his hands, he tortured Adherbal to death and permitted the killing of captured combatants,
no matter who they were or where they came from. The news
that Jugurtha had not spared the Italians in Cirta forced the Senate
to act, although at first, they delayed, as usual. Sallust gives the
impression that every time the Senate hesitated it was because of
the pressure of Jugurtha's friends. Actually, many senators were
worried about any commitment of troops overseas, and especially
because of a possible threat to Italy posed by the movements of
northern tribes southward toward the Alps.

Finally, in 111 B.C., an army was dispatched to North Africa
under the consul Lucius Calpurnius Bestia, who was once entrusted with allotting land in Africa under the Gracchan plan.
Sallust tells a different story. He says that Bestia had "many excellent qualities of mind and body . . . all nullified by avarice"
(XXVIII. 5). Instead of punishing Jugurtha for his crimes, he
made peace with him in return for large donations to himself and
his chief aide and a rather small compensation to the Roman state.
There was consternation even in the Senate about this sudden and
unexpected peace, but it was the temper of the Tribal Assembly
which prompted a praetor to be sent to bring Jugurtha to Rome.
If he had indeed surrendered to the Romans, then he was the
person to explain how he managed to come off so well. If, as was
suspected, the consul and his friends had taken bribes, the people
wanted to hear about it.

Jugurtha came to Rome exuding humility in dress and manner. He had no intention, however, of testifying, nor did he have
to. His money had reached a tribune who was willing to halt the
proceedings in the Assembly and so frustrate the public will to
bring Bestia to account. What followed was worse. A cousin of
Jugurtha was in Rome seeking the throne of Numidia. He had
already won the support of Spurius Albinus, one of the consuls for
the year 110. Jugurtha was audacious enough to pay to have his
rival murdered even in the capital. When an aide, implicated in this

crime, was allowed bail before standing trial, Jugurtha quickly sent
the man back to Numidia. He himself soon followed. As he was
leaving Rome, he is reported to have called it "a city for sale." This
dramatic statement is probably a later invention, but Jugurtha
could no doubt have spoken the words with authority.

Jugurtha continued to hold the Romans at bay for another
five years. In 110, the determined consul Albinus took an army to
North Africa, but both he and his brother Aulus were in turn
deceived by Jugurtha's familiar tactic of alternating overtures for
peace with surprise attacks. Albinus and Aulus each on occasion
trusted Jugurtha, and to him that was as good as a bribe.

The Tribal Assembly at Rome, angered and frustrated by
the failure of the government to bring Jugurtha to terms, voted to
have all those accused of trafficking with him brought to trial.
Sallust doubts the sincerity of this move. He writes that the Assembly "passed the bill with incredible eagerness and enthusiasm,
rather from hatred of the nobles, for whom it boded trouble, than
from love of country: so high did party passion run" (XL. 3).
Sallust considered party passion as the real reason for ineffectual
government at Rome. Amid the current hysteria, certain senators
of high standing, Bestia and Opimius among them, were found
guilty and sent into exile.

Not until 109 did the consulship fall to a nobleman worthy
of the trust. Metellus was an aristocrat, haughty, unbending, and
suspicious of the crowd, but also a brilliant leader and honest
beyond question. His appointment came in time to save the Romans from disaster. The report that he was not a man who could
be bribed was bad news for Jugurtha, whose overtures for peace
were eyed by the new commander with unusual caution. Jugurtha's reputation had preceded him. Indeed, his own tactics were
now being used against him, for while Metellus pretended to be
interested in negotiations, he continued making elaborate plans for
war.

In describing Metellus' invasion of Numidia, Sallust mentions that the officer in charge of the cavalry was Gaius Marius. It
is a casual introduction to the man who would one day, in his
own way, conquer both Metellus and Jugurtha. In the beginning,
however, Marius was simply another loyal aide badly needed in
the struggle with the crafty Numidian.

It was not easy to find Jugurtha. His penchant for turning
up unexpectedly kept Metellus off balance. Winning battles was

not the same as winning the war, and effective guerrilla movements helped to even the contest. Metellus' intention to fight to the finish was good news to the Romans, who had long since grown weary of the war. But hopes at Rome for an early solution were premature and opened the way to disappointment. Metellus, fearful of any reverses, became less daring and the pace of the war was slowed. Jugurtha continued to lose battle after battle, but he was not captured. Marius had time to consider how he might do a better job. To have the chance he would have to return to Rome and stand for the consulship. Dare Marius try it? Dare any man from the ranks without a distinguished ancestry to recommend him?

Marius had been born in the district of Arpinum (modern Arpino), about sixty miles southeast of Rome. To him it was a fortunate beginning. Others might seek to escape from the rigors of the simple life, but Marius equated his background with the best in the Roman tradition. The folk heroes were his models; he wanted to be like them. His first chance came while serving in the war against the Numantines in Spain. Scipio the Younger marked him there as a young soldier with exceptional self-discipline. Later, in Rome, Marius became well known as a steady shoulder-to-the-wheel type of citizen. The people considered him a natural choice for the tribuneship. But Marius was his own man—as a praetor in 115 B.C., he refused to cater either to the interests of the populace or to the Senate. He did not hesitate to oppose any faction when he felt the circumstances warranted it. Aside from providing this clue to Marius' nonpartisan attitude, his early public career was not noteworthy. Before his appointment to Metellus' staff, his marriage appears to have been the most significant event of his life. For a "new man" he did very well. His wife belonged to the ancient and honorable Julian clan. By marriage, Marius later became an uncle of Julius Caesar.

The decision of a "new man" to be a candidate for the consulship was a daring move in the late second century. Despite the recent political upheavals, as Sallust reminds us, the nobles still "passed the consulate from hand to hand within their own order" (LXIII. 6). The old families in Rome were gracious toward a talented man in Marius' position so long as he recognized and accepted the limits set for him by his humble birth. Metellus admired Marius, but he considered it a defect in him to want to rise above his proper place. His reply to Marius' request for leave was not even tactful. "It will be soon enough for you to be a candidate when my son becomes one," he said (LXIV. 4). His son was about twenty. Marius was forty-nine.

Plutarch, in his biography of Marius, looks at all this from Metellus' side. He thinks the trouble between the two men involved more than Metellus' haughtiness, as Sallust would have it. Metellus apparently felt himself betrayed by a man he trusted. Marius was not merely a humble man of ability trying to make his way in the world; Plutarch shows that he could be ruthless and deceitful on occasion if it would serve his purpose.

The letters which Marius' soldiers and friends were sending to Rome, urging that Metellus be replaced, were part of a campaign to undermine a man whose performance in the war had been the best to date. Among Marius' most willing supporters were Roman businessmen in North Africa who were losing money because of the war. Their letters spread the word at Rome that Marius would be the best choice to finish off Jugurtha. News of reverses helped Marius' cause no matter how they happened. For instance, in the town of Vaga, the celebration of a general holiday was used to catch the Romans stationed there off guard. Unarmed soldiers, enjoying a day off and taking part in the native festivities, were suddenly attacked and killed. Metellus punished the Vagenses severely, but the event hurt him at home. The war dragged on and, rightly or wrongly, Metellus became the victim of a growing demand for better results.

Marius was allowed to leave for Rome in 108, shortly before the scheduled election for the consulship. In Rome, he intensified his campaign to discount Metellus' capacity to get the job done in Numidia. His boast that he could bring Jugurtha back to Rome in chains, with only half the resources now being used, carried with it the suggestion that Metellus had been dragging his feet. The attack was unfair—especially so since the proconsul was not present to defend himself. But Marius stood before the people as more than a replacement for Metellus. He was the champion of a new order altogether.

In Athens, over three centuries earlier, the famous statesman Pericles had said in his *Funeral Oration:* "If we look to the laws, they afford equal justice to all in their private differences; if to social standing, advancement in public life falls to reputation for capacity, class considerations not being allowed to interfere with merit; nor again does poverty bar the way: if a man is able to serve the state, he is not hindered by the obscurity of his condition" (Thucydides II. 6. 37). Marius wanted this to be true in Rome. A citizen must be judged according to his individual worth. It is worth noting that he was talking about equality of opportunity among "citizens." Neither he nor Pericles thought in modern egalitarian terms; they were not saying that all men are created equal. On the contrary, they were stressing the varying capacities of men and saying that the state would be best served by those of natural talent rather than by men who had inherited a famous name but were lacking in ability. In Europe in the early years of the twentieth century, men were led into battle by officers born to good families and trained in the best schools who were incompetent and in some instances probably stupid. That was precisely what Marius was saying about the erratic conduct of the Jugurthine War. The voters agreed with him.

Marius was elected consul for the year 107; however, he would not automatically receive the command against Jugurtha. A majority of senators, better informed about events than the average man, had voted to extend Metellus' proconsulship. They thought his chances for bringing the war to an end looked promising. The voters in the Tribal Assembly believed Marius would get quicker results. The decision of the Senate was thus countermanded when the Assembly voted to relieve Metellus of his duties in North Africa and transfer the command to Marius. The Assembly's action was not routine. Another significant precedent had been broken; another important senatorial prerogative had been ignored.

The news was a shock to Metellus. His victory, which he felt to be close at hand, would be claimed by another—by a commoner, which was especially humiliating. Addressing the people in Rome, Marius vigorously attacked the aristocracy and their tradition of privilege. Reporting the occasion, Sallust offers a speech which in substance if not in style is presumably faithful to Marius' intention. Marius wanted to destroy altogether the awesome reputation of the nobility, which for so long had held the people in check. As recently as the Gracchan crisis, the habit of respect for even the names of prominent families had kept many men from helping the reformers in their time of need. Marius was not after new laws only, but a whole new attitude:

Compare me now, fellow citizens, a "new man," with those haughty nobles. What they know from hearsay and reading, I have either seen with my own eyes or done with my own hands. What they have learned from books I have learned by service in the field; think now for yourselves whether words or deeds are worth more. They scorn my humble birth, I their worthlessness; I am taunted with my lot in life, they with their infamies. . . . But if they rightly look down on me, let them also look down on their own forefathers, whose nobility began, as did my own, in manly deeds. . . . The more glorious was the life of their ancestors, the more shameful is their own baseness. . . . I cannot, to justify your confidence, display family portraits or the triumphs and consulships of my forefathers; but if occasion requires, I can show spears, a banner, trappings and other military prizes, as well as scars on my breast. These are my portraits, these my patent of nobility, not left me by inheritance as theirs were, but won by my own innumerable efforts and perils. (LXXXV. 13–30)

Marius singled out Albinus and Bestia as examples of men who belonged to the best families but were not the best of sons. Undoubtedly the crowd was thrilled to hear him openly vilify the aristocracy, naming names, and exposing weaknesses. He played to the crowd, employing the "I am one of you" technique so familiar to politicians in a democracy:

My words are not well chosen; I care little for that. Merit shows well enough in itself. It is they who have need of art, to gloss over their shameful acts with specious words. Nor have I studied Grecian letters. I did not greatly care to become acquainted with them, since they had not taught their teachers virtue. . . . They say that I am common and of rude manners, because I cannot give an elegant dinner and because I pay no actor or cook higher wages than I do my overseer. This I gladly admit, fellow citizens; for I learned from my father and other righteous men that elegance is proper to women but toil to men, that all the virtuous ought to have more fame than riches, and that arms and not furniture confer honour. (LXXXV. 31–40)

It was easy for Marius to arouse ill feeling toward the nobility. Winning continued support for the war was more difficult. The Numidian affair was not popular with the Romans. Marius' speech was intended to boost morale and encourage enlistments. Heretofore those who did not own property had been excluded from service because they were considered unsettled and therefore unreliable. In the earliest time, to serve in the army had been considered a privilege. During the Second Punic War and after, service became a burden, as we have seen, particularly to the small landholder. Now Marius proposed to sign up men of the lowest class—men with nothing to lose and booty to win. In the recent elections the poorest citizens had given him his strongest support. He now offered them a chance to win something in return. Knowing the desperate need for new recruits, Marius was willing to enlist and train men who were destitute. In that sense his new army was an invention of necessity, but Marius was in fact creating an army of men who would be totally dependent on him for their future welfare. They would have nothing to come home to except what he would give them. Would such veterans have a greater loyalty to him than to the state? This may not have been what Marius intended, yet in the coming civil wars the armies on both sides, each loyal to its own commander, owed something to Marius' example. He took the first step when he gave the poor hope of a share of empire, not, as the Gracchi had done, through land laws, but by joining the army.

Marius was as good as his word. He was a rough and ready warrior, hardened by experience and proud of his Spartan manliness. He saw the world through the eyes of a soldier. His disdain for the niceties of a formal education gave him common ground with his men. This he needed, for it took much to convince raw recruits that rugged training was for their own safety and forced marches were good for conditioning. To increase speed and maneuverability he required each man to carry his own pack. His discipline was both fair and severe. Nor was Marius any harder on others than he was on himself. He never asked his men to eat food he would not share, to sleep where he would not lie down himself, or to work at any task he would not try. To be the best soldier of all gave him the right to lead. Marius believed in obedience to orders, willingness to endure hardships, and courage in the face of danger. With those qualities went an undeniable thirst for power.

By the time Marius took charge of the war in Numidia, Jugurtha's days appeared to be numbered. Certainly Metellus thought so. Because of his resentment toward Marius, who would now steal his victory, Metellus refused to meet him and left the transfer of command to an aide. Some of Jugurtha's supporters, even his closest friends, also sensed that the end was near and began to look ahead. Jugurtha kept moving from place to place in constant fear of being betrayed. Meanwhile, Marius took one Numidian stronghold after another. Because of his reputation and the new vigor he brought to the war, a few towns gave up without a struggle. Yet it was not by arms alone that the war would be won.

Bocchus, the king of Mauretania (modern Morocco), was Jugurtha's father-in-law and a man he trusted. Suspecting that Jugurtha's cause was doomed, Bocchus let Marius know that he wanted to discuss their mutual interests. Marius sent two officers to listen to the king's proposal. Bocchus had asked that one of them be a young man he already knew, Lucius Cornelius Sulla (138–78 B.C.), who was a quaestor at the beginning of his public career. Marius considered Sulla to be a dedicated young soldier and a friend. Before long he would have reason to be suspicious. Marius might well be wary of an ambitious aide, having been one himself to Mettelus.

Various negotiations were begun with Bocchus, who at times seemed to be wavering in his willingness to make a deal with the Romans. Sulla played an influential role in the effort to keep the king from going back on his promises. For Bocchus, it was a question of whom to betray. Undoubtedly he preferred the friendship of the Numidians to the sufferance of the Romans, who would scarcely treat him as an equal. On the other hand, although Jugurtha was his son-in-law, Bocchus was secretly worried lest he would not be easy to control should he successfully elude the Romans. As with other minor monarchs of the time, Bocchus' fear of Rome helped him to make up his mind. In secret meetings with Sulla he revealed a plan for capturing Jugurtha. Bocchus invited the Numidian king to a conference, to which Jugurtha came expecting to have Sulla handed over to him. The ambush went the other way. Bocchus traded Jugurtha to the Romans in return for future favors. Sulla gave himself credit for the capture, and he was supported by all those who had any reason to dislike Marius. To commemorate the victory, Sulla ordered a seal to be made showing who was present at the betrayal. So began the open rivalry between Marius and his able young lieutenant. Jugurtha was taken to Rome, displayed as a prisoner in Marius' triumph, and executed about a week later.

Italy in Danger

In 105 B.C., the Romans had something else on their minds besides Jugurtha. Anxiety about the threat to Italy by tribes from northern Europe had given way to panic. Later historians, men like Sallust, looked back and saw in the Jugurthine War a warning about the future. At the time, when the war in Africa ended, the Roman people were simply grateful to have a leader like Marius whom they could trust to save them from a greater danger, closer to home.

The fall of the Roman Empire evokes a picture of hordes of barbarians sweeping down from the north in the fifth century of the Christian era. Actually, throughout a thousand years of their history, the Romans were never free from this threat. Time and again, tribes came pressing southward in search of better land. The Gauls sacked Rome in the early fourth century B.C. Now, in the late second century, the Romans were badly frightened again. Year by year, the Cimbri and the Teutones, who came from the lands near the North Sea, had been moving steadily southeastward toward Italy. These tall, grey-eyed warriors, who brought with them their women and children and everything they owned, were arriving in southern Gaul in startlingly large numbers. That was part of the bad news from beyond the Alps. The rest was even worse. The first Roman commanders sent to stop them had failed miserably and so given the barbarians further encouragement.

As in the early stages of the Jugurthine War, the Romans appeared to be defeating themselves. There was a breakdown in discipline and morale. The failure of the proconsul Quintus Servilius Caepio to coordinate his plans in Gallia Narbonensis with the consul, Gnaeus Mallius Maximus, was particularly damaging. Mallius' performance is evidence that not all of the "new men" coming to the fore were of the same capacity as Marius. In 105, at Arausio (modern Orange, about thirteen miles north of Avignon), an ill-managed battle cost the lives of an estimated 80,000 men. It was the worst disaster for Rome since Cannae.

The Roman people, seeing themselves deceived by faltering leadership, again called on Marius to save them. They elected him consul for 104 and reelected him for 103, even though tradition decreed that a man should not serve in successive years and that he should not be chosen in any case while absent from the city. Once the barriers were broken, choosing Marius for the consulship became a habit. He was elected five times in succession (104–100 B.C.). The tribune Lucius Saturninus was the man credited with soliciting the votes which helped Marius to achieve this enviable record, and the debt Marius incurred would later prove embarrassing. Much would go wrong for Marius in the years ahead;

meantime, his luck held out. The Cimbri and Teutones unexpectedly turned toward Spain and so provided him with some badly
needed time.

When it became necessary to defend the approaches to Italy,
Marius was ready. Cautious about taking any action, deliberate
when he did, he employed tactics that proved exactly right. On
one occasion he taunted the barbarians into racing uphill to face
his soldiers, who then had the advantage in forcing them back-
ward down a steep incline; at the bottom were other troops hidden behind their position. Marius knew that the barbarians were
easily excited and hence prone to confusion. Their numbers were
frightening, but that only meant a higher toll when they gave way
to panic. Plutarch repeats an old tale that near Massilia the local
farmers built fences made of bones around their vineyards.

After Marius had stopped the Teutones from marching
along the Mediterranean coast toward Italy, he joined his fellow
consul, Catulus, who had been less successful in keeping the Cimbri from moving through the Alpine passes. Together they
blocked the barbarian advance at the Po River. Sulla was also
there, serving with Catulus; later, in his *Memoirs* he made some
observations about that battle. The *Memoirs* are no longer extant,
but Plutarch quotes him as saying that the Roman victory was
partly due to the heat and dust of an August day. The Cimbri,
coming from a northern climate, had not been bothered by the
snow of the Alps, but they found the sun unbearable in the plains.
Sulla also suggested that it was fortunate the dust kept the Romans from seeing the vast hordes approaching; otherwise they
might have been discouraged out of their victory. He adds that
Marius arranged the Roman formation to favor himself and his
army; Catulus apparently thought so too. Marius received the
major credit at home for this second victory and he was willing to
accept it because his colleague had not fared well before his arrival. He did share the triumph with Catulus. Perhaps, as Plutarch
observes, Catulus' soldiers would not have had it otherwise. Besides, Marius could use their votes as he prepared to seek a sixth
consulship.

Marius in Rome

A military man used to giving orders is often ill at ease in canvas-
sing for votes among the rank-and-file. Marius was proud of

being a blunt soldier, straightforward in his speech. He could well have been embarrassed by what he had to say and do to be elected in peacetime. Yet he was a man too covetous of power and fame to live quietly and out of sight. His old enemy Metellus, whom he had replaced in North Africa, was exactly the opposite. He would not cater to the crowd and had only scorn for the demagogues who promoted Marius' candidacy.

Saturninus and his friend Glaucia stirred class strife to a fever pitch by their harangues. Marius depended on these men to deliver the votes needed for his election and that of a hand-picked colleague. Rumor had it that Marius also spent part of his newly acquired fortune to bribe the electorate. His enemies claimed that he would not let anything stand in the way of his ambition.

The murder of a newly elected tribune, Nonius, was particularly shocking. In 101, Nonius had dared to expose the collusion between Glaucia, then a praetor conducting the election for the tribuneship, and Saturninus, who was running again for the office. Both men had previously been condemned for their bad character by Metellus (now called Numidicus), but he was unable to move against them because his fellow censor refused to agree. They knew they would not be so lucky if Nonius became tribune. As soon as he was elected, they attacked him with a mob of followers and killed him. The following morning, amid threats of further trouble, Glaucia rushed through the election of Saturninus to fill the vacancy. Violence had served its purpose in getting him elected, and it is not surprising that he followed the same course in pressing for the legislation he wanted.

A bill for dividing the land in Gaul recently won from the Cimbri was particularly troublesome. It favored the Italian allies and the rural citizens, who were among Marius' strongest supporters. Saturninus used agitators from outside the city to stir up trouble and frighten off the urban voters who opposed him. The bill was passed in a mockery of the legislative process.

Saturninus was also the chief instigator of a maneuver to drive Marius' enemy Metellus out of Rome. In a rider added to the land law which had been so hastily adopted, all senators were required to take an oath to abide by whatever the people should decide concerning the distribution of land. As might be expected, Metellus was vehement in his opposition to the oath. Saturninus fed the fears of the rural voters by telling them they would lose their allotments if this influential official did not agree. Although

the urban voters rallied to Metellus' defense, he voluntarily left
the city in order to avoid further disorder or bloodshed.

The exile of this respected man was less of a boon to Marius
than it might have seemed. With his arch-enemy out of the way
he was left with the question of how much lawlessness he could
himself permit. Success made Saturninus reckless. In the year 100,
the elections were again marred by the murder of a candidate.
Memmius, a rival of Glaucia for the consulship, was killed. He
was not waylaid in the street as Nonius had been but was attacked
in the Tribal Assembly by henchmen of Saturninus and Glaucia,
whose intention was to terrify the voters. At last the people were
terrified enough to strike back. They had support from every
quarter. Senators and equestrians, who were seldom on the same
side, decided to join forces against Saturninus. Nor could Marius
any longer resist the call for law and order. He sided with the
Senate against Saturninus and so in a sense against himself. His
own veterans were used to force the surrender of Saturninus and
his mob of followers. Glaucia and Saturninus surrendered to Marius, but he could not protect them or their ruffians from an
aroused citizenry, who killed them in a wild outburst of civic
revenge. The Senate was again triumphant. Metellus returned to
the city the following year. Circumstances had forced Marius to
join those who liked him least.

At this juncture the Senate lost a rare opportunity for a
reconciliation of factions. Instead of making an accommodation
with Marius in the hope of forestalling further civil strife, the
Senate rejoiced that he had been forced to eliminate his own supporters. Marius travelled to Asia Minor, where he had a firsthand
look at the trouble brewing in that part of the world. Mithridates,
the dynamic ruler of the small kingdom of Pontus, was the prime
mover behind an effort to drive the Romans out of the Aegean
region. For the present, however, polite relations were still maintained; Marius was a distinguished visitor, and Mithridates gave
him a cordial welcome. Behind the scenes, preparations continued
in anticipation of the right moment to rally all those opposed to
Roman power. That would come while Rome was preoccupied
with yet another domestic crisis.

The War with the Italians

The debate over the demands of the Italian allies had been going
on for a long time, and patience was no longer the answer. Ap-

pian says: "Fulvius Flaccus in his consulship (125 B.C.) first and foremost openly excited among the Italians the desire for Roman citizenship, so as to be partners in the empire instead of subjects" (III. 1. 34). It appears, however, that soon after he brought up the subject he was sent overseas on assignment by senators who preferred to think of other things. Later, in 122, when Flaccus and Gaius Gracchus were tribunes, the matter was revived. Nor did it lapse after both of them were killed. Agitation continued into the first century. In 91 B.C., the controversy reached a climax during the tribuneship of Livius Drusus, whose liberal views would have shocked his father, a man well remembered for his vigorous opposition to Gaius Gracchus. Actually, the younger Drusus was trying to avoid partisanship, and his promotion of the Italian claim for citizenship was part of a larger plan. He wanted to give a prize to everybody. It was apparent to him that many men are less inclined to think about the merits of an issue than they are to feel that somebody is getting ahead and they are falling behind. In that respect his program recalls the policy of Solon, the early Greek lawgiver, who had sought to give every faction in Athens something, to keep any group from having everything.

To balance citizenship for the Italians, Livius Drusus proposed that needy plebeians who were already citizens be sent to new colonies overseas; to placate the upper classes, he suggested that about three hundred new members be appointed to the Senate. They were to be chosen from among the equestrians, and future judges were to be selected from this new mixed group in the Senate. So business interests were to be given an equal voice at the highest level of government, and at the same time the senators were to regain their old role in the judiciary. This was the program of a man of good will who sought harmony through compromise. What he was asking for was mutual good faith, but he was the only one who seemed to have it. As Appian says, "both the Senate and the knights [it will be recalled that in early Rome, the *equites* were cavalrymen], although opposed to each other, were united in hating Drusus" (III. 1. 36). Moreover, despite his other generous proposals, citizenship for the Italians continued to be an unpopular idea with the citizenry at large. One night, while in a crowd, Drusus was stabbed and mortally wounded. No one knows who killed him.

Not everybody would agree with the above version of Drusus' career. It is possible, while admitting his ability, to speak of his arrogance and to suggest that his program, like that of his father, was designed to keep the oligarchy in power and everybody else quiet. All can agree, however, that the death of Drusus ended the last hope for a peaceful settlement of the Italian question. An extremely bitter war followed between Rome and her former friends—the so-called Social War (from the Latin *socii,* allies), from 91 to 88 B.C. It ended with the ex-allies surrendering to Rome and receiving in return the citizenship which they had sought in the first place—a conclusion which surely makes that war one of the most futile exercises in the annals of man.

In the Social War, Rome had the help of her loyal allies, including certain Italian cities which did not join the rebels. The challenge to her authority, however, came from the most tenacious fighters in the peninsula—those who lived in the central mountainous region, an area which had been the most difficult for Rome to subjugate in earlier centuries. Now, in addition to native aggressiveness, the Italians could count on the experience of native officers who had had their training under Marius during the war against the Cimbri and the Teutones. Appian's account of the war is little more than a catalogue of battles; yet it amply conveys the bitterness of a struggle between former friends. Appian spends most of his time telling us about the operations conducted by Sulla and by Pompeius Strabo, father of the more famous Gnaeus Pompeius, called Pompey the Great. Marius, home from the East but out of favor with the Senate, played a less prominent role.

The Italians were strong in spirit but short on resources; time was on the Roman side. Furthermore, the confederates fought at cross purposes. Some sought autonomy and the end of all ties to Rome, but most continued to hope for the citizenship the Romans had denied them in peacetime. With this in mind the Roman Senate decided to discourage further defections by granting citizenship to the Etruscans and Umbrians and, in fact, any Italians who had remained loyal. The unprecedented gesture was obviously unsettling to the confederacy. Although it appeared that rebellious allies would also be well treated if they returned to the fold, that did not actually occur. The new citizens were not to be assigned to the thirty-five tribes but rather grouped in new tribes (how many is not certain), which in the nature of things would vote at the end of the roll call. With each tribe having one vote, the voice of the newcomers was muted, and the Tribal Assembly continued to express the will of the "original" citizens. This ar-

9. Coin of the Italian Confederacy. A bull, representing the former allies, attacks the Roman wolf. Courtesy of the Trustees of the British Museum.

rangement would invite trouble at a later date, and, in fact, only lasted a few years; but, for the time being, the new people were happy to be included at all.

As time passed, continued Roman successes prompted almost all of the Italians to lay down their arms and take up citizenship. Only the Lucanians and Samnites held out to the bitter end. To optimists at Rome the solution to the long standing citizenship problem was a hopeful sign. Pessimists could argue that this issue was peripheral to the real trouble, and they were right. The war with the Italians was an interlude in the drift toward civil war within the entire Roman state. The traditional machinery for solving domestic problems was simply no longer working as it had before the Gracchan crisis.

Civil War

At about the time the Social War was ending, according to Appian, money lenders killed a praetor during the performance of his duties. Usury at Rome had long been a touchy issue; an ancient law forbade the practice, yet time-honored custom sanctioned it. The praetor Asellio, seeking to have the matter resolved in the

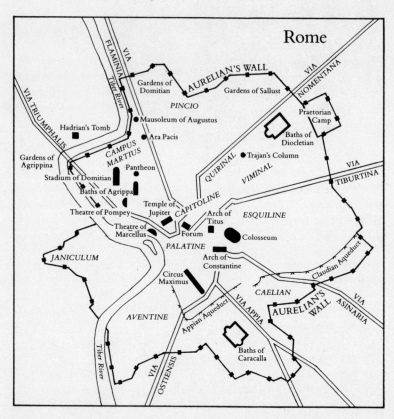

courts, was murdered by men who saw his meddling as a threat to their business. A magistrate killed while making public offerings in a temple! There could not have been a worse scandal. The Senate's investigation of the matter, however, was blocked because no witness could be found, and the case was dropped without anyone being convicted. The event may seem unimportant, for it did not concern a man with a name like Tiberius Gracchus or Julius Caesar, and yet that is precisely the significance of it. The Republic did not collapse because one or two famous men were killed, it was ruined by many men who were determined to take the law into their own hands and kill those who for whatever reason stood in their way. Isolated instances of unresolved murder preceded a general upheaval.

For over three decades, reformers had included citizenship for the Italians as a major plank in their platforms. That they were at last vindicated on this score did not mean that they were right about everything, yet it was now easy for them to think so. They were determined to reorder the existing system and, as they saw it, the place to begin was the Senate. This body should divest itself of members who were in debt for more than 2,000 denarii. New citizens should be distributed evenly among all thirty-five tribes rather than remain in the extra tribes which had been created for them. Finally, the reformers wanted Marius to be given the assignment against Mithridates.

As mentioned earlier, Marius had had a private interview with Mithridates in the year 99, during which the two men had had what is known as an exchange of views. Since then, Rome's relations with Pontus had steadily deteriorated. The neighbors of this small kingdom on the southern shore of the Black Sea counted Mithridates' early successes a mixed blessing. When the Greek cities in the Chersonesus Taurica (modern Crimea) were threatened by Scythian and Sarmatian tribesmen, they asked for his aid and received, as usual, considerably more. By acting as a permanent protector, he brought the Black Sea area and its trade within the orbit of his power. Any effort to expand his sphere of influence meant trouble, of course, with Rome, for she had agreed to guarantee the security of weaker kingdoms within his reach. For example, for over fifteen years Mithridates played a cat-and-mouse game in Cappadocia, in eastern Asia Minor. In 104, while the Romans were fighting off the northern invaders, he had entered Cappadocia, where he remained until the Senate sent him a

10. Mithridates in lion's-head helmet. Courtesy of the Louvre.

sharp eviction notice in 95. In 93, his son-in-law, Tigranes, the king of Armenia, took over Cappadocia for a year, but withdrew under pressure from Sulla, who in 92 was the governor of neighboring Cilicia.

When the war with the Italians began, it was easy to predict that Mithridates and Tigranes would again take advantage of Rome's domestic troubles. Cappadocia was again occupied and the more important kingdom of Bithynia, in northwestern Asia Minor on the Black Sea, was also seized. This was the third time Mithridates had defied the Romans, and despite the war on their doorstep they decided to take drastic action. Instead of relying on a local governor, the Senate sent Manius Aquillius, a man of proven military capacity, to drive Mithridates back within his own borders. Aquillius was given charge of the army stationed in the province of Asia, and all allied soldiers available. He did not have sufficient forces for a showdown with Mithridates; yet the king withdrew because he was still hesitant about beginning a full-scale war with Rome. Aquillius misjudged him, however, when he urged Nicomedes, king of Bithynia, to invade Pontus. Aquillius would accept whatever booty was won in return for services rendered in restoring Nicomedes to his throne. It would therefore appear that Mithridates was goaded into a counterattack. He was amply prepared. Once he started to move, Aquillius never had a chance of containing him. Mithridates reoccupied Bithynia in 88, and then invaded the province of Asia (formerly, kingdom of Pergamum), where he was received as a conquering hero by the cities long chafing under Roman rule. Once he had control of Asia, the rest of Asia Minor was his by default. Only a few cities in the south were determined to fight for their autonomy.

Mithridates' lightning strike at Asia was an act of war which sealed the fate of all the peoples of this region. Though Rome had befriended and supported the native kings, the city dwellers of the province of Asia knew the Romans only as ruthless tax farmers and exploiters. At a prearranged time they suddenly seized and murdered every hated foreigner they could lay their hands on; innocent and guilty were slain alike in what has been called the "Asiatic Vespers." The number who died in the massacre is usually given as 80,000. Those who wielded the daggers bound themselves to Mithridates and his cause. Now it was to be Rome's turn.

Ironically, the struggle over who would conduct the campaign against Mithridates led to political paralysis in the capital and then a brief civil war. The command of this expedition was a coveted prize because it would give the man who headed it a chance to build a new personal following. Moreover, at the time, there seemed to be little conception of how difficult a war with Mithridates would be. The Senate had given the assignment to Sulla. They had every reason to do so, because he was the consul in 88, and also the man least likely to be a threat when he came home.

The threatened intervention of the Assembly in this matter revived the rivalry between Marius and Sulla which went back to the day when Jugurtha had been captured. Although Marius had been publicly at odds with Metellus, it was always Sulla from whom he had the most to fear. During the Social War Sulla's star had risen. Marius gave a good account of himself and had won at least one major battle, but illness had forced him to give up his command before the war was over. He might now have gracefully retired from politics, being in his late sixties; yet a man so long at the center of attention often loses track of the time. He cannot believe that he is not needed, and so he listens to those who would encourage him as much for their own purposes as for his. Businessmen, who were at odds with the nobility, backed Marius because he was useful in their campaign against the Senate. They were not always interested in his popular causes. As the Gracchi had learned earlier, support from that quarter was easy to get if the going was good, but hard to keep if it was not.

For the moment Marius felt encouraged. He took up a regular regimen of exercises, although this meant standing alongside youths whose lithe torsos were a sharp contrast to his own distorted body. Sulpicius Rufus, a tribune, was supporting him with the same illegal tactics Saturninus had used earlier. Three thousand ruffians stood ready to silence anyone who opposed Sulpicius or to break up meetings if they were not going his way. Marius, however, needed broader support than this if he was to regain his old power, if not his glory, and Sulpicius enlisted some six hundred equestrians who were fanatically opposed to the Senate. The forging of this alliance brought about renewed agitation on behalf of the reform program dormant since the assassination of Livius Drusus. The Senate, which had been managing the affairs of state since the recall of Metellus, now looked to Sulla, fifty years old, as a man who could be trusted to block any radical moves. Sulla, a proud patrician, further enhanced his position among the nobility when, in this same year, he married a daughter of Metellus Numidicus.

Sulla had no sooner been chosen to oppose Mithridates than Marius began to devise means for upsetting the appointment. He used Sulpicius to advance a proposal for reassigning the new citizens to the original thirty-five tribes. That would cinch their support. A sharp reaction by those opposed to this move led to fighting in the streets and prompted the consuls to postpone a vote on the question until tempers could cool. Sulpicius, who had nothing to gain from calm deliberation, pressed for an immediate decision. He and his followers carried out a planned uprising in the city, which sent all their opponents running for cover. Sulla's son-in-law, who was the son and namesake of the other consul, Quintus Pompeius Rufus, lost his life during this sudden terror. According to one account, Sulla managed to save himself by hiding at Marius' house. If so, we can only conclude that although the old general did not repudiate Sulpicius, as he had Saturninus earlier, he did not want Sulla's blood on his hands. Perhaps there is no truth in the story at all. Sulla denied it in his *Memoirs,* and Appian says that Sulla was not even aware of any immediate danger to himself when he left the city. There is no doubt that Sulla managed to leave Rome and make his way to Campania, where six legions stood in readiness for the war against Mithridates. Sulla led them against Marius instead. According to Appian, the decision to march on the capital was prompted by the news that Marius had been given the Eastern command, which Sulla felt was legally his. The soldiers assembled at Capua were probably eager to support Sulla, for it was possible that Marius might recruit others to go in their place and so deprive them of what they considered a prosperous adventure.

Sulla's march on Rome sent a chill throughout the city. If ever there was a sacred prohibition, it was the one against bringing an army into the city. Who could be happy to see that precedent broken? Many citizens showed their displeasure at Sulla's arrival by throwing stones from the rooftops. Sulla responded by setting their houses on fire. He had little trouble taking Rome. Appian writes: "Marius and Sulpicius went, with some forces they had hastily armed, to meet the invaders near the Esquiline forum, and here a battle took place between the contending parties, the first regularly fought in Rome with bugle and standards in full military fashion, no longer like a mere faction fight. To such extremity of evil had the recklessness of party strife progressed among them" (III. 1. 58).

In desperation, the Marians offered freedom to slaves who would help them, but slaves usually had an uncanny knack for knowing which way things were going and did not respond to the offer. Finally, Marius and his friends were forced to make their escape as best they could. Sulla, in his own eyes, was a liberator. It was predictable that others would see the event differently. He was faced with the immediate problem of restoring order even in his own legions. Looting, a familiar by-product of chronic violence, was a special problem. Sulla acted quickly to make public examples of those caught in the act.

Recent legislation was declared null and void, and laws which Marius and Sulpicius had sponsored did not survive their departure. The legal pendulum swung abruptly in the opposite direction. In times of trouble, it is customary to hear that current problems are a result of recent changes. The solution is simple, men say. Restore all power to the hands of those who held it in times past and destroy any means by which their authority might be challenged. Sulla is without doubt the classic example of the stalwart reactionary who insists that the best is what used to be. He ignored the Tribal Assembly, which from the time of the Gracchi had become increasingly radical in its demands. As of old, all proposals were to be taken to the Centuriate Assembly, where safe responses were more predictable; there wealth still counted for something, and the poor could not order what they pleased simply by being the most numerous group, as in the Tribal Assembly. The power of the majority, in Sulla's opinion, was the chief source of recent instability. He favored returning to the pre-Gracchan custom which required all questions to be debated in the Senate before being put to a vote by the people. The veto power of the Senate over legislation and elections was again acknowledged. To shore up the sagging reputation of the Senate, three hundred new members were added from among citizens of the better class whom Sulla felt he could trust.

Marius and those who had fled with him were outlawed. Their murder was sanctioned by the state; they could be killed by anyone, anywhere. Sulpicius was soon caught and executed. So were certain tribunes who were known to have supported Marius. Plutarch gives a lively account of Marius' narrow escapes as he sought to find a refuge. On one occasion, when close to being taken by a band of pursing horsemen, he plunged into the sea and with the help of servants managed to reach a ship nearby. His reception on board was cautious. Common folk, seamen, and farmers had respect enough for Marius to hide him for a time, but there would be danger in protecting him too long. Provincial governors did not want to see him at all. Abreast of the news from Rome, they had to be especially careful about welcoming the wrong old friend. When Marius arrived in the province of Africa, the governor, Sextilius, gave him a rude reception. He was warned to leave immediately or be executed. His son, who had failed to find a refuge in Numidia, joined his father on the small island of Cercina near the coast of Africa. There for a time they could rest.

In the year 87, Sulla finally departed for the East. His going was by no means a sign of stability at home. Quintus Pompeius, his fellow consul, had been killed when he tried to assume command over the forces which guarded Italy. Their previous commander was reluctant to give them up, and although his responsibility for what happened is not clear, the legal transfer of command was thwarted and another shocking episode was added to the list of recent unsavory events.

Even Sulla could not be sure of everybody. He guessed wrong about Lucius Cornelius Cinna. In an attempt to placate the citizenry and assure a stable government, he nominated Cinna as consul. Yet Cinna was popular with the people precisely because he did not share Sulla's reactionary views. The alliance between these two men was shaky at best; however, Cinna was willing to swear allegiance at the time in return for Sulla's support. The best explanation for Sulla's trust of him is that Sulla was in a hurry. Cinna was immediately at odds with the other consul, Gnaeus Octavius, over the question of placing the new citizens in the thirty-five tribes, where they would have a greater voice. He agreed with those who argued that this redistribution would forestall further trouble. Octavius, true to Sulla, favored the status quo, as did the majority of the "old citizens." Some of them backed Octavius in the Forum with their fists and crude weapons.

Cinna's first move set in motion a familiar chain reaction. So long as he remained a reform-minded leader interested in laws beneficial to the majority of the citizens, he was popular. When, like the Gracchi or Drusus, he began to philosophize about how good it would be in the long run for the majority to share their gains with others, his popularity disappeared. Daggers were drawn and the Forum stained with blood before Cinna fled for his life. The Senate hastily stripped him of his consulship. Here was a man who needed Marius, and Marius was on the way. Informed of events at home, he had left his refuge on the island of Cercina and sailed for Italy.

Landing in Etruria, Marius proceeded to muster his loyal veterans, and he added to their ranks local shepherds and even runaway slaves willing to take a chance. There was widespread sympathy for Marius among men whose fortunes were poor. His were too. In rude clothing and on foot, the old general, now past seventy, made his way toward Rome for the last great comeback of his life.

Cinna had been travelling widely among the Italian cities where the new citizens lived, telling them that he was fighting for their cause and needed their support if he was to take Rome. Late in 87, he joined forces with Marius, and together they challenged the consul. Octavius declared himself too honorable to press slaves into service against the law. Instead, he relied on the guidance of soothsayers to save him. Plutarch, in a rare quizzical mood, wonders why Marius so often profited by their advice but Octavius did not.

The gods had forsaken the city altogether. Cinna and Marius successfully cut off the food supply and burdened the Senate with a hungry populace. Rome was taken without a battle. Cinna was then returned to the consulship, having won the office, so to speak, a second time. The tribunes quickly lifted the order of banishment against Marius. Although it was only a formality, he insisted on it, having been greatly insulted by the decree, in view of his previous service to Rome.

Both Marius and Cinna assured Octavius that he would not be harmed. However, they seemed unable to control their supporters, who were angered to see Octavius accompanied by lictors and still insisting that he was the legal consul. All signs indicated that the city was not safe for him, yet he refused to leave. He was slain amid an orgy of violence; his head was cut off and displayed in the Forum as an ornament. So foul an indignity had been inflicted on a consul for the first time. Only a few years before it would have been unthinkable.

Marius and Cinna presided over a reign of terror marked by a capricious cruelty usually associated with the more decadent emperors of the centuries ahead. Appian writes: "They killed remorselessly and severed the necks of men already dead, and they paraded these horrors before the public eye, either to inspire fear and terror, or for a godless spectacle" (III. 1. 71). Sulla's supporters were put to the sword in an atmosphere of impatient hysteria. Plutarch tells us that no matter how high an office a man might hold, if his salute to Marius was not returned by the general the man was liable to be killed on the spot. Even Catulus, who had served with Marius in the war against the Cimbri, was driven to suicide. He had made the mistake of not joining Marius in exile, and those who had not helped then might not hope for mercy now.

Cinna joined in the ruthless suppression of all opposition, but his bitterness did not run as deeply as did that of Marius, nor apparently his thirst for blood. Certain slaves, declared free by Cinna when he first challenged Octavius, had enrolled in Cinna's army. They now took vengeance on their former households and killed their one-time masters. Cinna, who had expressly forbidden them to use his service for private revenge, promptly put them to death. As usual, amid the horrors, there were selfless acts of heroism by those who hid their hunted friends. One man was saved by his slaves, who found a body and set it afire, explaining to those who hunted their master that he had committed suicide and that they were dutifully burning the corpse. There were also cruel betrayals by those who sought favors from the victors of the moment.

For the second time in two years the city was at the mercy of an army. When Sulla seized the city he had abrogated the laws passed by Sulpicius. Now *his* laws were in turn overruled, and he was declared banished even as Marius had been. According to one of the new traditions, his house was burned.

Marius had achieved his long-hoped-for seventh consulship and in the process set two new records. He was the first man to have gained the office a seventh time, and, with Cinna, shared the honor of being the first consul to serve without an election. With the heads of their opponents on display in the Forum, there was no need for a campaign; Marius and Cinna simply announced that they were the new consuls (86 B.C.). For Marius, the old soldier and one-time savior of Rome, the success was a hollow one. His revenge-filled days were brief. Sick, unable to sleep, often drunk, he died on the seventeenth day after he took office.

In a speech mentioned earlier, Marius had compared himself to those ancestral heroes who had established the names of Rome's great families. During his early career he was truly one of them—a man of bold spirit and generous intention. Attempting a comeback at a time when virtue had lost its charm, Marius fought fire with fire and succumbed to all the baseness he had once abhorred. Yet it would be wrong to take leave of Marius at his worst. Plutarch tells a story which illustrates his better self. On one occasion he gave the "freedom of the city" to men from Camerinum who had fought to save Rome from the threat of the Cimbri and the Teutones. The act was contrary to law, but Marius thought they deserved a reward. When he was criticized for this, he replied that he had not heard the letter of the law amid the din of the battle. There are other such stories—enough to justify Plutarch's conclusion that Marius was a good man ruined by his ambition to be great.

With Marius dead and Sulla a long way from home, three years of relative calm followed, during which Cinna and the Senate were locked in a standoff. Cinna was strong enough to appoint the man he wanted to serve with him. In 86, after choosing Valerius Flaccus as his colleague, he gave him orders to lead an army against Mithridates—a move obviously designed to undercut Sulla in the East. When Flaccus was killed, Cinna gave the consulship in 85 and 84 to Gnaeus Papirius Carbo, who was next in his favor. There were no elections; the Senate could only bide its time. Sulla would someday be home. In the meantime, Cinna finally managed to redistribute the Italians throughout all the tribes. There would no longer be any second-class citizens. Those who lived elsewhere in Italy still had to travel to Rome to vote. Once there, they were equal in all respects.

Sulla

By the time Sulla and his legions reached the East, Mithridates held sway over the richest portions of Asia Minor, the islands of the Aegean, and even Greece. The majority of the Greeks were eager to join in the new alliance. At Athens, the rebellion stirred memories of a former greatness; this city alone among the Greek states refused any formal acknowledgement of Sulla's presence. Her defiance compelled Sulla to spend precious time in besieging the city. The cost was paid by the rest of Greece. Her famous shrines, even Delphi, were plundered by Sulla's agents. Nor were the Romans the only foreigners guilty of looting defenseless towns. Forces loyal to Mithridates, unmindful of their mission, joined the devastation. The first century B.C. was disastrous for Greece.

The fall of Athens, followed by a bloody purge of its people, was satisfying to Sulla personally. The later crucial victory at Chaeronea over a group of armies sent by Mithridates was a more direct blow at the enemy. Sulla celebrated that event with joyous feasting. Another triumph followed at Orchomenus. Success in Greece was of no help to Sulla at home, however. On the contrary, it inspired urgency among those who wished to prevent his returning victorious. Word that Flaccus had been sent with an army was only a part of the alarming news from Rome. Sulla's family and friends fled to him with the latest grim details of Cinna's rule.

In former times, the stability of Rome's domestic affairs had constituted an advantage over her enemies. Now, as in the Jugurthine War, political uncertainties at home seriously hampered Roman ventures overseas. Sulla saw that he would have to scale down his plans to make the best settlement he could in order to return as soon as possible to Italy. Nothing could have been more welcome than an overture for peace from Mithridates, which came through the king's general, Archelaus, whom Sulla had defeated at both Chaeronea and Orchomenus. Some delay ensued before Sulla and Mithridates met face to face. As both men were seeking peace without a full surrender, each side tested the other for any overeagerness which might betray a weakness which could be exploited. Mithridates knew how anxious Sulla was to return home to face his enemies. All the same, the war had been going badly for the king and it was apparently going to get worse. He was faced by the prospect of an attack by Fimbria, who had replaced Flaccus after the consul was killed in a mutiny. Under the circumstances Sulla's terms seemed generous. In return for an indemnity and the evacuation of certain strategic areas, Sulla was willing to leave Mithridates secure in his place as the most powerful king in the Aegean world—and even to announce that he was an ally of Rome. These terms were an embarrassment to the Romans, but Sulla had for the time being at least checked Mithridates' power. At Dardanus, near the Hellespont, the two men met and sealed their bargain with an embrace and a kiss. Each betrayed his present cause for the chance to win something better at a later day. Fimbria had gambled that Sulla and Mithridates could not conclude a peace. When they did, he killed himself.

As Sulla hastened homeward, Cinna and Carbo sought feverishly to rally their forces. Their soldiers did not relish a fight with Sulla's veterans; in fact, their feelings ran so high against Cinna that he was killed suddenly in what amounted to little more than a casual riotous incident. When a lictor walking ahead of the consul struck a man in the way, he was in turn attacked by a soldier. During the attempt to seize the offender, a general melee broke out. Cinna was stabbed to death—the third consul to be assassinated in four years.

Since the omens were against an election to replace Cinna, Carbo stood alone in the consulship. In the following year, 83 B.C., the consuls Gaius Norbanus and Lucius Cornelius Scipio, inherited Cinna's war with Sulla. Carbo joined them in the struggle (which lasted for three years in Italy and even longer overseas) between the so-called Marians and the partisans of Sulla. The great toll of lives is reflected in Appian's remark that "the war ruined everyone" (III. 1. 82).

At first, there was widespread horror in Rome at the thought of a Sullan victory. The citizenry had cooperated with the Marians who had burned Sulla's house and declared him an outlaw. Outside the city, the Italians were willing to fight against Sulla, for he had never shown any interest in the progressive features of the Marian program. In the beginning, most men remained loyal to the government in power, but disappointment in their commanders later prompted large numbers of them to change their minds. Sulla was particularly encouraged by the wholesale defection of soldiers under the command of the consul Scipio.

In 82, Carbo was consul again, along with Marius' adopted son and namesake, who was heir to his father's policies. They were no match for Sulla. The younger Marius was besieged at Praeneste, and Carbo, greatly discouraged, sailed to Africa in hopes of holding at least that province. Other generals were eager to follow, but not all of them managed to escape.

Ironically, the stiffest opposition Sulla faced came from the Samnites and the Lucanians, who fought him near the walls of the capital and nearly kept him from taking the city. Thus the oldest enemies of Rome played a major role in her destiny. Although the fear of the Roman citizenry that they would fall into the hands of their most ancient foes was not realized, what happened to some of them was another kind of nightmare. They were saved by Sulla, a professed friend, who then unleashed within the city a furious retribution on all those whom he suspected of ever having opposed him.

Before long, besieged Praeneste surrendered. The younger Marius committed suicide before he could be captured. Sulla ordered that his head be placed on display in the Forum. Other enemies still alive, Carbo among them, were to be hunted down and killed. The crucial mission of destroying Carbo and his friends in North Africa and in Sicily was given to Pompey, who had gained his first laurels during Sulla's last campaign. So began the career of the renowned Pompey the Great. Sulla relied on him in spite of his youth.

While Pompey was engaged in silencing opposition abroad, Sulla acted with severity against his enemies at home. The mass murders he perpetrated seem more horrible than those of Marius because they were more systematic. Appian says that Sulla drew up a list of about forty senators and sixteen hundred members of the equestrian order who were to be killed on sight. Describing Sulla's thoroughness, Appian writes: "He seems to have been the first to offer a formal list of those whom he punished, to offer prizes to assassins and rewards to informers, and to threaten with punishment those who should conceal the proscribed. . . . Some of these, taken unawares, were killed where they were caught, in their houses, in the streets, or in the temples. . . . Others were dragged through the city and trampled on, none of the spectators daring to utter a word of remonstrance against these horrors" (III. 1. 95).

Plutarch in his *Life of Sulla* tells more of the story:

> Nor did the proscriptions prevail only at Rome, but throughout all the cities of Italy the effusion of blood was such, that neither sanctuary of the gods, nor hearth of hospitality, nor ancestral home escaped. Men were butchered in the embraces of their wives, children in the arms of their mothers. Those who perished through public animosity or private enmity were nothing in comparison of the numbers of those who suffered for their riches. Even the murderers began to say that "his fine house killed this man, a garden that, a third, his hot baths." Quintus Aurelius, a quiet, peaceable man, and one who thought all his part in the common calamity consisted in condoling with the misfortunes of others, coming into the Forum to read the list, and finding himself among the proscribed, cried out . . . "My Alban farm has informed against me." He had not gone far before he was dispatched by a ruffian, sent on that errand. (P. 570)

The bad fortune of some was a boon to others. Men of all classes had won Sulla's favor, and they were now generously rewarded from the great wealth obtained in the proscriptions. The former exiles among the nobility had the best reason for gratitude. They had returned in triumph and were happy to serve the man who had reprieved the old regime.

Although the average man in Rome had little cause for rejoicing, the terror which struck the rich and the famous showed that there was one advantage at least in being poor and anonymous. Besides, Sulla promised a better day for those who were wise enough to submit to his orders. By cruel suppression of some and largesse to many the new regime planned for a period of quiet cooperation. That was Sulla's first goal, and he was not long in achieving it. He insured himself an extra margin of safety by freeing 10,000 slaves formerly owned by proscribed persons and giving them the name Cornelius, thus acquiring a large and loyal family all his own. Sulla used the same means of consolidating his power in the rest of Italy. By requisitioning the property of proscribed Italians and distributing the land to his soldiers, he made them at once guardians of his power and of their own interests throughout the peninsula. There remained the anti-Sullan forces active in Spain. Sulla sent Metellus Pius to deal with them.

Sulla and Marius were both born and raised in humble circumstances, but Sulla was never eager to talk about it. He was a member of an old patrician family which had fallen on bad times. Unlike Marius, who took pride in the rugged life of his forebears, Sulla was preoccupied with restoring his family to its former status. The lifelong support he gave to the senatorial faction leaves no doubt that Sulla was proud of his name and of his class. He recouped the family's finances by acquiring a small fortune in the early years of his public service, a fact which did not escape the notice of his contemporaries. Some of his money came from legacies he received from at least two women. One was a stepmother; the other, a wealthy woman who was on the list of Sulla's many admirers. If Plutarch's information is correct, Sulla's adventures with women of all classes would make a long story. He was married five times and had several children. His marriage to Metella, a woman of high social position, was apparently the most sincere of these arrangements, despite its political implications. After her death and shortly before his own, he married a much younger woman whom he had met by chance at the games. The daughter she bore after his death was called Postuma, as was the custom in such a circumstance.

All that we hear about Sulla suggests that he was a man who worked hard and played hard. His success lay in keeping these occupations apart. Friend and foe alike were startled by the difference between the shrewd and sober man they met on one occasion and the boisterous drinker they saw on another. Even when Sulla was attending to business, there could be subtle and sudden shifts from one mood to another. His decisions at times appeared capricious. He could treat with raging cruelty a man who had committed a small error and soon afterwards behave graciously toward a man responsible for a serious blunder. By such unpredictable behavior, he kept those around him alert and grateful for small favors. By insisting that other men should have no moods of their own and be always subservient to his, Sulla reveals himself as the brand of tyrant who, if not widely loved, yet proves to be an able administrator.

With the state at his disposal, Sulla found it convenient to reinstate the old custom of appointing a dictator in times of emergency; yet he did not reinstate the ancient six-month limitation on such service. A dictator had not ruled for over a century, but with the "consent of the people" Sulla was given the office. The vote was not important. Dictator, tyrant, or king, he had the military force to reorder the constitution as he pleased, and he did so. At the same time, the staggering loss of life and property during the anarchy of recent years made a firm hand welcome. Men were happy to see order restored under any circumstances. Sulla's intention was to reconstitute the power of those ancient families which had long dominated Roman affairs. This was clearly seen in his attack on the power of the plebeian tribunes. By denying those who served as tribunes the right to be candidates for any higher office, he discouraged men of talent or ambition from serving in that capacity. Also, to forestall any man (except himself) from garnering too much power or holding it too long, he made the *cursus honorum* inflexible by ordering a strict step-by-step progression from quaestor to consul and reinstated the rule which made a ten-year interval mandatory before an official could hold the same office a second time. This limitation naturally did not apply to Sulla; he took the consulship in 80 and could have had it again in 79 if he had wanted it. His "technical" changes in the constitution made little practical difference. He had acquired his enormous power by extralegal means, as would future generals who followed his example.

Sulla added to the Senate rich equestrians who were politically orthodox by his standards and therefore safe. He wanted that body to remain the guardian and anchor of the state. It was as if a drama were being staged in which time moved backwards and all groups were replaying their former roles. The honored old families were to hold power by inheritance, the new moneyed class would cooperate, and the common citizens would be grateful. The realities of the times were suspended for so long as Sulla ruled.

One of the great surprises of history is that he decided not to rule very long. Sulla's retirement in 79 is one of those unpredictable events which help to keep historians honest in judging their own worth as prophets and seers. Who would suppose that Sulla, especially Sulla, would step down at the height of his power? At a much later date, Appian still considered the decision to be almost unbelievable, but concluded that he abdicated because "he was weary of war, weary of power, weary of Rome" and "finally fell in love with rural life" (III. 1. 104). Maybe so.

Although no one would put Sulla on the same list of wise men with the Greek sage, Solon, there is a parallel. Both men reordered the constitutions of their respective states, and both decided to withdraw at the height of their success. Solon of course had acquired power because he was trusted rather than because he was feared. He was understandably disappointed to see what happened to his program, and Sulla would have been similarly disappointed, had he lived.

In contrast to the hard deaths he had inflicted on so many other men, Sulla's own passing was relatively easy, even if he did suffer toward the last from an unpleasant intestinal disorder. He always insisted that good fortune had given him the best of everything. He was not called Sulla the Great, but Sulla Felix—the Fortunate. In the epitaph which he wrote for himself he claimed to have taken care of both his friends and his enemies. Plutarch had the last word when he wrote that for all Sulla's talents he "owed his rise to the hatred which the nobility bore Marius" (p. 514).

Sulla's death came at his country estate near Cumae in 78 B.C., at the age of sixty. His state funeral was dominated by soldiers loyal to his name and enhanced by the multitudes attracted to a great occasion. Sulla's supporters would not have settled for less than a magnificent spectacle. History has given him a colder eye. If we see the story of the last century of the Roman Republic as a tripartite tragedy, the fanfare of Sulla's funeral contributes only a final scene to an inconclusive second act.

VIII

The Competitors:
Pompey, Lucullus, and Crassus

Sulla's last will and testament gave the Romans something to talk about: he had remembered all his friends except one. Pompey was not mentioned—a small omission, perhaps, and yet a clue to Pompey's career. Pompey did not fare well with Rome's famous dictators. Sulla gave him his start, but probably never cared for him. Julius Caesar brought his life to a sad end. He had trouble knowing who his friends were. Even his father disappointed him.

Customarily, at Rome, a father was a teacher-model to his son. It is seldom mentioned that a youth might learn the most from a bad example. While serving in the army, Pompey saw how an otherwise successful general could make himself hated by soldiers and civilians alike. Strabo was a selfish man with little feeling toward those who took orders from him. The numerous stories of his petty cruelty explain why he occasionally faced a rebellion in the ranks. During one mutiny, Pompey's pleas saved his father's life.

Pompey won a better reputation. In his own career he sometimes acted with abrupt harshness, but this seems to have been toward men who deserved it. He was not a vicious man who went out of his way to hurt others. Once in power, he did not

11. Pompey. Courtesy of the Ny Carlsberg Glyptotek, Copenhagen.

consider a wholesale murder of his enemies to be necessary. He never had that many. Precisely because he was of such a mild temperament, even indecisive at times, the firm-minded Cicero was often irritated with him. Pompey wanted to be honored in the grand manner of the Old Roman. He was willing to work hard for that. If at the same time certain of his actions contributed to the collapse of the Republic, he would have been the last to be aware of it. A much less favorable opinion of Pompey can be found in Sir Ronald Syme's *Roman Revolution*. Syme views Pompey as not just a man of excessive ambition but as a perfidious person, especially when he was young, who would not have cared even if he had known what the consequence of his acts would be. But, in either ancient or modern times, it is not surprising that judgments vary about a man of Pompey's prominence.

Strabo left Pompey considerable land holdings in Picenum on the Adriatic side of the peninsula, northeast of Rome. There his friends and neighbors belonged to the upper strata of society—men who felt threatened by the demagoguery of Cinna and Carbo. They lost no time in joining Sulla when he returned from the East. Pompey came later, bringing soldiers whom he had recruited for his own service. On his way, in three encounters with forces loyal to Carbo, he successfully scattered them or won them over to his own command. At the time he was twenty-three.

Sulla was amazed at the presumptuousness of the young Pompey, but he had a sharp eye for ability, and ability excuses many things. He greeted him with unusual generosity, returning salute for salute. Pompey was a model of courtesy. Those who witnessed the scene could be proud; it was a Roman performance.

Later, the triumphant Sulla gave Pompey his first major assignment, sending him to track down members of the Marian party and any refugees who had fled Italy to escape the proscriptions. In Sicily, Pompey captured Carbo and gave him a humiliating tongue-lashing before he was executed. Carbo had been consul three times and was Sulla's most conspicuous enemy. It would be noted in Rome who had captured him and put him to death. Less important men caught in the net were allowed to sneak away unharmed.

From Sicily, Pompey sailed to North Africa, where success was foretold by the defection of thousands of soldiers serving the rebel commander Domitius. One decisive battle, fought during a violent rainstorm, ended all resistance. Pompey's forces overran the enemy camp and killed Domitius. After the pacification of provincial Africa was completed, there followed a whirlwind march through nearby kingdoms to remind their rulers that they were indeed the clients of Rome.

Pompey had completed his mission in Sicily and North Africa with record speed. When he returned to Rome, flushed with victory, Sulla addressed him as Pompeius Magnus. He may already have been "Pompey the Great" to his forces in Africa. Now the title was official. For a reward Sulla considered it enough, but Pompey saw himself as a conquering hero and asked for a triumph—a glorious procession with all the trappings. Because older men had fought longer campaigns without receiving as much, Pompey's insistence was awkward. Sulla, disapproving, embarrassed, but partly amused, finally agreed to the occasion. A grand occasion it was for a man too young to sit in the Senate.

Pompey remained in Rome during the last calm years preceding Sulla's retirement. Sulla's enemies were quiet, but he had not forgotten who some of them were. Marcus Aemilius Lepidus topped the list. Pompey resisted Sulla's attempt to persuade him that Lepidus was dangerous and even supported Lepidus in his campaign for the consulship which he won for 78 B.C., the same year Sulla died. There was soon reason to regret the choice.

As others had predicted, Lepidus lost no time in attacking

the Sullan constitution. Widespread discontent gave him encouragement. The poor in the city demanded a return to the old
practice of a cheap grain price supported by the government. The
relatives and friends of men whom Sulla had proscribed were
anxious to see an end to the hated regime which bore his name.
Farmers who had been driven off their land to make room for the
dictator's veterans were eager to regain their former property.
When these discontented groups rallied around Lepidus, they
offered proof that, given the times, any hero would do. He was
certainly a tarnished one. Although a nobleman, Lepidus had been
little concerned about his family's good name. Nor was he worried about the welfare of others when quick money was to be
made in the topsy-turvy land market during the Sullan proscriptions. His record as a governor in Sicily was marred with scandal.
Conservatives in the Senate called him two-faced for his current
catering to the crowd. Earlier, Lepidus had lost favor with
Pompey by trying to block the plans for Sulla's elaborate public
funeral. Pompey's objections carried the day on that occasion, but
he did not interfere with Lepidus' offer of amnesty to all the old
enemies of Sulla. Exiles during the recent troubles, including the
young, as yet unsung, Julius Caesar, were allowed to return.

Lepidus favored a low price for grain and backed a proposal
to return the tribunes to their former power and prestige. In view
of this activity, the Senate was happy to send him to quell an
uprising in Etruria, where displaced farmers were now up in arms
against Sulla's veterans. That tactic backfired. Lepidus went first
to Cisalpine Gaul, where he recruited new troops. He followed
this move with a demand that he be allowed to seek reelection as a
consul in the following year. When the Senate refused, he invited
the rebels in Etruria to join him in a march on Rome. A century
earlier, an assault on the capital would have been unthinkable.
Since then, Marius and Sulla had shown the way.

The Senate could be grateful there were two consuls. Quintus Lutatius Catulus, a steady loyalist, drove Lepidus back to
Etruria. In the meantime, Pompey had been sent to northern Italy
to block Marcus Junius Brutus (father of the more famous Brutus), one of Lepidus' chief aides. Brutus was quickly defeated and
executed. When Lepidus tried a second time to lead his army to
Rome, he was defeatd by Catulus in a battle near the Janiculum
Hill. His revolution was over. Lepidus fled to Sardinia along with
his frightened followers and died there a short time later.

Pompey was now serving the Senate the way he had served Sulla and making it as difficult for that body to refuse him any favor in the future. At the moment they needed him in Spain. Since 80 B.C., Sertorius, a general of rare talents, had held the Spanish provinces as the last stronghold of the Marian party. Efforts to dislodge him only made matters worse. His camp became the sole rallying point for officers and soldiers who for any reason were at odds with the government. The latest commander sent to destroy him was the aging Metellus Pius, well respected but growing somewhat soft in his habits. The Senate decided toward the end of 77 to reinforce Metellus by sending Pompey, despite the reservations of senators who considered him to be a dangerously ambitious young man. Sertorius also noted Pompey's youth, and when comparing him to Metellus remarked that he had nothing more to fear from a boy than from an old woman. Actually, Sertorius took his opponents more seriously than that. Still, he was not wrong about his superiority. He defeated Pompey twice. If Metellus had not become familiar with Sertorius' tactics, the two armies sent by the Senate might not have been able to contain him at all.

Sertorius was one of the finest warriors Rome ever produced; and yet, except for the good he did in Romanizing the Spaniards, his best years were spent to little purpose. Earlier, he had served under Marius in the war against the Cimbri and later against the Italians. During the Civil War the Marian leaders preferred to send him to Spain rather than to use him against Sulla. Perhaps his strong voice for moderation made him appear unreliable. He was a tough soldier opposed to political extremes, insisting always that his war was only against the Sullan regime. After Sulla's death, an unforgiving Senate, faithful to Sulla's memory, doomed any chance for reconciliation. Sertorius' only choice was to continue the struggle against the home government. He even sought to foment trouble for Rome by sending veteran officers to train Mithridates' forces. A sad affair! This excellent man, a valiant Roman, allied with a foreign king. In 72, his own string of brilliant victories came to nothing when he was assassinated by men in his inner circle. Their leader, Marcus Perperna, had arrived in Spain after the defeat of Lepidus.

Perperna was a commander whom Pompey could defeat, and the sedition in Spain soon ended. The captured Perperna boasted that he had come into possession of Sertorius' correspondence, which included letters from high-ranking persons in Rome anxious to have Sertorius return and raise their banner of revolt. This revealing information could have been used in various ways, and who could predict the trouble it might cause? Pompey executed Perperna and burned the entire correspondence without looking at it. A craftier politician would have at least read it. A meaner one would have kept it. Pompey was really not much of a politican at all.

The generous terms given to the Spaniards who had served with Sertorius reveal Pompey's spirit of good will. For that he deserved honor when he returned to Rome. The people also gave him full credit for the victory. It was really more than he deserved, but he did not choose to share the glory with Metellus.

Lucullus

While Pompey was in Spain, the tempo of events in the East had quickened. Sulla's settlement with Mithridates had only been a breather for both sides. The harsh indemnities and taxes which the Romans imposed on "disloyal" cities were in themselves a guarantee of future trouble. Almost any new development would serve to upset an uneasy truce. In 75 B.C., Nicomedes IV of Bithynia died, leaving his kingdom to Rome. Having no heirs of his own, Nicomedes could only foresee a struggle for power unless the Romans gave the area their special brand of peace. The Romans were ready. Bithynia would serve as a buffer state between Pontus, where Mithridates ruled, and the Aegean area which he would, if he could, liberate from Rome's control. Mithridates saw the challenge. His invasion of Bithynia in 74 began a second war with the Roman Republic which lasted off and on until his death in 63. This time, the man who received the prized command against him was Lucullus, a consul in 74 B.C.

Lucullus had a career which poets would find interesting—a mixture of success and failure, with many strange twists of fortune. He belonged to a once prominent family, which kept its pride and hopes alive by remaining loyal to the rule of the best. Lucullus had served Sulla as a commander on land and sea during the first war with Mithridates. They were close friends and confidants. In his will, Sulla named Lucullus as the guardian of his son. Earlier, he had dedicated his memoirs to him. Yet it seems strange that these two men were friends at all, they were so different from each other. Sulla's usual associates were a rough lot. His admiration for Lucullus, a young aristocrat of good breeding, was the exception. Lucullus spoke and wrote Greek with ease, and his humanistic learning gave him a cosmopolitan outlook often lacking in generals who represented Rome abroad. This was shown in the sympathetic way he treated provincials, as compared to the heavy-handedness of Sulla. Some men considered Lucullus to be soft-headed, but they would have had to admit that he knew his way around in Roman politics.

When Pompey asked that reinforcements be sent to Spain, Lucullus eagerly favored the request. Without further help Pompey might come home to be a serious contender for the assignment against Mithridates. Even so, Lucullus only won the post by chance. At first, the Senate gave him the governorship of Cisalpine Gaul. The unexpected death of the governor of Cilicia created an opening there, which Lucullus was appointed to fill, with the command against Mithridates added by the Senate. The other consul, Marcus Aurelius Cotta, was given the governorship of Bithynia and made commander of the Roman fleet operating in the northern Aegean.

In the East, Lucullus sought to alleviate the suffering of those caught in a familiar squeeze between Roman tax collectors at one door and money lenders at the other. As usual, to satisfy the first the natives had to pay exorbitant interest rates to the second. Certain cities in the province of Asia had borrowed money to pay Sulla's indemnity and were now being strangled by debt. Interest charges had multiplied to six times the amount of the principal. Lucullus pared down the balance owed and helped the cities restructure their tax systems so as to plan for the liquidation of the remaining debt within four years. Henceforth the maximum rate of interest would be twelve percent, and Lucullus further stipulated that no person be compelled to pay a money lender more than a fourth of his income. These humane and sensible directives reflect Lucullus' conviction that Roman mismanagement evoked much of the ill-feeling now being faced in foreign lands. The outrageous practices of some Roman investors would have invited rebellion with or without Mithridates' assistance.

The provincials hailed Lucullus as a savior. That did not help his stock in Rome, where powerful politicians joined their business associates at dinner in denouncing him as a meddler. His sympathy for the provincials, they said, was weakening Roman control abroad. He might not have withstood this pressure if there had not also been much talk about his spectacular success on the battlefield.

In 72 B.C., Mithridates suffered a crippling defeat at Cabeira in Pontus. Two years after his bold invasion of Bithynia, Lucullus had forced him to flee empty-handed to Armenia, where he sought the protection of the king, who was also his son-in-law. Tigranes was the most powerful ruler in the Middle East, and when he called himself the King of Kings a majority of the senators at Rome were impressed. It was never their intention that Roman rule in Asia Minor should precipitate a war with him, nor did Lucullus make any move in that direction for two years. Domestic problems in the province of Asia kept him occupied.

In 70 B.C., Lucullus, acting on his own authority, ordered Tigranes to surrender Mithridates. A rude reply prompted him to cross the Euphrates in 69 and invade Armenia. It was a crucial decision; not only did he lack the support of the Senate, but he led an army which even before the battle of Cabeira was grumbling about his decisions. Lucullus preferred the peaceful surrender of a city through negotiation to the burning and looting which proved so profitable to soldiers. If he felt he had to take a city by force, he would let his soldiers plunder it, but such occasions were too infrequent to satisfy them. This same general was now leading them into a strange mountainous country, farther away from home than the Romans had ever fought before. The terrain was rough and the weather was bad. Lucullus pressed on, not realizing that the soldiers who would destroy him were not ahead but marching along with him and becoming more dangerous with every mile. A showdown was only postponed because Tigranocerta, the showplace capital of Armenia, was too big a prize to miss. Since the first army Tigranes sent against Lucullus could not stop him, the king left Tigranocerta to join forces with his allies. From the south came Arabs and from the east Medes to mingle with other peoples of the region whose kings were pledged to assist Tigranes. The result was a polyglot army—a great dragon, slow to move, sluggish in action, and easy to kill. Tigranes, seeking to lift the siege of Tigranocerta, was convinced that his numbers alone would win the day. Observing Lucullus' relatively meagre forces, the king commented that "they were too many for ambassadors, and too few for soldiers" (p. 612). Plutarch slyly places this remark immediately before the account of the king's disgrace. Tigranes was lucky to escape with his life. He was soon united with Mithridates, who had reason to be sympathetic.

In spite of continued murmurings in his army, Lucullus pressed on against Tigranes and was determined to take Artaxata, the second capital of Armenia. Although Tigranes and Mithridates had recovered sufficiently to challenge him, it was soon demonstrated again that their native troops were no match for seasoned Romans. They fled with Lucullus in pursuit. His men soon found themselves fighting an early winter. One day they refused to go on. Why, after months of grumbling, did they mutiny at that moment? Perhaps it was the sight of bleeding sinews on horses' legs cut by jagged ice.

In 68, Lucullus was forced to turn back from Artaxata, and although in retreat his men captured the city of Nisibis, a venture which offered them some profit, they refused to serve Lucullus any longer in the war against Tigranes and Mithridates. All that had been won was in jeopardy.

Mithridates returned to Pontus. Tigranes again attacked Cappadocia. When agents of the Senate arrived to oversee the pacification of areas they thought had been secured, they were in for a surprise. Lucullus' victories added up to considerably less than had been promised by the good news reaching Rome. Now he was helpless to command either his officers or his men. The Senate had sent its congratulations to a failure. One by one he was stripped of his provinces, first Asia, then Cilicia, and finally Bithynia.

Centuries before, the mighty Alexander had found that no army could defeat him save his own. Like Alexander, too, it was Lucullus' own self-confident determination that had taken him so far. He was a brilliant man of good intentions, who treasured the satisfaction of a job well done. He was especially proud that his campaign had not cost the government a single sesterce. Did a man need more than virtue and skill for success? His officers and men thought so. Having worked hard and risked their lives, they wanted something to show for it. Lucullus forgot that they had hearts and minds of their own. Whether that particular lapse was a fault or not, it ruined him.

Crassus

While Lucullus was winning his way closer to defeat, Pompey continued to know only success. He returned from Spain in time to help crush a massive slave revolt which began in 73 B.C. The rebellion could hardly have been a surprise. Romans had been talking about a slave uprising for a long time. Half a century earlier, the Gracchi had worried about it, but over the years politicians in Rome had done little more than hope it would not happen. Against this hope was the hostility of a growing number of workers enslaved in the fields and in the mines. A few were trained to be gladiators. Household slaves, particularly those serving as tutors, had a better life than most and were more likely to be freed in time. But a well-educated and sensitive captive could not be entirely disposed to service at the whim of a wealthy, even if pleasant, master. A slave was a piece of property, no matter who he was.

In ancient times, slaves were usually soldiers defeated and captured in battle. Obviously, they were men of varying experience and abilities and not necessarily of a different race, much less color. Even a very exceptional man might be placed on sale in one of the busy slave markets which dotted the Mediterranean world. Pirates who traded in human cargo were by no means respecters of persons. Stories about the Greek philosophers Plato and Diogenes having been captured and offered for sale may be apocryphal, but they suggest what was possible.

The slaves in Italy needed only the right leadership and organization to become a formidable threat to the established order. Spartacus gave them both. He was a slave whose talent put him far above the gladiator's role for which he was in training at a school in Capua. The Thracians and Gauls chosen for this place were spirited fighters scheduled for vicious combat with each other. On a signal from Spartacus they became brothers. In a daring escape, seventy-eight men armed with kitchen knives began the revolt which sent a shock through Italy. Hoards of enslaved farmhands and herders fled the land to join them. With makeshift swords, they overwhelmed the feeble forces in their path. Better weapons were plucked from the Romans. Soon, attacks on slave prisons brought desperate men and arms together. The Senate assigned one praetor after another to suppress the rebellion before deciding to send consular armies into the field—all to no avail. The casualties mounted in the encounters with Spartacus' irregulars, who numbered now between fifty and one hundred thousand. Finally, it was evident that the crisis warranted a single commander of proven skill. At

the time Pompey was still in Spain. Marcus Crassus was everybody's second choice.

Crassus had stood beside Pompey and Lucullus among
Sulla's trusted lieutenants. When the rest of Sulla's forces were
faltering in the crucial battle outside the Colline Gate, it was Crassus who had saved the day with his victory on the right wing.
Sulla was always grateful for that, but never gave him as much
attention as he did Pompey or Lucullus. Both as soldier and politician Crassus fitted well into the best of the second rank. In only
one direction did he outdistance his rivals. He had a rare gift for
making money. While Pompey was busy tracking down the enemies of Sulla in Sicily and North Africa, Crassus was at home
paying low prices for their confiscated property. In Rome he was
the man to see about real estate. It was a lucrative business even
without the help of civil disorders. The careless use of lamps or
stoves in multi-storied wooden structures meant frequent fires. A
man whose house was burning, or even a neighbor who felt his
property was endangered, was tempted to sell out low to Crassus
or to one of his agents who offered ready money. After a deal was
made, Crassus would quickly send into action the gangs of fire-
fighters he had standing nearby.

Crassus never seemed to have time for amusing himself, or
for spending his money. He made it and he kept it. His interest in
philosophy was not expensive. When going on a trip, he would
occasionally take an Aristotelian scholar along for company and
conversation. The man was poor, and so Crassus would supply
him with a cloak to wear while they were traveling. Upon their
return, Crassus took the cloak home.

If there was any ill feeling because Crassus made his millions
through the misfortune of others, he seems to have balanced it by
being generous with loans. Many senators owed him money. The
indebtedness served him well, but it was not his only advantage in
politics. He was an affable person and generally well liked. Although Crassus was usually occupied with business, no one ever
accused him of trying to shirk his duty. He had a good military
record. Even so, the slave revolt was his first chance to manage a
major campaign. When he took over from the Roman consuls, he
immediately established his authority by severely punishing any
lapses in discipline. This gave him one advantage over Spartacus,
whose major problem was the unruliness of his followers.

Originally, Spartacus planned to leave Italy as soon as possible and strike for the Alps; but easy victories gave his men a chance to plunder, and they were in no hurry to escape toward home. It was obviously a mistake to give the Romans time to bring their full weight to bear on the rebels. In 71, Spartacus and his army were trapped in the toe of Italy, near Rhegium. Using a snowstorm for cover, a third of the slaves were able to flee. Then another group broke away, and the end came quickly after that. Crassus pressed for a decisive victory, and Spartacus was unable to restrain his depleted army from fighting the set battle which the Romans wanted. In the midst of an uneven fight, he died as the gladiator he was trained to be.

As many as five thousand slaves fled from the battle scene and headed northward. Pompey caught and destroyed this remnant in Etruria, whereupon he gave himself credit for having saved Italy. Crassus kept his thoughts to himself. His best chance to be elected consul for 70 B.C. was to stand alongside the ever popular Pompey, now due a second triumph for his victory in Spain. Crassus could expect an ovation and he, at least, was in line for the consulship. Pompey was not. He was six years under the age for qualfication, and had never served in any lower office, which by custom was required of a candidate. Still, he expected the Senate to approve his candidacy, and he stood waiting outside the city with a battle-tested army. The Senate, armed with legalities, chose not to challenge him. Pompey's popularity with the citizenry insured his election. By openly soliciting votes for Crassus, he carried him in too.

Pompey was a man of good will, innocent except for the example he set. The first time he came to the Senate was as a presiding officer, and his scholarly friend Marcus Terentius Varro had to tell him what to do. Those who remembered Marius and Sulla, their obsession for power and their abuse of it, were apprehensive. They need not have been. Pompey lacked the instincts of a ruler. He was guilty only of being conspicuously exceptional in a society struggling to live by law and custom. His insistence on the highest honors at the youngest age broke the barriers for other men who were ambitious for more than fame.

The partnership of Pompey and Crassus did not disturb the relative calm which Rome had known in recent years. Pompey was anxious to please the general run of citizens, among whom he had always counted his stongest support. His sponsorship of a law which gave the tribunes their full pre-Sullan status was a popular move. A revamping of the courts followed. The number of senators chosen as jurors was drastically cut, thereby ending the monopoly of the judiciary which Sulla had given them. The weight of opinion on future juries would rest with men of more modest means.

Neither the restoration of the tribunate nor the court reform were considered radical. As the Sullan constitution had been altered bit by bit for the past five years, the latest changes evoked little hostility. Crassus was on the friendliest of terms with the Senate, and Pompey's alliance with the people was motivated less by philosophy than by gratitude. Besides, these two old rivals had no intention of marching far together. When the term of consulship ended, Crassus returned to his business interests. Pompey stood ready for further service, with well-planned appearances in the Forum to remind the people that if they needed him he was ready. The Senate remained skeptical, especially because his chief supporters were members of the restored tribunate.

Pompey's Best Years

From the coves of ancient Cilicia to the shores of modern Tripoli, piracy was a problem in the Mediterranean Sea. In the fifth century B.C., Athens built an empire on her guarantee of safe sea lanes in the Aegean. Later, the wealthy trade-minded Rhodians used their fleet and maritime law to keep seaborne highwaymen at bay. In the second century, however, Rhodes began to support Rome's enemies and Rome in return, as we saw, deliberately undercut the prosperity of this once friendly island. The decline of Rhodes meant an end to the regular policing of the Mediterranean, and thereafter piracy enjoyed a prosperous revival.

Mithridates encouraged pirates to prey on Roman traders and even hired their fleets to serve his cause. The Romans, preoccupied with a series of domestic crises, had made only sporadic attempts to deal with this menace. From 76 to 74 B.C., Roman forces stationed in Asia Minor had been used to stamp out pirate bases in Lycia, Pamphylia, and Cilicia, but the attack by Mithridates in 74 meant a new priority. In the same year, in North Africa, the territory of Cyrenaica, sometimes called the kingdom of Cyrene after its capital city, finally became a province and the Romans were able to clean up at least that section of the Mediterranean coastline. When the island of Crete was made a province in

67 another base of pirate operations was closed. In spite of these
efforts, however, the number of pirate ships roaming the seas had
grown to a thousand and more. Flagstaffs painted gold and oars
painted silver were an index of good business. The wealthy
temples of coastal cities, far from being respected, were inviting
targets. Daring gangs of pirates even made raids on farms and
villages at some distance inland. Finally, they became bold enough
to attack ships bringing grain to Rome. The resulting shortage of
food meant a corresponding rise in prices, and a cry soon went up
for drastic action. In 67, the tribune Aulus Gabinius proposed that
a single commander be given charge over all ships in the Mediterranean Sea as well as armed forces in coastal areas up to a distance
of fifty miles inland. Since this authority would supersede that of
provincial governors in the affected districts, it would constitute
an unprecedented grant of military power.

There was strong opposition in the Senate to authorizing
such an extraordinary command, although there was ample precedent for doing so. In 74, a similar but less inclusive commission
had been given to a praetor, Marcus Antonius, with orders to
sweep the seas. The debate this time was enlivened by an open
secret: Pompey was the man Gabinius had in mind for the assignment. For that same reason common citizens favored the bill and
their support ensured its passage. As usual, Pompey behaved with
conspicuous modesty, thereby undercutting the notion that the
honor would spoil him. He was given five hundred ships, 120,000
soldiers and 5,000 horsemen. Twenty-four experienced generals
served under his command in thirteen areas of operation. Within
forty days the western Mediterranean was made safe for shipping.
In the East, a battle off the coast of Cilicia ended all resistance.
When the pirate leaders saw the hopelessness of their position they
quickly surrendered their fortifications on the shore.

No one had expected the curse of piracy to end in so short a
time. Pompey's treatment of his prisoners was another surprise.
Ordinarily they would have been put to death. Pompey was of a
different mind, and Plutarch credits him with some generous
thoughts:

> Therefore wisely weighing with himself that man by nature is not a
> wild or unsocial creature, neither was he born so, but makes himself
> what he naturally is not by vicious habit; and that again, on the other
> side, he is civilized and grows gentle by a change of place, occupation,
> and manner of life, as beasts themselves that are wild by nature be-

come tame and tractable by housing and gentler usage, upon this consideration he determined to translate these pirates from sea to land, and give them a taste of an honest and innocent course of life by living in towns and tilling the ground. Some therefore were admitted into the small and half-peopled towns of the Cilicians, who, for an enlargement of their territories, were willing to receive them. (p. 759)

Pompey's success came at an embarrassing time for Lucullus. As we have seen, he had not captured Mithridates, and he had lost the support of his own soldiers, who in great numbers now left his camp to return home or to go and join Pompey. The final humiliation came in 66 B.C., when his command against Mithridates was transferred to Pompey.

When Lucullus returned home he was allowed a triumph for his past victories. It was a small but richly adorned procession—the Roman equivalent of a retirement banquet. Lucullus' many enemies could agree to that. Yet those who had lost money because of his high-minded reforms in the East were not consoled to see him return a rich man, even if in muted glory. In fact, in the years ahead they watched him set a new standard for luxury. "Living like Lucullus" became a byword. The dinner parties he gave for his kind of people—the leading poets, artists and philosophers of the day—were sumptuous indeed, still, no more so than when he sat down alone.

Lucullus had often talked about his great days in the East. He claimed that his campaigns had so weakened Mithridates and Tigranes that Pompey with his much greater resources had little more to do than round them up. He was at least half right. Tigranes readily submitted to Pompey without a fight. He would even have been willing to debase himself on his knees had not the magnanimous Pompey caught him before he went too far. Mithridates would not be caught in such a position, nor indeed be caught at all. He eluded Pompey twice before being forced to fight near the Euphrates River. There he was again lucky to escape from a losing battle in the company of a few companions. Pompey went searching for him in the region of the Caucasus Mountains, where amid uncertain terrain he became embroiled with natives of the area to little purpose on either side. That experience prompted him to reconsider the wisdom of using a whole army to track down one man; so he headed southward, leaving his enemy time to make a mistake. Later, when Pompey was in Syria, news came that Mithridates was dead. In his haste to rebuild an army in the Crimea, the king had been too harsh on new recruits. Even his son Pharnaces turned against him. The rebellion robbed Mithridates of his last hope, and he ended his own life. Not since Hannibal had one man caused the Romans so much trouble; now it was over. Mithridates' body was sent to Pompey as a trophy, but he refused to look at it and ordered the hastily embalmed corpse shipped to Sinope for burial in Mithridates' native soil. Pompey was bringing order to the lands of the East. The proper place for a dead king was in a royal tomb.

Pompey had now brought the presence of Rome to the vicinity of the Parthian Empire, whose borders with smaller kingdoms on her western frontier were as impermanent as shifting sands. Alliances made and broken allowed the Parthian kings to choose the time and place for expansion. Pompey had remained noncommital about this problem so long as he was busy in Asia Minor. In the Roman style, he preferred to invade the area and let a conquest establish the borders. To conquer Syria was no problem. The Seleucid dynasty which had ruled the land for about two hundred and fifty years had fallen on sad times during the latter part of the second century. Founded by Seleucus, an energetic young general who had served Alexander the Great, this proud house had once claimed the greater share of Alexander's empire extending eastward to India. In recent years, internal power struggles, marked by frequent battles and quiet poisonings, had sapped the strength of the Seleucids to the point where they had lost all their holdings save Syria. Even this now was disputed among claimants for the throne who were no more than leaders of small mercenary armies. In 64, Pompey brought the sorry tale to an abrupt end by making Syria a Roman province.

The next stop was supposed to be Petra, the capital of the Nabataeans. These people controlled the profitable trade routes which ran through their territory in northern Arabia, bringing the luxuries of the East from ports in the south to the crossroads of Damascus. But as Pompey headed in that direction his attention was diverted by a civil war in Judaea. He never managed to get back on the road to Petra.

The Jews had freed themselves from Seleucid control in a series of successful revolts, 175–164 B.C., spearheaded by members of the Hasmonaean family, better known as the Maccabees. Their success won them some valuable support. In 161, the Roman Senate was still anxious to curb Seleucid power, which at the time remained formidable. Assurances of aid were given to Judah Maccabaeus in his fight to restore Judaea to its ancient status as an independent kingdom under God. The renewal of this treaty in 134 gave the Jews enough encouragement to launch a counterattack on Seleucid territory. Sufficient land was seized to restore the kingdom of their ancestors. What they lacked was another David. Their fight for independence and the chance to govern themselves led to suicidal struggles for power among various factions and even within families.

When Pompey arrived in Palestine in 64, he found two brothers, John Hyrcanus and Aristobulus, locked in a bitter contest over the throne. They were the sons of Alexander Jannaeus, the first Jewish priest-king, who ruled 103–76 B.C. The brothers were willing to accept Pompey as an arbiter, but their followers were not. The temple precinct in Jerusalem was held firmly by the supporters of Aristobulus, and that meant a three-month siege of the temple walls before Pompey could have his way. The Jewish historian Josephus writes:

> Now, here it was that upon the many hardships which the Romans underwent, Pompey could not but admire not only the other instances of the Jews' fortitude, but especially that they did not at all intermit their religious services, even when they were encompassed with darts on all sides; for, as if the city were in full peace, their daily sacrifices and purifications, and every branch of their religious worships was still performed to God with the utmost exactness. . . . And now did many of the priests, even when they saw their enemies assailing them with swords in their hands, without any disturbance, go on with their divine worship, and were slain while they were offering their drink-offerings, and burning their incense, as preferring the duties about their worship to God before their own preservation. (I. 7. 4–5)

Pompey was impressed by the religious zeal of the Jews, joined as it was to stubborn military resistance. This same combination would give the Romans trouble for the next two hundred years.

In 64, after the temple was taken, Pompey, with a Roman eye for inspection, went in to look around, even entering where only the high priest was intended to go. The Jews were properly shocked, but they were now at Pompey's mercy. He favored John Hyrcanus, the elder and less dynamic of the brothers, to govern Judaea. As high priest, Hyrcanus would be obedient to

Rome, and the Jews were expected to be obedient to him. Quarreling over the kingship was ended by eliminating it. The royal line of the Hasmonaean family was thus brought to an end, even as the Romans had extinguished the Antigonid line in Macedon, and the Seleucid in Syria. The last of the Attalid kings had died childless.

Pompey enlarged the province of Syria at the Jews' expense. He then headed home, bringing with him the defeated Jewish prince Aristobulus and his family, along with the son of the king of Armenia. These royal prisoners would grace Pompey's triumphal procession. Treasure too was expected, and no one had ever brought home more than Pompey did. He also issued a report of his improvements in provincial administration. The provinces of Asia Minor had been divided and regrouped so as to provide greater stability. In addition, he had either founded or restored forty cities in the East. There was now a better chance for peace and prosperity in the region and everywhere a salutary respect for Roman rule. Pompey was properly proud of these unprecedented accomplishments, which had been achieved in the short span of four years, 66–62 B.C. Only the Senate seemed unimpressed.

During Pompey's absence, the nobility at Rome had regained their old sense of importance. This was reflected in the Senate, which delayed ratification of Pompey's arrangements in the East, and refused to provide the land allotments he had promised his soldiers. Neither his victories nor the money he had poured into the treasury could make them forget that he had gained so high a place without their support.

Not since the Gracchan crisis had the Senate been so confident of its power. The members in general were not much better than their predecessors, except for two of them who, standing together, made a difference. The dynamic orator Marcus Tullius Cicero had given the Senate a new prestige and a strongwilled Cato the Younger knew how to use it.

IX

The Guardians:
Cicero and Cato the Younger

It is not easy to be brief about Cicero. He was rarely brief himself, and much that he said survives. For that reason we know him better than any other personality in ancient times. Seven-hundred-and-seventy-four of his letters have been preserved (along with ninety letters written to him). Relatives and close friends away from the city were kept informed about events almost daily. Many of the letters went to his brother Quintus and to his long-time friend, and publisher, Titus Pomponius Atticus. What Cicero wrote has a special value because he did not have a chance to edit his letters or even to know that they would be published. The pros and cons of difficult decisions were discussed, and at times Cicero reported what he was saying in public along with what he was thinking in private. The letters, together with fifty-seven of his speeches, supply a rare close-up of Rome during a period of almost forty years, from about 81 to 43 B.C. If there is anything which obscures the view it is Cicero himself. He would have no one forget that he was an outspoken defender of Old Roman virtues, who placed a high value on public service. His writings show him to be all of that and also very vain—a man to be

12. Cicero. Courtesy of the Museo Vaticano, Rome.

watched on matters which touched on his own career. Plutarch calls his vanity an "ungrateful humour like a disease, always cleaving to him" (p. 1054).

Cicero was born January 3, 106 B.C., in Arpinum, about sixty miles southeast of Rome. It was the year after Marius' first consulship, and as a child Cicero could enjoy the reflected glory which the great commander brought to his native district. As a young man, Marius had gone to Rome to join the ranks of the "new men" who lacked influential family connections. Later, Cicero shared that much with him, but little else. It was never Cicero's intention to make a career out of his provincialism. On the contrary, from his earliest days he was known for his scholarly interests and fondness for poetry and the other arts by which he might distinguish himself. His family was of perhaps better than average means. In any event, the money was there for a good education, and his obvious abilities made him welcome in the best circles in Rome. He served for a short time in one of Sulla's armies, but his body was not equal to the robust life and his mind was on other things. Livy said of him, "No man could possibly have been less born for war." If he impressed a general it was by his oratory. Julius Caesar was once so moved while listening to him that he dropped some papers he was holding.

Cicero's failure to build a military reputation and acquire a following of veterans was a serious handicap in Roman politics.

He sought to make up for it by becoming the capital's best lawyer. Throughout antiquity, imitation was the better part of learning. Cicero listened carefully to the leading orators and attended sessions of the law courts as was customary for a young man preparing for a career in public life. In both Athens and Rhodes he became acquainted with the leading philosophers of the day.

Cicero was always an enthusiastic student of history, and his works are valuable sources precisely because he so often used historical illustrations to prove a point. "To be ignorant of what happened before you were born," he said in the *Orator,* "is to live the life of a child forever. For what is man's life, unless woven into the life of our ancestors by the memory of past deeds?" Cicero's painstaking preparation for public service explains how he felt about men who came to power by way of the army or through family connections. He loved to extol the virtues of tradition in education. There was a favorite line from Homer: "Strive always to excel; be ever foremost in the race." Those who listened could count him as either a man of high standards or a middle-class snob.

Although well remembered as the prosecutor in a case of official wrongdoing, Cicero began his career as a defender of persons who had involved themselves in unpopular causes. He once successfully defended a man who had lost favor with Sulla, and that victory may account for one of his long sojourns to Greece.

Cicero entered public life three years after Sulla died. He served as quaestor in 75 B.C. at the age of thirty-one. His first assignment was in Sicily, where he performed his duties with uncommon diligence. Six years later, the experience proved invaluable. His role in the trial of the notorious Gaius Verres, an ex-governor of Sicily, gave him the first major break of his career.

The Trial of Verres

The trial of Verres was an exposé of corruption in the provinces—a singular example of what some governors had been getting away with. Nothing is known about Verres except what we read in Cicero's speeches condemning him, but his name has ever since been a byword for Roman administration at its worst.

Verres may not have been less scrupulous than other Roman governors, but he was certainly less lucky. He was accused of extortion at the very time when senatorial juries were becoming unusually sensitive to criticism. Sulla had restored jurisdiction to the Senate in such cases, and the equestrians continued to press for legislation which would return the juries to their hands. If a jury of senators failed to convict a member of their own class who was guilty of flagrant abuses, they would in effect be condemning themselves. Cicero never let them forget it. In his opening statement he said, "And now, at the moment of supreme danger for your Order and your judicial privileges, when preparations have been made for an attempt, by means of public meetings and proposals for legislation, to fan the flames of senatorial unpopularity, Gaius Verres appears, to stand his trial before you: a man already condemned in the world's opinion, by his life and deeds; already acquitted, according to his confident assertions, by his vast fortune" (*Verrine Orations,* I. 1. 2).

Pressures were applied from another quarter. As mentioned in the last chapter, Pompey had asked that the power of the plebeian tribunes be fully restored. Cicero said that there would not have been such urgency to do so had the senatorial courts remained honest. The common people again felt the need for protectors of their rights. According to Cicero, the senators had only themselves to blame for this renewed agitation to have a strong and effective tribunate. "It is the present trial in which, even as you will pass your verdict upon the prisoner, so the people of Rome will pass its verdict upon yourselves" (I. 16. 47).

For Verres, it was especially bad luck to have Cicero serving as the prosecutor. Someone else might have been intimidated by the reputation of the man defending Verres. Quintus Hortensius was the best known and most successful orator of recent years. Far from being put off, Cicero felt challenged. By his performance, he did, in fact, replace Hortensius as the leader of the bar in Rome.

Verres was at Cicero's mercy. Public records were on the table, and victims were standing by to testify. Cicero relished every piece of evidence. He had a keen eye for details in the wall he built around Verres. The attack was brilliant and relentless. But Cicero could also be a bore. With monotonous regularity he spoke of the righteousness of his cause. He never felt that others were giving him sufficient recognition for his public service and kept telling the Roman people why they should be grateful to him. He did not seem to realize that many of them could feel indebted without liking him enough to say so.

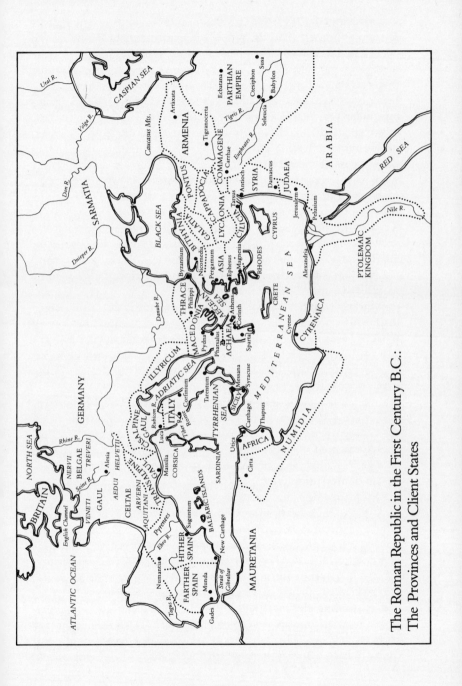

The Roman Republic in the First Century B.C.:
The Provinces and Client States

During the trial, Cicero was as much concerned with corruption at home as he was with mismanagement abroad. It was an open scandal that wealthy men could escape punishment because of the general tolerance of bribery in the courts. Cicero admitted this sad state of affairs: "Since the whole of our poorer class is being oppressed by the hand of recklessness and crime, and groaning under the infamy of our law-courts, I declare myself to these criminals as their enemy and their accuser, as their pertinacious, bitter, and unrelenting adversary" (I. 12. 36). Things had come to such a pass, he said, that men could no longer even trust those who were taking bribes. He mentioned a case in which one senator serving as a juror took money from a defendant to vote one way and from the prosecutor to vote the other.

In the most famous passage of the *Verrine Orations* Cicero declares that Verres had planned in advance to use the profits of his first year as governor of Sicily for himself, those of the second year to pay for his defense at Rome, and the third year's income to bribe the jury. Under the circumstances, Cicero observed, the provincials would be better off if the Romans did not have a court for trying extortion cases. Then they would suffer the loss of what a governor might want for himself without having to incur any further expenses. "They feel that they may meet the demands of a greedy man's cupidity, but cannot meet those of a guilty man's acquittal" (I. 14. 41–42).

It should be understood that not all of Cicero's *Verrine Orations* were actually delivered. The attack was so devastating that the accused fled from Rome before the bulk of the evidence had been presented. Cicero did, however, publish his speeches as though they had been presented; and quotations from them leave an "in court" impression.

Cicero began his attack by recalling events in Verres' unsavory past. "His term of service as adjutant was a disaster to the whole of the provinces of Asia and Pamphylia, where few private houses, very few cities, and not one single sanctuary escaped his depredations" (I. 4. 11). That was a warm-up for the great crimes he would commit during his three years as governor of Sicily. Cicero had spent fifty days in Sicily interviewing Verres' victims and examining the local records, some of which had telltale erasures. Verres' outrageous abuse of power extended into every corner of Sicilian life. He insisted on the final word in all court cases. Where a legacy was worth his attention he might openly transfer it to his own pocket. Native farmers were squeezed by ingenious new regulations, each designed to produce revenue for Verres and his cronies. Even the rights of Roman citizens were ignored.

It was Verres' abuse of loyal subjects of Rome which aroused Cicero's greatest fury. The governor entered into profitable deals with pirates whereby rich towns were left defenseless and at the mercy of marauders, who gave Verres a share of the spoils. Who could forgive this betrayal by the very man sent to protect subject peoples? Verres' own agents did not hesitate to steal art treasures, even from the most sacred sanctuaries of Sicily. In this recital of crimes Cicero occasionally hesitates. Good taste would not allow him to mention everything, and he draws a curtain around Verres' sexual offenses. But his gesture was not wasted. Cicero's reticence allowed the jurors' imagination to evoke more guilt than his words might have proven.

As Cicero's case against Verres unfolded, it was obvious that more was involved than the theft and extortion of a corrupt official. Verres had destroyed overnight the time-honored arrangements by which the Sicilians had become loyal subjects of Rome. The established policy in Sicily had been to respect local traditions and retain the familiar means of collecting taxes at the same old rate. The Romans simply substituted their own treasury for that of former rulers. In so far as possible, self-rule was encouraged. This wise concern for native feelings and interests bolstered morale among the Sicilians as it had done with other provincials. The Romans even took the time to arrange special treaties with different cities of the island where special circumstances prevailed. A generous policy for Sicily was especially important. The island contributed a large share of the grain upon which the Romans had come to depend. Verres' callous disregard of old procedures was a serious break with Roman policy going back over a century. The result was panic and despair among the Sicilians.

Cicero had a question for Verres. Why did a successful system have to be changed? "Did your powerful brain detect some fault in it?" Cicero could see none. Under the old order the claims of Rome were safeguarded, and so were the interests of the farmers who paid their taxes in grain. Verres made changes to suit himself. He replaced the local tax-collecting machinery with his own appointees. New tax rates were entirely at the whim of these chosen henchmen. One of them, Quintus Apronius, had caught

Cicero's eye: "It is he who was Verres' right-hand man in his debaucheries, in his sacrilegious robberies, in his filthy carouses. . . . Apronius sat next his chair of office, shared the privacy of his chamber, and was the master spirit of his festive gatherings—notably when, with the governor's young son present, he proceeded to dance stark naked before the company" (III. 9. 23).

Where could a farmer complain about harrassment from this unsavory tax collector? Would it be to a jury of peers composed of small landholders? No, because Verres said they were all prejudiced against tax collectors. They could only appeal to a jury appointed from among Verres' close friends. The advantage of this arrangement was that no one came to complain. They were better off to stay home and pray that they be cheated of a small amount rather than make trouble and lose everything.

A means of extorting more grain from a farmer was to charge that he had reported too little acreage. Even though falsely accused, the man was usually frightened enough to pay what was asked. But how long could farmers keep paying more than they could afford? Some began to give up, and the landscape was soon marked by abandoned farms. Cicero says, "When I arrived in Sicily after a four years' absence, it had to my eyes the look we associate with countries that have been the seat of a cruel and protracted war. . . . The year before had dealt the farmers a staggering blow; this last year had ruined them altogether" (III. 18. 47).

Cicero was ready with specific cases. He named names of formerly prosperous farmers driven from the land. Not only had the frustrations of Verres' rigged courts forced a man named Xeno to pay an exorbitant tax—he received a threat of violent treatment into the bargain. Cicero cited actual instances of brutality:

> Polemarchus, a good respectable inhabitant of Murgentia, was ordered to pay a tithe of 700 bushels on a farm of 50 acres. Because he refused, he was marched off to appear before Verres, in Verres' own house; and as our friend was still in bed, the prisoner was brought into the bedroom, a privilege otherwise extended only to collectors and women. There he was knocked about and kicked so brutally that, after refusing to settle for 700 bushels, he promised to pay 1,000. (III. 23. 56)

The case against Verres was built of facts and figures, including accounts of the ruination of whole towns. Finally, there was something horrible about the indignities which Verres and his henchmen heaped on the aged. The humiliation of one old man tells it all. Cicero describes the confusion of the victim and the arrogance of his smirking tormentor: "Lollius was led in, or rather dragged in, by the slaves, just as Apronius had come back from the playing-fields and laid himself down by the dinner table he had spread for him in the marketplace of Aetna. . . . This old Roman knight of nearly ninety was made to stand, as I tell you, before this festive gathering of Apronius, who meanwhile proceeded to smear his own head and face with perfume. . . . Quintus Lollius was constrained, by his humiliating treatment, to fall in with the terms and conditions imposed by Apronius. Age and infirmity have prevented his being able to come here and give his evidence" (III. 25. 61–63).

There were many such cases. More than enough to give a dramatic edge to Cicero's question, "Is this the government of Rome?"

As explained earlier, Verres was finished even before this question was asked. He left the city at the height of his trial and spent the rest of his life in exile. Hortensius was obviously embarrassed by his client's departure. Nor did the senators on the jury save themselves by condemning Verres. Pompey's reform measure was passed to end senatorial control of such juries. Only Cicero emerged victorious.

The Catilinarian Conspiracy

Cicero was elected to an aedileship. Little is known of his conduct in this office, but it must have been honorable, or his enemies would surely have used the evidence against him. That they had nothing to say may account for the fact that he next ran at the top of the poll for the praetorship. In 66, he would preside over the court which handled extortion cases, where he had received so much favorable publicity. As praetor, Cicero's powerful voice gave him considerable influence in the policy making of the day. His speech *On the Manilian Law* praised the law which would give Pompey supreme power in the East. Cicero was often the spokesman for the businessmen of the city who strongly supported Pompey. They were soon rewarded by his prompt action against the pirates who plagued their trade routes.

While Pompey was in the East, Cicero was elected consul for 63. Although he had curried favor with whoever could help his cause and had said whatever had to be said to be elected, he still considered the office a reward for his conscientious service. But that was not why he was chosen. In the eyes of most voters, especially among the nobility, he was simply the least objectionable of a poor list of candidates.

Cicero surprised everybody by surviving a tumultuous year in heroic style. He was marked for assassination from the moment he took office. A disappointed rival in the election, Lucius Sergius Catilina, and his companions plotted to kill the chief officials at Rome and seize control of the government. The conspiracy is described in detail by Sallust in his first historical monograph, *The War with Catiline*. This sensational episode has always been a focal event for those interested in the intrigue and mixed motives of Roman politics.

Catiline's secret plan was outrageous. That was its chief advantage. There was no proof of anything, and honest men are not prone to act against an evil they cannot see. In fact, it is still not possible to be certain of the seriousness of this crisis, because there is no way of knowing exactly how widespread the conspiracy had grown or who exactly was involved in it. There were many rumors at the time and some of them persisted in later years. Perhaps one of Sallust's reasons for writing *The War with Catiline* was to help clear his friend Julius Caesar, whose name had been erroneously linked by gossip to this affair. Caesar's reluctance to join Catiline and his friends can be easily understood. He had much more to risk than they did. His skill as an orator was obvious, and his career in public life looked promising. Catiline had been defeated twice for the consulship, and most of the men who joined him were also tainted by failure. Some of them were aristocrats who had allowed their taste for high living to outdistance their inheritance. Debt and disgrace were urgent reasons for joining with the poor who were clamoring for a cancellation of debts. In Etruria, some of Sulla's old veterans joined the cause. These rough soldiers had failed to make a go of farming on the land alloted to them. A period of general disorder would give them the chance for some old-fashioned plunder.

The Catilinarians gathered support not only from men who had failed but also from those who had never had a chance in the first place. The luxuries of the East were plentiful in the markets of Rome, but available to only a few. The pleasures enjoyed by elite families incited the envy of all. No one could doubt the sincerity of the complaints about high prices, high interest rates, and low income. At the same time the men who led the conspiracy were unlikely heroes of social reform.

Sallust describes Catiline as a keen and courageous criminal with a superior mind full of evil intent. He would employ any means, no matter how devious, so long as it served his purpose. Although born to privilege, he had never settled into a comfortable life but spent his time and money in a careless pursuit of excitement. By temperament he was impatient with the conventional life of the Old Roman whom Cicero extolled. His models were not ancestral heroes of the dim past but the victorious politicians of the present. Had the powerful Sulla been a virtuous man? How did Crassus acquire his millions? Catiline and other men of his generation insisted that the few wealthy men who controlled the government were no better than the ruthless Sulla or the shrewd Crassus. Why not rally all those dissatisfied with their lot and root out this deceitful clique so that the spoils of empire might be shared by all? Catiline's call for a cancellation of debts was not just a slogan. It was widely believed that moneylenders were in collusion with the courts and that the courts were operated by an oligarchy of wealthy men who passed the reins of government from hand to hand. In short, the revolution gained momentum as a convenient outlet for legitimate complaints, which desperate men could use to serve their own ambitions.

Many sober-minded men of good standing in the city could appreciate the feelings of those who criticized the government. They could not, however, sympathize with a foolish urge to destroy the system unaccompanied by any idea of what would happen next. Sallust belonged to this group. Although his monograph was written after Caesar was assassinated in 44 B.C., he had lived through the earlier times, and his mood in describing them is grim. At all levels of society the time-honored virtues of honesty, loyalty, and steadfastness were no longer useful in the stampede for money and power. If "distinguished" officeholders were commonly known to have bribed and bullied their way ahead, how could anyone expect a Catiline to remain true to honor? Yet Sallust could not agree that corruption could be cured by disorder. The solution was rather to be found in better leaders, and he was not hesitant to name them. If Sallust could later sympathize with Julius Caesar's overthrow of the government, it was because he felt that Caesar was the right man to build a new order. Catiline was not. Sallust recognized that Catiline had surrounded himself with hardened toughs because he needed the muscle, but found it unforgivable that he so callously exploited youths who qualified for his service only by their lack of either experience or good judgment. Some of them had been duped by wild promises of money and pleasure. But Sallust notes that many well-to-do young men flocked to Catiline's banner neither for principle nor gain, but out of sheer malice: "Although in quiet times they had the means of living elegantly or luxuriously, they preferred uncertainty to certainty, war to peace" (XVII. 6–7).

The ringleaders of the conspiracy were members of both the senatorial and equestrian orders who had for one reason or another become estranged from the ruling circle. Catiline was having private talks and laying plans with these men as early as the summer of 64. In the meantime, he was keeping up appearances by engaging in politics as usual. He had nothing to lose by running for the consulship. In fact, he felt there was enough dissatisfaction among the citizenry that he might come to power legally and so arrange all matters to suit himself and his fellow conspirators without the trouble of a coup. When he failed to be elected, the more radical course was ready to hand. Weapons were being collected at various places in Italy. Sympathizers in the towns and countryside were organized quietly for local uprisings. These would be timed to coincide with prearranged disorders at Rome. In the city, fires would be set at twelve strategic places in order to create a panic. Amid the confusion, Cicero and the other leaders of the government were to be murdered. Sallust says that some young men were assigned to kill their fathers. He seems to accept this report as true, although elsewhere he admits that he could not verify all the tales he had heard.

The conspirators were certainly aware that chances for a coup in 63 were better than usual. Pompey and his army were far away in Syria. Most senators felt comfortable with the reliable Cicero as consul and were unbothered by rumors. The very fact that three years earlier a plot to murder the consuls had come to nothing made these senators complacent about any new talk of conspiracy. Gnaeus Piso, an incompetent young nobleman, had been in charge of the earlier misadventure, but Catiline had been privy to the intrigue, and so in the light of later events it has been called the "first conspiracy" of Catiline. Some members of the Senate remained more worried about the threat which Pompey's power posed than about agitators such as Piso and Catiline. Amid the crosscurrents of Roman politics, it was even suggested that these rebels might somehow be turned against Pompey.

Given the number of people involved, it would have been surprising if the details of Catiline's plan had not reached Cicero before long. Quintus Curius, a disgraced nobleman, who had been ejected from the Senate, boasted to his mistress of better days ahead. Fulvia, a woman of mixed loyalities, told Cicero of her suspicions. Through her he made a deal with Curius for information. It was Fulvia who brought the warning which saved Cicero during the first attempt on his life.

At about the same time, it was learned that Catiline's colleague Manlius was raising an army in Etruria. As soon as the Senate heard the news, the consuls were authorized to take whatever measures they deemed necessary to protect the state. According to this declaration, the *senatus consultum ultimum,* the power of the consuls was now comparable to that of the dictators appointed for emergency purposes in the earlier years of the Republic and so amounted to what we call martial law. Theoretically, this power was to be shared by the consuls, but it was Cicero who was in charge. He had turned over to the other consul, Gaius Antonius, the governorship of Macedonia for the following year. Antonius dearly wanted this province instead of Gaul, which had come to him by lot. He in turn was willing to let Cicero receive the praise, or the blame, for the conduct of affairs during their consulship.

Catiline's plans in Rome depended on Gaius Manlius' raising a sufficient force in Etruria to threaten the city. The reports of smaller forces being assembled elsewhere in Italy, even if vague and unconfirmed, were sufficient to prompt the Senate to dispatch loyal soldiers in several directions. Tension mounted in the capital. Special security guards were assigned to key locations to watch for unusual nighttime activity. Magistrates were heavily protected. Violence in the streets had become the worst of Rome's traditions. In the days of the Gracchi, men looked about for makeshift weapons to use in a sudden riot. Now they went from their homes already armed and aware that other men with daggers stood waiting.

Events came to a climax when Cicero delivered his stirring *First Oration Against Catiline.* The Senators were highly excited by Cicero's warnings, and Catiline, sensing their temper, fled from the city to join Manlius in Etruria. An army must be rushed to the city at once if the plot was to succeed. Publius Lentulus Sura was left in charge of the conspirators in Rome. His major commission was to kill Cicero.

With a clash inevitable, there were self-righteous claims on both sides. Cicero, speaking for the senatorial order, insisted that all that was sacred was being threatened and must be saved. He neglected to mention that much corruption and political self-serving would be preserved in the process. For his part, Catiline claimed that false accusations against him and the greed of certain men had driven him to champion the cause of the unfortunate. If some of these same unfortunates had dared hope that the mere threat of violence would suffice to bring relief, they were due for a disappointment. Cicero's resolute words had stiffened the Senate's backbone. There would be no discussion of proposals during the present threat. The consul Antonius was directed by the Senate to march against Catiline and Manlius, whose activities were now labeled as treason. The constitution must be obeyed, and for now the constitution was on the Senate's side.

Many stalwart citizens viewed the Senate's "patriotism" as a blind for its own power; but for the moment they remained quiet, waiting to see what would happen. Cicero was worried about these moderates and wanted to keep them uncommitted. To do so he had to expose the sedition within the city as soon as possible. So long as there were no overt moves by the conspirators, it would be difficult. No one could be arrested for what he might be thinking. There had to be proof of a treasonable plot. By one crucial miscalculation, Catiline's overanxious lieutenants supplied exactly what was needed. In fact, it was a little more than Cicero might have hoped for.

There happened to be in Rome representatives of the Allobroges, a Transalpine Gallic tribe, who were seeking relief from the greedy magistrates sent to govern them. Their complaints and frustrations were widely known, and the conspirators never doubted that they would be useful allies. On Lentulus' orders, they were approached and given the impression that in return for their present help they would be richly rewarded after the conspiracy succeeded. It was an inviting bargain, good enough to convince the Allobroges that they were now in a position to make an even better one with Cicero and the Senate. When Cicero heard that the envoys were willing to betray the conspirators, he instructed them to obtain some proof of the plot. They did so by insisting that Lentulus and his friends give them a signed statement which they could take back to their people. When this document was brought to Cicero, he ordered the arrest of the ringleaders. That he had caught the conspirators plotting with foreigners was a bonus. Cicero now enjoyed a sudden shift of public sentiment in his favor. Men implicated in the plot ran for cover. The Senate began to receive more evidence than it needed from those seeking immunity. One defector hinted that Crassus, who earlier had welcomed Catiline's support, might have been involved; but Cicero protested that this could not be true. Sallust wonders if Cicero, despite his actions, started the rumor himself in order to put Crassus on the defensive. Crassus apparently thought so. The attempts of Julius Caesar's enemies to involve him in the plot were not successful. Sallust dismisses the accusers as petty and vengeful men.

Most senators experienced an exhilarating relief. It had been a narrow escape. The Gallic ambassadors who had set the trap were treated as heroes. There was only cold anger toward the conspirators. The Senate declared them all guilty of treason without the formality of a trial, which was not necessary under the *senatus consultum ultimum*. Those in custody were prominent citizens and a decision about punishment was urgent, for there was still the danger that die-hard partisans might try to free them. A quick vote would have meant an immediate death sentence. In the end it came to that, but not until Julius Caesar had delivered a brilliant plea for clemency. Sallust makes Caesar look very good indeed. In the midst of hysteria he stands as a confident man of thirty-seven who knows how to keep his head. A remark at the onset of his speech sets the tone: "No mortal man has ever served at the same time his passions and his best interests" (LI. 2–3).

The argument against the death penalty was based on the Porcian Law, which stated that a condemned Roman citizen should not be put to death without the option of going into exile. Caesar was worried that executions would take place without a trial or due process. His advice was sound and not unfamiliar. He said, in effect, that the lawlessness of others should not provoke men to break the law in order to satisfy their passions of the moment.

Caesar knew that some senators, including Cicero, "our distinguished consul," considered the unusual danger of the conspiracy to be an adequate excuse for unprecedented action. He asked them to think about the future. "All bad precedents have originated in cases which were good," he said, "but when the control of the government falls into the hands of men who are incompetent or bad, your new precedent is transferred from those who well deserve and merit such punishment to the undeserving and blameless" (LI. 27). This was what had happened under Sulla. He had begun by executing men whose past wickedness aroused little sympathy for them, but he later let matters get out of hand by allowing the proscription of good men whose only fault was to have a valuable piece of property. Such are the dangers of precedents.

Caesar proposed a compromise. The prisoners should be permanently imprisoned in cities away from Rome. Though his arguments were sound, few could remember them after hearing Cato the Younger's scathing reply. How could Caesar dare to find room for pity? The state remained in grave danger precisely because there was, he said, too much "gentleness and long-suffering" and not enough iron in dealing with men who would have shown no mercy had their vile plot succeeded. Cato did not object to following the example of ancestors, but he said Caesar did not go back far enough. Before the time of the Porcian Law, the Romans had set a better precedent of putting to death men who for any reason endangered the welfare of the state, even those who were not traitors. Did not the present conspirators much more deserve to die for their treasonable plot with the Allobroges? In those earlier times magistrates were not so confused about what was right and what was wrong. For this reason they could act with quick and firm discipline to preserve order. Cato added:

> In very truth we have long since lost the true names for things. It is precisely because squandering the goods of others is called generosity, and recklessness in wrongdoing is called courage, that the republic is reduced to extremities. Let these men by all means, since such is the fashion of the time, be liberal at the expense of the allies, let them be merciful to plunderers of the treasury; but let them not be prodigal of our blood, and in sparing a few scoundrels bring ruin upon all good men. (LII. 11–12)

Cato concluded with the warning that this was not the time for the half-measures which Caesar proposed. The execution of the conspirators was the best safeguard against others who would take their place. The Senate agreed, and Cicero took charge of the details. Lentulus and the four other ringleaders were strangled before nightfall.

The news from Rome was shattering to the army which Manlius and Catiline had assembled. Recruits who had eagerly joined for the promised rewards departed as quickly when they heard what had happened. Nothing was left to Catiline except to lead his hard-core supporters out of Italy. Even that failed. His route was known to the loyalists, and he soon found himself trapped between forces to the north and to the south. Short of supplies, he had to fight or surrender. He chose to challenge the army which was pursuing him under the consul Antonius, but the situation was altogether desperate. The rebels fought like heroes as Catiline had exhorted them to do, in a last-ditch struggle. Manlius was killed first, and then, according to Sallust, Catiline, seeing the hopelessness of his cause, committed himself to a quick death by seeking the heat of the battle and dying sword in hand.

In a letter to Atticus, Cicero asks if there were ever a moment in history so glorious as his handling of the Catilinarian conspiracy, but then adds, "I hope you do not object to my blowing my own horn." In Rome, he was suddenly a hero—the first person in history to be called the "Father of His Country." He had his victory. It was a great day. He never saw a better one.

There are many positive things to be said about Cicero. He was not opposed to change if it could be brought about by an orderly, even if slow, process. On occasion he might not agree with a particular measure favored by the equestrians, but if he felt it would serve the cause of unity he would vote for it. He acted the same way toward certain pet measures of the senatorial class. Yet this intelligent man with a flair for practical politics failed in his ambition to unite the Romans by the aura of his leadership. Ironically, although famous for his oratory, he was probably hurt as much by the sharpness of his tongue as by anything else. Cicero's ready wit was augmented by an excellent memory for items of gossip. A man who had once been accused of poisoning his father with a piece of cake boasted about the "invectives" he intended to direct at Cicero. "Better these," said Cicero, "than your cakes." On another occasion, when a rival called attention to Cicero's common birth by asking, "Who was your father?" Cicero replied, "Your mother has made the answer to such a question in your case more difficult" (Plutarch, p. 1056). Pompey and Crassus would have smiled and Caesar would have laughed aloud.

But while Cicero's agile wit was much admired within his own circle, among the rank and file the great orator seemed only to make the unprofitable impression of being too clever.

Cato the Younger

Those who think of Cicero as the typical bullheaded Old Roman have probably never heard of Cato the Younger. Had it not been for him, Cicero might have accepted Caesar's plea for the conspirators' lives. Cicero publicly extolled inflexible principles, but behind closed doors he knew how to come to terms. Cato's relentless obstinacy made Cicero look good. As a child, he was serious beyond his years. At thirteen, when most boys would have felt privileged to enjoy the luxuries of Sulla's household, Cato had only a sharp eye for the severed heads being carried in. Aware of Sulla's many enemies, he asked his tutor, "Why does nobody kill this man?" "Because they fear him, child, more than they hate him," he was told (Plutarch, p. 919). Cato announced that he would do it himself. His teacher surely raised his eyes to heaven and took careful watch of his young charge. Cato would exasperate many men in the years ahead. Obviously, the pattern of his life was set early and was perhaps as much a matter of temperament as anything else. Virtue was a vocation which left little room for joy. Cato rarely smiled and almost never laughed. The traditions of the past weighed heavily on his shoulders; the present was devoted to public service; the future, of course, looked dim. He sounds like his dour great-grandfather, Cato the Elder. Both took to politics with a missionary zeal. Cato the Younger was a self-appointed foe of all tyrants. Liberty should be circumscribed only by traditions, but never by men, he thought. There could be no distinction between one tyrant and another whether they be selfless men or self-serving, reactionary or progressive, a Sulla or a Caesar.

It is not surprising that Cato was attracted to Stoicism and enjoyed the company of its leading practitioners. A philosophy which downgraded emotions and preached a universe governed by unchanging principle suited him exactly. Stoicism did not change his point of view, but simply confirmed it. The Stoics were fond of tracing their intellectual lineage to Socrates. Cato, in some ways, imitated him. Study and contemplation were valued as other men might value business. Cato was also known to disregard either heat or cold, exercising in all kinds of weather, and so showing himself the master of circumstances rather than their victim. He had no interest in fashion. To him money was important only for what could be done with it. Although considered generous by his relatives and friends, Cato supposedly declined their praise with the argument that those who give away material things do not offer very much. Duty and honor were everything. A man in public service should never sacrifice his reputation for the sake of private gain. Plutarch tells several stories about the career of this honest man in breathless pursuit of those who were not honest. His portrait of Cato was undoubtedly true to the public impression of the man. Yet it was not the way Cato's brother saw him. Caepio knew that despite Cato's reputation for rigorous self-discipline, he might sit up all night talking and drinking wine even as Socrates used to do. Cato did not appear cold and reserved to his brother, with whom he shared a deep bond of affection. They were inseparable when they were young and served in the army together during the slave war. Later, when Cato heard his brother was seriously ill in Thrace, he hurried to his bedside at great expense and at some risk to himself. After Caepio died, Cato surprised even his closest friends by an excessive display of grief at an uncommonly elaborate funeral.

Publicly, Cato stood alongside Cicero. They were both champions of the old school. They had carefully prepared themselves for their responsibilities and took their duties seriously. Cato did not stand for the quaestorship until he had become thoroughly familiar with the operations of the treasury. Once in office he surprised long-time bureaucrats who expected a new quaestor to be as ignorant of the job as his predecessors had been. Inefficient or corrupt staff members were sorted out in a housecleaning which gave the public a new confidence. Cato especially delighted in collecting debts owed to the government and kept a sharp eye out for favoritism by which senators might try to help their friends. He was the watchdog of the treasury, even out of office. It was exceedingly rare for anyone to doubt his honesty. "I would not believe it, even if Cato said it," became a familiar saying.

In 62, the year after Cicero's suppression of the Catilinarian conspiracy, Pompey arrived home from the East. It was Cato who led the opposition to the proposal that his veterans be used to repress any further uprisings. As Cato saw it, the prevention of one coup might be the means of another. It was like him to declare that he would rather die than allow Pompey's army in the city. He was of course strongly supported by Lucullus, who incidentally was married to his sister—a family alliance which each man found useful.

Cato's opposition to Pompey was a fateful turn of events for the Republic. He sought to save the state from subversion, but this move was to have the very opposite effect. Cato's relations with Pompey had never been easy. When Pompey was at the height of his power, he had treated the younger Cato cordially whenever he came to see him, but, as Plutarch has it, was never sorry to see him go. A man of Cato's strict habits, who never missed a single session of the Tribal Assembly or the Senate—he was the first to arrive and the last to leave—made the more easygoing Pompey uncomfortable. Out of political considerations, Pompey had once sought to ally himself to Cato by marrying one of his daughters or nieces. Cato rebuffed him. "I will not give hostages to Pompey's glory against my country's safety" (Plutarch, p. 935). Caesar would. He gave his daughter, Julia, to Pompey. If the forging of this new alliance posed a grave threat to the Republic, Cato was himself partly to blame. The Senate had listened to him and turned its back on the mild, indecisive Pompey, who then became a partner of the more determined and more dangerous Julius Caesar.

X

Julius Caesar and the First Triumvirate

In a short history of Rome, the name of Julius Caesar would light up the page like a comet. The credulous among his contemporaries thought his soul left that way en route to heaven. Actually, his career was a long time in building. Only with time did his capacity for leadership become obvious to others and, more important, to himself. The skillful writings of his mature years show him to have been a man of keen intelligence. But there was always something special about him. Ancient authors speak of his charm. Even as a young man he had a style—a presence. What he lacked was self-discipline.

Caesar's vices may have helped to save his life. His name reminded the almighty Sulla of various old enemies, Marius for one, an uncle to Caesar by marriage. Caesar himself had married Cornelia, daughter of the Cinna who had betrayed Sulla and nearly destroyed him. Although proud of his famous uncle and father-in-law, Caesar kept quiet. Even so, influential aristocrats found it necessary to defend "this boy" to Sulla, who listened only half-heartedly. He saw in Caesar "many a Marius." Others saw a young man who drank too much and gambled beyond his means. How could he injure anyone except himself? That ques-

251

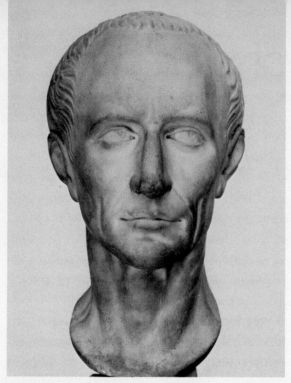

13. Julius Caesar. Courtesy of the Trustees of the British Museum.

tion may have saved him from Sulla's henchmen, but it was well that he kept out of sight.

Caesar hid in the Sabine country before he went to the East to serve as an aide to Marcus Minucius Thermus, the governor of Asia. In this capacity he was sent as an envoy to Nicomedes, king of Bithynia, to seek help in equipping a new fleet. Caesar won that but picked up a bad reputation in the process. His extended visit at Nicomedes' court spawned a rumor that his relations with the king had gone beyond diplomacy. Whether true or not, the episode gave rise to numerous sly remarks in the years to come. Bibulus, Caesar's unwelcomed colleague in the consulship of 59 B.C., called him "the Queen of Bithynia." Cicero helped to keep the scandal alive. Once when Caesar was speaking of his "obligations" to Nicomedes, Cicero interrupted him to say that there was no need for an accounting: "We all know what he gave you, and what you gave him in return" (Suetonius, I. 49). In spite of these embarrassing references, Caesar, over the years, was popularly known as a ladies' man; his affairs with women of both noble and common standing were as well known as his three marriages. The encounter with Cleopatra was in a class by itself. But Caesar became too famous for incidents of the past to be forgotten. Long afterwards, the elder Curio called him "every woman's husband and every man's wife."

Caesar's early adventures also included being held by pirates for thirty-eight days until his aides could bring a ransom, which he laughingly said was set too low for a man of his quality. On another occasion, he seethed with anger about the inconvenience of being held captive and vowed that he would one day crucify his "hosts." They had heard such threats before and let him go, expecting him to consider himself luckier than others had been. That estimate left out of account a youthful impetuosity and a man's share of iron. Caesar raised ships in Miletus, captured the very pirates who had held him captive, and crucified them exactly as he said he would. Those who knew Caesar as an appealing young orator at Rome found this steeliness in check, but later observers saw it often in the man who conquered Gaul.

When Caesar returned to Rome after Sulla's death, those who opposed the old regime saw him as a natural ally, thinking him sympathetic to popular causes. Yet Caesar was not a man for other people's risks. He stood aloof from the uprisings led by Lepidus and Catiline. These adventures did not look profitable to him. As mentioned earlier, there was an effort to link him to Catiline, but Cicero would not have it. Caesar had told the government all he knew of that plot and was obviously too clever to become entangled in Catiline's clumsy alliance of malcontents. He was really not a likely suspect. His easygoing manner was in refreshing contrast to the tense and cautious ways of men whose ambitions were more obvious. There is nothing to suggest that the young Caesar considered himself a giant among men. Plutarch says that Cicero was the first who "saw the designing temper of the man through this disguise of good humor and affability." But the sharp-eyed Cicero was still not sure. "When I see his hair so carefully arranged, and observe him adjusting it with one finger, I cannot imagine it should enter into such a man's thoughts to subvert the Roman state" (p. 856).

Caesar took his time and his turn in the lower offices. In 69 B.C., nine years after Sulla's death, he began his public career as a quaestor in Spain. In 65, he served as a curule aedile. The public knew him as a generous producer of gladiatorial contests as well as other entertainments. He spent government funds lavishly and matched them with money of his own, even if often borrowed. Caesar was always generous, always in debt, and always popular. In 63, he was elected *pontifex maximus,* with the help of a law which renewed the Domitian Law of 104 and so took the choice away from the priests, where Sulla had placed it, making it a popular selection by seventeen tribes. The defeat of two older men who could boast of distinguished careers showed what could be accomplished by extravagant expenditures. Caesar's elevation to the highest priestly office in Rome also says something about the perfunctory character of Roman religion. His writings suggest that he did not have much reverence for the gods, if indeed he believed in them at all. Caesar reserved his praise for men of great deeds. When serving as an aedile, he restored statues of the unforgettable Marius to public view. Aristocrats might be shocked by this veneration of an old enemy, but common citizens were grateful to see their hero back in place. They were perhaps less well-informed about Caesar's having expressed regrets if any senator's feelings were hurt.

Caesar operated skillfully on both sides of the political fence. This may explain his equivocal stand in the midst of a scandal which arose during his praetorship in 62. One night religious rites which were held at his house were open to women only. There came a young man, dressed as a girl, who was presumably anxious to visit Pompeia, Caesar's second wife. It is not certain that he came with Pompeia's knowledge, although a maid was willing to inform her mistress quietly that he was there. When another servant detected a false note in his voice, he was chased from the house with the assembled women in full cry. The pitch was probably set by Caesar's mother, Aurelia, who kept a suspicious eye fixed on her daughter-in-law. The next day, those who heard the story were quick to guess that Publius Clodius Pulcher was the man involved. He was an obstreperous young patrician who had been in numerous scrapes. Punishment for his latest escapade might have been swift if the case had been kept free of politics. But when the aristocracy disowned Clodius with unseemly haste, he became a hero to the crowd. During his trial for sacrilege, jurymen said they feared there would be trouble if he was convicted. Cicero suggested that they had been paid for their anxiety. In his own testimony he swore that Clodius had visited him at his house on the day in question, and so undercut the alibi that he was out of the city. Upon acquittal, Clodius boasted that Cicero's testimony had not been believed by the jurors. To which Cicero replied, "Yes, five-and-twenty of them trusted me and condemned you, and the other thirty did not trust you, for they did not acquit you till they had got your money" (p. 1058).

Caesar did not attend the trial. There was no proof of any relationship between his wife and Clodius. Facts were needed in a courtroom. Not so at home. Caesar divorced Pompeia immediately and so insured her everlasting fame as the wife who had not kept herself above suspicion.

In 61 B.C., Caesar went as a propraetor to Spain. There he carried Roman banners to the Atlantic Ocean, subduing tribes heretofore free of Roman domination. In administering local matters, Rome's most famous debtor finally found good use for his considerable expertise on matters involving credit. Most of his own debts had been cleared up, with the help of Crassus, before he left for Spain. When he returned home with money to spare, there was widespread speculation about his overseas operations. He could not, however, be forced to answer charges connected with his recent governorship while he remained in office. To be elected to the consulship for 59 would give him that protection. The office was in a sense seeking him, for circumstances in 60 were conveniently favorable to his candidacy.

In the years immediately following the Catilinarian imbroglio, a reactionary Senate, seemingly under Cato's spell, had refused to cooperate with any of the major military figures of the day. This caused men who might not otherwise have been friends to look to each other. When Pompey returned from the East late in 62 B.C., his behavior could not have been more conciliatory. The disbanding of his army was a great sacrifice, in view of his triumphant campaign and the wealth he was bringing home. Yet, as mentioned earlier, instead of the Senate's rewarding him for his success and subservience, they delayed a confirmation of his settlements in the East and did not provide the land allotments he had requested for his veterans. Pompey was obviously embarrassed. Cato, his most vociferous opponent, excused this rude treatment by saying that the government feared the power which great military commanders were acquiring. Nor did he believe any of them could escape being corrupted by such power. But Pompey, on his performance, was a man whom conservative senators could have trusted. Before long they would wish they had done so.

Crassus was upset by recent judicial decisions because of his strong ties to the business community. A bill to suppress bribery among equestrian jurymen was considered a slap at the entire order. In addition, Crassus strongly favored relief for tax "farmers" (*publicani*), investors in private companies which held contracts with the government for the collection of taxes locally and overseas. These men often found themselves committed to pay the state more money than they could collect. Crassus wanted their payments scaled down. When Cato blocked a bill for this purpose, Crassus, like Pompey, began to look around for political allies.

Cato's policies kept the senatorial and equestrian orders from an accommodation. Yet that was exactly what Cicero thought was needed. He actively supported cooperation between these groups, the one which prided itself on old names and the other on new money. Joining together in a solid front, these Optimates, "best people," could prevent the rise of demagogues who might arouse the more radical instincts of the masses. In the recent past, when the equestrian order had supported Marius and the senatorial order backed Sulla, there was a civil war. On the other hand, when the two classes cooperated against Catiline, catastrophe was averted. Now, with these powerful factions disunited, there was an unusual opportunity for political maneuvering; an unusual man, Julius Caesar, took advantage of it.

In recent years, Caesar had generally held a flexible enough position to keep men guessing about the direction of his politics. Now was the time to take a stand, and he took it firmly on the side of the Populares, leaders whose concerns, broadly speaking, were those of the poor rather than the privileged. In this course he needed strong allies, and the Senate's intransigence provided them. Pompey and Crassus joined Caesar in the arrangement, called the First Triumvirate. Caesar was the link between these two old rivals. The three of them, in an unofficial alliance, would soon manage the affairs of the state to suit themselves.

During the election for 59 B.C., only Cato and his friends were openly hostile. They rallied the aristocracy behind Marcus Calpurnius Bibulus and managed to elect him as the other consul instead of Lucius Lucceius, whom Caesar had preferred as his colleague. Both sides passed out bribes more freely than usual. It is taken as a measure of Cato's fear of Caesar that he would countenance dishonest tactics on this occasion.

The triumvirate was never stronger than in its first year. Caesar and Pompey had become related through Pompey's marriage to Caesar's daughter, Julia. Crassus, the realist, was a friend of the family. Cicero, who rejected Caesar's overtures, and Cato, who presumably never received any, were left outside. In the fashion of city bosses, the triumvirs sought to please as many voters as possible. Unemployed fathers with three or more children were favored in government allotments of land. Tax farmers who had overestimated their collections were allowed a reduction in their debts to the treasury. From the first, Caesar, in particular, showed an interest in reform. He began the practice of publishing the daily proceedings of the Senate and the courts. The Romans were thus given at least a sampling of the democracy which they never knew in fact.

In spite of the positive aspects of their rule, the triumvirs, with Clodius' collusion, were quick to use force whenever it suited them. The lictors who led the way for Caesar's colleague in the consulship, Bibulus, were attacked, and the poor man even had excrement hurled at him as he was entering the Forum. Later, the presence of Pompey's veterans in the Forum made it unsafe for Bibulus to venture there for business. So he remained at home and limited himself to giving out notices about omens which, if they had not been ignored, could have interfered with the plans of the triumvirs. He had been accused of seeing signs in the sky which nobody else saw. Each side, of course, said much about the trickery of the opposition, but the triumvirs obviously had the last word. In 59, some may have joked about it, but there was truth in the sly comments about the consulship of Julius and Caesar.

Cato was outraged by recent events and openly defiant. The triumvirs demanded that all senators take an oath to uphold their new legislation, including the distribution of land to the poor. At first, Cato refused to take the oath, but Cicero helped him change his mind. He said that Cato's martydom would be a hollow gesture and rob the constitution of one of its staunchest defenders. "For though Cato have no need of Rome yet Rome has need of Cato, and so likewise have all his friends' (Plutarch, p. 936). Cato reluctantly took the oath. Still, nothing could prevent an early clash with Caesar. While others remained silent, Cato continued publicly to denounce the consul's actions until Caesar in a rare moment of pique had him seized. But Cato kept talking as he was being taken away, and Caesar was embarrassed by the number of people who went along to listen. Aware of his mistake, he directed one of the tribunes to use his veto to release him. Thus was Caesar, not Cato, saved from humiliation. At a later date, a different tribune, Gaius Trebonius, tried to jail Cato illegally and met with the same difficulty. Public opinion saved Cato. He was not much loved, but was greatly admired. If he was to be silenced there would have to be some more pleasant way to do it.

The triumvirs were generous to their followers, but Caesar gave himself the richest prize of all. As a proconsul, his command for the following five years would include Cisalpine Gaul, the area on the Italian side of the Alps which had been settled by northerners, and Illyricum, a rich recruiting area for soldiers. The Senate then added Transalpine Gaul when the governor there died, and so Caesar was given all the opportunities which the vastness of Gaul could offer.

To make sure that his interests would be protected during his absence, Caesar promoted the election of Piso as consul for the following year and Clodius as tribune. As Caesar had recently married Piso's daughter, Calpurnia, his ties there were firm. Clodius was a risk. He had given up his patrician status in order to become a tribune and so better serve his plebeian supporters. He was also eager to serve the triumvirs so long as he was given a free hand in dealing with his enemies. Clodius had managed by obvious demagogic means to become the hero of the city's rabble. Many men were afraid of him, and Caesar had little reason to be proud of this connection. Still, he needed a vigorous spokesman in Rome while he was away. Marius had had his Saturninus and later Sulpicius. Now Caesar had his Clodius—and the embarrassment that went with him.

Clodius was bent on revenge. He of course had a personal grudge against Cicero, but it would be easier to attack him if the voluble Cato could be gotten out of the way. Here he succeeded where Caesar had failed. Clodius, with mock sincerity, praised Cato as the man who could be most trusted as the governor of newly annexed Cyprus. The offer of this relatively insignificant post, a long way from Rome, was an insult, yet how could a loyal public servant refuse it? The Tribal Assembly gave Cato his orders—it was legal—and he had to go.

Suddenly the haste with which Cicero had put five conspirators, including the praetor Lentulus, to death in 63 B.C. was remembered as a crime. At the time, the action had been excused because of the turmoil and danger of the moment. Now the illegality of the act was all that Clodius needed as he launched a campaign to drive this "criminal" from the city. Caesar was busy making preparations to leave for Gaul, and may have hurt Cicero by his public silence. His private concern and offers of help may have been turned down by Cicero because he feared they would compromise him politically. Would Pompey help? He left his house by one door when Cicero arrived at the other.

Afraid to stay and fight, Cicero felt compelled to steal away from his beloved Rome under cover of darkness. In exile, too, he was wounded by old friends who avoided him. Still there were others who ignored Clodius' threats and made Cicero's passage easier. In Greece he was treated like visiting royalty. All the same his spirits remained low. Cicero saw himself as an ardent patriot and once savior of Rome. Especially galling was the ingratitude of ordinary citizens, who made no effort to stop the pillaging and burning of his house on the Palatine and two of his villas. For a man who was supposed to have a stolid philosophical outlook he took his misfortune very hard. Plutarch observes that "the desire of glory has great power in washing the tinctures of philosophy out of the souls of men" (p. 1060).

Caesar in Gaul

Julius Caesar stands preeminent in both history and drama as a man of extraordinary self-confidence. It was in Gaul that he discovered how far he could go. Success on the battlefield was only part of the story. Year after year Caesar had to contend with crucial supply problems. He also had to face sharp ups and downs in morale and, worse, his allies often gave him as much trouble as the enemy. In the end, he was totally triumphant. He knew why better than anybody else, and his *Commentaries* tell the story.

Among those who call warfare an art, Caesar is acknowledged as one of its great practitioners. Even a pacifist would agree that he could write. This rare combination of talents served him well. Absent from Rome, he kept his name alive by writing skillful accounts of his campaigns. The style is as simple as an arrow on target.

Factual truth was in Caesar's favor and required little embellishment. If the Romans had had daily newspapers, his *Commentaries* could have been serialized for easy reading by a mass audience. Not the least of Caesar's talents was his capacity to communicate with men at all levels. The *Commentaries* have a "this is exactly what happened" tone. If he is in doubt about something he admits it. On one occasion, speaking of an excuse given to him by a native tribe, he says, "Whether this was the true reason I do not know, and therefore abstain from any positive assertion" (p. 118). He made an observation now and then without sounding opinionated. Like the renowned Greek historian Thucydides, Caesar spoke of himself in the third person. That device gave his account an impersonal tone. But the candor, made possible by his brilliant victories, the steady nerve—the impression of a man who knows exactly what he is doing—are as apparent to a modern reader as they were to a contemporary. If it was Caesar's intention to impress a mostly hostile Senate by his exploits in the service of Rome, his propaganda may have succeeded too well. Some senators grew more fearful of his power.

Caesar left Rome early in 58 B.C. The eight books of the *Commentaries* are concerned with the next nine years spent in Gaul and Britain. He wrote the first seven himself, but whether these books were written in installments and sent to Rome year by year is still a matter of debate. The eighth book, covering the years 51 and 50, was added later by his friend and confidant Aulus Hirtius. It served as a transition to the three books which Caesar wrote about his war with Pompey. The *Commentaries* end with the battle of Pharsalus and Pompey's death in 48 B.C. The accounts of Caesar's later adventures in Alexandria and the campaign in Asia Minor were probably written by Hirtius. It is not known who wrote the extant material on the campaign in North Africa. The author who wrote the on-the-spot account about Spain knows the story well enough, but nothing else is known of him except that he was poorly educated. In this chapter and the next, the quotations which describe the conquest of Gaul are taken from the *Commentaries* as translated by John Warrington, who says in his Introduction: "Caesar following a convention, and not because of any Olympian aloofness, wrote in the third person. I have allowed him to speak directly in the first person: the narrative becomes thereby more vivid, and difficulties in reported speech are overcome" (p. xix).

Caesar offers an impressive, if monotonous, string of battles, which required his constant attention from spring to fall. Each year, after his soldiers had been settled down for the winter,

14. Amphitheatre at Arles (top) and the theatre (in the foreground) are examples of the substantial structures of Roman Gaul. Courtesy of the French Government Tourist Office, New York.

he would return to Cisalpine Gaul. There he met with his friends and agents, who brought the latest news from home and returned to the capital with his advice.

Crassus and Pompey were well aware of the power base which Caesar was building in Gaul. Victory succeeded victory, and where an opportunity for one was lacking it could be created. The tribes of the region, numbering fifty or more, appealed to Caesar for help against one another. Caesar admits that the Romans occasionally provided some trouble of their own where it might be useful.

The three parts of Gaul were occupied by the Belgae, the Aquitani, and the Celts, whom the Romans called Gauls. Each of these peoples spoke a different language, followed different customs, and obeyed different laws, but, in general, they were each ruled by a dominant aristocracy loyal to an heroic code. There might also be a king. Some tribes were more aggressive than others. A few of them produced outstanding leaders who managed to attract support far beyond their immediate neighborhood.

In 58, Caesar fought two campaigns. The first was against the Helvetii, who considered themselves the toughest tribesmen among the Gauls—an evaluation which was widely appreciated. They had moved out of their own territory, along with three neighboring tribes, in search of space. More prosperous and settled peoples in the way were hit hard. Villages of the Aedui, Ambarri, and Allobroges were burned and their fields stripped. These allies of Rome sent urgent appeals for help. Caesar had another reason for intervention: the Helvetii, flushed with their early victories, had violated the frontiers of the Roman province between the Rhone and the Lake of Geneva. When they sent a commission to Caesar to forestall any Roman moves, he sent back stern terms. They would have to repay the Gallic tribes whose property had been damaged by their invasions, and they must surrender hostages to insure that their agreements would be kept. The seriousness of the situation was obvious. Caesar even felt called upon to mention the gods. He told the Helvetii: "When the immortal gods mean to punish guilty man they often grant him all the more prosperity, all the longer impunity, simply that he may suffer the more when his good fortune is reversed" (p. 7). The Helvetii were not interested in either the terms or the advice. Caesar was short of grain and they knew it. They also knew that he was having trouble with his closest allies, the Aedui. Allies of

15. Another view of the theatre at Arles. Courtesy of the French Government Tourist Office, New York.

the Helvetii, on the other hand, came to their aid, and the Romans had two battles to fight at once, which made their victory all the more conclusive. After an unconditional surrender, Caesar took hostages, recovered his escaped slaves, and ordered the Helvetii to return to their original lands. They had to rebuild the villages they had burned and settle down peaceably under Roman protection. Caesar would in the meantime see that they did not starve. The Allobroges were ordered to feed them until their next harvest. Caesar easily assumed the role as arbiter of Gallic affairs and protector of Gallic interests. What some Gauls had feared was now upon them. Others were more worried about an invasion from the north.

Recently, the Germans had been crossing the Rhine in increasing numbers, partly by invitation. The Gauls, quarreling among themselves, bought the services of German fighters for use against one another. These mercenaries found more than money in Gaul. News of rich farmland and a better standard of living attracted their relatives to join them. Caesar heard that 15,000 mercenaries had grown to approximately 120,000 settlers, with more on the way. It was also reported to him that when Ariovistus, the Germanic king, appropriated Gallic land he took the best. Caesar made sure that everybody heard about Ariovistus' practice of capturing enemy children and torturing them with all manner of cruelties until his demands were met. Caesar calls him "savage, passionate and reckless." More to the point, he was pushing Gallic tribes off their land and upsetting the status quo. What would be the end? The danger a half century before from other Germans, the Cimbri and the Teutones, was easy to remember. Caesar had to act before there was a threat to Italy, but his request for a conference with Ariovistus brought only a rude reply: "If I wanted anything of Caesar, I would go to him: if Caesar wants anything of me, he should come to me" (p. 17). Caesar was patient. He sent a letter telling Ariovistus that as the governor of Roman Gaul he was under orders from the Senate to protect such Roman allies as the Aedui. Ariovistus must return their hostages, and he must also stop the flow of Germans across the Rhine. Back came a reply written with the politeness which one aggressor might reserve for another. In effect, Ariovistus told Caesar to mind his own business. When he said, "For fourteen years my Germans have not known a roof over their heads" (p. 19), he was not complaining. Caesar's soldiers had been hearing about the boasts of these proud barbarians.

Caesar was calm. His officers were given straightforward talk. The Romans had beaten Germans before, and the forces they now faced were no fiercer than the Cimbri and Teutones. Besides, had not the already subjected Helvetii defeated the Germans in recent years? Caesar showed some irritation. Others had been talking about the need to postpone action because of bad roads and short supplies. He was in command and he would make the decisions. It was his decision to search out Ariovistus and, if negotiations failed, to bring him to terms by force. His self-confidence was infectious. Morale was further strengthened when Caesar, pointedly singling out the soldiers of the Tenth Legion as the most loyal, gave the others a reason to deny rather than to excuse their weaknesses.

Within a few days, the Roman army stood near enough to Ariovistus' camp to suggest to him the wisdom of a conference.

Both sides made elaborate plans for security. Ariovistus insisted on the precaution that he and Caesar talk while on horseback. The arrangements guaranteed a tense atmosphere. When they met, neither had much to offer except self-justification, although one remark by Ariovistus stands out. He suggested that many important persons in Rome would thank him if they never saw Caesar again. It may not have occurred to him that by the same token Caesar could greatly increase his stature at home by killing him. Ariovistus wanted another conference, but Caesar refused. There would have to be a battle. It came about a week later.

Caesar had aroused the spirits of his troops by telling them stories of German arrogance and treachery. On the other side, morale was not a problem. Behind the German lines were wagons filled with wives, screaming that their husbands spare them the humiliation of captivity. The hand-to-hand fight was savage; for a time the battle could have gone either way. The right move by the Roman cavalry made the difference. As the Germans fled toward the Rhine, both of Ariovistus' wives and one of his daughters were killed. The king escaped. Nevertheless Caesar's mission was accomplished. The defeat of Ariovistus was a warning to every other German to stay where he was.

When the campaign was finished, Caesar settled his forces in winter quarters and headed for Cisalpine Gaul. The first year was over; and although he must have felt much satisfaction, his report continues matter-of-factly and with the kind of understatement which a very proud man might use.

In the spring of 57, Caesar was faced with a Belgic mobilization. His victories over the Celtic Gauls and the intruding Germans alarmed the Belgae, who, as we saw, occupied a third of Gaul. They feared they would be next. News of the size of their conglomerate army was enough to make Caesar proceed with extra caution; yet he also saw a possible advantage. The leaders of these loosely related tribes were easily frustrated, and Caesar fought only from well-selected sites. In the early summer, after a costly engagement with the Romans at the Axona River (modern Aisne) in northern Gaul, the coalition split up, with each tribe returning to defend its home ground. Caesar easily disarmed the Suessiones and Bellovaci, took hostages, and then left both tribes free to pursue their daily life within the bond of friendship which the Romans called peace. Caesar often speaks of his "well-known forbearance and magnanimity." But he was not through with the Belgae yet.

The Nervii were the Spartans among them—a people strongly disciplined by strict laws. Caesar says that "they admitted no traders and imported no wine or other luxuries, regarding such commodities as effeminate and destructive of the warlike spirit" (p. 35). In a battle at the Sambre River they put Caesar and his legions to one of their severest tests. Not unexpectedly it was Caesar's Tenth Legion which stood around him and turned back the attack with a frightful massacre of the Nervii. The few survivors were ordered back to their homeland; Caesar gave warning to their neighbors to leave them alone. The Atuatuci, who had hoped to join with the Nervii in their struggle with the Romans, were not so fortunate. They were trapped in a fortress around which Caesar built the siege devices which never failed to amaze the enemy: "The Gauls, of course, are notoriously contemptuous of our stature, which is small in comparison with their own huge physique; and they were puzzled to know how those little men with their puny hands and feeble arms imagined they were going to lift a heavy tower on to the top of a wall. They were seriously alarmed, however, by the strange, uncanny spectacle of the thing in motion, approaching their own walls" (p. 41). Their response was to feign total submission. When they surrendered they gave up their weapons, except for about a third, which they buried for use in a surprise attack planned for the middle of the night. Caesar anticipated it and easily caught them unaware. He did not forgive their treachery; the entire tribe, 53,000 in all, was sold into slavery.

At the end of 57, Caesar again returned to Cisalpine Gaul, happy to know that news of his success had been so well received in Rome, a point which suggests that his *Commentaries* were dispatched to the capital year by year. In 56, the defeat of the Aquitanian tribes meant that the last of the three famous regions of Gaul had been brought under Roman control. Yet it was too early to think that the Gallic peoples had become reconciled to Roman rule. Caesar frequently mentions the unpredictable behavior of the Gauls, their willingness to take great risks on information no better than rumor, and the ease with which they made and broke agreements.

For the next few years Caesar and his lieutenants were confronted with a series of uprisings in all parts of Gaul. In any region where the army was undermanned or short of rations, local tribes were sure to make trouble. As usual, a few of them were quick to invite the Germans back to join their resistance movement. Others were kept quiet by Caesar's practice of taking the near relatives of Gallic leaders as hostages. Of course such tribes as the Aedui remained faithful voluntarily, at least for the moment.

Britain

Caesar's campaign in 56 B.C. against the Veneti and other tribes living along the coast of Brittany induced him to build ships serviceable in northern waters. It was not, however, until his invasion of Britain during the late summer of 55 that he discovered what kind of ships he needed.

Caesar's first visit to Britain was brief and merely for the purpose of reconnaissance, or so he said, perhaps with hindsight. He was by no means welcome. It took about nine hours for eighty ships to cross the channel and sight the great cliffs. The natives stood ready with their eyes and spears fixed on the beaches. When a more level landing site was found, it was still not easy to go ashore until the Britons had been forced to retreat inland. Caesar was then able to win oaths of allegiance from the tribal chieftains, but when closer observation assured these same leaders that the Romans had not arrived in any great force, they changed their minds and made a sudden attack. Caesar was impressed by the maneuverability and speed of the British chariots. The season, however, was too late for large-scale action, and his first encounter with the Britons was not conclusive. Nevertheless, he declared himself the winner and demanded that hostages from the various tribes be sent to him on the continent. Once he was gone, only two chieftains remembered their promise. The Britons never took the giving of a man's word any more seriously than the Gauls. In part, Romanization was the lesson that civilized living depended on mutual trust. Caesar would teach these peoples that they must abide by their oaths, and he considered the lesson to be a favor.

In 54 there was a second crossing of the channel. During the past winter, about six hundred ships had been built especially for the mission. This time they were broader, to accommodate more pack animals, and shallow because the waves of the channel were not so high as those encountered on the Atlantic or the Mediterranean. Both oars and sails were available. Boulogne, the port of departure, was only twenty-eight miles from Britain.

Early in July, the Romans set sail and landed about noon on

the seventh, meeting no resistance from the natives. However, a storm that night wrecked about forty Roman ships and left the others badly in need of repairs. At the same time the Britons began to gather nearby. Cassivellaunus was their leader, although most of them had earlier been at odds with him. Despite the healing of their differences, they were still no match for Caesar's legions or cavalry. The Romans clearly had the best of it in a series of brief encounters and set battles. The native alliance then fell apart, with individual tribes seeking a settlement. Before long Cassivellaunus asked for terms. Caesar was eager to oblige, for the summer was ending and the situation in Gaul was too tense for him to remain longer in Britain. He took hostages, arranged for an annual tribute, and warned that tribes friendly to Rome should not be molested because of that friendship.

Caesar's invasions had been too short to effect any permanent change in Britain. He had no intention of establishing a province. He had come to see what was there, with an eye to trade possibilities. He also wanted to make a show of Roman power. That surely had been accomplished.

Gaul Again

In the winter of 54–53 B.C., Caesar was forced to spread his legions in Gaul far apart because of a scarcity of food. This was a risk, and the trouble which followed was not surprising. What did amaze Caesar was a decision by one of his officers. At Tongres, the Roman commander, Sabinus, was advised by an Eburonian leader, Ambiorix, that he was in danger and that for the safety of his forces he should break camp and join the nearest Roman contingent. Unwilling to give credence to his colleague's suspicions about the source of this good will, Sabinus stubbornly led a legion and five cohorts into a deadly ambush. His next move was even more amazing. He was willing to go unarmed to Ambiorix to seek terms. He could not believe that this man who gave his word not to harm him would use that trust to betray him again. Perhaps just before he was murdered he recognized the ease with which evil disguises itself. Caesar would never have made such blunders; yet he had lost considerably by Sabinus' naiveté. Not only had the Romans suffered severe casualities, but the unnecessary losses had given encouragement to other Gallic tribes ripe for revolt.

Gallic resistance grew steadily during 53, and in spite of all he had won, Caesar still had his stiffest tests ahead of him. He was sufficiently alarmed to ask Pompey to send additional legions, hoping to impress the Gauls with the depth of Roman manpower. Challenged by a coordinated revolt, Caesar adopted the strategy of striking at the strongest of the Gallic tribes to scare off the rest. The Treveri, his chief target, were defeated by his lieutenant Labienus, who feigned a retreat and drew them into a trap before their German allies could arrive to help them. The slaughter which followed prompted the Germans to return home without making contact. Caesar crossed the Rhine to warn the Germans about the provocations they were creating by their interference.

As winter approached, Caesar felt satisfied enough with the events of the year 53 to return to Cisalpine Gaul, where he hoped to remain until early spring. He was anxious to hear the news from Rome. During the past six years he had kept in close contact with events and had even had a powerful influence on them, particularly in 56 B.C.

Events in Rome

Caesar had left Rome about the time that Cicero went into exile in 58. Both missed the excitement of Roman politics and eagerly awaited the news which told of old alliances broken and new intrigues taking form. After Cicero's sixteen months of exile, a shift in the wind paved the way for his return: Clodius made the mistake of attacking Pompey.

In Caesar's absence, Pompey was expected to attend to the day-to-day problems in Rome. In this capacity he soon manifested his dormant conservative sympathies. He was particularly annoyed by the agitation of certain tribunes, especially the popular Clodius. His earlier ties to this man had resulted from a bad bargain, made at the time when the Senate had insulted Pompey and he had turned to Clodius and his radical supporters. Pompey's name could have lent respectability to their cause, but Clodius' wild promises and terrorist tactics undercut that possibility. Nevertheless, Pompey had turned his back on his old friend Cicero for this unscrupulous man, and he soon regretted it. Clodius took Pompey for granted, and even ridiculed him in public. This was partly Pompey's fault. Lacking interest in administrative duties, he had allowed the affairs of the city to drift during successive consulships of friends who were unable to check Clodius' excesses. Pompey's decision to bring the sharp-tongued Cicero home from exile was clearly a slap at Clodius and his friends. Cicero's brother rallied support and received Pompey's backing by way of his friend Milo, who was served by some roughnecks of his own. Rioting ensued, and men were killed on both sides before Clodius withdrew from the Forum.

In a letter to Atticus, Cicero describes the joyous celebration of his return on the fourth day of September in 57. The public, which had treated him so rudely only a short time before, was now happy to see him again, and Cicero warmed to the occasion—as pleasant as it was rare. Soon after his return, Cicero sought to challenge Clodius by arranging a rapprochement between Pompey and the Senate. For this purpose a severe shortage of grain was a blessing in disguise. With the Senate's approval, Pompey was given an extraordinary command to oversee the entire grain market. It was like old times. Such an assignment was more suited to Pompey's talents than the complex and subtle workings of the city. He personally took charge of the operations in Sardinia, Sicily, and Africa, which resulted in plentiful supplies of grain, not only for Rome but other parts of Italy. By this action Pompey enhanced his standing in the Senate, and Cicero was hopeful that the members of the triumvirate might now become divided. But Caesar, hearing of Cicero's maneuvers, arranged a reunion with Pompey and Crassus in the spring of 56 at Luca, a town near the border between Cisalpine Gaul and Italy proper. Ostensibly, the purpose of the meeting was to publicize the harmony of their partnership, but jealousies and suspicions among the three triumvirs lingered close to the surface. Plutarch's statement, "Caesar grew great and famous with his wars in Gaul" (p. 776), says it all. Caesar was fast becoming one of the greatest war heroes in Rome's history. From time to time he mentions in his *Commentaries* the days set aside at Rome to commemorate one of his victories. These references appear casual, but an experienced eye could readily see that he was building for the future. A loyal army of experienced soldiers stood ready for his orders in Gaul. Officials of all ranks and their wives were proud to count themselves among his friends. Two hundred senators were among the crowd who came to Luca to see him. Like the manager of an elaborate spoils system, he welcomed everyone and, with an eye to the future, offered many promises. To Pompey and Crassus he promised that he would send soldiers home to vote for them when they sought the consulship for 55. They in turn agreed that his assignment in Gaul was to be extended for another five years.

Pompey and Crassus expected to be elected consuls for 55 without opposition. Cato's brother-in-law, Lucius Domitius Ahenobarbus, whose announced intention was to have Caesar recalled from Gaul, was the only candidate who refused to step aside. Later he changed his mind, after some of Pompey's partisans attacked him as he walked with Cato and a few companions. One of Ahenobarbus' friends was killed in the affray. At the same time Cato was frustrated in his bid for a praetorship. His supporters charged that bribes were being used against him. The use of a false omen to disrupt the voting was something novel. When Pompey cried that he heard thunder all agreed, and the election was postponed. On another day when Cato claimed to have heard thunder, he and his followers were driven from the Forum.

By agreement with Caesar, Crassus was given Syria as his province. He would have charge of Rome's relations with Parthia, and in view of his ambitions that meant an Eastern war. Pompey was given Africa and the two Spains, but decided to assign these areas to subordinates and remain in Rome. Again he had chosen routine tasks which had no real attraction for him, and again he neglected his duties in the city. Plutarch thinks he was now more interested in spending time with his young wife Julia, whom he sincerely loved. All the greater was the shock in 54 B.C. of her untimely death in childbirth. A newly born daughter did not long survive her. The loss of Julia broke a link between Caesar and Pompey. In the following year there was more bad news for a shaky alliance.

Death of Crassus

Crassus was impatient for a great victory. Only vanity could have impelled a sixty-year-old man, who Plutarch says "seemed older," to try to match the glory Caesar had won in Gaul. At the moment, the Parthians did not appear to threaten Rome's eastern dominions, and there was little enthusiasm for a war with them. Nevertheless Caesar and Pompey gave Crassus their support, for he had given them his. This give-and-take was what the Triumvirate was actually all about.

At the outset, Crassus' haste to leave Brundisium, a naval station in southeast Italy, cost him some ships during bad weather. His first venture in the East was to enrich himself at the expense of Mesopotamian cities which could scarcely hope to withstand him. Then he returned to Syria for the winter. There he made himself unpopular by heavy exactions from cities which were hitherto considered to be friendly. These people were easy to rob, but the time was ill spent, for the Parthians were busy preparing for an invasion. Caesar would never have given them the chance. Any available time would have been spent learning more about the geography of the region and the habits of the local people. Crassus was poorly informed about both, and when he did seek advice it came from a risky source. Ariamnes was an Arabian chieftain who had years before befriended Pompey and now relied on that connection to deceive Crassus. He told him that the Parthian king, Orodes, was fleeing eastward and Crassus must give chase immediately if he was to have his victory. This meant abandoning a route along the Euphrates River and giving up the cover of protective hills. Although his lieutenants were suspicious of this advice, Crassus decided to take it. Plutarch says he led his army "into vast plains, by a way that at first was pleasant and easy but afterwards very troublesome by reason of the depth of the sand; no tree, nor any water, and no end of this to be seen; so that they were not only spent with thirst, and the difficulty of the passage, but were dismayed with the uncomfortable prospect of not a bough, not a stream, not a hillock, not a green herb, but in fact a sea of sand, which encompassed the army with its waves" (pp. 664–65). Having brought Crassus and his army into this difficult passage, Ariamnes left under the pretext of going to mislead the enemy, but it was the Romans who were misled. Not long afterwards, the Parthians attacked with sudden fury. Crassus was undecided whether he should fight in a spread formation or a closely knit square. It did not really matter. Either way his men were at the mercy of arrows which came at them from all directions. Nor did the assault slacken, for the Parthians kept great supplies of missiles on nearby camels. The Romans were especially terrified by the small darts which struck them like hail.

Orodes had placed his noblest warrior in charge of the attack. Although Surenas was only half Crassus' age, he was a man far more experienced in the subtleties of warfare. When Crassus first sighted the Parthian army, he was unduly optimistic. Surenas kept most of his forces hidden until after his drums had done their work. "For the Parthians do not encourage themselves to war with cornets and trumpets, but with a kind of kettle-drum, which they strike all at once in various quarters. With these they make a dead, hollow noise, like the bellowing of beasts, mixed with sounds resembling thunder." Plutarch writes that the Parthians had "very correctly observed that of all our senses hearing most confounds and disorders us, and that the feelings excited through it most quickly disturb and most entirely overpower the understanding" (p. 666). That passage remains a topical message from ancient drums.

Amid the noise and excitement, the Parthians revealed their true strength and, led by the "magnificent" Surenas, they

> raised such a dust that the Romans could neither see nor speak to one another, and being driven upon one another in one close body, they were thus hit and killed, dying, not by a quick and easy death, but with miserable pains and convulsions; for writhing upon the darts in their bodies, they broke them in their wounds, and when they would by force pluck out the barbed points, they caught the nerves and veins, so that they tore and tortured themselves. Many of them died thus, and those that survived were disabled for any service . . . their hands nailed to their shields, and their feet stuck to the ground, so that they could neither fly nor fight. (p. 667)

Crassus' son, Publius, trapped and wounded, ordered an aide to kill him. The Parthians, cutting off his head, carried it on a spear to taunt the Romans. The sight of the living Crassus was more demoralizing. His efforts to rally his soldiers by recalling their great victories of the past was a sad mistake. They could only be reminded of better leaders than the one they had. Julius Caesar always had the confidence of his soldiers. Crassus had blundered into a horrible trap through ignorance and impatience. Only the coming of darkness offered any safety.

Under the cover of night, leaving the dead and dying behind, the fleeing refugees, a tired general, and the remnant of his army reached Carrhae (modern Harran). Eventually, some officers and legionaries managed to escape, but Crassus was caught and killed by Surenas' bodyguard. His head and right hand were cut off and sent to Orodes. Plutarch writes of a bizarre postscript to this disaster. He says that an actor amused the Parthian king by using the head of Crassus for the severed head of Pentheus while reciting lines from Euripides' *Bacchae*.

Later, in a fit of jealousy, Orodes murdered the triumphant Surenas, and the king was in turn strangled by his own son. But these men are cardboard figures compared to the once likeable and at the last pitiable Crassus. Before the final battle, we see an aging Roman trying to carry on. At a sacrifice, his hands shook and he lost hold of the entrails. Quickly he said to those around him, "See what it is to be an old man; but I shall hold my sword fast enough" (p. 663). He was finished then. Caesar, in his place, would have faced the fact.

XI

Julius Caesar:
Alone at the Top

The First Triumvirate was dead with Crassus. Now who would be heir to the power it represented—Caesar or Pompey? It was soon evident that if the Senate were to choose, it would be Pompey. A man was preferable to a superman. From Pompey there was less to fear. His weaknesses endeared him to the leaders of the Senate. Had he been an autocrat at heart, he would not have so neglected the management of Rome that by 53 B.C. near anarchy was a threat to all.

Cato was among those who had their differences with Pompey, but he too considered Caesar far more dangerous. It would be easy to come to terms with Pompey. He was warned that "he was setting Caesar upon his own shoulders, who would shortly grow too weighty for him" (Plutarch, p. 942). Cato's overture was a complete reversal of his former position. As usual, he insisted that he did what was in the best interest of the state.

It is not certain exactly when Pompey began to drift away from his arrangement with Caesar so as to become again the champion of the Senate. Perhaps he was not sure himself. His new relationship with the hard-eyed Cato was not easy to sustain.

Pompey on the one hand ordered magistrates not to send messages to the courts on behalf of their friends, and on the other hand did precisely that himself. There sat Cato among the jurymen, holding his hands to his ears for fear of hearing what Pompey had written.

Cato was enough encouraged by recent events to stand for the consulship himself. There are various suggestions as to why he was defeated in an unusually quiet election. Perhaps his zeal in preventing bribery had cost too many men a petty profit, and they resented it. Cicero thought Cato lost because he would not make any promises to the public which, though compromising and even dishonest, were nevertheless expected. With characteristic candor, Cato said that he had been defeated because the people did not like him. He was probably right. Neither he nor Cicero, nor even Pompey for that matter, possessed the personal magnetism of Julius Caesar.

Cato repeatedly attacked Caesar on the floor of the Senate in an effort to counteract the glowing reports about his successes in Gaul. Some senators agreed that Caesar was more dangerous to Rome than the barbarians he was fighting. But such talk was nonsense to the general public. Ordinary citizens were repeatedly told by Clodius that Caesar's critics were jealous of his success and anxious to preserve the power of their own clique. Clodius also outbid Pompey for the favor of the poor by sponsoring a law enacted in the Tribal Assembly for the distribution of free food. Whenever and wherever Clodius spoke, passions were aroused and trouble was close at hand. To keep Pompey from maintaining order in the city served Caesar's cause. Certainly, by comparison, Caesar's triumph in Gaul looked better than Pompey's management of Rome. The man who came to Pompey's aid was Titus Milo, a staunch friend of Cicero. During the fifties, Milo had served as a tribune and a praetor. He was Pompey's most loyal supporter from the time they had joined forces to bring Cicero home. Milo was a man who did not shrink from giving Clodius some of his own medicine. Hired toughs exchanged blow for blow with rival gangs in the streets.

One of Clodius' devices for irritating Pompey was to instruct mobs to shout Pompey's name over and over whenever Clodius asked who was responsible for some recent calamity. This inane trick made Pompey uncomfortable wherever he went in the city. Although he was angered by the chanting, there was little he could do about it. For a time he simply stayed home, and let Milo's men bloody the mouths of the opposition.

The turmoil reached a climax early in 52 B.C. Milo and his bodyguard encountered Clodius with some of his followers on the Appian Way outside Rome. Fighting broke out and Clodius was wounded. Milo ordered him killed. The uproar which followed plunged the city into wild disorder. Clodius' wife Fulvia joined the tribunes in harangues which kept the mood of their followers at fever pitch. Dio writes: "They took up the body of Clodius and carried it into the Senate-house, laid it out properly, and then after heaping up a pyre out of the benches, burned both the corpse and the building" (XL. 2–3). They would have burned down Milo's house too, had it not been defended by his partisans, including some equestrians and senators. So the fighting went on. A strong hand was needed. Since Pompey was at his best on short-term assignments, the Senate decided that he should be sole consul for 52 in order to quiet things down. Without having to consult with a colleague, he would have free rein to suppress the hired gangs of hoodlums, who roamed the streets on behalf of their patrons and drove decent citizens to cover. Even Cato supported the Senate's decision as being required by the times. Since it was exactly the kind of honor which Pompey cherished, he gave Cato profuse thanks for his backing. Not unexpectedly, Cato made the sour reply that he sought to serve Rome, not Pompey.

Special courts were set up to try those responsible for the recent disorders. Milo's guilt was so patent that even Cicero, who intended to defend him, was at a loss for words. When he sat down Milo was quickly convicted. In spite of the high feeling against him, he was only sent into exile at Massilia (moder Marseilles), where he could at least enjoy the mullets. And he thanked Cicero for the unusual silence which made it possible.

Caesar in Gaul

Caesar knew how easily the Gauls were excited by the slightest news of any trouble the Romans might be having among themselves. When they heard about the murder of Clodius and the continuing disorders in Rome, another and more serious uprising occurred. But the Gauls underestimated Caesar. They guessed that he would be too concerned about events in the capital to return for another campaign. He came back in the dead of winter, with his men clearing the way even where there were six-foot snowdrifts. When he arrived, he found that the Gauls had at last found a hero around whom they could rally. The young Vercingetorix was a fiery warrior with a surprising talent for public speaking and a savage temper. Caesar had heard about his discipline: "Serious cases were punished with torture and the stake, while those guilty in a less degree were sent home without their ears or perhaps with one eye gouged out, to serve as a warning to others of the stern penalties a delinquent might expect" (p. 118).

In spite of the fact that the Romans had been fighting for six years in Gaul, all would have been lost had not Caesar persevered in 52. He defeated Vercingetorix three times in the region of Aurelianum (modern Orleans) in north central Gaul. His enraged enemy then punished everybody with a scorched-earth policy. Caesar was again reminded of how tenuous was his hold on Gaul, and a short time later, in the south central region, he received a severe setback at Gergovia. Ironically, the eagerness of his own troops spelled trouble. Gergovia was a town-fortress strategically situated on high ground. After Caesar had begun the siege, he changed his mind and decided to withdraw before he was himself attacked by encircling tribes. Lest it appear, however, that he was unduly worried or about to flee in panic, he ordered a limited attack on the walls, but once begun he could not get it stopped. His officers obeyed but his men did not, and so suffered heavy casualties.

During the retreat from Gergovia, Caesar's position was more precarious than at any time since his arrival in Gaul. Even his old friends the Aedui were in open revolt and urging others to join them. By killing hostages which Caesar had given them to guard, they broke their ties with the Romans completely. They were even willing to take orders from Vercingetorix, whom they had previously scorned.

Caesar gathered all his forces. He sent to Narbonensis for more recruits, and he was now even willing to employ German cavalry as mercenaries against the powerful Gallic horsemen. Vercingetorix, after his cavalry had been routed in a large-scale engagement, took refuge within the fortress at Alesia in northeast Gaul. Caesar established eight camps around the hillsite. His elaborate plans for keeping the Gauls penned in meant that Alesia would be the decisive battle. The enemy sent fast horsemen to urge their fellow tribesmen to surround and attack the Romans from the other side. Vercingetorix calculated that his supplies could last for a month if rationed and he was satisfied to wait out the Romans. Caesar kept on building siege towers.

When the Roman position was attacked simultaneously by those under siege on the one side and newly gathered troops on the other, Caesar was prepared. "The enemy were hurled back, and as their mounted divisions fled, the archers were cut off and slaughtered. The rest of our horses galloped up from other parts of the field, and chased the fleeing squadrons right up to their camp, giving them no chance to rally. Vercingetorix's men re-entered the town, bitterly disappointed and almost in despair" (p. 153). Two days later, there was another effort to penetrate the elaborate Roman defenses, but this too failed. Vercingetorix saw his forces defeated a third time and knew that it was hopeless to try again. Although insisting that he had championed the war for all the Gauls rather than for selfish ends, he was willing to be executed by the native chieftains if they considered he deserved to be punished for this final humiliation. The defeated Gauls asked Caesar what to do and he told them that their most prominent leaders, including Vercingetorix, must be handed over to him and the weapons of the Gauls also given up. The best Gallic effort had come close but was not enough. The Aedui returned to the fold like disobedient children. In 46 B.C., after Caesar celebrated his Gallic triumph, Vercingetorix was executed.

The rest of the story in Gaul was an anticlimax, and less important events were related by Aulus Hirtius. Much of what he wrote was told to him by Caesar, whom he greatly admired. In fact, he was rather self-conscious about his role as a collaborator. In a prefatory letter he made a graceful aside: "But here I am, collecting evidence to excuse the comparison of myself with Caesar, and thereby proving my own arrogance in imagining that anyone is likely to compare us!" (p. 158).

Hirtius described Caesar's success in discouraging further trouble during 51. By marching swiftly against individual tribes he made each of them too concerned about their own safety to join in any general engagement. They rarely knew he was coming, because his strict orders forbidding fires along the way eliminated the smoke by which the Gauls were usually alerted. To prevent further problems, Caesar also eliminated certain trouble-makers among the tribal leaders. The assassination of a chieftain during a conference was a useful tool for keeping the peace. So, apparently was cruelty, when it was used to set an example. After the successful siege of Uxellodunum, all who had defended this town had their hands cut off and became a widespread advertisement of Caesar's irritation with continued resistance. Finally it was over. The Gauls were tired and quelled by fear. No significant engagements were recorded for 50 B.C.

The Opposition in Rome

Pompey in the past two years had solidified his position in the capital. On balance, in 52, he had given Rome a good year's service in restoring at least a deceptive calm. His own behavior was so natural, even nonchalant, as to dispel the notion that he was scheming for greater power. Certainly a man with a plan would have avoided Pompey's clumsiness. First, he married the widow of Crassus' son, a girl young enough to be his daughter. Plutarch says his celebration of the event was sadly out of tune with the somberness of the times. With a business-as-usual air, Pompey also went out of his way to do favors for his friends, both in and out of the courts. He flattered his father-in-law by inviting him to share his unusual consulship for the final five months of the term.

It was what Pompey did for himself which set the stage for a civil war. He arranged to have his command in Africa and the two Spains extended for another four years. The Senate, in ratifying the request, seemed to give Pompey a vote of confidence. Cato led the faction which blocked any similar favor for Caesar, who had also asked for an extension. Caesar needed the time so he could seek the consulship for 48 without having to leave office. He also asked to be excused from the requirement that he appear personally in Rome during the campaign, and that much was granted under a law of 52. Pompey spoke in favor of these requests, but he did not fight for them. In fact, he gave the impression of having spoken only for the record.

When the Senate ordered both Caesar and Pompey to contribute a legion apiece to the war with Parthia, Caesar lost two. He would have to send the one he had previously borrowed from Pompey along with one of his own. When they arrived, in 50 B.C., the consul Gaius Claudius Marcellus cancelled the Parthian order and turned both legions over to Pompey. Hirtius wrote: "That there was a conspiracy against Caesar was now undeniable"

(p. 183). But Caesar was not surprised to hear that the legions had remained in Italy. He had made certain that they would remember him, no matter where they were, by paying them handsomely before they left his service.

Caesar, in his *Commentaries* on the civil wars, said that he repeatedly sought a reconciliation with Pompey. It is not surprising that he wanted to justify his own position. He claimed that constitutional regulations were being manipulated in Pompey's favor; yet he doubted that this was being done for Pompey's sake. He recognized that a strong party led by Cato opposed both partners of the old triumvirate, and sought to use them one against the other. Pompey would be left to the mercy of the Senate if Caesar was ruined. Why should Pompey submit to senators whom they had both opposed in the past? Caesar decided that it was because he could not endure an equal. Or was it that he feared he would not be an equal? Although Pompey was older than Caesar, he may well have guessed that he would always be a junior partner. So, he wrapped himself in the mantle of a just cause and talked about "the defense of liberty." His recent role as a triumvir gave the slogan a hollow ring.

Cicero's Agony

The time had come to choose sides, and Cicero agonized over the choice. He had recently returned to Rome from a tour of duty in 51 B.C. as governor in Cilicia. His appointment had resulted from a new law which forbade ex-consuls from serving as governors until five years had elapsed after their consulships. Cicero, who had been consul in 63, was asked to fill one of the numerous vacancies. He prepared himself by reading everything available on Cilicia. His administration was as clean as a hound's tooth. No gifts or favors were accepted even though such gratuities were now commonly winked at. A few victorious encounters with mountain tribesmen prompted him to feel he was entitled to more than a decree of thanksgiving when he returned home. However, few agreed with his exaggerated account of what had happened. Cicero had other disappointments. Soon after his return, he divorced his wife Terentia after thirty years of marriage. He had never liked her bad temper and was now disgruntled with the way she had handled his property while he was in Cilicia. When he remarried at sixty, it was to a girl, Publilia, as young as his own daughter, but much wealthier. The gossip which followed was not necessary to make the marriage unhappy. Cicero loved his daughter Tullia most of all, and when she died he was unconsolable. There followed a separation from his second wife. The marriage had lasted seven months.

There is not much to be said about Cicero's son and namesake until after the great orator's death. In his youth, he seems to have sat in his father's shadow and drunk more than his share of wine, but those were his student days. Later, he performed well as a cavalry officer, was a consul in 30 B.C., and then a successful administrator in the provinces. He had had his first knowledge of provincial affairs at fourteen when his father took him to Cilicia during his governorship.

That Cicero remained a dominant figure in Rome is shown by Caesar's hope for his support or at least his neutrality. Cicero chose Pompey. His enemies would say it was because Pompey could be controlled, and Cicero had the most to gain from him. His friends would say that Cicero felt Pompey offered the least danger to the state.

Cicero was a man of the middle class all his life. He opposed the selfish interests of a senatorial oligarchy and the selfish interests of Populares, who had their way in the Tribal Assembly. When one side appeared to have the upper hand, he leaned toward the other. He was very conscious of a decadent ruling class which insisted on its right to rule regardless of whether it ruled well or not. The demagogues of Clodius' stripe were even more frightening to him, and most of the time their activities kept him estranged from the people.

The old Roman days of honor and virtue were almost beyond recall to all save men like Cicero, who, however, realized that the men of the nobility, either through corruption by wealth and power or poor education, could no longer provide the necessary leadership. It would be hard to find a group of people willing to forego their own personal or class interests to save the state. But to find one man willing to do so seemed possible. In an essay, *De Republica,* which summed up his thoughts on government, Cicero's central argument was that final authority should rest in an assembly led by an enlightened man who sought not his own but the best interests of all. In agreement with Plato and Aristotle, his ideal government would be one directed by a godlike individual whose wisdom and self-sacrifice would inspire men of all stations to accept his guidance. At one time or another, Cicero must have had Caesar or Pompey in mind for the job, but came to despair of them both, and in the final analysis might have had to admit that he was his own best candidate. Yet while he speculated, worried, and wrote letters, events were catching up with him.

Civil War

The open opposition to Caesar by the consuls and Pompey's followers, if not Pompey himself, forestalled any solution of the crisis. A motion in the Senate that Caesar be ordered to give up his army or face a charge of treason brought on a tense debate, with feelings running so high that a vote was delayed until the following day. Then, according to Caesar, "The Senate was packed with consuls' friends, Pompey's relations, and all those who bore me a grudge; with the result that the weaker members were awed into silence, those who could not make up their minds had it made up for them, and the majority were too scared to express an opinion" (p. 186). Caesar again and again insisted that the majority of the senators favored his offer to disband his army if Pompey would do the same, but were coerced by a spiteful and selfish few who put their own ambitions ahead of the welfare of all and so forced a civil war. According to Caesar, these were men like Lentulus, badly in debt, and Scipio, Pompey's father-in-law, who were looking for the gift of lucrative provincial commands from a victorious Pompey. One of the consuls in 49 B.C., Gaius Claudius Marcellus, whose cousin of the same name had been consul in 50, was unalterably opposed to dealing with Caesar except on the strictest terms. On January 7, the Senate called upon the officials of the state "to provide for the public safety." Marcellus asked Pompey to take command of the government's forces and was supported by Cato, who successfully blocked Cicero's efforts toward a compromise solution. The call to arms made Pompey the man of the hour. Cato was shocked to learn that he was not ready. Caesar was. He had rallied his forces with blunt talk. In the time-honored fashion of the Roman politician, he proclaimed himself the defender of tradition. Beside him stood the spokesmen of the people, two tribunes of the plebs, Quintus Cassius and Marcus Antonius, better known as Mark Anthony. They had seen Caesar's enemies fomenting hysteria in Rome. Should

Caesar submit to unlawful men who sought his destruction or should he defend himself?

On January 10, 49, Caesar stood in a thoughtful pose at the Rubicon, but not for long. This small river, which flows into the Adriatic, was part of the boundary between Caesar's province of Cisalpine Gaul and Italy proper—the boundary between loyalty and a treasonable invasion of the homeland. Once across that river, he never stopped and in two months swept through the entire peninsula. Many units previously loyal to Pompey defected to Caesar as he moved southward.

Pompey left Rome on January 17 and went directly to Apulia, the heel region of the Italian boot, where the two legions obtained from Caesar on the pretext of war with Parthia were awaiting their orders. At the moment, his strongest arm was a navy, which enabled him to transport his army to Greece. He was ill-prepared for a fight with Caesar's Gallic veterans.

Caesar entered Rome only days after Pompey left and expropriated the treasury left behind. By the ninth of March he had reached Brundisium, but without ships he could not follow Pompey to Greece. Actually, he was more worried about the strength of Pompey's forces in Spain which might be a threat to Gaul and Italy; so he turned his attention to what was behind him before moving ahead.

Pompey was never safe from his supporters. A majority of the Senate went with him to Greece; he never lacked for advice. It was like a modern American general's having Congress with him overseas. Unfortunately, the man who could have advised him best was now his enemy.

Cato was supposedly supporting Pompey but not without strain. In the first place, he thought of Caesar as a creature of Pompey's making. Moreover, it perturbed him greatly that, although Pompey had answered questions confidently in the Senate, he had not really been ready for war. Cato's assignment had been to keep Sicily loyal; but lacking the necessary troops, he gave it up and joined Pompey in Dyrrachium (modern Durres), a seaport on the Adriatic coast of what is now Albania.

When Cato had heard that Pompey had abandoned Italy, he was greatly alarmed about the future. What had happened to Pompey's magic? During the period of his extraordinary commands in Spain, against the pirates and in the East, all had gone very well. Now, when he was entrusted with saving the Republic, he seemed less sure of himself. But even Cato was not sure that a decisive victory over Caesar was the answer. There was still hope that a clash might be avoided. He abhorred the thought of Romans killing Romans. Pompey's realization that Cato supported him only out of fear of Caesar was no comfort. He decided not to give him charge over his navy or any large complement of men. It was a precaution. If Caesar was defeated, Cato might use any forces at his disposal to turn on Pompey.

Although Pompey was obviously caught off guard by Caesar's whirlwind campaign, he had made one prearrangement. That concerned Massilia. Caesar had apparently hoped that this strategic city would at least remain neutral. But a small contingent of ships loyal to Pompey arrived first and bolstered the support Pompey claimed from members of the nobility there. Caesar, en route to Spain, stopped long enough to order the building of siege towers. He then went on leaving the work in the hands of one of his lieutenants, Trebonius.

The Spanish provinces were under the command of three generals loyal to Pompey. Caesar's men knew they were in for heavy fighting. They had not anticipated an acute shortage of grain and miserable weather. The floods which swept away their bridges also drowned their chances. As soon as the bad news reached Rome, there began an exodus of officials headed for Greece, eager to assure Pompey that they had been with him from the beginning. Later, Caesar delighted in referring to those who had put such small faith in him and lived to regret it. His luck never stayed bad for long.

Before long, Caesar caught the combined armies of Afranius and Petreius in a trap, and there was no way out except by abject surrender. Caesar was extremely generous. He only asked that they disband their armies and cease all resistance to him. His clemency greatly impressed the captured soldiers and, more important, their relatives at home. Caesar counted on that.

Marcus Terentius Varro, the third commander in Spain, was impressed with how many cities in western Spain were willing to welcome the victorious Caesar. When one of his own legions deserted, he anxiously turned over the other one. Caesar saw to it that all the local inhabitants who had had their property confiscated because of their early and open support of him would now enjoy restitution.

With Spain secure, Caesar headed back to Massilia and arrived in time to preside over the surrender of the city. But his victorious return to Rome was marred by bad news from North Africa. Curio, who as a tribune had been one of Caesar's staunchest supporters, had taken an army to Africa. There he had faced the governor, Publius Attius Varus, who favored Pompey, and his ally King Juba of Numidia, whose father had been a friend of Pompey. The wily Juba had tricked the Romans into a trap. Curio died with his legions, which were totally wiped out.

Eventually, Caesar would have to go to Africa to face Juba and a host of Pompeians. For the present, there were pressing matters in Rome. He was made dictator and presided over the elections, in which he was given the consulship for 48. This was what he had asked for in the first place; it was a long way round but he had made it. Before giving up his dictatorship on December 13, he sought to ease the strain between debtors and creditors in Rome. All property was to be assessed at prewar value. This was reasonable, and debts were thus more likely to be paid. He also sought and received the support of the Tribal Assembly in cancelling the judgments made by Pompeian courts against persons accused of bribery. Caesar claimed that these men had actually only been guilty of giving him their support too soon.

Rome was never quiet in Caesar's absence, and he was always anxious to remain there, but he could not settle down until Pompey and his partisans had been brought to terms. It was almost a year since his war with Pompey had begun and there had not yet been a single direct engagement with him. On January 5, 48, Caesar crossed the Adriatic with seven legions, and managed to land safely at Palaeste in Epirus. It was the only harbor not held by Pompey's fleet, which was spread out along the coast.

Caesar continued to send messages to Pompey with the hope of negotiating a settlement. One note reminded his old colleague that they both had suffered severe losses. Pompey had abandoned Italy, and Caesar had lost the entire army under Curio in Africa. Why not reach a settlement while hopes on both sides remained high and the scales had not yet been tipped one way or the other? Caesar again proposed that they disband their armies and be obedient to the Senate and the Assembly. In effect, this meant that Pompey, embraced by the Senate, would be at the mercy of Caesar, who was enormously popular with the people of Rome. Then there was Pompey's pride. He was reported to have said: "I care nothing for life, or even for my country's welfare, if the world is going to believe that I owe both to Caesar. And the world cannot believe otherwise as long as it is thought that I left Italy only to return at his victorious summons" (Caesar, p. 253).

Early in April, Caesar decided to deprive Pompey of his principal supply center at Dyrrachium. He led his men at top speed in a nighttime march and reached the city ahead of Pompey, who had been fooled by Caesar's trick of first marching in one direction and then suddenly shifting to another. Both sides encamped near the city and in the days ahead contested for the heights nearby.

At this time Caesar, having lost his first defectors to Pompey's camp, took pains to explain how this could happen. Two of his cavalry officers were Allobrogians, who had served him well but had mistreated their own kinsmen, holding back their pay and denying them a fair share of the booty. Caesar tried to smooth over the matter. He valued the officers as first-rate soldiers and attributed their behavior to their success in his service and a "short-sighted pride . . . so characteristic of uncivilized peoples" (p. 276), which caused them to look down on their own followers. But Caesar could not protect these men from the angry remarks of other soldiers, and they soon felt they would be safer in Pompey's camp. There they were received with a great show. Later, at Pharsalus, after a pre-battle skirmish, Caesar mentioned that one of these officers was found among the enemy dead. He could never forget them.

The information which the Allobrogians had given Pompey about the weak spots in Caesar's defenses was far more serious than the loss of two officers. Pompey immediately took the offensive. In the action which followed, first one side and then the other had the upper hand, but in the end Caesar said of his army: "Not one man stood his ground." Only Pompey's hesitation to pursue, fearing an ambush, saved Caesar's army from annihilation. It was a rare setback, and all the more provoking in that Caesar considered the loss to be in no way his own fault. He told his army so in plain language: "You may attribute your failure to any one you like, but not to me. My tactics were perfectly sound: we gained our objective, overcame the enemy's resistance, and drove them from their position. I do not know what it was that snatched an apparently certain victory from our hands: it may have been your own fear, or an error of judgment on someone's part, or perhaps the intervention of Fortune herself" (p. 283). That having been said, the ever unabashed Caesar then predicted

that victory would be theirs nonetheless. His confidence was
never in doubt. There were those beside him who would need
time to recover theirs.

Being short of food, Caesar marched to Thessaly. Late in
July, 48, he arrived at a site near Pharsalus and set up camp. He
had hardly dared to hope that Pompey would follow him, and
thus lose the advantage of his seapower near the coast. But
Pompey did just that. His decision decided the war.

There had been much division of opinion in Pompey's camp
about what to do. His soldiers, encouraged by their recent success,
were anxious for a battle. Pompey felt that time was on his side and
wanted only to besiege and harass Caesar, without the agony and
risk of a battle. It was a cruel fate to be caught between Caesar and
those in his own camp whom he distrusted. But Pompey could not
hold out against the pressure of close associates and the numerous
magistrates in his camp. Certain men surrounding Pompey were so
sure of victory they had already sent payments to Rome for houses
near the Forum in anticipation of politics as usual in the near future.
Against his better judgment Pompey was persuaded to fight a set
battle. That was exactly what Caesar wanted.

In Pompey's camp, too little time was given to considering
how formidable an embattled Julius Caesar could be. He was busy
preparing surprises for them. Because his cavalry was badly outnumbered, he trained some young and daring javelin-throwers to
coordinate their attack with the horsemen. He gambled that the
enemy cavalry would be unprepared to respond to these units
working together. His plan worked exactly the way he wanted it
to. Pompey had massed his cavalry on the left wing to strike at
the much publicized Tenth Legion. His battle plan was based on
the superiority of his cavalry. It was to attack the right wing of
Caesar's line and, smashing through with its greater superiority,
to come around behind the enemy's position. To counter this
move, Caesar hid six cohorts behind the Tenth Legion and
ordered them not to move until Pompey's horsemen had established contact. Then, rather than hurl their spears, they were to
run forward and "strike them upwards into the eyes and faces of
the enemy"—an ingenious strategy but this time against fellow
Romans, not Gauls. Plutarch has a pensive comment:

> Only some few of the noblest Romans, together with certain Greeks
> there present, standing as spectators without the battle, seeing the

armies now ready to join, could not but consider in themselves to what a pass private ambition and emulation had brought the empire. Common arms and kindred ranks drawn up under the selfsame standards, the whole flower and strength of the same single city here meeting in collision with itself, offered plain proof how blind and how mad a thing human nature is when once possessed with any passion; for if they had been desirous only to rule, and enjoy in peace what they had conquered in war, the greatest and best part of the world was subject to them both by sea and land. (p. 790)

Caesar estimated Pompey's forces at 45,000 men and his own as 22,000. On the ninth of August, 48 B.C., the two armies were drawn up facing each other, with Caesar holding a position opposite to Pompey. The morning air gave fair warning that it was going to be an unusually hot day. Although Pompey's forces outnumbered Caesar's two to one, the battle hinged on the single maneuver which Caesar had planned. Momentum was important to him. He wrote that "Nature herself has implanted in every man as it were a spark of enthusiasm which is fanned to flame in the excitement of battle, and which a general must try to keep alive rather than to quench" (p. 293). On signal, his horsemen on the extreme right drew back and let the six cohorts rush forward to attack Pompey's cavalry by ramming their javelins into their faces. Those assaulted whirled around and fled as Caesar had predicted they would. Attacked from two sides, Pompey's exposed left wing collapsed and with it Pompey's pride. He returned dazed to his camp, and then fled from his own headquarters as Caesar's men closed in. Many of Pompey's supporters were caught. With overconfidence they had decorated their tents in advance; Plutarch says there was "a great slaughter" amid a festive scene.

Caesar usually took full credit for his own accomplishments. He did not credit the gods with any favors. Once, during a sea battle, a sudden shift in the wind had prompted him to comment on "the fickle character of chance," but otherwise his point of view was entirely practical. Yet, perhaps as much out of custom as anything else, he did record on this occasion the strange happenings which men of ancient times usually associated with great events. "It was established after a careful reckoning of dates that on the very day of Pharsalus a statue of Victory, which stood facing that of Minerva in her temple at Elis, turned of its own accord and faced the main entrance to the shrine" (p. 300). Such stories were among the prizes given to the successful, and Caesar accepted his without comment.

Pompey made his way to the sea, and there, just beyond the Vale of Tempe, spent the night in a humble cottage. The next day he was taken aboard a Roman merchant ship by a captain who Plutarch says had dreamed that he would rescue Pompey. At Mytilene, Pompey was joined by his wife Cornelia and their young son. When the citizens of the city sought to hail him, he told them "to be obedient to the conqueror and fear not, for that Caesar was a man of great goodness and clemency" (p. 794). Sorrowful and depressed, Pompey had little hope of recovering his former position. Then news came that Cato had managed to reach Africa with loyal forces. The fight against Caesar could go on. There was the chance of a comeback. Pompey needed a place to rest and to make new plans. He and his senatorial supporters had little choice about where to seek refuge, for places like Rhodes or Antioch in Syria were quick to favor Caesar by refusing admission to his enemies. Egypt seemed a likely choice; Pompey sailed to Pelusium on an inlet of the Mediterranean at the eastern end of the Delta. The young Ptolemy XIII was expected to show some gratitude for how well Pompey had treated his father. The king, however, was not old enough to have escaped the intrigues of his experienced ministers, who took it upon themselves to decide Pompey's fate. When they heard that he was coming, they were faced with an obvious dilemma. To welcome Pompey would offend Caesar and to send Pompey away would mean risking his revenge on a later day. It did not take the king's wily advisers long to decide what to do. Pompey would be welcomed and then murdered. "A dead man cannot bite." They thought that Caesar would be pleased.

On the following day, the twenty-eighth of September, the day after Pompey's fifty-eighth birthday, he left Cornelia and his son aboard a galley and went ashore in a rowboat with a few companions and an Egyptian escort. He was now at the mercy of foreign soldiers and nervously tried to make small talk. When there was little response, he sat quietly studying the brief speech he intended to make when he landed. His wife and friends anxiously watched his progress. They were encouraged to see the Egyptian officialdom move forward to greet him. Pompey saw them too and that was all. A sword struck him from behind, and as he fell other blows came from both sides. Those nearby could hear Pompey groan. Everybody heard Cornelia scream.

Pompey had had neither the mind nor the spirit of a tyrant; yet this was a tyrant's death—a cruel and undeserved fate. The petty men who had planned his murder soon discovered their mistake. On his arrival, Caesar was horrified to see Pompey's head. He would have forgiven his old friend and would have sought to patch things up. Caesar considered the malicious ministers at Ptolemy's court akin to his own enemies in the Roman Senate. Two of the officials responsible for Pompey's murder were put to death. The rest fled for their lives. Pompey's corpse was burned where he fell on the shore. Later, on a quieter day, Cornelia took his ashes home to Rome.

Caesar in Egypt

Following the climactic struggle with Pompey, Caesar's adventures in Egypt would have seemed almost ridiculous, had he not been short of men and supplies and in serious danger. The ministers of Ptolemy XIII were plotting against him.

If Caesar had to sit up all night to save his life, he at least had lively company. Cleopatra was one reason for the predicament of a man who rarely took risks. Plutarch says she was brought to him secretly wrapped in a bedspread. He was greatly amused. She was less than half his age, but possessed an unusual charm, and from the outset Caesar shared more with Cleopatra than the same enemies. Before long it was decided that she should be a queen and rule jointly with her brother, Ptolemy XIII. For this purpose, Caesar fought the Alexandrian War, 48–47 B.C., which nearly cost him his life.

It is surprising that barbers play so small a part in history, given the wealth of their information. It was Caesar's barber who relayed to him the details of a plot on his life. Caesar struck first, killing Pothinus, the ranking eunuch of the Egyptian court. He was then besieged by Ptolemy's general Achillas, whose overwhelming forces made an unusual escape plan necessary. To keep from being trapped in the harbor, Caesar set his own ships afire as a diversion. The docks were burned too, and a library which stood nearby was also said to have been destroyed. Amid the smoke and confusion, a daring Caesar swam to safety. On a later day, he defeated the Egyptians in a battle which left Ptolemy XIII missing and presumably drowned in the Nile.

Cleopatra was now safe as a co-ruler with her younger brother, Ptolemy XIV, and she and Caesar celebrated by taking a vacation floating on the Nile. They might have floated all the way to Ethiopia had not Caesar's soldiers appeared impatient. With more pressing matters at hand, his dalliance does seem extraordinary. The histories of democracies lack such casual episodes, but Caesar was on his own time. When Cleopatra had a son she named him Caesarion. Not everyone believed the paternity, but enough did to make the child's existence significant, and later, after Caesar was gone, his death mandatory.

From Egypt, Caesar marched through Palestine and Syria, receiving honors and bestowing them as befitted a conqueror. Only Asia Minor remained a trouble spot. Pharnaces, a son of Mithridates, had successfully defied the Romans in taking Bithynia and Cappadocia. But the natives had no sooner been reminded of his father's previous performance than Caesar arrived. The so-called Second Battle of Zela (Lucullus had fought there earlier) has never attracted as much attention as Caesar's laconic description of his victory: "I came, I saw, I conquered." The phrase was not only matter-of-fact but carried with it an air of nonchalance which unsettled even his friends. After the defeat of Pharnaces, Caesar returned to Rome late in 47 for a brief stay. Before the year was over, he had crossed to Sicily en route to North Africa for an assault on the Pompeian forces gathered there.

Cato was on his way to Egypt when he learned about Pompey's death from Sextus, the younger of Pompey's two grown sons. Those loyal to Pompey's name were now assembling in the province of Africa, where they could count on the support of the neighboring King Juba, the most powerful man in the region. Unfortunately, at the moment the cause was without a leader. Quintus Metellus Scipio, Pompey's father-in-law, Attius Varus, his choice as governor of Africa, and Labienus, the best of Pompey's generals, were often at odds with each other. Cato preferred to see Scipio take the command and at first supported him. In return, he was given charge of Utica, which had a strategic value in the fight for North Africa. Afterwards, these two quarreled bitterly over the best policy to follow. Cato hoped that time would retard Caesar's momentum and wanted to avoid a showdown with him for as long as possible. Scipio would not wait.

King Juba's skilled horsemen were expected to be an advantage. In the initial skirmishes they were, but then Caesar's army struck three allied camps near Thapsus with lightning speed, and his daring gave him the crucial victory. Both Scipio and Juba were defeated. Several captured officials who had fled Italy with Pompey killed themselves without waiting for Caesar's mercy. They knew that Caesar's clemency was not for everybody.

Cato now stood alone and refused to surrender. There was still the hope that an uprising under the younger Pompey in Spain or trouble in Rome would prompt Caesar to leave North Africa. Cato tried to rally the leading citizens of Utica, mostly Roman businessmen, to stand firm if an assault did come. At first, his patriotic oratory kept them nominally loyal, but second thoughts about their risk turned them around. These men were primarily interested in doing business under whatever government might be established. Many of them considered Caesar to be the best bet. Those senators who had fled to Utica were Cato's staunchest supporters, but now they felt themselves endangered. The Utican population was mostly Carthaginian, and they too were leaning toward Caesar. These factions now engaged in noisy quarrels. Cato's claim that he was growing deaf could not excuse him from knowing it for very long. The city was doomed by its division.

Preparations were hurriedly made for the escape of the senators and all others who dared not face Caesar. The gate toward the sea remained open for that purpose. Cato and his son and a few close companions remained in the city. When they gathered together for the evening meal, all eyes were on Cato. It seemed certain that he too would refuse to face Caesar, but no one dared to voice his thoughts.

That night Cato missed his sword and realized that it had purposely been removed from his room. He angrily insisted that it be returned and chided his son that he had dared to keep his father from having command over himself. Before this incident, and then again afterwards, he read the *Phaedo,* Plato's discourse on the soul. Toward dawn, Cato's inquiry about the safety of those who had fled the city caused his friends to think that he might now be free from any thoughts of self-destruction. But the good news that his friends had escaped was all he was waiting for. He dismissed his aide and, with the same strong will by which he had lived, took his sword in hand and killed himself. He was forty-eight. The Uticans, for all their troubles, found the time for an impressive funeral. Plutarch says the statue they erected of Cato still stood in his own day, a century and a half later.

Caesar had lost another chance to display his clemency. He

had no more wished to have Cato dead than he had wished to have Pompey murdered. Of Cato, he said, "I grudge you your death, as you have grudged me the preservation of your life" (Plutarch, p. 959). Later, however, he often remarked how much he disliked Cato personally.

It was not from fear but from pride that Cato had committed suicide. This stubborn man refused to owe Caesar anything, even his life.

Only Spain now held out against Caesar; there Pompey's sons, Gnaeus and Sextus, stood ready to make a last stand. Before leaving Rome, Caesar was made consul a fourth time. He celebrated his recent victories with his soldiers and the Roman people. Gladiatorial shows and free entertainments offered temporary relief from the continuing wars which left the future still unsettled. If he won in Spain, there would be peace and reform. It was a close call; Caesar later admitted that he had had to fight for his life. Many of his best trained soldiers died in a furious battle which raged near Munda in southern Spain. Pompey's elder son, Gnaeus, was killed. Sextus escaped.

In four years, Caesar had triumphed in Italy, Thessaly, Egypt, Asia Minor, North Africa, and Spain. No man in armor could kill him or defeat him. After Munda he was master of the Roman world, and in the following year, 44, the Romans acclaimed him dictator for life. On the surface there was an air of reconciliation, although underneath bitter resentments still simmered. Caesar had risen to the top on the corpses of his fellow Romans. No amount of free grain, new colonies, or entertainments could heal the scars of what had been a bitter civil war. Nobody had hated Pompey or his sons. The relatives of those who had died to keep Caesar at bay would not be easy to win over. But Caesar tried. He showed respect for Pompey's name and even for the memory of Sulla, by restoring statues which his partisans had damaged. Cassius and Brutus, greatly respected for their support of Pompey, were given praetorships.

Cicero was among those whom Caesar had pardoned. In fact, in Cicero's case, a magnanimous Caesar was especially courteous and kind. The two met at Brundisium where, after Pharsalus, Cicero had waited about ten months for Caesar's return from the East. Plutarch says that Cicero was apprehensive about the meeting and perhaps feared at least some form of public humiliation. And maybe Caesar guessed this when he left his aides and took Cicero alone for a walk down a nearby road. Nobody knows what he said, but it is safe to guess he offered Cicero a pleasant future in return for his support, or at least silence, on political matters. In the days ahead Cicero produced most of his philosophical works and two of his famous writings on oratory, the *Brutus* and *Orator*.

Cicero was a better speaker than statesman and a better writer than philosopher. He is to be admired for what he wanted to do with his skills. His writings enlightened others about the wealth of guidance available in Greek literature.

Caesar displayed in peacetime the same diligence and intelligence as he had shown on the battlefield. He recognized the need for reforms in the municipal governments throughout Italy and immediately set about standardizing and streamlining cumbersome local operations. His reforms and his concern for more efficient government foreshadowed the best intentions of later rulers. There was another hint of the future in his generous bestowal of Roman citizenship on his Gallic veterans. It was a convenient device for uniting diverse peoples. One day future emperors would themselves come from the provinces.

In Rome, Caesar made plans for a Greek and Latin library to be gathered under the direction of the scholarly Varro, who had been perhaps the least enthusiastic of Pompey's generals in Spain. There were plans too for the codification of the laws and for greater government interest in education, especially by giving citizenship to Greek teachers in order to encourage them to come to Rome. Proposed construction projects were aimed at improving Rome's trade by sea, particularly by making Ostia a safe and seaworthy port. Of all his proposals, the only one Caesar lived to see was a new calendar. We still have that and July to remind us where it came from. As might be expected, his calendar did not rely on the priests whose manipulations, or lack of them, had wrought such havoc in the old system. Caesar gave the job to astronomers and mathematicians. A slight change in the calendar they devised was promulgated by Pope Gregory XIII in February, 1582, and eventually adopted in England and America in 1752.

While Caesar busied himself with solutions of current problems, the public and the politicians continued to speculate about the possibility of his becoming a king. As dictator, he held a constitutional office, but in 46 it was declared to be for ten years and now in 44 he held it for life. His enormous power made small matters loom large. A failure to stand up when approached by other dignitaries was considered an affront and part of a "kingly" attitude. It may have been that he simply did not want to be bothered. When Antony on the occasion of a public festival offered him a diadem he refused it, to the cheers of the crowd. However, Plutarch says, he was unhappy when two tribunes made a public issue of the kingship. What he really thought on the subject we will never know. He was making plans for a spring campaign against the Parthians and probably wanted to wait until his return before making a decision. At the same time he kept hearing rumors of plots against his life. It was only to be expected that he would be blamed for frustrations or injuries, real or imagined, but he did not take the talk very seriously. Even so, Plutarch has him looking around, summing up, and furnishing future playwrights with a dramatic line: "I do not like Cassius," he said, "he looks so pale."

The Romans called the fifteenth day of certain months the Ides. In 44, as the Ides of March approached, there was mounting tension. Caesar's wife, Calpurnia, sensed it both awake and in her dreams. Her anxiety almost persuaded Caesar to stay at home on a fateful day, even though he was not a superstitious man. Caesar paid only enough attention to soothsayers to make jokes about their solemn prophecies. One of them had warned him about the Ides of March. When Caesar passed, surrounded by a crowd of clients, he made a point of chiding the seer that the day had come. "But not gone," the soothsayer called after him as he made his way toward the place where the Senate was to meet. The building was one of those which Pompey had given the city. To the ancients this was fate, not irony.

As he came in, Caesar might have had a stout defender alongside him had not one of the conspirators detained Antony in conversation. The Senate stood as Caesar made his way to his seat, showing his usual impatience with the fawning subservience of petitioners asking for favors. Suddenly, someone pulled at his cloak. Casca stabbed him in the neck. Caesar was stunned and angrily grappled with his assailant. It was too late. He was trapped. As many as sixty men crowded around to attack him. The assault was so furious some of those attacking him wounded each other. The remaining senators looked on with shock, but no one moved to help. Caesar struggled, staggered, and finally fell mortally wounded at the foot of Pompey's statue. He had been stabbed twenty-three times. It was said that Caesar cried out only once during the attack. "You, too, my son?" he asked in astonishment as Brutus raised his dagger. While the line has given rise to much speculation, it is not generally believed that Brutus was an illegitimate son, but simply, in Caesar's eyes, a beloved companion. Standing over Caesar were others besides Brutus whom he had trusted. Every enemy on the battlefield had been outmatched. There was no defense against his friends.

Why was Caesar killed? Jealousy was surely part of it. There was also a genuine fear, especially on the part of men like Brutus, that Caesar's power meant the end of republican institutions. Caesar could have understood such motives, but doubtless he would have been surprised to learn how deeply others resented him for simply being the kind of man he was. A seemingly unimportant incident suggests an answer. Plutarch says that once during a battle which was going poorly Caesar caught hold of a panic-stricken standard bearer running in the opposite direction. He turned him around with the pointed instruction that "the enemy is the other way." The young man, probably frightened and embarrassed, may have laughed nervously and run on ahead. The story is typical of Caesar who, like a teacher, seemed always to be directing affairs in a world of children—chiding one, patting another—yet too far above them all to care about hurting any. To less gifted men, however, his aloofness, even if mixed with kindness, was thought to be patronizing. They could not believe that in his heart he really cared about them. Caesar never bothered to ask for another man's opinion. He lacked the tact by which a talented person might reassure others that they have worth too. Pardons, jobs, or favors did not completely satisfy the recipients' craving for attention. Nor did men he had pardoned love him for it. *Clementia* displayed the indulgence of a superior; and not all of Caesar's peers, some of them from more distinguished families than his own, were willing to acknowledge the role he gave to himself.

Caesar, at fifty-five, was a supreme egotist wrapped in his own sense of well-being and good service to the state. When the daggers were drawn against him, he was genuinely startled. For all his experience and sophistication, he had never learned how ungrateful men can be—especially those who feel ignored.

Cicero was not active in the conspiracy against Caesar, but it is hard to believe that he did not know about it. Moreover, after the deed, his enthusiastic support of the "liberators" showed his contempt for Caesar's one-man rule. Yet Mark Antony now emerged as a worse threat, for he had none of Caesar's redeeming virtues. "The tyrant is dead," Cicero said, "but the tyranny lingers on."

The Man of a Thousand Follies

During his lifetime, Mark Antony (*ca.* 83–30 B.C.) set an unenviable record for choosing the wrong friends and lovers. He is Plutarch's man of "a thousand follies." A prominent career was due to one good choice. He was unswervingly loyal to Julius Caesar, to whom he was related through his mother.

Plutarch thinks that Antony's rugged good looks and personality were advantages which helped to offset his generally poor judgment. He had a coarse boyishness about him which appealed to soldiers and courtesans alike. There was always time for playing practical jokes and laughing at one on himself. The niceties were omitted. On the contrary, he adopted a self-conscious air of casualness, as for example, in the way he dressed—"his tunic girt low about the hips." Enemies branded him as a sloppy eater and noisy drinker. Cicero called him vulgar by his very nature. Plutarch softens the picture by describing him as essentially an overgrown boy who had little time for stuffy people with their hypocritical manners—Cicero for instance.

In his early years, Antony fell in with the younger Curio and his circle of friends, who were noted for having much money and no morals. His choice of a political base was equally bad. He became a follower of Clodius, whose platform of violence was self-defeating. It was later, as a soldier, that Antony found himself. He had command of the cavalry during military campaigns in the East under the ex-consul Aulus Gabinius. His skill was crucial both in the defeat of Aristobulus, who had escaped from Rome and was then leading a Jewish rebellion, and in the restoration of Ptolemy XII to the throne of Egypt. Antony was remembered not only for taking Pelusium, but also for a rare act of political sagacity in preventing a slaughter of Egyptians by the revengeful Ptolemy.

In Rome, during the hectic days before Caesar invaded Italy, Antony, now a tribune of the plebs, was one of his outspoken defenders. He took Caesar's case directly to the people by reading letters in public which the senators had refused to hear. Eventually, the quarrel with Cato and the consuls who supported Pompey caused him to flee the city in disguise and join his hero in the north. When Caesar learned that men who favored his "just" proposals of mutual disarmament were being silenced, he knew what he had to do. Following his initial success, Caesar left Antony in charge of the Italian operation while he went to deal with Pompey's forces in Spain. Antony was a poor manager. He was insensitive about the suffering created by the war and short-tempered toward everybody except other men's wives. Caesar was embarrassed, but apparently found Antony valuable enough as a general to be endured for almost everything else.

Antony commanded the left wing at the battle of Pharsalus and shared the credit for that victory. Before leaving for Egypt, Caesar, as dictator, made him his Master of the Horse. Again, Antony ruled Rome—badly. He usually played politics as a grudge sport with little concern for issues. Antony knew how to speak, for he had studied in Greece, but his style was bombastic, in what Plurarch calls the "Asiatic taste," and lacked the steady logical quality which Roman orators used to build an argument.

Antony divorced his first wife, who was also his cousin, because he suspected her of having an affair with the tribune Dolabella, who was at the same time his political enemy. His second wife was the widow of Clodius, a strong-willed woman named Fulvia, who kept him in line. Because he disliked Dolabella, who was trying to get debts cancelled, he opposed the measure and lost favor with the common citizens. Nor did the better classes who benefited care for him. Antony went far on his wits, but such a man soon loses all his friends. His worst personal enemy was Cicero, who knew how to ruin a man's reputation, and did a better job on Antony than he had on Catiline. The cause of their enmity dated from an earlier time. Antony's stepfather, Lentulus, was one of the men Cicero had executed at the time of the Catilinarian conspiracy. Later, Cicero in his *Philippics* described Antony's revolting behavior at the height of his power. The *Second Philippic* is one of the most devastating pieces of character assassination ever written.

When Caesar returned from the East, Marcus Aemilius Lepidus, younger son of the Lepidus who had sought to overthrow the Sullan constitution, was chosen as his colleague in the consulship. Antony got the message, and for a time began to behave. But he was not really out of favor. Caesar seems to have enjoyed his company, and while he appeared to be annoyed by the way Antony played up to him, he may not have disliked it altogether.

Those who were united in the conspiracy against Caesar were divided about Antony. He was too loyal to be included in the plot, and yet to kill him would have offended Brutus, who insisted that what must be done, be done for principle. It was decided to detain Antony at the door so that he would not be present during the attack on Caesar. Ironically, in the short run, he gained the most from Caesar's death. Upon learning that Caesar was the sole target, his first reaction was to act as a conciliator. He was much praised on the one hand for winning the Senate's approval of his proposal to send Brutus and Cassius on assignments out of the city and, on the other hand, for confirming all that Caesar had done. But if the conspirators had been unwilling to see the city ruled by Caesar, would they accept Antony? The calm which accompanied the shock of Caesar's death gave way to the hysteria which surrounded his funeral. Antony saw his chance. He bitterly denounced Brutus and Cassius and their co-conspirators. They fled from the wrath of the plebs who adored Caesar. Antony took the helm, briefly. He had scarcely begun to busy himself with Caesar's property, with the papers which Calpurnia had turned over to him, with making appointments to offices, and issuing orders, when Caesar's legal heir arrived in Rome. If Antony was the protector of Caesar's legacy, what could be done about the eighteen-year-old Octavian, Caesar's grandnephew? Neither ridicule nor threats could discourage this young man, who knew exactly the strength of his position. Antony's enemies, especially Cicero, readily supported Octavian, if only for their own ends. The plebs and the soldiers, who revered Caesar, now gave Octavian their allegiance. It was Cicero who rallied the Senate and succeeded in getting Antony condemned as an enemy of the people (*hostis publicus*). At a battle site near Mutina (modern Modena), the consuls, Hirtius and Pansa, were both killed, while their legions were defeating Antony's veterans. Octavian survived the fight, but little had been decided.

After a difficult trip through the Alps, a beaten and worn Antony proved that he could still rally an army. When he arrived in Gallia Narbonensis, where Lepidus' forces were stationed, he was welcomed by the men in the ranks as though he were one of them. Lepidus followed his army. He was thereafter doomed to be a prominent man without power and has been dubbed as "history's most forgettable character."

When Antony returned to Italy with renewed strength, he already knew that he would not need it. There had been overtures from Octavian, who realized that he had been a stalking horse for Cicero and the Senate. How would they have treated him with Antony out of the way? He decided to take the other course, and so with Antony and Lepidus formed the Second Triumvirate which, unlike the first, was formalized by a law of November, 43. There was a marriage to seal the alliance. Octavian married Clodia, Antony's stepdaughter by his marriage to Fulvia.

Cicero was doomed. Each of the triumvirs had his own list of enemies to be killed, even though they were friends or relatives of one of the other two partners. Although Octavian distrusted Cicero, he respected his great ability. Yet he let him die, for he was surely the first name on Antony's list. So, too, Antony allowed his uncle to be proscribed (although he may never have actually been killed). Even Lepidus' brother was condemned. There were about three hundred others whose blood would seal the bond among the triumvirs. Plutarch speaks with horror of this deadly pact: "I do not believe anything ever took place more truly savage or barbarous than this composition, for, in this exchange of blood for blood, they were equally guilty of the lives they surrendered and of those they took; or, indeed more guilty in the case of their friends, for whose deaths they had not even the justification of hatred" (p. 1115), though of hatred there was enough. Antony had Cicero's head and right hand cut off and displayed on the rostra in the Forum. If there existed a picture of that awful scene, it would say more about Antony and his times than words could ever do.

Without Caesar's gentle curbing, Antony returned to his old loose habits in Rome amid "players, jugglers and drunken flatterers." In the field, he was as usual a masterful soldier. Near Philippi, he fought separate battles with Cassius and Brutus. Both were beaten. Their suicides marked the end of the conspiracy. Octavian was at the battle site, but was generally made inactive by bad dreams and illness. He gave no hint that there might be a "Caesar" in him. He would in his long life depend on others of greater military capacity, Marcus Vipsanius Agrippa in particular.

Octavian also lacked the sturdy body which gave Antony his amazing perseverance. What he did have in abundance was luck. It was his good fortune that Antony did not return to Rome, but went on a triumphal parade through Greece and the East. Always a good target for conniving flatterers, he paid little attention to details, and so wasted his fortune and his time. He finally succumbed to the woman who was nearly a match for Caesar and surely more than a match for him.

Cleopatra

The Romans hated and feared Cleopatra, for unlike Hannibal or Mithridates who had to face their legions, she threatened to take the Empire one man at a time. Cleopatra's unusual life proves that fascination exists without beauty. Her existing portraits are not flattering. What events tell us is that she was remarkably intelligent, with a consummate sense of timing—subservient when she had to be, shrewd when she could afford to be, and, at the end, defiant with an asp at the breast in the nick of time. Her hold on the mighty Caesar recommends her best. The fact that she was the only Ptolemaic ruler who learned Egyptian says something else. But most of all it was her personality which held the greatest attraction. She could converse with the urbane Caesar or relax and join in coarse banter with Antony.

Antony first met Cleopatra when she was a young girl. In 41 B.C., while in Cilicia, he ordered her to appear before him to answer the charge that she had recently sent aid to Cassius. It was an opportunity she might have arranged for herself. She was the one who would be doing the testing. Plutarch said, "She came sailing up the river Cydnus, in a barge with gilded stern and outspread sails of purple, while oars of silver beat time to the music of flutes and fifes and harps. She herself lay all along under a canopy of cloth of gold, dressed as Venus in a picture, and beautiful young boys, like painted Cupids, stood on each side to fan her. Her maids were dressed like sea nymphs and graces, some steering at the rudder, some working at the ropes" (p. 1118). That extravaganza set the tone for Cleopatra's happy days with Antony. She soon had him back in Alexandria, where they played dice and drank together, spent a prodigious amount of time feasting, and in quieter moods went fishing. In the meantime, his campaign against the Parthians, who were even threatening Syria,

16. Cleopatra, a likeness which in profile is similar to that of her coins. Courtesy of the Trustees of the British Museum.

was delayed, and his wife, Fulvia, was trying to maintain his influence in Italy against the ambitious Octavian.

Fulvia and Antony's brother, Lucius, did not fare well, and were forced to leave Italy. The situation in Italy had deteriorated to the point where Antony felt it necessary to return with the forces he had mustered against Parthia. His suspicions that the impetuous Fulvia had mismanaged matters were confirmed by those who had recently left Italy and met him on the way. He might have had difficulty with her himself had she not died in Sicyon while en route to join him. Her death made things easier. Octavian was also willing to blame her for their troubles. Consequently, according to agreements reached at Brundisium in 40 B.C. and Misenum in 39 B.C., they divided the Mediterranean world, with Octavian taking the West and Antony the East. Lepidus was given the province of Africa. Pompey's son Sextus was left in charge of Sicily and Sardinia. He would presumably be left alone as long as he sent grain to Rome and kept the pirates in his region in check.

Again the bargain was confirmed with a marriage. Antony, now a widower, married Octavian's half-sister, Octavia, herself a widow. At the time it appeared to be a politic arrangement, but Octavia was a woman much admired in Rome and that boded ill for the future. Antony's attentions to Cleopatra might not offend the irascible Fulvia, but Octavia was a Roman woman of the highest standing. Still, the marriage began well enough. Octavia bore Antony a daughter, and she and the baby accompanied him to Greece. By the time she had had another daughter, and was pregnant a third time, Antony was again worried that Octavian was growing too strong in Italy. So, there was another conference at Tarentum. Antony was powerful on the sea and Octavian on the land. They exchanged some forces and reaffirmed their pact—for the last time.

Octavian now felt free to attack Sextus, in order to bring Sicily under his own rule. Antony, after many delays, was ready to attack Parthia. Yet, en route, he met Cleopatra in Syria and proceeded to undo all that was accomplished at Tarentum. He turned over to her Phoenicia and Cyprus. Cleopatra in turn presented him with the twins she had had since their last meeting. He gave the girl the title *Selene,* moon, and the boy *Helios,* sun—a fair approximation of Cleopatra's ultimate ambition for herself and her children. As Plutarch tells the story, she failed because she ruined the man she hoped would make her dreams come true.

Plutarch blames Antony's poor preparation for his invasion of Parthia on his infatuation with Cleopatra. In short, she had bewitched him. Such is the romance of history, and it may in part be true. But Antony, while superb in set battles, had never before planned such a difficult campaign. His judgment about what it would take to win or the toughness of his opposition may simply have been faulty. He began without the necessary equipment. Time and again he was surprised by the movements of the Parthian king, Phraates.

Antony had sent an advance army under Ventidius to keep the Parthians from advancing too far west. The amazing success of this general in two major battles was all the more significant because Antony failed so miserably when he took over. His grand invasion floundered badly, as had the campaign of Crassus, because he was at the mercy of a terrain the Parthians knew so well. The morale of his men was slowly drained; some of his allies, the king of Armenia for instance, took their armies, including much

17. Octavia. The Louvre. Photograph courtesy of Maurice Chuzeville.

needed horsemen, and went home. Antony won some battles, but it appeared from the outset that he was not going to win the war. It is a testimonial to his skill as a leader that his soldiers stood by him for so long. They were often without food or water. After he had to give up the siege of Phraaspa, a major city of Media, he was too embarrassed to address his soldiers when they began their retreat. Yet on the hard march back he retained his popularity with the ordinary footsoldier, for he comforted the sick and the wounded with tears in his eyes. Plutarch said they felt more sorry for him than for themselves.

The Parthians repeatedly attacked during the desperate twenty-seven day retreat. But worse things happened. Roman soldiers were given to assaulting each other in the night, even killing for money. Such incidents are rarely mentioned, but in a large army it was only to be expected that there was a certain bad element which caused widespread suspicion and turmoil. Another enemy was disease. It was estimated that, of the twenty thousand footsoldiers and four thousand horsemen lost, at least half died from drinking foul water or from assorted ailments.

It was not until Antony led his men into Armenia that they were safe. "They kissed the ground for joy, shedding tears and embracing each other in their delight" (Plutarch, p. 1133). Yet they were still far from home, and before Antony had led them to the coast of the Mediterranean, near Sidon, several more thousands were dead.

The kings of Media and Parthia fell to quarreling among themselves after their joint success against the Romans. Antony later allied himself with the Median ruler by a marriage between the king's daughter and Alexander, one of his sons by Cleopatra. But the destiny of Antony and Cleopatra would be decided not in a magnificent palace in the East, but in the chamber in Rome where senators crowded together to listen to Octavian's complaints. His sister, taking gifts and supplies, had gone to Athens to await Antony. But her husband preferred the company of the despised Cleopatra. Octavia returned to Rome and presided over Antony's household with great dignity. She cared for Fulvia's children as well as her own, and her goodness damned Antony more than a brother's accusations could ever do. Nothing damaged Antony more in the eyes of the Roman public and officialdom than his own actions. In Alexandria, amid pomp and ceremony, he parceled out the East between Cleopatra and two of the sons she had given him. Egypt, Cyprus, Libya and Coele-Syria were hers. One son, Alexander Helios, was to have Armenia and Media. The other, Ptolemy Philadelphus, would rule Phoenicia, Syria, and Cilicia. Antony had the further audacity to accuse Octavian of not giving him his fair share of Sicily, which he had recently taken from Sextus in 36. In that same year, Octavian had removed Lepidus as a partner. He let him be the *pontifex maximus* and that was all.

When word reached Rome that Antony wanted Octavia and her children out of his house, the final bond of the Second Triumvirate was broken. A new civil war was inevitable.

Cleopatra's money would pay for the battle with Octavian, and she was determined to be there to oversee her investment. Antony reluctantly agreed. It was repeatedly charged in Rome that he was too much under Cleopatra's influence. Ironically, for Octavian, that was the best possible luck. The Roman soldiers serving Antony resented Cleopatra as deeply as did their fellow citizens at home. Her presence lowered morale more than Antony dared to guess. Surely, however, the defection of high-ranking officers to the other side must have given him warning of his shaky position. Obviously, they feared Cleopatra more than they loved him. On the other hand, the stories of Antony's subservience to the Egyptian queen may have been exaggerated by his enemies. Those who left him possibly used her as an excuse when they guessed that Octavian would be the ultimate victor. With hindsight, there were said to have been many ill-omens foretelling Antony's doom. For instance, the swallows would not remain nesting on Cleopatra's flagship. The great celebrations he and Cleopatra held at Samos and Athens before the pending battle seemed inappropriate, as they certainly proved to be.

Sizeable land forces were present on both sides, but Antony's fleet was stationed at Actium on the west coast of Greece, and that was where the decision was made. The long awaited event was something of an anticlimax, scarcely any contest at all. Those who manned Antony's ships were in many instances ill-trained recruits impressed from among the Greeks and lacking spirit for the fight. Octavian not only had the better fleet, he had the best commander. Agrippa would for the years ahead remain his right hand man in military affairs.

According to Plutarch, it was Cleopatra who insisted that the decision be at sea rather than on land, where Antony was obviously better prepared. The sea offered her the best way to escape if things went wrong. Whether the assumption that her judgment prevailed over Antony's is correct or not, it is true that at Actium she was the first to flee, and she took sixty ships with her. Whether she left too soon is another question. It may have appeared obvious that Antony's large, well-armored vessels were too bulky and slow to match Octavian's smaller and faster ships. No matter: her leaving caused such a panic that even Antony became disheartened, and followed her in a single ship. What remained of his fleet was left to be destroyed. The story goes that although he joined Cleopatra he did not speak to her for three days, but sat brooding. His army remained loyal for a short time and then surrendered to Octavian. The eastern allies, Herod of Judaea among them, made great haste to join the new "Caesar."

Antony was left with the choice of where and how to die. It was in Alexandria that he stabbed himself with a sword. That much may be a fact. The melodramatic stories surrounding the event are no more certain than his age. He may have been fifty-three or fifty-six. Was he falsely informed by Cleopatra's own orders that she was already dead? Did he learn the truth and manage to reach her for one last embrace before he died? It appears doubtful that Octavian wept when he heard the news. Antony did not live to see the Empire, but through his children by Octavia his blood was in the royal family. He was the great-great-grandfather of another man whose follies became more notorious than his own—the Emperor Nero.

Once Octavian had cornered his two enemies in Alexandria, his main goal was to take over Cleopatra's treasury before she could abscond with it or destroy it to spite him. As for the queen herself, he would have her in chains to grace his triumph, a delightful sight for the Romans! Octavian spoke pleasantly to the Alexandrians and praised their city. They perhaps were given the first hint of the magnanimity he would show once his enemies were overcome. There seemed to be a few left, however. Antony's eldest son (by his marriage to Fulvia), Antyllus, was a threat and was put to death shortly after Octavian's arrival in Alexandria. Another was Cleopatra's child Caesarion. who had been Caesar's one son. For Octavian one was too many. At the time, not everybody believed Cleopatra's claim that the boy was Caesar's son, but Octavian obviously thought so. When Caesarion, who had been sent away by his mother, returned to Alexandria under the false hope that he was safe, he too was executed in 30 B.C.

Octavian's first meeting with Cleopatra was proper, polite, and business-like. She countered with her usual histrionics, but he quickly put an end to that. They spent most of their time inspecting a ledger of her wealth. She said the jewels reported to him as missing from the list were intended as presents for his wife and sister. By this false confession she tricked him into believing that she intended to live. He was put off guard long enough for her to pay a last visit to Antony's tomb. Then she killed herself rather than face those hungry eyes in Rome.

Most men, including Octavian, believed Cleopatra committed suicide by letting an asp bite her; the asp was after all a symbol of royalty. But there were rumors that she had for some time been experimenting with poisons on other people, and it is possible that she used one of these. Nevertheless, the best story will remain the one about the asp brought to her in a water-jar or a basket of figs, or maybe flowers, even though what actually happened will probably never be known. The only witnesses were two serving women, and they died with their mistress.

18. Octavian. Courtesy of the Museum of Fine Arts, Boston.

Octavian, the richest and most powerful figure in the Mediterranean world, began his triumphal journey to Rome. He now had everything Caesar had, to which he added at least a pretense to modesty and a willingness to listen to the opinions of others, in short, tact—and so began a reign of forty years as the first of the Roman emperors.

XII
Laughter, Love, and How to Die

As the Roman Republic passed into history, so did the words of its most eminent spokesmen, and some of them have been quoted in the preceding chapters. Unfortunately, they might leave the impression that war and politics were all the Romans ever thought about. Of course we know that many Romans were often thinking about where their next meal was coming from. But, again, it was the politicians and historians who wrote about that and not the poor themselves. War, politics, hunger—there is a grimness about it all so well reflected in the solemn faces of Roman portrait busts. Little wonder that those writers who wrote lighthearted comedy, passionate poetry, or, like Cicero, contemplative essays, turned to the Greeks for inspiration in the arts and philosophy. Talented Romans gave proof of that inspiration.

Bad times are good for comedy. In particular, the grimness of war needs a remedy. At Athens, the greatest comic writer of all times, Aristophanes, produced his best plays during the long and disastrous Peloponnesian War. In Rome, it was Plautus who kept audiences laughing during the last years of the struggle with Hannibal.

Livy, Cicero, and Vergil may have earned the best reviews

in Roman literature, but Plautus (*ca.* 254–184 B.C.) had the largest audiences. Today, Emerson, Whitman, and O'Neill are part of the roster of Americans in college literature courses, but more people have probably seen the popular television performance of *A Funny Thing Happened on the Way to the Forum* than have read the three authors just mentioned. The play is an adaptation of parts of at least three of Plautus' comedies. His plots were themselves borrowed from Greek plays. But much of the fun, especially the boisterous banter, is pure Plautus. Fun fitted him better than wit. There is none of the sophistication of a drawing-room comedy. Almost all of the action took place in the street, and if Plautus' characters ever went indoors it was as likely as not into a brothel. The traditional scenery for Roman comedy was simply a backdrop on which the facades of a few houses were painted.

Plautus was well acquainted with the assorted characters in the streets of Rome. He was often looking for a job. The early years of his life had many ups and downs. He did not begin to write until after he was forty-five. Although his birthplace, Sarsina, in Umbria (central Italy), was once the great city of the Umbrians, it never had a more famous native than Plautus. He was born there in about 254 B.C., and left for Rome when he was twenty-four to find something besides the poverty he already knew. Curiously enough, one of the first jobs he found was working as a clown in rustic theatricals. A more formal theatre was only just beginning under the direction of Livius Andronicus (*ca.* 284–204 B.C.), a Greek epic poet and playwright, famous for his Latin translations of Homer, as well as of Greek tragedies and comedies. One of his contemporaries, Gnaeus Naevius (270–199 B.C.), wrote an epic on the First Punic War and also used Greek plots in "Roman" productions, in addition to turning out some original plays.

Attic comedy and tragedy were presented in Rome a decade before Plautus came to the city. During his lifetime, the cultural leaders of the city who had travelled or served in the army overseas were partial to all things Greek in the arts. They, however, had intellectual interests as befitted their aristocratic station. Plautus would give the people Greek comedy on their own terms. After a short and unsuccessful career as a merchant, which meant some travels of his own, he returned to Rome to work as a lowly mill hand. In his spare time, he began to read the plays of the Greek comic poet Menander for diversion. He was soon writing his own comedies, and his instant success freed him from the necessity of other work. He had spent the better part of his life looking for money, and some of his plays have a slipshod quality, as if he turned them out quickly indeed. Consequently, some ancient and modern critics have seen him as a literary hack, writing for profit. But what he wanted to produce was laughter, not literature, and no Roman ever excelled him at that.

Plautus was awarded Roman citizenship toward the end of the third century B.C., undoubtedly as a reward for the enormously popular entertainment he was providing for the city. Since his home town, Sarsina, was an ally of Rome, he had probably fought with auxiliary troops during the war against Hannibal. Now he was Titus Maccius Plautus, instead of simply Titus, as he was known in Sarsina, or Plautus, as he was nicknamed, because of his large flat feet. In his heyday he might have been tagged with a number of names.

The Comedy of Asses is typical of the thin plots which Plautus used as a setting for his jokes. The story is about a henpecked husband, Demaenetus, who wants to subsidize his son Argyrippus' love affair. The youth is hopelessly smitten with a girl, Philaenium, whose mother, Cleareta, happens to be the "madam" of a house where money comes before romance. In brief, the son needs a few hundred drachmas or so if he is to enjoy the company of his girl exclusively for the following year. And there is at least one rival who might put the cash down first. So much for suspense. Because Argyrippus' mother, Artemona, controls the family purse strings, Demaenetus must engage the services of two of his own slaves to cheat the household out of money. Their scheme calls for one of them to pose as the family business manager in order to receive a payment for two asses purchased by an out-of-town buyer. This involves a considerable amount of horseplay, with the imposter beating his accomplice to prove he is the one in authority. When they finally bring the money to Argyrippus, there are more "sight gags" before the money is handed over in exchange for Demaenetus' being allowed to spend the evening with the girl friend in question. All are agreed that it is a good bargain. But the rival suitor finds out and sends a lackey to tell Artemona the latest news. She arrives and listens at the door, where her husband, son, and Philaenium are enjoying drinks, to the following dialogue:

PHILAENIUM:	Do tell me, there's a dear—your wife's breath isn't bad, is it?
DEMAENETUS:	I'd rather drink bilge water, if it came to that, than kiss her.
ARTEMONA:	(*aside*) So? You would, would you? Good gracious, sir, that fling at me will cost you dear. Very well! just you come back home, sir! I'll show you the danger of vilifying a wife with money.
PHILAENIUM:	Goodness me, you poor thing!
ARTEMONA:	(*aside*) Goodness me, he deserves to be!
ARGYRIPPUS:	Look here, father. Do you love my mother?
DEMAENETUS:	Love her? I? I love her now for not being near.
ARGYRIPPUS:	And when she is near?
DEMAENETUS:	I yearn for a death in the family.

(Act V, sc. iii)

Artemona bursts in and hauls him off, having decided that her sweetest revenge will be plenty of kisses in the future.

Earlier in the play, when Philaenium's mother and Argyrippus are quarreling over her recent demand for money, she chides him for his naiveté and gives a description of a profession which was already old:

CLEARETA:	This profession of ours is a great deal like bird-catching. The fowler, when he has his fowling-floor prepared, spreads food around; the birds become familiarized: you must spend money, if you wish to make money. They often get a meal: but once they get caught they recoup the fowler. It is quite the same with us here: our house is the floor, I am the fowler, the girl the bait, the couch the decoy, the lovers the birds. They become familiar through pleasant greetings, pretty speeches, kisses, cooey, captivating little whispers. If he cuddles her close in his arms, well, no harm to the fowler. If he takes a naughty kind of kiss, he can be taken himself, and no net needed. You to forget all this, and so long in the school, too?

(Act I, sc. iii)

Plautus' *Amphitryon*, also probably written early in the second century B.C., has even less plot than *The Comedy of Asses*. It is a story about the unusual homecoming of Amphitryon, commander-in-chief of the Theban army, who is returning from his triumph over the Teloboians. During his absence, Jupiter, the father of the gods, has taken a fancy to his wife, Alcmena, and accompanied by his son Mercury, has paid her a visit. He comes disguised as her husband, which a god can do if wants to, and Mercury looks exactly like Sosia, one of the family slaves now away with his master. The *deus ex machina* was a familiar device in Greek plays wherein a god arrived toward the end of a play to straighten everything out. In this instance it is Jupiter who begins the mischief—and he will be around at the end playing the familiar role of peacemaker. In the meantime, Alcmena wonders why her husband pretends to be just arriving when he has visited her just a few hours earlier. He accuses her of having either delusions, or an affair with another man, or both. The slave Sosia's encounter with Mercury, who looks exactly like himself, is another uproarious scene. The whole business is very much contrived and does not amount to much, aside from Plautus' clever dialogue. In the end, Alcmena gives birth to twins. One walks at birth and so obviously belongs to Jupiter. The other is her husband's child. Amphitryon says: "I make no complaint at being permitted to have Jove as partner in my blessings" (Act V, sc. i). To which the god responds: "Live again in fond concord as of old with thy wife Alcmena: she has done naught to merit thy reproach; my power was on her. I now depart to heaven" (Act V, sc. ii). A happy ending. All that mattered were the laughs along the way. The audience came to the theatre knowing what to expect of Plautus. If he was not the greatest of artists it was, perhaps, in part because he was so predictable.

For centuries Plautus remained Rome's favorite writer of comedy. His plays were frequently revived and, as mentioned before, they still are. By the first century B.C. he had had many imitators, and there was some confusion about which plays were actually his. Varro, scholar, antiquarian, and friend of Julius Caesar took it upon himself to choose twenty-one plays as authentic. His choice still stands.

Here and there in Plautus' plays are references to events of the day. The Carthaginians are mentioned, and there are remarks about efforts to have laws repealed which put a limit on how much a woman should spend on her clothing. But his plays were written exclusively as a diversion and lack the political overtones of Aristophanes' comedies. Almost devoid of seriousness, let alone reverence, Plautus' plays were a worry to moralists. The

old-time strictness was only slowly being relaxed at Rome. In
what Plautus wrote, vice was something to cause a smile instead
of a long face, all of which undoubtedly made old Cato the Censor frown.

The great literature of the Romans was primarily about the
sober and serious men who sat in the Senate. Plautus' plays have
historical significance for bringing to life the livelier characters in
Rome. He was one himself.

Plautus died in 184 B.C. At that time, his foremost successor, Publius Terentius Afer, better known as Terence, was still a
child.

Terence

Terence (*ca.* 190–159 B.C.) was brought to Rome as a slave. He
was only a boy when he was bought in Carthage by a wealthy
Roman, who liked him enough to see that he received a first-rate
education. It was not wasted. By the time he was twenty-four,
Terence was an established figure in the Roman theater and a free
man. Scipio Aemilianus was one of his patrons, and that meant
entrée to the best circles in Rome. His talent for adapting Greek
comedies to the Roman stage had made him a celebrity. Then
suddenly he was gone. He died during a trip to Greece when he
was about thirty. During that brief career, however, Terence had
established himself as a writer of comedy second only to Plautus.
Yet his most successful works closely followed the original comedies written by the Greek playwright Menander (*ca.* 342–291
B.C.), so much so that unfriendly critics call him a mere transla-
tor. A more generous opinion would see a certain degree of innovation in his adaptations written for Roman audiences. Yet he was
not as inventive as Plautus, and his plays were certainly less entertaining. His cast of characters were the familiar stock figures
which Menander used so successfully: wealthy old men betrayed
by rascally sons and clever servants, daughters pursued by all
manner of suitors, courtesans living by their beauty and wits, and,
of course, wives and mothers kept in a state of nervous apprehension by all the rest. The hopes and schemes of the main characters
are largely abetted by hangers-on and layabouts who will do anything for money. As in Menander, so in Terence, the plots depended on farcical misunderstandings as a result of disguises or
events known to some persons while kept secret from others. By

frequent asides the characters kept the audience informed of everything. The dialogue was usually at a high pitch; somebody was either intensely in love, outrageously deceitful, or almost uncontrollably angry. To say that Terence's comedies were less bawdy than those of Plautus does not mean that they were more subtle. His plays, like those of Plautus, seem short by modern standards. They were written to be performed without intermissions; separation of the plays into acts was the work of scholars who issued new editions in later times.

The Eunuch, produced in 161 B.C., won for Terence his highest acclaim and was typical of his output. Its plot concerned two brothers. The elder one, Phaedria, was a pleasant fellow, in love with the courtesan Thais. She was presumably in love with him, but at the moment, for a good hearted reason, pretended to love a blunderbuss of an officer named Thraso. Her mother had once been served by a young girl, Pamphila, who, although well born, had been kidnapped by pirates at so early an age that she did not know her homeland. In time, when the mother died, Thais' uncle sold the girl to Thraso. Now Thais wanted him to give her Pamphila as a present so that the girl could be reunited with a brother who had appeared. To counteract his rival's gift, Phaedria purchased a servant girl and a eunuch whom he would give to Thais. In the meantime, Phaedria's younger brother, Chaerea, had fallen in love from afar with the beautiful girl owned by Thraso and used any means to be near her. He intrigued with Parmeno, one of Phaedria's servants, to pass him off as the eunuch. By that time the girl he loved had been turned over to Thais by the officer. Chaerea, as the "eunuch," was given charge over her. With the bedroom door locked he proceeded to rape Pamphila. As Thais later confessed, when the truth was known, she had "set the wolf to keep the sheep!" There was a considerable amount of outrage on all sides until it was discovered that Chaerea really loved Pamphila and would marry her. Thais was, of course, now free from her obligation to Thraso, but the two brothers agreed that the officer was so full of conceit as to be easily deceived by Thais and so continue to supply gifts, including money, for the benefit of everybody except himself.

The play has some amusing twists and turns. The dialogue, however, is not hilarious. Parmeno encounters Gnatho, a "parasite," who served Thraso and pretended to be an admirer of his although, in fact, he loathed him. Nonetheless, Gnatho was in Thraso's service and at the moment was bringing Pamphila as a gift to Thais. This he thought would surely cut Parmeno's master Phaedria out of the competition. The fun is at the following level:

GNATHO: (*jeeringly*)	My own dear friend! Gnatho's thy very humble servant. Well, what are you upon now?
PARMENO: (*surlily*)	Upon my legs.
GNATHO:	I see that . . . But don't you see something here that offends your eyesight? (*Pointing to Pamphila*)
PARMENO: (*surlily*)	Yes, yourself.

(Act II, sc. ii)

Roman comedy at its best began with Plautus and ended with Terence. Their plays were continually revived in later times and enjoyed a special popularity during the troubled last years of the Republic. Cicero was not always making speeches in the Senate and Caesar was not forever reviewing his legions. Sometimes they were sitting in the great stone theatre which Pompey built, laughing along with the crowd at a play by either Plautus or Terence. In Cicero's essay "On Friendship," he twice used examples from Terence's *The Eunuch* to illustrate human traits. Gnatho was the base flatterer who would say anything to anybody in order to win some favor. His habitual insincerity ruled out any degree of friendship. And Thraso, of course, was so puffed up with self-importance that the only kind of friend he wanted was one who would pour compliments in his ear, no matter how exaggerated they might be.

In his essay "On Old Age," Cicero contrasted the ways in which two brothers had faced the problems of advancing years. The manner in which Cicero referred to characters in Terence's plays leaves no doubt that his readers knew them well.

Catullus

During the time when Julius Caesar was coming to power, Catullus was the foremost poet in Rome. Recent editions of his poetry have given him a minor revival in the mid-twentieth century. The poems addressed to his friends are secular and candid. Put in modern idiom by Frank O. Copley (*Gaius Valerius Catullus—The Complete Poetry*, published in 1957), the lyrics have a tone which is clearly flippant and rebellious. The breakdown of the Republic was accompanied by a sharp reaction against the tried and true or maybe just time worn subjects and forms of the old poetry. Catullus, who was born sometime in the eighties and died young sometime in the fifties, belonged to a circle of poets who delighted in being different. Their outrageous verse was, as might be expected, more interesting to themselves than to the general public. Catullus' works managed to survive. They reveal him to have been a well-read poet with a caustic wit and passion to spare. It is not surprising to learn that he translated Sappho. Whether writing of himself, his friends, or the gods, his themes are loves won and lost, jealousy, and revenge. Now and then he is deliberately obscene. Almost nothing is known about Catullus except the hints he gives in his poems. For instance, he made more than one unflattering remark about Caesar who, as governor of Cisalpine Gaul, had been a guest of Catullus' father. That suggests a wealthy background. It is not certain what caused the trouble between Caesar and Catullus, but apparently they became reconciled before Catullus died.

That Catullus had a great love affair with a woman he calls Lesbia there can be no doubt. In the standard Loeb Classical series, a prose translation with Victorian overtones, poem forty-three appears this way:

> I greet you, lady you who neither have a tiny nose, nor a pretty foot, nor black eyes, nor long fingers, nor dry mouth, nor indeed a very refined tongue, you mistress of the bankrupt of Formiae. Is it you who are pretty, as the Province tells us? is it with you that our Lesbia is compared? Oh, this age! how tasteless and ill-bred it is!

Copley updates it in free verse:

> Hi there, sweetheart!
> that nose of yours is not too small
> your feet—well, hardly pretty
> your eyes—well, hardly snappy
> your fingers—not too long
> your lips—you wiped your mouth yet?
> your tongue—well, shall we say not the most elegant
> aren't you Dickie-boy's girl—that chiseler from Formiae?
> you mean to say that out in the sticks
> they call you pretty?
> you mean to say they've been comparing you
> to Lesbia—my Lesbia?
> O what a tasteless witless age!

Lesbia, of course, has been identified with Clodia, the sister of the Clodius who was Cicero's arch foe and for a time a useful ally of Julius Caesar. She was an extraordinarily beautiful woman whose many extramarital affairs gave her a wicked reputation. She probably deserved it. Given the low morals of the age, such notoriety was not easy to come by. In any event, she seems to have given Catullus his one great love—and much grief. According to Copley, poem seventy should read:

nobody
my Lady says there's nobody
she'd rather marry than me
not if Jove himself should come asking her
so she says
but what a woman says to a lover
that wants her
she should write on wind and running water

Some readers might prefer the translation of this poem by Reney Myers and Robert J. Ormsby in *Catullus: The Complete Poems for American Readers,* published in 1970:

My love says she would marry only me,
And Jove himself could never make her care.
What women say to lovers, you'll agree,
One writes on running water or on air.

The present-day preoccupation with antiperspirants and colognes deals with an old problem. The Copley translation of poem sixty-nine has a pungency of its own:

Rufus!
you got no business bein' surprised
if there's no dame that wants to lay
her nice white smooth leg under yours
not even if you break her down
by buyin' 'er some fancy clothes
or maybe a pretty-pretty, say,
that's got a big fat sparkler on it.
you know what 'tis that's hurtin' you?
well, there's a story goin' 'round
—jus' tellin' you what people say—
you got a goat, a stinkin' goat
lives in your armpits—yeah, that's what
the dames is scared of—and why not?
a goat's a dirty beast, no girl

is gonna wanta sleep with that

so either kill the thing that kills their noses
or quit wonderin' why they run away

It is not a subject which Cicero would have considered appropriate. That is the point about Catullus. Copley tries to keep up with him. Certain of his translations could offend the easily shocked. The choice of four-letter words by C. H. Sisson in his 1966 edition, *The Poetry of Catullus,* definitely would. On the other hand, Sisson provides a beautiful modern rendering of poem five, which alone might justify the claim that Catullus was the greatest of the Latin lyric poets:

Living, dear Lesbia, is useless without loving:
The observations of the censorious old
Are worth a penny every piece of advice.
One day follows another, the sun comes back
But when once we have gone away we do not;
Once night comes for us, it is night for ever.
Give me a thousand kisses, and then a hundred,
Then give me a second thousand, a second hundred
And then another thousand, and then a hundred
And when we have made up many, many thousands
Let us forget to count. Better not to know—
It will bring someone's jealous eye upon us
If people know we give so many kisses.

Cicero's Essays

Cicero has received the rare honor of having a literary age named after him. He was the foremost writer of the middle years of the first century B.C. His orations and letters have already been mentioned for their historical value. He also wrote a series of essays intended to instruct or comfort. Instruction was derived from history. Cicero was devoted to lessons from the past. Philosophy supplied the consolation.

Cicero, although a declared adherent of the skeptically inclined New Academy, did as much as any other Roman writer to propagate Stoicism. Zeno, probably a Phoenician, was the founder of this philosophy. He taught in Athens during the late fourth and early third centuries B.C.; his teachings took a strong hold among the Greeks. In the mid-second century B.C., Greek teachers like Panaetius brought these ideas to Rome. Blossius, the tutor of the Gracchi, was a Stoic. It was mentioned earlier that the emphasis on a radical adherence to principle accounted for the uncompromising stand taken by the Stoics. Certainly, it was one of the reasons for the rigidity of Caesar's foe Cato the Younger. Cicero was more flexible, but his writings show that his outlook was generally Stoic. His essay "On Old Age" is a good example. He dedicated it to his old friend Atticus. They were both getting along in years, and Cicero hoped that his musings about what lies ahead would be a comfort to them both.

The essay is composed in the style of a dialogue with the venerable old Cato, when he was eighty-three, as the principal speaker. He talks to the sons of two of his late friends. Like Socrates' students, they are an agreeable and appreciative audience. While Cato would undoubtedly have agreed with the sentiments expressed, the actual words are, of course, those of Cicero. The essay is unflaggingly optimistic, somewhat repetitious, but pleasant for all that.

Nature is mentioned at the outset, and the word suggests one of the two major themes in the essay. "Now it cannot be supposed that nature, after having wisely distributed to all the preceding periods of life their peculiar and proper enjoyments, should have neglected, like an indolent poet, the last act of the human drama, and left it destitute of suitable advantages" (p. 219). Here is the Stoic emphasis on the harmony and order of a universe governed by Reason or Providence, in which man finds serenity so long as he is reconciled to what must be. The second main theme is that if men do not enjoy their old age or, in fact, if they find it painful, "the true grievance . . . lies in the man and not in the age" (p. 221). Toward the end of his essay Cicero writes, "What a striking contrast, for instance, between the two old men in Terence's play called *The Brothers!* Micio is all mildness and good humor; whereas Demea, on the contrary, is represented as an absolute churl. The fact, in short, is plainly this: as it is not every kind of wine, so neither is it every sort of temper, that turns sour by age" (pp. 251–252). There are those who complain of a loss of physical powers and sensual gratifications or seem lost without the attentions they once received. Cicero writes: "They whose desires are properly regulated, and who have nothing morose or petulant in their temper and manners, will find old age, to say the least of it, is a state very easily to be endured, whereas unsubdued passions and a froward disposition will equally embitter every season of human life" (p. 221).

As might be expected, Cicero insists that wisdom qualifies the aged for public service long after their physically active years are over. With his penchant for historical evidence, he can name a number of old heroes whose valuable counsel gave them a second career in later life:

> Appius Claudius was not only old, but blind, when he remonstrated in the Senate with so much force and spirit against concluding a peace with Pyrrhus, to which the majority of the members appeared strongly inclined. . . . This celebrated harangue, which is still extant, Appius delivered seventeen years after his second consulate, between which and his first there was an interval of ten years, and prior to both he had exercised the office of Censor. It is evident, therefore, that he must have been a very old man at the time of the Pyrrhic war. And, indeed, the tradition received from our forefathers had always represented him as such. (pp. 225–226)

Cicero adds: "It is not by exertions of corporal strength and activity that the momentous affairs of state are conducted; it is by cool deliberation, by prudent counsel, and by that authoritative influence which ever attends on public esteem, qualifications which are so far from being impaired, that they are usually strengthened and improved by increase of years" (p. 226). Ancient Sparta, the dominant land power in Greece for two centuries, was always a ready example of the strong leadership provided by its elders.

Answering the claim that age may impair creativity, Cicero points to Sophocles, who was still writing great tragedies in his eighties. Talent, like a good memory, is something a man maintains for himself: "For the faculties of the mind will preserve their powers in old age, unless they are suffered to lose their energy and become languid for want of due cultivation" (p. 228). Cicero asks:

> Did length of days weaken the powers of Homer, Hesiod, or Simonides of Stesichorus, Isocrates, or Gorgias? Did old age interrupt the studies of those first and most distinguished of the Greek philosophers, Pythagoras or Democritus, Plato or Xenocrates? Or, to descend into later times, did grey hairs prove an obstacle to the philosophic pursuits of Zeno, Cleanthes, or that famous Stoic whom you may remember to have seen in Rome, the venerable Diogenes? On the contrary, did not all of these eminent persons persevere in their respective studies with unbroken spirit to the last moment of their extended lives?" (pp. 228–229)

And not only do men of age retain their talents; they even add new ones. Socrates at the last began to play the lyre, and Cicero allows Cato to boast that it was in his old age that he learned to read Greek. Cicero concedes that age does bring a slackening of physical vigor, but this too is often tempered by moderation earlier in life: "This imbecility of body is more frequently occasioned by the irregularities of youth, than by the natural and unavoidable consequences of long life. A debauched and intemperate young man will undoubtedly, if he live, transmit weakness and infirmities to his latter days" (p. 232). Otherwise, the weakness that does occur must be accepted as part of nature's process. "Nature conducts us, by a regular and insensible progression, through the different seasons of human life, to each of which she has annexed its proper and distinguishing characteristic" (p. 234). It is of great importance that the mind should remain active. "As I love to see the fire of youth somewhat tempered with the gravity of age, so I am equally pleased when I observe the phlegm of age somewhat enlivened with the vivacity of youth; and whoever unites these two qualities in his character, may bear, indeed, the marks of years in his body, but will never discover the same traces in his mind" (p. 236).

When Cicero returns to the question of whether men should not properly be upset to lose the pleasures of the senses, his arguments are summed up in two passages. First, he says, "If age renders us incapable of taking an equal share in the flowing cups, and luxuriant dishes of splendid tables, it secures us too from their unhappy consequences—from painful indigestions, restless nights, and disordered reason" (p. 240). Then, after again referring to the works of ageing scientists and poets, he asks, "Tell me now, can the gay amusements of the theatre, the splendid luxuries of the table, or the soft blandishments of a mistress, supply their votaries with enjoyments that may fairly stand in competition with these calm delights of the intellectual pleasures?" (p. 243). Cicero does not wait for an answer, but piles argument upon argument in a similar vein. If a man does have need of physical activity, let him find it in farming. "I am principally delighted with observing the power, and tracing the process of Nature in these her vegetable productions" (p. 244).

Finally, the most difficult problem: How should a man face the nearness of death? Cicero's answer combines two propositions long ago offered by the Greeks—one by Epicurus, the other by

Socrates. Death "is an event either utterly to be disregarded, if it extinguish the soul's existence, or much to be wished, if it convey her to some region where she shall continue to exist for ever. . . . What then have I to fear, if after death I shall either not be miserable, or shall certainly be happy?" (p. 252). Cicero agrees with Socrates, particularly with his arguments for immortality as presented by Plato in the *Phaedo*. The soul is a prisoner of the body, and when released by death is free to go to a far better place. No man should resent the prospect. "Every event agreeable to the course of nature ought to be looked upon as a real good, and surely none can be more natural than for an old man to die. . . . I shall at length find a happy repose from the fatigues of a long voyage" (p. 254). In the meantime, age has many advantages. This is especially true for those who can "look back with self-approving satisfaction on the happy and abundant produce of more active years." Age also lends fortitude. Referring to history again: "Accordingly Solon, it is said, being questioned by the tyrant Peisistratus, what it was that inspired him with the boldness to oppose his measures, bravely replied, 'My old age' " (p. 254).

Yet even these advantages have their term. "Now when this state of absolute satiety is at length arrived, when we have enjoyed the satisfactions peculiar to old age, till we have no longer any relish remaining for them, it is then that death may justly be considered as a mature and seasonable event" (p. 256). At the very end of his essay Cicero again refers to nature. "For Nature has appointed to the days of man, as to all things else, their proper limits, beyond which they are no longer of any value" (p. 261).

Cicero's friend the poet Lucretius (*ca.* 94–*ca.* 55 B.C.), in his remarkable work *De Rerum Natura* (*On the Nature of Things*), stressed that death was not only natural but also absolutely final. He was the spokesman to his time of the philosophy of Epicurus (341–270 B.C.), mentioned above, whose message about a totally materialistic universe was intended to rid men of their fears either of the gods or of any terrors beyond the grave. The proposition that all that existed was composed of atoms, and so void of Platonic Ideas or immortal souls, was older than Epicurus. He used it to promote a gospel which taught that death offered not heaven nor hell but oblivion. This point of view, the Epicurean believed, could bring peace of mind to fearful men if only they could accept "what is" and abandon any hope for "what might be." Lucretius, in six books, offers a brilliant poetical exposition of this material world which men could see and enjoy if they followed Epicurus' advice to avoid superstitition and have prudence in their daily lives. On the other hand, Cicero, at least in his later years, held to the Socratic vision of a better world after death. On a less controversial subject, however, he did agree with Epicurus. Both of them spoke warmly of the great value in having friends in the here and now.

Cicero's essay "On Friendship," slightly longer than the one on old age, treats the enjoyment of friends as a precious experience. There is his usual emphasis on excellence—what the few can know and enjoy. He writes for well-bred gentlemen. Who else would have the time or inclination to reflect on the nature and the rules of friendship? And even among such men true friendship is shared by only a few. "I desire it may be understood . . . that I am now speaking, not of that inferior species of amity which occurs in the common intercourse of the world (although this, too, is not without its pleasures and advantages), but of that genuine and perfect friendship, examples of which are so extremely rare as to be rendered memorable by their singularity" (p. 179).

The theme of the essay is that only the virtuous can achieve true friendship: "The first endeavor should be to acquire yourself those moral excellences which constitute a virtuous character, and then to find an associate whose good qualities reflect back the true image of your own. Thus would the fair fabric of friendship be erected upon that immovable basis which I have so repeatedly recommended in the course of this inquiry" (p. 206). He has indeed. Cicero had the lawyer's, or professor's, predilection for driving home the same point again and again. He carries this practice into his essays. There are pleasant aphorisms along the way: "Without friendship, life can have no true enjoyment" (p. 208) and "without sincerity, friendship is a mere name" (p. 210).

The essay is an imaginary dialogue, almost a monologue, between Gaius Laelius, a noted orator of the second century B.C., who had recently lost his dear friend Scipio Aemilianus, and two younger men who are Laelius' sons-in-law. "This kind of dialogue," Cicero writes, "where the question is agitated by illustrious personages of former days, is apt, I know not how, to make a stronger impression on the mind of the reader than any other species of composition" (p. 168).

Laelius begins with some reflections on the death of Scipio. The passage gives Cicero a chance to rebuke the Epicureans of his day, who denied the immortality of the human soul. "For I am by no means a convert to the new doctrine which certain philosophers have lately endeavoured to propagate; who maintain that death extinguishes the whole man, and his soul perishes with the dissolution of his body" (p. 173). While he is not entirely positive about the matter, he obviously leans, as mentioned earlier, toward the Socratic doctrine "that the human soul is a divine and immortal substance, that death opens a way for its return to the celestial mansions, and that the spirits of those just men who have made the greatest progress in the paths of virtue find the easiest and most expeditious admittance" (p. 174). Laelius does not grieve for Scipio, much less for himself. "I derive so much satisfaction from reflecting on the friendship which subsisted between us, that I cannot but think I have reason to congratulate myself on the felicity of my life, since I have had the happiness to pass the greatest part of it in the society of Scipio." He adds, "To express at once the whole spirit and essence of friendship, our inclinations, our sentiments, and our studies were in perfect accord" (p. 175).

Cicero sees friendship as a kind of passionless marriage. Friends, he states:

> can scarcely, indeed, be considered in any respect as separate individuals and wherever the one appears the other is virtually present. I will venture even a bolder assertion, and affirm that in despite of death they must both continue to exist so long as either of them shall remain alive; for the deceased may, in a certain sense, be said still to live whose memory is preserved with the highest veneration and the most tender regret in the bosom of the survivor, a circumstance which renders the former happy in death, and the latter honoured in life. (pp. 179–180)

There are certain attributes encouraging to true friendship. A prime virtue is "steadiness and constancy of temper" (p. 198). Then there is self-confidence. A man who finds worth in himself can more easily be attracted to it in others. Frankness and a willingness to serve a friend's need are also valuable. Adversity, of course, is the age-old testing ground for friendship. Good manners are important, also humility. "It frequently happens that there is a great disparity between intimate friends both in point of rank and talents. Now, under these circumstances, 'he who has the advantage should never appear sensible of his superiority'" (p. 201). But there is more than that. "It is not sufficient, therefore, merely to behave with an easy condescension towards those friends who are of less considerable note than oneself; it is incumbent . . . to bring them forward, and, as much as possible, to raise their consequence" (p. 202).

Another good attribute is manliness. "There are numberless occasions which may render an absence between friends highly expedient; and to endeavour, from an impatience of separation, to prevent it, betrays a degree of weakness inconsistent with that firm and manly spirit, without which it is impossible to act up to the character of a true friend" (pp. 203–204). Here, of course, Cicero recalls the age-old Roman emphasis on *virtus,* manly excellence, which, as he suggests, includes not only courage but poise.

There are, on the other hand, motives damaging to friendship: calculation for gain would be one of them. Perhaps even worse is for someone to ask a friend to join him in an illegal or immoral venture. Cicero was firm. "I lay it down, then, as a rule without exception, 'that no degree of friendship can either justify or excuse the commission of a criminal action' " (p. 187). Condemned too is a person "capable of taking an ill-natured satisfaction in reprehending the frailties of his friend" (p. 189).

True to his Stoic principles, Cicero finds friendship a part of man's nature. Thus, "it derives its origin . . . from a distinct principle implanted in the breast of man; from a certain instinctive tendency, which draws congenial minds into union" (p. 182). So, he writes, "It is the total disparity between the disposition and manners of the virtuous and the vicious that alone renders their coalition incompatible" (p. 203).

Cicero takes time out to attack current philosophies which offered different views on friendship from his own. In particular, he denounced the Cynics, whose love of total self-sufficiency led to an unwillingness to rely on friends, let alone get married. The Cynics renounced all possessions, including friends. But for Cicero a friend is different: "A true friend is a treasure which no power, how formidable soever, can be sufficient to wrest from the happy possessor" (p. 195). The Hedonists were worse for, although they embraced others, it was only for what they could get and never for what they could give. Cicero disapproved of this hardening of the heart: "Extinguish all emotions of the heart and what difference will remain, I do not say between man and brute, but between man and a mere inanimate clod? Away then with those austere philosophers who represent virtue as hardening the soul against all the softer impressions of humanity" (p. 192).

Yet, like it or not, that has always been one of the chief criticisms levelled against Cicero's own beloved Stoicism. As one modern critic put it, "The Stoics turned their hearts to stone and called it peace."

Most of the essay is about attachments which abide. But friendships can be broken. Perhaps the best passages in Cicero's essay deal with this problem. He advises that if there has to be a break, let it be by stages, a gradual cooling off without rancor. Cicero's gentleman retains his poise, no matter how trying the circumstances. There is no doubt that an abrupt termination of a friendship could mean ill temper and rash accusations. If possible, insults should be received with silence. True to Stoicism, Cicero believes that the mistakes of others should not compel us to make any of our own.

He concludes his essay by returning to his theme: "Let me only again exhort you to be well persuaded that there can be no real friendship which is not founded upon virtuous principles, nor any acquisition, virtue alone excepted, preferable to a true friend" (p. 215).

Cicero's standards were extraordinarily high. Yet he might well have understood why others settled for less, since he elsewhere admits "Human nature . . . is so constituted as to be incapable of lonely satisfactions" (p. 208).

XIII

Government by the Emperor for the People

Amid the political turmoil of the times in which they were written, Cicero's essays were remarkably quiet and reflective. But with the assassination of Julius Caesar, Cicero was back on stage again for one final influential role before he too was murdered on December 7, 43 B.C. Thus, one by one, did the major figures of the later Republic pass from the scene. Finally, after a brief war with Antony, Octavian stood alone. He had been born in 63 B.C., the year Cicero was consul, and represented a new generation and a new hope.

Octavian was lucky. When he returned to Rome from Egypt in 29 B.C., nearly everybody was longing for peace, after the century of intermittent civil war. The Roman people gave him an uncommon welcome, and the Senate ordered the gates of Janus closed. Even though Octavian fell ill, an elaborate celebration went on for days. The Romans had a habit of rating these occasions by the number and variety of animals slain. This time a rhinoceros and hippopotamus added new excitement.

In the following year, Octavian and his friends mulled over the kind of settlement which should be arranged now that he had become the new "Caesar." Among his closest advisers were

19. Agrippa. The Louvre. Photograph courtesy of Maurice Chuzeville.

Agrippa and Maecenas, a wealthy patron of the arts, both sound men of experience. In the past, when he was out of the city, he had trusted them to read and revise his letters to the Senate. They did not always share the same opinion, and on the question at hand they again gave him contrary points of view. Octavian had to weigh the consequences of giving up his absolute control, as Agrippa advised, or find a way of keeping it, as Maecenas suggested, without allowing the impression that he wanted to be a king. Octavian realized the constitution of the Republic could no longer operate without controls. Too many men of the present generation had grown up under the sway of military rulers rather than their own laws. Nevertheless, the idea of a king, or maybe just the name, was repugnant to the Roman people.

Dio Cassius, in his *History of Rome,* attributes to Agrippa a long speech in which the dangers of a monarchy are discussed. In brief, he warned that a claim to all power had the appearance of evil, whether in fact the government was wicked or not. Octavian chose the appearance of goodness. He loudly disavowed all power. At the same time, to guarantee stability, he retained a military force sufficient to make his influence irresistible. His own version of this arrangement was later given in his *Res Gestae,* a statement of "things accomplished." The original bronze inscription which stood in front of his mausoleum in Rome has been lost, but copies were fortunately set up elsewhere in the Empire. One was discovered in the sixteenth century on the walls of a temple at Ankara in Turkey (ancient Ancyra in Galatia). The statement was prepared when the Emperor was seventy-five and nearing the end of his life. It is more of a long epitaph than a short autobiography. He remembered nothing unpleasant. The following is a key passage: "After I had put an end to the civil wars, having attained supreme power by universal consent, I transferred the state from my own power to the control of the Roman Senate and people" (Lewis and Reinhold, Vol. II, p. 19). This was not the whole truth. Dio Cassius tells the real story. When Octavian and Agrippa, using their consular *imperium,* held a census some years earlier, they used the occasion to remove persons allegedly "without merit" from the Senate. Octavian, with the Senate's concurrence, also advanced several families to patrician status, since many of the old families had been wiped out during the civil wars and some in the proscriptions, including his own. Those promoted were given a seat in the Senate. They knew whom to thank. It was to this Senate that Octavian made a crucial speech during his seventh consulship in 27 B.C. His friends were there, and some of them knew what he would say. It was that although he possessed supreme power and had widespread support, he was determined to resign:

> I give up my office completely, and restore to you absolutely every-thing,—the army, the laws, and the provinces,—not only those which you committed to me, but also those which I myself later acquired for you. . . . Since, then, Fortune, by using me, has graciously restored to you peace without treachery and harmony without faction, receive back also your liberty and the republic; take over the army and the subject provinces, and govern yourselves as has been your wont. (LIII. 4.3, 4; 5.4)

Denying that this was a great self-sacrifice, he asked, "Will it not add most to my renown to resign so great an empire, will it not

add most to my glory to leave so exalted a sovereignty and voluntarily become a private citizen?" (LIII. 6.3,4). This was Octavian's
grand gesture towards the Senate and the People of Rome—*Senatus Populusque Romanus*—symbolized by the letters SPQR, which
are still prominent in the city.

The senators who took his words at face value were probably a small minority. The rest either knew or suspected that he
intended to have the Senate grant him special powers—and with
ostensible willingness. A majority shared Octavian's private view
that to restore the old republican system intact would be an invitation to renewed factionalism and civil war. A firm hand was
needed. The government would have to be managed. Octavian's
urge to be humble suggested he was the man for the job; at least
there was no one willing to suggest anybody else. The senators
who were made uncomfortable by his "cunning" kept their embarrassment to themselves. Others, Dio says, "kept applauding
him enthusiastically." By giving up all power, he received it back.
A congenial big lie resulted in a unique arrangement.

Among Octavian's first acts was a division of the provinces,
giving the Senate charge of the peaceful ones and taking under his
own supervision any which might foment trouble. He of course
retained the ultimate control over all provinces, for he later
switched them around, taking some away from the Senate and
giving it others as the need for military forces changed with new
circumstances. If this meant sharing the responsibility and the
problems, it also meant keeping the Senate from having any military power. He reserved for himself supreme command of the
armed forces. There would be no civil wars, because there would
be no other armies.

In 29, when Octavian was consul for the fifth time, he took
the title Imperator. He had already been designated Imperator
twenty-one times because custom allowed the title to be conferred
on a general for his victories. Now, however, Octavian took it as
a permanent title, "which signifies the possession of the supreme
power." Julius Caesar had also used it so. To enable him to direct
domestic affairs, Octavian was later, 23 B.C., given tribunitial
power for life (although he was never actually a tribune). Since, in
addition, he called himself *Princeps,* a polite way of saying he was
the most distinguished of the Roman statesmen, it all added up to
precisely the authority which he purposely disavowed. The essential difference was the way he behaved. He lived in a modest

house and walked the streets of Rome like any other magistrate. The fact that he played a special role in the government was simply noted by a title no one else had ever had. He was called Augustus. The name had a connotation of sacredness and put him in a class by himself. Suetonius wrote that "sanctuaries and all places consecrated by the augurs" were known as "august." Caesar's calendar was changed. The month Sextilis became August. It was the month in which Augustus had held his first consulship at the age of nineteen. He preferred to commemorate that event rather than his birthday in September.

In the *Res Gestae,* his description of his unique role in the state had a kind of theological ambiguity. He said, "I excelled all in authority, but I possessed no more power than the others who were my colleagues in each magistracy" (Lewis and Reinhold, Vol. II, p. 19). No more "power," but certainly more influence. And he used it shrewdly, for the Senate felt free on occasion to vote against his opinion.

In 23 B.C., the Senate voted that Augustus (who had resigned his ninth consecutive consulship early to enable others to hold the office that year) "hold once for all and for life the office of proconsul, so that he had neither to lay it down upon entering the *pomerium* (from earliest times a strip of unoccupied sacred land which separated the areas of civil and military jurisdiction) nor to have it renewed again, and they gave him in the subject territory authority superior to that of the governor in each instance" (Dio, LIII. 32.5–6).

To see Augustus in the best light would be to recall the old Platonic dream of intelligence ruling the world for the common good. A less sympathetic view would make him the front man for a quietly efficient inner circle, or oligarchy, composed of his closest friends. Others might prefer to call him a constitutional monarch. Whatever the arrangement, it worked. His settlement with the Senate produced the Principate, a government which lasted, in theory at least, until A.D. 285, when it gave way to the autocratic rule of Emperor Diocletian. Noting the difference in the reigns of Augustus and Diocletian, Edward Gibbon wrote: "It was the aim of the one to disguise, and the object of the other to display, the unbounded power which the emperors possessed over the Roman world" (Vol. I, p. 332). Yet in some respects the trend was toward despotism even from Augustus' own day.

In view of the many honors showered on Augustus—and he

even refused a few—it would be difficult to deny that he was a paternal figure. The *Res Gestae* states: "For successes achieved on land and on sea by me or through my legates under my auspices the senate decreed fifty-five times that thanksgiving be offered to the immortal gods" (Lewis and Reinhold, Vol. II, pp. 10–11).

History is more than events, laws passed, and speeches given. It is also the subtle hints of what is really happening. During the Augustan era, there were signs of a gradual slackening of personal responsibility. Some senators began to wonder if it really mattered what they thought or did. In 17 B.C., Augustus was worried about the number of senators who straggled into the Senate after a session had begun. He began to exact heavier fines from those who could not give a satisfactory explanation for being late. By 11 B.C., so many senators were absent altogether that he had to permit business to be conducted by even fewer than four hundred members out of six hundred, although that had not been allowed before. To keep members of the Senate awake and attentive, Augustus dropped the old rule of the members' speaking according to seniority and began to call on them at random, hoping to avoid the evasion they sometimes practiced by simply announcing, "I agree with the last speaker." As mentioned earlier, Julius Caesar during his first consulship in 59 B.C. had introduced the practice of publishing the proceedings of the Senate. Augustus ended this and so cut off one of the few remaining democratic aspects of the Republic.

Because of men's growing reluctance to serve on juries, Augustus ordered the age qualification to be lowered from thirty-five to thirty. He was also disturbed because almost nobody was interested in standing for the tribunate. His own tribunitial power had actually made the office an empty title; yet he was determined to maintain the constitutional facade. Those already holding the office were required to nominate men who would, like it or not, stand for election to the post. Unlike the situation in the early centuries of the Republic, when the Romans were slowly learning how to participate in government, the early centuries of the Empire saw them learning how to give it up.

Paternalism can also be seen in the energetic effort Augustus made to restore to Roman life the moral tone of bygone days. On the practical side, the dwindling proportion of Roman citizens to the rest of the population of the Empire foreboded ill. Among the upper classes in particular, too many men and women were remaining single, too many married couples were having few if any children, and both groups were seemingly engaged in outrageous promiscuity. Augustus' laws were designed to take the pleasure out of everything but normal family living. Bachelors were not permitted to hold public office, and neither they nor spinsters were allowed to attend public entertainments, except as they were later permitted to do so on Augustus' birthday. There were also limits on what legacies they could receive. On the other hand, married couples with three or more children were greatly favored. A man with three legitimate children was excused from the age qualification for public office and could serve more often, as he was also excused from the required interval between terms. There were thus positive inducements for a man to get married and settle down; and, the law was strict on adultery. Either a husband or father-in-law could kill the man involved. A father could kill his daughter. Exile was an alternative. Augustus made that choice for his own promiscuous daughter, Julia. In 2 B.C., she was sent to the island of Pandateria (northwest of Naples); he never let her return to Rome. Suetonius writes: "He kept Julia for five years on the prison island of Pandateria before moving her to Reggio in Calabria, where she received somewhat milder treatment" (II. 65). Her daughter, the younger Julia, was exiled ten years later for "indulging in every sort of vice."

Augustus was apparently among the last to hear of his only child's drunken orgies; according to Dio, he never recovered from the shock. Among the instructions he left to be read after his death was one excluding Julia from being interred with the other members of the family in his tomb. If Julia did not measure up to her father's expectations, she probably had reason for some complaint of her own. She was at the center of Augustus' dynastic plans. First, there was a childless marriage to her cousin Marcellus, who died in 23 B.C., then she bore five children during her marriage to Agrippa, who died in 12 B.C., and finally at her father's orders there was a marriage to the humorless Tiberius, from whom presumably she sought some escape.

If Augustus could not manage the morals of his own daughter, what could he expect from the society which Livy had said "could stand neither its vices nor their cure?" The attempt to outlaw vice was Augustus' most conspicuous failure. Perhaps he was in part to blame himself. Dio Cassius repeats the rumor that a certain coolness developed between Augustus and Maecenas because of the Emperor's attentions to the latter's wife. If true, he was not following the advice Maecenas had given him earlier. According to Dio, Maecenas pointed to one of the main reasons for the failure of the Republic—the corruption which began at the top. He is reported to have told Augustus: "Whatever you wish your subjects to think and do, this you should always say and do yourself. . . . one finds it easier to imitate that which is good when he sees it actually practised than to avoid that which is evil when he hears it forbidden by mere words" (LII. 34.1–2).

Augustus was proud of his generosity and kept accounts of the money he had distributed on various occasions. In the *Res Gestae* he says that, obeying Julius Caesar's will, he gave three hundred sesterces to every Roman plebeian. Later, in 29 B.C., of his own volition, he gave them four hundred apiece, and the same amount was given twice again in subsequent years. Twelve times at his own expense he made a special gift of grain. He does not mention that the city proletariat and the veterans were especially vocal in their demands, but he does record the extra amounts he gave to these groups. Ex-soldiers were undoubtedly his greatest personal expense. Not only did he give them bonuses from time to time, but he actually paid for the Italian or provincial land where he set up colonies of those men who had been mustered out of service.

There was an extensive building program under Augustus. He built a dozen temples and repaired eighty-two others. Repairs and additions to existing government buildings, roads, aqueducts, and bridges were made. But Augustus initiated fewer new structures of this kind; temples were his main concern. He was anxious to restore the old-time religion and took membership in several priestly colleges, helping to revive some of them. After the death of Lepidus he became *pontifex maximus*.

Gifts to the people, support for the treasury, entertainments, and a major building program were necessary and, at the same time, calculated to buy good will. Augustus certainly offended no one. More citizens than ever before began to feel grateful for the paternal care of the imperial administration. After several generations, who could remember when they had not been?

20. Pont-du-Gard, near Nîmes, in southern France, one of the best preserved Roman aqueducts, built in the last quarter of the first century B.C. Courtesy of the French Government Tourist Office, New York.

Keeping the Peace

Under Augustus, the limits of the Roman Empire were determined wherever possible by geography. A perimeter of rivers, seashores, and desert surrounded the Mediterranean basin. In his long regime, Augustus allowed very few campaigns outside these defensible boundaries. A successful one was an invasion of Ethiopia led by his first legate in Egypt, Gaius Cornelius Gallus. Gallus succeeded in temporarily ending the troubles along Egypt's southern frontier and set up a buffer area south of the first cataract. Nine years later, however, Augustus had to send a stronger expeditionary force into Ethiopia to insure compliance with Roman authority in the area. Earlier, Gallus had maintained internal peace in Egypt, particularly around Thebes, ever a center of native restlessness. Unfortunately, success was his undoing. He had inscrip-

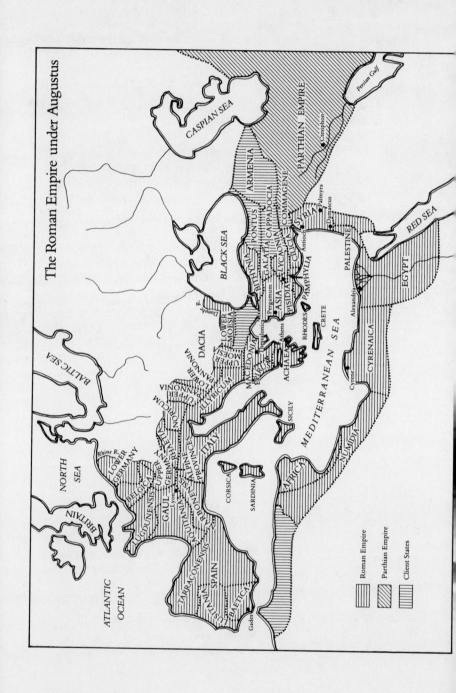

The Roman Empire under Augustus

tions boasting of his accomplishments carved everywhere, even on pyramids, and erected several statues of himself. Apparently, he had missed Augustus' message about who should receive the glory for all endeavors. Augustus dismissed him in a hurry, whereupon Gallus killed himself. Under the Empire, suicide became an acceptable, even expected, form of apology.

In the Near East, Augustus preferred diplomacy to warfare and sponsored numerous successful claimants to the Armenian and Parthian thrones as a means to keeping the peace. Besides negotiation, however, threats were needed to get back the Roman standards lost by Crassus and Antony to the Parthians. Augustus was fortunate to recover them as easily as he did, for it was unlikely that he wanted a war with Parthia. He was sensitive about past experiences; the Romans had never seen much success in the barren spaces east of Syria. Augustus was content with the Euphrates as the Eastern frontier, and that restraint did not detract from his reputation. He mentioned in the *Res Gestae* that embassies came from distant India to seek his friendship.

A successful campaign in Germany by Augustus' stepson Drusus carried Roman standards to the Elbe River, and, in 9 B.C., when Drusus died in camp after a fall from his horse, he and his descendants were given the name Germanicus by the Senate. His brother, Tiberius, sought to consolidate the gains made in the area, but, later, a three year war with the Pannonians (A.D. 6–9) taxed the Romans' resources, and they were unable to stabilize their claim in Germany. After the loss of three legions by the general Quinctilius Varus in the Teutoburg Forest (A.D. 9), Augustus let his hair and beard grow as a sign of mourning. "Quinctilius Varus, give back the legions!" he was said to have cried. His despair was heightened by the fact that Varus, now another suicide, had behaved with "haste and recklessness," two qualities Augustus had often criticized in his military commanders. In any event, he now accepted the Rhine as the best place to stop.

Three times during the Augustan regime the gates of the Temple of Janus were closed, to symbolize the state of peace throughout the Empire. Only twice before had the gates been shut. But apparently not every Roman was happy at the prospect of his sons serving in the noble cause of keeping the peace. Suetonius says a certain equestrian cut off the thumbs of his two sons to keep them from enlisting in the army. Augustus punished the man by confiscating his property.

Augustus worked hard at being a responsible ruler. It was sometimes late in the evening before he finished all his paper work. He was his own inspector-general, made frequent tours of the provinces to see for himself what was going on, and managed to visit every province in the Empire except Sardinia and Africa. One of his aims was to make the roads and seas of the Empire safe for everyday travel. In areas where highwaymen were known to operate he posted armed guards.

At Rome, better security was achieved by dividing the city into fourteen districts with local supervisors. In an effort to combat the loss of life and property in nighttime fires, Augustus placed watchmen around the city like modern air-raid wardens to keep an eye out for fires and alert the brigades when necessary. Also, armed guards were stationed at regular posts to keep hoodlums from harassing people on deserted streets. This was the first police department Rome ever had.

The Altar of Peace

In 13 B.C., the Senate voted to erect in the Campus Martius an Altar of Peace (*Ara Pacis*) to commemorate Augustus' pacification of Gaul and Spain. In modern times, the first fragments of this monument were found in 1568, but it was not until 1937 that a reconstruction was undertaken and the restored altar housed in a building by the Tiber, near Augustus' mausoleum.

The Altar of Peace is a rectangular block of marble surrounded by a wall twenty feet high. The north and south sides of the wall are approximately thirty-five feet in length. On the east and west sides, which are about thirty-eight feet long, there are broad doorways. Steps at one end lead to the platform where the altar stands. Compared to the enormous arches and columns of the imperial period, the Altar of Peace seems restrained and refined. The reliefs decorating the outer walls contribute to this impression. They are among the best examples of Roman sculpture; the treatment of the drapery is especially fine. Although these reliefs may have been executed by Greek artists, they show distinctly Roman taste. The allegorical figures, Earth, Wind, and Water, are harmoniously grouped in a single panel, reflecting the universality of the Augustan peace. Wheat stalks, flowers, and resting animals add a pastoral touch.

In the main scene, Augustus and his family and friends are

shown walking in a procession en route to a sacrifice to the goddess of Peace. The figures are grouped as in a crowd the way they might have actually appeared. Athenian artists of the Greek classical period put balance and beauty before realism. The Romans were inclined the other way, and even included children in their processional scenes, although the smaller figures upset the balance of the composition.

Augustus the Man

The title of Emperor may bring to mind an imposing figure in opulent robes enjoying the luxury of a sumptuous palace. This was not Augustus' style. One of the vignettes Suetonius offers is of a lean figure with rather delicate features, wearing a simple wool gown, outstretched on a low couch with his hand over his eyes, catching a few winks after a light lunch. Many Roman businessmen lived a richer life. Augustus may have been one of the mightiest men of all time, but the life he lived was middle-class. He was born on the twenty-third of September in 63 B.C., the year Cicero was consul. The house of his birth later became a shrine. His family was of respectable equestrian stock and fairly well-to-do. Augustus was four when his father died. He lost his mother during his first consulship when he was twenty. Both his father and his maternal grandfather had held praetorships and performed other public services. More important, however, was the fact that his maternal grandmother was Julius Caesar's sister.

As happened frequently in ancient times, a person who had achieved the heights which Augustus had was sooner or later furnished with a divine paternity. In his case it was said that a god in the guise of a serpent had visited his mother in the Temple of Apollo nine months before he was born. The story served to explain his special fortune as well as to flatter him. It was also commonly believed that an astrologer had proclaimed at his birth, "The ruler of the world is now born." Suetonius comments at some length about the numerous portents in Octavian's childhood which foreshadowed the majesty of the Augustus he would become.

The real Augustus was rather bland. During his long reign he seems not to have aroused men's feelings one way or the other. There was of course a wide range of individual reaction. Dio says Augustus "received praise from the people of good sense and was even given the right to convene the Senate as often as he pleased; but some of the others despised him" (LIV. 3. 3–4). While his modesty and moderation won him great praise, in the *Res Gestae* the list of the many honors he received sounds perfunctory and formal. Nevertheless, he succeeded in reestablishing the order which had been disrupted by the more exciting personalities of the past century. The contrast is an argument against glamour in politics. He seems to have deliberately avoided a cult of personality. On the other hand, such a cult may not have been possible. Augustus did not have Julius Caesar's sophistication, imagination, or charisma. Upon his arrival in Egypt, local officials were anxious to show him their treasures and sacred places. He went to see the corpse of Alexander the Great and even succumbed to the tourist instinct of touching it. But when invited to visit the shrine of the precious bull calf, the god Apis, he declined, saying that he did not care to see any cattle. In any evaluation of the man, that particular statement is hard to forget.

Augustus occasionally lost his temper, even in public, and needed the restraining counsel of his friends to keep him from acting rashly. That he easily took such advice, especially from Maecenas in the early years, and was grateful for it, shows one of his most admirable qualities. His eagerness to enjoy the good opinion of other men was exactly the opposite of the attitude of the brilliant, but self-satisfied, Julius Caesar. Augustus liked to know the reaction of the Assembly to legislation he was proposing so that he could amend it to conform to public opinion. He also regularly discussed his ideas with a small group of senators and a select number of public officials before taking up certain matters with the full Senate. Elections continued to be held, although when Augustus nominated anybody it was equivalent to victory. As for the other candidates, he wanted only to be certain that they were qualified.

Another of Augustus' good traits was his appreciation of other men's talents. The affection, praise, and honor he lavished on Agrippa showed Augustus to be sincere as well as practical. Agrippa was a superior military man. He took Sicily from Sextus and later managed the victory at Actium. Augustus was dependent on him during the early years of the Principate. When Augustus was gone from Rome, he had Agrippa take charge. To seal the bond, Agrippa was required to divorce his wife and marry Julia. When Agrippa died in 12 B.C., the Emperor began to rely more on his stepsons Tiberius and Drusus, and later to a limited degree on his grandsons Gaius and Lucius.

In time, according to Dio, Augustus became reconciled to the dangers which a man in his position must face. During a forty-year reign there were bound to be conspiracies born of intrigue, and occasionally a man was executed for being involved in overt action against the Emperor. Not all the attempts on Augustus' life, however, resulted from plots in high places. Humble persons acting on their own, and being possibly deranged, tried now and then to get near him in what may have been attempts at assassination. When it was once suggested in the Senate that the senators themselves should guard Augustus, one of them said he would have to be excused from sleeping at the Emperor's bedroom door because his own snoring might keep the Emperor awake.

Augustus preferred a fine or exile as the punishment for those who wrote or said anything insulting toward him and was apparently not unduly offended. Again, he was usually faced with individuals acting on their own and not representing any faction. All-powerful as he was, he could afford a mild rebuke from the Senate now and then. Once when a sharp disagreement developed in the Senate over one of Augustus' appointees, a senator shouted, "A man is entitled to his own opinion." Augustus let that stand, as the senator had the courage to speak for himself. The Emperor bore down harshly, however, on anyone who issued a statement under a false name. Augustus recognized the ineffectiveness of large-scale purges to stop envy or suspicion. Dio quotes him as saying, "Indeed, we should be equals of the gods if we had not troubles and cares and fears beyond all men in private station. But precisely this is what causes my grief,—that this is inevitably so and that no remedy for it can be found" (LV. 15. 2).

Dio's generally favorable treatment of Augustus is occasionally varied by an unflattering story. The Emperor seems to have been somewhat revengeful, forgetting Maecenas' advice. Antony's old friends still had reason for fear. Octavian said that he had burned all of the letters which Antony had kept locked up. Actually, Dio says, he kept most of them, and later "did not scruple to make use of them."

Augustus always had an alert mind, but never a strong body. The famous statue of him as Imperator, found in Livia's garden at Prima Porta, was quite flattering. The sculptor gave him a physique akin to that of Polycleitus' renowned *Spearbearer;*

21. Augustus, the Imperator statue found in 1863 in his wife Livia's villa at Prima Porta near Rome. Courtesy of the Museo Vaticano, Rome.

actually, Augustus had weak legs. Suetonius says that as a soldier, when still very young, Augustus had injured a leg and both arms when a bridge collapsed. Over the years, he was frequently ill, being especially bothered by colds, accompanied by diarrhea, bladder trouble, and finally rheumatism. As mentioned earlier, he was incapacitated during part of the welcoming ceremonies when he returned to Rome in 29 B.C. Again in 25, he was too ill to attend the marriage of Julia to Marcellus. Agrippa had to preside in his place. In 23, he became so ill that death seemed imminent. His physician, Antonius Musa, gave him successful treatments involving cold baths and cold potions. For this Musa was well paid and received permission to wear a gold ring, a distinct honor for a freedman.

In spite of his uneven health, Augustus lived a long life and was married three times. Early in the Second Triumvirate, he married Antony's stepdaughter, Clodia. He soon divorced her and married Scribonia, and so gave himself a better tie to one of her relatives, Sextus Pompey, at a time when he needed it. That marriage also ended in divorce, but not before his only child, Julia, was born. His third marriage to Livia was for love and for life. Yet Suetonius adds that it was common knowledge that Augustus often had extramarital affairs. Whether the story contradicts his legislation against adultery or was prompted by it cannot be known.

A man in his position would have attracted gossip no matter what he did. Actually, Augustus appears to have lived a rather routine life. It was certainly not exotic. His interest in younger women as he grew older cannot be considered a particularly exceptional diversion. He never drank much; and if it could be said that he had a major vice, it was gambling, but he could afford that. And certainly he could have enjoyed a larger house with finer furnishings if he had wanted them. His modest house on the Palatine Hill, later called the Palatium, was by no means a palace, although that is where the word comes from. Augustus ate simply and dressed comfortably rather than ostentatiously. Heavy soled shoes to make him appear taller supplied the only touch of vanity.

Aside from occasional outbursts of temper, Augustus was a mild man whose pleasant smile set others at ease. His congenial and natural manner made those who might have been stiff in his company relax and enjoy themselves. He did not need flattery and had a well-known stern look for flatterers. He was a man of average intelligence, wise enough not to try to pass himself off as brilliant. His many superstititons were those of the common men of the day, not the intellectuals. It was "bad luck to thrust his right foot into the left shoe as he got out of bed." He did not speak well extemporaneously and did not try to. He usually wrote down in advance anything he had to say, and according to Suetonius, aimed at clarity with a simple and direct style. He occasionally wrote some prose and a little poetry, but apparently nothing particularly outstanding. His taste in reading ran to moralistic treatises; he had no time to spare for the *avant garde*. One thinks of today's man who tacks pithy slogans on a bulletin board. Augustus did, in fact, send his aides brief passages copied from the books he read.

The many sculptural portraits of Augustus do credit to his face. He was a handsome man with pleasing, if somewhat delicate, features. In stature he was small and slight. (Suetonius thought his quoted height, equivalent to our five feet seven inches, was an overestimate.) This is the Augustus who is remembered, not the aged ruler with yellowing hair, decaying teeth, and dimming eyesight. In his declining years, he made few public appearances; he rarely left his house, even to go to the Senate.

The Emperor as Patron

Before age curtailed his activities, Augustus frequently visited persons of high standing on their birthdays and went to see them if they were ill. He entertained a wide circle of officials at dinner parties. The tone was one of Periclean formality without extravagance. He had few close friends; however, he was generous with his patronage, and among those who benefited were two of the major poets of the day.

Publius Vergilius Maro (70–19B.C.) would have been the poet laureate of the early Empire, had such a title existed. His great epic, the *Aeneid*, telling of the adventures of the legendary Aeneas, glorified the time-honored virtues which Augustus was anxious to restore to Roman life. Some passages seemed to suggest that the Emperor was himself the living example of the good Old Roman. In Vergil's earlier poetry Augustus could also find much to his liking. The pastoral poems, the *Eclogues* or *Bucolics,* and especially the four books of his *Georgics,* described the simple life of the land and its rewards. Amid the hustle of Rome's commercialism and its jaded social whirl, Vergil's verse was clean, clear, and nostalgic as an old song.

Vergil was born on a country estate near Mantua, in Cisalpine Gaul, and that is where he grew up. After losing his property in the confiscations following Philippi, he was fortunate to have Maecenas, Augustus' companion, consider him a promising poet. In fact, Maecenas became his patron, and the sensitive, somewhat retiring Vergil was able to spend the rest of his life near Naples, writing the poetry which gave him the best reputation a Roman poet ever earned. Some critics stress the optimism of the *Aeneid,* others its pessimism. Vergil had the good sense to include both. He credited courageous men with great deeds; and yet, while sympathetic toward the human condition, he was aware of the tragic gulf between what most men want to be and what they are. Augustus was not concerned with the philosophic undertones of Vergil's work. The obvious message was one of destiny and duty, and that was what he wanted to hear.

Vergil introduced Quintus Horatius Flaccus (65–8 B.C.) to Maecenas' literary circle; Horace, too, came to enjoy the patronage of the Emperor. The tone of his poetry was never as patriotic as Vergil's, for he retained his republican sentiments, but satirical thrusts at upper-class decadence were in keeping with Augustus' complaints:

> But as wealth into our coffers flows in still increasing store,
> So, too, still our care increases, and the hunger still for more . . . .
>
> *(Odes,* III. 16)

His *Odes* in particular matched the sentiments Vergil expressed about the good life of the land. Mixed in was a familiar poetic theme:

> And fret not your soul with uneasy desires
> For the wants of a life, which but little requires;
> Youth and beauty fade fast, and age, sapless and hoar,
> Tastes of love and the sleep that comes lightly no more.
>
> *(Odes,* II. 11)

Horace began to write after he had retired from politics. As a young man, he had taken his chances with Brutus at Philippi and lost. After Maecenas gave him a farm in the Sabine Hills, he settled down to a quiet literary life, which enabled him to view with tolerance the foibles and fancies of man. There was nothing bitter about his comments. Who would want to argue with his tongue-in-cheek observation that:

> The trouble with all singers is, when
>   you want them to sing,
> They're not in the mood, but when you
>   just wish they wouldn't
> They can't refrain.
>
> *(Satires,* I. 3)

Augustus did not like Ovid—Publius Ovidius Naso (43 B.C.–*ca.* A.D. 17). His poems mirrored the sophisticated pleasures of the upper classes from the standpoint of a man who was in on the game. His *Amores* and the later *Art of Love* were out of tune with the Augustan program for moral reform. These impertinent

22. Horace, in section of marble frieze. Courtesy of the Museum of Fine Arts, Boston.

love poems gave Ovid a bad reputation, one which served him ill. It was rumored that he belonged to the unsavory crowd surrounding Augustus' granddaughter Julia, who was sent into exile. So was Ovid. He languished in the town of Tomi (modern Constanţa in Romania) on the Black Sea, and sought by any means possible to return to Rome, including revising the *Fasti,* a sober poetic review of Rome's festivals and today a valuable source on Roman religion. Still, he died in exile, about A.D. 17. A famous lament by Medea from his *Metamorphoses* summed up his life:

> I see, approving,
> Things that are good, and yet I follow
> worse ones.

(VII. 20–21)

The Last Problem

Julia's marriage to Agrippa gave Augustus five grandchildren: Gaius, Lucius, Agrippa Postumus, Julia the Younger, and Agrippina. The Emperor adopted the first two boys as his own sons and had great plans for their future, but they both died young. He then adopted his last grandson, Agrippa Postumus, but was soon disgusted by his despicable actions and disinherited him. Reluctantly, then, he was forced by circumstances to accept Tiberius, Livia's son by a previous marriage, as his heir. Since Tiberius' father was a member of the Claudian gens and Augustus belonged to the Julian, their successors are known as the Julio-Claudian dynasty.

In A.D. 14, after a brief vacation at Capri, Augustus was on his way home when he became ill at Nola, about sixteen miles from Naples. Tiberius was summoned, and it would be revealing to know what the Emperor said to him during their long final visit together.

Augustus' last problem was how to insure the peace by a smooth succession. But there was perhaps not much to worry about with the strong-willed Livia on hand as the chief promoter of her son. The Emperor had made it plain to the army that he wanted Tiberius to be his successor. He proclaimed the choice to the citizens in Rome when he gave him the tribunitial power. Nevertheless, as Augustus grew weak in his last years there continued to be speculation about alternatives. Anyone who dreamed of preventing Tiberius' succession was at a disadvantage by not knowing when to act. Livia managed Augustus' final days. Announcements of his condition remained optimistic until a sudden bulletin said that he was dead. Augustus died quietly in the mid-afternoon of August 19, A.D. 14. Livia was with him. At that moment, Tiberius became the new Emperor.

Augustus' body was borne with due solemnity to Rome, and after eulogies by Tiberius and his son, Drusus, was cremated in the Campus Martius. The remains were placed in the mausoleum which he had prepared for himself. Tiberius had warned that he would not allow hysterical outbursts at the funeral. Guards were posted to prevent a repetition of what had happened when Caesar's body was burned. Tiberius did not like public displays of emotion; he never made any himself.

The principal heirs were Livia and Tiberius. There was also a distribution of silver to the people and to the army, the Praetorian Guard being especially favored. In another sense, his real legacy to the Romans was the greater security which Dio said he had given the world. Dio commented reflectively that whereas under the Republic there had been conflicting reports about the same event, hereafter there seemed to be only one version—the

1. The Julio-Claudian Succession

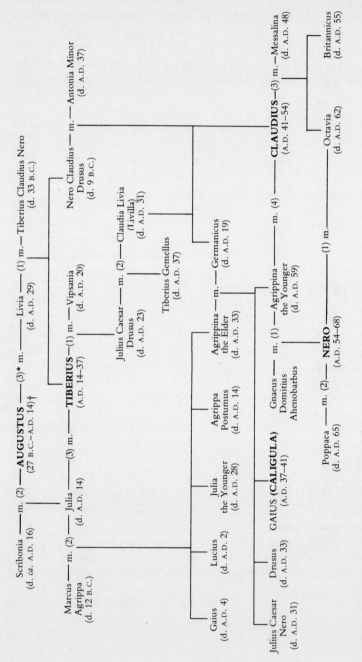

* The notation (3) on Augusutus' side of the "m." indicates it was his third marriage.

† Inclusive dates refer to length of reign.

official one approved by Augustus. Whoever disagreed would be a threat to security. That was the price the Romans paid for peace and unity.

Augustus was dutifully declared to be a god, and a temple was erected in his honor. Henceforth, emperors who followed his example by ruling constitutionally would join the ranks of the deified Caesars. Tiberius would not be one of them.

XIV
Power without Glory

Augustus' was a hard act to follow. Nobody could have expected to take his place. Tiberius always spoke of him with fulsome praise and worked at carrying on his program for peace and prosperity. Yet all that Tiberius did was lost in the face of his failure to maintain the political climate which Augustus had created. Tiberius never evoked respect, much less love. He dealt with the Senate as though he were engaged in a fencing match. The senators had good reason to be cautious, for Tiberius early gave evidence of his spitefulness. Any speaker who even inadvertently offended him was quick to correct the error before he sat down. There were those who suggested that Augustus had protected his own memory when he chose Tiberius, for he was surely "the worst of possible comparisons" (I. 10). So said the historian Tacitus (*ca.* A.D. 55–120), who wrote in his *Annals,* a fascinating account of Tiberius and his reign.

Tacitus wrote roughly a century after Tiberius' time. He admitted that his picture was clouded by rumor, mostly unfavorable to the Emperor. The *Annals* covered not only Tiberius' reign but those of Gaius (Caligula), Claudius, and Nero. That parts of it are missing is unfortunate not only in the historical sense but because Tacitus was one of the greatest stylists of ancient times. Of his *Histories,* which treated the emperors in the latter third of the century, even less remains. For that period especially, it is necessary for the most part to depend on Gaius Suetonius Tranquillus who was born about A.D. 69 and probably lived for some years after his dismissal from the service of the Emperor Hadrian in 121. Previously, he had had access to imperial files, but he was not noted for his studiousness. His *Lives of the Twelve Caesars* is intact, but much less reliable than the works of Tacitus. The *Lives* are crammed with gossip, some of which sounds sensational even today. Tacitus knew that those who "listened at the door heard some secrets and invented more," but Suetonius hardly cared.

Neither Tacitus nor Suetonius lifted his sights much beyond the imperial household, and modern critics have been greatly exercised about their failure to consider sociological and economic aspects of the empire during the first century A.D. That would certainly have made their works more complete, but far less interesting. As it is, they focus on individuals, most of whom Tacitus found depressing. Yet his story was necessary, he said, because "the proper function of history, as I conceive it, is to insure that merits are not passed over, and that base words and deeds will have occasion to fear the judgment of posterity" (III. 65). It can be added that his works offer a rich store of notes on the social mores of the times.

Another reason Tacitus wrote was to set the record straight. While certain emperors were alive, contemporary historians felt constrained to give them a good press. He tipped the scale the other way. Presumably free to write as he pleased, his story was a stern indictment of men whom he believed to have been corrupted absolutely by power. At the same time Tacitus was honest. He repeated passages from excellent speeches Tiberius made in the Senate, even though they undercut his own almost totally negative view of the man. When he said he was writing "without prejudice or partisanship," he meant that he was not doctoring the evidence, although much of it was probably already corrupted by those who had passed it on. But he made no attempt to hide his personal distaste for Tiberius. Nor did he like the Emperor's mother, Livia, any better. In short, Tacitus had strong opinions based as much on intuition as on history.

Tiberius' reign began on a grim note. The murder of Augustus' grandson, Agrippa Postumus, was quick and quiet. He was an unruly youth, perhaps on the slow side, and in any event not suited for the succession. Yet his blood was "royal," and he might have been a rallying figure for disaffected persons. Tiberius probably wanted it to be believed that Augustus had ordered his grandson's death, and maybe he did. But everybody knew Livia hated the boy and Tiberius distrusted him. Who gave the order to a centurion to kill him remains a mystery; the affair was hushed up. If Tiberius had been more willing to talk about it, he might not have been so grossly accused. Afterwards, his critics could recall the deed as a forecast of the Emperor's secretive, often sinister ways. More of that later. First to something positive.

The Better Side

Tiberius' appointments were generally excellent, giving consideration to merit along with the usual prejudice in favor of selecting men from the "best" families. He was, however, slow in making his choices. Faced daily with new decisions, the burden often caused him to procrastinate. Too much depended on the Emperor. He occasionally told the Senate to stop bothering him with every question which came up and to take some initiative. His impatience was understandable. At one time the senators were in an uproar over a quarrel between an ex-praetor and a young nobleman about who should have a certain seat at the gladiatorial games.

As an administrator, Tiberius ran a taut ship. He kept a sharp eye on provincial officials and quickly punished corruption. State funds as well as his own were carefully guarded. His court was run with a modest staff and in most respects, his sexual tastes aside, he lived quietly as Augustus had done. Unlike his predecessor, he spent very little money on building projects. When major fires in A.D. 27 and 36 gutted large areas of Rome, however, Tiberius won widespread praise by supplying funds to rebuild the homes burnt out. As with Augustus, so with Tiberius, the place to turn in time of need was to the Emperor. That habit helped to rule out a return to republicanism. So did Tiberius' attendance at trials where he occasionally questioned the accused. One of them, it was said, felt it wrong to let the Emperor ask questions for nothing and so confessed a little. Although the Emperor "was acting in the interests of truth, the effect was to diminish freedom" (I. 75). It happened in the Senate, too. A senator asked him, "When are you going to vote? If first, you set me an example to follow: if last, I am afraid I may unintentionally disagree with you" (I. 74). Such remarks lend credence to Tacitus' evaluation of Tiberius' reign as a "thoroughly corrupt period, deeply tainted by servility" (III. 65). But Tiberius was himself disgusted at the degree to which men fawned on him. He called the senators "men ready to be slaves!" (III. 65). On this point Tacitus gives Tiberius his due: "He was no friend of civil liberty, but even he found such a degree of self-abasement intolerable" (III. 65). In short, from one standpoint, the Principate was a government the Romans deserved.

Tiberius insisted that some matters be left to the Senate's deliberations. Charges were made in the Senate that some roads in Italy were becoming impassable because of "the frauds of contractors and the slackness of the authorities." Prosecutions and convictions correct the notion that the Romans built roads for eternity. There were other instances of faulty construction. In A.D. 27, at Fidenae, an amphitheatre built by an unscrupulous contractor collapsed. Thousands were killed. The Senate began to regulate how and where such enormous structures should be built.

The Senate was often vexed by social or moral questions. In A.D. 21, at least one senator was alarmed about the new freedom which women had acquired in Roman society. He was against provincial governors taking their wives abroad: "The presence of women stimulates extravagance in peace, timidity in war. . . . The female sex is not only weak and unable to endure hardship, but, given encouragement, cruel, avaricious, and greedy for power. . . . Once they were restrained by the Oppian Laws and other legislation; now they have cast off their chains and dominate our homes, public business, the army itself!" (III. 33). This line of attack did not get very far. It was argued that the old laws did not suit the times, and besides women were no more addicted to "power or wealth" than men. The debate took place in A.D. 21, the year that Tiberius was consul for the fourth time and his son Drusus for the second. It was Drusus who had the final word when he said he would only leave Rome on military assignments "in a very grudging spirit if you intend to separate me from my dear wife, mother of all our children" (III. 34). Shortly thereafter, however, Tacitus mentions that Drusus was often criticized for leaving his "dear wife" while he went carousing at night.

On another matter, Tiberius' duel with the Senate showed his astuteness. Many voices had been raised about the failure of the old sumptuary laws to check the extravagance of living. In

A.D. 22, food prices on the black market soared. Without debate, the senators asked Tiberius to do something. He replied that he could well understand their own reluctance to tackle the problem. Those in favor of a crusade against vice could look virtuous while the Emperor who carried it out would reap the blame from prominent persons in the state whose wealth enabled them to be the worst offenders. Tiberius was not fooled. Would stricter enforcement do any good anyway?

> And if I have to get back to the old standards of simplicity, where do I start? With the enormous mansions and their polyglot hordes of slaves? With their heavy gold and silver plate, their masterpieces of painting and sculpture? With men's clothes—undistinguishable from women's—or with that special feature of feminine extravagance, the transfer of Roman currency to foreign, often hostile nations, for the purchase of jewelry? (III. 53)

In effect, he was saying that these were the times. And they were certainly not what they used to be. He suggested that the Senate expel certain dancers from Italy for putting on obscene shows. That was about as far as he went as a guardian of public morals.

Tacitus added comments of his own. If past events had brought on this laxity in living, then different circumstances would cause a reversal. Later in Tiberius' reign, when persons of great wealth were suspected of being involved in conspiracies, modesty became a safeguard. As time went on, prominent men from the Italian municipalities and provinces brought simpler tastes to the capital. Later in the century, when the rugged Vespasian became Emperor, it was wise to follow his moral example. Tacitus said: "It may well be that there is a kind of cycle in human affairs, and that morals alternate as do the seasons" (III. 55).

Tiberius consistently denied requests from overseas that temples be erected in his honor or that he be given divine honors. Although he allowed an exception in the province of Asia, his usual answer was that further temples and rites would attenuate the worship of the deified Augustus. Whether he was sincere or not, that was true. He preferred to await a verdict on his own divinity until he too had departed. As events showed, he waited too long.

Finally, Tiberius should be credited for shunning gladiatorial games, although not because he had any particular aversion to cruelty. Tacitus thought that he stayed away either because of his distaste for crowds or because of what he calls "his gloomy temperament."

23. Gladiators, from a third century mosaic. Galleria Borghese, Rome.
Courtesy of Gabinetto Fotografico Nazionale, Rome.

24. Gladiators, from a third century mosaic. Galleria Borghese, Rome.
Courtesy of Gabinetto Fotografico Nazionale, Rome.

25. Arch of Tiberius, Orange, built in the first century A.D., perhaps *ca.* A.D. 25. The decorations include reliefs commemorating the earlier victories of Julius Caesar in Gaul. Photograph courtesy of Arthur W. Forbes.

Keeping the Peace

During his twenty-three year reign, Tiberius generally managed to preserve the Augustan peace. There was a conspicuous display of legions in all parts of the Empire. Ironically, the most serious disturbances during the early years of Tiberius' reign were among his own troops in Pannonia (now parts of Hungary and Yugoslavia) and in Germany. The soldiers on the frontier were the forgotten men of the Empire. Peacetime chores gave them time to think about it. Demands followed. They wanted more pay, an end to the bribery necessary to get a leave, earlier retirement (after sixteen years), and something better than "a muddy swamp or stony hillside" as part of their pension. They were jealous of the Praetorian Guard at Rome, who were paid more and did not have to "live among savages." The recent succession of a new Emperor

26. Amphitheatre at Nîmes, built in the first century A.D., seating more than 20,000 spectators. Courtesy of the French Government Tourist Office, New York.

was in itself an incentive to trouble. Some of the discontent was, as always, blamed on the lazy, bad-tempered "scum of the army."

Tiberius depended on his son by his first marriage, Drusus, and his adopted son, Germanicus (his dead brother's son), to deal with the rebels. Although they were his personal representatives, they were more likely to cajole the troops by evoking the memory of Augustus. Germanicus had further help. His wife Agrippina and son Gaius were with him. When the trouble was at its

27. Maison Carrée, Gallo-Roman temple, built about 16 B.C. Photograph courtesy of Wayne Andrews.

28. Theater at Orange. Courtesy of the French Government Tourist Office, New York.

worst he sent his family away for safety. The soldiers were so chagrined to hear that Augustus' granddaughter and great-grandson felt threatened, they asked Germanicus to bring them back. The young Gaius was a favorite with the soldiers. They nicknamed him "Caligula" or "Little Boots," after the imitation army boots he wore. The name's connotation of a frolicsome child of course lost its meaning later during a short and disastrous reign.

In the case of the Fifth and Twenty-first legions, it was the loyal majority which suddenly attacked those soldiers known to be mutinous. When Germanicus arrived he was horrified and called it a massacre; nevertheless, he now had two strong legions and he needed them. The Germans often fought the Romans to a draw and even beat them now and then, but, as usual, quarrels among tribal leaders had a weakening effect. By comparison, Germanicus kept Roman morale high despite bad weather, short supplies, and rations "stained with mud and blood." Finally, in A.D. 16, he had his victory. The occasion was marked by an inscription: "This monument was dedicated to Mars and Jupiter and the deified Augustus by the army of Tiberius Caesar after the conquest of all the tribes between the Rhine and the Elbe" (II. 22). It was something of an exaggeration. There would be more fighting, even though the major resistance of the enemy had been broken. Yet Tiberius insisted that Germanicus return to Rome for a triumph and leave the rest of the war to Drusus, who could use a victory or two. Tiberius often praised Germanicus, but always appeared more sincere when speaking of his own son. Tacitus comments that Germanicus "was being deprived, through jealousy, of the honors he had won." Later, he says that Drusus managed to "provoke" trouble with the Germans so that he could finish them off and take credit for the pacification. Still, Drusus and Germanicus remained friends. Perhaps Germanicus' good nature guaranteed that. When he was recalled, there was much praise for him. Riding in triumph through the streets of Rome with five of his children crowded beside him in his chariot, he was the darling of the public.

In A.D. 21, there was trouble among desperate Gallic tribes, driven to act because of their heavy debts and poverty. When it was over, Tiberius wrote a letter telling the Senate "the war was begun—and finished." It is a good example of his secrecy. In North Africa, there was guerilla warfare. Tribesmen living near the desert were led by Tacfarinas, who had also once served with the Romans. Like Jugurtha of old, he seemed not to be worth an all-out effort, and yet managed to outsmart the local commanders. It was not until A.D. 24 that he was finally cornered and killed. In Thrace, a struggle between an uncle and a nephew whom Augustus had made kings in different parts of the country broke the peace. When the uncle, Rhescuporis, murdered his nephew, Cotys, Tiberius sent the governor of Moesia to Thrace to conduct the errant king to Rome. He was eventually sent into exile at Alexandria and other relatives were given power in the divided kingdom. Such events were typical of the housekeeping in the client kingdoms which added to Tiberius' busy schedule.

Elsewhere, provincial governors generally took care of local problems on their own with garrison soldiers on hand. In a disturbance in Judaea caused by a controversy over the claims of a Messiah among the Jews, Pontius Pilate, the Roman procurator, was determined to keep the peace. He found no fault with Jesus but it was expedient to quiet those who did. Judaea was a small, relatively unimportant province in the Roman Empire. What happened there received little notice in Rome.

Tacitus described Tiberius' wars as "petty" compared to the great struggles of the past. It was easier for Tiberius to keep peace in the Empire than in his own household, and this, in part, was due to his resentment of his adopted son Germanicus. Nobody served him better overseas, but that did not mean that the Emperor was grateful.

Germanicus

Germanicus is one of the most attractive personalities in Roman history. He was a handsome, good-natured man, who had great stamina, even if perhaps weak legs. Among the soldiers, "Some spoke of their general's noble birth, others of his physical beauty; all agreed about his endurance, his charm of manner, the level temper he kept in jest or earnest" (II. 13). There was much about him to remind older men that he was the grandson of Mark Antony, although he had far better sense. In the ruling classes, a happily married man who had had nine children and no scandal seemed a rarity. He was extremely popular with nearly everybody except the Emperor and his mother. Germanicus held a place in the hearts of the people which they knew they could never enjoy. Also, possibly, his goodness offended them. Certainly Tiberius had reason to be jealous. His own life was just the opposite, for he had been forced to divorce a woman he loved and marry the notorious Julia, who disliked him intensely. Julia died in A.D. 14, the same year as her father Augustus. She was still in exile, and her passing was of no concern to Tiberius. He was saddled, it was said, with a tyrannical mother, whom he resented but could never bring himself to break with. His own son, Drusus, was no match for the heroic Germanicus. His not so secret vices involving young boys were anything but those of a family man. Tacitus speaks of "the bleak and solitary life of Tiberius, with its gloomy vigilance and evil intentions" (III. 37).

In A.D. 17, Tiberius sent Germanicus to the East as a trouble-shooter. He was to rank above all the governors in the region—serving as a stand-in for Tiberius, who was reluctant to follow the Augustan example of making tours of inspection. At the same time, Tiberius sent a former confidant of Augustus, the proud and ambitious Gnaeus Calpurnius Piso, to be governor of Syria. Piso was as jealous of Germanicus as was Tiberius himself. The matching appointments were a prelude to trouble. As usual, Germanicus made himself popular wherever he went by the informality of his manner and the fairness of his policies. Then, suddenly in Syria, he fell ill. Before long, at thirty-three, he was dead. It was widely believed that Piso had poisoned him. Germanicus had censured Piso for his mismanagement of the province, but it occurred to many that the plot was larger than that. Nor was it necessary to think Piso had acted on Tiberius' direct orders. He may simply have assumed that Tiberius would be pleased. Very likely he was, but that did not guarantee gratitude.

Tiberius made an outward show of grief, even if it was highly restrained. At the same time the Roman people were sincerely shocked by Germanicus' death. Great memorials were dedicated to him, and he was richly eulogized. Agrippina carried the ashes of her husband in her bosom on the long trip home. All through the provinces people came from far and near to watch the mournful procession, "the standards undecorated, the fasces reversed." Every town offered its own funerary sacrifices. Germanicus' relatives, the consuls, the Senate, and crowds of ordinary people left Rome to meet Agrippina. Tacitus records that Germanicus' seldom-mentioned brother, Claudius, was there.

Tiberius and Livia kept out of sight. They were of course

well aware of the great outpouring of love for Germanicus. Perhaps, to give Tiberius the benefit of the doubt, he felt that his presence as Emperor might distract from the attention rightfully focused on Germanicus. (Tacitus' bias against Tiberius is most obvious in his refusal to allow him any good motives.) As Tacitus has it, Tiberius and his mother had already focused their jealousy on Agrippina, for she was now a symbol of the glory which was gone from the Julio-Claudian house.

Germanicus was not accorded a state funeral. In a simple ceremony, his ashes were placed in the mausoleum of Augustus. Yet the people of Rome turned out in such numbers that he was given a greater tribute than the old rites could have provided. Germanicus would have known the difference. That was why there was a feeling of emptiness when he was gone.

Tiberius took a neutral position about Piso, who was left to the mercy of the Senate and brought to trial within earshot of people clamoring for him to be put to death. Actually, the charge that he had poisoned Germanicus at a dinner party was never proved. With Tiberius standing aside, and the people inflamed, it did not need to be. From the mood of the senators who one after another denounced him, Piso knew he was doomed. Did he slit his own throat before the verdict or was he killed by someone sent to silence him? There were many rumors; Tacitus as a young man had heard some of them from men who remembered the event. Had Piso withheld evidence which could have implicated Tiberius? Was there a bargain by which he was betrayed? Tacitus admits that it was by no means certain what had really happened to Germanicus. He was candid about his sources: "Obscurity always surrounds great issues. Some people are ready to take on trust what is only hearsay; others falsify the truth; the passing of time amplifies both kinds of distortion" (III. 19).

The Last Years

There is no obscurity about why Tiberius failed as Emperor. His reign became increasingly infected by a poisonous atmosphere of intrigue, spying, trials, executions, and suicides. Basically, it was his own fault. All that might have been added up in his favor was hopelessly outweighed by the terror which he permitted during the latter years of his reign.

During the Republic, there had been a law to punish acts of

treason against the army or the state. Augustus included as treasonable what men might write; Tiberius even added whisperings. In the second year of his reign, certain men had been charged with spreading scandalous stories about the Emperor's private life. Fortunately for them, acquittal was still possible after a hearing. Others were not so fortunate, later on. In A.D.16, one Marcus Scribonius Libo Drusus became involved with astrologers, whose dire predictions could be encouraging to secret plans. Aside from hearsay, the most telling piece of evidence against Libo was a document wherein he was alleged to have written "mysterious symbols" next to the names of the ruling house. Because it was contrary to tradition for slaves to be tortured while giving evidence against their masters in such a case, Tiberius arranged for Libo's servants to be sold so that they could be technically free from the ban. (According to Dio, Augustus had set the precedent for this.) At the same time, Tiberius maintained an aloof, seemingly disinterested air toward Libo's pleas that he was the victim of unscrupulous informers. When Libo's own relatives deserted him for fear of implication, he killed himself. Then Tiberius let it be known that he had intended to pardon Libo if he had been found guilty. Surely no one present was bold enough to smile when he made the announcement. Even trivial offenses could be cause for danger. "Speech was indeed constrained and hazardous under an Emperor who dreaded freedom and loathed flattery" (II. 87).

Tacitus says it was in the year A.D. 23 that "Tiberius' principate took a decisive turn for the worse" (IV. 6). Nor had he any doubt about the reason. "The root and cause of the change sprang from Aelius Sejanus, commander of the Guard" (IV. 1). Tiberius found in this man a willing tool with whom he could share his secrets. Sejanus had a secret of his own. "In him were blended servility and arrogance; behind a mask of modesty there was an unbridled appetite for power" (IV. 1). Tacitus' story unfolds with Sophoclean suspense. The reader knows all along that Sejanus is conspiring to succeed Tiberius himself, but the Emperor continues to praise and trust him—calling him "the partner of my labors."

Sejanus was a man in the shadows, where the truth about him still lies. Tacitus records all the rumor and scandal. It was said that at the time Sejanus was having an affair with Tiberius' daughter-in-law, Livilla, the wife of Drusus. Of course nobody could better have furthered his designs if she told him of Drusus' every word and act.

In A.D. 22, following Augustus' example, Tiberius had conferred the tribunitial power on his son Drusus and thus designated him to be his successor. That he hoped would put an end to speculation. So it did, and in the process gave Drusus a new priority as the object of the recurrent plots against the throne. But when Drusus died in the following year, after a long illness, the Emperor did not suspect anything. Eight years later, he was told that a eunuch named Lygdus, who attended Drusus, had administered small amounts of poison from time to time. With Drusus out of the way, Sejanus turned his attention to undermining the already shaky reputation of Germanicus' wife, Agrippina. Her impetuousness and frank ambition gave him a head start. She never let anyone forget that she was Augustus' granddaughter and that her sons stood in line for the succession. They were a threat to Sejanus. Nor was it difficult to make Tiberius suspicious of them, obsessed as he was by thoughts of treason. As long ago as Germanicus' early campaigns in Germany, Agrippina had gone among the soldiers tending the wounded. Tiberius wondered then why she went out of her way to make herself so popular with the army.

For eight years, Sejanus kept Tiberius' suspicions focused elsewhere. Otherwise he might have accepted the kind of moderate safeguards which could have salvaged the reputation of his regime. Many senators worried about the informers, who had become a pack of bounty hunters, since they received rewards out of a condemned man's estate if it had been proven that he said or did what they had reported. One senatorial suggestion was to refuse a reward when a man committed suicide before he was sentenced to death. But Tiberius vetoed this modest curtailment of the informers' business. " 'Better cancel the laws than remove their watchdogs!' he said. So, the informers, a class of men bred for the ruin of the state, and never checked by any form of punishment, received incentives to productivity" (IV. 30).

Tacitus said Sejanus was made incautious by success. He asked Tiberius for the hand of Livilla, Drusus' widow, if the Emperor planned a second marriage for her. Tiberius was careful. To elevate Sejanus, an equestrian, would cause more trouble with Agrippina, and there was enough family dissension already. Furthermore, Tiberius said, there was much resentment toward Sejanus, and they should guard against increasing the criticism which affected them both. But, he added, in effect, that he would look out for Sejanus and that he should not worry. Apparently Sejanus *was* worried, however, and now applied himself to a new approach. He knew how weary Tiberius had grown of Rome and its official routine. Tiberius also had reason to be embarrassed by the trials for treason which he attended in the Senate. There, a string of witnesses would carefully, with great detail, spell out what the accused had said against the Emperor. Tiberius had to sit through hours of insulting criticism in order for the case to be properly disposed of—and everybody present knew that much of what was said was true. If he lived elsewhere, he could be spared the experience. Moreover, there could be nothing pleasant said about his family life in Rome. Agrippina, knowing that the charges of adultery and treason being brought against her friends were really aimed at her, spoke sharply about this to Tiberius. For a time she felt safe, but the signs were ominous. Before long, at dinner, she refused to eat food, untasted by her slaves, which the Emperor had offered her. Did she cast a glance of hatred as she passed up the dish?

One reason why Tiberius left Rome in A.D. 26 might have been to get away from his mother. Tacitus calls Livia a "disaster" as a mother and a "calamity" as a stepmother. When he is inclined to find some excuse for Tiberius, he thinks about Livia. Some at court had reason to be grateful to her, for she occasionally intervened on behalf of her friends. Tiberius did not like to cross her in matters where she had strong feelings. She never ceased to remind him what he owed to her, and she lived into her eighties. Once she was dead, he did not even bother to attend her funeral.

Tiberius might have left the city to pursue his perverse enjoyments with greater secrecy. Or, did he withdraw from public view because his vanity increased with age? His thin frame, bent with the years, his hawklike face marred by running sores, he no longer looked like the all-powerful ruler of a mighty empire.

Once Tiberius left Rome he never set foot there again for the remaining eleven years of his reign. He spent a year in Campania and then enjoyed a quasi-retirement on the beautiful island of Capri, where he continued his pastime of bathing with small boys he called his "minnows." The practice was a devastating and yet pathetic confession of his adult inadequacies. Tiberius was within himself a lonely man, whatever that may excuse.

With Tiberius away from Rome, Sejanus began pressing his plots against Germanicus' sons. Since he was now the man who controlled appointments in Rome, there were many who stood ready to do his bidding. Unfortunately, a fragment is all that remains of Tacitus' Book V of the *Annals*. Missing is his account of how Tiberius discovered that the trusted Sejanus was really the man who had arranged the death of his son Drusus. The downfall of Sejanus in A.D. 31 is recorded by Suetonius. All those who had had any connection with Sejanus were executed in the worst purge of Tiberius' reign. Even Germanicus' son, also named Drusus, died in prison, having been accused, ironically, of conspiring with Sejanus. He apparently had been left to starve to death, and did so after eating the straw on his bed. His mother Agrippina was a suicide a brief time later.

By the end of Tiberius' reign, almost anyone could be convicted by the charges levelled by reckless informers. Concerning A.D. 32, Tacitus wrote: "Of all the calamities of that age this was the worst—that leading senators were willing to serve as the basest informers" (VI. 7). On one occasion, "three Roman senators squeezed themselves in between the roof and the ceiling—an ignominious hiding place for a detestable trick—and put their ears to chinks and cracks. . . . People refused to talk, even to their own kin: all meetings and conversations were avoided: they shunned the ears of friend and stranger alike. Walls and ceilings—dumb things though they are—came under suspicion" (IV. 69). Commenting on a prominent official who died a natural death, Tacitus says it was "a remarkable occurrence in a man of his eminence" (VI. 10).

At times, wives followed their husbands in suicide. Even children were caught up in the intrigues of their parents. The children of Sejanus were both murdered. It was said that his eleven-year-old daughter was raped by the executioner to circumvent the law which forbade the execution of virgins. The story may not be true, but in those days it was believed to be possible. That much is history. What sounds true is Tacitus' touching description of a frightened innocent being led to her death. She "kept saying, 'What have I done? Where are you taking me? I won't do it again!'" (VI. Fr. 4). By A.D. 37, Macro, who replaced Sejanus as head of the Praetorian Guard in 31, was wielding great power in affairs of the state. With the Emperor old, ailing, and absent, Macro continued the terror for his own purposes.

Tiberius thought he should choose his successor, but events were to decide between his grandson, was Tiberius Gemellus, who Drusus' son and still a child; Caligula, now a young man; and Germanicus' brother Claudius, who, Tacitus says, was considered weak-minded. One man who committed suicide while being hounded by Macro in A.D. 37 said before doing so: "If Tiberius, with all his experience, has succumbed so completely to the corruption of absolute power, what of [Caligula]? . . . Will he change for the better under Macro's tutelage? Macro was chosen as the greater villain, to suppress Sejanus: he has committed more crimes and done even more harm to the state" (VI. 48).

On March 16, A.D. 37, Tiberius breathed his last difficult breath. He had been taking his time dying, and somebody gave orders for him to be smothered. Was it Macro or the young Caligula? In any event, nobody of any importance seems to have objected. For twenty-three years Tiberius had managed to survive without a hand being laid on him. But nobody liked him, for all that.

Caligula the Monster

Tacitus' account of Caligula's reign has been lost. But if he was repelled by Tiberius, who at least, until possibly toward the end, had his wits about him, it can be imagined what he thought of the erratic, if not at times unbalanced, Caligula, who ruled from A.D. 37 to 41. Suetonius' gossipy report survives, and although not entirely reliable, at least gives an impression of a man whom he frankly calls a monster.

Caligula's brutish instincts were obvious from an early age, and Tiberius was presumably aware of them. Whether or not he ever said, "I am nursing a viper in Rome's bosom" (IV. 11), it was still an understatement. The citizens of Rome were unaware of what manner of viper they were getting. After the grim Tiberius, Caligula seemed a relief. The people remembered his father Germanicus with great fondness. The Senate, with the consent of the Romans, gave Caligula the powers which Augustus had once given to Tiberius. He was also Macro's choice.

Although historians have devoted little space to Caligula's administrative capacity, certain of his acts were apparently commendable. His reign began with an amnesty toward all exiles or prisoners in Rome who had been charged under Tiberius' regime.

He also restored certain constitutional practices lost under Tiberius. A budget was again to be published as under Augustus, magistrates were to be elected again and given their old power to make independent decisions about sentences. More jurors were added to speed up the courts. These orders allowed some men the false hope that "Rome had now been born again."

According to Suetonius, Caligula played host to all of Rome, in his effort to be popular. He held banquets for the families of the senators and equestrians and entertained the whole city with elaborate shows, including nighttime spectacles. He was fond of gladiators, boxers, and actors and was something of a showman himself, with a taste for elaborate costumes. Suetonius says he fancied himself as a "gladiator, as a singer, as a dancer . . . and drove chariots in many regional circuses." Both in Rome and abroad, people were amused to see such exuberance after the austerity of Tiberius' reign. Nobody as yet seemed to raise any question about where the money was coming from. There seemed to be enough for several building projects, and plans for more than Caligula lived to see.

Compared to his account of Caligula's administration, Suetonius writes over five times as much about Caligula the monster. There is not a redeeming note in any of it, aside from the suggestion that he may have been the world's first major collector of sea shells. It was also true that the Romans did not suffer any major earthquakes, fires, or other catastrophes during Caligula's reign. He was the only disaster they needed.

Caligula's initial popularity may have prompted him to promote himself as a god. Or the reason could have been sheer vanity. Either way, he originated his own cult and apparently desired to have images of himself set up everywhere. An embassy of five Jews, headed by the philosopher Philo Judaeus, had an audience with Caligula in A.D. 40 and asked him not to require worship from the Jews, but to no avail. The procurator in Judaea wisely hesitated about installing the Emperor's likeness in the temple at Jerusalem. Caligula was dead before the objectionable order had to be carried out.

Caligula treated his relatives cordially at the beginning of his reign, but soon fell into Tiberius' habit of getting rid of them one by one. His rudeness toward his grandmother Antonia was rumored to have been accompanied by poison. His young cousin Tiberius Gemellus was murdered outright on the pretext that he had insulted the Emperor by taking "an antidote against poison." Nobody could have blamed him for that, although Suetonius says it was only medicine which Caligula noticed on his breath. Fate continued to protect Caligula's uncle Claudius. He was not taken seriously and, as he admitted later, he found safety as a fool. Old friends received rough treatment. Of Macro and his wife Ennia, Suetonius says, "Their very loyalty and nearness to him earned them cruel deaths" (IV. 26).

In sexual enthusiasm Caligula has been a well-known case history. Nobody was left out, not even his three sisters. His favorite died early. He ordered the other two into exile after accusing them of plotting against him. He also had a number of homosexual liaisons with men of both high and low birth. And he conferred himself on one of Rome's best-known prostitutes. More often, he appropriated other men's wives and used his authority to subject these helpless victims to his perverse tastes. To have forced his corpulent bulk on them may in itself have given him a not unintentional pleasure.

Whether or not Caligula happened to be married at the moment never bothered him. Suetonius says, "It would be hard to say whether the way he got married, the way he dissolved his marriages, or the way he behaved as a husband was the most disgraceful" (IV. 25). Of one of his unfortunate wives, Suetonius writes, "For his friends he even paraded her naked; but would not allow her the dignified title of 'wife' until she had borne him a child, whereupon he announced the marriage and the birth simultaneously" (IV. 25).

Suetonius' account of Caligula's brief reign continues with a catalogue of sadistic horrors. He amused himself at other people's expense, and that his power allowed him to do so was the greatest weakness of the Principate. Did he really have the awnings removed during gladiatorial contests and insist the spectators sit in the broiling sun? Maybe, but far more serious were the reports that he scheduled contests which pitted old or weak or physically handicapped persons against one another. Added to this was his insistence that fathers and mothers witness the execution of their sons. Nor were such killings quick. Caligula delighted in slow torture, sometimes, Suetonius says, "while he was eating or otherwise enjoying himself" (IV. 32). No physical or mental pain of another human being was beyond his enjoyment.

Given his capricious cruelty and frivolous satisfaction of

every whim, it is a wonder he lasted as long as he did. Bank-
ruptcy was part of his downfall. He spent a fortune and then
began a frantic effort to raise funds by any means possible. His
auctions of slaves and gladiators, furniture and jewels, were one
thing. Worse was the revival of a practice dating back to Sulla's
day of making outrageous accusations against persons whose property could be confiscated after they were executed. New taxes,
including a "charge of two per cent on the money involved in
every lawsuit and legal transaction whatsoever," added more
revenue. That at least was legitimate.

If at first Caligula appeared to be a boon and afterwards a
joke, his behavior was soon to convince everyone that he was at
times mentally unbalanced. He probably knew it himself.
"Whispered conversations" with an image of the Capitoline Jupiter were part of his increasingly odd behavior. Wracked by
superstitious fears, plagued by insomnia, and beset with intrigue,
he showed by his wild extravagances that he knew his time was
short. His bizarre, often effeminate clothing, his obscene speech
and agitated manner when he spoke were all signs of a man whom
Philo called a "fidgety neurotic."

Nowadays there would be many excuses offered for Caligula. Unquestionably, he had an unsettled childhood, living
sometimes at the frontier, later shifted from place to place to stay
with relatives who might be busy with plots against one another.
Nor could it be doubted that he had inherited his mother's notorious temper. Suetonius says that as a boy he suffered from
epilepsy.

Caligula's gross appearance could perhaps be used to explain
something of his peculiar ways. He had a hairless head on a hairy
body, which sat too heavily on thin legs. His physique, mind, and
personality added up to a man who might have thought about life
and dreamed of revenge. Yet it was the horror of the times that
this twisted person could become the first citizen of Rome. It was
a wonder that the Augustan system could survive him, a blessing
that his reign was so short.

"On those he loved he bestowed an almost insane passion."
That included horses. Perhaps the best-known, if wildest, rumor
about him was that he intended to make his favorite horse, Incita-
tus, a consul. Suetonius adds, with a degree of understatement:
"Such frantic and reckless behavior roused murderous thoughts in
certain minds" (IV. 56).

The final plot against Caligula's life was supported by persons who felt their own lives in danger. Among them were officers of the Praetorian Guard, who killed him about noon on January 24, A.D. 41. He was twenty-nine years old and had ruled three years, ten months, and eight days too many.

Claudius the Scholar

Ancient historians were not obsessed with finding a cause for every event. Luck was too ready an answer. The elevation of Claudius offered a good example. Tacitus writes: "Whether in public opinion, his own hopes, or the respect felt for him, the most unlikely candidate for the Principate was precisely the man whom fortune was keeping up her sleeve" (III. 18).

Claudius, the brother of Germanicus, was born at Lyon on the first of August, 10 B.C. Their father, Drusus, who died the following year, was a stepson of Augustus by his marriage to Livia. Augustus was also a great-uncle because his sister Octavia was Claudius' grandmother. As a child, Claudius was sickly and had none of Germanicus' vigor. He was different in other ways. His serious interest in books allowed him from time to time to surprise his relatives with a display of erudition. That did not alter their opinion that he was a daydreamer without ambition. Augustus looked at him and shook his head. But he was wrong in his estimate of Claudius. Among the members of his family who succeeded him, Claudius was the best.

During Tiberius' reign Claudius lived quietly and made few public appearances. He gave up asking if there was something for him to do when he realized that Tiberius shared Augustus' opinion that he lacked the power of concentration. Under his nephew Caligula, he was given a consulship, but largely as an honorary matter. It was surprising he attained even that. Usually Caligula gave him only insults.

When Caligula was assassinated, Claudius feared for his own life. He was hiding behind some draperies when the Praetorian Guard took him into protective custody. They were the first to hail him as the new Emperor, and he promptly rewarded each of them with a donation. At the same time, the Senate was wrangling over the possibility of restoring the Republic. The discussion came to an end as soon as Claudius had purchased the allegiance of the guards. Even the record of the debate was destroyed.

29. Claudius in the oak leaf headdress of Jupiter. Courtesy of the Museo Vaticano, Rome.

Claudius was fifty, and apparently one of the better looking members of his family, although a clumsiness in the way he walked detracted from his otherwise distinguished appearance. He was tall and had a great mane of white hair—not as handsome as his brother Germanicus, but still an imposing figure, unless he became excited. Then, Suetonius says, he would slobber and stammer and display an obvious facial tic. Usually, however, in the Augustan style, he conducted himself with great restraint and modesty, soliciting the good will of the Senate by frequent requests for approval of his acts. There were nevertheless conspiracies against him, and he maintained tight security by having visitors searched and keeping armed guards at hand. But the plots were neither as frequent nor as frightening as those which kept Tiberius and Caligula in constant fear. Claudius was more genuinely affable than they were, and he had a much more sensible approach to his position. His informality when he was among the people was more like that of a democratic politician than an emperor. Ironically, a sympathetic manner invited a greater degree of rudeness toward him than might have been risked with other emperors.

Claudius boasted that he never wanted to be angry for long, and if he ever felt offended it had to be for a good cause. Yet he was unpredictable and there was a vagueness in his manner. His conversation was often wandering and nobody was surprised if his speech in the Senate was not on the subject being debated. He was often absentminded. It might be questioned, however, whether, as reported, he went so far as to ask at dinner where his wife was, after having had her executed in the afternoon.

Temperamentally, Claudius was more concerned about the spirit of the law than a rigorous rule by the book. During his five consulships, four of them during his own reign, he worked seriously at being a good judge, and his rulings showed an uncommon amount of common sense—when he was awake. A common complaint in the Claudian family was insomnia. Claudius was more likely to be asleep in court during the day than he was in bed at night.

Claudius was at his best when giving advice about one of the crucial problems facing the Empire. History records over and over again the story of "ins" against the "outs." At Rome, there were first the patricians grudgingly conceding offices to the plebeians, next, the bitter struggle over full citizenship for the Italian allies. In the early Empire there were sharp discussions over the admission of Gauls to the magistracies and the Senate. Some of them had been given citizenship by Julius Caesar. Claudius sought to speed up the process with a speech in the Senate. His words were preserved on a bronze inscription at Lyon. Tacitus improved the speech somewhat in the *Annals,* but the message remained the same. Claudius showed the emptiness of the argument that inclusion of Gauls would debase Roman public affairs:

My own ancestors, going back to Clausus, who, though of Sabine origin, was made a Roman citizen and a patrician at one and the same time, induce me to follow the same policy in public affairs—to import excellence, from whatever source. I recall that the Julii came from Alba, the Coruncanii from Cameria, the Porcii from Tusculum. Leaving aside these venerable parallels, Etruria, Lucania, and the whole of Italy have sent men to the Senate. . . . our founder Romulus had the wisdom to treat several peoples as first enemies, then in the same day, as Roman citizens. We have had foreign kings. That the sons of freedmen should be elected to office is not, as is often alleged, an innovation; it happened often in early times. . . . Look back over all the wars we have fought, and mark how the Gallic wars took the shortest time

to finish. They were straightway followed by a peace that has endured. They are linked to us in customs, culture, and marriage; let
them bring their gold and wealth, rather than keep it separate. Members of the Senate, everything that now seems ancient was once a
novelty. Plebeians held magistracies after the nobility, Latins after the
plebeians, the other peoples of Italy after the Latins. This, too, will
grow customary with time; what today we justify by precedent will
be a precedent in its turn." (XI. 24)

The most erudite of all the Roman emperors, Claudius
wrote voluminously on Roman, Etruscan, and Carthaginian history. His works were still being read and appreciated in the
second century A.D. Along with other scholars of his day, he
spoke and read Greek as well as Latin. But the scholarly Claudius was no military man. He did little more than make an
appearance in Britain, which was nevertheless added to the Empire as a result of a six-month campaign. Much of the time was
spent going and coming. Suetonius writes: "He had fought no
battles and suffered no casualties, but reduced a large part of the
island to submission" (V. 17). An elaborate triumph in Rome
was one of the highlights of his career. In general, his reign was
a quiet one on the frontiers, for Claudius was very cautious. In
A.D. 47, according to Tacitus, he "forbade all further advance in
Germany, even ordering the withdrawal of garrisons from across
the Rhine" (XI. 19).

Claudius was at his best in handling domestic problems.
Food, water, and entertainments remained the necessities of
Rome. Otherwise, the people would become restive. A new supply of fresh water was available from an aqueduct which had been
begun by Caligula but was completed by Claudius and named
after him. Among his other public works was the construction of
a harbor at Ostia, a project which had been contemplated by
Julius Caesar. The practice of keeping the Romans happy with
grandiose spectacles, including shows with gladiators and exotic
animals, was continued. No emperor could hope to hold the
people's loyalty without them. Spectators were particularly
thrilled by mock battles. One gigantic show which depicted the
conquest of Britain was possibly more exciting than the event
itself.

There is no doubt that Claudius wanted to follow Augustan
policy exactly. He did not like people to be late to, much less
absent from, court sessions. He was particular about religious

30. Claudian Aqueduct near Rome, as it appeared prior to recent building projects in the area. Courtesy of the Italian Government Travel Office, Chicago.

matters and customs in general. He also revered the orderliness of the old class lines and was concerned about the presumptuousness of certain prominent freedmen. Suetonius writes: "Any freedman who tried to pass himself off as a knight found his property confiscated" (V. 25). On the other hand, Claudius gave so much responsibility and power to his own trusted freedmen that he actually did more to advance the status of this group than any other emperor.

Although Claudius showed great respect for the Senate, it was during his reign that the government was effectively transferred to the imperial household. The magistracies became more and more honorary. For instance, Claudius established courts in Rome and the provinces to handle trust cases which had formerly been judged by magistrates. The bureaus of the government were now run by the Emperor's appointees who, as might be expected, carved out their own domains and built their own followings. Narcissus, one of Claudius' favorites, was put in charge of imperial correspondence, a vantage point which gave him great influence. Pallas, in charge of finances, shared with Narcissus the privilege of standing near to the Emperor. Both were top-grade bureaucrats who served the state well, and themselves too. Suetonius says they wound up with more money than Claudius.

Suetonius let stand side by side two traditions about Claudius, one friendly, the other hostile, without any effort to explain or reconcile them. It is likely, however, that the less favorable view of Claudius stems from the last years of his rule. At one point, Suetonius tells a story which suggests that the term *humanitarian* might be used of the Emperor. Claudius heard that certain ailing old slaves had been confined on an island in the Tiber so their owners would not have the expense of looking after them. He promptly freed them and declared that in the future any man who tried to dispose of an ailing slave in this fashion was to be charged with murder. On the other hand, Suetonius offers a contrasting judgment about Claudius when he says: "His bloodthirstiness appeared equally in great and small matters" (V. 34). By this account he was presumably preoccupied with tortures and wildly enthusiastic for gladiatorial bloodshed, even going so far as to order all contestants who tripped and fell to be killed. This may only have been as typical of the times as was his excessive eating, which appears to have been a habit at least of the upper classes. It is not surprising to learn that Claudius suffered from stomachaches.

Elsewhere, Suetonius records that Claudius had so many senators and equestrians executed that he could not remember who they all were. This cruelty, however, may have resulted from the influence exerted over him by his various wives and counselors. Tacitus felt that Claudius was easily influenced and says that "anything was possible with an Emperor whose likes and dislikes went according to what was suggested or dictated to him" (XII. 3).

Claudius married four times. His single-minded fondness of women and lack of sexual interest in boys or men also set him apart from several of his relatives. He divorced his first two wives. His third wife, Messalina, was very much in love with somebody else. She even went so far as to arrange a wedding ceremony with Gaius Silius while still married to the Emperor. He was apparently the last to know about her outrageous unfaithfulness. Pallas hesitated, but Narcissus took the risk of telling the Emperor not only about the present scandal but also about Messalina's other affairs. The news reached Claudius while he was out of the city at Ostia; he saw it as part of a plot to unseat him. In a bewildered state, he asked his guards, "Am I still Emperor?" He was, and Messalina was put to death for all the unpunished crimes which had encouraged her to commit the last one. Narcissus' calculated risk had paid off, and now he outranked Pallas and the other freedmen in Claudius' service.

It has often been remarked that Claudius married once too often. The scramble among Claudius' freedmen to find him a new wife, once Messalina was dead, has a parallel in the efforts of those who served Henry VIII. His fourth wife was Agrippina the Younger, the daughter of his brother Germanicus. She was favored by the freedmen Pallas and Callistus. Among the Romans it was considered incestuous for an uncle to marry his niece, but neither Agrippina nor Claudius showed any reservations about their relationship. Suetonius says that Agrippina "had a niece's privilege of kissing and caressing Claudius, and exercised it with a noticeable effect on his passions" (V. 26). A *senatus consultum* passed by the Senate declared that such marriages were allowable, after all.

Claudius' children by Messalina were Octavia and Britannicus. When he married Agrippina the Younger, he adopted Nero, her son by her previous marriage to Gnaeus Domitius. With Agrippina's prodding, he advanced Nero by placing him above his own younger son for the succession and giving him Octavia as his wife. This was also at Pallas' urging, for he was now tied to Agrippina the Younger both politically and personally. Another man who advanced because of Agrippina's influence was Afranius Burrus. He was made commander of the Praetorian Guard.

Tacitus said that Agrippina, the daughter of Germanicus, as "a sister, wife and mother of Emperors, held a position which remains unrivaled to this day" (XII. 42). Of the year A.D. 53, he wrote, "Claudius was now constantly goaded into acts of savagery by the wiles of Agrippina. She brought down Statilius Taurus, famous for his wealth, whose gardens she coveted" (XII. 59). Agrippina was not above using her power for petty purposes; she especially connived at the downfall of any women who had in the past or present won any attention from Claudius. She was surely pleased when he established a Roman colony in her honor at a favorable site on the Rhine. Colonia Agrippinensis became the modern city of Cologne.

The consensus about Claudius' death is that Agrippina feared he was having second thoughts about the choice of her son Nero as his successor and poisoned him with mushrooms before he could change his mind. Or she may have been taking seriously the threats against her which he dared voice while he was drinking. The poison was slow-acting; Claudius was already in a stupor with wine. But by noon on the thirteenth of October, A.D. 54, he was dead, at sixty-three. Nero became Emperor, having been hailed by the Praetorian Guard. Following Claudius' precedent, Nero rewarded them by a gift of money. The Senate agreed to accept Nero, and the armies in the provinces acquiesced on hearing the news.

Besides Augustus, Claudius alone of the Julio-Claudian rulers was deified. His funeral was on a grand scale, equaling that of the first Emperor. Once he was dead, there was nothing Agrippina would not do for him.

Nero

Nero was born at Antium on December 15, A.D. 37, the year of Tiberius' death. Suetonius describes Nero's father, Gnaeus Domitius, as "a wholly despicable character," who even predicted that his own son "was bound to have a detestable nature and become a public danger" (VI. 6). Nero was eleven when he was adopted by Claudius. His marriage to Claudius' daughter Octavia was part of Agrippina's plan for the succession. At sixteen, he was the youngest emperor the Romans were to have before the fourteen-year-old Elagabalus was elevated to the purple by his relatives in the third century A.D.

The early years of Nero's reign, before he decided to rely on his own judgment, went rather well. He was guided by Sextus Afranius Burrus, the praetorian prefect, and Lucius Annaeus Seneca, a statesman and dramatist, who was his tutor. The reign began with a promise of justice for all and a show of deference toward the Senate. His early appointments were based on merit rather than favoritism. It was a good beginning. Nero apparently was both affable and gracious, with even a hint of kindness now and then. He allowed the tax structure to be revised and even some reductions to be made. In addition, all information regarding taxes was to be posted for the public to read. Cases against tax collectors were to be handled promptly everywhere in the Empire, and delinquent taxes were not collectable after twelve months. Tacitus adds, "There were other excellent provisions, which were observed for a time, and then lapsed" (XIII. 51).

Nero delighted in presenting shows for the people and began a new festival, the Neronia, which included contests in music, poetry, and athletics. He fancied himself a musician, poet, and athlete. It never concerned him whether the profuse flattery he

31. Head of youth (detail of Figure 32). Courtesy of the Detroit Institute of Arts.

32. Youth in toga, possibly Nero. Courtesy of the Detroit Institute of Arts.

received for his performances was sincere or not. Nor did he ever seem to get enough of it. In this respect his life was comical, but the smile does not last. There was a vicious streak in Nero. If his early public acts gave some promise of good behavior, his private life did not. Suetonius writes that "there was no family relationship which Nero did not criminally abuse" (VI. 35). Although married to "the noble and virtuous" Octavia, he became enamoured of an ex-slavewoman named Acte. This curious affair was the beginning of his estrangement from his mother, who had nothing to fear from the demure Octavia, but worried lest Acte's power exceed her own. After her friend Pallas was dismissed by Nero, she began to hint that maybe Claudius' son Britannicus would have made a better Emperor. As time passed, she became increasingly critical. At the outset of Nero's reign she had had things her way. The death of Claudius had hardly caused her even to hesitate in her intrigues. One old enemy, Junius Silanus, was poisoned, and the formerly powerful Narcissus was forced to commit suicide. Only the restraint of Burrus and Seneca had stood in the way of another reign of terror. Ironically, she had taught Nero how to get rid of people. Now she was to be among his victims. If he had, as rumor had it, committed incest with her it was because of passion, not love. In A.D. 55, he began to see less of Agrippina and even insulted her by removing her guard of honor. She was being eased out. Tacitus comments: "Nothing in human affairs is so transitory and precarious as the reputation for power without the means to support it" (XIII. 19). Agrippina began to divide her time between the places she owned in the country at Tusculum or Antium, staying out of Nero's sight. But according to Tacitus, "At last he decided that, wherever she was, she was intolerable" (XIV. 3).

One night, Nero invited his mother to a celebration at Baiae and then after fond kisses ushered her aboard a ship which Suetonius says had a cabin roof "weighted with lead so that it would collapse while she was en route home." It did, but she managed to swim to safety. One of her freedmen informed Nero that she had survived, whereupon the Emperor had a dagger thrown at the man's feet, and quickly claimed that his mother was behind an assassination plot. Henchmen were sent to kill her. It would be announced that she had committed suicide, although no one who saw the body would have been deceived.

Nero's conscience was reported to have bothered him, but

not enough to keep him from arranging the death of his aunt, Domitia Lepida, who had helped to care for him after his mother was exiled by Caligula. Then followed the execution of his wife Octavia. Privately he admitted she only bored him, but publicly he charged her with adultery. Earlier, he had poisoned Britannicus while the family was at dinner. Tacitus' description of that event shows superb descriptive powers:

> Now it was the custom for the young princes of the imperial house to dine with others of their age at a separate table, where the fare was simpler and they were under the eyes of their relations. There sat Britannicus, but he had a special attendant who tasted his food and drink. A trick was therefore invented which would allow the custom to be observed, without betraying the crime by the death of two persons. A cup of mulled wine, previously tasted, and so far without poison, was handed to Britannicus. But it was too hot to drink, and he refused it. The poison was then put in with some cold water. Its action was so immediate on his whole system that he at once lost the power to speak or breathe. The other guests were appalled. Some were foolish enough to rush out of the room, but the more intelligent waited, their eyes fixed on Nero. (XIII. 16)

Nero made his debut as a singer in Neapolis (Naples) where the Greeks were properly enthusiastic even over a voice which Suetonius frankly called "feeble." After his performance, the theatre collapsed. If the earthquake which caused it was a hint from the gods, Nero ignored it. On the contrary, since the people had left and nobody was killed, Nero viewed the event as a sign of divine favor.

Nero loved to sing in public; once he got started there was no stopping him. At one contest, he sang so long the other artists did not have a chance to perform. If there was any sound he preferred to his own voice, it was applause. He arranged for large groups of young men to be trained to clap their hands in unison as a claque. No one was allowed to leave his recitals. The story goes that women gave birth to babies while entrapped on these occasions, and men pretended to fall dead in order to be carried out. The reports sound exaggerated, but there can be little doubt that Nero imposed his artistry on friend and foe alike. A criterion for friendship was lengthy and loud applause. Nor was he above letting other actors and singers know that he would resent any effort to outmatch him. It was not only the theatre which attracted Nero. He also raced as a charioteer at the circus and appeared as a gladiator in the arena. One unfriendly tradition has his opponents tied up during the contests. Another had Nero appearing naked, as Hercules, in combat with a lion.

Tacitus says it was considered degrading for Nero to take part in chariot races or sing to the lyre in public. "Burrus grieved—and applauded." Nero and his partisans were blamed for a sharp decline in public morals, particularly among the young. Those at the top were again setting the worst example. It had always been considered a mark of ill-breeding for a member of the upper classes to perform in public. The heroic Roman was a soldier and a magistrate. Actors, singers, and dancers, with their loud and coarse manners, had low status. For the Emperor and members of the Senate to mingle with them and even perform alongside them was viewed as condoning indecency.

The year A.D. 62 marked the beginning of the end for Nero. Burrus was dead, possibly by poison, and Seneca was under attack. For all their shortcomings these men at least made a pretense of morality. Tacitus writes that during the first year of Nero's reign, the Emperor "bound himself to clemency in a number of speeches which had been put into his mouth by Seneca, who wished to publish to the world through the mouth of the Emperor what excellent advice he gave—or what a good orator he was" (XIII. 11).

There seems to be little doubt that Seneca had profited from his position, but the increasing viciousness of Nero's acts made him uncomfortable and put him at odds with the inner circle. Sensing the undercurrents, Seneca asked Nero if he might give to the Emperor all he had earned in his service, including gifts of magnificent gardens, and retire to a life of contemplation. Nero pretended to be upset by the offer; yet he did let him go. Ironically, Seneca thus left the way open to power for Burrus' successor as praetorian prefect, Ofonius Tigellinus, whose blatant wickedness seemed to amuse the Emperor. The shift in favor would soon cost Seneca his life. He was a Stoic, and Tigellinus considered such men to be hypocrites in their preachments about the simple life. He called them "that arrogant sect of provokers of sedition and meddlers in politics." He may have been partly right. Tacitus says that for a time Nero purchased silence from certain reputable men, giving them property which seemed to assuage for a time their Stoic predilections for austerity.

In contrast to his earlier years, Nero now showed his contempt for the Senate and even the people of Rome. That stemmed in part from his knowledge of how much they disliked him. Suetonius says he was "universally loathed." Many of the jokes enshrined on walls for all to enjoy had to do with his penchant for enlarging his palace and grounds at everybody else's expense. But he was hardly as touchy as Tiberius had been about those who insulted him to his face. They were sent into exile. He was actually more severe toward those who sought to help him improve than to the insolent ones who seemed to forswear any hope for reform, as indeed he may have himself.

Nero liked to wear a loosely flowing dressing gown which, probably more for comfort than out of kindness, hid his flabby and pustular body. His best feature was his face, although it too lacked strength. He had a blondish, blue-eyed prettiness. Sometimes he dressed flamboyantly in "a Greek mantle spangled with gold stars over a purple robe." This outfit, with his hair set in rows of curls, gave him a foppish appearance that matched his personality. Some people seem to have found him attractive, although physical charm was not necessarily the grounds for his marriages to three women, one man, and a eunuch. Of these Poppaea Sabina, who had long been his mistress, was possibly the only one he really cared for. Yet, during a rage, he kicked her to death while she was pregnant. It was a curious ending for the beautiful and clever woman who had schemed at length to become his wife.

Nero was indulgent of his own vices, among them eating and drinking. His banquets could continue from noon to midnight. Surprisingly, his health remained good and he was never seriously ill. The common people of the city were not so fortunate. While he wasted money on silly and stupid expenditures, they watched for the arrival of grain ships from Egypt so they could eat. One anxiously awaited vessel came loaded instead with sand for Nero's wrestlers. It was said that the Emperor never put on the same garment twice and made ridiculous bets at dice. His greatest folly was a palace noted for its ostentatious tastelessness. When the imperial treasury was emptied with this foolishness, the usual abuses followed in Nero's attempts to keep himself solvent. The Greek cities were asked to send back the presents he had given them, and even the temples in Rome were robbed.

The Fire

The well-known caricature of Nero "fiddling while Rome burned" is out of Suetonius. He does not doubt that Nero had men set fire to the city in A.D. 64 in order to proceed with urban renewal. According to Suetonius, while Nero watched the fire he sang "The Fall of Ilium" (Troy). Since he would have been accompanying himself on the lyre, modern references have him "fiddling." Fires were frequent in Rome. Crude stoves and lamps were a permanent hazard in the wooden tenements where the poor lived. The fire of 64 was the worst holocaust to date. A sharp wind kept the flames moving, and a wide area of the city was completely burned out. Included in the loss were many works of art and a whole library.

Tacitus was by no means certain that Nero was at fault and puts more emphasis on his prompt measures of relief for the victims of the fire. "As a refuge for the terrified, homeless people he threw open the Campus Martius and the buildings of Agrippa. He also opened his own gardens, and constructed emergency huts to house the thousands of helpless refugees. Supplies were brought in from Ostia and the neighboring towns" (XV. 39).

The city was carefully rebuilt after the fire. The streets were to be wider and the houses and apartments held to a specified height. Nero was a generous contributor, and the new city was undoubtedly more attractive than the old one. But there were still complaints that it was not so cool. Before the fire, tall tenements along narrow streets had afforded good protection from the sun.

The Christians

Nero, aware of the rumors that he had set the fire, had to blame somebody else. He did not have far to look for a scapegoat. The Christians in Rome were extremely unpopular. Nero did not create any prejudice against them, he simply exploited it. The earliest Christians generally belonged to the lowest segments of the population: poor and uneducated, and some slaves. The hope for them was for something in the next world, not this one. They had no more than a rudimentary organization, kept to themselves, saying prayers and performing simple ceremonials to commemorate the Last Supper. Because of their withdrawal from the world of affairs and their peculiar way of life, there was gossip about them. They were suspected of practicing cannibalism ("eating the body of Christ") and incest. Their refusal to perform any religious obligation to the Roman gods, including the deified Caesars, meant that they would not serve in the army or the government where such ceremonies were a patriotic gesture. It was galling to the Romans that these lower-class people thought themselves to be superior, and became martyrs as well. The Christians saw themselves as a humble band of believers following their conscience. They considered their simple life to be more moral than that of other men. This made them self-righteous, but failed to bear out the popular view that they were actually carrying on secret crimes. Tacitus writes: "Those who confessed to being Christians were at once arrested, but on their testimony a great crowd of people were convicted, not so much on the charge of arson, but of hatred of the entire human race" (XV. 44). Suetonius says that during Nero's reign "a great many public abuses were suppressed." He adds: "Punishments were also inflicted on the Christians, a sect professing a new and mischievous religious belief" (VI. 16). But the viciousness of Nero's attack on them resulted in a certain amount of sympathy. "Dressed in the skins of wild beasts," Tacitus says, "they were torn to pieces by dogs, or were crucified, or burned to death: when night came, they served as human torches to provide lights" (XV. 44). Their martyrdom was a message. Many were amazed at the courage of these men and women. What must be in their faith which made them stand so fast? Soon there were more converts. Irenaeus, a bishop of Lyon (ancient Lugdunum) in the second century A.D., would one day say, "The blood of the martyrs is the seed of the Church."

After Nero's time, the persecutions of the Christians were usually localized, depending on circumstances. They did not end altogether until A.D. 311. It was not legal to be a Christian until 313. For much of this time the opinion of educated men was that of Tacitus, who called Christianity an "abominable superstition." Only very gradually after his time did that attitude change.

Conspiracy

Early in A.D. 65, a conspiracy developed against Nero. In view of the many men and women of all classes and ages involved, Tacitus found it hard to believe that it could have been hidden so

long. Yet that may have been a measure of the hatred of the
Emperor. Most of those involved wanted to replace him with a
more attractive figure, Gaius Calpurnius Piso, who came from a
noble family and was handsome and popular, with a happy personality. But Piso was not sure of everybody. There was some
hesitation and discussion among the conspirators over how and
when to act. Suddenly it was too late. A slave in a household
where the plot was known decided to use his knowledge for
whatever reward it would bring. He went to see one of Nero's
freedmen. Arrests, tortures, and executions followed—a replay
of the last years of Tiberius' reign, except for one major difference. Many of Tiberius' enemies were scoundrels themselves.
Almost all of Nero's victims were persons of ability and virtue—
the best people in Rome. There were many suicides, Piso among
them. Tacitus says, "Now virtually the whole city was under
arrest." The most famous victim was Seneca, who may not have
been involved at all. On the contrary, the evidence against Seneca revolved around a single conversation he had had with a
friend who was actually complaining about his not seeing Piso of
late. Nevertheless Nero ordered his old tutor to commit suicide.
Seneca accepted death and cut his own veins with Stoic calm. He
had known for a long time about Nero's cruelty to others. It
was now his turn to suffer.

Tacitus' judgment on Nero was dramatically expressed by
an officer of the guard, who confessed his complicity to Nero and
told him: "I hated you, though you never had a more loyal officer, while you deserved loyalty. I began to hate you when, after
the murder of your mother and your wife, you paraded yourself
as a charioteer and an actor and an incendiary!" (XV. 67). Flavius
was not a man to mince words. While he was waiting to be
executed, a trench for his burial was being dug nearby. He looked
it over and remarked "Slovenly again, as usual!" His head was cut
off with "a blow and a half."

Tacitus continues at length the account of Nero's victims
and then pauses to wonder if his readers will not find it all "wearisome and repetitious":

> But now such passive servility, such a prodigal effusion of blood in
> times of peace, paralyzes the mind and dulls the sense of pity. The
> only concession I would ask from my readers is that they permit me
> not to despise these inglorious victims. . . . These were famous men,
> and let us grant this concession to their memory: that as their funeral

rites distinguish them from the common herd, so each shall have his own memorial in the narration of his end. (XVI. 16)

A man of talent was not safe in Nero's circle. Gaius Petronius was witty and well enough acquainted with the refinements of vice to make him popular at court. He was the author of the *Satyricon,* an insider's view of the high cost of low life in Nero's time. His capacity for indulgence made him Nero's favorite, but aroused Tigellinus' jealousy. So Petronius was a victim of the familiar arrangement whereby other men saved themselves by accusing him and supplying the testimony.

Unlike Augustus, who had toured almost all the provinces as his own inspector-general, Nero went only to Greece to offer himself to a wider audience. Suetonius has him say: "The Greeks alone are worthy of my genius; they really listen to music" (VI. 22). He had reason to expect a warm reception. The cities of this province had long been sending him the prize for lyre-playing in contests at which he had never appeared. During his stay in Greece, contests were set up out of season for his convenience; he spent money lavishly on his effusive hosts. At Olympia, he fell out of a chariot pulled by ten horses, was hoisted back in, failed to finish the race, and won the prize. Affairs at Rome were of course neglected during this grand tour, and if there is a single reason for his eventual failure it was his carelessness about events which would have warned a wiser man.

The Empire Under Nero

The most serious foreign troubles Nero faced were in Britain and Armenia. Claudius had annexed Britain, but had not pacified it. A rebellion there in A.D. 60 was all the more brutal because of the realization that the Roman reaction would be severe. The Roman citizens and their allies living in Britain caught the main brunt of the natives' anger. Seventy thousand of them were slaughtered before a decisive battle restored order.

A war between Rome and Parthia was fought over which side would include Armenia within its sphere of influence. At the moment, Tiridates, the brother of the Parthian king, Vologases I, was on the throne. The Roman general Gnaeus Domitius Corbulo felt that the campaigns of Lucullus and Pompey had given the Romans a better right to control the land, but he was not really trying to overthrow the king. He simply wanted him to admit that his rule was dependent on Roman permission. When the Parthians became preoccupied with trouble elsewhere, that became the best solution for Tiridates, who was obviously not going to be left alone.

Nero took credit for any success in Britain and Armenia. What he was really responsible for was the revolt of his own commanders in Gaul and Spain.

Nero's Last Days

When Julius Vindex, the legate of Gallia Lugdunensis, dared to call Nero a "bad lyre-player," there was no doubt the Emperor was in trouble. At first, Nero pretended to be unconcerned and failed to make any realistic moves to maintain his authority over military commanders who were all too aware of his unpopularity in Rome. He even made light of the threat by Vindex when he said he would have some new water organs installed in the theatre "if Vindex [had] no objection." When he heard that Servius Sulpicius Galba in Spain had declared himself to be the legate of only the Senate and the Roman people, he was panic-stricken.

By the time Nero decided to go to Gaul in an attempt to win back the loyalty of the troops there, it was too late. They were now sworn to their provincial commanders. It was precisely the kind of situation which Augustus had warned was the prelude to civil war. Nero's unpopularity and his neglect of state affairs had led to this open defiance. The news from other quarters was equally bad. Former promises of allegiance to him proved to be hollow. Once the revolt against him began, his power evaporated overnight. Like the last of the Romanoffs, he was suddenly a nobody.

Nero ran through the palace, screaming hysterically. The guard, even most of his servants, deserted him. Only a few members of his household, possibly sharing his disbelief at what had happened, stayed to serve him. A freedman, Phaon, suggested they flee to his own villa four miles from the city. It was there in the slave quarters that Nero was trapped. The Senate had condemned him as a public enemy and ordered him to be executed. As cavalrymen closed in, Nero was caught between fear and cowardice. He asked one of his staff "to set him an example by committing suicide," but the man seems not to have felt obliged. Nero's hand was held on a dagger by a scribe and guided into his throat. By tradition, he was reported to have cried, "Dead! And so great an artist!" (VI. 49). It was Rome's misfortune that he wanted to be remembered more as a singer than as a successor to Augustus.

Nero was given a proper funeral amid "widespread general rejoicing" and his remains were placed in the family tomb of the Domitii Ahenobarbi. He was only thirty years old.

XV
Disorder and Recovery

The three short-term successors to Nero might be called emperors of a city, not of an empire. Only the first of these rulers ever held the allegiance of all the troops, and then for only half a year. Servius Sulpicius Galba (*ca.* 3 B.C.–A.D. 69) was past seventy by the time his chance came. His wife and two sons were dead. He was totally bald and badly crippled from arthritis, yet boasted of his "vigor" and apparently was not indifferent about sex, even if he was about his partners.

It seems strange to call a man of Galba's age a disappointment, but it is true to say that he did not live up to expectations. Or, as Tacitus said, with a certain acerbity, "all would have agreed that he was equal to the imperial office if he had never held it" (*Histories,* I. 49). One reason he lasted less than seven months was his failure to realize that soldiers who had promoted a general could as quickly break him. Galba did not take the necessary steps to reform an unstable army. He was too easily ensnarled in the politics of Rome where indulgence toward his friends was matched by revenge on enemies old and new. During a public career in which he rose, as his father had before him, to a consulship, Galba distinguished himself as a military commander but was best known for his justice, and for his mercilessness toward the guilty. When he was a governor in Spain, a convicted murderer condemned to be crucified sought leniency because he was a Roman citizen. "Let this citizen hang higher than the rest" was Galba's reply.

Galba had previously served in Germany and Africa. The morale and alertness of his troops had won praise and rewards from Caligula. He served Nero in Spain until called upon to "rescue humanity" from the man who had appointed him. He might have hesitated to take the risk if he had not learned that Nero had already ordered him killed. His troops, soon to be swelled by Spanish recruits, hailed him as Emperor. His acceptance was symbolized by the appointment of a special guard to protect him while he was asleep.

Nero's death left the way open to Rome. On the road, Galba's harsh treatment of those who did not share his rejoicing tarnished his image as a savior. In Rome, it was not long before the image vanished altogether. The men he chose to advise him were a mean and petty lot who proved to be more interested in their own future than in his. It was palace politics as usual. Even the much hated Tigellinus, who had served Nero, was given imperial protection. As Emperor, Galba's justice was still quick but no longer fair.

Suetonius writes that Galba "outraged all classes at Rome; but the most virulent hatred of him smouldered in the army." When reaching for power, he made grandiose promises of rewards to those who would support him. Having succeeded in his ambition, he made the curt statement, "It is my custom to levy troops, not to buy them" (VII. 16). Predictably, the soldiers stationed in Germany began to look for a new imperial candidate. Even the sacred chickens forsook Galba and at the worst possible time. They took their departure while he was making a sacrifice. The news that his curule chair in the Senate was found turned toward the wall may be a good example of how men could arrange for an omen when they needed one. There were other warnings. Then suddenly, like a replay of Nero's demise, Galba's power vanished. A false report that the rebellious guards had been suppressed drew him into a trap in the Forum. Those around him fled for their lives. Galba was cut down by horsemen, who abandoned his corpse as though he had been some worthless animal.

Otho

Galba never knew how close he was to the end. His successor Otho did. He was a man of thirty-seven, about half Galba's age, who would only reign about half as long, a little over three months. He was a member of a family which had only become prominent under Claudius, but was well connected in the upper circles.

Otho was twenty-two when Claudius died. Nero was the first emperor he knew well. He was for a time his closest confidant, and in that capacity was supposed to look after Poppaea Sabina, whom Nero had seduced away from her husband. But Otho fell in love with Poppaea himself and married her. So, as Suetonius said, he put Nero "on the wrong side of the bedroom door." Then, curious to say, Suetonius declared that Nero only took mild retaliation because of his fear of scandal. He merely annulled the marriage and gave the ex-bridegroom a governorship in Lusitania (modern Portugal).

If Otho was not a man of personal accomplishments, he at least knew how to wait for others to make mistakes. Ten years later, when Nero lost his grip, he eagerly joined Galba's cause. He had to wait only a few months for Galba to blunder. The childless Emperor decided to adopt Piso Licinianus as his heir and announced his decision to the Praetorian Guard without promising any donation for their support. That was Otho's chance. Although badly in debt, he managed to distribute enough money to win over the soldiers stationed in Rome.

Even on the morning of his last day, Galba, unaware of what was going on, greeted Otho warmly at the palace. Otho had already placed his men "at the gilt milestone near the Temple of Saturn." Part of that landmark remains in the Roman Forum today.

In the past, loyalty of the Praetorian Guard had been sufficient insurance for an emperor, but now the troops in the provinces were more important. In Germany, they hailed Vitellius. For the first time since the days of the Second Triumvirate, there was the spectacle of rival armies fighting for control of Rome. When Otho's troops were defeated by Vitellius' army at Bedriacum, Otho's ceremonial reign was over. Yet tradition says the suddenness of the end resulted from Otho's own lack of resolve, or distaste for civil war, rather than any reluctance of his loyal followers to fight. Suetonius added a personal note. He said that his father, who had served with Otho, had given him a favorable view of the man—at least in his final days. It would seem that Otho was praised more for a decision to kill himself and the grace with which he did so than for anything else in his life. His behavior was methodical as though he were carrying out a policy decision. He gave orders not to punish deserters, wrote letters, distributed money, and had all of his private papers burned so that no man would suffer for having secretly supported him. Finally, he had a good night's rest. In the morning, he plunged a dagger into his side. For that he was a hero at last.

Vitellius

Compared to Galba and Otho, tradition treats Vitellius as something of a joke. There are doubts about Vitellius, including the quality of his ancestry, but no question that eating was his hobby—and he looked it. During his regime, it was good politics to set before him a sumptuous table. He ate four times or more a day and it was recorded that he once ordered up a dish composed of "pike-livers, pheasant-brains, peacock-brains, flamingo-tongues and lamprey-milt." But that was not because he was a gourmet. Vitellius would eat anything, including the sacrificial meat off an altar.

Galba had been unfaithful to his army supporters; Vitellius was lenient and fraternized with his troops. He even made light of their unruliness in towns where they took their leisure and anything else they could lay their hands on. It was a disastrous policy. Vitellius' eagerness to please and reluctance to punish may have won the hearts of those who marched with him, but it was a bad sign to everybody else. Many could recall that in earlier days he was not above stealing from temples in order to relieve some of his constant debts.

Although he had not been present at the crucial battle of Bedriacum, Vitellius marched to Rome as a conqueror. Suetonius says that "he had himself carried through the main streets of the cities on his route, wearing triumphal dress; crossed rivers in elaborately decorated barges wreathed in garlands; and always kept a lavish supply of delicacies within reach of his hand" (IX. 10). In Rome, he decided to become a consul for life. Within eight months, his life was in serious danger. While Vitellius was violating "all laws, human and divine," the troops stationed in Moesia,

Pannonia, Syria, and Judaea decided on a better choice. Vitellius' abuse of power had not gone unobserved. It was evident in the cruel revenge he took against those who had once tried to collect any money he owed them. Executions were carried out before his eyes, and anybody who pleaded for the victims risked death by so doing. Even Vitellius' mother became disgusted. Some said she died of her own will; others were not so sure.

When the forces of Vespasian, a provincial commander, closed in on Rome, Vitellius started to flee, "accompanied by his pastry cook and chef," but turned back and was finally found hiding alone in the palace. Vespasian's soldiers hauled him to the Forum where he was ridiculed by the crowd before finally being put out of his misery with a series of stab wounds. Like Galba's, his corpse was just another carcass treated with contempt. An ignominious finish for the mighty is one of Italy's least celebrated traditions: in the twentieth century, a dead Mussolini was hung upside down by his ankles.

The Flavians: Titus Flavius Vespasianus and His Sons

If stability was to be restored, it would probably be under an Emperor who preferred the smell of garlic to perfume. That is the kind of man Vespasian was, and he said so. Nor did he mind being called a mule-driver. He had once sold mules to recoup his finances, and he was not ashamed of it. Ancestors on both sides of his family had been solid citizens of small towns, middle-class people, raising families and obeying the law. A praetorship was the highest office reached by any of them. Vespasian never forgot his childhood days when he lived with his grandmother. He often went back to the homestead he loved. Later, as Emperor, he promoted a search for old inscriptions. His interest in Roman history and tradition was a quality he shared with Augustus and Claudius, and like them he proved to be one of the best emperors of the first century.

During his career, Vespasian was flattered by an invitation to the palace, but was ill-suited to join the company there. His habit of falling asleep while Nero was singing led to a temporary retirement. Earlier, he had been more successful in keeping in Caligula's favor, and began his career by serving in Thrace, Crete, and Cyrenaica. Under Claudius, he saw duty in Germany and won honors for his victories in Britain. Finally, he became the first member of his family to attain the consulship (A.D. 51). His later service as proconsul in Africa gave him service in all parts of the Empire except the Eastern provinces.

During the latter part of Nero's reign there arose a need for a top commander to put down a rebellion in Judaea. Despite Nero's personal feelings, Vespasian was obviously the right man. Suetonius said he "had given signal proof of energy and nothing, it seemed, need be feared from a man of such modest antecedents" (X. 4). It was one of the best appointments Nero ever made and a fortunate one for Rome.

Trouble in Judaea

Judaea was one of the smallest of the Roman provinces, but it had the greatest potential for trouble. Most Judaeans were strongly opposed to Roman rule and made no attempt to hide their feelings. Jewish unrest went much deeper than the usual complaints about tribute heard from other provincials. Indeed, while the Jews were expected to pay their taxes, the Romans excused them from military service and did not require them to worship the state gods. These exemptions gave the Jews a privileged status which did not endear them to their neighbors, particularly the Greeks and the Syrians, with whom they had frequent squabbles.

To the Jews, however, privileges were no substitute for independence, which would allow them to have a theocratic state, free from outside interference. The hope for this goal was somewhat dimmed by the divisions amongst themselves. Sadduceeism, with its emphasis on freedom of the will, had the strongest hold among the better-educated Jews. It was also this class, including traders and wealthy landholders, which traveled most and was more cosmopolitan. They could find reasons for an accommodation with the Romans. Small farmers, dominated by the Pharisees with their strict adherence to ceremonial and ancient law, were the real seed bed of revolt. True, many of the Essenes, monastics famed for the Dead Sea Scrolls, came from this group, but from it also arose a party of Zealots determined to win independence by force if necessary. Their efforts to rally the rest of the population were helped by the kind of officials whom the Romans customarily sent to Judaea. Since it was not economically or militarily an important province, they were likely to send mediocre men. By and large, these officials were insensitive to the deep religious feelings of the Jews, and their actions helped to precipitate the

uprising which began in A.D. 66. The Jewish cause was hopeless
from the beginning. Many wanted to desert to the Romans and
did; but those who stood fast until the end in A.D. 73, including
the valiant defenders of the fortress at Masada, bore testimony to
a fervent faith that they would win. The greatest Jewish writer of
the era did not think so. Joseph ben Mattias, better known as
Flavius Josephus (A.D. 37–*ca.* 100) was a traitor; but, as often
happens, he considered himself to be doing his people a favor. His
writings parallel those of Polybius, the friendly hostage who became an apologist for the Romans to the Greeks. Josephus, who
earlier had been sent as an envoy to Nero, believed that the Romans were best suited to rule the Mediterranean world and in any
event were destined to do so. That decision was made presumably
while he was serving as an officer during the siege of Jotapata, in
Galilee, in A.D. 67. To him it was better to submit and enjoy the
benefits of the Roman peace than it was to die. As a friend of
Vespasian's son Titus, he was richly rewarded for his opinion. He
received Roman citizenship, adopted the name Flavius, and was
given land in Judaea plus a pension.

Despite Josephus' unpopularity with his own people, he was
in a sense their Livy. In the period A.D. 75 to 79, he wrote a *History
of the Jewish War,* published first in Aramaic and then in Greek.
About twenty years later, he completed another history, *Antiquities
of the Jews,* which covered their history from the Creation to A.D.
66. Another work, *Against Apion,* was a defense of the religion of
the Jews. His *Autobiography* served to defend himself.

In 67 and 68, Vespasian led a Roman army into Judaea, which
forced the Jews to retreat into a few fortresses and into the well-
fortified Jerusalem, where those who crowded inside, though short
of food, were prepared for a long siege. One of the strongholds
which Jewish resisters controlled was a mountain fastness that in
former times was the palace of Herod the Great (*ca.* 73–4 B.C.).
The plateau on top of this mountain was thought to be impregn-
able, and it was until the Romans arrived. When at last the Jewish
defenders found themselves in danger of capture, they resolved to
kill one another rather than be taken alive. "Let us therefore make
haste, and instead of affording them so much pleasure, as they hope
for in getting us under their power, let us leave them an example
which shall at once cause their astonishment at our death, and their
admiration of our hardiness therein" (VII. 8.7). Josephus thought
that the Jewish resistance was a lost cause, but he never denied that

33. Masada. Three Roman camps and their siege ramp to the crest of the mountain can still be seen. Courtesy of the Consulate General of Israel, Chicago.

it was courageous. In 1955, Israeli archaeologists began work at Masada. Later, Yigael Yadin, who directed the excavations there from 1963 to 1965, published *Masada: Herod's Fortress and the Zealots' Last Stand.* The historical background for the work at this memorable place must come from Josephus, who provided a description of Herod's impressive buildings.

Vespasian's Regime

While Vespasian was faithfully doing his duty with great success in Judaea, he was not unmindful of the contest for power between Otho and Vitellius. Would he serve under either of these less capable men who had chanced to be closer to Rome? His omens were as good as theirs. The gods sent signs by plants as well as

34. Vespasian. Courtesy of the Ny Carlsberg Glyptotek, Copenhagen.

animals, and he had both. A tree said to be sacred to Mars had had a new sprout every time his mother became pregnant. The branch which appeared when Vespasian was born fared much better than those of her other two children. Later on in life, an ox which broke into Vespasian's house seemed to do obeisance to him. But signs aside, the soldiers who hailed Vespasian in Moesia, Egypt, and Judaea were supporting a general who, they felt, could win the title of Emperor and stay on top. The strategy he adopted proved them right. An army which had declared for Vespasian was sent under Gaius Licinius Mucianus, the governor of Syria, to challenge Vitellius in Italy. Vespasian wisely headed for Egypt, where he could cut off the grain ready to be shipped to Rome. As it happened, that strategy was not needed. Marcus Antonius Primus, who publicly supported Vespasian, brought his Danubian armies into Italy and defeated Vitellius' forces even before Mucianus arrived. Vitellius was killed; and with his corpse in the Tiber, the shrewd Vespasian marched on Rome unopposed. He was obviously, and finally, the right man. His son Titus was left in charge of the siege of Jerusalem.

Meaning to stay in power, Vespasian moved quickly to re-

store the fibre of the Empire's armed forces, which had recently
been so sorely weakened. He knew, as Augustus had known, and
Nero had forgotten, that the army must have close supervision by
a single commander-in-chief. Equally important, the Emperor
and his personal representatives should be worthy holders of their
power. Vespasian wanted a good job done and intended to see to
it that it was done. Commanders were reshuffled and some dismissed outright. The same treatment was applied to senatorial and
equestrian officeholders in Rome. Both groups were purged of
men who were not only incompetent, but lacked integrity and so
disgraced the system by holding any rank at all. If he found better
men in the provinces than in Rome, Vespasian, like Claudius,
promoted them.

The "second founder" of the Roman Empire was not a second Augustus. The difference showed in Vespasian's face and his
sturdy, muscular body. He was a tough army commander, who
had made his way in the world by hard work. In contrast, the
handsome but sickly Augustus needed men like Agrippa to guide
him so that he might use the mighty Caesar's name and fortune to
advantage. Vespasian stood on his own. His closest aide was his
son Titus, who did what he was told. The simple practicality and
common sense of the Old Romans at their best returns in Vespasian. He was neither eloquent nor elegant. His talk was coarse and
his humor generally earthy because he liked it that way. Yet, the
collection of his memorable remarks shows a dry wit. It shows
too that he had seen too much of the world to take anybody,
including himself, too seriously. That asset alone gave him a distinct advantage over his predecessors.

If Vespasian always had a somewhat strained look on his
face, it was very likely because he was constantly forcing himself
to be patient with officials less competent than himself. The trace
of foxiness revealed by his portrait busts is confirmed by one of
the best anecdotes about him. A member of his household had
been selling favors to outsiders. On one occasion he tried to persuade Vespasian to appoint a man who, he claimed, was his
brother. The Emperor called the fellow in and sold him the job
himself. Later, he told his servant: "Go and find another brother.
The one you mistook for your own turned out to be mine!" (X.
23). Behind this amusing story is the fact that Vespasian was
indeed serious about money and had no qualms about where it
came from. When Titus complained about a tax on the urinals in

Rome, Vespasian is said to have retorted, "Money does not smell." Vespasian imposed new taxes and higher rates on the old ones during his regime and kept a close eye on tax collectors. Officials caught building up their bank accounts by cheating received their punishment; Vespasian got the money. If there were higher assessments on the provinces, there were also more taxpayers to collect them from. Rhodes, Byzantium, and Samos lost their independent status as federate states by being incorporated into nearby provinces, thereby providing more revenue.

Vespasian, like Augustus, put in long hours at the job of being Emperor. And he went about it in an unassuming fashion. In fact, while Augustus might be accused of being calculating in his air of modesty, Vespasian was merely being himself. He thrived on keeping busy setting things right. The virtue of industriousness had become old-fashioned during Nero's theatrical regime. Now, if the courts were better managed and cases handled more quickly, it was because Vespasian took a hand in all branches of government. His orders were sensible.

Vespasian's private life was quiet. He had lost his wife and a daughter early in his career. Thereafter, he lived with a series of mistresses, and one favorite in particular, Caenis. Of his two sons, Vespasian always favored Titus, who served with him in Judaea. The younger son, Domitian, was more or less an outsider until his father and brother were dead.

In the best tradition of great leaders from Pericles to Augustus, Vespasian was rarely provoked into taking harsh or revengeful action against those who tried to bait him into acting rashly. His self-confidence saved him from an ostentatious display of temper or the pomposity of some of his predecessors. He generally kept a sense of humor toward those who were discourteous to him and let them be condemned by their own rudeness. But he was human, and it is recorded that once after great provocation he did lose his temper and condemn a man to death. He soon regretted it, but because of a misunderstanding his message arrived too late to prevent the execution. Suetonius says that case was exceptional and he was not aware of any instance when Vespasian knowingly allowed a man to suffer unjustly or under any circumstances took joy in another man's death.

Although Vespasian was not personally interested in the arts, he felt that it was his duty to encourage them. He shored up the cultural life of Rome with subsidies to teachers of rhetoric and prizes to poets, sculptors, and even actors. His contribution of a new stage for the Theatre of Marcellus, built by Augustus, allowed for its reopening. Parts of this structure are still standing. Given his caution with money, such expenditures must have seemed a sacrifice to him. It is also certain that Vespasian was intolerant of long-winded intellectuals who were short on practical experience, but nevertheless critical of the way the Emperor was managing affairs of state, including his intention to have his sons inherit the imperial power. Certain philosophers, Helvidius Priscus for instance, were ordered out of the city, not because Vespasian had any firm philosophical position of his own, but because he felt he knew how to run the Empire better than they did.

Vespasian died in his seventieth year on the twenty-third of June, A.D. 79, after a brief bout with an illness we would probably call flu. Pericles on his deathbed is reported to have said he wanted to be remembered for never having used his power for a selfish or petty purpose; Vespasian could have said the same. Instead, he preferred to joke about how he was about to become a god. No emperor since Augustus had died so peacefully. He was deified, and Titus succeeded him. Titus Flavius Vespasianus and Sons was a sound corporation.

By one means or another, Vespasian restored the imperial treasury to a firm condition. Many complained about his sharp practices, but nobody could fault him for how he spent the money. It was certainly not on himself. He built new temples to please the gods. He ordered work begun on what was to become the world's most famous amphitheatre. The Colosseum, as it was later called, has become more famous than its builder.

It had a major advantage over modern sports arenas: people found it easy to get in and out. At the ground level, the elliptical facade of the amphitheatre offered access from any direction through eighty archways. Once inside, the spectator was dwarfed by massive square columns made of solid blocks of stone which supported the upper tiers of seats. Following the corridor which encircled the building, he found an aisle by which he could reach his seat in a hurry. Still, today, the visitor senses the dramatic contrasts of the Colosseum. The dark and cool interior corridor offers a refuge from the blazing sunlight of the street or arena. In ancient times, awnings were used to give the spectators some protection; holes where the poles were inserted can still be seen. The compact strength of the building

35. Colosseum. Photograph courtesy of F. Warren Peters.

helps to account for its survival, albeit its future will be less secure without costly maintenance.

In the first century B.C., fifty thousand spectators sat in a oval mass around the relatively small area of combat. If there is horror to contend with in the memory of the Colosseum it is that the atmosphere was one of a cock fight, not a ball game. No one missed the sight of blood spilled on the sandy floor of the arena. Today, the floor is missing and so exposed to view are the animal dens and narrow corridors, like cattle runs, through which condemned prisoners and hopeful gladiators passed on their way to die in the sunlight amid the savagery of a public entertainment.

Titus

Titus ruled for only a little more than two years. His untimely death about two weeks before his forty-second birthday evoked

more genuine grief than for any other emperor, including even
the aged Augustus. His complete devotion to his father was a
virtue the Romans admired. When Vespasian went to Rome from
the Near East, it was Titus who joined in the thick of the fight
and completely subdued Judaea. His own triumphal return to
Rome was commemorated by the Arch of Titus, fifty feet high,
which still stands at one end of the old Forum. Inside the single
archway is a relief of Titus in a trimphal chariot, with Victory at
his side. The panel on the other side depicts, with lively realism,
his troops carrying the treasures from the temple in Jerusalem,
including the golden seven-branched candelabrum.

People were anxious about what would happen when Titus
became Emperor, but their fears were premature. His new responsibility brought out the best side of his character. Titus was a
close companion of Britannicus and was, in fact, at the table when
his friend drank the poison Nero had arranged for him. When
many years later Titus sat in Nero's place he only gently chided a
person who had conspired against him and sent a message to the
man's mother telling her not to worry about her son. Titus' devotion to the problems of the Empire and concern for the suffering
of others made him popular in a way no Emperor had been before
him. The limits he set on his own enjoyments, the dismissal of his
mistress Berenice for instance, were particularly impressive because he had never had a reputation for denying himself anything.
In contrast to his father's rather spare life, Titus had been a handsome, dashing "prince" given to sports and parties, interested
enough in music to play the harp. The report of an ill-spent
youth, however, may be exaggerated, as it was one of a parcel of
stories about the young blades who survived the vice at Nero's
court.

Titus was good-natured like his father. But, unlike his
father, he was generous with money. There could have been no
greater test of his open-heartedness than after the multiple disasters which marked his short reign. The most famous of these
catastrophes occurred on August 24, A.D. 79. The eruption of
Mount Vesuvius, near Neapolis (Naples), buried the towns at its
base. Titus set up a far-reaching relief and rehabilitation program
and paid for much of it himself.

Suetonius only mentions the eruption of Vesuvius in passing.
Presumably, there was a long account by Tacitus in a section of his
Histories, which has been lost. We know about it because one of

36. Arch of Titus. Photograph courtesy of F. Warren Peters.

37. Relief, Arch of Titus, showing the great candelabrum being brought from Jerusalem to Rome along with other treasures. Photograph courtesy of F. Warren Peters.

Tacitus' friends, a survivor of the catastrophe, answered the historian's request for information by writing what he remembered in two letters which have survived. The writer was Pliny the Younger, whose published correspondence is a major literary source for the late first and early second centuries A.D. He is called Pliny the Younger, to distinguish him from his scholarly uncle, whose *Natural History* in thirty-seven volumes is one of the enduring works of the first century A.D. In the summer of A.D. 79, young Pliny, then seventeen, was with his mother at Misenum, where his famous uncle was the commander of the fleet. In his first letter to Tacitus, Pliny repeated the stories he had heard from those who had accompanied his uncle on a rescue mission during the eruption. Ironically, while hundreds of persons were evacuated by the navy, its commander was lost in the operation. He stayed too long ashore, and died at Stabiae from suffocation, as did so many others. The younger Pliny described how it happened:

> My uncle decided to go down to the shore and investigate on the spot the possibility of any escape by sea, but he found the waves still wild and dangerous. . . . Then the flames and smell of sulphur which gave warning of the approaching fire drove the others to take flight and roused him to stand up. He stood leaning on two slaves and then suddenly collapsed, I imagine because the dense fumes choked his breathing by blocking his windpipe which was constitutionally weak and narrow and often inflamed. (VI. 16. 17–20)

When another request for information about his own experience came from Tacitus, Pliny wrote about how he and his mother fled along an open road:

> We had scarcely sat down to rest when darkness fell, not the dark of a moonless or cloudy night, but as if the lamp had been put out in a closed room. You could hear the shrieks of women, the wailing of infants and the shouting of men. . . . a gleam of light returned, but we took this to be a warning of the approaching flames rather than daylight. However, the flames remained some distance off; then darkness came on once more and ashes began to fall again, this time in heavy showers. We rose from time to time and shook them off, otherwise we should have been buried and crushed beneath their weight. I could boast that not a groan or cry of fear escaped me in these perils, had I not derived some poor consolation in my mortal lot from the belief that the whole world was dying with me and I with it.
> At last the darkness thinned and dispersed into smoke or cloud; then there was genuine daylight, and the sun actually shone out, but

yellowish as it is during an eclipse. We were terrified to see everything
changed, buried deep in ashes like snowdrifts. (VI. 20. 14, 16–19).

Today there are fast interurban trains from Naples to the
excavations (*scavi*) at Herculaneum, situated at the northwest foot
of Mount Vesuvius, and Pompeii, just south of the mountain,
which along with Stabiae (modern Castellammare di Stabia on the
Bay of Naples) were destroyed in the holocaust of A.D. 79. These
doomed places had not yet recovered from an earthquake in A.D.
62 before the eruption of Mount Vesuvius buried them.

The areas open to visitors at both Herculaneum and Pompeii
have benefited in recent years from improved landscaping and the
addition of helpful identification signs. Although these neighboring towns have many similarities, as might be expected, Pompeii
offers more to see, for over half of the ancient site has been
excavated. A typical forum, theatres, amphitheatre, baths, and
temples can be seen to good advantage. Herculaneum is buried
beneath the modern town of Resina; to expand the site there
would be very expensive. The area open to visitors is compact,
however, and the restoration work exceptionally well done. The
streets at Herculaneum are somewhat narrower than those at
Pompeii, but the original polygonal slabs of stone used for surfac-
ing are still to be seen in both places. There were small shops
opening onto the sidewalks. For long stretches, only small doorways in undecorated walls provide an entry into houses standing
side by side. Those which belonged to the wealthy had large
rectangular areas, generally in the center of the house, open to the
sky. In that usually sunny climate, people liked to be outdoors
enjoying flowers, pools, and fountains, even when at home. The
arrangement offered privacy besides. The peristyle surrounding
the innter courtyard consisted of columns on all sides supporting
the roof of sheltered walkways, off which the rooms of the house
opened.

At Herculaneum, the second floors of some houses have
been skillfully restored. Also to be seen are the typical low beds of
the time, which take up about half the space of the very small
rooms. Some of these houses with upper stories have attractive
balconies overhanging the street. In the fashion of the day, the
walls, particularly of the better houses, were painted with scenes
which gave each room its own distinctive theme. Some remains
of these colorful paintings are still visible. On the walls of public

38. Street scene, Herculaneum. Photograph from the slide collection of the Detroit Institute of Arts.

39. Odeon, Pompeii. Photograph from the slide collection of the Detroit Institute of Arts.

buildings and in the baths, numerous graffiti and election slogans have been found—mute testimony to busy hands which suddenly came to a stop. In the museum at Pompeii, glass cases exhibit casts of dead figures, sprawled on their hands and knees, the way they were caught by poisonous gases amid burning ash and lapilli. The Naples National Museum also has extensive collections of paintings, bronzes, and mosaics from the excavations at Pompeii and Herculaneum.

The end of Titus' reign was distinguished by other acts of mercy. He was equally concerned for the victims of another great fire in Rome in A.D. 80. Finally, in that same year, there was an epidemic which struck the city and ran its course despite Titus' frantic efforts to find a remedy or evoke a miracle. Suetonius wrote that Titus "showed far more than an Emperor's concern: it resembled the deep love of a father for his children" (XI. 8).

Titus' own death on the thirteenth of September, A.D. 81, was another disaster for the Roman people, not only because they lost him, but because it brought to power his younger brother Domitian, whose eventual death at forty-four would not be thought untimely.

Domitian

When Charles II of England was warned by his brother James to beware lest he be executed as their father had been, he was reputed to have replied, "They will never kill me, James, to make you king." The line might have been used by Titus to his younger brother Domitian, except nobody would have wanted to kill Titus. Domitian (A.D. 51–96) had neither his brother's charm nor his father's affability. He had administrative capacity but was unfit as a man. He was often compared to Tiberius, being both contentious and humorless. Domitian was taller, but neither so handsome as his brother nor so strong in appearance as his father. He did share their angular features. Suetonius mentioned that he had "large, rather weak eyes." He was touchy about his baldness, but a man does not have to be an emperor to feel that way. On balance, Domitian apparently did not look as sinister as his cruelties might have suggested. He was extremely jealous of his brother and worked against him in every way possible. His feelings were obvious when he left Titus' deathbed before the end. Yet he was credited with completing the Arch of Titus as a memorial.

The story that Domitian liked to sit alone sticking flies with the end of his pen might at first seem all we need to know about him. But this idiosyncrasy is misleading. He was undoubtedly neurotic, with some curious quirks, but the record of his administration is surprisingly good. Suetonius says that during Domitian's regime the standard of justice was generally admirable. He gives full credit to Domitian, who, like his father, insisted that the machinery of the government function well. It was not, however, out of any particular love for those who benefited.

Domitian had never been much of a military figure, and the campaigns during his reign were minor. It was his domestic policies which made a favorable impression during the early years of his rule. Foreshadowing the humanitarian outlook of the good emperors of the following century, he issued an order against castration and sought to curb the traffic in slave eunuchs. His severity with officials or jurymen caught taking bribes gave the plebs an unusual degree of confidence in his courts. Like his father, he wanted members of the senatorial and the equestrian classes to conform to moral standards or at least to avoid public scandal. He strictly enforced a law forbidding unnatural sexual practices, and watched over the purity of the Vestal Virgins, whose indiscretions showed a corrosion of morality at the innermost circle of the state cult. Three of these maidens were convicted of breaking their vows during his regime. The last one convicted was buried alive in the Campus Sceleratus, following an ancient custom. Under Domitian's correct regime, the gods were not to be mocked.

It seems ironic that Domitian, who was so severe in curbing both moral and political corruption among his subjects, should turn out to be common murderer himself. Like the morality of some other despots, his was only a means to achieve order, not a reflection of his true character. The catalogue of his crimes is long, and tradition says that, like the worst of his predecessors, he capriciously inflicted death on young and old alike. Even senators were condemned for the merest slight to the Emperor. It is hard to believe that Domitian put a man to death for commemorating the birthday of an uncle, who happened to be the former Emperor Otho. Yet Suetonius includes this story along with others describing the empty pretexts Domitian used for getting rid of people he suspected of disloyalty.

The historian Tacitus was an eye-witness to the poisonous

atmosphere at court, and it surely affected his point of view when early in the second century A.D. he at last felt free to write a history of the first century. To be quite fair, Domitian had reason to fear conspiracies against his life. The man at the top inevitably feels lonesome and apprehensive. As Domitian once observed, the people never seem to take an emperor's fears seriously until he is assassinated.

Although merciless toward suspected plotters, Domitian was strangely lenient in his response to one actual attempt to unseat him from the throne. He reacted to an abortive revolt among the troops stationed on the Rhine by raising the pay scale in the army, an action which actually was long overdue. His one precaution was to restrict the amount of savings which could accumulate in any single legion's camp, as he had learned with some surprise that that kind of money made the attempt to overthrow him possible.

Domitian's generosity to the army, along with his building program, returned the imperial treasury to the depleted state in which "stingy" Vespasian had found it when he became Emperor. In collecting taxes, however, Domitian, like his father, was mindful of every penny. Suetonius injects a personal note when he testifies that as a boy he once saw a ninety-year-old man forced to expose himself in court so that it could be a matter of record whether or not he was circumcised. Domitian did not intend one Jew to evade the tax which Jews paid for the privilege of worshipping their own God.

As the years passed, the Emperor grew more fearful for his life, and he seemed to demand worship as well as loyalty. He called himself "Lord God" and spoke of himself as divine. Scholars have speculated that he decided to promote himself as a divinity while he could, since he foresaw that he would never be proclaimed a god after his death. Each succeeding year of his reign, which was longer than that of his father and brother, brought new cause for regret. His time eventually ran out. Suetonius writes that "finally his friends and freedmen conspired to murder him with [his wife] Domitia's connivance" (XII. 14). The alliance was born of desperation; if Domitian could kill his cousin Flavius Clemens, who was in no way a threat to him, nobody knew who would be next. The way to end the suspense was obvious.

As might be expected, the story of his final days includes a variety of ominous signs. One conscientious if foolhardy astrologer gave Domitian the news of impending doom and met his own end earlier than he might have expected. But Domitian's personal fears could not be allayed by killing an astrologer. One day, when offered some apples, he said: "Serve them tomorrow—if tomorrow ever comes" (XII. 16). He was murdered early the next morning. The plotters used his well-known anxiety about conspirators, which made him willing to see his niece's steward, who posed as an informer bringing a list of names. While Domitian was reading it, the steward stabbed him in the groin. The Emperor put up a struggle, but four other assailants appeared to join in the kill. His passing was not mourned by the people. The Senate ordered the images of him to be defaced, and even condemned his name by a formal decree, the *damnatio memoriae*. Only a well-paid army seems to have regretted his death, and an "old nurse" carried his ashes to the Temple of the Flavians.

Throughout the ensuing centuries, parts of Domitian's buildings have remained and some are still to be seen today. His marble-faced fountain, which stood near the Colosseum, is gone. Mussolini tore it down.

XVI
The Good Years

When those who killed Domitian backed a prominent senator to succeed him instead of an army man, they were opting for consensus among the leading citizens rather than civil war. Marcus Cocceius Nerva (*ca.* A.D. 30–98) was the Senate's man. He was chosen for his excellent record and his advanced age. If, at sixty-six, he proved to be a bad choice, time would be on the Senate's side. In those days, sixty was much older than it is now. Pliny said of a recently deceased friend: "I know he had lived to the end of his sixty-seventh year, a good age even for a really sound constitution" (I. 12. 11). True, Vespasian had ruled until he was seventy, but he was a sturdier man than Nerva. There were other considerations. Nerva had experience, having lived through the best and worst days of the Flavian dynasty. Everyone hoped that he would restore the good feeling of Vespasian's time, but at the outset no one was sure. The uneasiness in the early months of his reign is reflected in one of Pliny's letters. In the Senate, Pliny had vigorously attacked a high official whom he considered to have been guilty of crimes during the reign of Domitian. Privately, he was asked if he was not being too bold; but Pliny guessed that he was safe, and he was right.

40. Nerva. Courtesy of the Museo Vaticano, Rome.

Nerva voluntarily limited his own power. He promised that he would never put a senator to death without the Senate's concurrence, and furthermore he allowed philosophers and others noted for their often savage criticisms to return to Rome. Pliny spoke reverently of Nerva and rejoiced that men could once again speak their minds. It is ironical, however, that he later mused about how little there was to talk about. For the time being it was possible to hope that in the future there would be an open discussion in the Senate about a successor. Nerva might have allowed for some constitutional system of succession had he not had to worry about the unruly Praetorian Guard, so long pampered and now grumbling about a loss of power. They received a perfunctory donation, but that would not satisfy them for long. Out of necessity, then, Nerva needed a forceful partner, a military man who would take a firm hand with the soldiers stationed both in Rome and on the frontiers. Whoever was chosen would of course be Nerva's successor; and in Rome, by tradition, a successor was also a son. In October, A.D. 97, Nerva, who had no children of his own, adopted a forty-four-year-old general—Marcus Ulpius Trajanus (A.D. 53–117), who had been born to Roman parents near Seville in Spain. Trajan was exceptionally well suited to the job at hand. The Senate acquiesced in his selection and named him Caesar, which amounted to calling him crown prince. Nerva had found a practical solution for the problem of succession. After him, each Emperor chose the next, to produce five excellent rulers in a row. Then the otherwise remarkable Marcus Aurelius committed a rare blunder by letting his worthless son Commodus succeed him.

Nerva, Trajan, Hadrian, Antoninus Pius, and Marcus Aurelius are called the "good emperors." Although restrained by little more than their own consciences, these men gave the Empire honorable service because each personally wanted to. If there was any justification for enormous power, that was it. Not every one of their actions was well-intentioned; but compared to stretches of the Julio-Claudian and Flavian periods, theirs was a time of enlightened leadership. The eighteenth-century historian Edward Gibbon, famous for his history of Rome's decline, looked back to the second century and wrote a rapturous, often quoted statement: "If a man were called to fix the period in the history of the world during which the condition of the human race was most happy and prosperous, he would, without hesitation, name that which elapsed from the death of Domitian to the accession of Commodus" (Vol. I, p. 70).

Civilization reached a higher level in the second century A.D. than would be known again before the Renaissance, itself a revival of all things classical. The vitality of the cities during the time of the good emperors was evident in the number of new constructions everywhere in the Empire. Bridges, aqueducts, and baths were being built at such a rate that several projects got into financial trouble. Hotels, like the one discovered during the excavations at Ostia near Rome, made it easier for businessmen or tourists to travel long distances. Presumably more people were going off to see the sights of other lands during this period than ever before or afterwards in ancient times. The capital itself remained the most popular city for the provincials to visit. Many of those who could afford to leave Rome headed for Greece and Egypt. Guidebooks were available. The most famous was that of the second-century geographer Pausanias. His *Periegesis of Greece* has helped modern archaeologists to find ancient monuments which had long since been buried.

Available to a reading public now interested in the past history of Greece or Rome were two new works which are still extant. First, there were the popular *Parallel Lives* by Plutarch (*ca.* A.D. 46–*ca.* 120) who was himself an inveterate traveller, and also the author of the *Moralia,* sixty essays which, like the better modern magazines, touched on a variety of subjects. The *Roman History* of Appian (*ca.* A.D. 95–*ca.* 165) displayed none of the artfulness of Plutarch's works but made interesting reading on the great events and personalities of the now long ago republican times, especially the civil wars of the first century B.C.

Readers of sophisticated tastes who preferred lighter fare could sample the wit of the extraordinary Lucian, a native of Samosata in Syria. His short satires included the *Dialogues of the Gods* and *Auction of Philosophers.* The Roman Empire of the second century with its bustling cities and well travelled roads furnished a cosmopolitan audience for Lucian, whose clever, secular, and somewhat cynical comments were the smart talk of his age.

Apparently, among the private enterprises of cities of any size were bookshops. In one of his letters, Pliny mentions that he was surprised to hear his books were being sold as far away as Lyon in Gaul. Collections of the satiric verse by Pliny's contemporary Martial were bestsellers in Rome. In one of his epigrams, Martial named Atrectus' bookstore across from Caesar's Forum as a place where his books were readily available. His works, like Pliny's, were also sold in distant cities throughout the provinces, and Martial mentioned that, too.

Perhaps the most significant indication of the high level of civilization reached in the second century was the unusual concern for the suffering of the helpless in Roman society, unusual because throughout ancient times the misery of great masses of poor people was accepted as a condition which had always been and would always be. Above all, what was good about the good emperors was their effort to alleviate the suffering of those who by circumstance could not help themselves. This was done, in part, by edicts providing minimal rights, for slaves for instance, to be mentioned more fully later. It also included programs which would today be classed as social welfare. The children of the poor were a special concern. They were the beneficiaries of a plan whereby the government made low-interest loans to Italian farmers and used the income in the local communities for the care and education of needy children. This *alimenta* system begun by Nerva was kept in operation by his successor. Trajan's role in the expansion of the program is commemorated in a relief on a great triumphal arch built at Beneventum. The decoration includes a tableau showing children perched on their fathers' shoulders, amid crowned figures who personify the various towns receiving the *alimenta* funds. The Arch of Beneventum also marked the opening of the Via Traiana, which ran to Brundisium but was not actually completed until Hadrian's reign.

Many wealthy men followed the government's example and thereby won favor with the emperors. Self-interest sweetened the joy of giving, as with modern tax deductions. They set up *alimenta* funds of their own, akin to present-day charitable foundations. These usually benefited the needy children of their home towns. Local gratitude is well attested by the numerous inscriptions set up in various places throughout the Empire, thanking these men for their generosity. An inscription dating from the mid-first century shows how old this practice was and that it had been used by a few philanthropists even before Nerva made it a state policy. The example of the good emperors led to greatly increased private donations.

Pliny described such an arrangement with his home town:

> Personally I can think of no better plan than the one I adopted myself. I had promised a capital sum of 500,000 sesterces for the maintenance of free-born boys and girls, but instead of paying this over I transferred some of my landed property (which was worth considerably more) to the municipal agent, and then had it reconveyed back to me charged with an annual rent payable of 30,000 sesterces. By this means the principal is secured for the town, the interest is certain, and the property will always find a tenant to cultivate it because its value greatly exceeds the rent charged. I am well aware that I appear to have paid out more than the sum I have given, seeing that the fixed rent charge has reduced the market value of a fine property, but one ought to make personal and temporary interests give place to public and permanent advantages, and consider the security of a benefaction more than one's own gains. (VII. 18. 2–5)

The humanitarianism of the good emperors had its practical side. Nerva and Trajan were particularly concerned about the welfare of Italy. The Roman Empire had become a kind of common market. Certain places became noted for specialized products, glass at Cologne for instance, which were distributed over a wide area. The provinces had long since become competitive with Italy in wine and olive oil. Labor costs had become higher in Italy because of a decline in the population, and because slaves were less plentiful as a result of the suppression of piracy and the end of the wars of conquest. So, the government's program was designed to help the local farmers and to encourage the raising of families.

There is no continuous account of the best years of the second century. Much of the story is pieced together from the plentiful inscriptions of the period, wherein the good emperors take credit for their building projects, charitable works, and triumphs over Rome's persistent enemies. The best literary source is Pliny the Younger, who so vividly described the eruption of Vesuvius. The replies to Tacitus' inquiry were among the hundreds of artful letters which he published with joy and pride. The first nine books of the *Letters* are largely personal. Most of them were written to friends and a few to his relatives. The tenth book contains his correspondence with the Emperor Trajan, while serving as his special emissary in Bithynia.

Pliny's *Letters* are those of a man of quality, born to wealth, well-educated and devoted to duty. He left his native Comum (modern Como, twenty-four miles north of Milan) as a young man to continue his education in Rome under the famous Quintilian, a Spaniard who had taught oratory there since early in Vespasian's reign. The soundness of Pliny's training was soon in evidence in the Centumviral Court in Rome, where he began his career at eighteen and spent most of his time in the years to follow. This court, which handled cases primarily dealing with wills and inheritances, met in the Basilica Julia. Today, in the Forum there remain the ruins of this enormous administrative building begun by Julius Caesar and completed by Augustus. It is noteworthy that the only service in the army Pliny performed was quartermaster duty. Finances were his lifelong specialty.

Pliny occasionally referred to the evil times under Domitian, when his own career was taking shape. He does not spell out how he escaped the Emperor's wrath in spite of his association with certain philosophers who were put to death by Domitian. There can be no doubt that he was at times in danger during his praetorship in A.D. 93. On one occasion he went to visit a man who was under suspicion and even lent him money when others were reluctant to do so. Seven of Pliny's friends had already been exiled or executed, and he later wrote that he had himself stood on dangerous ground. On the other hand, one senses in Pliny's letters that he was a man given to serving the powers that be and that he was by no means sympathetic to philosophers in general. He said of a man he admired that his sterling qualities were rather rare among the philosophers of the day. Still he did not approve of Domitian's purge. Rather it was that his temperament enabled him to forego martyrdom. How he escaped that fate is suggested in a story he told about a man who was perhaps the only genuine enemy he ever had. Though others may not have agreed, Pliny considered Marcus Aquilius Regulus to be a henchman for Domitian. On one occasion, a certain Modestus, whose testimony would have been important during a trial in which Pliny and Regulus took opposing sides, was not available, having been sent into exile by Domitian. Regulus demanded to know Pliny's opinion of the man. The truth would have sorely offended the Emperor, and a lie would have disgraced Pliny before his friends. He replied that no one need state an opinion about a man already convicted. Such agility seems to have served him well during a dangerous season.

Pliny spent most of his life in Rome. Both Nerva and Trajan were emperors with whom Pliny could feel comfortable, and he held several posts at their requests. But his roots were always in Comum, and he showed this constantly in letters to friends living there and by his generosity to the town, particularly its children. The *alimenta* fund he set up has already been mentioned. Comum was also a major beneficiary in Pliny's will. During his lifetime, he supported a school, built a library, and helped the indigent. In a letter to Tacitus, he described the stipulation he set for any money he would contribute to a school. The parents had to raise two-thirds of the total themselves. If they were spending their own money he felt they would be more cautious with his. He wanted the parents to select the teachers and asked Tacitus to send the names of some likely candidates. It is ironic that Pliny, who placed such strong emphasis on local control of local matters, was later a key figure in the Emperor's plan to oversee municipal operations in distant Bithynia. There were reasons for the interference. But in the long term the drift was toward increasing centralization of powers and less local responsibility.

"A Good Life and a Genuine One"

Pliny worried about the time wasted in Rome on what he called trivialities, and although he would never have dreamed of abandoning his duty he occasionally allowed himself the luxury of complaining about his routine activities in Rome. He liked to get away to his house at the sea. "There is nothing there for me to say or hear said which I would afterwards regret, no one disturbs me with malicious gossip, and I have no one to blame—but myself—when writing doesn't come easily. . . . I share my thoughts with myself and my books. It is a good life and a genuine one, a seclusion which is happy and honourable" (I. 9. 5–6).

Pliny enjoyed writing about the comforts of his various villas: the place at Laurentum, near Ostia, about seventeen miles from Rome, was his favorite. He wrote about this house as though he were fingering a fine piece of cloth, mentioning the location of each room and how it was affected by the sea breezes or by the passing sun. Typically, the house was built around a courtyard. The slaves' quarters were at one side. Two dining rooms and the main bedrooms looked toward the sea. The larger dining room had "folding doors or windows as large as the doors all round, so that at the front and sides it seems to look out on to three seas." One of the bedrooms "lets in the morning sunshine with one window and holds the last rays of the evening sun with the other." There was of course a more complicated way of getting heat by means of "a floor raised and fitted with pipes to receive hot steam and circulate it at a regulated temperature" (II. 17. 5–6, 9). A luxurious feature of the house was a heated swimming pool from which swimmers could see the sea.

Back in Rome, among the more elegant forms of entertainment were poetry readings, either in public or in private for friends, by invitation only. One April, there was a new reading almost every day. Pliny, a familiar figure on such occasions, was appalled at the manners of some of the others who attended, particularly those rude persons who left early. There were other dangers at public hearings, even from the best of company. A man named Paulus began by flattering his dear friend Javolenus Priscus with the phrase "You bid me, Priscus—." "Indeed I don't," was the waspish reply. The program never recovered from the laughter.

Pliny had no interest in the popular entertainments of the city. He found nothing amusing about dancers, mimes, or clowns, but added "I can put up with those who do." At a modern American university, he would have spent his Saturday afternoons in the library, far from the roaring crowd at the stadium.

The ruins of the great imperial Circus Maximus, where the races were held, still stand in the area between the Palatine and Aventine hills. Pliny had a particular aversion to the chariot racing which took place there:

> I have been spending all the last few days among my notes and papers in most welcome peace. How could I—in the city? The Races were on, a type of spectacle which has never had the slightest attraction for me. I can find nothing new or different in them: once seen is enough, so it surprises me all the more that so many thousands of adult men should have such a childish passion for watching galloping horses and drivers standing in chariots, over and over again. (IX. 6. 1–3)

Pliny was more interested in writing letters than most of his friends, and he frequently complains about not having heard from them. His own letters included advice to his friends about what they should be reading, and, to a few, whether he considered their writings worth publishing. He also asks advice and shares it with friends about where and when to buy property. The weather was a familiar topic because many of his friends depended, as he did, on the income from their farm lands.

Pliny was frequently consulted by fathers seeking suitable young men to marry their daughters. As might be expected, he recommended only those whom he knew personally and whose families had an impeccable reputation, as well as money. After all a man had to have a certain amount of wealth to be admitted to the Senate.

Good connections, whether by marriage or friendship, were always important among the Roman upper classes. Pliny depended on them. One of his correspondents received this: "Your command of a large army gives you a plentiful source of benefits to confer, and secondly, your tenure has been long enough for you to have provided for your own friends. Turn to mine" (II. 13. 2–3).

Pliny often refers to his speeches. He liked to give readings, publish them, and send copies to his friends even as a scholar today distributes offprints. The only oration which is extant is the *Panegyricus,* delivered in A.D. 100 to thank Trajan for an appointment as consul. The present version is the one Pliny revised and expanded for publication. In addition to being a mountain of praise for Trajan, it offers a valid historical contrast between the regimes of Domitian and Trajan. The Emperor must remain constitutional in the Augustan sense by restraining himself. Pliny spoke for all those who saw this arrangement as the best solution for the problem of power. Pliny was of course grateful for the better atmosphere. Ability was now rewarded, rather than being envied and so punished. But elsewhere his comments on the tribunate betray a subtle cynicism. In answer to a friend's question about how to act in his new office, he wrote: "It depends entirely on the view you take of the tribunate—an 'empty form' and a 'mere title,' or an inviolable authority which should not be called in question by anyone, not even the holder. When I was tribune myself, I acted on the assumption (which may have been a wrong one) that my office really meant something" (I. 28. 1–2).

Some Realities of the Times

The good life of a well-to-do gentleman of the second century A.D. was made possible, in part, by slaves, who were also a source of anxiety. Pliny complains that his servants treated him with "indifference," taking advantage of his kindness to them. He seems to have been lucky. A friend of his went on a trip, taking his slaves along, and was never heard from again. Pliny feared the man had been murdered by his servants, who had then run off. Such murders happened often enough. Not unexpectedly, the treatment of slaves varied from inconsiderateness or outright cruelty on the one hand to generosity, including early freedom, on the other. Pliny said he never kept the slaves on his farms in chains. At the same time, he did not trust the looks of a man he was purchasing, but preferred to have a recommendation from former masters. No one discussed the morality of buying and selling people; it was not a moral question. The use of slaves was so well established in the social order that it was taken for granted. Pliny's criticism of a vicious slave owner would be the equivalent of condemning a reckless driver today. His overall view of slavery was probably typical and is candidly expressed in an excerpt from one of his letters:

> This horrible affair demands more publicity than a letter—Larcius Macedo, a senator and ex-praetor, has fallen victim to his own slaves. Admittedly he was a cruel and overbearing master. . . . He was taking a bath in his house at Formiae when suddenly he found himself surrounded; one slave seized him by the throat while the others struck his

face and hit him in the chest and stomach and—shocking to say—in his private parts. . . . at least he died with the satisfaction of having revenged himself, for he lived to see the same punishment meted out as for murder. There you see the dangers, outrages and insults to which we are exposed. No master can feel safe because he is kind and considerate; for it is their brutality, not their reasoning capacity which leads slaves to murder masters. (III. 14. 1–2, 4–5)

Pliny allows that the master was cruel in the case cited, but then concludes that it made no difference because the slave's brutality caused the trouble. Historically, this mixed statement probably shows how most men of his class looked at the problem.

That corruption, even criminality, still occurred in the governing provinces during even the best of times can be seen in cases which Pliny described. Both he and Tacitus represented the province of Africa in the trial of an ex-governor and former consul, Marius Priscus, who had not only stolen money but taken payments from certain men in return for summarily ordering the executions of their enemies. Pliny was of course horrified and called such deeds monstrous. If at times he sounded self-righteous, he had good reason to. Whether he spoke for the prosecution or the defense in a court action depended on which side had the better cause. He felt contempt for men who went fee hunting or sought to win a case regardless of its merits. Pliny did not take fees and was happy to be free from the obligations thrust on those who did. From time to time he did inherit money from friends. But any services he had rendered them would have been part of a lifetime of devotion. It is no use saying that Pliny's substantial income from renting out his farm properties, particularly in Tuscany, allowed him to stand on principle. There were men of far greater wealth who had no scruples. Pliny's letters show how pleased he was to have a reputation as a virtuous man. The Emperor Trajan evidently thought he was, for he trusted Pliny implicitly, although he may at times have tired of listening to him.

At Priscus' trial before the Senate with the Emperor presiding, Pliny admitted to being nervous, but warmed to his subject:

My speech lasted for nearly five hours, for I was allowed four water-clocks in addition to my original twelve of the largest size. . . . The Emperor did indeed show such an attentive and kindly interest in me (I should not like to call it anxiety on my behalf) that more than once, when he fancied I was putting too much strain on my rather delicate physique, he suggested to my freedman standing behind me that I should spare my voice and lungs. (II. 11. 14–15)

And perhaps the Emperor?

In publishing the speech which he delivered at the official opening of the new library he gave to Comum, Pliny was worried lest he was simply seeking self-glorification in doing so. "Fame should be the result, not the purpose of our conduct, and if for some reason it fails to follow, there is no less merit in cases where it was deserved. But when people accompany their generous deeds with words they are thought not to be proud of having performed them but to be performing them in order to have something to be proud of" (I. 8. 14–15). His self-analysis showed the influence of Stoicism, with its greater concern about why a man was doing something than with the act itself. Pliny's moralizing in his *Letters* has a Stoic tone. For instance, he once remarked that "a duty performed deserves no gratitude if a return is expected." Yet Pliny was not a dedicated Stoic unto death, as were some others. During Domitian's reign, his words had apparently been motivated by the desire to stay alive.

Most of Pliny's letters concern the good life of the gentleman, whether in the country or in the city. But he also talked of death, speaking of more than one aging friend who, faced with the agony of a terminal illness, decided to die by refusing all food. As such a person grew weaker the will to refuse became stronger, for the escape was near. These quiet suicides were probably a common enough event at a time when the aged especially were beyond medical help. "The news has just come that Silius Italicus has starved himself to death in his house near Naples. Ill-health was the reason, for he had developed an incurable tumor which wore him down" (III. 7. 1–2).

Martial

Pliny mentioned the death of the poet Martial, but did not say how he died. It was presumably from natural causes. The letter began on a note of sorrow and then went on to generous praise of Martial as an entertaining poet. It was also mentioned that when his old friend was returning to his home town in retirement, Pliny gave him money for the journey. There was more in common between these two men than their mutual literary interests. Both managed to survive Domitian's dangerous regime. Martial had apparently avoided risks by engaging in outrageous flattery toward the Emperor. Maybe as a thirty-four-year guest in the city he felt no need to do anything else.

Martial came to Rome from Bilbilis in Spain. His career in the city was that of an observer who displayed an uncommon talent for writing epigrams which wrapped up human nature in neat little packages. At times, his wit fell flat, but it was more often very clever and on occasions devastating. There is no translation, archaic or modern, which can obliterate his meaning when he is on target. "What I hate about a fellow tippler is a perfect memory" (I. xxvii).

His caricatures with words were not intended as a message for or against anything. They were moral in that they preached tolerance for the human condition both funny and sad, good and bad. He persistently mentioned hypocrisy, the foibles of the *nouveaux riches,* and often made cutting remarks about the looks of certain persons, although he did not always use actual names. To be mentioned in one of Martial's popular verses was to win a small degree of fame, no matter what he said. Pliny was flattered and was at the same time apparently one of the few men toward whom Martial showed any deference. Commenting on one of the poems Martial wrote about him, he said: "The poet is addressing the Muse, telling her to seek my house on the Esquiline and approach it with respect" (III. 21. 5). On the other hand, it might be questioned whether these two men were really close friends, for they had quite different tastes and temperaments. Pliny spoke of Cicero with reverence and awe except for one curious remark about the orator's relationship with his freedman Tiro. Martial called Cicero a "profounder bore" than Vergil. He did not erect any pedestals. The barber who worked so slowly that another beard was growing while he was shaving one off was as worthy of Martial's bite as the young interns whose "two hundred chilly paws assailed my brow; I had no fever, but I have one now" (V. ix). And it might even be wondered how far from his mind was the longwinded Pliny when he wrote about a certain Caecilianus:

You ask for seven water clocks
As time in which to plead.
The judge is none too pleased with this,
But sourly says, "Agreed!"
So you go on, and on, and on,

And heated by your task,
You pause for one long, lukewarm swig
Of water from your flask.
Cecil, for God's sake, kill two birds
With just one stone, or rock,
And end your thirst and speech alike—
Drink from the water clock!

(VI. xxxv)

Martial returned to his home town in Spain in A.D. 98 and
died there about six years later.

The Pliny-Trajan Letters

The tenth volume of Pliny's letters begins with a letter wishing
Trajan "health and happiness" on his accession to power in A.D.
98. Pliny's obsequiousness sometimes borders on the servile, but
it must be remembered that he did sincerely admire Trajan as a
man of many talents.

The Emperor's letters to Pliny maintain a distance. He kept
aloof, lest he be overwhelmed by requests, and he had much
flattery to contend with. Pliny often began a letter with a courteous formality about the Emperor's kindness and generosity, continuing with a suggestion how Trajan's kindness could be extended.
If Pliny received most of what he asked for, it was because Trajan
considered him to be a valuable aide, but the Emperor was cautious. Once, after receiving an elaborate explanation from Pliny
about a decision which might have been misunderstood, Trajan
sent a brief reply: "You have acted rightly both as a citizen and as
a member of the Senate in obeying the just demands of that distinguished body, and I am sure that you will perform the duties you
have undertaken in accordance with the trust placed in you" (X.
3B). It was polite and reassuring. No more, no less.

Pliny's early letters to Trajan indicate the kind of detail for
which the Emperor found time. Pliny was thankful for having
received "the privileges granted to parents of three children," an
honor instituted by Augustus. Pliny had no children, even though
he was married three times. Almost nothing is known of his first
two wives. His beloved third wife, Calpurnia, had a miscarriage
which left her unable to bear children. She was in all other respects exactly what he wanted in a wife, as two excerpts from his
letters suggest: "She is highly intelligent and a careful housewife,

and her devotion to me is a sure indication of her virtue." And: "If I am giving a reading she sits behind a curtain near by and greedily drinks in every word of appreciation" (IV. 19. 2–4).

Pliny sought a friend's promotion to "the dignity of senatorial rank." And for freedmen or women who had served him or his relatives and friends, he sought to use his good standing to acquire citizenship. These were not matters handled through some separate bureau of government, but had to be carried to the Emperor, although his secretaries prepared the answers. Pliny felt free to advise the Emperor on appointments, and one of his letters asks that a well-qualified associate be given the honor of a praetorship. In another letter, he sought a priesthood for himself.

When Pliny built a temple for Tifernum he placed in it likenesses of recent emperors, including Nerva. Beforehand, he asked Trajan if he might also erect a statue to him. The Emperor was gracious in replying that although he did not want to encourage such deeds, he would accept this one as a token of Pliny's loyalty.

Trajan sent Pliny to Bithynia to straighten out the affairs of its municipalities. The year is not certain; it could have been as early as 109. Problems had been building up there for several years. A primary concern was finance. Pliny was especially well qualified because he had earlier served twice in defense of governors charged with corruption by the Bithynians. His investigations acquainted him with Bithynian affairs; and while he considered the governors innocent, it was nevertheless apparent that the province needed better management. There were other problems with which Pliny was less familiar, and he wrote often to Trajan asking for his advice. The Emperor's answers carried the force of law.

Imperial rescripts were only one means by which the emperors were now making the law. Their edicts pronounced what the law would be and their judgments in important cases which came before them showed how laws should be interpreted. Finally, there were administrative orders concerning a multitude of details which might not previously have been covered by legislation.

During the Republic, to a lesser degree, the elected praetors had shaped Roman law. When these officials took office they added to the praetor's edict handed down to them any new grievances for which they would issue writs and also any innovations in court procedure they intended to follow. This process allowed for a certain fluidity which, however, gradually dried up under the Principate, when to make any changes became more and more the Emperor's prerogative. Trajan's successor, Hadrian, finally had the various edicts of the praetors refined and consolidated into a single document by a prominent jurist, Salvius Julianus. His work, in effect, blocked further innovation from this source, and indeed there had been very little for a long time. Under the good emperors, leadership was remarkably enlightened; but, nonetheless, a steady drift toward an unrestrained autocracy continued.

Pliny quickly discovered that a scandalous state of affairs existed in Bithynia: "I am now examining the finances of the town of Prusa, expenditure, revenues, and sums owing, and finding the inspection increasingly necessary the more I look into their accounts; large sums of money are detained in the hands of private individuals for various reasons, and further sums are paid out for quite illegal purposes" (X. 17A. 3–4). His subsequent investigations in other towns confirmed how widespread the problems were. If the municipalities of the Roman Empire eventually found themselves under the thumb of an all-powerful central bureaucracy, it was partly their own fault. Too many seemed unable to manage their financial affairs. Pliny wrote to Trajan about the huge sums of public money which had gone into the construction of two aqueducts at Nicomedia without any water in the city to show for it. Both constructions were halted before completion, and the first one was even torn down altogether. Trajan was of course suspicious and ordered an immediate investigation to determine where the money went and who might have profited. There was apparently similar waste in projects for a theatre and gymnasium at Nicaea. Trajan was aware that part of the problem resulted from towns trying to build what they could not afford: "These poor Greeks all love a gymnasium; so it may be that they were too ambitious in their plans at Nicaea. They will have to be content with one which suits their real needs" (X. 40. 2–3).

Hearing from Pliny that some towns were spending money for unnecessary junkets, the Emperor responded: "You were quite right, my dear Pliny, to remit the 12,000 sesterces which the citizens of Byzantium were spending on a delegate to convey their loyal address to me. Their duty will be fulfilled if their resolution is simply forwarded through you. The governor of Moesia will also forgive them if they spend less on paying their respects to him" (X. 44).

Pliny was forever asking Trajan to send him more assistance, but only occasionally did he receive any. In reply to a request for an architect, the Emperor showed some impatience: "You cannot lack architects: every province has skilled men trained for this work. It is a mistake to think they can be sent out more quickly from Rome when they usually come to us from Greece" (X. 40. 3). Trajan's letters to Pliny set down policy guidelines. More than once he told Pliny that he should keep to a minimum the number of soldiers relieved from active duty in order to serve in some civilian capacity. For instance, Pliny asked if he should use soldiers instead of public slaves as prison guards. Trajan said the slaves would do. "Their reliability depends on your watchfulness and discipline" (X. 20. 2). In response to a request by an official for more soldiers to be placed at his disposal, Trajan wrote privately to Pliny that he feared the man was only seeking to enhance his position and added the admonition that "the public interest must be our sole concern" (XXII. 2). The sincerity of that remark was borne out by Trajan's administration. The laudatory *Optimus Princeps* which appeared on his coins was a genuine title.

Trajan kept a sharp eye on developments in the provinces which might lead to political disorders. In his reply to Pliny's suggestion that a volunteer fire department be organized in Nicomedia, the Emperor was candid about his reservations. Such groups elsewhere had become political in character and centers of agitation. Trajan thought it was better to provide equipment and instructions for its use to the townspeople as a whole rather than rely on a special crew. Thus was the *Pax Romana* maintained. In the roughly two hundred years between 27 B.C. and A.D. 180, the Romans kept the peace of the Mediterranean world by the prompt suppression of disorder. A paragraph from one of Trajan's letters to Pliny reflects the stern tone of the official attitude: "If people commit a breach of the peace they must be arrested at once; and, if their offenses are too serious for summary punishment, in the case of soldiers you must notify their officers of what is found against them, while you may inform me by letter in the case of persons who are passing through on their way back to Rome" (X. 78. 3).

Ironically, all of those who were peaceful were not necessarily law-abiding. In that respect, the Christians continued to be a worry.

Trajan and the Christians

As mentioned earlier, religion for the Romans was not a matter of creed but of respect for the gods. It did not matter to Trajan what the Christians chose to believe or what other gods they might choose to worship so long as they were obedient to the law in showing reverence to the state deities, including the deified Caesars. To pour a libation of wine before a cult statue was equivalent to citizens' today standing for a national anthem or saluting a flag. However, since non-citizens were required by the Romans to conform to the state worship it was not so much an act of loyalty in the modern nationalistic sense as an evidence of willingness to cooperate in a religious act considered beneficial to all. The well-pleased gods would protect Rome and Rome would protect everybody else. The few who refused to join in the ceremonials appeared at the very least ungrateful. They offended the gods and put the majority in jeopardy. The result was anger and retaliation. Yet for a Christian to pour a libation before the image of a deified Caesar was a denial of his one true God, and he would cease to be a Christian if he complied. Caught in this dilemma, the uncooperative Christian was guilty of obstinacy. If he wanted to escape punishment, he had to keep his identity secret.

In writing to Trajan for advice about the Christians, Pliny said he was unfamiliar with many aspects of the problem. He did not know how far he should go in seeking to identify them or precisely how they should be tried and punished when found. Should the young be held as responsible as their parents? Should a man who first confessed he was a Christian and then renounced his faith be let go without punishment? In other words, are people really guilty by the mere fact that they call themselves Christians or must they be charged with specific acts? By the time Pliny elicited a ruling from Trajan on these questions, he had already executed some non-citizens. They had admitted to being Christians and even kept on admitting it when asked three times in a row with an accompanying warning about the punishment due for stubbornness. Citizens of course had the right to be tried in Rome. Pliny presumably sent these "fanatics" to the capital, whether they requested it or not.

The ever-increasing number of persons who were denounced as Christians, many of them by anonymous accusations, alerted Pliny to the possibility that vengeful relatives or neighbors could be using the charge as a blind for their own motives. Pliny thus instituted his own test, which included a denial by the accused of any affiliation at any time with the Christians, a willingness to pray, pour wine, and burn incense before images of Trajan and the state gods, and finally to denounce Christ. "Genuine" Christians, he said, would stubbornly refuse.

When those who renounced Christianity told Pliny about the Christian ceremonials, he relayed the information to Trajan:

> They had met regularly before dawn on a fixed day to chant verses alternately among themselves in honor of Christ as if to a god, and also to bind themselves by oath, not for any criminal purpose, but to abstain from theft, robbery and adultery. . . . After this ceremony it had been their custom to disperse and reassemble later to take food of an ordinary, harmless kind; but they had in fact given up this practice since my edict, issued on your instructions, which banned all political societies. (X. 96. 7–8)

Pliny did not want to alarm the Emperor, but he felt he should be aware of this growing problem and reported that persons of all ages and classes both in the urban centers and in the country were joining "this wretched cult."

Trajan's brief reply to Pliny is probably the best known letter of ancient times. Mild in tone and judicious in content, it is Trajan at his very best:

> You have followed the right course of procedure, my dear Pliny, in your examination of the cases of persons charged with being Christians, for it is impossible to lay down a general rule to a fixed formula. These people must not be hunted out; if they are brought before you and the charge against them is proved, they must be punished, but in the case of anyone who denies that he is a Christian, and makes it clear that he is not by offering prayers to our gods, he is to be pardoned as a result of his repentance however suspect his past conduct may be. But pamphlets circulated anonymously must play no part in any accusation. They create the worst sort of precedent and are quite out of keeping with the spirit of our age. (X. 97)

The Dacian Wars

Of the five good emperors, only Trajan consciously sought to increase the holdings of the Empire, by his wars in Dacia (the region of modern Romania), Armenia, and Mesopotamia. Nerva

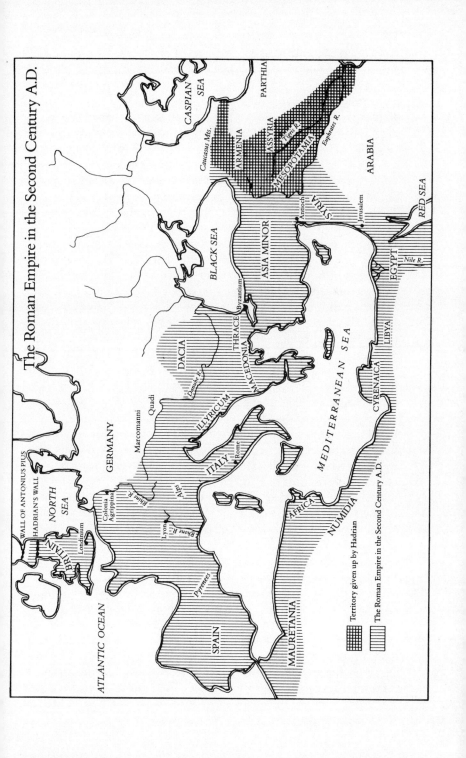

The Roman Empire in the Second Century A.D.

Territory given up by Hadrian

The Roman Empire in the Second Century A.D.

was concerned with internal order. Hadrian, Antoninus Pius, and Marcus Aurelius were kept busy maintaining existing frontiers.

Domitian's treaty with the Dacians in 89 had included sending engineers to help king Decebalus construct better defenses. This looked like appeasement, but, to be fair, Domitian was buying time with which to deal with other unruly tribes and was in fact able to achieve peace on the Danube by 93. Still, many senators considered any assistance to the restless Dacians as a dangerous policy, and Trajan agreed. It is not known what excuse he used for invading Dacia in 101. In any event, the result was inconclusive. It was the campaign in 102 which caused Decebalus to accept Roman terms for peace. In effect, Dacia became a client kingdom, and Decebalus was expected to have the same friends as Rome and even assist her against her enemies. Trajan also retrieved the Roman technicians. But Decebalus kept his ambitions. Three years later, in 105, he wiped out the token Roman garrisons in Dacia and attacked the Iazyges whom the Romans were pledged to protect. Trajan was now determined to convert Dacia into a Roman province. His clear-cut victory in 106 was climaxed by the suicide of Decebalus. The Roman people hailed Trajan's triumph in Dacia with the longest, most expensive celebration in their history. Trajan had not conquered as large a territory as Gaul, nor did the Romans hold it after A.D. 270, but his daring and self-confidence were reminiscent of Julius Caesar. Instead of a detailed account of his campaigns, like the *Commentaries,* he left behind a remarkable monument telling the story of his conquest in sculptured reliefs. Trajan's Column, which dates to A.D. 113, consists of drums of marble resting one on the other to a height of about one hundred feet. It stands on a square base, which is well below the present street level, in that small part of Trajan's Forum which has been preserved. Today, the column alone testifies to the grandeur of the most impressive forum built by any of the emperors. There are remains of the libraries and the great basilica which once stood in this monumental complex, but no trace survives of the Arch of Trajan, his equestrian statue, and the Temple of Trajan. Even Trajan is gone from atop his column, having been replaced in modern times by a statue of Saint Peter, whose life was scarcely compatible with the scenes of war below. Spiralling upward around the column, like a scroll, are 155 scenes of bas-relief in a frieze 650 feet long and three feet high, which depict Trajan's campaigns. Surprisingly, the sculptures have survived

41. Trajan. Courtesy of the Ny Carlsberg Glyptotek, Copenhagen.

more than eighteen centuries of wind and rain, although the signs of wear are plain to see.

The story begins with the Romans crossing the Danube and follows a chronological sequence, including a panel which shows Decebalus killing himself as a Roman cavalryman lunges at him. In contrast to the numerous scenes of figures crowded together on the march or in battle, ingenious landscapes are interspersed, showing fortresses and cities in miniature.

The Emperor has the dominant role in the sculptured narrative. He is shown making offerings to the gods, speaking to his troops who stand before him amid a cluster of legionary standards, leading them in battle, receiving ambassadors, and accepting the surrender of the Dacians, who humble themselves at his feet. The crowded scenes of Roman soldiers setting up their own defenses or attacking those of the enemy are remarkable for their

42. Trajan's Column, Rome. Photograph courtesy of F. Warren Peters.

authenticity in armor and weaponry. That cruelties were inflicted by both sides is also vividly shown. The Romans eagerly chopped off Dacian heads and in one scene are shown presenting their "trophies" to the Emperor. In another, the heads are impaled on pikes. There is also a scene in which Dacian women inflict horrible tortures on captured Romans shown naked in their agony.

Considering the enormous time and effort which must have gone into the design and execution of this immense sculptural work, it is unfortunate that the artist remains unknown. Trajan's personal architect, Apollodorus of Damascus, directed the Emperor's greatest building adventures, including this magnificent new Forum in Rome and the great stone bridge across the Danube, which appeared on Trajan's coins and on his column. Although he accompanied Trajan on the Dacian campaign and may well have made sketches of fortifications, it is impossible to know whether he also deserves recognition as the master hand and supervisor in decorating his own structures. Whoever was responsible deserves to be ranked among Rome's greatest artists. Trajan's Column is distinctly Roman—a proclamation of imperial power restrained by the simple dignity of the design. In some respects, it is the most impressive monument to be seen in Rome. As long as it stands, Trajan cannot be forgotten.

Trajan's great celebration marked the Roman Empire at its height. It would never again know such glory. His own later Eastern campaign to stabilize the border with the Parthians was not successful and indeed marked a kind of ebb tide.

Disappointment and Death

For a decade, A.D. 106–116, the Romans took the offensive in the East, but ultimately they had little to show for it. In the region between the Roman and Parthian domains there were petty kingdoms, which each side sought to control. Roman forces had already overrun the old kingdom of the Nabataean Arabs (converted into the province of Arabia) by the time Trajan arrived in 114. He quickly added Armenia. Since Nero's time, there had been a Roman puppet on the Armenian throne, but the Parthians had replaced him in A.D. 110 with their own appointee. Trajan's invasion ended the monarchy and brought this ancient land inside the Roman Empire. To the south, beyond the Euphrates and especially on the far side of the Tigris, he claimed new territory by creating the provinces of Mesopotamia and Assyria. His initial success was largely due to the weakness of the local opposition and the absence of the Parthians, who were busy with internal problems. By the time the Parthians were able to mount a counteroffensive in A.D. 116, Trajan was faced with a domestic crisis of his own. In 115 a widespread rebellion began in the Jewish communities of various provinces, including Egypt. At first, the hostility was toward local neighbors, particularly the Greeks, but the Messianic dream of an independent Judaea was ever the ultimate goal. So, again, the Jews were at war with the *Pax Romana*. They of course benefited by the new threat from Parthia, which kept Trajan's forces occupied. That served to intensify Roman ill-feeling toward the rebels, whose resistance, inspired by Zealot leadership, made the ensuing struggle bitter in the extreme. Where Jewish forces had been successful, especially in Cyprus and Cyrene, there had been a horrendous massacre of Gentiles. When the Romans recovered control, they allowed the Greeks to have their revenge; the Jews were killed in such numbers that hence-forth their communities outside Judaea were no longer a source of worry to the Romans. Trajan's general Lusius Quietus, "the Moor," was able to restore order in Palestine, but the situation in the Jewish homeland remained dangerous.

Trajan's last days were bitterly disappointing. He had pushed the boundaries of the Empire to their greatest extent, and then saw his conquests slipping away as a result of revolts in Seleucia, Mesopotamia, and Assyria, which gave the Parthians a chance to regain their holdings. Trajan's Eastern policy was a conspicuous failure in a reign which had otherwise been a great success. Early in August, A.D. 117, he became ill in Antioch and set out for Rome, but his days were too few for the trip. He died in Cilicia.

It was reported that Trajan's final act was to name as his successor Publius Aelius Hadrianus, the general now in command in the East. Rival officers doubted the story. There were rumors that Plotina, Trajan's wife, had decided the succession. What actually happened is not known. But Hadrian was an excellent choice and that certainly argues for Trajan's having made the decision.

Hadrian

It was left to Hadrian to admit the failure of plans which had overtaxed Rome's resources. He made as good a settlement as possible in the East, in order to turn to other problems. In effect, the peace he made with Parthia reestablished the frontiers as they had been before Trajan's conquests. Assyria and Mesopotamia were abandoned. Armenia returned to her client status under Rome, although the king was chosen by the Parthians.

Trajan had broken with the Augustan policy of maintaining strong defenses along fixed frontiers. Hadrian, a distinguished military man in his own right, knew that was a mistake. Where a defensible barrier was lacking, as in Britain, he built one. Only parts of Hadrian's Wall are still in place. Over the years, much of the stone was used in other constructions. These included a road built in the eighteenth century, which travels for several miles where the wall once stood. Originally, the wall stretched for about seventy-five miles from Wallsend-on-Tyne in the east to Bowness-on-Solway in the west. Not all sections of it were built to exactly the same dimensions, but roughly it stood about

43. Hadrian. Courtesy of the Trustees of the British Museum.

twenty feet high, including the parapet, and was nine feet or so wide. This stone barrier was only part of a plan for keeping the Picts out of Britain. A ditch, nine feet deep and twenty-seven feet wide, was dug on the north side. At mile intervals along the wall were milecastles, about fifty-five feet by seventy feet, where fifty men could be stationed. Spaced in between the milecastles were two-man turrets, about twenty feet square. In addition, there were several forts, usually attached to the wall, which included stables, storehouses, large barracks, and the headquarters of the local commander. Other outposts were built north of the wall and along the Cumberland coast. Auxiliary troops raised in other provinces were stationed in the region, about 15,000 in all. The three legions in Britain were called only if these frontier soldiers needed help in an emergency.

The construction of Hadrian's Wall was most probably ordered when Hadrian arrived in Britain in A.D. 122. The barbarians to the north were not his only problem. The Britons themselves continued to be restless under Roman rule, and the troops stationed in the area were required to keep the peace on both sides of the border. That meant dealing with cattle rustlers on the south as well as the ferocious Picts on the north. A formidable ditch, dug along the south side of the wall, kept the Britons out of the fortification area. It was ten feet deep, with sides slanting from a width of twenty feet at the top to eight feet at the bottom. Earth embankments were built on either side of the ditch to make the whole an intimidating barrier.

Although Hadrian's Wall represented a considerable investment to the Romans, another less ambitious barricade was built some distance to the north during the reign of his successor, Antoninus Pius. It extended about thirty-six miles, from the Firth of Clyde to the Firth of Forth, and was built of turf rather than stone. Few traces of it remain. During the middle years of the second century when the Romans were relying on this shorter frontier, Hadrian's Wall was for a brief period practically deserted. On later occasions, when the governors of Britain used their troops to fight in civil wars, the fortifications were left unprotected and severe damage resulted. What remains today includes some reconstructions. Hadrian's Wall was abandoned altogether by the end of the fourth century, and it was not until fourteen centuries later that it was seriously studied as a prelude to its modern role as one of Britain's major tourist attractions. That would have pleased Hadrian. He was a man who would have been interested in archaeology and the promotion of antiquarian studies. In his own time he was an avid promoter of all sorts of creative endeavors.

Juvenal (*ca.* A.D. 60–*ca.* 130), one of the leading literary figures of his time, began his Satire VII on a rare optimistic note before plunging into his usual gloomy recitation of the ills of the day.

> All hopes for the arts today, all inducements to study, depend
> Upon Caesar alone. Who else spares a glance for the wretched
> Muses in these hard times, when established poets lease
> An out-of-town bath-concession or a city bakery
> To make their living, when hungry historians are quitting
> Helicon's vales and springs for the auction-rooms?

And further on:

> So at it, young men: your Imperial
> Leader is urging you on, surveying your ranks for talent
> That merits his support.

The Emperor is not named, but was most probably Hadrian, from whom long-suffering poets and historians could expect more support than from any of his predecessors. Hadrian was a man of sensitive tastes, well-read and well-travelled. He would have understood Juvenal's complaint about the poverty of writers, teachers, and lawyers, at a time when popular singers and jockeys were able to demand and receive enormous sums.

Hadrian used his own resources to assist the arts and was particularly generous with his patronage in Athens, where the great Olympieum, Temple of Zeus Olympius, was finally finished with his support. This did not win him any popularity with the Old Roman set in the Senate. But Hadrian was not a dilettante. He was a soldier with genuine cultural interests which were simply not common in the military. His aloofness toward officers in his camp or politicians in Rome stemmed from a difference in taste, and, without a doubt, of temperament. His long absences from Rome, 121 to 126 and 129 to 132, reflected a cosmopolitan outlook. At the same time, his tours of the provinces were in the best Augustan tradition. He was as much interested in all facets of the imperial government as was Trajan. Yet, his serious interest in Greek studies made him a very different sort of man. Trajan was more the Roman idea of an Emperor. This may, in part, explain why he did not earlier designate Hadrian as his successor. They were related by both blood and marriage, and Hadrian had even at one time been Trajan's ward, but their differences made the relationship correct rather than close.

The variety of his interests made Hadrian the most exciting personality among the good emperors. In addition to his genuine delight in the arts, he was a shrewd general who managed to maintain both strict discipline and excellent morale in the army. At the same time, he was a skillful administrator. His search for greater efficiency prompted him to place Latin and Greek correspondence under separate bureau heads. It was during his reign that the government became more flexible in making appointments. In particular, equestrian officials moved from rank to rank in civil-service style without necessarily performing any military duty as a prerequisite. The innovation was useful in recruiting non-military personnel for government service, but eventually contributed to an unproductive rivalry between civilian and military officials.

On the other hand, there was a soft side to Hadrian. He was given to personal satisfactions quite unlike those of the other good emperors. One example was the lavishness of his attentions to the young Antinous, whose good looks are attested by statues which the Emperor commissioned. The fascination extended to naming a new city in Egypt after him. Hadrian was heartbroken when his

favorite, who was nineteen or perhaps twenty years old, committed suicide presumably by drowning in the Nile.

Another of Hadrian's extravagances was the villa he built
about twenty miles from Rome, near Tibur (modern Tivoli). The
ruins are a tourist attraction today. The term *villa* implies a certain
pretentiousness, but that would still be an understatement in view
of what has been uncovered at the site. Hadrian's estate had
theatres, baths, libraries, and a palaestra (gymnasium)—all the
joys of a small city without the annoyance of a population. Some
of the structures were copied from the famous buildings of the
world which the Emperor had visited—ranging from the *Stoa
Poikile* in Athens to the sanctuary of Serapis at Alexandria. There
was apparently no particular plan for the arrangement of these
structures. One comparison might be a cluster of pavilions at a
modern world's fair. However, the imperial palace was roughly
the center of the complex, which included a variety of walkways
leading through gardens with pleasant summer houses. A section
of the palace was given over to guest rooms, and in another part
there were barracks for the guards.

During the ten years, A.D. 125–135, it took to build this
elaborate project, Hadrian was collecting works of art from all
parts of the world, and his villa was very probably the greatest
private museum of ancient times. Excavations at the site began as
early as the sixteenth century and have provided European muse-
ums with some of their finest pieces. Decorating the villa was
surely Hadrian's hobby, if *hobby* is the word for anything so expensive. In recent times, the multimillionaire William Randolph
Hearst took thirty years building San Simeon in California, which
by intention, if not in taste, is reminiscent of Hadrian's villa.

Hadrian's extravagances were balanced by redeeming characteristics. His most attractive side was his humanitarianism. No
one can doubt that he was sensitive about the welfare and feelings
of those he thought subject to ill-treatment. Yet there are inevitably reservations about certain improvements, for the solution of a
problem may give rise to unexpected consequences. Hadrian's
steps to reduce the power of a father over the members of his
household were truly revolutionary, for they aimed at freeing
sons from the strictness of the home and gave the family a looser
construction than it had had in the Old Roman mold. This move,
however, probably contributed to a general decline of the discipline in Roman society which, for better or for worse, had been a

part of its success. There would be less controversy about Hadrian's attitude toward slaves who by chance found themselves at the mercy of cruel masters. He went beyond Pliny's regrets. The Emperor's concern was undoubtedly shared by other educated persons, who nonetheless accepted the system the way they found it. Hadrian issued an edict holding any master accountable for the wanton killing or torturing of a slave. He also forbade the castration of male slaves or the selling of male or female chattels to those who would force them into prostitution. Not only was castration a barbarous practice in Hadrian's eyes, but circumcision was, too. His prohibition of this practice was taken as a further provocation by the Jews and contributed to their intransigence in the brutal war of suppression which the Romans waged against them, A.D. 132–135.

The attack on Jewish law was part of Hadrian's answer to continuing trouble in Judaea. He decided that assimilation was necessary. As a beginning, outsiders were placed alongside the Jewish population of Jerusalem, renamed Colonia Aelia Capitolina, and a shrine was built for Jupiter Capitolinus on the site of the Jewish Temple. As three centuries earlier Judah Maccabaeus had led a popular revolt against the attempt of the Seleucid king Antiochus IV to Hellenize the Jews, so now under the inspired leadership of Bar-Kokhba, "Son of the Star," there began a struggle unto death. As it often happens when rebels have the advantage of surprise, Jerusalem was taken and a Roman legion annihilated. But when Hadrian returned to Syria and began assembling a mighty army, the Jews were doomed. They were soon surrounded and outnumbered, but the choice between their faith and the Romans allowed no hope for compromise. Hadrian put the Roman forces under the command of Gaius Julius Severus, who had formerly been stationed in Britain. His soldiers doggedly pursued the Jewish resisters, and it is estimated that the local Jewish population suffered half a million casualties. Yigael Yadin, in his book *Bar-Kokhba,* tells of the archaeological work in caves on the west bank of the Dead Sea, where many Jews were trapped by the Romans in A.D. 134. Among the discoveries were the letters of Bar-Kokhba, which give solid historical evidence about this hitherto legendary figure. Coins, utensils, and beautiful glassware were also recovered, along with baskets full of skulls. Whole families starved to death in the caves rather than surrender to the Romans.

44. Tomb of Hadrian (Castel Sant'Angelo). Photograph courtesy of the
Italian Government Travel Office, Chicago.

45. Pantheon. Photograph courtesy of the Italian Government Travel Office, Chicago.

The Last Days of Hadrian

Hadrian's reign ended as it began—under a cloud. In the beginning, the Senate had quickly suppressed the opposition to him led by certain army officers whose own ambitions had given way to conspiratorial plans. They were executed by the Senate for creating a threat to the peaceful continuity which Hadrian represented. However, as time passed, his oath not to put a senator to death without a trial did not suffice to prevent strained relations. The Emperor's diffidence resulted in a coolness which turned eventually into hatred on both sides. Toward the end of his reign, certain senators openly opposed the Emperor, and his retaliation might well have cost him deification had it not been for the dutiful insistence of his heir and successor.

Despite his problems with the Senate, Hadrian, ailing and childless, looked there for the best man to succeed him. After his first choice, Lucius Ceionius Commodus, died, he adopted Titus Aurelius Antoninus (A.D. 86–161), a native of Lanuvium, whose family came from Narbonese Gaul. Respect for his "father" won for Antoninus his title Pius, and he showed his devotion when, in 145, he built the Temple of Hadrian. Today, one side of the cella including eleven Corinthian columns of this structure is to be seen as part of the building which houses the modern stock exchange in Rome. Because Antoninus was already in his early fifties when Hadrian adopted him in 138, he in turn was required to adopt a pair of successors: his nephew, Marcus Aurelius, and also Lucius Verus, the son of the earlier designate who had died. The succession was thus arranged for two generations.

Hadrian's tomb, near the Vatican, is a tourist attraction in Rome. It has been called the Castel Sant'Angelo since the sixth century, because Pope Gregory the Great reported that he had seen a vision of an angel there. This enormous structure, completed in the year after Hadrian died, looks like a fortress; it was so used from the time of the early Middle Ages. Today, much of its space is given over to a military museum.

Another of Hadrian's famous buildings, the Pantheon, has also served different purposes. The original Pantheon, a temple to all the gods, was built by Agrippa. After a fire, it was restored by Domitian and then during Hadrian's reign replaced by the present domed structure, although the inscription, restored in modern times, still gives credit for the building to Augustus' faithful aide and son-in-law. Like the Parthenon in Athens, originally a glorious temple to Athena, the Pantheon became a Christian church during the Middle Ages. In troubled times toward the end of that period, it served as a fortress and is now a national shrine of Italy, where an artist like Raphael can be buried with kings. The portico, with pediment and Corinthian columns, and the massive rotunda are impressive, but the interior has grandeur. The height of the dome and the diameter of the building are almost the same, about 142 feet. The only light comes from an opening, over 28 feet wide, in the dome. To walk inside this vast space is an awesome experience. There have been changes in the decoration from what Hadrian saw when the building was completed about A.D. 128, but like the Colosseum, this structure is indelibly Roman and imperial.

Antoninus Pius

Antoninus Pius reigned for twenty-three years (A.D. 138–161), and yet we know little more of him than of Nerva, who reigned for less than two. Both men were quiet, respectful toward the Senate, and carried out their duties without grandiose gestures or words. Neither was a great statesman or warrior. Antoninus deserves praise for his encouragement to those who were gradually humanizing Roman law, but such workaday business did not win any fame equal to Trajan's dramatic conquest of Dacia.

Antoninus was a hero at least to his adopted son Marcus Aurelius who wrote a glowing statement of what he had learned from his father: "mildness, and an unshakeable adherence to decisions deliberately come to; and no empty vanity in respect to so-called honours; and a love of work and thoroughness; and a readiness to hear any suggestions for the common good." Marcus particularly admired Antoninus for the manner in which he bore pain: "After his spasms of violent headache he would come back at once to his usual employments with renewed vigor" (I. 16). These passages are from a long tribute, which remains the monument to Antoninus Pius. If Marcus described him correctly, it was probably more than he would have wanted.

The *Pax Romana* was never more secure than during Antoninus' reign. He continued Hadrian's policy of strengthening the Rhine defenses. The only major project undertaken anywhere was the previously mentioned new wall he built in Scotland. There were the usual border problems, in Mauretania for instance, but even the Parthians did not give Antoninus any serious trouble. He warned them away from Armenia, and they went.

Finally, the succession did not involve the complications it had for his predecessors. Marcus Aurelius, the elder of Antoninus' two adoptive sons, had been given the title of Caesar as early as A.D. 139. About 145, he married the Emperor's daughter Faustina, which gave him preeminence over Lucius Verus. In view of his superior talents, he scarcely needed it. It was a measure of Marcus' character that, after Antoninus died in 161, he took Lucius Verus as his colleague, even though he might have safely ignored him.

46. Temple of Diana, Évora, Portugal, second century A.D. Photograph courtesy of Wayne Andrews.

Marcus Aurelius

The Romans had seen several generals and a few fools as emperors. Marcus Aurelius was the first philosopher. The *Meditations*, thoughts he wrote down in Greek from time to time wherever he happened to be, is one of the best sources for the philosophy of Stoicism. As a child, Marcus Aurelius spent much of his time alone with his books. For companionship, he turned to his father and mother or to older teachers, especially Fronto, his senior by about twenty years, rather than boys his own age.

The scholarly Marcus Cornelius Fronto, whom Marcus so much respected, undoubtedly enjoyed a far greater reputation in his own day than he has since. During a routine political career, his eloquence in the Senate and the courts attracted attention. His primary assignment at the palace was to teach Marcus and his younger brother Lucius Verus how to write and speak the best possible Latin. Later, his letters offered further instruction on oratory. He was the authority of his time in matters of language, even as Cicero had been two centuries before him. Both were champions of high standards. On the other hand, no one would argue that Fronto could have matched wits with the remarkable man whose works he studied and gave to his pupils to read.

A correspondence between teacher and student began during periods of separation, when Marcus was in his teens, and lasted until Fronto's death about A.D. 166. Their letters have been arranged in chronological order, as far as could be determined, in two volumes, and translated by C. R. Haines. Fronto was interested in language and literature, but not at all in philosophy. Indeed the large number of letters mentioning the aches and pains which at one time or another afflicted all parts of his body have no philosophical tone whatsoever. Certain brief letters are simply a list of complaints. It was another teacher, the Stoic Rusticus, who guided Marcus' training in philosophy.

Unquestionably, the self-discipline Marcus learned through Stoicism made him the man he was to become. Still, Fronto saw in him an innate goodness from the beginning. In a letter written a few years before he died, Fronto told Marcus, now the Emperor:

> To begin my comparison of yourself to yourself with your dutiful-ness, I will mention your bygone devotion to your father, and contrast it with your present attention to duty. Who does not know that, when your father was unwell, you used to discontinue baths in order to keep him company, deny yourself wine, even water and food; that you never studied your own convenience in the matter of sleep or waking or food or exercise, but sacrificed everything to your father's convenience? (II, p. 127)

Fronto often flattered the young crown prince as might be expected, but he would also take him to task occasionally for some error in composition. Marcus was grateful for this, and, far from being smug about his high status, repaid his teacher compliment for compliment. In his *Meditations,* he says he learned from him "to note the envy, the subtlety, and the dissimulation which are habitual to a tyrant; and that, as a general rule, those amongst us who rank as patricians are somewhat wanting in natural affection" (I. 11).

The Meditations

In Book I of the *Meditations,* Marcus recounted the virtues he learned from his relatives and teachers. His search for goodness matched the moral idealism of the Stoics. "Cease to be pulled as a puppet by thy passions." An obsessive urge to overcome the slightest shortcomings exposed the Stoics to the complaint that they lacked human qualities.

In the *Meditations*, Marcus repeats to himself the tenets of Stoicism, which by his time were already centuries old. The founder of Stoicism, Zeno of Citium in Cyprus, had taught in Athens in the third century B.C. Later practitioners of the doctrine brought it to Rome, where it became a part of the education of certain public figures, beginning with the Gracchi brothers. Seneca and Epictetus, a lame ex-slave who reached out to fellow sufferers, were the most prominent proponents of Stoicism in the first century A.D. The works of Epictetus in particular influenced Marcus strongly during his formative years. Nevertheless, in his *Meditations*, he occasionally voiced an opinion at odds with Stoic doctrine, as for instance his contention that the wrongs caused by lust were worse than those caused by anger. Normally, the Stoics did not make that kind of distinction.

True to Stoic mentality, Marcus sought moral alertness— being prepared for whatever might happen so as not to make any mistakes. "The business of life is more akin to wrestling than dancing, for it requires of us to stand ready and unshakeable against every assault however unforeseen" (VII. 61). There is another significant passage at the beginning of Book II:

> Say to thyself at daybreak: I shall come across the busy-body, the thankless, the overbearing, the treacherous, the envious, the unneighborly. All this has befallen them because they know not good from evil. But I, in that I have comprehended the nature of the Good that it is beautiful, and the nature of Evil that it is ugly, and the nature of the wrong-doer himself that it is akin to me, not as partaker of the same blood and seed but of intelligence and a morsel of the Divine, can neither be injured by any of them—for no one can involve me in what is debasing—nor can I be wroth with my kinsman and hate him. (II. 1)

Why does the Emperor, a solitary man of studious habits, attend so conscientiously to the perplexing problems facing him? He tells himself why:

> Every hour make up thy mind sturdily as a Roman and a man to do what thou hast in hand with scrupulous and unaffected dignity and love of thy kind and independence and justice; and to give thyself rest from all other impressions. And thou wilt give thyself this, if thou

dost execute every act of thy life as though it were thy last, divesting thyself of all aimlessness and all passionate antipathy to the convictions of reason, and all hypocrisy and self-love and dissatisfaction with thy allotted share. (II. 5)

Throughout his writings Marcus stressed the all-governing power of Reason, which the Stoics equated with Nature or Providence. Echoing Cicero, he shows the importance of Stoic thought in the argument for a natural law which applied to all men and mitigated the harshness of laws on the books:

If the intellectual capacity is common to us all, common too is the reason, which makes us rational creatures. If so, that reason also is common which tells us to do or not to do. If so, law also is common. If so, we are citizens. If so, we are fellow-members of an organized community. If so, the Universe is as it were a state—for of what other single polity can the whole race of mankind be said to be fellow-members? (IV. 4)

So it was he wrote: "All that is in tune with thee, O Universe, is in tune with me!" (IV. 23).

Every man should be guided by divine reason throughout his life. Indeed, a man might use his reason to decide when it was time to die. The Stoics approved of suicide under certain circumstances. As for life, it is a matter of bearing up in tune with a providential order: "Let the god that is in thee be lord of a living creature, that is manly, and of full age, and concerned with statecraft, and a Roman, and a ruler, who hath taken his post as one who awaits the signal of recall from life in all readiness" (III. 5).

Marcus found solace in contemplating death. "A little while and thou wilt have forgotten everything, a little while and everything will have forgotten thee" (VII. 21). Death puts to rest all the trivialities and petty hurts; so why not be done with them today? "This is the mark of a perfect character, to pass through each day as if it were the last, without agitation, without torpor, without pretense" (VII. 69). To accept the vanity of worldly things saves a man from the worries of the days ahead before death makes it finally so. Besides, according to Stoic teaching, what we now behold is part of a cycle which endlessly repeats itself. All that is now has been before and will be again—precisely so—not just in the ordinary sense of history repeating itself. Although Marcus Aurelius, the Emperor, had to be engaged in the business of the world, he did not want it to disturb his inner calm. The Stoic takes part, does his best, but is not disturbed by the results. It is the doing that matters. From this follows the Stoic emphasis on motive. To do what is right because it *is* right is all that counts. "For without a purpose nothing should be done" (VIII. 17). There is no expectation of a return. "For when thou hast done a kindness, what more wouldst thou have?" (IX. 42. 5). By this process the Stoic is spared disappointment. He frees himself from the unpredictable behavior of others. He controls his own motives and his own actions. That is the guarantee of satisfaction and tranquillity.

Marcus recognized that nature's gifts were uneven. He admitted he was not given a clever wit. But it was important to make the best of what one did receive and to exhibit those attributes which were possible: "sincerity, dignity, endurance of toil, abstinence from pleasure. Grumble not at thy lot, be content with little, be kindly, independent, frugal, serious, high minded" (V. 5). Time and again in various ways, he reminds himself: "I do my own duty; other things do not distract me" (VI. 22). He emphasizes self-sufficiency. Marcus found great solace in the realization that at any time he could retire into himself and be totally unperturbed by what others might say or do against him. It was the man who sought to do harm who had the problem, for he was only injuring himself by his malevolence. When Marcus writes, "The unjust man is unjust to himself, for he makes himself bad" (IX. 4), he echoes Socrates' statement to the jury which condemned him when he told them that he did not blame men for harming him, only that they wanted to.

The *Meditations* is often repetitive, as are modern tracts espousing New Thought, which keep the reader's mind so filled with morally fit ideas that there is no room for self-destructive hatred or impurity. More than once Marcus remarks that it is "thinking which makes it so" (II. 15; XII. 8). The warfare was in the mind, and he never gave up. Only his body, wracked with disease, succumbed. His soul went on. He was not quite sure where or how; nevertheless whatever happened would be according to nature and therefore for the best.

The essential weakness in Stoicism is its refusal to come to terms with irrationality, which is simply to be tolerated in others, as if jealousy, hatred, and selfishness could be bypassed by the

Stoics themselves. Their desire to overcome these destructive tendencies is of course commendable, but their failure to recognize the power of these urges in the development of human events gave them an unrealistic view of the world. Thus, toward the end of his reign, Marcus was undoubtedly surprised by the disloyalty of his best general in the East, Gaius Avidius Cassius. The usual human reaction would have been anger; but he, being a Stoic, had to avoid that. "For the nearer such a mind attains to a passive calm, the nearer is the man to strength. As grief is a weakness, so also is anger. In both it is a case of a wound and a surrender" (XI. 18). It was his duty to the Empire to go to the East and suppress the revolt. But the real struggle was with himself, to avoid feelings of disappointment or frustration. Speaking of the true Stoic, he wrote: "What others may say or think about him or do against him he does not even let enter his mind, being well satisfied with these two things—justice in all present acts and contentment with his present lot" (X. 11). And so, "Put an end once for all to this discussion of what a good man should be, and be one" (X. 16).

Marcus as Emperor

Marcus sorely needed the consolation of his philosophy. He faced mounting problems on all sides. Some were of the kind which would sap the strength of the Empire until the end of its days. Trouble in the East was an old story. Again the Parthians took the offensive. Marcus sent his colleague to command the Roman forces, but the presence of the ineffectual Lucius was little more than symbolic. Credit for counterattacking and winning a settlement belonged to Statius Priscus, and especially to Avidius Cassius, then legate in Syria, who had captured and destroyed the Parthian stronghold at Ctesiphon.

Despite their success, the Romans decided to occupy only a portion of northern Mesopotamia, rather than attempt to hold the territory which Trajan had once claimed. In the meantime, Armenia had changed hands twice again, and was finally restored as a Roman client state. Ironically, the triumph of Roman arms in the East was counterbalanced by a dreadful consequence. Returning soldiers carried home the contagion of a disease that was presumably smallpox. The epidemic which swept through the military camps in Europe caused widespread disorder and death. This was the first of the plagues which sharply depleted Roman manpower in the later centuries of the Empire and so made more difficult the problem of defense.

There was already a shortage of soldiers when a crisis on the Danube foreshadowed the future in another way. Several tribes in southern Germany, including the Quadi and the Marcomanni, crossed Rome's northern frontier in A.D. 167 and headed south, partly in search of land, and partly because they felt threatened by their neighbors. The Roman defenses, minus the forces sent to the East, gave way before the onslaught, and the barbarians penetrated as far south as Aquileia, a fortified town, twenty-two miles northwest of modern Trieste. Marcus Aurelius stopped this invasion. By A.D. 175 most of the barbarians had again been confined to their former homes. Some, however, were allowed to settle on available land in the provinces. They had long since learned the settled life of farming and were no longer nomads. It was of course not so much farmers as soldiers that the Empire needed. To face the crisis just passed, Marcus had pressed slaves and gladiators into service and even hired Scythian mercenaries. The newly-settled Germans would now help in the fight to keep their relatives out. This barbarization of the Roman army was slight but prophetic. The process would expand in years to come, gradually weakening the Empire. At the time, however, the Danube frontier had been restored. The German tribes were not really to be trusted, but Marcus' pacification plans had to wait. He was being challenged by the first usurper in over a century.

Marcus had stood alone in power since the death of Lucius Verus in 169, during the campaign to push the barbarians out of the provinces of Noricum and Pannonia. In 175, Avidius Cassius, using as a pretext a false report of the Emperor's death, declared himself in power, and claimed the allegiance of several Eastern provinces. Marcus had to act quickly, but as it happened the incident cost him only time. As soon as the Emperor arrived in the East, Avidius Cassius' hopes were over. He was executed by his own officers.

Marcus returned to Rome at a time when new uprisings along the Danube made necessary another campaign against the Quadi and Marcomanni. He had to spend the last years of his life amid the worldly struggles he would so readily have foresaken as a private citizen. He died where his duty had taken him, in Vindobona (modern Vienna), March 17, 180.

Marcus Aurelius and the Christians

Consternation has often been expressed over the fact that one of the most violent persecutions of the Christians in the second century occurred during Marcus Aurelius' reign. The high-minded sentiments of the *Meditations,* espousing a morality closely paralleling that of the Gospels, would seem to rule out such a possibility. But Marcus, like the other good emperors, did not look at the Christians philosophically. He knew them as citizens, and he considered them to be bad ones. His impression of them was based partly on false information, which was nonetheless widely believed even by the best-educated Romans. Because the Christians refused to worship the state gods, they were called atheists, as though they had no God at all. Their asceticism, as mentioned earlier, caused the Christians to stand aside from ordinary society and left them open to charges of secretly practicing all manner of crimes, including incest and cannibalism. That was scandal enough; but what really concerned Marcus Aurelius, as it had Trajan, was their stubborn disobedience. They would not do what they were told, and so created a disunity which seemed all the more intolerable as the external dangers to the Empire mounted. Marcus Aurelius may not have been directly responsible for the forty-seven Christians killed in Lyon; he may even have privately respected the martyrs who stood by their convictions. Christians and Stoics were alike in their display of steadfastness. In political terms, however, the example of these cultists, if unpunished, might inspire further disobedience.

Justin, called "the Martyr" (*ca.* A.D. 100–*ca.* 165), presumably executed at Rome about A.D. 165, was the most prominent Christian to be killed during Marcus' reign. It is noteworthy that by this time the Christians could claim leaders of scholarly standing. Justin was also known as "the philosopher," for he had been active in correlating the Platonic and Stoic philosophies with Christianity. The career of this early Father of the Church who became a saint suggests the great attraction which Christianity held for men of learning. Though it remained dangerous for any man to proclaim himself a Christian, men like Justin were bound to win respect for Christianity in the years ahead. But, at the time, it remained a despised sect in Rome and throughout the Empire. Besides the persecutions in Rome and Gaul, there were also Christians martyred in Africa, specifically in Numidia. In

47. Marcus Aurelius. Photograph courtesy of F. Warren Peters.

his *Meditations,* Marcus describes the Christians as atheists who do not support the government in troubled times and "who do their deeds behind closed doors" (III. 16).

The Succession

If there is one thing great fathers seem unable to do, it is to produce great sons. Marcus Aurelius and the only one of his six sons to survive are a good example. Commodus was a muscular bully, who imagined himself another Hercules. He forgot, if he ever knew, that that man who became a god had more than brute strength to recommend him. After the brief scare created by Avidius Cassius in the East, Marcus named his son co-emperor, in the interest of a smooth succession. Commodus was only sixteen at the time, and Marcus obviously overestimated him.

It would have been better to have chosen an experienced

man of proven capacity, as in the past, but then none of the other good emperors had any blood heirs who might have tempted them to make a father's mistake. Still, there is something else to say about Commodus. Was his father's strict self-discipline a burden to those around him, particularly his son? Perhaps Commodus, like Nero who found the strictness of Burrus and Seneca too much for him, decided to give up the race and run the other way.

Commodus at least honored his father's memory with a triumphal column, which now dominates the Piazza Colonna in Rome. It was erected to commemorate the Emperor's victories on the northern frontiers. Marcus Aurelius is the dominant figure in the reliefs which encircle this marble monument, built and decorated like Trajan's Column, although the workmanship of the designs was not as inspiring. In this instance, a statue of Saint Paul is now to be seen on the pinnacle, replacing the original figures of Marcus Aurelius and his wife, Faustina. But Marcus appears elsewhere in Rome today. In the Piazza del Campidoglio on the Capitoline Hill stands the only remaining bronze equestrian statue of the ancient world. Marcus Aurelius, as a conqueror, sits on a horse which looks far from sleek or fast. There is no evidence here that an Arabian strain had as yet been introduced into the West. Presumably, the raised hoof of this exceptionally stocky horse once rested on the back of a prostrate barbarian, who has since disappeared.

In retrospect, the good emperors, from A.D. 96 to 180, had provided the Roman Empire with its best years and, curiously, also contributed to the dismal age to come. As was true of Augustus, the goodness of their rule was a blind, or even an excuse, for an assumption of enormous power which, being enshrined in the office, was unfortunately transmitted to men who did not have good intentions. So the evil which lived after the good emperors was a tightly controlled executive and judiciary under the sole authority of the Emperor, without any means of checking tyranny except by assassination.

The Senate by the end of the second century was more representative of the provinces than of Italy, especially those of the East, precisely because the good emperors had swelled its ranks with valuable new members. Those appointed were respectable men of wealth who liked the status quo. As in Nero's day, the Senate had again become an instrument of the Emperor. At that former time, the senators were mostly an unsavory lot, led by one of their own kind. Now the Senate was composed of better men, sympathetic to a government which had achieved desirable goals. Yet an institution which had become increasingly subservient in the good years of the second century was ill-prepared to take a leading role amid the troubles of the third. Inexorably, it would seem, the Principate was moving toward an absolutism more in keeping with Eastern than with Western tradition.

XVII

In the Shadow of the Army

Although Dio Cassius' lengthy history of Rome has particular value for the Augustan period, Dio also wrote about his own time, the early third century A.D. Unfortunately, the story of the events he knew best has been preserved only in fragments or in the epitomes made by later historians. A continuous account of the years after the reign of Marcus Aurelius comes from Herodian, a contemporary of Dio, whose *History,* written in Greek, covers the fifty-eight year period A.D. 180 to 238. He concentrated on the events of his own lifetime, but neither the year of his birth nor that of his death is certain. Almost everything about Herodian is problematical. Since he kept himself out of his history, it is not even definitely known where he came from, although he was possibly from Syria or Bithynia. He mentions his government service; apparently it was in the Eastern provinces, although he did not hold a high-ranking office. It seems unlikely that he ever sat with Dio in the Senate.

Herodian's work has the moralistic tone traditional in Roman history. Good men and bad are delineated as in a melodrama. But the *History* makes pleasant reading about personalities and events. There is little commentary. On the rare occasions when Herodian

does appear agitated, he probably reflects a general public concern.
It is possible that, like other freedmen of modest means, he feared
the influence exercised by men of great wealth or high birth. He
also worried about the growing emphasis on the military, as being
against the interests of the rest of the population.

Careful studies of Herodian's *History* have revealed errors in
his chronology and geography. Still, these details, or the lack of
broad perspective, do not detract from an obvious sense of dedication. The work by no means measures up to his Thucydidean
model; but at least he aimed at the best, and for that he deserves
credit. "My policy has been not to accept any second-hand information which had not been checked and corroborated. I have
collected the evidence for my work with every attention to accuracy, limiting it to what falls within the recent memory of my
readers" (I. 1. 3). There are discrepancies between the material
available from Dio and what Herodian wrote, but in the main
their stories are the same. C. R. Whittaker's notes to the Loeb
edition of Herodian offer useful cross-references to Dio. Whittaker calls attention to Herodian's possible borrowings from Dio
and also to his disagreements with him.

One other possible source of information is the *Historia Augusta,* which purports to be a product of six authors writing in the
fourth century A.D. It offers a chronological series of biographies
of the emperors of the second and third centuries, more exactly
A.D. 117 to 284. While this compilation may sound useful, it has
actually been under severe critical attack for almost a century.
Internal evidence suggests that the work was written by only one
man, perhaps more for amusement than for any other purpose.
Some of the documentation is unverified by other sources and
indeed, as has been frequently suggested, the *Historia Augusta* may
in fact be an outrageous forgery. Given this possibility, Herodian,
with all his faults, is here chosen as a better guide.

Herodian began his *History* with the death of his hero, Marcus Aurelius. The career of the virtuous Marcus set a high standard by which all other emperors were to be judged, and quotations from him helped to sustain his reputation. Marcus had been
"worn out not just by age but also by hard work and worries."
Herodian included a deathbed scene in which Marcus offered a
final word of caution to relatives and officials, with special reference to his son Commodus, who stood at his side. "There is a
danger that he will be carried away and dashed against the rocks

of evil habits because he has an imperfect experience of what to do. You who are many must be fathers to him in place of me alone. Take care of him and give him sound advice" (I. 4. 3–4). The passage was dramatic in its foreshadowing; precisely what the Emperor feared came to pass.

Commodus

After his father died, March 17, 180, Commodus made a donation to the soldiers in camp, and, according to Herodian, delivered a speech in which he emphasized that he was a blood heir, and not merely adopted as recent emperors had been. That he was a true son of the much-loved Marcus would also account for the warmth of his welcome when he returned to Rome from the Danube frontier. But the fact that he returned so soon after his father's death was a clue to the kind of son Marcus had left behind. At first, Commodus listened to the best advisers his father had appointed to guide him, but before long became privately intrigued with suggestions about the grandeur and pleasures awaiting him in Rome, where, if nothing else, the weather would be better. There were advisers near him, petty-minded men of bad habits, who encouraged his longing to leave the rigors of the frontier and looked forward to accompanying him home. He first announced that he was leaving and then changed his mind after a pleading speech by his older brother-in-law, Pompeianus, that he stay and do his duty. Commodus was, however, only detained briefly. He turned the campaign against the barbarians over to his generals, who, presumably, by successive victories forced some of the enemy to terms and, with Commodus' approval, appeased others by granting large sums of money in return for peace. It was an unfortunate precedent.

Great throngs accompanied the Senate in going out to greet Commodus as he approached the city. Marcus' son was a handsome youth with a powerful physique, bright-eyed and golden haired. The Romans liked him best at that moment when they knew him the least. Only the first years of his thirteen-year reign were tolerable. After that, he fell under the dominance of his praetorian prefect, Tigidius Perennis, who recognized how easily Commodus could be diverted into sensual pursuits. Perennis gained an even greater grip on the Emperor after an assassination attempt in which leading members of the Senate and even Commodus' elder sister Lucilla were involved. He was saved by an uncommon piece of luck. The actual attempt on his life was left to a voluble young senator who, with dagger in hand, proceeded to deliver a dramatic speech which gave the bodyguards all the time they needed to take him in hand. The execution of Commodus' sister and anyone else associated with the plot created a tense atmosphere in which Perennis flourished, only too well. Before long Commodus became convinced that Perennis was a threat to his own power and had him beheaded. The sudden execution of Perennis was indicative of Commodus' executive performance. He usually became aware of problems only after they had gotten out of hand, and then reacted impulsively. The rapid turnover in praetorian prefects betrayed the instability which pervaded his reign.

Seldom does Herodian break away from the story of the palace to describe incidents elsewhere. But he does mention a roving band of ex-soldiers, deserters among them, who were joined by impoverished provincials and plain criminals in attacking farmsteads and even towns in Gaul and Spain. The leader of this growing army, Maternus, was viewed by Herodian as an ambitious freebooter who aimed at nothing less than the overthrow of Commodus. That was looking at the problem from the narrow viewpoint of his own times. It seems apparent that Maternus and his followers were part of a disturbing development. The government, increasingly preoccupied with the frontiers where soldiers were most needed, could offer less and less protection, as time passed, to local areas left to the mercy of armed gangs, whose ranks were swelled by prisoners they had released and recruited. Commodus sharply rebuked provincial commanders for letting an intolerable situation develop. For a time the disturbances were suppressed and the ringleaders executed. But when Commodus' reign was over, these same generals were too busy fighting each other to be able to protect the countryside. Herodian, who died probably about the middle of the third century, cannot be faulted for failing to see the consequences of the events he was describing. Eventually, certain regions within the Empire would have to find the means of protecting themselves. The decentralizing process took a long time, but was part of the decline of the Empire. Though the end was a long way off, signs of dissolution were beginning to appear. In other words, Herodian's description of what was happening allows the modern reader to see what was *really* happening.

48. Commodus, in the style of Hercules. Museo Capitolino, Rome.
Photograph courtesy of Aldo Reale.

At Rome, Commodus grew increasingly fearful of plots among those prominent persons who were obviously disappointed by his style and performance. He had seemingly given up any hope of living up to his father's strict moral standards and so had abandoned them altogether. Now, like Nero, he increasingly disliked anyone who even reminded him that he had ever sought after virtue. And, like Nero, he took to the arena, where he displayed great skill in killing wild beasts with spears. He also evoked disgust for the way in which he was demeaning his position: "He took off the dress of a Roman emperor and took to wearing lion skin and carrying a club in his hand. Or he would dress himself up in purple and gold, making himself a laughing-stock by wearing clothes which gave the impression of a feminine extravagance and heroic strength at the same time" (I. 14. 8). He was certainly no hero. The people saw not only a disgraced Emperor but many portents of his downfall. The most significant was a fire, perhaps caused by lightning, which completely gutted Vespasian's Temple of Peace, described as "the largest and most beautiful of all the buildings in the city." The fire burned out a whole section of the city and was only ended after several days by rain. This catastrophe was generally reckoned as a divine judgment on the ruthlessness with which Commodus had been disposing of his suspected enemies. By chance, a list of prominent persons whom Commodus had slated for execution fell into the hands of one of them. Commodus was murdered that same night with the collusion of his mistress, Marcia, who was also on the list. Since the poison she gave him in his wine seemed ineffective, a powerful athlete was brought in to strangle him. It was New Year's Eve, 192.

Pertinax

As when Domitian died, those who killed Commodus needed a respected man of excellent reputation to replace him and lessen the shock of the sudden change. Pertinax, one of Marcus Aurelius' most trusted aides, was the obvious choice. He was a cautious man who lived simply, and at sixty-six had a record of honorable service in the army and numerous government posts. As the son of a freedman, he was not likely to be received enthusiastically by the nobility, but, that aside, Pertinax looked safe.

It was given out that Commodus had died of apoplexy. The people who heard the news were too overjoyed to bother about the details. Their enthusiasm forced the praetorians to give at least a grudging welcome to Pertinax when he came to their camp. The assembled soldiers went through the motions of saluting him as Emperor, but they knew the favor they had enjoyed under Commodus was not likely to be continued under the sober Pertinax.

In spite of his low birth, Pertinax was well received by the Senate, where a majority recognized the value of his age, experience, and modesty. If Pertinax, like Nerva, had found a Trajan in time to assist him, he might have survived. As it was he lasted less than three months. Herodian gave him unrestrained praise for his efforts to restore the principles of good government which had existed under Marcus Aurelius. He quickly suppressed abuses by the soldiers in the city by strict orders against any further unwarranted attacks on civilians. Ironically, the new atmosphere Pertinax had promoted provided the opportunity for his early downfall. One day, a number of angry praetorians appeared suddenly in the palace. Though Pertinax's dignified presence and noble words held most of them at bay, a few of these men, sworn to protect him, lunged forward as he spoke and killed him on the spot. They were the ones who had remained loyal to the easygoing Commodus. They could not abide the conscientious Pertinax. By their act, he was given the distinction, for what it was worth, of being the first Emperor who was a far better man than the men who murdered him.

Julianus

Little time need be spent on Pertinax's successor, Marcus Didius Julianus. Although he had seen service in the army and held various provincial governorships, he was better known for his wealth and heavy drinking, and, finally, for a kind of pathetic stupidity. The reckless murder of Pertinax gave the city a shock which was compounded by the praetorians' blatant offer of their support to the highest bidder for the throne. Julianus, with the urging of his wife and daughter, "bought the Empire" by promising the guardsmen even more money than they had expected, or that he could ever afford to pay. The usual formalities were carried out by the Senate, but it was an empty show. Julianus was in the palace only because the praetorians put him there. The Roman people displayed their contempt for him by catcalls whenever he made an appearance. As might be expected, when the news of the scandalous happenings in Rome reached the provincial commanders, there was an immediate lifting of banners. Both Septimius Severus (*ca.* A.D. 145–211), who commanded troops in Pannonia, and Gaius Pescennius Niger, the governor of Syria, made a bid for power, but Severus was nearer to Rome. Niger was hailed as Emperor by his legions, and their support apparently gave him a false sense of optimism. When Severus invaded Italy, now unprotected, with his army of provincials, it became apparent that there was no choice. Herodian says Niger's delay in setting out for Rome, caused by celebrations in his honor, was a crucial mistake. There was a contest, of course, as there had been in 69, but by the time it came, Severus was the Emperor of record, putting down a usurper.

The Severan Dynasty

In Herodian's description, Severus offers a contrast with Niger. Severus was a decisive man of action with a no-nonsense approach

2. The Severan Succession

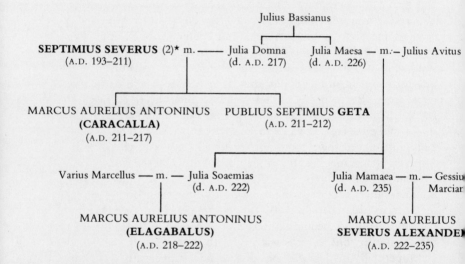

Julius Bassianus

SEPTIMIUS SEVERUS (2)★ m. —— Julia Domna   Julia Maesa — m. — Julius Avitus
(A.D. 193–211)   (d. A.D. 217)   (d. A.D. 226)

MARCUS AURELIUS ANTONINUS   PUBLIUS SEPTIMIUS **GETA**
(CARACALLA)   (A.D. 211–212)
(A.D. 211–217)

Varius Marcellus —— m. —— Julia Soaemias   Julia Mamaea — m. — Gessiu
(d. A.D. 222)   (d. A.D. 235)   Marciar

MARCUS AURELIUS ANTONINUS   MARCUS AURELIUS
(ELAGABALUS)   **SEVERUS ALEXANDE**
(A.D. 218–222)   (A.D. 222–235)

★The notation (2) indicates this was the second marriage of Septimius Severus to both domestic and foreign affairs. The tradition said he was also blessed with dreams which he claimed were divinely inspired. Rallying the northern provinces in behalf of a campaign to avenge the murder of Pertinax and depose the hapless Julianus, he set out for Rome, where his personal ambitions would also, coincidentally, be fulfilled. From the outset his rapport with his soldiers was a clue to the direction of his regime. According to Herodian, Severus lived the way his men did, and if the food was poor he endured that, too. Sallust had once said the same about Marius in his day.

Julianus reigned only a little more than two months. The scant support which he could muster evaporated when Severus and his army approached the city. Deserted by the guards, who felt that he had cheated them, Julianus made a bid to resign and so save his life, but this pitiful act only made his position worse. The senators voted to send word to Severus that they formally accepted him as Emperor. They gave proof of their allegiance by ordering the execution of Julianus. According to Herodian, a military tribune found the unprotected old man cringing in the palace and murdered him on the spot. Thus, in June, 193, began a new dynasty, which would last for over forty years, until 235. This was long enough to make the government obedient to the army rather than the other way around.

Septimius Severus' decisions after he was in power were mostly aimed at staying there. The new Emperor was eager to do or say whatever was necessary to win an advantage of the moment. This policy of expediency accounted for the strong favor he showed the military in general and the frontier troops in particular. He was born in Lepcis Magna in Libya, had spent most of his career in the provinces, and was married to a well-educated Syrian woman, Julia Domna. To reign in Rome and be a part of its traditions remained the *sine qua non* of imperial power. Severus knew that and adopted himself into the Antonine family. He was nevertheless the first Emperor whose favor seems to have been more directed toward the provinces than toward Italy.

Severus' first act as Emperor was to disarm and disband the troublesome Praetorian Guard and to replace it with the best men of his own Pannonian army. The Italian dominance of the imperial corps was now gone, along with their preferential role in the Roman army, which had disappeared long before. The new Emperor sought to lull any lingering fears in the Senate by echoing

49. Julia Domna. Courtesy of the Ny Carlsberg Glyptotek, Copenhagen.

the sentiments of the "good emperors." He would not summarily execute any senator and he would not condone informers. That was what the Senate wanted to hear. For the people there were spectacles; for the army, money. A loyal capital was behind him as he left to deal with Niger. To keep the other provincial commanders in line, he followed Commodus' practice of taking their children into custody. Those who supported Niger were thereby given a good reason to defect. Winning cooperation by fear rather than loyalty was part of the drift toward absolutism in the later years of the Principate.

The only provincial governor who seriously worried Severus was Decimus Clodius Albinus, a rich nobleman stationed in Britain, who was known to be ambitious and might have been the senators' choice, if they had had one. Severus kept Albinus at bay by giving him the title of Caesar, which, in effect, made him the heir apparent. Albinus, whom Herodian called "vain and rather simple," may have been completely fooled by this stratagem. In any event, he waited his turn, so to speak, while Severus went to face Niger in the East.

Niger had requested and received soldiers from the kings of Parthia and Hatra, a powerful commercial city in southern Mesopotamia. But a large part of his army was made up of raw recruits from Antioch, who were no match for Severus' veterans. The

Emperor's superior forces won a series of battles in Asia Minor and made their way slowly toward Syria. Even in the territory he held, Niger was in trouble; not all of the cities supported him. The long-time rivalry between Antioch, his capital, and nearby Laodicea caused the latter city to support Severus, which prompted Niger to use severely repressive measures, thus undercutting his popularity in the whole region. Severus later was generous in subsidizing the rebuilding of the cities which Niger had wrecked. Niger was defeated at the battle of Issus in A.D. 194, where "the rivers of the plain carried more blood than water down to the sea" (III. 4. 5). Finally, his recruits broke and ran. Niger escaped, too, but was later captured near Antioch and beheaded.

Herodian's handling of the chronology of events in Severus' reign is not sound. It is possible, however, to elicit from his account a general idea of the Emperor's various orders and campaigns. After the defeat of Niger, Severus decided to postpone a campaign to punish the Parthians and the king of Hatra for the aid they sent to his enemy. He returned to Rome briefly and then left for Gaul, where a contest with his other major competitor, Albinus, was imminent. With Niger out of the way, he had no further need to tolerate Albinus' ambitions. In 196, Severus gave his elder son, Caracalla, the title of Caesar. Albinus was thus pushed aside and, indeed, would have been killed had he not remained wary of all messengers sent to him by Severus. Everybody was searched for weapons before being admitted to see him. He declared himself Emperor and busily mustered support for the inevitable showdown. It came at Lyon in Gaul, where the estimate Severus gave his troops concerning Albinus' British forces proved false. They were daring fighters, and Severus' army was saved only by the late arrival of one of his generals, Laetus, who brought reinforcements. Albinus, who remained in the city while the battle raged, was captured and, according to variant accounts, either committed suicide or was beheaded as Niger had been. In any event, only his head reached the Rome he longed to rule. There it was on display as a sign of hostility toward all those who had supported him. Severus knew who they were, for he had also captured Albinus' private papers and correspondence; consequently, the victory celebration in Rome, in June 197, which included a distribution of money to the people, had a grim side. Severus soon put to death not only Albinus' supporters but also persons known to have favored Niger.

Severus' soldiers had won him his unchallenged position, and to them he gave the greatest rewards and favors. Their pay was raised substantially, which set a precedent for later emperors, whether the treasury could afford it or not. Inevitably, taxes had to be raised and currency debased in an effort to keep up with demands for more money. As a consequence, the civilian population, especially the middle class, was being squeezed for the sake of the military. Herodian was sharply critical of the concessions which had made army life more attractive and comfortable. He feared a decline in discipline, and later observers saw his predictions come true.

Severus' decision to allow frontier soldiers to marry and raise families away from camp on their own land was part of an effort to maintain morale and commit local forces to the defense of their own property. In time, however, soldiers settled in one place were reluctant to be transferred for duty elsewhere, even in times of emergency. Those who lived along the Rhine-Danube frontier were particularly unhappy about having to fight in the East against the Parthians, or later the Persians. They worried that, while they were absent, the barbarians in the north would break through weakened defenses and ravage their own homeland. In the mid-third century that is exactly what happened; discipline problems, including frequent mutinies, which later emperors had to contend with, were spawned by Severus' solution of a pressing need in his own time.

The Romans had become used to the emperors being absent from Rome for long periods, attending to the problems of the frontiers. Severus returned to the capital to be greeted by crowds waving laurel branches. He spoke to the Senate and provided money for spectacles. But for all that, he was somehow a remote figure, increasingly more like an oriental despot and much less in the image of Augustus.

Severus' second campaign in the East was aimed at punishing the city-kingdom of Hatra and the Parthians for their aid to Niger. The attempt to take Hatra was very costly to the Romans and had to be abandoned because of the heat and high casualties. Severus compensated for this setback by suddenly attacking the Parthian capital, Ctesiphon, on the east bank of the Tigris. The unsuspecting Parthian king managed to escape, but in such a hurry he left his jewels behind. That victory over the Parthians gave Severus his chance at last for a genuine triumphal celebration

in Rome. His previous successes had been over Roman commanders, and for those a formal triumph did not seem appropriate. The triple Arch of Septimius Severus which stands on the
northwest side of the Forum is decorated with reliefs which commemorate his Eastern campaign.

This time, Severus remained in Rome for a relatively
lengthy stay of two years, while he attended to domestic problems which had hitherto been neglected. He also watched his two
sons grow into manhood, and with some justifiable apprehension.
Both were spoiled by their servants and the attention they received as crown princes. To make matters worse, they developed
an intense rivalry in their childhood which lasted until the day the
elder son Caracalla stabbed his brother Geta to death. Severus
never lived to see that day, a day, in fact, hastened by his own
death. He hoped in vain for a reconciliation.

In A.D. 208, Severus took his sons with him on a campaign
to put down a rebellion in Britain and deal once more with the
turmoil along the northern border. The experience, he hoped,
would improve his sons' characters and give them closer ties to
the soldiers. Time and again, he told his sons that all they needed
to retain power was the army if they could learn to live with each
other. Severus, now past sixty, was so badly crippled by gout that
he had to be carried on a litter by the time he and his sons reached
Britain. The rebels were eager to make amends when faced with
the overwhelming weight of imperial power, but Severus insisted
on punishing them. The war was a desultory affair, with the
natives using guerrilla tactics to postpone the inevitable pacification the Romans sought. Severus had hoped to return in triumph
to Rome once more, but he died at York early in February, 211—
a sad ending to a career which, militarily at least, had had its great
moments. Severus was probably aware of Caracalla's eagerness to
have him out of the way. Caracalla later executed the doctors who
refused to hasten Severus' departure.

In the short run, the continuing enmity between Severus'
sons was detrimental to the Empire. Beyond that, he had given
the army a more powerful role in Roman society. In a sense it was
the new privileged class. Caracalla distributed gifts to the officers
in the hope that he could win the army to his side and exclude his
brother. But the memory of Severus' wish that the two reign
together was too strong. They were hailed as co-emperors. Yet
carrying their father's ashes back to Rome for burial in Hadrian's

mausoleum, and having him deified, was probably the only time they cooperated about anything, aside from perfunctory ceremonials. Dining together was out of the question, for they both worried about being poisoned. The palace was divided as between two armed camps, with doorways walled up and separate guards. The two brothers never wanted to see each other and rarely did. Public officials belonged to one faction or the other, and even charioteers rode as partisans. Julia Domna heard talk of dividing the Empire, but she persuaded her sons to drop that idea. She could not get them to agree on appointments, however. They also clashed over important trials by supporting one side against the other. Caracalla's violent temper finally ended the impasse. Only in his mother's presence could he catch Geta unawares. Late in February, A.D. 212, according to Herodian, "Geta was mortally wounded and died spilling his blood on his mother's breast" (IV. 4. 3). Caracalla told the soldiers in Rome that he had been the target of a plot by Geta, but had managed to save himself. They soon heard otherwise, but by this time another pay raise, which the treasury could ill afford, made them content with a murderer as Emperor.

Caracalla

Caracalla, in speaking to the Senate, stuck to his story of having been surprised by Geta's attempt to kill him and even had the audacity to recall that Romulus had defended himself against Remus. The speech was followed by a bloodbath in which anyone ever associated with Geta, as a servant or senator, was executed. The patrician families were again decimated, for they had been the chief supporters of Geta. Even one of the revered Marcus Aurelius' daughters, who had dared to weep over Geta's murder, was slain.

Caracalla possessed little administrative capacity but interestingly enough the most famous decree of his reign was an edict concerning internal affairs. By the *Constitutio Antoniniana* issued in 212, Caracalla gave citizenship to all those of free status in the Empire. On the surface this generous pronouncement completed the process by which provincials were given equality, but its real purpose was undoubtedly to bring more money into imperial coffers. Roman citizens paid a five percent inheritance tax, and now there would be more of them to pay it.

50. Caracalla. Courtesy of the Metropolitan Museum of Art. Samuel D. Lee Fund, 1940.

The soldiers stationed in Rome found in Caracalla another Commodus, who let them run roughshod over the people and steal what they wanted. Unlike Commodus, however, who delighted in the pleasures of Rome, Caracalla went to live among the troops on the northern frontier. He was a short, husky man who delighted in pleasing the soldiers with feats of great strength. He even won the hearts of the Germans across the Danube. To please them, Herodian says, the Emperor wore a blond wig and German-style clothing, including the cloak which gave him his nickname. Consequently, the Germans were flattered to serve him. The most powerfully built among them became his bodyguard. As for his relationship with his Roman soldiers, Herodian wrote: "He claimed that he loved being called a comrade instead of emperor by them." It was a sign of the times. Caracalla fancied himself another Alexander. Herodian says he saw "ludicrous pictures" of one body with the head divided, being half Alexander and half Caracalla.

Caracalla traveled to the East not merely to inspect the provinces and issue orders but also to seek a cure for some unspecified

ailment at the healing shrines there. In the summer of A.D. 215,
the Emperor arrived in Alexandria, ostensibly to visit the tomb of
Alexander and worship at the Serapeum, a grandiose temple of
Serapis, a god of healing. His real purpose was to catch the city
off guard and sacrifice its young men to his vanity. According to
Herodian, Caracalla bore a grudge against the Alexandrians for
their many jokes about him. They thought his comparison of
himself to the tall and handsome Alexander the Great was ridiculous. Making fun of the high and mighty was an established pastime in Alexandria, an echo of the old Greek comedy when no
public figure was safe from ridicule. Caracalla had heard about the
sport made of him by the Alexandrians, but saw nothing funny in
it and plotted his revenge carefully. Upon his arrival in Alexandria
he made ceremonial visits to the Serapeum and the tomb of Alexander and kept his true feelings well hidden amid the elaborate
festivities with which the Alexandrians welcomed him. Then,
pretending to honor the city by creating a special corps to be
named for Alexander, he had the young men gathered together so
that he could inspect them in person. It was of course a trap, but
even the relatives of the youths assembled had no reason for suspicion. As the Emperor spoke to each of the youths in turn, his
soldiers slowly formed a ring around them. Suddenly Caracalla
withdrew and the slaughter began. This was his punishment of
the Alexandrians for their little jokes. Then he moved on; and that
episode was followed by another deceit practiced on the Parthians.
Caracalla offered a new kind of peace to Artabanus, the king of
Parthia, proposing marriage between the Roman Emperor and the
king's daughter, and a military alliance whereby the two empires
would conquer all peoples not yet under their domination. He
also offered a free exchange of goods between their two peoples.
Artabanus at first hesitated and then agreed because of the numerous gifts Caracalla sent as a sign of his sincerity. When the Romans crossed into Parthia to meet the king, they were greeted
with a colorful celebration at which the Parthians drank and
danced with joy, having put aside their weapons for the occasion.
Without warning, the Romans attacked and slaughtered great
numbers of them, who were hobbled by their long, voluminous
garments. The Parthian king was saved by his bodyguard, but
only a few others managed to get away. Herodian says Caracalla
now "marched throughout the length and breadth of the Parthian
territory, until even his soldiers were exhausted from looting and

killing, and he returned to Mesopotamia" (IV. 11. 8). The Senate soon "voted him full triumphal honors out of fear and flattery."

If Caracalla could feign friendship while plotting the massacre first of the Alexandrians and then of the Parthians, what could be expected from him by his officers? He was fearful of plots, seeking advice from soothsayers in Rome and elsewhere about who his enemies might be. One day, a dispatch from Rome brought the warning that a praetorian prefect named Marcus Opellius Macrinus was dangerous. It was to Macrinus, however, that Caracalla had entrusted that day's communications for perusal to see if there were any important matters to be brought to the Emperor's attention. So the message, possibly part of a conspiracy to eliminate Macrinus, became a death sentence for the Emperor. Macrinus hurriedly enlisted the services of a young, disgruntled centurion who was told to strike when he could. It was not easy to get near the Emperor because of his German bodyguard. However, according to the story Herodian tells, when Caracalla was on his way to visit a shrine near Carrhae, he found it necessary to retire from company to relieve himself. While the guards stood with their backs turned, the centurion caught the Emperor with only one servant nearby. The assassin plunged his dagger into Caracalla's back, killing him on the spot. He was himself slain by the Germans. Macrinus was able to stand with others and weep at the sight of the Emperor's body.

The army was shocked at the death of their comrade, whose ashes were sent to his mother in Antioch. Not long afterwards, Julia Domna, out of power and out of favor, committed suicide.

Macrinus

That Macrinus now received widespread support from various officials and was elevated to the purple supports the view that the conspiracy against Caracalla was wider than the story would suggest. With the news that the Parthian king, Artabanus, was ready to avenge his people treacherously slain by Caracalla's orders, there was little time to debate Macrinus' merits. The ensuing hostilities were not conclusive. But peace was finally achieved after the Parthian king learned that his primary enemy, Caracalla, was dead and that Macrinus, disapproving of his predecessor's perfidiousness, was willing to pay for the damage which Roman forces had inflicted. The Parthian king was satisfied. For the remainder of Macrinus' one-year reign, his enemies were behind him. He was a Mauretanian who had risen through the equestrian ranks and was considered a usurper by the patricians in the Senate. Macrinus was the first Emperor who was not a senator. Nevertheless, he was by all odds a more reliable ruler than Caracalla, and for that they could be grateful. In a letter to the senators, Macrinus asked what the noble birth of Commodus or Caracalla had ever availed them? His theme that merit was worth more than a name or ancestry was reminiscent of Marius' famous speech reported by Sallust. Virtue or no, Macrinus' failure to become a comrade to the army as Caracalla had been led to grumbling. If they needed someone to replace him, why not Caracalla's own son? The sister of the late Julia Domna was Julia Maesa, a native of Emesa in Phoenicia, who had grown used to power and wealth when her brother-in-law Septimius Severus and his sons ruled. She had two daughters, Soaemias and Mamaea. Each daughter had given her a grandson, both of whom, she was prepared to say, were sired by Caracalla. The elder, Bassianus, is better known as Elagabalus, after the Phoenician name for the sun god whom he served as a priest. At fourteen, this exceptionally good-looking boy found the exotic garments and dances of a sun cult more to his taste than soldiering, or anything else for that matter. The claim that Elagabalus was Caracalla's son, combined with Maesa's generous promises, prompted rebellious soldiers to support him. Macrinus tried to resist; but, when his followers deserted him in a battle with the rebels, he was forced to flee. Later captured, he was killed as was his son Diadumenianus, who had shared his father's hopes and now his bad luck. With Macrinus dead, the army united in hailing Elagabalus as Emperor. This time they had chosen not just a fool but an absurdity.

Elagabalus

Nothing says more about the helplessness of the civilian government than that the Senate accepted this bizarre youth as Emperor. Elagabalus' insistence that the name of his cult god be given precedence over Jupiter was a clue to what Rome was in for. What officials in the capital thought of his daily ritualistic performances can only be imagined. "Around the altars he and some Phoenician women danced to the sounds of many different instruments, circling the altars with cymbals and drums in their hands"

(V. 5. 9). To many prominent Romans it was simply a bad joke. The seriousness of it, however, was apparent when those whose hostile views became known were executed. Elagabalus' grandmother was able to arrange for payments to the people and unusual shows to amuse them, but she could not prevent her stubborn grandson from making himself the greatest spectacle of all. "He used to go out with painted eyes and rouge on his cheeks, spoiling his natural good looks by using disgusting make-up" (V. 6. 10).

Julia Maesa, fearful that the exotic Elagabalus would not hold the loyalty of the troops for long, decided to shore up her own position by having him adopt his cousin, Alexander, son of her daughter Mamaea. In A.D. 221, the Senate accepted the arrangement whereby the sixteen-year-old Augustus became the "father" of a Caesar who was about five years younger. To protect Alexander from the religious fanaticism at court, his mother saw to it that he practiced wrestling and was taught at least the rudiments of a normal education. Elagabalus, angry about the attention given Alexander, ordered the execution of his cousin's innocent teachers. As further proof of his unfitness, he began to make outrageous appointments to high offices, including even actors, dancers, and charioteers. Ultimately, his attempt to downgrade Alexander was his undoing. Mamaea had apparently been quietly winning the soldiers by passing out money. They hardly needed it to turn them against Elagabalus, whom they now considered disgusting. When, on March 13, A.D. 222, in their camp, he issued orders against those who favored Alexander, they killed him and all who had accompanied him, including his mother Soaemias. According to Herodian, the bodies of Elagabalus and his mother were "handed over to those who wished to drag them around and desecrate them. After being dragged through the city for a long time and mutilated, they were thrown into the sewers which run down to the River Tiber" (V. 8. 9). Amid changing times, one tradition was holding.

Severus Alexander

In the years ahead, the young Alexander was completely pliant to the wishes of his grandmother and mother. By a concatenation of circumstances, the affairs of Rome were, for the first and only time, in the hands of women. Strange as that may seem, these two experienced and well-educated Syrian women gave the Empire the best rule it had known since the days of the good emperors. Sixteen highly respected senators were selected to give guidance. Herodian says that their role was a serious one and that nothing was said or done without their advice. Maesa and Mamaea, whose ties to the army were weak, courted the favor of the Senate and gave this body its best years of influence. The return to normalcy was also marked by a housecleaning in the administration. Those foolishly appointed by Elagabalus were turned out. Even statues of the gods were put back in their rightful temples, after having been displaced according to the whim of some previous ruler. Without doubt the greatest glory of Alexander's fourteen-year rule was his strict adherence to the law and the absence of arbitrary orders for executions. Herodian wrote that Alexander was by nature a kind and considerate person. His high praise for this regime can be understood in the light of both what came before and what would follow.

It is ironical that Alexander's "gentleness," which contributed to the mildness of his reign, was also a reason for his downfall. He was too subservient to his mother, who after Maesa's death took over the sole management of her son's affairs. She arranged a marriage for him in which he seemed content and attached to his wife. That, of course, was not to Mamaea's advantage, and she sent her daughter-in-law into exile. The outward calm of this regime was obviously not a true image of the imperial household. Alexander was also disturbed about his mother's preoccupation with obtaining money, at times illegally. Her argument was that she needed it to take care of the soldiers, but he was aware that she also was taking care of herself. However, Alexander was apparently helpless. Herodian wrote: "Completely dominated by his mother, he did exactly as he was told. This was the one thing for which he can be faulted; that he obeyed his mother in matters of which he disapproved because he was over-mild and showed greater respect to her than he ought to have done" (VI. 1. 10).

A sudden change of affairs in the East propelled Alexander into problems of warfare which neither he nor his mother were prepared to manage. The Persians under their king Artaxerxes had successfully overrun the Parthian kingdom. They were now sufficiently inspired by their dynamic leader to dream of retaking the lands which once belonged to the mighty Persian Empire conquered by Alexander the Great five-and-a-half centuries earlier.

The present Alexander possessed the name only and was not likely to discourage them. He was reluctant to fight and tried to come to terms with Artaxerxes by diplomatic means, but to no avail. The king was determined to recover Syria and even Asia Minor. Alexander was thus forced to fight, and not the least of his worries were mutinies by contingents of his own army, who would rather have a new Emperor than face the Persians under Alexander. Worse, many of those who were willing to fight lost their lives in a disastrous campaign in 232. Alexander had a feasible strategy, but did not follow it himself, and Herodian frankly attributed his failure to timidity and the influence of Mamaea. The Roman armies retreating from Parthia suffered further losses because of illness and lack of food. Nevertheless, despite their defeat when Alexander had failed to arrive with the forces under his command, they fought hard enough to deter a further effort by Artaxerxes. That was fortunate, for by this time the Germans had broken through the defenses of the Rhine and the Danube. They were ravaging towns as they moved southward and even posed a threat to Italy. Many of Alexander's soldiers had left their families behind in that region, and their fears for what had happened at home further lowered their morale. By the time the major part of the army reached the northern frontier to deal with the new threat, Alexander was sufficiently frightened by the prospect of a war along such a long border that he attempted to buy the Germans off rather than punish their violations of the frontier. By this time, too, his personality and policies were in sharp contrast to those of one of his leading officers, Gaius Julius Verus Maximinus (A.D. 173–238), a powerfully built Thracian of reputed low birth, who was a born fighter. Mamaea had been skimpy with donations of late; Maximinus, now hailed as Emperor, promised to be more generous. Deserted by his army, Alexander was killed in his tent while sobbing in his mother's arms. On Maximinus' orders Mamaea was killed, along with her friends. That slaughter, early in March, 235, brought the Severan dynasty to an end. Except for the first ten years of Alexander's reign, it had been mostly a time of troubles. What was to follow would be worse.

The Barracks Room Emperors

In the fifty-five years since the death of Marcus Aurelius in A.D. 180, every emperor had been murdered or executed, except Sep-

timius Severus, and even then there were rumors that Caracalla had
tried to poison him. The reigns of Pertinax, Julianus, Macrinus,
and Elagabalus were little more than interludes. Alexander Severus
was another victim of the chronic military disorders. It would seem
that a purple cloak had become standard equipment in legionary
supply vans to be taken out and draped over the shoulder of a
commander, willing or not, whenever the occasion seemed right.
The rapid turnover at the top contributed to feelings of instability
and a crumbling of old patterns throughout Roman society. Even
the poorest, least educated peasants, who had ordinarily held to a
routine obedience, were slowly being affected by events which
gave a sense of temporariness to all things. The confidence inherited from the second-century apogee of the Empire was giving way
to a pervasive sense of fear. Compared to what has happened to
modern nations in the course of a decade or two, the process was
gradual, but it was still discernible.

The impact of events on the predominantly rural population
of the Empire was, of course, not immediately so great as in the
cities. Moreover, the time it took for news, let alone an army, to
arrive in one part of the Empire from another retarded the pace of
change. Still, in the succeeding fifty years, after the death of Alexander Severus in 235, a series of shocks cracked even the veneer of
the Principate, which by then was all that remained of what Augustus had arranged. Eighteen to twenty-six emperors, more or
less legitimate, discovered that the highest honor, was, if anythng,
a near guarantee of an early death.

Herodian's *History* ends in 238. There is no contemporary
account of the years that follow. A resumé based on the available
information, while running the risk of becoming a monotonous
catalogue of names, dates, and places, contributes to what can be
surmised about the agonies of this half-century.

Events show how increasingly difficult it now was for one
man to manage the problems of the Empire. The long frontiers
and the many provinces would soon have to be divided for purposes of defense. When the division became state policy at the end
of the century, it was born of a half-century of experience.

The Senate had gained enough self-confidence during Mamaea's time to take the unusual step of defying Maximinus in
A.D. 238 and recognizing Marcus Antonius Gordianus (A.D. 158–
238), the popular eighty-year-old proconsul in Africa, as Emperor. He insisted on sharing this role with his son Gordianus II

(A.D. 192–238), who was perhaps better known for reputedly having sixty children than for his brief term in power. Both father and son were said to have been killed fighting the Numidians that same year, although the elder Gordian may have been a suicide. The Senate then declared two of its members, Marcus Clodius Pupienus and Decius Caelius Balbinus, co-emperors. Fortunately for them, Maximinus was killed by his own followers after he led them in an invasion of Italy; but that is all the luck they had. They were shortly murdered by the Praetorian Guard, who insisted on their own nominee Gordianus III (*ca.* A.D. 224–244) as sole Emperor. He was about fifteen at the time. The year 238 alone had seen six claimants to the throne.

The young Gordian, with the aid of his father-in-law, Timesitheus, a praetorian prefect who died in 243, was successful against the Goths and the Persians, but was eliminated in an uprising led by an officer, Marcus Julius Philippus, known as Philip the Arabian. It was this man—curiously enough, given his ancestry—who was destined to preside in A.D. 248 over the celebration of the one thousandth anniversary of the founding of Rome.

Philip's peace with the Persians was not in Rome's interest, and it did not help his popularity, which remained low at Rome in any case. His reign was cut short by the troops along the Danube, who saluted their commander Gaius Traianus Decius (A.D. 201–251) and, according to tradition, forced him somewhat reluctantly to invade Italy. Philip was killed at a battle near Verona in 249. However, this internal quarrel had left the frontier exposed and had given the Goths an opportunity to invade the Empire. Decius was killed in 251 during the fight to repel them. His aide and successor Gaius Trebonianus Gallus (*ca.* A.D. 205–*ca.* 253), who followed him, lasted two years before being murdered by his own troops.

The army then chose Publius Licinius Valerianus, who, as if the law of averages demanded it, turned out to be an Emperor of superior talents. Seeing the wisdom of separate commanders for the western and eastern frontiers, he made his son Publius Gallienus a co-emperor in command of Europe, while he went to the East to deal with the Persians. In the West, the Alamanni had long been a problem along the Rhine, but now Gallienus had a new force to deal with. A powerful coalition of various elements of old tribes had come into being, the Franks, whose role in the future of Europe was destined to be the greatest of all those peoples whom

51. Valerian, kneeling before Shapur I, a rock-relief at Naqsh-i Rustam,
Iran. Photograph courtesy of William H. Peck.

the Romans called barbarians. In the East, Valerian was able to
drive the Persians under their Sassanid king, Shapur I (reigned
A.D. 241–272), out of Syria. Valerian then lost a battle at Edessa
and later, during negotiations, was taken captive. He was still in
captivity when he died about A.D. 260.

Gallienus ruled alone after his father was captured, or it
might be better to say he had hoped to. There were more contenders for power during his reign than at any other time, although not all of the officers hailed by their troops were grateful
for the honor, considering the risk. The man who was most successful, Marcus Latinius Postumus, carved out a small empire of
his own, including Gaul, Spain, and Britain. It was fortunate for
him that Gallienus faced too many emergencies in the East to be
able to deal with one in the West. Postumus cut his ties to Rome
by setting up a Senate for his *imperium Galliarum*. By this time, the

Franks had securely settled themselves in parts of Gaul and Spain. The new regime was kept busy trying to prevent other German tribes from following their example. By confining his efforts to a smaller area, Postumus succeeded in establishing order in his realm until he was himself cut down in A.D. 268 by his own soldiers. There followed a succession of claimants to power—a Gallic edition of the old story known so well at Rome.

For Gallienus, try as he would, nothing seemed to work. Beset by numerous challengers, he saw a need for changes in the officer corps. Too many provincial commanders were desk men lacking solid military experience, who carried the politics of the Senate into the field and allowed themselves to be misled by the whims and ambitions of their soldiers. Gallienus sought to recruit a more professional staff, particularly from the equestrian middle class; but in assembling a superior group of officers, he surrounded himself with men who ultimately decided they could manage better without him. In A.D. 268, he was murdered as a result of a plot by the very men he had chosen for their talent. One of them, Marcus Aurelius Claudius (A.D. 214–270) became the new Emperor. He won the title "Gothicus" for maintaining Rome's hold on the Balkans, and putting an end to the Gothic threat, which had begun in 267 with a wholesale invasion of this area. Gallienus had scored a great victory over the Goths at Naissus (modern Nish) in Upper Moesia, a province south of the Danube, but he was unable to do more because of a rebellious officer, Aureolus, who threatened his authority in Italy. He succeeded in defeating his enemy, but was then killed by his friends. Claudius II, after pacifying the areas which the Goths had overrun in the Balkans, allowed some Goths to settle where there was available land, for instance in Thrace and Macedonia. Thus, gradually, during the middle years of the third century, barbarians moved into the Empire, both in the East and the West. During this same period, Saxons were crossing the North Sea to Britain.

In the third century, the Empire was the land of promise for the hungry barbarians without property, who lived beyond the frontier. These were not simply marauding tribes moving restlessly from place to place looking for booty. The Germans were now used to a settled life of farming. What they wanted was land. But the Romans never had a policy of immigration. The provincials, long since Romanized with cities and a relatively stable commercial life, feared the consequences of allowing these less advantaged people to cross the border. By comparison, in the twentieth century, the peaceful tide of immigrants to the United States from Europe, which reached a million a year in the period 1900 to 1914, was a miracle made possible, in part, by an industrialization unknown in ancient times.

At Rome, the decline in influence of the Old Roman patrician class had coincided with the emergence of the non-Italian provincials, Spaniards, Syrians, and Libyans, for instance. They became a new force in the government, particularly in the army. Roman society as Augustus knew it was disappearing long before the arrival of the northern peoples in any great numbers. Before the third century the Romans had hired German tribesmen from time to time, particularly for military service. Even Julius Caesar had used them in an emergency. The arrival of hundreds of families coming bag and baggage, like the Franks and the Goths, presented a new problem in the third century. While these newcomers had had contacts with the skills and products of Roman civilization before their arrival and were further Romanized once inside, they were not subject to modern inducements to assimilation. These new people became the nuclei from which separate barbarian kingdoms gradually emerged. In the fifth century A.D., when the shell of the western half of the Roman Empire cracked, disintegrated, and disappeared, new kingdoms were already there, as indeed they had been for a long time. That is why talking about the fall of the Roman Empire as though it were a single event makes little sense. It was a process, in which there were periods of calm, order, and retrenchment, but overall a drift toward dissolution, best pictured, perhaps, by a graph with minor spurts upward and a few long plateaus but gradually a downward trend.

In the third century, besides the invasions, another enemy was disease. Sporadic epidemics, which had been a serious problem since the time of Marcus Aurelius, continued to decimate the army camps, and even reached the tents of the mighty. Claudius Gothicus died at Sirmium during a plague in A.D. 270.

The man who replaced Claudius was Lucius Domitius Aurelianus (*ca.* A.D. 212–275), another of the Illyrian conspirators who had killed Gallienus. With great energy, strict discipline, and a willingness to take some risks, he was able to put the Empire back together again and provide one of those plateaus mentioned above. Before attempting to recover the western provinces which had seceded under Postumus, it was necessary to stabilize the eastern front. There the Persian thrust toward the Mediterranean had been blunted by the counteroperations of the powerful city of Palmyra, situated in an oasis which dominated the region between Syria and Babylonia. In an age of caravans, this great trading city had strong ties to Antioch, a major center of Graeco-Roman culture, and its educated class had become Romanized, as had the Syrians. Palmyra had been a colony of Rome for a long time before her commercial life began to be affected by the resurgence of Persian power in the Near East. In 260, forces under the command of Septimius Odaenathus were successful in distracting the Persians and relieving the pressure on Rome's eastern provinces. Gallienus, in return, recognized Odaenathus as the king of Palmyra and gave him charge over Rome's eastern defenses. When Odaenathus died about six years later, his ambitious and beautiful widow, Zenobia, ruled Palmyra, although the title passed to an infant son, Vaballathus. Rather than remain dependent on the Roman Emperor, Zenobia began to play the Persians off against him. She did not expect Aurelian to lead an army across the desert. Yet, with a daring reminiscent of Rome's old heroes, he did just that and put Palmyra under siege. Zenobia was captured when she left the city in search of Persian help. She later walked as a prisoner in Aurelian's triumph, but was treated respectfully and managed to survive. Palmyra did not. In A.D. 273, when Aurelian heard that the soldiers whom he had stationed there had been murdered, he returned and laid in ruins this city, which by one account had been built by Solomon. Today, there is only the tiny village of Tadmor at the site of the once thriving Palmyra, which had dominated the trade route from Egypt to the Persian Gulf.

In Europe, the elderly Gaius Pius Tetricus reigned as Emperor over the domain Postumus had established. He was, however, unwilling to risk much to maintain himself. His soldiers were willing to fight, but he soon gave up and eventually walked with Zenobia in Aurelian's triumph in Rome. The celebration had a special significance, for the Empire had been reunited. Aurelian took the grandiose title *Restitutor Orbis,* Restorer of the World. The inscription appeared on his coins, but he was not deceived by his own propaganda. During his reign there began the construction of a great wall to protect Rome, twenty feet high, twelve feet thick, and twelve miles in length, long sections of which are still to be seen. For some time there had been serious fears that the city itself was in danger of attack by the barbarians, who were making increasingly deep penetrations toward the south. By this time, a large band of Vandals had crossed the Danube and commenced to earn for themselves their unsavory reputation. Aurelian defeated them decisively in Pannonia and drove them off, but their distant descendants would one day breach the wall he had begun to build for Rome. The Emperor might have gone on to other victories over the Persians had he not been cut down in A.D. 275 by his staff officers in a plot according to a now familiar scenario.

In the last decade of the Principate, A.D. 275 to 285, there were six emperors: Marcus Claudius Tacitus, Marcus Annius Florianus, Marcus Aurelius Probus, Marcus Aurelius Carus, and his sons, Marcus Aurelius Numerianus and Marcus Aurelius Carinus. Under Tacitus, the Senate was treated respectfully and for a brief time regained part of its old status, but Carus did not even bother to seek its recognition. He accepted the army's support as the final word. Thus, the Senate's traditional right to confer legitimacy on an Emperor was allowed to lapse. That was merely the latest in a series of setbacks for the one remaining institution of the Republic which had retained any viability at all. Gradually, because of the recurring invasions, the Senate's appointees had been replaced by military men serving the Emperor. In that respect too, the partnership which Augustus had established for the management of the Empire thus came to an end. If followed that the Senate lost its chief source of funds. Aurelian took away even its right to issue coins.

A battle in A.D. 285 between the forces loyal to Carus' elder son Carinus and the praetorian prefect Gaius Aurelius Diocletianus was like all the earlier contests between contenders since A.D. 69. But this time the victorious Diocletian not only emerged as Emperor but proceeded to put the capstone on a governmental structure which had for a long time been taking shape inside the moribund Principate. Now the ruler was an unrestricted autocrat in the old Oriental-Hellenistic style of kingship, having more in common with the earlier pharaohs of Egypt than with Augustus.

Christianity in the Third Century A.D.

Throughout the third century, Christianity remained on trial. Persecutions were infrequent; but, technically speaking, the Christians continued to practice their faith outside the law, and were liable to suppression at any time, either by local officials or by imperial order. The policy toward the Christians varied with the attitudes of individual emperors. Under Decius at mid-century, for the first time an edict was issued calling for an empire-wide effort to stamp out the Christian communities. All citizens were required to prove, if asked, that they had poured a libation before the images of the gods of the state. It was a simple ritual, and certificates could be obtained from a temple showing that the act had been performed before witnesses. Suspected persons were well advised to carry such a paper with them so long as feelings ran high in their particular community. Papyrus documents preserved in Egypt dating to Decius' reign reveal the perfunctory character of these forms:

> To those superintending the sacrifices of the village of Theadelphia, from Aurelia Bellias, daughter of Peteres, and her daughter Capinis. We have sacrificed to the gods all along, and now in your presence according to orders I poured a libation and sacrificed and tasted of the sacred offerings, and I request you to subscribe this for us. Farewell. (Signatures)

> We, Aurelius Serenus and Aurelius Hermas, saw you sacrificing. Signed by me, Hermas. Year 1 of the Emperor Caesar Gaius Messius Quintus Trajanus Decius Pius Felix Augustus, Payni 27. (Lewis and Reinhold, Vol. II, pp. 596–97)

Valerian also ordered a widespread persecution of the Christians beginning in A.D. 257, with the same result as in the past. Certain bold Christians who heroically proclaimed their faith, particularly writers or those in the clergy, were martyred. Others preferred to abjure Christianity for the time being and managed to survive. But the majority of Christians, being anonymous people in the lower classes, simply went underground until the present danger passed. It did under Valerian's son Gallienus, who showed remarkable leniency in allowing the Christians to hold open meetings in buildings of their own and to bury their dead in their own cemeteries, in their own way. His edict in A.D. 260, which gave toleration, if not legal recognition, to the Christians, meant a respite from persecution of almost forty years. The next attempt at suppression—the last serious threat—began under Diocletian in 299. When that effort failed, it was only a few years before Christianity would finally be recognized as a legal religion. By this time the Church was already a well-established institution. In fact, as early as Trajan's reign, in the early second century, there had developed a hierarchy of command. Two bishops, Saints Ignatius of Antioch and Simeon of Jerusalem, were martyred at that time.

Earlier, in the first century A.D., fledgling Christian flocks were guided by elders like those Saint Paul talks about in his letters, some of whom he appointed. These men were also called presbyters, and gradually a rather informal office evolved into that of a priest, as the clergy became more clearly separated from the laity. Soon a bishop (*episcopos,* or overseer) emerged as the chief official in a given area with several congregations under his jurisdiction. Today, in Christian churches, bishops still preside over dioceses. The term was long used by the Romans to designate an administrative unit.

It was natural for the Christians to seek a greater solidarity and strength by joining in larger groups. By the third century, the churches of a given province were subject to the metropolitan bishop who lived in the principal city. Certain of these bishops could claim that the see they occupied had been founded by an apostle, and eventually those who presided in Alexandria, Jerusalem, Antioch, Constantinople, and Rome took the title of patriarch. The bishops of Rome contended as early as the second century that because their apostolic founder was Saint Peter they should be given precedence. The Eastern bishops did not agree. The controversy has a special interest because it is one dispute which arose in ancient times that is still unresolved.

XVIII
*Could the Old Problems
Be Solved?*

That Diocletian reigned for twenty years, A.D. 285 to 305, was in itself exceptional. His eventual resignation was even more so. Yet it was part of a plan for achieving an orderly succession and preventing further civil wars. In 286, he appointed Marcus Aurelius Valerius Maximianus, actually a better general than he was, to be his partner. In 293, two younger men, also of proven military ability, were given a share of power which marked them as being next in line. Diocletian and Maximian each held the title of Augustus. Their subordinates, with the rank of Caesar, were Flavius Valerius Constantius, known as Constantius Chlorus, "the pale," and Galerius Valerius Maximianus. The Caesars were both adopted sons and also became sons-in-law, for Galerius married Diocletian's daughter and Constantius married Maximian's. The Empire was thus to be ruled by four men instead of one, each in charge of a given area. That meant a stronger system of defense. Although "divine" edicts were signed by the four members of the Tetrarchy, Diocletian was the guiding hand. His reign began the period of Roman history known as the Autocracy (A.D. 285–476).

From the outset of the Empire, the authoritarian position of

489

52. Tetrarchs, St. Mark's Basilica, Venice. Photograph courtesy of F. Warren Peters.

the emperors had never been far from the surface. Three centuries earlier, Augustus had walked the streets of Rome behaving like any other magistrate, in keeping with the fiction that the Republic had been restored. He and certain of his successors, Claudius for instance, were anxious for the cooperation and support of the Senate. Yet the overriding power, which every emperor did in fact possess, made tyrannical abuses possible under Tiberius, Caligula and Nero. Obviously, the temperament and talent of a given emperor influenced the course of events. But regardless of who the emperor happened to be, the old republican institutions gradually eroded. First, the assemblies ceased to function, and then the magistrates began to lose their importance. Only the Senate retained any vitality. During the reign of Alexander Severus, his grandmother and mother found that body a more reliable ally than the army. Consequently, some semblance of constitutionality remained even as late as the Severan dynasty. The ties to the past were not yet entirely broken. By convention, then, the

Principate, in which the emperor was theoretically the top man in a highly bureaucratic system, did not end until A.D. 285. But earlier, Aurelian's coins had carried the inscription *Dominus et Deus Natus,* "Born Lord and God." That announcement showed that the Principate was disappearing. Suffice it to say that by Diocletian's day it was gone.

Aurelian may have called himself a god, but Diocletian began to act like one. Actually, he claimed only to have been the choice of Jupiter and thereby to be ruling as the god's agent. Calling down heaven to support some form of earthly rule was of course a very old device. The divine rulers of the Ptolemaic kingdom in Egypt, 323 to 30 B.C., and the Seleucid Empire, based in Syria, 312 to 64 B.C., were only following the example of Alexander the Great, who had declared himself Pharaoh, that is, a god, in Egypt.

In ancient times, the line between the human and the divine was shaded by myth and superstition. A ruler who was also a god was presumably beyond criticism. Such a power motif was still evident in early modern times. The divine-right kings were believed to have been selected by God to rule, at least until more enlightened men began to question why so many foolish ones had been chosen.

A divine ruler of the ancient world, who was worshipped by diverse peoples, was his own source of unity. That was an advantage in the numerous eastern territories which the Seleucids inherited from Alexander. The same practice would be useful to the Roman emperors. During the Republic, certain prominent generals had been deified, but only locally, as for example, in Greece. Augustus had refused to let deification interfere with his magisterial posture in Italy, but did allow the cult of Roma and Augustus to flourish in the provinces, where it would provide men of different backgrounds with a common object of loyalty. Moreover, deposed chieftains could be given a form of patronage by appointment as priests in a local cult. The arrangement, however, was a matter of expediency, and the worship of Augustus in the provinces did not impair the modesty he affected in Rome. By contrast, Diocletian purposely set about creating an aura about himself and his court. Although a stern and sensible man, he was yet willing to wear garments of gold reminiscent of the gaudy costumes worn by the foppish Nero. The diadem on his head was also for show. The splendor of his dress and the use of elaborate ceremonials served to create a distinct gulf between him and his subjects. Those admitted to his presence were required to prostrate themselves. Diocletian was to be viewed with reverence, and above all he was to be obeyed.

To mention Augustus in one sentence and Diocletian in the next is easy enough to do, but it should be emphasized that there were three centuries dividing them. During that time, each succeeding generation had grown more accustomed to accepting the will of the emperor and his chosen officials. By the time Diocletian assumed "sacred" power, the Roman mentality had already become subservient, and indeed had been so long enough to make such a state of mind appear natural. In other words, circumstances alter what has been called the "collective mentality" of a people. It is tempting to illustrate this by noting the shift in attitudes in the United States in the course of a single century. The contrast would be between the rural, small-town view of the role of government in the lives of its citizens in the mid-nineteenth century and the degree of interference commonly accepted in the industrialized, urban society of the mid-twentieth century.

In Diocletian's time it was not a rapidly expanding economy which created new problems calling for new plans, but just the opposite. The barbarian invasions and internal disorders of the previous fifty years had seriously disrupted the commerce of the Empire. Repeated devaluations of the currency by one emperor after another had produced uncertainty and fear. Diocletian sought to stabilize a shaky economy by a whole series of measures. The most famous was his Edict on Prices of 301, designed to curtail a runaway inflation. The edict began with an indignant attack on greedy tradesmen who kept raising their prices and acquiring exorbitant profits without any concern for the public welfare. The government was particularly worried about its soldiers, whose pay bought less and less as time passed. Workers and farmers, whose income did not vary from year to year, were also at the mercy of profiteers, described as "uncontrolled madmen." By placing the blame on those who were becoming rich at other people's expense, Diocletian wrapped his program in moral righteousness, as economic planners are at times inclined to do. What he said was true, but it was not the whole truth. His own depreciation of the coinage and the recent political upheavals which had reduced productivity were both reasons for the continuing inflation.

Since Diocletian knew that prices would vary according to circumstances in different provinces, the edict did not fix the price of a given item. It simply listed maximum prices for items sold throughout the Empire. Anybody who asked for more than the set amount was liable to be executed. There is no mistaking the tone: "For rarely is a situation beneficial to humanity accepted spontaneously; experience teaches that fear is the most effective regulator and guide for the performance of duty" (Lewis and Reinhold, Vol. II, p. 466).

Earlier, it was mentioned that Diocletian's regime was more like that of a pharaoh in ancient Egypt than of Augustus. Certainly his tax system was reminiscent of the pharaonic genius for squeezing the maximum amount of income from the land. Diocletian demanded the state's share in kind, rather than in his own uncertain coinage. The assessment against every property owner throughout the Empire, including Italy, was based on the amount of land he held, plus the number of peasant tenants, plus the amount of livestock. Allowances were made for the fact that some areas were not as productive as others; one man might owe as much for five acres of good fertile land as another would for ten acres of rocky soil. Since part of the government's income came from counting the persons working a given piece of property—and they were necessary for production besides—it was important to keep people where they were. Thus, the hereditary status of the farm worker resulted from a series of contingencies. First, the emperors had ever increasing needs for more funds. Each of them, of course, inherited the dole to keep the needy from starving, and the tradition of providing large-scale entertainments. The oriental-style court established by Diocletian, with its hierarchy of specialized attendants, was a financial burden known earlier, but only occasionally, under emperors like Nero. The enormous palace Diocletian built at Salonae in Dalmatia was that much more expense. Besides, there were the costs of large-scale public buildings. Indeed, it might be said that the unwarranted extravagances which Trajan had tried to keep from bankrupting the municipalities were now threatening the imperial treasury. But the greatest expense of all came from an expanding civil and military bureaucracy.

Diocletian divided the frontier provinces into smaller units, which increased the efficiency of the defensive system while decreasing the power of possibly ambitious local commanders. The

result, however, was to add many more officials to the government payroll. Above all, there was the rising cost of an army
which kept growing in size while declining in efficiency. The
steady decline in Roman manpower, primarily because of warfare
and disease, had made it necessary since Marcus Aurelius' time to
hire barbarians in increasing numbers. Some of them were actually captives. Others were volunteers who crossed the border
alone, or came in groups, to earn a living fighting their former
neighbors. The so-called barbarizing of the army, so pronounced
during the fourth century, was not, however, necessarily the
prime reason for its decline in quality. Actually, some of the
barbarian recruits rose though the ranks to become officers. A
more telling cause of weakness was the decision to conscript the
peasantry by demanding a quota for the army from the great
landowners. There was no reason to expect that they would send
their best workers. Consequently, the army's ranks were increased, to little purpose, by many unhealthy, and certainly unhappy, draftees. So, it was as a result of the government's own
policies that the greater need for income arose. That in turn meant
more state regulation of the economy in order to keep the productivity high enough to support the required taxes. Under the circumstances, fixing persons in their occupations seemed at the time
a natural enough solution. Later, Diocletian's famous successor,
Constantine, required the sons of soldiers to enter the army. He
was simply following a standard practice of maintaining stability
by eliminating choices.

Still, the developments under Diocletian and Constantine
did not produce a thoroughgoing system of state socialism with
individual initiative entirely curtailed. Rather, it was a matter of
an autocratic state's skimming money, goods, and services from
the top and letting the large landowner or enterprising business-
man operate as he always had with what was left. The indulgence
of these two influential groups was part of another problem. In
practice, the system as it evolved tended to accentuate the differences between classes. Those with the lowest income were im-
mobilized by being required to stay in their jobs, no matter how
they fared. The middle class was particularly hard hit by the new
tax system. Only those who had been prospering all along, the
large landowners and high officials, managed to continue doing
so, either by a privileged status which excused them from taxes or

because they knew how to avoid them. The inequities and particularly the plight of the middle class boded ill.

If Diocletian's efforts to achieve economic stability were not entirely successful, it was because there were so many human propensities to deal with. The unscrupulous found crafty ways to avoid the intent of his laws. There is nothing new about tax loopholes or outright cheating. The very stringency of Diocletian's punishments for tax evasion show how serious a problem it was. His maximum price list eventually went by the board, partly because of the difficulty of enforcement. Nevertheless, he had restored a sufficient degree of public confidence to provide the Empire with at least a plateau of economic health which extended through the long reign of Constantine, although Constantine only managed to achieve sole power after another round of costly battles among contending generals.

When Diocletian, in failing health, retired in 305, he insisted that Maximian also step down to make room for Constantius and Galerius. Two new Caesars, Severus and Valerius Maximinus Daia, were duly chosen, but the honor was not worth much. When Constantius died in 306, the troops in the West favored his young son Constantine to succeed him, and Constantine, battle-tried, was ready. But Galerius was not ready for him and elevated Severus to be the new Augustus. For the time being, however, it was Constantine's good fortune that Maximian had decided to try a comeback. That meant trouble not only with Severus, whom Maximian defeated and may have executed in 307, but with Maximian's own son Maxentius, who by this time had a sizeable following of his own. This rivalry forced Maximian into Constantine's camp, where his prestige was useful for a time, as was his daughter Fausta, whose marriage to Constantine helped seal the alliance. It did not prevent Maximian from being caught up in a conspiracy against his young son-in-law, who now eliminated the old general who had previously eliminated his rival Severus. That left Constantine facing Maxentius. Their showdown battle is one of history's most storied events. It took place in A.D. 312 at the Milvian Bridge over the Tiber near Rome. On this occasion, a Roman army carried Christian symbols for the first time. The shields of Constantine's soldiers bore the Greek letters *chi* and *rho*, which begin the name *Christos* and so evoked the blessing and aid of the Christian God. There is no reason to believe that Constantine had by this time accepted the Christian belief in only one God. At the time, any god who could help him was welcome. Yet he must surely have been impressed by the survival of Christianity and by its widespread acceptance among all classes despite its former reputation. His sensational victory over Maxentius' forces convinced him that the Christian God did indeed possess great power. In the ancient world, that was the kind of god to support. Putting spirit and doctrine aside, the battle of the Milvian Bridge was also a great victory for Christianity.

In the meantime, after Severus' death, Galerius had next selected Valerius Licinianus Licinius to be the new Augustus. Again the appointment was only a license to fight for the title. After Galerius died in 311, Licinius, temporarily allied with Constantine, became embroiled with Daia, one of the Caesars appointed when Diocletian resigned. The death of Daia in 313 left Licinius in full command of the East. Constantine already controlled the West. In the following year, 314, Constantine won a battle with Licinius in Pannonia, which only served to define more sharply their areas of power.

Licinius became Constantine's brother-in-law, and they cooperated in dealing with common problems, although uneasiness grew between them in the years to come. After nine years, their rivalry again led to open warfare. Again Constantine was victorious. Licinius quit his claim to the Empire shortly after this defeat and gave himself up to Constantine, expecting that he could at least keep his life. That was taken too.

Constantine ruled the Roman Empire alone between 323 and 337, when he died. As usual, he had relied on the army as his chief support. There was added for good measure the help of the Christian Church.

The decision on Christianity was the sharpest break which Constantine made with Diocletian. Otherwise their policies were much alike. Both showed a preference for the Eastern half of the Empire. At the time that Diocletian had made the allotment of territories among the members of the Tetrarchy, he had taken the Eastern sector for himself and transferred the seat of his operations to Nicomedia in Bithynia. Shortly after becoming sole emperor, Constantine decided to build a new imperial palace at the site of the ancient Greek colony of Byzantium—and to build a new city to go with it. In 330, Constantinople, a city named for himself,

53. Constantine, the remains of a 30-foot seated statue. Photograph courtesy of Aldo Reale.

was dedicated, and begun a period of over eleven hundred years as an imperial capital and one of the great cities of Christendom. Today, as Istanbul, it is a center of Moslem culture and Turkish commerce and the seat of a patriarch of the Greek Orthodox Church.

Constantine enhanced his glory by having a city of his own, but the decision involved some very practical considerations. The Empire had for some time an East-West axis, and the new city on the Bosporus was more central to that arrangement than was Rome. The region was also less vulnerable to the barbarian threats than was Italy. Rome was still the mother city of the Empire;

history dictated that. But geography made Constantinople the *de facto* capital, and Constantine set up a new Senate there if only for appearance's sake. As in Rome, it consisted of an elite having wealth and prestige. The senators listened to whatever the Emperor had to say and praised him in any case.

Christianity under Constantine

Constantine and Licinius had for a time cooperated on a joint policy toward the Christians. Galerius had shown the way. Beginning in 311 the Christians were freed from the fear of persecution. In that year, Galerius declared in his Edict of Toleration that they could practice their religion unmolested and could restore churches damaged in the persecutions under Diocletian. In 313, Constantine and Licinius appear to have agreed to recognize Christianity as a legal religion, a step beyond mere toleration. The decision came as a result of a meeting in Milan, but it is generally doubted that there was a formal edict. Rather, it appears that the two rulers reached an understanding which each communicated to his provincial governors. It included a decision to return confiscated property to the various Christian churches.

Constantine never ceased to be a strong supporter of Christian interests thereafter, but Licinius reneged on their agreement and actually began putting pressure on the Christians again as in the past. The reversal in his attitude did not help matters in their touchy relationship.

The Council of Nicaea

In the Gospel according to Saint John it was written that Jesus in reply to certain Jews who were questioning him said, "I and my Father are one" (John 10:30). The statement was blasphemous to his listeners and they hurled stones at him because "thou, being a man, makest thyself God" (John 10:33). The Jews, abhorring polytheism, had been bitterly opposed to the proclaimed divinity of the exalted rulers of Egypt and the Seleucid Empire. For the humble Jesus to declare himself "one" with God was equally repulsive. The earliest Christians, on the other hand, although also dedicated monotheists, were unbothered by the implications of that Gospel declaration. They were mostly unlettered believers who did not speculate about philosophical questions, much less the possible meanings of the sayings of Jesus. Theirs was a Christianity of daily living, faith, hope, and charity—a religion unencumbered by the intricacies of theology. The sum of faith was to love your neighbor as yourself. There was no difference of opinion about that. Only gradually did Christianity begin to appeal to more educated persons, some of them Stoics, already committed to the ideals of the simple life and concerned about the welfare of their fellow man. Among the converts, however, were able writers and orators who used their talents in defense of a beleaguered Christianity. The apologists for the new faith vigorously defended its teachings against its learned critics. In short, they were writing, talking, and so arguing *about* Christianity as well as, presumably, practicing its simple precepts.

Justin Martyr, who considered himself a philosopher, had investigated Stoicism, Pythagoreanism, and Platonism before turning to Christianity. He was therefore well prepared to challenge other thinkers on their own ground and at their own level. In the process he stressed certain ideas which would appeal to the philosophically minded. For instance, Christ was also the Logos, equated with the divine reason which the Stoics insisted ruled the world. But one of the strongest arguments for Christianity was not intellectual at all. Its truth was manifest in the goodness and purity of the Christians themselves. In other words, Christianity could be justified on the practical grounds that it literally produced a better kind of man.

The apologists were especially anxious to have their message reach the Roman officialdom; certain of their writings were addressed to a particular emperor. For instance, *The Apology* of Aristides was dedicated to Antoninus Pius. At least one foreign ruler, Tiridates III (A.D. 261–317) of Armenia, was converted to Christianity before any Roman emperor decided to accept its blessings. Justin Martyr's *Dialogue with Trypho* was aimed at convincing Jews that their conversion to Christianity was their sole hope for salvation. In attempting to convert Jews and Gentiles as well, Justine stressed the claim that the prophecy of the Old Testament was fulfilled in Christianity.

Tatian, Athenagoras, and Theophilus, a bishop of Antioch, were among the other apologists of the second century whose works survive. They argued, like Justin, that the teachings of Christianity were very old, having been taught by the prophets, and so sought to counter the claim that their religion was only one more of the many cults which had recently sprung up in the Near East. For the most part, the writings of the apologists were in agreement with one another. Nevertheless, differences of opinion about how to interpret and defend Scripture were bound to arise. Divisions remained minimal as long as there was the greater need of unity during the nearly three hundred years that Christianity was considered illegal. The internal stability of the developing Church owed something to external enemies. Once, however, the Church was safe, in the early fourth century, the danger of a schism over doctrine became a reality. An educated and hierarchical clergy had by this time taken upon itself the task of interpreting Scripture to the faithful; yet they disagreed about what should be taught. For instance, what did Jesus mean when he said, "I and my Father are one"?

The belief that Christ was truly God was clearly espoused by Irenaeus, Apostle of the Gauls, a bishop of Lyon in the second half of the second century. In his work, *Against Heresies,* he argued that this doctrine was necessary for the redemption of men. It was only God who could bring about their salvation on earth: "Unless it had been God who had freely given salvation, we never could have possessed it securely. And unless man had been joined to God, he could never have become a partaker of incorruptibility." He also wrote: "That it should not be a mere man who should save us, nor (one) without flesh. . . . And that He should Himself become very man, visible. . . . That He is God, and that His advent was (to take place) in Bethlehem" (Roberts and Donaldson, Irenaeus, III. 18. 7, 20. 4). Irenaeus' writings echoed the letters of Ignatius, bishop of Antioch, who was martyred in Rome under Trajan. He too had spoken of Christ as God and of the "partaking of God" as necessary for salvation. At the same time in his letters he did not equate the Son of God and God the Father. Nor had the apologists like Justin Martyr taught such a doctrine. They taught that the Son of God was divine, as was commonly believed by the earliest Christians, but they viewed him as a separate being altogether. They did not believe that God himself had appeared on earth. It was only the Son, the Christ, who was born of a virgin, although Justin admitted that not all Christians in the second century accepted the tradition about Mary.

Irenaeus was said to have been martyred under Septimius Severus. Thereafter, some accepted his position; others rejected it, whether for intellectual reasons or simply because such a proposal went beyond their primarily ethical interests. The man whose name has been most identified with the opposition was the devout and scholarly Arius, a presbyter (from the Greek for "elder" whose function resembled that of a priest) in Alexandria. He owed much to his teacher, Lucian of Antioch, who had also opposed the idea that Christ was God. But Arius' fame resulted from a quarrel with Alexander, bishop of Alexandria, and therefore his superior. The bishop believed in the divinity of Christ; his conflict with Arius on this point became a focal point to all willing to take a stand publicly. The dispute was among the clergy. Arius did not really object to the faithful's worshipping Christ as a divine being, for that met the needs of their simple piety. He accepted Christ as a revelation or manifestation of God, but the laity were not much interested in the theological difference.

What Arius opposed was a formal declaration that the Son and the Father were the same God, or, to be more exact theologically, that they were of the same "essence." The most vocal opposition to his position came from Athanasius, a deacon in the Alexandrian Church who supported Bishop Alexander. To most churchmen the alarming animosity generated by this conflict, so un-Christian in character, was of greater moment than the issue itself. This moderate group, led by Eusebius, bishop of Caesarea, sought a formula which would be acceptable to both sides and bind the wounds. Constantine strongly supported the moderate majority, for the Church torn by doctrinal disputation was of little use to him politically, and that was his major concern. That the controversy had gotten out of hand was evident when in 321 a synod sponsored by the bishop of Alexandria removed Arius from his position and excommunicated him. The bishops of Egypt and Libya were thus on record against the Arian doctrine, but a different group of bishops convened in Nicomedia and supported Arius.

Constantine sent out a call for a general conference of bishops to convene at Nicaea (today, the small Turkish town of Iznik), and there they met in June, 325. Because of the distance, not only geographical but also to some degree emotional, most of the Western bishops did not come. Among those absent at this first council, interestingly enough, was the bishop of Rome. However, observers were sent to report. The council of 318 bishops was therefore overwhelmingly dominated by Eastern churchmen, whose penchant for theological debate had a Greek flavor as against the Western preoccupation with Church law and organization. There were administrative matters before the Council of Nicaea, but the crucial question was the debate over the relationship of the Son and the Father. Arius and Athanasius were present to support their positions, but since neither was a bishop they were not actually voting members of the assembly. Presiding was Emperor Constantine, who did not countenance any institution of the Empire as independent of his authority. Eusebius, in his *Life of Constantine,* describes the Emperor's arrival on the scene as "dazzling the eyes of all with the splendor of his purple robe and sparkling with fiery rays, as it were, adorned for the occasion as he was with an extraordinary splendor of gold and jewels" (Lewis and Reinhold, Vol. II, p. 610).

Eastern Christianity never recovered from that glorious entrance. Constantine's presence at Nicaea set the pattern for church and state relations in the long history of the Byzantine or Eastern Roman Empire. The two institutions were inextricably bound together with the Emperor acting as a kind of guardian, who might appoint and depose patriarchs, but did not assume any spiritual powers akin to those of the Roman pope. So it is today in those countries where the Greek Orthodox Church is predominant. On the other hand, the collapse of the Western half of the Empire and the disappearance of the imperial authority presented the bishop of Rome with the opportunity to assume temporal power and in fact to rule the city. Thus, a very different set of circumstances in the West gave the Latin Church an independence which in medieval times created a rivalry with emperors and kings.

Eusebius in his writings found it hard to mention Constantine without describing him as "most pious." His *Life of Constantine* was so patently flattering as to contribute little to our knowledge of what the Emperor was really like. However, there is sufficient evidence elsewhere to show that he was not the saintly character of Eusebius' rhapsody. Constantine's role at Nicaea, the glitter aside, was like that of a political boss who insists that factions in a party agree on a platform agreeable to as many as possible. What happened was that the Arian position was first voted down. Then Eusebius offered a moderate creed which was amended to suit those supporting Athanasius. The result was a compromise which both the moderates and anti-Arian forces could live with. The Nicene Creed, which proclaimed the Trinity, was actually signed by all except two dissenting bishops:

> We believe in one God, the Father Almighty, maker of all things visible and invisible; and in one Lord Jesus Christ, the Son of God, the only-begotten of his Father, of the substance of the Father, God of God, Light of Light, very God of very God, begotten, not made, being of one substance with the Father. By whom all things were made, both which be in heaven and in earth. Who for us men and for our salvation came down (from heaven) and was incarnate and was made man. He suffered and the third day he rose again, and ascended into heaven. And he shall come again to judge both the quick and the dead. And (we believe) in the Holy Ghost. And whosoever shall say that there was a time when the Son of God was not, or that before he was begotten he was not, or that he was made of things that were not, or that he is of a different substance or essence (from the Father) or that he is a creature, or subject to change or conversion—all that so say, the Catholic and Apostolic Church anathematizes them. (Percival, p. 3)

The Nicene Creed as it is known today differs somewhat from the original version because of new wording which crept in and became accepted, even if never adopted at a formal council.

The two bishops who refused to bow to the agreement which Constantine, catching the spirit of the times, called "the will of God," were excommunicated. Arius, the arch-offender, was sent to Illyria. Now a Christian must offer proof of his orthodoxy. Even as in the past a pagan in good standing was one who poured oil before the images of the deified Caesars, so now a Christian must sign a creed. The genuine Christians were presumably those who accepted the Trinitarian principle. The Arians were heretics. Thus, the Council of Nicaea marked the culmination of tendencies which had been giving Christianity a different direction for over a century. There had been a gradual emphasis on doctrinal questions over the necessity for a simple and quiet life. An elaborate Church organization and an increasingly complex ceremonial were part of an institution quite foreign to anything in Jesus' simple ministry. Now the noisy and bitter disputes over the relationship of the Son and the Father resulted in behavior altogether divorced from the simple tenets of love and forgiveness taught by the Son under discussion. Again, as history so often shows, success brought problems for Christianity. The

Christian Church had survived its long struggle against the world only to succumb to many of the same shortcomings which the earliest Christians strove so hard to escape.

Over the years, the gradual shift away from the insistence on how a Christian must behave to the less burdensome commitment to what a Christian must believe facilitated the rapid growth of Christianity. In the first century, the Christians, few in number, were a "peculiar" people cut off from others by their determination to "come out from the world and be separate." By the fourth century, not only were the dangers gone, but so was the former abhorrence of wealth or possessions. Now anybody who accepted the doctrine could be a Christian, because the Christians behaved like everybody else. Indeed, in the years ahead their persecution of the pagans and destruction of their temples would be no worse than what had once been done to them—it merely seemed worse because of what Christianity had once stood for. Perhaps the most startling development was that Constantine would one day be honored as a saint in the Greek churches of the East. The execution of Licinius could be justified on the grounds of a plot, but Constantine was also responsible for the murder of members of his own family, including his son Crispus and his wife Fausta. Their condemnation for adultery may have been in keeping with Constantine's harsh penalties for sexual impropriety, but the same charge had been used by the worst emperors as an excuse for getting rid of unwanted relatives. In any event, Constantine's severity was worse than Augustus', and certainly lacking in Christian mercy or forgiveness.

Centuries earlier, Alexander the Great, also noted for a bad temper, had been deified, though he was capable of killing one of his companions with his own hand. In other words, the old religions were used to bolster political power, not to mitigate its cruelty. Now that Constantine had seen the Church as a prop for his rule, he threw his full weight behind an effort to crush the wickedness which Christianity condemned. Lost in the process was the kind of compassion Jesus exhibited toward sinners. Even as Christianity was providing a profound civilizing influence on the throngs converted to its teachings, it was also being corrupted, in part, by the violent methods of the world it had supposedly won.

Constantine has often been called the first Christian emperor because he was, in fact, baptized. That the ceremony was not performed until his deathbed was not in itself unusual, for it was customary for men to exercise as late as possible the option which wiped out all previous sin. It is more significant, however, that Constantine did not seek to supplant the other religions of his time with Christianity. His practical inclination to use policies which worked meant an accommodation to the religious sensibilities of all of his subjects. He kept the title of *pontifex maximus* and all of the paraphernalia of the old state religion, including the sacred fire of Vesta. His promotion of Sunday as a day of worship without work could satisfy the votaries of the sun as easily as the believers in Christ. On the other hand, he made no concession whatsoever to the Christian condemnation of the atrocities which passed for sport in the arena. The gladiatorial games went on at Rome and were introduced at Constantinople, along with the grain dole, as part of what every large city, or at least capital, had a right to expect.

The Price of Security

Since republican times, private associations (*collegia*) had been organized by members of a trade or profession who joined together for social events and to protect common interests. For the very poor, including slaves, having a proper funeral was almost the only event they could afford to think about. They paid dues into their burial clubs, an insurance for being taken care of when the time came. The "good emperors," as might be expected, encouraged such associations as useful for the public welfare.

Beginning in the latter half of the second century A.D., about the time of Marcus Aurelius, worsening times created concern about the supply of goods and services required by Rome. Consequently, there began to be closer cooperation between the government and associations of bakers, meat sellers, etc. During the time of Alexander Severus the state took over those *collegia* considered essential to the life of Rome and the army. In effect, baking bread became a public duty. A baker was a public servant. The new obligation was alleviated by concessions on other duties or taxes, but the fact remained that a former entrepreneur was now working for the government. Later, under the Autocracy, membership in many associations had become hereditary by government order so as to insure a steady supply of craftsmen or tradesmen in businesses where state demands and regulations had discouraged initiative. A man could not leave his occupation and was required to apprentice his sons to the same work.

In the meantime, much of the rural work force of the Empire was gradually sliding into serfdom. As early as Commodus' reign in the late second century there had been concern about the future of the tenant farmers (*coloni*) of the great imperial estates. The superintendents of these lands were making an inordinate demand for labor from their tenants, and in 182 Commodus sought to put a stop to it. But during the tumultuous third century the "barracks room emperors" were too busy fighting each other to keep close supervision over imperial estates, let alone the vast landholdings of the very wealthy. In fact, while the number of imperial domains increased due to confiscations, some of the old ones dwindled in size. The latifundia, private holdings of the rich, expanded at the expense of neglected or devastated state properties and began to absorb the small farms of less fortunate neighbors. The best hope for protection in these dangerous times was to become a tenant farmer and work for a man who offered some kind of fortified refuge against brigands or barbarians.

Not all of the new tenants came from smaller farms. The deteriorating conditions in the cities, plus the oppressive tax obligations, prompted a migration back to the land. But few of those who left the city had the capital to begin anew on abandoned land, as the emperors from Septimius Severus onward hoped they would. Most became tenant farmers who began in debt on the imperial or the private estates. The relationship between the landowner and his tenant was more than a business arrangement. Circumstances made the tenant a ward. He was not only to be protected but also to be guaranteed justice in any dispute. Part of the growing independence of the wealthy landowners was derived from preempting the imperial court system. These powerful men set up local courts and dispensed justice as if ruling a small principality of their own. The need for a stable labor force on the land prompted them to insist upon contracts binding a tenant and his descendants to a given piece of property. The tenant farmer had little bargaining power, and in bad times there was much to gain from such a proposition. Still, it amounted to serfdom. In technical terms this meant that those who worked a piece of land no longer had the option of doing anything else. They were not themselves property, like slaves, but if the land was sold they went with it as part of the bargain.

The practice grew despite government objections. Even so, it had been legal since A.D. 247 to force a man to stay on his land until his tax arrears were paid, and in some cases that meant permanently. In addition, the government had given certain of the barbarians untilled land to cultivate and in return expected them to remain there. This condition contributed to an emerging society wherein people were fixed in their places, doing what they had always done. More significantly, the state came so to depend on the large landowners, especially for food supplies and taxes, that no serious efforts were made to stem the drift to serfdom. Moreover, many high officials in the bureaucracy were themselves benefiting from the new system.

Consequently, during the third and fourth centuries, the Roman free laborer lost his freedom and was confined to an estate which was becoming increasingly self-sufficient and much like the more isolated units which would in the Middle Ages be known as manors. Serfdom was well-established before Constantine came to power, and there was no turning back. Indeed, in his day it was legal, and thereafter it began to assume the time-honored status which made it appear so natural in the Middle Ages.

The distress of the middle class in the fourth century can be seen in the problems of city council (*curia*) members, the *curiales*. Traditionally, the members of this income bracket were the solid citizens of any town who possessed enough property to belong to the local senatorial order. The councilors were made responsible for the collection of taxes in their district and liable for any difference between the amount they took in and the total assessment owed to the imperial government. When the property qualification for this class was reduced to fifteen acres, there were men included who could not afford to bear any extra burden. In desperation many of them tried to get away, but Constantine made their status hereditary. Some of them with influential connections probably managed to escape into the bureaucracy or some other privileged haven, but most of the councilors were left in the unenviable position of being squeezed from above while trying to squeeze the poor below.

Thus it happens in history that free societies may attempt to solve their inevitable problems by returning to a more static, more structured condition, while tightly organized systems may

54. Mosaic from Carthage, showing a fortified villa surrounded by scenes of seasonal occupations. Courtesy of Musée du Bardo, Tunis.

look for solutions in the direction of more freedom. Neither can escape problems, and neither has any way to go except in the other direction. There was nothing about Diocletian's and Constantine's autocracy which committed it to failure. It actually succeeded in the East, where the Byzantine Empire continued as an autocratic state, highly bureaucratized and closely allied with the Christian Church. In the West, however, there was too much that went wrong for any simple, or single, explanation of the collapse.

The anxieties of the Roman world under Diocletian and Constantine were reflected in the landscape, as the memory of the quiet and security of the *Pax Romana* grew faint. Travelers set out from the walls of one city and looked forward to seeing those of the next. Soldiers lived in forts strung out along the frontiers. In times of emergency they would be supported by reserves stationed here and there in the Empire, ready to rush to whichever sector needed them. Still, the barbarians managed to break through and threaten the people dwelling in the countryside, whether in Britain, Gaul, or Italy. An army of 25,000 or so might not sound like much today, but these marauders could frighten people in a wide area before they were checked. A fortress style of architecture evolved from necessity. The great landowners built their villas with thicker walls and narrower windows than heretofore. The world was going inside and locking up.

XIX
The End of the Story

Constantine left the Empire to three sons, with two nephews in minor roles. In the thirteen years A.D. 337 to 350, everybody except the second eldest son Constantius II was eliminated in one way or another. The two nephews, Delmatius and Hannibalianus, originally assigned small domains in the East, were murdered almost immediately by the army. Since Constantius then ruled this region alone, his connivance in their deaths is assumed. The other two Augusti clashed in a battle in 340 because Constans resented his elder brother's assumption of preeminence. When Constantine II was killed at Aquileia, Constans became the sole ruler of the West. For ten years he held the enemy at bay along the frontier, but by this time there were barbarians in back of him too. One of them, Magnentius, who had risen from the ranks, led a mutiny which resulted in the death of Constans. Reminiscent of events in the mid-third century, Magnentius was hailed as Emperor by Constans' forces. He was, however, only one of three usurpers whom Constantius had to face. The other two, Nepontianus and Vetranio, were eliminated within a year. It was not until 353 that Magnentius, having been defeated twice, committed suicide.

A.D. 353 is the same year with which the extant eighteen

books of the history of Ammianus Marcellinus begin. The whole work by this Greek native of Antioch originally consisted of thirty-one books in Latin, which he published as a continuation of Tacitus' history, beginning with the reign of Nerva. What remains covers the twenty-five years from 353 to the death of Emperor Valens in 378.

Ammianus was a writer of little sophistication but great sincerity. "So far as I could investigate the truth, I have, after putting the various events in clear order, related what I myself was allowed to witness in the course of my life, or to learn by meticulous questioning of those directly concerned" (XV. 1. 1). He dressed up his text with imagery and frequent quotations from earlier writers and included many references to Greek history, especially to Herodotus. Sometimes he uses a passage from one of the writings of Cicero which has been lost and so preserves that much more of the great orator's sayings.

The more one reads Ammianus, the more likeable he becomes, although certain of his melodramatic devices are unintentionally amusing. In describing times of stress, often before a battle, he reports much gnashing of teeth either among the barbarians or the Romans or both. On one occasion an angry Emperor Julian is portrayed also grinding away. Since Ammianus was in military service, he was now and then, as he mentioned, an eyewitness to events—a rare contribution to the history of the Empire. Also, not being a Christian, he was able to give a rather objective, if not completely well-informed, view of the history of Christianity in the fourth century. His description of Constantius is candid. He said that the Emperor kept the "dignity of imperial majesty" by never wiping his nose or spitting in public. Constantius was careful about his appearance, always well shaven and well groomed. There was never any scandal about his private life. He lived simply and quietly, taking his principal relaxation in sports, although he did not look much like an athlete. His torso was very long and his legs exceptionally short. Those who knew him were alerted to his moods, particularly in times of stress, when his expressive eyes bulged from his head in a dramatic, even terrifying, manner.

Gallus

The available portion of Ammianus' history begins with a report on the activities of Gallus, one of Constantius' two surviving cousins. Gallus had been made Caesar by the Emperor in 351 and given charge of the Eastern sector. According to Ammianus, if there was anything good about him it was his looks, highlighted by his attractive golden hair. Otherwise, there was nothing to say except to recount his violent deeds. Specifically, he and his wife, Constantia, sister of the Emperor, were guilty of gross abuse of their power in capricious executions of persons unhappily caught in the web of intrigue at the court in Antioch, she being as blood-thirsty as he was.

Constantius, busy subduing the Alamanni, a confederation of Germanic tribes, who continued to attack Gaul along the frontier, heard reports of dissension and executions in Antioch. It was not, however, solely for this reason that he decided to eliminate the twenty-eight-year-old Gallus. After all, Constantius had himself been responsible for the cruel deaths of those who had supported Magnentius. It was rather that Gallus was an irresponsible Caesar with a "disordered mind."

In telling the story of Gallus' career and downfall, Ammianus interspersed several passages relating events elsewhere or offering some topical information as a means of diversion. He included accounts of the Isaurians, a restless people who occasionally left their homes in the mountains and raided the valleys and coast of southern Asia Minor. They were the reason travel was no longer as safe as it used to be in that part of the Empire. Small groups of them would set up roadblocks and rob unlucky wayfarers. Gallus finally had to send troops to clear out these people, who had successfully outwitted the local forces.

One of Ammianus' longer digressions was about life in Rome, where he spent most of the last ten years of his life. The date of his death is not certain, but he probably died after A.D. 393. He wrote his *History* in Rome; his friends there included some of the leading citizens of the day, including Symmachus, a highly respected stateman and spokesman for paganism, whose letters are a source for the period. Ammianus saw Rome as "declining into old age," having experienced a once glorious "youth and manhood." Constantinople had become the heart of the Empire. Ammianus' complaints about life in Rome echo, in part, those of writers and moralists in every age. There was too much concern with fine clothes and sumptuous banquets and not enough simple courage and virtue. It followed that "the few houses that were formerly famed for devotion to serious pursuits now teem with the sports of sluggish indolence. . . . In short, in place of the philosopher the singer is called in, and in place of the orator the teacher of stagecraft, and while the libraries are shut up forever like tombs, water-organs are manufactured and lyres as large as carriages, and flutes and instruments heavy for gesticulating actors" (XIV. 6. 18). If that was the condition of the better classes, what could be expected of the poor? Ammianus' picture is one of Hogarthian squalor, drunkenness, gambling, and fighting—sometimes all through the night. Almost everybody was addicted to chariot racing, thinking about it "from sunrise until evening, in sunshine and in rain." Ammianus concluded, "These and similar things prevent anything memorable or serious from being done in Rome" (XIV. 6. 26). Today, the intellectuals who grieve over Rome's decadence have much to say about soccer.

Ammianus' description of Rome provided an interlude from the monotonous record of wars, negotiations, and internal politics which occupied the Emperor and his officials. Elsewhere in his history, he included long geographical discussions covering the Eastern provinces, the Aegean and Black Sea areas, and the Persian domains. Some of his material is inaccurate, since it was based on faulty sources, but much of his information was firsthand. For instance, his account of Egypt, its great monuments and varied animal life, is a travelogue, for Ammianus had been there. His service as an aide to Ursicinus, a prominent cavalry officer, took him to various parts of the Empire. Other sections of Ammianus' work have to do with suggestions about the causes of earthquakes, plagues, eclipses, and rainbows. And, as Ammianus said after a digression, "I shall now resume the thread of my narrative."

The death of Gallus was followed by a ruthless purge of all those who had carried out his cruel orders. It was conducted by officials serving Constantius who, Ammianus said, were no better than the men they put to death. One of them was called "the Chain" because of his success in ensnaring others. Another was the so-called Count of Dreams, who reported to the Emperor whatever he heard that men had seen in their dreams. Given the superstitions of the Emperor, this could result in a serious charge against the dreamer. In a rare display of good humor, Ammianus slyly wrote: "Since rumor exaggerated these reports and gave them wide currency, people were so far from revealing their nightly visions, that on the contrary they would hardly admit in the presence of strangers that they had slept at all" (XV. 3. 6).

In addition to these internal affairs, Constantius was continually occupied with the Alamanni, who showed an equal facility for making and breaking peace treaties. He was also faced with a usurper, a Frankish officer, Silvanus, in 355. This man had been sent to Gaul at the head of an army to put an end to the "bitter massacres, pillage, and ravages of fire" in this region. While there, he became the victim of a plot by an enemy, who with clever forgeries sought to convince Constantius that Silvanus was a traitor. Fearing he would not receive a fair hearing, Silvanus proclaimed himself Emperor; whereupon an arrangement for his assassination in Cologne was carried out, ending the possibility of an invasion of Italy. Ammianus, who was among those sent to deal with Silvanus, wrote with sympathy of this officer's predicament, but was nevertheless loyal to his orders. He felt that what was done was necessary under the circumstances. As usual, there followed the elimination of all Silvanus' associates.

Julian

In early November, A.D. 355, Constantius decided to take his remaining cousin, Julian, "by the right hand" and present him to the army as a Caesar who would "share in pains and perils" (XV. 8. 4, 13). He then sent Julian to Gaul to deal with the continuing raids by the Germans, a task he no longer relished himself.

If there is a hero in Ammianus' history it is Julian. This twenty-four-year-old, fresh from his studies in the philosophical schools in Athens, took on a challenge which might have unnerved a much older and experienced man. He had been an avid student of philosophy, poetry, and history, but in Ammianus' opinion it was Julian's extraordinary character, not his education, which brought him to such a resounding success. Ammianus admitted in one place that his report of Julian was almost a "panegyric." He compared him to the best of the former emperors, in having "foresight" like Titus, "glorious" in war like Trajan, "mild as Antoninus Pius," and in his quest for truth a follower of Marcus Aurelius (XVI. 1. 3–4). And like those of Marcus, Julian's writings are a valuable source for his times.

Although Julian had been given strict training as a Christian, he publicly renounced his religion in A.D. 361. His conversion to paganism had been kept a secret for some time. The decision to renounce Christianity was all the more telling because of his intellectual standing and his reputation for virtue. Intensely curious and opinionated, Julian the Apostate comes alive in the pages of Ammianus. His vibrant personality showed in his eyes, "at once terrible and full of charm." He was of average height, with a sturdy build accentuated by his heavy neck and broad shoulders. His pronounced features did not blend into handsomeness; an angular nose contrasted with a rather voluptuous mouth, which was rarely closed, for Julian had much to say.

Before leaving for Gaul, Julian married Constantius' sister Helena; the bond was expected to bring them closer together, yet the Emperor's persistent suspicions, bordering on paranoia, prevented his wholehearted support of Julian. On the contrary, included in the young Caesar's retinue was at least one secret agent assigned to spy on him.

While successfully repelling the Alamanni and chasing them back into their own lands, Julian also made himself popular in Gaul by his just and merciful rule, including a reduction in taxes. He also ordered "that the powerful should not grasp the property of others, or those hold positions of authority whose private estates were being increased by public disasters" (XVIII. 1. 1). He was especially concerned about the quality of justice and that the necessary evidence substantiate any charge, for "Can anyone be proved innocent, if it be enough to have accused him?" (XVIII. 1. 4).

As early as 357, Julian's army first hailed him as Augustus, and so Imperator. Despite his vigorous refusal to accept the promotion and his efforts to restrain his soldiers from such outbursts, news of the event, or any of his successes for that matter, was disturbing to the ear of the proud Constantius. In fact, the Emperor was upset enough to release bulletins in which he placed himself in the heat of battle and gave himself credit for a victory which took place at a distance of "forty days' march" from where he was at the time.

In the meantime, Julian continued to pursue and punish the Alamanni and frequently to arrange the truces which allowed at least for temporary periods of peace. In Ammianus' opinion, Julian's sporadic war with the Alamanni could stand comparison with those against the Carthaginians and Teutones in earlier times. Julian and his generals also made short work of the roving bands of Franks who occasionally surprised them. Nevertheless, his reports of success to Constantius were ridiculed by persons at the court who "turned Julian's well-devised and successful achievements into mere mockery by endless silly jests of this sort: 'This fellow, a nanny-goat and no man, is getting insufferable with his victories,' jibing at him for being hairy, and calling him a 'chattering mole' and 'an ape in purple,' and 'a Greekish pedant,' and other names like these . . . railing at him as a lazy, timid, unpractical person, and one who embellished his ill success with fine words" (XVII. 11. 1).

In accordance with the tradition that a great general suffers the same hardships as his men, Ammianus credited Julian with toiling more strenuously than even the lowliest soldiers. Nevertheless, Julian did not escape their anger at times, especially if food was low and they were hungry. Then "resorting to outrageous threats, they assailed Julian with foul names and opprobrious language, calling him an Asiatic, a Greekling and a deceiver, and a fool with a show of wisdom" (XVII. 9. 3). Yet their anger toward Julian was usually short-lived and the desire to hail him as an Augustus remained strong. In 360, Constantius issued an order which provoked Julian's forces, particularly his Gallic followers, to rebellion. Certain legions were ordered to the Eastern front to face a new threat by the Persians, led by King Shapur II, called "the Great," who reigned from A.D. 309 to 379. Their departure would of course reduce Julian's strength, which the Emperor now feared as much as he did that of Shapur. The men to be sent to the East were angry at being asked to fight so far from their own threatened homeland. Moreover, the effort to recruit barbarian volunteers would be set back if the promise that they did not have to serve beyond the Alps was not kept. Julian was sympathetic to the complaints of his army, but tried to resist their rebellious acclamation of him as Augustus. In the end, Julian recognized that he really had no choice, and that his life was actually in danger if he continued to refuse. He tried to explain to Constantius in a letter what had happened, but the Emperor was enraged at his presumption and stared his envoys down with eyes perhaps bulging even more than usual, insisting that Julian remain Caesar. Julian's soldiers would not obey. Thus, Julian was compelled to rebel against Constantius, whose long-standing suspicions were confirmed by the news that Julian had now accepted the title Augustus.

In the meantime, Shapur had begun his campaign to regain

Mesopotamia by crossing the Tigris and taking the stronghold of Singara. Other fortified towns were then attacked. Ammianus tells a particularly interesting story about the siege of Bezabde. The local Christian bishop, eager for an end to the killing on both sides, was allowed to consult with the Persian king and urged him to withdraw lest worse slaughter ensue. Shapur refused. It was later rumored that the bishop, in the interest of bringing matters to an end, revealed secrets about where the city's walls were weakest, so that it might be quickly taken. Ammianus did not want to believe the story, but admits that it looked suspicious when those very spots along the walls were vigorously attacked by the Persian siege-engines. It was surely not the bishop's intention that when the city was taken "the swords of the infuriated enemy cut down all that they could find, children were torn from their mothers' breasts and the mothers themselves were butchered" (XX. 7. 15). But that is what happened.

Constantius did not know whom to fight first, Julian or Shapur, but finally decided that to win in the East would strengthen him against his cousin, who was now a usurper. So he took the offensive against the Persians. Ammianus repeats the rumor that Constantius induced one of the Alamannic kings to disrupt the peace from time to time to keep Julian occupied in Gaul. Although Constantius had no success personally against the Persians, at times his generals did. The overall result of a great Roman effort, however, was very disappointing.

In 361, a battle for supremacy seemed inevitable. Julian left Gaul and headed toward the East. Constantius was anxious to defeat the Persians before having a showdown with his defiant cousin. As it turned out, Shapur, learning that various signs were against his fortunes in war, withdrew from the frontier. While the Emperor was in the East, Julian took over his capital at Sirmium in Western Illyricum. Among those who gained Julian's favor was Sextus Aurelius Victor, a writer whose short history of the emperors is partly extant. He was made a consular governor of Lower Pannonia.

In the manner of earlier historians, Ammianus usually recounted the omens which foretold any great event. There were signals, "almost as plain as words," which gave warning of the death of Constantius. He was taken ill with a fever during the march westward and died at Mopsucrenae in Cilicia on the third of November, A.D. 361. It was said that toward the end he named

Julian as his successor. Apparently he did not object to Julian's
becoming an Augustus so long as he was not there to see it happen.
Constantius, although only thirty-seven when he died, had had one
of the longest reigns of all the emperors—twenty-four years. He
had consciously kept himself aloof from his subjects, in keeping
with the style of rule first established by Diocletian.

With Constantius gone, all power passed to Julian. He
marched joyously to Constantinople, accompanied by many relieved officials. His entry into the city was a triumph, and "all
ages and sexes poured forth, as if to look upon someone sent
down from heaven" (XXII. 2. 4). On a less exalted plane they
were simply welcoming home a native son, for Julian had been
born in Constantinople. He was praised for his justice and hu-
maneness, but in the aftermath of his arrival in Constantinople,
there was undue haste in bringing to account and executing those
who had advised Constantius. Perhaps in this instance Julian left
too much to others.

Once in full power, Julian no longer sought to hide his true
religious feelings. Earlier, when the contest with Constantius
seemed in the offing, he had dutifully worshipped the Christian
God in an effort to win as widespread support as possible. Now,
he openly supported the worship of the pagan gods, including the
usual sacrifices. His advice to the Christian bishops that each
should observe his own beliefs was not calculated to be helpful,
for such freedom could only lead to further internal quarrels
among the Christians. Julian could expect that any opposition to
him would be hopelessly divided, "knowing as he did from experience that no wild beasts are such enemies to mankind as are
most of the Christians in their deadly hatred of one another"
(XXII. 5. 4). This was a devastating comment by one of the
foremost pagan writers of the day. Yet it was in part true, for the
bitterness had dawned early with the typically Greek intellectual
disputes over doctrine which had led inevitably to some typically
Greek animosity.

Julian did not persecute the Christians. On the contrary, he
flattered them by suggesting that pagan priests adopt some of
their practices. In particular, he wanted to see the priests hold
daily rites and be more studious. In short, they were to start
competing more vigorously with the energetic Christian clergy.
While Julian did not remove any Christians from official positions
they might hold, he forbade them to teach, arguing that it was

wrong for them to use "our own books" as weapons. On this point, Ammianus broke with him completely: "This one thing was inhumane, and ought to be buried in eternal silence, namely, that he forbade teachers of rhetoric and literature to practice their profession, if they were followers of the Christian religion" (XXII. 10. 7).

One of Julian's inheritances from Constantius was the continuing struggle with the Persians. In 363, he began to assemble an army and supplies necessary for a campaign to punish Persian "misdeeds in the past, knowing and hearing as he did that this savage people for almost three score years had branded the Orient with the cruelest records of murder and pillage, and had often all but annihilated our armies" (XXII. 12. 1). Julian told his soldiers: "We must wipe out a most mischievous nation, on whose sword-blades the blood of our kinsmen is not yet dry" (XXIII. 5. 19).

The omens looked promising to Julian in the early days of his campaign, after he had crossed the Euphrates. One of them, however, illustrates how a fine mind could be swayed by superstition. His horse, Babylonius, was wounded and fell to the ground with "its ornaments, which were adorned with gold and precious stones," falling all around. Julian joined others who witnessed this in happily proclaiming it was an omen of the fall of Babylon "stripped of all its adornments" (XXIII. 3. 6).

In keeping with his omens, Julian had some early successes, taking and destroying several fortresses, but heavy winds and floods were among his enemies, as was the intense heat. He considered captured Persian girls to be another danger for "he refused to touch a single one or even to look on her, following the example of Alexander and Africanus, who avoided such conduct, lest those who showed themselves unwearied by hardships be unnerved by passion" (XXIV. 4. 27).

Finally, as Ammianus would say, Julian lost his luck. The Persians scorched the earth, and the Romans turned back, desperate for food. They were repeatedly harassed during their retreat. One day, the rear guard was attacked, setting off a general assault along the Roman lines. Julian impetuously rushed into the battle without his armor, and although the enemy was repulsed, he was fatally wounded by a spear, which went through his ribs and into his liver. Carried back to his tent, he was immediately surrounded by his grief-stricken officers, to whom he delivered a long farewell address. He chose not to name a successor before "in the gloom of midnight he passed quietly away in the thirty-second year of his age" (XXV. 3. 23). Julian died on July 26, A.D. 363. He was later buried at Tarsus according to instructions he had left behind.

As mentioned earlier, Ammianus found much to praise and little to blame in Julian. Indeed he found him "older in virtue than in years." The purity and simplicity of his private life expressed a kind of asceticism, for Ammianus says the Emperor "did not indulge in pleasure, even to the extent which nature demanded." He was temperate in other ways, for "he more frequently threatened men with the sword than actually used it" (XXV. 4. 6–8).

Ammianus, though a pagan himself, calls Julian "superstitious rather than truly religious," adding that if the Emperor had returned victoriously from the Persian campaign he would have offered so many sacrifices as to put a strain on the cattle market. Julian was also faulted for excessive vanity in wanting the praise of all men, even to the extent of currying favor with otherwise worthless persons.

In the scramble for power after Julian died, there were several qualified men who each had strong support. While they quarreled, a dark horse, so to speak, carried off the prize.

Jovian

Jovian, who was neither brilliant nor very energetic, was in charge of the Emperor's personal guard. He probably was as surprised as the next man that he was hailed as Emperor by "a few hot-headed soldiers" eager to be marching, but the momentum of that sudden salute carried him into power. It was an odd sight, perhaps, for he was too tall for any available imperial cloak to fit him properly. Maybe that was an omen. He was a short-term ruler. Jovan was best remembered for having made one of the most humilating peace treaties in Roman history. Hoping to extricate himself entirely from the Persian danger, he ceded much that the king had long sought to acquire, and even turned over to him the great fortress city of Nisibis, which the Persians had repeatedly tried but failed to capture. It must be admitted that an acute shortage of food forced his hand. Even so, the treaty need not have been as generous as it was. Moreover, his generosity only served to whet the Persian appetite for more, but that nearly predictable development was left for his successors to handle. Jo-

vian had scarcely taken his young son Varronianus as his colleague
before he died under curious circumstances. Some said his death
was accidental, having resulted from an improperly vented char-
coal stove. Others thought he might have been poisoned or strangled. Ammianus adds, "At all events he died in the thirty-third
year of his age." He had reigned only eight months.

Ammianus' opinion of Jovian was generous. He considered
him a handsome and happy man who, having been elevated by
chance to a position for which he was not suited, was not really to
blame for the shortcomings of his reign. At least the Christians
were satisfied with him, for he was dedicated to their doctrine;
but his private life was no credit to their moral standards. Ammianus calls him "an immoderate eater, given to wine and women."

Valentinian

There was little trouble selecting a successor for Jovian. Valentinian, a seasoned Pannonian officer, was strongly favored. He was
tall, powerfully built, and dignified. Grey, unsmiling eyes revealed his seriousness. He was quickly accepted as the new Emperor. As usual, the bargain with the soldiers was sealed with a
donation.

The favorable consensus toward Valentinian in the officer
corps and in the ranks did not extend to his brother. The suggestion that Valens be appointed co-emperor prompted an observation by one of Valentinian's commanders: "If you love your relatives, most excellent Emperor, you have a brother; if it is the state
that you love, seek out another man to clothe with the purple"
(XXVI. 4. 1). Events proved him right, but Valentinian chose his
brother. He felt certain that Valens would do as he was told, and
seemingly that was all he wanted to know.

Both men were kept busy with the same problems that had
confronted their predecessors. Valentinian faced the severest problems in the West, where he was based at Mediolanum. It cannot
be said that he ever neglected his duties or was without plans. He
carried out a great building program for the defense of Gaul,
which resulted in a series of "fortresses, castles, and towers" all
along the Rhine. His eagerness to protect the frontiers prompted
him to put an outpost even across the Danube, where the Quadi
lived. These people, recently less threatening than formerly, were
upset by this, and then outraged when their king, Gabinius, was

murdered while unsuspectingly accepting the hospitality of a Roman general, Marcellianus. Ammianus does not hesitate to repeat the misdeeds, some of them stupid, by which Roman commanders were often themselves to blame for the turmoil along the frontiers.

The Alamanni began their new campaign with a great burst of energy, and before they could be stopped two Roman generals were among those dead in the onslaught. Valentinian remained in Paris and eventually received the news that his commander of the cavalry had reversed the tide. The Emperor's decision to ally himself with the Burgundians against the Alamanni was a telltale sign of growing Roman dependence on some barbarians to help them against others.

In A.D. 367, during an acute illness, Valentinian decided to give his nine-year-old son Gratian the title of Augustus and so make sure of the succession. Nobody objected to the selection of this bright-eyed youth with his appealing wholesomeness. Ammianus says he might have become one of the best of the Roman emperors, "had this been allowed by the fates and by his intimates, who, by evil actions, cast a cloud over his virtue, which was even then not firmly steadfast" (XXVII. 6. 15). There had never been such a hope for Valentinian, whose bad temper resulted in many ill-advised orders, including having persons burned to death for some minor infraction of the law. This happened because he did not allow his friends to correct him as Julian had done, and of course his enemies were disinclined to say anything. Ammianus says that Valentinian placed a high value on his own ideas. During his reign, almost the only subject over which he did not lose his temper was religion. He was undisturbed by the controversies of his day, and expected all sides to share his respect for different opinions.

Recent events in Africa would have been a test of any emperor's patience. The Moors overran Roman territory and plundered at will, because of corruption in the Roman army and among the government officials, who were too busy stealing from the local population to handle the situation adequately. In part, what happened was Valentinian's own fault, for he had been much too lenient with his officers, and they, because of their greed, greatly abused the civilians. So, as Ammianus was wont to put it, "Justice wept again"—and went on weeping, for Valentinian was greatly deceived about the true events in the African province of Tripolitana. The commanding officer of his troops made excessive demands on the natives in return for protection against marauding tribesmen. Some of those who lied to Valentinian about what was going on were not brought to trial until after the Emperor's death, at which time Gratian was better informed.

Valentinian died at fifty-five, in 375, from apoplexy, while he was dressing down some representatives of the Quadi, whom he considered to be making feeble excuses for their rampages. He had lived a clean life, with little extravagance, and had worked hard for the Empire during the past twelve years, but had been so often unpleasant about it that his passing was not much mourned. The crowd at his bedside was there primarily to provide witnesses enough to swear he had not been murdered. Shortly after Valentinian's death, his younger son, Valentinian II, four years old, was hailed as Augustus. He thus joined his brother Gratian in maintaining the dynasty, but it was not to last long.

In the East, Valens, the uncle of the young Augusti, was easily tricked by the flattery of those around him. The target of several plots, he was persuaded to listen to accusations reported by those who sought to ingratiate themselves at court. Thus "some learned that they had been condemned to death before knowing that they were under suspicion" (XXIX. 1. 18). But according to Ammianus' usual practice of ascribing most events to fate, Valens was preserved until the great disaster which overtook him at Adrianople.

In the meantime, many innocent men were somehow fated to die because of Valens' capricious condemnations. Ammianus reported there were so many that the arms of the executioners grew tired. These horrible massacres in which human life was spent so cheaply can hardly be considered unusual in a society which had so long condoned the savagery of the gladiatorial games. The blood lust of the Romans was only slowly assuaged after the dawn of Christianity; but eventually the greater value accorded to human life by the Christians (and even some of them forgot it) helped to mitigate the inhumane aspects of Roman society. Christianity was a vehicle for bringing to the mass of citizens a moral code akin to that held by philosophers, especially the Stoics. The philosophers, however, had always insisted that men arrive at their conclusions by reasoning, a process very difficult, or at least unpleasant, for most men, who more readily accepted the signs and miracles of religion. So it was that all the philosophers of the ancient world taken together never had the impact which the simple teachings of Jesus eventually made on the majority of the people in the Empire.

Disaster at Adrianople

Another reason the barbarians crossed the frontiers, aside from the provocations of Roman generals, was that they were at times being pushed by less pleasant people behind them. That, to be sure, is an understatement when talking about the Huns. Little was known about these warriors because they were always on the move. In fact, they disliked ever having a roof over their heads. Ammianus says that their children did not know where they came from, being "conceived in one place, born far from there, and brought up still farther away" (XXXI. 2. 10). Many different peoples, to their peril, had seen what they looked like: "They all have compact, strong limbs and thick necks, and are so monstrously ugly and misshapen, that one might take them for two-legged beasts or for the stumps, rough-hewn into images, that are used in putting sides to bridges" (XXXI. 2. 2). Even their horses were ugly, and they were rarely off them. The Huns allegedly had neither laws of their own nor regard for those of others. The Goths, a Germanic people who had migrated from southern Scandinavia and were now living north of the Danube, learned these violent tribesmen were headed in their direction. One group of this Teutonic family, the Visigoths, besought Valens to let them come peaceably inside the Empire, preferably to Thrace, promising to be busy farmers and good soldiers in the Emperor's service.

Ammianus called the arrival of the Visigoths "the ruin of the Roman world." Then he contradicted himself by reporting abuses inflicted on them by irresponsible officials, suggesting that they might have kept their bargain if they had not been driven to despair. The migrants were desperately in need of food, and the commanding general in Thrace kept them that way, so as to acquire them and even their children as slaves, in return for bare sustenance. The ruthlessness with which other officials took advantage of the Visigoths drove them to a rebellion which, as usual, was made fiercer by what they considered to be the justice of their cause. The pillaging by these barbarians, who in the process gathered in Roman weapons, aroused Valens to counterattack. He would also face the Ostrogoths, who had earlier been driven from the Ukraine by the Huns, and now followed the Visigoths across the Danube, although without permission.

Valens' nephew Gratian, disturbed that so many barbarians were loose inside the Empire, set out to bring help. But Valens, envious of Gratian's success against the Alamanni and fearful that a victory might be stolen from him, decided to deal with the Goths alone. The battle at Adrianople in Thrace, early in August, 378, was of momentous significance. For the first time, legions of Rome were defeated inside the Empire. Valens was killed in the thick of the battle, and his body was never found. The rash move which had cost him his army and his life was characteristic of his rule. While generally a conscientious and honest man, he was weak in judgment. Moreover, he often took a long time coming to a bad decision.

Valentinian had apparently inherited the best features of his family. Valens, shorter, "knock-kneed and somewhat pot-bellied," was an ungainly-looking Emperor at a time when kings were expected to be warriors. As an Arian, he did not follow Valentinian's policy of tolerance and meddled in affairs of the Church to the extent of sending again into exile the bishops restored by Julian.

The barbarian victory at Adrianople left the way open to Constantinople, but the city was safe, for fresh Roman troops arrived. Many Goths, on promise of being given money, assembled only to be slaughtered. Thus peace was restored by treachery, the same way as the war had begun.

Theodosius

The man most responsible for the recovery after Adrianople was Theodosius (*ca.* A.D. 346–395), a Spanish general who, having won Gratian's confidence, was appointed Augustus by him early in 379. He managed to drive the Ostrogoths back across the Danube, but let the Visigoths settle down to form one of the proto-kingdoms within the Empire which would one day share in its displacement altogether. The Visigoths were treated as allies rather than citizens. It is estimated that Theodosius took about 40,000 of them into his army.

In August, 383, Gratian was murdered near Lyon. Ammianus described him as "a young man of splendid character, eloquent, self-restrained, warlike and merciful" although, under the

influence of his companions, at times given to "frivolous pursuits" (XXXI. 10. 18). He was killed during an unsuccessful attempt to suppress a revolt led by one of his officers. Magnus
Maximus, as a matter of expediency, was accepted as a new Augustus both by Theodosius and the supporters of the young Valentinian II. In that same year, Theodosius had given the highest
title to his sons, Arcadius and Honorius. For five years there
were, in name at least, five Augusti. Then, as in the past, a gradual elimination occurred. In 388, Maximus lost a contest with
Theodosius and was beheaded. In 392, Arbogast, a Frankish officer under Valentinian II, was powerful enough to replace the
twenty-year-old Emperor with his own choice, Eugenius, who,
like Maximus, was eliminated by Theodosius. In A.D. 394, Arbogast committed suicide.

In spite of these challengers, Theodosius was the dominant
figure in the Empire from A.D. 383 until his death at fifty, early in
395. Ammianus called him "a most glorious emperor." He had
served as a general in Upper Moesia, while still so young that his
beard was only just starting to grow. Part of the reason for his
early start was that his father before him had had a distinguished
military career, much of it spent in Britain.

For nearly a decade Theodosius had fought to bring the
Empire under his own rule, with his sons as the heirs apparent.
He succeeded shortly before he died. In the meantime, he brought
about religious unity, at least officially, by making Christianity
the sole state religion. By ordering the pagan temples closed and
the traditional sacrifices ended, Theodosius declared the old gods
to be dead. Particularly in the East, overzealous monks went a
step further and wrecked the pagan places of worship. Many
simple folk, particularly of the rural regions (*paganus,* peasant,
from *pagus,* a country district) bitterly resented these assaults and
even challenged the soldiers, who eagerly joined in the attack.
Prominent among the Christian leaders who incited their followers to destroy pagan symbols was Marcellus, a Syrian bishop,
who was killed during the violence and so won martyrdom for his
efforts.

To declare the Empire Christian did not make it so. Yet
Theodosius had his way with the trappings of the old religion
which Constantine had not cared to tamper with. At Rome, the
sacred fire of Vesta no longer burned. The statue and altar of
Victory had been removed from the Senate, first by Constantius,

and again by Gratian after Julian had restored it. The protest of the orator Symmachus had been to no avail. Gratian also renounced the title *pontifex maximus*. Elsewhere the great Serapeum of Alexandria, which was used as a kind of fortress by the pagans, was shut down, and in Greece the Olympian Games, with their pagan altars, were ended. Whereas it was once a punishable offense to be a Christian, now it was declared a crime to venerate the statues of the old gods.

In 391, the Emperor commanded all his subjects to submit themselves to the dictates of the Christian Church. Significantly, he discovered that he was expected to do the same. His lesson came from Ambrose, the powerful bishop of Milan, whose *Letters* are among the valuable sources for this period. Since Gratian's time he had been highly influential in urging an end to pagan symbols and fought any effort to reverse the trend. He twice brought Theodosius to terms. The Emperor had angered some of his subjects, particularly in Eastern cities, by placing Gothic officers in high positions. Resentment toward these foreigners led to a serious revolt in Thessalonica, in which one of the officers was killed. Theodosius retaliated by ordering a brutal assault on the citizenry in the amphitheatre of the city, which amounted to a massacre of the innocent with the guilty. Thereupon Ambrose shut not only his church door but also presumably the door to heaven to the Emperor. Theodosius was compelled to do penance in order to be absolved from his crime.

Does this story (which not everybody believes) support the historian Edward Gibbon's contention that Christianity, with its exalted virtues and idealism, took the steel out of the Roman Empire? Actually there is another report which contradicts him. On a different occasion, Theodosius, angry about the destruction of a Jewish synagogue in Mesopotamia, ordered the local bishop to be punished. In this instance, Ambrose compelled the Emperor to change his mind. It is not, then, certain that the influence of a determined Christian bishop was entirely on the side of the peacemakers. That it represented a new power in the world, which grew stronger every year, is certain.

Christianity: Success and Problems

During the fourth century, the Christian Church attracted some of the best minds in Roman society. Formerly, intellectuals had

55. Relief, Christ with Saint Peter and Saint Paul (detail of Figure 56). Courtesy of the Rev. da Fabbrica di San Pietro in Vaticano.

56. Early Christian sarcophagus of Giunio Basso, fourth century. Courtesy of the Rev. da Fabbrica di San Pietro in Vaticano.

found in philosophy a refuge from noisy strife and materialism. Now, in increasing numbers, they were converted to Christianity. Other men who might in earlier times have had prominent careers in the government or the military were now finding a vocation in the Church. It is tempting to characterize a society by the activities which attract its most qualified members. Today, business and particularly the sciences are foremost in gathering talent. When the Church did the same we speak of the Middle Ages. The fourth century Fathers, like Ambrose, Augustine, and Jerome, point the way.

Augustine

The career of Saint Augustine (A.D. 354–430) argues for the regenerative power of Christianity. He was an admitted sinner, who became the greatest of the Latin Church Fathers. Although his mother, Monica, was a Christian, and had given him some simple instruction when he was a child, he was not baptized until he was thirty-four.

Augustine's writings not only helped to shape the theology of his own time but had a far-reaching influence on such later thinkers as Zwingli and Calvin. He was particularly governed by the Old Testament, as was evident in his emphasis on an omnipotent God and the necessity for man to be absolutely obedient to Him. Predestination was of less interest to his contemporaries than to later Protestant reformers. Even they broke with him on certain aspects of his doctrine.

Augustine's works are historically valuable. In defense of the orthodox faith he wrote at length about competing sects. It was not strange that he had much to say about Manichaeism, for he had himself for nine years been a Manichaean, attracted by its vigorous morality. Manichaeism was founded by a mystic, Mani (A.D. 216–277), who had spent some time in India and taught that only those who practiced a severe asceticism could escape from the wearisome cycle of rebirth. As a young man, Augustine had a strong desire to escape the vice and folly of the world, with which he appears to have had considerable acquaintance, and an illegitimate child to show for it.

In his *Confessions,* Augustine recounts his long and arduous search for satisfaction in one or the other of the competing philosophies or religions of his day. Manichaeism was apparently too extreme for him. The advocacy of celibacy for all men meant that having children at all was an evil. The eradication of mankind was scarcely an edifying goal. Abandoning the logic of the Manichaeans, Augustine next became a skeptic, wondering if man could know anything at all. He was, however, soon attracted to Platonism, with its emphasis on the other world, the real world of Ideas. That concept had been given new currency in the Neoplatonism of Plotinus (*ca.* A.D. 205–270) in the third century. For Augustine, Plotinus' writings were the philosophical counterpart of Saint Paul's message concerning "things not seen." Eventually, he concluded that right reason and the true faith were joined in Christianity. But according to his *Confessions,* it was an ecstatic experience in a garden which marked his conversion. In any event his later remembrance of that day is one of the most appealing passages in Western literature:

> I flung myself down, how, I know not, under a certain fig-tree, giving free course to my tears, and the streams of mine eyes gushed out, an acceptable sacrifice unto Thee. And, not indeed in these words, yet to this effect, spake I much unto Thee—"But Thou, O Lord, how long?" "How long, Lord? Wilt Thou be angry for ever? Oh, remember not against us former iniquities"; for I felt that I was enthralled by them. I sent up these sorrowful cries—"How long, how long? To-morrow, and to-morrow? Why not now? Why is there not this hour an end to my uncleanness?"
>
> I was saying these things and weeping in the most bitter contrition of my heart, when, lo, I heard the voice as of a boy or girl, I know not which, coming from a neighboring house, chanting, and oft repeating, "Take up and read; take up and read." . . . So, restraining the torrent of my tears, I rose up, interpreting it no other way than as a command to me from Heaven to open the book, and to read the first chapter I should light upon. . . . I grasped, opened, and in silence read that paragraph on which my eyes first fell—"Not in rioting and drunkenness, not in chambering and wantonness, not in strife and envying; but put ye on the Lord Jesus Christ, and make not provision for the flesh, to fulfill the lusts thereof." No further would I read, nor did I need; for instantly, as the sentence ended—by a light, as it were, of security infused into my heart—all the gloom of doubt vanished away. (*The Confessions,* VIII.12)

Augustine abandoned his profession as a teacher and devoted himself to Christian interests. He did not, however, give up his interest in classical writers. Cicero was his favorite. After his baptism by Ambrose in Milan, where he had taught rhetoric, he returned to his birthplace, Tagaste (modern Souk-Ahras in Algeria) in eastern Numidia and became a priest. Later he was made the bishop of nearby Hippo Regius (the ruins of which are one mile south of modern Bône) and he retained the post from 396 until his death in 430.

Augustine's writings are a valuable source on various heresies, including Donatism and Pelagianism. He was not altogether fair to them, but then truth is not always kind to opinion. Nor in those days would anyone have expected him to be totally objective. The heresies were among the thorny problems the Church faced from within once it had overcome its enemies from without.

The quarrel with the Donatists was over a clear-cut issue. They insisted that the sacraments, the vessels of God's grace, could only be valid if the priests dispensing them were morally fit. In the early fourth century, Donatus, bishop of Carthage, led a separatist movement which insisted on purity, and went so far as to set up a "true church" with sanctity as a qualification for membership. The movement became particularly strong in North Africa, but spread little beyond that region.

Augustine agreed with the point of view of the Roman Church that the validity of the sacraments depended solely on God, and not on any human contingency. Otherwise, how would the faithful be assured of salvation, unless they knew the private life of every priest they had contact with? The Donatist ideal, if adopted, would have kept the Church forever small, as compared to the prevailing larger Church which could welcome even barbarians, and leave the final judgment to God. Although the Donatist movement lasted for over a century, and its ideals were commendable, it was not suitable for the needs of most men.

In the Donatist controversy, as in other matters, the Church of Rome was practical. Practicality was also in evidence during the earlier quarrel over the readmittance of Christians who had lapsed from the faith under the threat of persecution. A Church of dead or living martyrs would also have been a small community. Furthermore, an accommodation with human weakness could be defended on theological grounds.

Pelagius (*ca.* A.D. 360–*ca.* 420) was a native of Britain, a monk and a theologian. He decided that the decline in morals among Christians was, of all things, being encouraged by certain doctrines currently taught in the Church itself. The emphasis on original sin, inherited sin, and more recently Augustine's advo-

cacy of predestination appeared to relieve man of any responsibility for his own condition. How could he help himself? Pelagius,
denying that any of these doctrines was true, insisted that man
had to decide for himself between good and evil. He even argued
that it was possible for men to live without sinning and furthermore they did not require God's help in their effort. Did man then
not need the Church's sacraments? Pelagius did not say that, but
he and his followers were obviously on dangerous ground. Augustine, the foremost defender of the Church as the sole means of
salvation, was appalled at Pelagius' liberation of man from God's
omnipotence. In his attack on Pelagius he stressed his own doctrine of predestination.

A synod in Carthage in 418 condemned the Pelagian position, and in that same year Emperor Honorius drove both Pelagius and his closest follower Coelestius into exile. The Council of
Ephesus, in 431, declared Pelagianism a heresy, and so it has
remained. Regrettably the controversy tended to obscure Pelagius'
outstanding moral quality and good intentions. But he was cling-
ing to the ancient Graeco-Roman conception of man at the center
of things. Augustine gave God that place, and made all else subservient to him. Thus did the mentality of ancient times yield to
that of the Middle Ages.

Augustine's *City of God* was written to contradict the claim
that the Christians were responsible for the sack of Rome in 410.
It was claimed that they had cost the city its patronage and protection from the old divinities. For Augustine, all that happened
belonged to the one God's divine plan; even disastrous events
served a purpose. Ultimately, the city of God, a world of goodness, which Augustine identified with the Church, would triumph
over the earthly city, a world of wickedness, especially the Roman
Empire, but including all other states and institutions. The enmity
between them had begun in the struggle among the angels and
continued among men. Yet it was an uneven contest, for the trials
and tribulations of the earthly city prepared men for the glorious
city of God. Thus did Augustine admonish Christians to accept
the blessings of orderly societies on earth and to obey their laws.
However, his identification of the Church with the city of God
clearly implied that earthly powers must be obedient to the
Church's dictates. That powerful idea gave the popes of the
Middle Ages more protection than either wealth or armies could
supply.

J. B. Bury, in his *History of the Later Roman Empire,* suggests that Augustine was also to some extent responsible for involving Christianity on the side of violence. In one of his letters, Augustine wrote an answer to a question from a senator, which was of crucial importance. He was asked if a Christian might use force on behalf of a good cause. His answer was yes. Indeed it was a favor to those who fall into immorality that they be punished and so for their own benefit be compelled to correct their ways. Thus, according to Bury, did Augustine establish "unintentionally a dangerous and hypocritical doctrine for the justification of war, the same principle which was used for justifying the Inquisition" (Vol. I, p. 311). Yet it is only fair to say that Augustine was inconsistent on this point. In the bitter struggle with the Donatists, he was willing to have the state put them down forcibly if necessary. As he grew older, however, Augustine became inexorably opposed to the use of force to suppress heresy.

Jerome

During the controversy with the Pelagians, Augustine had some powerful allies. One of them was the dour and cantankerous Saint Jerome (*ca.* A.D. 348–420), who was the foremost scholar of his day. In the degree of his bitterness he even exceeded Augustine's capacity for confronting the heretics. His lasting fame comes from his Vulgate Bible, skillfully translated from the original sources.

Jerome was deeply pious—strict with himself and with others. He thundered against sexual incontinence and strongly advised celibacy, which he practiced himself. If one man were to be chosen among the early Fathers who would be least in sympathy with the recent reforms within Catholicism it would be Jerome. He confronted those who made similar suggestions in his own time. Among his contemporaries was one Vigilantius, who was highly skeptical about the numerous martyrs, of varying character, who were being declared saints. He wondered if paganism was not creeping into the Church. Another writer, Helvidius, was worried about the attention being given to the Virgin Mary. Then there was Jovinian, who saw nothing to be gained by either virginity or fasting. To Jerome, who risked his health in a life of self-denial, who venerated like-minded men who had become saints, and who was especially devoted to Mary, these critics were an abomination. And he was victorious over them. The ascetic

mood even triumphed in Christian art, for Jesus came to be depicted as having a weak and emaciated body, much in keeping
with the ideal of those who found holiness in the mortification of
the flesh. Most of these men were monks; so was Jerome, who
pursued his studies in a monastery in Bethlehem. He was, in fact,
one of the foremost advocates of monasticism in his time.

Monasticism

As the Christians settled into the society around them, acquiring
property and gaining even political influence, it was natural that
certain of them would feel uncomfortable. Jesus had taught by
example, and his kingdom was not of this world. So it is understandable that at the time when the Church was becoming
stronger, some men saw in its success a weakness. The suggestion
has already been made that the disputatiousness surrounding the
Nicene controversy offered a startling contrast to the Christlike,
humble loving-kindness of the early Christians. They were no
more concerned than He was with the problems which are natural
to human institutions, religious or political. As time passed, there
was inevitably a reaction within the Christian movement, led by
men who wanted to live apart from the world, alone if necessary,
so as to remain untainted by earthly things. Those who sought to
escape were not all, to be sure, rebelling against the Church's
current involvement in the world. Some of them merely wanted
to avoid the miseries of their times. Yet all could agree that the
real victory over the world was to give it up, even as to gain one's
life one must lose it. The earliest monks were not interested in
even the Donatists' ill-fated attempt to build an ideal Church
among the holiest of men. Nor were they concerned with charity
and the alleviation of human suffering, which a thriving Church,
for all its faults, could provide. Theirs was a solitary quest for
salvation.

In the latter part of the third century, anchorites, hermits,
were living on the fringes of the desert in Egypt as a few monks
of the Coptic Church still do. The most famous of them was Saint
Anthony, who gained a wide reputation for holiness. Not all of
the ascetics who left the world remained unseen. In Syria, there
were the so-called "pillar saints." The most famous of them, Simeon Stylites (from the Greek *stylos,* pillar) was reported to have
spent thirty years on a platform atop a pillar sixty feet high. While

only a few disciples followed his example, many who came to see him were impressed by his self-sacrifice. Christian values were serving to alter radically the common opinion of what constituted heroism.

In Egypt, at an early date, certain of the anchorites recognized that loneliness was not necessarily an ennobling experience. They were therefore willing to submit to the rules for common living set down about 323 by an Egyptian, Pachomius, who was the founder of the first Christian monastic institution. The purpose of his community on an island in the Nile was still to have a life of meditation apart from the world, but an accommodation to at least one human need had been satisfied. It was in the latter half of the fourth century that Basil (*ca.* A.D. 330–*ca.* 379), bishop of Caesarea from 370 onward, gave a greater emphasis to daily labor among monks, and established a rule still used. This trend was followed in the West, when in the early sixth century Saint Benedict (*ca.* A.D. 480–*ca.* 543) founded the Monte Cassino monastery.

Both the desire of the monks to hide themselves away from the beaten path and to occupy themselves with the study and preservation of the great literature of the past were of incalculable value to European civilization. The barbarians did not scale every mountain or search out every forest. Buried away in remote places during the Dark Ages were the monks and their treasures, until Europe was ready for learning again. This familiar tribute to the great service of the monastic orders is the better side of the story. One commentator in the early fifth century, the Greek historian Zosimus, was appalled by the growth of the monastic movement and in his *New History,* on the period from Diocletian to A.D. 410, wrote about the uselessness of these men, who in perilous times served neither the army nor the government. He was also bitter because, while the monks were presumably not interested in material things, their monastic houses were growing wealthy. Legacies and gifts enabled them to dispense charity among their neighbors; but Zosimus, never a friend to Christianity, had reservations about how much wealth was ever shared. Many monks, of course, wandered from place to place in holy idleness, often making nuisances of themselves. For some, their greatest show of energy, as mentioned earlier, came in the desecration or even outright destruction of pagan temples and precious statuary. Such violence was another example of the profession of superior ideals being accompanied by unruly behavior. Conse-

57. Honorius. Courtesy of the Detroit Institute of Arts.

quently, practical minded bishops at the Council of Chalcedon in A.D. 451 had to order restrictions placed on the conduct of the monks, which would pave the way for a more productive life.

The Last Emperors

In the late fourth century A.D., the Frankish Arbogast's ill-fated adventure as the real power behind Valentinian II and then Eugenius forecast the future. In less than a century there would no longer be an emperor at Rome, or Milan or anywhere in the West. Beginning with Theodosius' sons, Arcadius (*ca.* A.D. 377–408) and Honorius (A.D. 384–423), the rulers were mostly titular figures. The major roles were played by German generals, who matched skills with each other and nominated puppet emperors until, it might be said, the reason why was forgotten.

Although Arcadius in the East and Honorius in the West considered themselves joint emperors, the Empire was never again united after their father's time.

Arcadius ranks as the first Emperor of the Eastern Roman Empire, albeit his inattentiveness to state affairs was an unhappy model. His officials and particularly his wife ruled him. It was the Empress Eudoxia who quarreled violently with the famous

John Chrysostom (*ca.* A.D. 354–407) and forced him into exile in 404. He was given his name Chrysostom for the Greek *chrysostomos,* goldenmouthed, because he was the foremost preacher of his day. His ascetic life in the desert near Antioch had not prepared him for the scandalous life at the court in Constantinople, where in 398 he became patriarch. Nor was the court ready for him. Despite his popularity with the people because of his charitable work, he was twice driven into exile. He died in Armenia in 407, leaving as part of his legacy numerous sermons which were considered models.

While the Eastern domain managed to survive, the Western half of the Empire slowly crumbled out of existence. It was not, however, immediately obvious that it would. Honorius was well served by a remarkable general, Flavius Stilicho (*ca.* A.D. 359–408), the son of a Vandal leader who had also been in Roman service. Stilicho, Theodosius' top commander, remained to manage affairs for Honorius, who became his son-in-law. It was Stilicho who took to the field. Honorius retreated to Ravenna. The surrounding marshes made it a relatively safe place.

Stilicho's major task was to keep the restless Goths at bay, particularly the Visigoths, inspired by their dynamic leader Alaric (*ca.* A.D. 370–410). Alaric, like Stilicho, had once served Theodosius, but, disappointed by the appointment offered him under Honorius, went back to his own people, who elected him their king. Under him, the Visigoths pushed their way into Greece, and alarmed both Arcadius and Honorius by their seeming freedom to roam at will. Arcadius offered Alaric the governorship of Illyricum, which he promptly used to build a better army by recruiting a number of mercenaries. In 400, he led an invasion of Italy, and for a couple of years the Goths plundered the countryside, until defeated by Stilicho at Pollentia (modern Pollenza) in central Italy, and again at Verona, as they retreated. It is significant that not only both generals were of German descent but also most of their soldiers. Honorius shared with Stilicho a triumph in Rome in 404. It was the ancient city's last great parade.

Honorius tried again with Alaric by putting him in charge of western Illyricum, but the Gothic king had too strong a following to be satisfied with a minor role. There was worse trouble ahead from him and his Visigoths.

In the meantime, Stilicho had ended another threat from a

different direction. A mixed horde of barbarians swept into Italy under Radagaisus, and besieged Florentia (modern Florence) in 405. They were defeated by Stilicho, who later captured Radagaisus at Faesulae (modern Fiesole) and executed him. A by-product of these threats in Italy was a disaster in Britain. Stilicho had had to recall most of the Roman forces there and leave the Romanized Britons on their own against their less civilized neighbors. By sea came the Angles, Saxons, and Jutes, who saved the land from the Caledonians but devastated it in the process. Roman Britain was buried beneath a Germanic culture. The newcomers borrowed little from the natives and at the outset had no trace of the refinements later to be associated with Englishmen.

The death of Stilicho in 408 was said to have resulted from his involvement in a plot against Honorius. But that may have been the Emperor's excuse, for he was known to be jealous of his general, and it would be easy to believe that Honorius connived at Stilicho's murder. There is no doubt Stilicho's death meant a crucial loss of leadership.

In the same year, Alaric again led his Visigoths into Italy and this time successfully besieged Rome, which had run out of food. The city was taken on August 24, A.D. 410. The Visigoths were nominally Christians, Arians at that, and they did not destroy the city's churches or massacre the people gathered in them. However, it was only after several days and nights of looting that they left. Alaric led them to southern Italy, where he died at Consentia (modern Cosenza) later that year. His brother-in-law, Ataulf, eventually established the Visigothic kingdom in Spain. By that time relations with the Emperor in Rome had become more stable. Ataulf not only made an alliance with Honorius, but also married his half-sister Galla Placidia.

In the early fifth century, while the Vandals carved out their own kingdom in North Africa, the Burgundians were settling in southeastern Gaul. With the Franks firmly established in central and northern Gaul, a new map of Europe was taking shape. By midcentury these various peoples, now semi-civilized and mostly Christian, were themselves faced with a barbarian invasion. The Huns under the fearsome Attila (*ca.* A.D. 406–453) had first threatened the East and received great sums in tribute from the frightened Theodosius II at Constantinople. Theodosius, son of Arcadius, had a long reign, (A.D. 408–450). The first six years were guided by his prefect Anthemius, who died in 414; thereafter he was assisted by his sister Pulcheria, who ruled with him for the rest of his reign. There were wars as usual with the Persians and also with the Vandals who had turned to piracy, but Theodosius II is best remembered for the Theodosian Code, a publication of imperial constitutions, all the enactments of Constantine and his successors which were still in effect. He was succeeded by Marcian (A.D. 392–457), who, by refusing Attila further tribute, prompted him to turn to the West. There a coalition was organized to stop the rampaging Huns.

The Roman general Flavius Aëtius (*ca.* A.D. 396–454) rallied the native provincials, who were joined by the Visigoths, Franks, and Burgundians under their own leaders. In a great effort at Châlons-sur-Marne, ninety-five miles east of Paris, in June, 451, the Huns were driven off. The next year, however, found them invading Italy.

There is a famous painting by Raphael (1483–1520) which shows Pope Leo I (looking like Leo X) astride a white mule, facing Attila outside Rome with Saint Peter and Saint Paul hovering overhead. The money-bags seen attached to Leo's saddle also presumably helped to turn the ferocious Huns away. The event actually took place in northern Italy, which felt the shock of the invasion. Venice is said to have been founded by those fleeing to a low-lying area to escape the Hun attack. Attila died suddenly in 453; the Huns never found another leader like him. He well represented what these people left as their legacy— a bad name.

The same was true of the Vandals, who sailed from North Africa in 455 under an able, if treacherous, king Gaiseric and took their turn sacking Rome. Among the treasures seized this time was the great golden candelabrum which Emperor Titus had carried back to Rome after the destruction of the Temple in Jerusalem nearly four hundred years earlier. In the following century, the Byzantine Emperor Justinian obtained it and for a time it was in Constantinople before being finally returned to Jerusalem. Its final destiny is not known.

After the second capture of Rome, its emperors were first selected by a Germanic chieftain of the Suevian confederation, Ricimer, who died in 472, and then by a Pannonian named Orestes. In 475, Orestes made his six-year-old son, ironically and mockingly called Romulus Augustulus, Emperor of Rome. Before long Orestes was slain by Odoacer (*ca.* A.D. 434–493) who led a band of German mercenaries, mostly Heruli. They deposed the young Emperor. Nobody ever bothered to name another. The year was 476. For those who demand to know the date Rome fell, that is it. Others will realize that the fall of Rome was not an event but a process. Or, to put it another way, there was no fall at all—ancient Roman civilization simply became something else, which is called medieval.

XX

*The Decline of Some
and the Rise of Others*

Rome, the eternal city, is now three cities in one. Visitors find themselves looking at ancient and medieval or, perhaps especially, Renaissance monuments in juxtaposition to a modern metropolis. The impressive evidence of the Roman Empire at its apogee is still there to inspire a seemingly eternal number of writers to struggle with the question, "Why did the civilization of ancient Rome decline and fall?" They would not be in business if the simplest explanation were accepted, which is that nothing in this world lasts. Leaving that answer to poets and philosophers, they plunge into a variety of special explanations.

If the man in the street were asked why Rome fell, he would probably reply that it was overrun by the barbarians. Yet, as it has been shown, when the collapse came, barbarians were already on the inside, many of them fighting for the Emperor. Moreover, the threat from the north had existed for a long time. The question narrows down to what internal weaknesses led to the breakdown of the western half of the Empire in the fifth century A.D.

Arthur E. R. Boak, in *Manpower Shortage and the Fall of the Roman Empire in the West,* developed the thesis that a decline in population beginning in the late second century, a result of inces-

sant warfare and plague, was one of the causes of the collapse of
the Western Empire. He argued that the emperors, beginning
with Marcus Aurelius, would not have adopted the dangerous
policy of recruiting barbarians for the army had there not been a
disastrous decline in the birthrate among the native population,
particularly in the rural areas. To this argument should be added
Edward T. Salmon's suggestion that another reason the barbarians
were needed was a lack of incentive on the part of the native
provincials. The reward of citizenship had once attracted great
numbers of them. As time passed, however, there were fewer
non-citizens to be recruited, for the sons of soldiers received citizenship as a result of their fathers' service. Caracalla's decision, in
A.D. 212, to grant citizenship to all freeborn persons in the Empire merely confirmed what was nearly true already. His edict,
however, removed altogether the major reason for volunteers
joining the army. Now the barbarians, mercenaries though they
were, became a necessary source of manpower. So, as Salmon
pointed out, it was an irony that Roman generosity in granting
citizenship had much to do with the barbarizing of the army.

In Boak's opinion, a shortage in manpower contributed to a
vicious circle. The fewer men available to work the land resulted
in lower productivity, which in turn meant a deplenished tax
base. The government's pressure on those who remained forced
more of them to flee the land, which resulted in even further
deterioration of the economy. Part of the drain, ironically, consisted of persons going into the civil service, where they might
join the tax-collecting units oppressing the ones who were left.
Lactantius, a Christian writer whom Constantine hired as a tutor
for his son Crispus, seems to have felt justified in voicing the
exaggeration that there were more taxcollectors than taxpayers.

A simple cause of the decline therefore would be that the
increasing number of barbarians hired during this crisis meant that
the western half of the Empire was so barbarized that it was
replaced altogether. But Professor Boak did not say that. He
stated emphatically that there was not a "single major cause" and
merely offered the manpower thesis as one which, until his time,
had perhaps been given too little attention. In passing, he mentioned other conditions, such as soil exhaustion, often cited for the
decline in agricultural productivity. While he agreed that erosion
may have affected some parts of the Empire, Greece and Italy in
particular, he thought it not significant elsewhere, and hence to be

considered a minor factor. Incidentally, the contention that there were any drastic climatic changes affecting productivity has also been generally refuted.

Was there any substantial deterioration of health or stamina due to malaria? How important is this contention? While it is generally conceded that towns in low-lying areas along the Italian coast, Paestum for instance, were affected by the unhealthy swamp areas in the vicinity, the problem was not widespread enough to be considered crucial.

The economic causes of the decline add up to a simple statement: the Empire went bankrupt. There has already been some discussion of this process in previous chapters, including the woeful fate of a struggling middle class. Fear about the future pervaded the whole society. The numerous hoards of coins for this period recovered by archaeologists show that wealthy men were burying their money, hoping for the better times which never came. There was no expanding gross national product which could support an increasing defense budget, as would be true today. On the contrary, as has already been pointed out, the instability of the late third century created a downward drift in commerce and in agricultural productivity, which was slowed but never actually reversed by the economic policies of the fourth-century emperors. The West was becoming impoverished at the very time taxes were going up. The result was catastrophic.

Historical scholar Tenney Frank asks if the cultural background of great numbers of new citizens might have had a weakening influence on the political structure of the Roman Empire in the long term (*American Historical Review*, 21 [1915–16], 689–703). His study of Roman inscriptions supports the often quoted observation by Juvenal, the second-century satirist, that "the Syrian Orontes was flowing into the Tiber." His studies show that in the early centuries of the Empire there was a substantial shift in population balance at Rome from a predominance of native stock to one of persons whose ancestry could be traced to the provinces, particularly those of the East. In part, this resulted from importing slaves, whose birthrate greatly exceeded that of the native population, and especially that of the educated aristocracy. What is important is that Frank does not suggest that this new stock was inferior, only that it was different. He does not deny the natural capacities of Syrians and Egyptians, whose ancestors had after all produced in their time great civilizations; but he holds that they lacked those qualities of mind peculiarly Roman, such as political acumen and the emphasis on duty—qualities of earlier generations of the Roman Republic, but not necessarily of the conquered provincials. The Syrians, for instance, were customarily less assiduous in civil affairs, and certainly less disciplined. The same observation might be made about the Greeks, who had ideas, compared to the Romans, who made plans. Frank would have agreed that the difference helps to explain why the Romans were more adept at managing the world for so long. The Greeks never ceased to quarrel among themselves, and so seemed in a constant state of disorder and disunity. That, at the same time, they produced the extraordinary Socrates does not make the proposition any less worthy of consideration. But to return to Tenney Frank's argument that the Eastern element in Rome's bloodstream had a negative effect on Rome's future: how can one then account for the success of the Byzantine Empire centered in Constantinople, where Eastern "characteristics" were surely even more pronounced? This kind of question keeps the discussion going.

What about the deterioration of morals among the Romans? It is true that Ammianus Marcellinus found the Romans of all classes in the late fourth century practically consumed with vice, with little time for anything else. He was a pagan observer without an answer. The Christian moralists were shocked, but at least had a remedy. But were conditions really any worse then than they had appeared to Tacitus in the first century or Juvenal in the second? Moreover, Rome was not the Empire. The average worker or farmer of the Mediterranean region undoubtedly had an earthiness about him which, while crude, was not unwholesome. He did not "laugh at vice" as Tacitus said the sophisticates at Rome did. Again, the difference between classes was as likely true in the fifth century as in the first or second. No, it was not so much a loss of morals that affected the people of the Empire as it was a loss of spirit, or, as it has been called, "a failure of nerve." In this connection, Diocletian's remark that fear was the best means of promoting duty is significant. In Roman society of the fourth century it was no longer expected that a man would do his duty because he wanted to, or because it made him a better man. Now he must be threatened. His personal sense of responsibility, his initiative, had been drained away by the increasing use of coercion by the government even if for what seemed desirable goals at the time. Inwardly there developed an awareness, which became stronger with each generation, that a man's destiny was out of his hands. The hard reality of this was in the drift toward serfdom. On the intellectual side, the triumph of Christianity meant that, as Pope Leo I (reigned A.D. 440–461) said in a letter to the priests and deacons of Alexandria, the truth of the church did not allow for any "variety." In the fourth century, the physical life of men became programmed by the state even as their spiritual life was now directed by the Church. In the world to be, Caesar would still have made a great king and Cicero a mighty bishop, but for a long time there would be no place at all for a Socrates.

The Goths

The last major writers of ancient times were Boethius (*ca.* A.D. 480–*ca.* 524) and his friend Cassiodorus, born about 490, who lived, amazingly, until about 583. Both these distinguished Romans served under Theodoric (*ca.* A.D. 454–526), who founded the Ostrogothic kingdom in Italy and reigned as king from 493. The Ostrogoths had been mercenaries in the pay of the Eastern emperors for some time. Theodoric, at home at the court in Constantinople, was by no means an ordinary, or rude, barbarian when the Emperor Zeno (reigned A.D. 474–491) sent him to bring Italy back inside the Empire. Theodoric defeated Odoacer at Aquileia and Verona in 489. It was not until four years later, when the chief of the Heruli was killed, that Italy fell completely under Ostrogothic control. The new kingdom was technically part of the Eastern Empire, although Theodoric set up his own capital and court at Ravenna. He proved to be the best ruler Italy had had since Theodosius. Although himself an Arian Christian, he generally showed respect for other beliefs, albeit he may have been less patient with the opinions of his high officials. During most of his career he appears to have been a fair-minded ruler who recognized the great value of Roman law. Two years before he died, however, he had Boethius executed. This was a particularly sensational event, for Boethius, whose father had been a consul under Odoacer, had heretofore been one of the king's most trusted officials, even his Master of Offices, the major administrative post in the palace. The charge against Boethius was conspiracy, specifically secret dealings with Eastern officials, but there may have been a private reason for the death of the king's learned ex-friend.

There has been much discussion about whether Boethius was a Christian. His primary interest was obviously in the pagan philosophers. It seems likely, however, that, as one of Theodoric's chief officials, he was at least nominally Christian although it could be that his partiality to the orthodox position put him at odds with Theodoric over Arianism. That may have been part of the trouble. However, the real reason for his downfall may have been his pride. He had studied in Athens and knew and loved the classics in the Ciceronian manner. There was perhaps on that account a gulf between him and the Gothic officials around him which his disposition, or theirs, was unable to bridge. An aloof manner, which gave him a superior air, could have caused deep resentment among Goths who had Theodoric's ear. It is unlikely, of course, that the king ever heard these same administrators tell of their anger at Boethius for his criticism of their oppressive tax policies toward the poor. The arrest of Boethius in 524 on a charge of conspiracy was perhaps a blind to give the king time to make up his mind about his former official. It was probably later in that year that he had him killed.

There is something very sad about Boethius sitting in his cell in a prison near Milan, seeking to reassure himself by writing *The Consolation of Philosophy*. His fame rests largely on this final work, which was to give so much comfort to others in the years ahead. It is a short dialogue, with Philosophy personified as a woman. In the course of the conversation, Boethius recalls the ideas of some of the greatest minds in a world which seemed to be dying with him. Despite his ill fortune, which he felt was so unjustified, he clung to the idea of a moral order in the universe. Whether it be based on Plato's notion of a perfect world of Ideas, Aristotle's teleological faith that all things have some good purpose, or Marcus Aurelius' idea of Providence, there was, Boethius believed, a goodness, a God, which must triumph over evil or mere chance. He does not mention Christ nor does he feel like a Christian martyr, although he was declared to be one in 1883. His outlook was akin to that of the tragic heroes in the plays written by the Athenian Aeschylus, who had lived a thousand years earlier. A man must stand on principle for its own sake and renounce any expediency which might win him some advantage in a world of vanities. It was on philosophical grounds that he would do God's will.

Philosophy comforts him in his struggle with himself:

So it is no matter for your wonder if, in this sea of life, we are tossed about by storms from all sides; for to oppose evil men is the chief aim we set before ourselves. Though the band of such men is great in numbers, yet it is to be contemned; for it is guided by no leader, but is hurried along at random only by error running riot everywhere. If this band when warring against us presses too strongly upon us, our leader, Reason, gathers her forces into her citadel, while the enemy are busied in plundering useless baggage. As they seize the most worthless things, we laugh at them from above, untroubled by the whole band of mad marauders, and we are defended by that rampart to which riotous folly may not hope to attain. (p. 8)

In his earlier, happier days, Boethius had prepared texts on music and arithmetic which were used by students during the Middle Ages. He was one of the major transmitters of the knowledge of ancient times—a man who had lived on into another age, and died there, somewhat out of season.

Cassiodorus

It would appear in history that when events offer a people new feelings of pride and destiny they are moved to discover a glorious past as a background for their present good fortune. The early logographers of Greece were kept busy supplying prosperous cities with adventuresome myths wherein gods and heroes figured prominently in the past. In the third century B.C., the century in which the Romans completed the conquest of Italy and twice defeated the Carthaginians, they too were in need of a history. By the time Livy and Vergil were writing, in the first century B.C., both could describe Rome's origins according to a well-established story, woven partly from Greek legends, but glorious to be sure. So it is not so strange that a great Gothic king ruling over Italy in the early sixth century would ask a learned aide to prepare a history of the Gothic people.

Cassiodorus was a well-educated young man about twenty years old when he first caught the eye of Theodoric. He was never thereafter out of the king's favor, and held a succession of offices which gave him an intimate knowledge of the Ostrogothic court and administration. Later, he published his official correspondence, the *Variae,* in which he displayed pride in his work. The old Roman sense of duty was alive in Cassiodorus, even though it served the ends of a Gothic ruler. Cassiodorus was more practical, more of a realist, than Boethius. The Goths were after all in

power, and Theodoric's loyal official felt it best for all concerned
to accept that fact and give full cooperation. His *History of the
Goths* was intended to shore up the reputation of the barbarians
who now occupied Italy.

He was by no means the first Roman writer to give praise to
the barbarians, however. Claudius Claudianus, a Latin poet who
had served on the staff of Stilicho in the early fifth century, has
been called the last of ancient Rome's notable poets. This honor
rests on more than his talent for singing the praises of the famous
Vandal general, but surely in that he could not be excelled. On the
occasion of Stilicho's consulship in A.D. 400, he wrote:

> Am I to recall his deeds of old and earliest manhood? His present
> deeds lure away my mind. Am I to tell of his justice? His military
> glory outshines it. Shall I mention his prowess in war? He has done
> more in peace. Shall I relate how Latium flourishes, how Africa has
> returned to her allegiance and service, . . . how Gaul has now nought
> to fear from a disarmed Germany? Or shall I sing of wintry Thrace
> and those fierce struggles whereof Hebrus was witness? Limitless is
> the expanse that opens before me and even on the slopes of Helicon
> this weight of praise retards my muse's chariot. (*On Stilicho's Consul-
> ship,* I. 14–24)

As the Romans had managed to relate themselves to the
valiant Trojans of long ago, so in Cassiodorus' history the Goths
were now to have a respectable ancestry among the Scythians and
other notable peoples of earliest antiquity. Cassiodorus' work has
been lost, but its purpose is plain in an abridgment made by
Jordanes, presumably Bishop of Crotona, about the mid-sixth
century, who is sometimes described as a pupil of Cassiodorus.
The original twelve books of Cassiodorus' history were distilled
into one very short one, to which was added some material from
other sources. In the process Jordanes made an unintentional contribution by supplying future readers with a good example of the
poor state into which Latin had fallen by his day. Jordanes, himself a Goth, was not a scholarly or even very well educated man.
His hope for a reconciliation of the Romans and Goths was somewhat sentimental. By the time he was preparing his condensation
of Cassiodorus' work, the Ostrogothic kingdom had already been
overthrown by the able general Belisarius (*ca.* A.D. 505–565), acting for Justinian (*ca.* A.D. 482–565), who reigned from 527 and
became the most famous of the Eastern (Byzantine) emperors.
Under whatever rule, it appeared that the Goths and Romans

would have to learn to endure each other. In the marriage of the widow of the last Ostrogothic king Vitigis, who ruled from 536 to 540, to Justinian's nephew Germanus, Jordanes saw a better future for everybody.

Cassiodorus had retired from public service before the fall of the Ostrogothic kingdom. Most of the rest of his long life was devoted to the preservation and advancement of knowledge. As a devout Christian, he would naturally turn to the monastic life as affording the best opportunity for meditation and service in a worthy cause. The two monasteries he founded in southern Italy were beehives wherein monks gave their lives to the task of making copies of, and so preserving, both the books sacred to the Christians and the writings of the great classical authors. These monasteries with their libraries and monks as teachers attracted students who sought training in theology. Such students, Cassiodorus believed, should begin by acquiring a basic education in the seven liberal arts. The educated Christian needed grammar and rhetoric. That meant wide reading in the pagan authors, whose books Cassiodorus and other like-minded men helped to save.

The literary legacy from Rome has appealed to men in different ages for different reasons. Nowadays there is a penchant for knowing how societies succeed and why they fail. The works of the ancient historians can still be read to remind us that long ago if a father was wont to advise his son to be a Roman it meant something. Those who read about the Romans today realize that they did not always live up to the challenge of that command. But there were many Romans who wanted to, and therein lies a greatness.

Roman society at its best was shaped according to tradition, education, and family pride, by which men were taught to discipline themselves. When that sense of discipline was lost and men lapsed into accepting themselves as they were, either for convenience or comfort, strength and vigor waned. The Jews had been trained by their Law, the Greeks by the *polis,* the Christians by their faith. The message seems to be that men must live according to the dictates of some formative power outside themselves. If that be a moral, then let it be so. Morality was after all what Roman writers had talked about from the beginning to the end of their histories of ancient Rome.

Appendix

A Brief Survey of the Ancient Sources
for Roman History

THE WRITTEN RECORD

Nowadays, people are inclined to search for answers to life's problems in future studies in psychology and sociology. In the ancient world, men looked to the past. The Romans read history. Historians, not novelists, were prominent among their great writers. Even the poet Vergil was at his best with legend.

Those who told Rome's story wanted to inform, entertain, and reform their readers, albeit not necessarily in that order. Moral uplift often took precedence over facts. A modern reader is apt to find the sermonizing tedious, particularly in contrast to livelier reading at hand. But he should not be surprised to find that the moralizing was accompanied by some sensational stories with the added attraction that many of them were true.

The bedrock of Roman history is supplied by the remarkable, if sometimes ponderous, Livy (59 B.C.–A.D. 17), living and writing during the last days of the Republic, whose work covered the previous five hundred years, or roughly the first half of the ancient Roman experience.

Where did he get his information? Most of it came from earlier writers beginning with Rome's first prose historian, Fabius Pictor, who was writing around 200 B.C. Pictor and his successors depended on a variety of sources which were also available to Livy. Among them were old stories which had been passed down orally from generation to generation; if they could not be verified, they were at least sanctified by age. Some tales had been enshrined in poetry. Long before Vergil's time, poets sang about the glory of Rome. Today, only fragments remain of the epics by Naevius (*ca.* 270–200 B.C.), who wrote about the first war with Carthage, and Ennius (*ca.* 239–169 B.C.), who retold in verse the story from the time of the kings to his own. In the interest of robust if not honest literature, Roman historians often borrowed passages from Greek histories to supply a dramatic turn where the native tradition was running thin. By the same token, if a speech or a letter would serve to make a point, Roman authors would invent what they needed and at the same time enliven their accounts with vivid writing. Such practices, of course, invite genuine skepticism about the worth of the historical tradition, particularly for the early Republic. However, documentary materials were also available. These included inscribed laws and treaties, lists of magistrates, and records of the chief priests, who from early times had duly noted the important wars, epidemics, and other significant events of each year. Specialists continue to worry about the possible errors or deliberate falsifications of these public records, but in general they were more reliable than the ancestral lore kept alive by proud families.

Almost all of the works of the earlier historians which Livy used were subsequently lost entirely or are now represented only by a few fragments. The notable exception would be the sizeable portions remaining of the *Histories* by Polybius (*ca.* 200–*ca.* 117 B.C.), the foremost of those Greek writers whose ancestors were writing history long before the Romans were writing at all. Understandably, the Greeks were fascinated with the events whereby Rome emerged as the foremost power of the Mediterranean world. The account of the last years of the third century and the first half of the second century B.C. by Polybius has a special value because in some instances he was describing events he had witnessed himself. That cannot be said for two of Livy's contemporaries, Diodorus of Sicily (*ca.* 80–*ca.* 29 B.C.) or Dionysius of Halicarnassus (*ca.* 60 B.C.–after 7 B.C.). Their material, which supplements Livy for the early centuries of the Republic, was dependent on secondary sources which later disappeared.

As suggested above, the inherited information about the early years of Rome down to the First Punic War (264 B.C.) which is found in Livy, Diodorus, and Dionysius is open to doubt. Nor could it be otherwise with the lapse in time and the many hands involved. Yet the vogue among modern scholars of arousing only doubt where there once was only trust has had its day. Recent archaeological studies serve to both correct and confirm some old facts. Suffice it to say that among ancient historians who exchange reputations by arguing such matters, Livy is acceptable again. If reservations remain about what he wrote, it is to be remembered that he had a few himself. Modern critics may still prefer their own reconstructions of Roman history to his and they may be more correct in some particulars, but they cannot replace the intrinsic value of Livy. They are not Romans. He was a Roman. And he remains the best example of how an educated Roman with a patriotic heart thought and felt. For that alone he is worth reading. Moreover, if the astute Machiavelli thought there was something to be learned from him, why shouldn't we?

Fortunately, the lost parts of Livy's account are summarized in available digests such as the *Periochae,* the essential contents of Livy's history. The *Epitome of Roman History* by Florus, who lived in the second century A.D., is another abbreviated version of Livy's work.

It was Plutarch (*ca.* A.D. 46–*ca.* 120) who in the second century wrote the biographies of selected Roman notables for the fashionable purpose of pointing out what was good or bad in human behavior. Earlier, Cicero's friend Cornelius Nepos published a voluminous work on the lives of illustrious men. His studies of two of Rome's staunchest enemies, Hamilcar and Hannibal, have been preserved.

Another Greek, Appian (*ca.* A.D. 95–*ca.* 165) wrote a history of Rome which provides a continuous record from the late second century B.C. through most of the first century before Christ. In this same period, Sallust's monographs on the Jugurthine War and the Catilinarian conspiracy spotlight two major events. The numerous letters and speeches of Cicero were written by a man inside Roman politics. Then there is Caesar's own version of the wars he fought in Gaul and his struggle with Pompey. His later campaigns were described by loyal aides who kept their commander's reputation intact. Cicero and Caesar were both more interested in promoting themselves than they were in history, but they did relay considerable information which would not otherwise be available.

On Agriculture by Cato the Elder (234–149 B.C.), written about 160 B.C., is not only a commentary on the management of large farms but also a source of information on slavery, social customs, and religious practices in the second century B.C. A supplementary work by Varro (116–27 B.C.), written in 37 B.C., although narrower in scope, describes in particular the livestock on farms as he knew them. Agriculture is again the subject of a book by Columella, who was writing in the mid-first century A.D. A Spaniard who owned farms in Italy, he sought to inspire others to turn to farming as an occupation and a good life, as did Varro earlier. Like Cato, he has something to say about slavery, and it is noteworthy that he comments on the increasing cost of such labor in his day.

The only existing book on Roman architecture is by Vitruvius, who served Caesar and Augustus and wrote not only from his own experience as an architect and military engineer, but also preserved what he had learned from the Greeks. Frontinus (*ca.* A.D. 30–104), who served as the superintendent of Rome's water supply under both Nerva and Trajan, prepared two volumes on the history and management (and frequent mismanagement) of Rome's aqueducts, which also furnish firsthand knowledge of Roman engineering.

There is no basic work comparable to Livy for the history of the Roman Empire. Tacitus (*ca.* A.D. 55–120) wrote abut the emperors in the first century A.D., and his available studies, especially the one on Tiberius, are worth reading for their own sake. The *Lives of the Twelve Caesars* (from Julius Caesar through Domitian) by Suetonius (*ca.* A.D. 69–*ca.* 150) is sketchy and lacks the literary value of Tacitus' work; yet it remains the only source for certain years. Only the first emperor, Augustus, left an account of his own deeds—good deeds. It was not to be expected that the *Res Gestae* (*Things Accomplished*) would record anything unfavorable to his reputation.

The *Compendium of Roman History* by Velleius Paterculus (*ca.* 20 B.C.–*ca.* A.D. 30) is a routine account of the years 146 B.C. to

A.D. 30, but it does include material on the Roman provinces and so occasionally escapes the customary focus on personalities in Rome. However, there was considerable praise of Tiberius, and that was certainly unusual. Of greater value than the *Compendium* for much of the same period is a history by Dio Cassius (*ca.* A.D. 155–*ca.* 230), who like Polybius was an historian who had been active in public life. Philo (*ca.* 20 B.C.–*ca.* A.D. 40) and Josephus (*ca.* A.D. 37–*ca.* 100), two Jewish scholars writing in the first century A.D., offer an "outside" view of Rome, albeit Josephus personally came to see the world from the Roman point of view.

Letters play a more important role in ancient history than they need to in modern times. As mentioned above, Cicero's correspondence gives the news about the times in which he lived. But there is much else available for that period. What makes the letters of Pliny the Younger (A.D. 61–*ca.* 114) of special importance for the late first and early second centuries A.D. (reigns of Nerva and Trajan) is that they are almost all there is to read. Although, to be sure, the amusing satires of Martial (*ca.* A.D. 40–*ca.* 102) and the gloomy tirades of Juvenal (*ca.* A.D. 60–*ca.* 140) provide some history on the side by calling to life a variety of characters and putting some action into Roman street scenes. Later, there are the letters between Marcus Aurelius and his tutor Fronto (*ca.* A.D. 100–*ca.* 167), which reveal why the young Marcus became one of the best of all the emperors. Otherwise the history of much of the second century must depend on the study of a fortunate number of inscriptions, coins, and decorated monuments.

Beginning in A.D. 180 with the accession of Marcus Aurelius' son Commodus (A.D. 161–192) it is again possible to follow a continual account of events. Herodian, about whom little is known, wrote a history which runs to A.D. 238 and covers the dynasty of the Severi. After that date there is again a patchwork of minor sources until reaching the edicts of Diocletian and Constantine, which speak for the newly founded Autocracy. By this time, too, there had been a growing body of Christian writers, beginning with Justin Martyr (*ca.* A.D. 100–*ca.* 165) on through Eusebius (*ca.* A.D. 260–340), who in addition to his *Ecclesiastical History,* a history of the Christian Church to 324 A.D., wrote a life of his hero Constantine. Although the Christian writers were primarily interested in defending their religion, they had much to say about the course of events. Lactantius (*ca.* A.D. 245–*ca.* 325) was particularly strong on Diocletian's crucial regime.

The earliest codifications of Roman law, prepared in the late third century A.D., have been lost. But the work of the first compilers was incorporated into the codes of Theodosius II, who reigned at Constantinople from A.D. 408 to 450, and Justinian, the great Byzantine emperor, from A.D. 527 to 565. Most of the Theodosian Code is available; but it has a limited scope, covering only the edicts of Constantine and his successors. The code of Justinian is not only intact but more comprehensive. The *Digest,* a section preserving the opinions of famous jurists, goes back as far as the late Republic.

The problems and mood of the fourth century are evident in the extant writings of Ammianus Marcellinus (*ca.* A.D. 330–400), whose account of the years A.D. 353 to 378 includes several digressions on subjects ranging from weaponry to the causes of earthquakes. His favorite subject was the Emperor Julian (A.D. 331–363), whose own letters and speeches add another source of information for the times. A similar period, A.D. 395 to 410, is covered in the *New History* by Zosimus, who lived in the fifth century and viewed with alarm the phenomenon of Christianity. His contemporary, Orosius, spoke for the winning side in his *Against the Pagans.* But neither Zosimus nor Orosius won the fame of Boethius (*ca.* A.D. 480–*ca.* 524). Imprisoned and later beheaded by the Ostrogothic king Theodoric, he wrote *The Consolation of Philosophy,* one of the last great books of the ancient Graeco-Roman world. In this work he remained true to the old intellectual tradition of reliance on philosophy rather than religion in a time of need. Rome had already fallen, but the old classical tradition lived on.

COINS

The Romans first used bronze bars for money as early as the fifth century B.C.; but, according to tradition, true bronze coins did not appear until the early third century. Silver appeared about 280 B.C. and finally, during the Second Punic War, gold; but it was not until the time of Julius Caesar that gold was used regularly. Some Roman coins are still in circulation. Collectors and tourists like to have them for private reasons; numismatists study them for their historical value. The place where Roman coins are discovered can itself be revealing. The location might indicate the extent of trade, whether in Scandinavia or India, or the amount of money being buried at home when the future looked grim. The metallic content of a given issue can also say something about the economic climate at the time it was minted. A side value of coins is that they allow for the dating within perhaps thirty years of the articles found with them, except for the reservation that the coins themselves may have been saved from a much earlier time.

Roman coins often carried a rough but distinguishable picture of a building or monument which has disappeared. The most frequent imprints were likenesses of notable persons, the emperors usually. With their portraits came some message they wanted carried to distant places. An emperor might boast of a recent victory or issue a coin with the likeness of his heir in order to give his designated successor some publicity. By the same token, a usurper who claimed a part of the Empire as his own needed a mint in a hurry to send out coins carrying his own picture, which in effect announced that he was in business for himself. Coins were the best means of putting propaganda in the hands of every citizen. For the emperor who wanted to boast of the security he had brought to the Roman world, the word PAX was a slogan. There was also the promotion of whatever deity or deities a particular emperor happened to favor. By the end of the fourth century, a latter-day ruler named Theodosius proclaimed the triumph of Christianity on bronze coins—a paradoxical tribute to a faith once so contemptuous of the things of this world.

PAPYRI

Historians who chronicle recent events have vast quantities of government records at their disposal, not to mention newspaper accounts. The ancient historian would have very little in the way of paper at all, if it were not for the sands of Egypt. It was in Egypt that papyri was produced, and because of the dryness of the land that was where almost all of it has been preserved. The production of papyri was an inexpensive process. Vertical strips cut from the stalk of a papyrus plant were placed across horizontal strips, and the resulting sheet was first moistened with size and then dried in the sun. Papyri was not as durable as parchment made from the skins of sheep and goats, but it was cheaper; and documents dating from the fourth century B.C. to the eighth century A.D. show that it served the same purpose as ordinary paper does today.

The public is only likely to see headlines about papyri discoveries when they offer long passages from some lost works of ancient literature. In this century, for instance, parts of three plays and one whole play by the Greek comedian Menander (*ca.* 343–291 B.C.) have been found. Patient papyrologists usually work with less newsworthy material, including personal letters, business records, and government documents. The many volumes which make this evidence available to the historian include much information about everyday matters. There is also considerable documentation of how the Romans governed Egypt when it was an imperial province. There are orders of Egyptian prefects and edicts issued by the emperors. In addition, certain of the papyri cover significant religious, magical, and scientific subjects in the Graeco-Roman period.

INSCRIPTIONS

Outside of Egypt, the records preserved intact from ancient times were usually engraved on stone. Metals, bronze in particular, were also used. The Romans followed the Greek practice of inscribing treaties, laws, and edicts on stone slabs, *stelae,* which were available for public inspection and more or less permanent. Then as now, the names of public officials and private philanthropists were duly recorded on buildings or monuments for which they were given credit. So, too, stone inscriptions were set up to announce publicly who was responsible for the construction or repair of a road. It was typically Roman to include the amount of money being spent and where it came from. It could be from the state treasury, the emperor's own funds, or appropriated from those living along the roads, or any combination of the three. Thus, the fabric of Roman history is sewn with thousands upon thousands of inscriptions, many more from the Empire than from the Republic, which offer the information which the Romans themselves thought worthy of being made permanent.

Bibliography

Paperbound editions are indicated by a dagger (†) following the date of publication.

Works Cited

References given after quotations in the text are to the following editions, listed by authors in alphabetical order of their most familiar names.

Ammianus Marcellinus. *The Surviving Books of the History of Ammianus Marcellinus.* 3 vols. Translated by John C. Rolfe. Loeb Classical Library. Cambridge, Mass.: Harvard University Press, 1963–64.

Appian. *Appian's Roman History.* 4 vols. Translated by Horace White. Loeb Classical Library. Cambridge, Mass.: Harvard University Press, 1913.

Augustine. *Basic Writings of Saint Augustine.* 2 vols. Edited by Whitney J. Oates. New York: Random House, 1948.

Aurelius, Marcus. *The Communings with Himself of Marcus Aurelius Antoninus.* Translated by C. R. Haines. New York: Macmillan, 1916.

Boethius. *The Consolation of Philosophy.* Translated by W. V. Cooper. Modern Library edition. New York: Random House, 1943.

Bury, J. B. *History of the Later Roman Empire.* 2 vols. London: Macmillan, 1889; New York: Dover Publications, 1958†.

Caesar. *Caesar's War Commentaries.* Translated by John Warrington. New York: E. P. Dutton, 1958†.

Catullus. *Catullus: The Complete Poems for American Readers.* Translated by Reney Myers and Robert J. Ormsby. New York: E. P. Dutton, 1970†.
————. *Gaius Valerius Catullus, The Complete Poetry.* Translated by Frank O. Copley. Ann Arbor: University of Michigan Press, 1957, 1964†.
————. *The Poetry of Catullus.* Translated by C. H. Sisson. London: MacGibbon & Kee, 1966; New York: Orion Press, 1967.
Cicero. *Offices, Essays, and Letters.* Translated by Thomas Cockman and W. Melmoth. Everyman's Library edition. New York: E. P. Dutton, 1909.
————. *The Verrine Orations.* 2 vols. Translated by L. H. G. Greenwood. Loeb Classical Library. Cambridge, Mass.: Harvard University Press, 1928–35.
Claudius Claudianus. *Claudian.* 2 vols. Translated by Maurice Platnauer. Loeb Classical Library. New York: G. P. Putnam's Sons, 1922.
Dio Cassius. *Roman History.* 9 vols. Translated by Earnest Cary. Loeb Classical Library. New York: G. P. Putnam's Sons, 1917.
Fronto. *The Correspondence of Marcus Cornelius Fronto.* 2 vols. Translated by C. R. Haines. Loeb Classical Library. New York: G. P. Putnam's Sons, 1919.
Gibbon, Edward. *The Decline and Fall of the Roman Empire.* 2 vols. Modern Library edition. New York: Random House, 1932.
Herodian. *History of the Roman Empire from the Death of Marcus Aurelius to the Accession of Gordian III.* 2 vols. Translated by C. R. Whittaker. Loeb Classical Library. Cambridge, Mass.: Harvard University Press, 1969–70.
Herodotus. *The Persian Wars.* Translated by George Rawlinson. Modern Library edition. New York: Random House, 1947.
Horace. *The Satires and Epistles of Horace.* Translated by Smith Palmer Bovie. Chicago: University of Chicago Press, 1959.
————. *The Works of Horace.* 2 vols. Translated by Sir Theodore Martin. London: William Blackwell & Sons, 1888.
James, William. *Pragmatism.* New York: Longmans, Green & Co., 1907.
Josephus. *The Great Roman-Jewish War: A.D. 66–70.* Translated by William Whiston. Revised by D. S. Margoliouth. New York: Harper & Brothers, Torchbooks, 1960†.
Juvenal. *The Sixteen Satires.* Translated by Peter Green. Baltimore: Penguin Books, 1967.
Lewis, Naphtali, and Reinhold, Meyer. *Roman Civilization.* 2 vols. New York: Columbia University Press, 1955; Harper & Brothers, Torchbooks, 1966†.
Livy. *From the Founding of the City.* 14 vols. Translated by various hands. Loeb Classical Library. Cambridge, Mass.: Harvard University Press, 1919.
Martial. *Selected Epigrams.* Translated by Rolfe Humphries. Bloomington: Indiana University Press, 1963.
Ovid. *Metamorphoses.* Translated by Rolfe Humphries. Bloomington: Indiana University Press, 1958.
Percival, Henry R., ed. *The Seven Ecumenical Councils of the Undivided Church, Their Canons and Dogmatic Decrees.* A Select Library of Nicene and Post-Nicene Fathers of the Christian Church, 2d series, Vol. XIV. New York: Scribner's, 1900.
Plautus. *Plautus.* 5 vols. Translated by Paul Nixon. Loeb Classical Library. Cambridge, Mass.: Harvard University Press, 1950.
Pliny. *Letters and Panegyricus.* 2 vols. Translated by Betty Radice. Loeb Classical Library. Cambridge, Mass.: Harvard University Press, 1969.
Plutarch. *The Lives of the Noble Grecians and Romans.* Translated by John Dryden. Revised by Arthur Hugh Clough. Modern Library edition. New York: Random House, 1932.
Polybius. *The Histories.* 2 vols. Translated by Evelyn S. Shuckburgh. Bloomington: Indiana University Press, 1962.

Roberts, Alexander, and Donaldson, James, eds. *The Ante-Nicene Fathers: The Writings of the Fathers down to A.D. 325.* Reprint edition. Grand Rapids: Eerdmans Publishing Co., 1953.

Sallust. *The War with Catiline* and *The War with Jugurtha.* Translated by J. C. Rolfe. Loeb Classical Library. Cambridge, Mass.: Harvard University Press, 1931.

Salmon, Edward T. *Samnium and Samnites.* Cambridge: Cambridge University Press, 1967.

Suetonius. *The Twelve Caesars.* Translated by Robert Graves. Baltimore: Penguin Books, 1957†.

Tacitus. *The Annals.* Translated by Donald R. Dudley. New York: New American Library, 1966.

———. *The Histories.* Translated by Clifford H. Moore. Loeb Classical Library. New York: G. P. Putnam's Sons, 1925.

Terence. *The Comedies of Terence.* Translated by Laurence Echard. Edited by Robert Graves. Chicago: Aldine Publishing Co., 1962.

Thucydides. *The Complete Writings of Thucydides.* Translated by Richard Crawley. New York: Modern Library, 1951†.

Books of Interest

REFERENCE WORKS

Hammond, N. G. L., and Scullard, H. H., eds. *Oxford Classical Dictionary.* 2d edition. Oxford: Oxford University Press, 1970.

Harvey, Sir Paul, ed. *The Oxford Companion to Classical Literature.* Reprint edition with corrections. Oxford: Clarendon Press, 1940.

Radice, Betty. *Who's Who in the Ancient World.* New York: Penguin Books, 1973†.

Sandys, Sir John E., ed. *A Companion to Latin Studies.* 3d edition. Cambridge: Cambridge University Press, 1921.

ATLASES

Grant, Michael, ed. *Ancient History Atlas.* London: Weidenfeld & Nicolson, 1975.

Treharne, R. F., and Fullard, Harold, eds. *Muir's Atlas of Ancient and Classical History.* 6th edition. New York: Harper & Row, 1963.

GENERAL WORKS

Africa, Thomas. *The Immense Majesty: A History of Rome and the Roman Empire.* New York: Thomas Y. Crowell, 1974.

Balsdon, J. P. V. D. *Rome: The Story of an Empire.* New York: McGraw-Hill, 1970†.

Barrow, R. H. *The Romans.* Baltimore: Penguin Books, 1949†.

Bourne, Frank C. *A History of the Romans.* Boston: D. C. Heath, 1966.

Cary, M. and Scullard, H. H. *A History of Rome down to the Reign of Constantine.* 3d edition. New York: St. Martin's, 1975.

Cook, S. A., and others, eds. *The Cambridge Ancient History,* Vols. VII–XII. 2d edition. Cambridge: Cambridge University Press, 1928–39.

Dudley, Donald. *The Romans: 850 B.C. to A.D. 337.* New York: Knopf, 1970.

Hadas, Moses, ed. *A History of Rome from its Origins to 529 A.D. as told by the Roman Historians.* Garden City, N.Y.: Doubleday, Anchor Books, 1956†.

Hamilton, Edith. *The Roman Way.* New York: Norton, 1932; New York: Mentor Books, 1957†.

Heichelheim, Fritz M., and Yeo, Cedric A. *A History of the Roman People*. Englewood Cliffs, N.J.: Prentice-Hall, 1962.
Rostovtzeff, M. *Rome*. Translated by J. D. Duff. First published as *A History of the Ancient World*, Vol. II, *Rome*, 1927. New York: Oxford University Press, Galaxy Books, 1960†.
————. *The Social and Economic History of the Roman Empire*. 2 vols. 2d edition. Oxford: Oxford University Press, 1957.
Sinnigen, William G., and Boak, Arthur E. R. *A History of Rome to A.D. 565*. 6th edition. New York: Macmillan, 1977.
Starr, Chester G. *The Ancient Romans*. New York: Oxford University Press, 1971.

ART

Bianchi Bandinelli, Ranuccio. *Rome, the Centre of Power: Roman Art to A.D. 200*. Translated by P. Green. London: Thames & Hudson, 1971.
————. *Rome, the Late Empire: Roman Art A.D. 200–400*. Translated by P. Green. London: Thames & Hudson, 1971.
Brilliant, Richard. *Roman Art: From the Republic to Constantine*. London: Phaidon, 1974.
MacDonald, William L. *The Architecture of the Roman Empire*. New Haven: Yale University Press, 1965.
Richter, G. M. A. *Roman Portraits*. New York: Metropolitan Museum of Art, 1948.
Swindler, Mary H. *Ancient Painting*. New Haven: Yale University Press, 1929.
Wheeler, Sir Robert E. M. *Roman Art and Architecture*. New York: Praeger, 1964†.

POLITICAL THOUGHT AND GOVERNMENT

Abbott, Frank F., and Johnson, Allan C. *Municipal Administration in the Roman Empire*. Princeton: Princeton University Press, 1926.
Adcock, Sir Frank E. *Roman Political Ideas and Practice*. Ann Arbor: University of Michigan Press, 1959.
Arnheim, M. T. W. *The Senatorial Aristocracy in the Later Roman Empire*. Oxford: Clarendon Press, 1972.
Broughton, T. R. S. *The Magistrates of the Roman Republic*. 2 vols. New York: American Philosophical Association, 1951–52.
Fritz, Kurt von. *The Theory of the Mixed Constitution in Antiquity*. New York: Columbia University Press, 1954.
Hammond, M. *The Augustan Principate in Theory and Practice during the Julio-Claudian Period*. 2d edition. New York: Russell & Russell, 1968.
Larsen, J. A. O. *Representative Government in Greek and Roman History*. Berkeley: University of California Press, 1955.
MacMullen, Ramsay. *Enemies of the Roman Order: Treason, Unrest and Alienation in the Empire*. Cambridge: Harvard University Press, 1966.
Smith, Richard E. *The Failure of the Roman Republic*. Cambridge: Cambridge University Press, 1955.
Taylor, Lily Ross. *Party Politics in the Age of Caesar*. Berkeley: University of California Press, 1949, 1961†.
————. *Roman Voting Assemblies from the Hannibalic War to the Dictatorship of Caesar*. Ann Arbor: The University of Michigan Press, 1966.
Wiseman, T. P. *New Men in the Roman Senate, 139 B.C.–A.D. 14*. New York: Oxford University Press, 1971.

THE PROVINCES

Jones, A. H. M. *The Cities of the Eastern Roman Provinces.* 2d edition. Oxford: Clarendon Press, 1971.

Levick, Barbara. *Roman Colonies in Southern Asia Minor.* Oxford: Clarendon Press, 1967.

Liversidge, Joan. *Britain in the Roman Empire.* London: Routledge & Kegan Paul, 1968.

Magie, David. *Roman Rule in Asia Minor, to the End of the Third Century after Christ.* 2 vols. Princeton: Princeton University Press, 1950.

Mommsen, Theodor. *The Provinces of the Roman Empire: The European Provinces.* Selections from *The History of Rome,* Vol. 5, Book 8. Edited by T. R. S. Broughton. Chicago: University of Chicago Press, Phoenix Books, 1968†.

Raven, Susan. *Rome in Africa.* London: Evans Brothers, 1969.

Richmond, Ian. *Roman Britain.* 2d edition. Baltimore: Penguin Books, 1963†.

Salmon, E. T. *Roman Colonization under the Republic.* Ithaca: Cornell University Press, 1949.

Stevenson, G. H. *Roman Provincial Administration till the Age of the Antonines.* 2d edition. Oxford: Oxford University Press, 1949.

Sutherland, C. H. V. *The Romans in Spain, 217 B.C.–A.D. 117.* London: Metheun, 1939; reprinted, New York: Harper & Row, 1971.

LAW

Garnsey, Peter. *Social Status and Legal Privilege in the Roman Empire.* New York: Oxford University Press, 1970.

Jolowicz, H. F., and Nicholas, Barry. *Historical Introduction to the Study of Roman Law.* 3d edition. Cambridge: Cambridge University Press, 1972.

Jones, A. H. M. *The Criminal Courts of the Roman Republic and Principate.* Edited by J. A. Crook. Oxford: Blackwell, 1972.

Watson, Alan. *Rome of the XII Tables: Persons and Property.* Princeton: Princeton University Press, 1975.

STUDIES IN ROMAN LITERATURE

Adcock, Sir Frank E. *Caesar as Man of Letters.* Cambridge: Cambridge University Press, 1956.

Bieber, Margarete. *The History of the Greek and Roman Theater.* 2d edition. Princeton: Princeton University Press, 1961.

Copley, Frank O. *Latin Literature: From the Beginnings to the Close of the Second Century A.D.* Ann Arbor: University of Michigan Press, 1969.

Duckworth, George E., ed. *The Complete Roman Drama: All the Extant Comedies of Plautus and Terence and the Tragedies of Seneca in a Variety of Translations.* 2 vols. New York: Random House, 1942.

———. *The Nature of Roman Comedy.* Princeton: Princeton University Press, 1971.

Duff, J. W. *A Literary History of Rome from the Origins to the Close of the Golden Age.* 3d edition. Edited by A. M. Duff. London: E. Benn; New York: Barnes & Noble, 1953.

———. *A Literary History of Rome in the Silver Age from Tiberius to Hadrian.* 2d edition. Edited by A. M. Duff. London: E. Benn; New York: Barnes & Noble, 1960.

Frank, Tenney. *Life and Literature in the Roman Republic.* Berkeley: University of California Press, 1930, 1956†.

Grant, Michael. *Roman Literature.* Revised edition. Baltimore: Penguin Books, 1964†.

Hadas, Moses. *A History of Latin Literature.* New York: Columbia University Press, 1952.
Highet, Gilbert. *The Anatomy of Satire.* Princeton: Princeton University Press, 1962.
——. *Juvenal the Satirist.* New York: Oxford University Press, Galaxy Books, 1961†.
Isbell, Harold. *The Last Poets of Imperial Rome.* Baltimore: Penguin Books, 1971†.

HISTORIANS

Laistner, M. L. W. *The Greater Roman Historians.* Berkeley: University of California Press, 1947†.
Syme, Sir Ronald. *Ammianus Marcellinus and the Historia Augusta.* Oxford: Clarendon Press, 1968.
——. *Emperors and Biography: Studies in the Historia Augusta.* New York: Oxford University Press, 1971.
——. *Sallust.* Berkeley: University of California Press, 1964.
——. *Tacitus.* 2 vols. Oxford: Oxford University Press, 1958.
Walbank, F. W. *A Historical Commentary on Polybius.* 2 vols. Oxford: Oxford University Press, 1957.
——. *Polybius.* Berkeley: University of California Press, 1972.
Walsh, P. G. *Livy: His Historical Aims and Methods.* Cambridge: Cambridge University Press, 1961.

RELIGION

Altheim, F. *A History of Roman Religion.* Translated by Harold Mattingly. New York: E. P. Dutton, 1938.
Bailey, Cyril. *Phases in the Religion of Ancient Rome.* Berkeley: University of California Press, 1932.
Cumont, Franz. *Oriental Religions in Roman Paganism.* London: Cecil Chambers, 1911; New York: Dover Publications, 1956†.
Ferguson, John. *The Religions of the Roman Empire.* Ithaca: Cornell University Press, 1970.
Fowler, W. W. *The Religious Experience of the Roman People.* London: Macmillan, 1911.
Grant, Michael. *Roman Myths.* New York: Scribner's, 1971.
Halliday, Sir William R. *Lectures on the History of Roman Religion from Numa to Augustus.* Liverpool: Liverpool University Press, 1922.
Jaeger, Werner. *Early Christianity and Greek Paideia.* Cambridge, Mass.: Harvard University Press, 1961; New York: Oxford University Press, Galaxy Books, 1969†.
McGiffert, Arthur Cushman. *A History of Christian Thought.* 2 vols. New York: Scribner's, 1947.
Markus, Robert. *Christianity in the Roman World.* London: Thames & Hudson, 1974.
Nock, A. D. *Conversion: The Old and the New in Religion from Alexander the Great to Augustine of Hippo.* Oxford: Oxford University Press, 1933; New York: Oxford University Press, 1961†.
Rose, Herbert J. *Ancient Roman Religion.* London: Hutchinson, 1948.
Staniforth, Maxwell, ed. and trans. *Early Christian Writings: The Apostolic Fathers.* New York: Penguin Books, 1975†.

SPECIAL TOPICS

Auguet, Roland. *Cruelty and Civilization: The Roman Games.* London: Allen & Unwin, 1972.

Badian, E. *Publicans and Sinners: Private Enterprise in the Service of the Roman Republic.* Ithaca: Cornell University Press, 1972.

Balsdon, J. P. V. D. *Life and Leisure in Ancient Rome.* New York: McGraw-Hill, 1969.

Barrow, Reginald H. *Slavery in the Roman Empire.* London: Methuen, 1928.

Burgh, W. G. de. *The Legacy of the Ancient World.* 2 vols. Revised edition. Baltimore: Penguin Books, 1953†.

Chevallier, Raymond. *Roman Roads.* Translated by N. H. Field. London: Batsford, 1976.

Clarke, Martin L. *Higher Education in the Ancient World.* Albuquerque: University of New Mexico Press, 1971.

Cochrane, Charles N. *Christianity and Classical Culture: A Study of Thought and Action from Augustus to Augustine.* Revised edition. New York: Oxford University Press, 1944, Galaxy Books, 1957†.

Cowell, Frank R. *Everyday Life in Ancient Rome.* London: Batsford, 1961.

Daube, David. *Civil Disobedience in Antiquity.* Edinburgh: Edinburgh University Press, 1972.

Grant, Michael. *The Jews in the Roman World.* London: Weidenfeld & Nicolson, 1973.

Harris, Harold A. *Sport in Greece and Rome.* Ithaca: Cornell University Press, 1971.

Hill, Henry. *The Roman Middle Class in the Republican Period.* New York: Macmillan, ·1952.

Kennedy, George. *The Art of Rhetoric in the Roman World, 300 B.C. to A.D. 300.* Princeton: Princeton University Press, 1972†.

MacMullen, Ramsay. *Roman Social Relations, 50 B.C. to A.D. 284.* New Haven: Yale University Press, 1974.

Marrou, H. I. *A History of Education in Antiquity.* 3d edition. Translated by G. Lamb. New York: Sheed & Ward, 1956; New York: Mentor Books, 1964†.

Pallottino, Massimo. *The Etruscans.* Revised edition. Translated by J. Cremona. Bloomington: Indiana University Press, 1975.

Percival, John. *The Roman Villa: A Historical Introduction.* Berkeley: University of California Press, 1976.

Perowne, Stewart. *The Caesar's Wives: Above Suspicion?* London: Hodder & Stoughton, 1974.

Pomeroy, Sarah B. *Goddesses, Whores, Wives, and Slaves: Women in Classical Antiquity.* New York: Schocken Books, 1975†.

Scarborough, John. *Roman Medicine.* Ithaca: Cornell University Press, 1969.

Scullard, Howard H. *The Elephant in the Greek and Roman World.* London: Thames & Hudson, 1974.

Toynbee, Jocelyn M. C. *Death and Burial in the Roman World.* Ithaca: Cornell University Press, 1971.

Treggiari, Susan. *Roman Freedmen During the Late Republic.* New York: Oxford University Press, 1969.

Vacano, Otto-Wilhelm von. *The Etruscans in the Ancient World.* Translated by Sheila Ann Ogilvie. London: Edward Arnold, 1960.

Warmington, B. H. *Carthage.* London: Hale, 1960; Baltimore: Penguin Books, 1964†.

Westermann, William L. *The Slave Systems of Greek and Roman Antiquity.* Philadelphia: American Philosophical Society, 1955.

Wheeler, Sir Robert E. M. *Rome beyond the Imperial Frontiers.* London: Bell, 1954; Baltimore: Penguin Books, 1955†.

MILITARY

Adcock, Sir Frank E. *The Roman Art of War under the Republic*. Revised edition. New York: Harper & Row, 1971.

Marsden, Eric W. *Greek and Roman Artillery: Historical Development*. Oxford: Oxford University Press, 1969.

Parker, H. M. D. *The Roman Legions*. 2d edition. Cambridge: Heffer, 1958; reprinted, New York: Harper & Row, 1971.

Starr, Chester G. *The Roman Imperial Navy, 31 B.C.–A.D. 324*. New York: Barnes & Noble, 1960.

Watson, George R. *The Roman Soldier*. Ithaca: Cornell University Press, 1969.

ARCHAEOLOGY, NUMISMATICS AND PAPYRI

Bass, George F. *Archaeology Under Water*. New York: Praeger, 1966.

Crawford, Michael H. *Roman Republican Coinage*. 2 vols. New York: Cambridge University Press, 1974.

Grant, Michael. *Cities of Vesuvius: Pompeii and Herculaneum*. London: Weidenfeld & Nicolson, 1971.

———. *Roman History from Coins*. Cambridge: Cambridge University Press, 1958.

Lewis, Naphtali. *Papyrus in Classical Antiquity*. Oxford: Clarendon Press, 1974.

MacKendrick, Paul. *The Dacian Stones Speak*. Chapel Hill: University of North Carolina Press, 1975.

———. *The Mute Stones Speak: The Story of Archaeology in Italy*. New York: St. Martin's, 1960; New York: Mentor Books, 1966†.

———. *Roman France*. London: Bell, 1972.

———. *Romans on the Rhine; Archaeology in Germany*. New York: Funk & Wagnalls, 1970.

Mattingly, Harold. *Roman Coins from the Earliest Times to the Fall of the Western Empire*. 2d edition. London: Methuen, 1960.

Sutherland, Carol H. V. *Coinage in Roman Imperial Policy, 31 B.C. to A.D. 68*. London: Methuen, 1951; reprinted, New York: Barnes & Noble, 1971.

Yadin, Yigael. *Bar-Kokhba: The Rediscovery of the Legendary Hero of the Second Jewish Revolt against Rome*. New York: Random House, 1971.

———. *Masada: Herod's Fortress and the Zealots Last Stand*. Translated by Moshe Pearlman. New York: Random House, 1966.

ECONOMICS

Charlesworth, Martin P. *Trade Routes and Commerce of the Roman Empire*. 2d edition. New York: Cooper Square Publishers, 1970.

Frank, Tenney. *An Economic History of Rome*. 2d edition. Baltimore: Johns Hopkins Press, 1927.

———, ed. *An Economic Survey of Ancient Rome*. 5 vols. Baltimore: Johns Hopkins Press, 1933–40.

Jones, A. H. M. *The Roman Economy*. Oxford: Basil Blackwell, 1974.

SPECIAL PERIODS

Arnheim, M. T. W. *The Senatorial Aristocracy in the Later Roman Empire*. Oxford: Clarendon Press, 1971.

Arragon, R. F. *The Transition from the Ancient to the Medieval World*. New York: Holt, 1936.

Boak, Arthur E. R. *Manpower Shortage and the Fall of the Roman Empire in the West.* Ann Arbor: University of Michigan Press, 1955.

Brown, Peter, R. L. *The World of Late Antiquity: From Marcus Aurelius to Muhammad.* New York: Harcourt Brace Jovanovich, 1971.

Burckhardt, Jacob. *The Age of Constantine the Great.* Translated by Moses Hadas. New York: Pantheon Books, 1949; New York: Anchor Books, 1956†.

Chambers, Mortimer, ed. *The Fall of Rome: Can It Be Explained?* 2d edition. New York: Holt, Rinehart & Winston, 1971†.

Charlesworth, Martin P. *The Roman Empire.* New York: Oxford University Press, 1951, 1968†.

Cowell, Frank R. *Cicero and the Roman Republic.* London: Peter Smith, 1948; Baltimore: Penguin Books, 1956†.

Dill, Sir Samuel. *Roman Society in the Last Century of the Western Empire.* 2d edition. New York: Macmillan, 1899; New York: Meridian Books, 1958†.

———. *Roman Society from Nero to Marcus Aurelius.* 2d edition. New York: Macmillan, 1919; New York: Meridian Books, 1956†.

Dorey, Thomas A., and Dudley, Donald R. *Rome Against Carthage.* London: Secker & Warburg, 1971.

Gruen, Erich S. *The Last Generation of the Roman Republic.* Berkeley: University of California Press, 1974.

Haskell, Henry J. *The New Deal in Old Rome.* New York: Knopf, 1939.

Jones, A. H. M. *The Later Roman Empire, A.D. 284–602.* 3 vols. Oxford: Blackwell, 1964. Abridged edition entitled *The Decline of the Ancient World.* New York: Holt, Rinehart & Winston, 1966†.

———. *The Prosopography of the Later Roman Empire.* Vol. I (A.D. 260–395). Cambridge: Cambridge University Press, 1971.

Lot, Ferdinand. *The End of the Ancient World and the Beginnings of the Middle Ages.* Translated by Philip and Mariette Leon. New York: Knopf, 1931; Harper & Brothers, Torchbooks, 1961†.

MacMullen, Ramsay. *Roman Government's Response to Crisis, A.D. 235–337.* New Haven: Yale University Press, 1976.

Marsh, Frank B. *A History of the Roman World, 146 to 30 B.C.* 3d edition. Revised by H. H. Scullard. New York: Barnes & Noble, 1963, 1971†.

Mattingly, H. *Roman Imperial Civilization.* London: Arnold, 1957; New York: Norton, 1971†.

Parker, Henry M. D. *A History of the Roman World, A.D. 138 to 337.* 2d edition. Revised by B. H. Warmington. New York: Barnes & Noble, 1969†.

Proctor, Dennis. *Hannibal's March in History.* Oxford: Clarendon Press, 1971.

Salmon, Edward T. *A History of the Roman World from 30 B.C. to A.D. 138.* 6th edition. New York: Barnes & Noble, 1968†.

Scullard, Howard H. *From the Gracchi to Nero: A History of Rome from 133 B.C. to A.D. 68.* 4th edition. London: Methuen, 1976; New York: Harper & Row, 1976†.

———. *A History of the Roman World from 753 to 146 B.C.* 3d edition. London: Methuen, 1961; New York: Harper & Row, 1969†.

———. *Roman Politics, 220–150 B.C.* 2d edition. Oxford: Oxford University Press, 1973.

Smith, Richard E. *The Failure of the Roman Republic.* Cambridge: Cambridge University Press, 1955; New York: Arno Press, 1975.

Syme, Sir Ronald. *The Roman Revolution.* Oxford: Oxford University Press, 1939; New York: Oxford University Press, 1960†.

Tarn, Sir William W. and Charlesworth, M. P. *Octavian, Antony and Cleopatra.* A reprint of chapters 1–4 of the Cambridge Ancient History, Vol. X. Cambridge: Cambridge University Press, 1965.

Walbank, Frank W. *The Awful Revolution: The Decline of the Roman Empire in the West*. First published as *The Decline of the Roman Empire in the West*. Revised edition. Liverpool: Liverpool University Press, 1969; Toronto: University of Toronto Press, 1969†.

BIOGRAPHY

Africa, Thomas W., *Rome of the Caesars*. New York: Wiley, 1965†.

Astin, A. E. *Scipio Aemilianus*. Oxford: Clarendon Press, 1967.

Balsdon, J. P. V. D. *The Emperor Gaius*. New York: Oxford University Press, 1934.

Beer, Sir Gavin de. *Hannibal: Challenging Rome's Supremacy*. New York: Viking, 1969.

Birley, Anthony R. *Marcus Aurelius*. Boston: Little, Brown, 1966.

———. *Septimius Severus: The African Emperor*. Garden City, N.Y.: Doubleday, 1972.

Browning, Robert. *The Emperor Julian*. Berkeley: University of California Press, 1976.

Buchan, John. *Augustus*. Boston: Houghton Mifflin, 1937.

Charlesworth, M. P. *Five Men: Character Studies from the Roman Empire*. Cambridge, Mass.: Harvard University Press, 1936.

Fuller, J. F. C. *Julius Caesar: Man, Soldier and Tyrant*. London: Eyre & Spottiswoode, 1965.

Grant, Michael. *Nero, Emperor in Revolt*. New York: American Heritage Press, 1970.

Haskell, Henry J. *This was Cicero: Modern Politics in a Roman Toga*. New York: Knopf, 1942.

Holmes, T. R. *The Architect of the Roman Empire*. 2 vols. Oxford: Oxford University Press, 1928–31.

Jones, A. H. M. *Augustus*. New York: Norton, 1970.

Kelly, J. N. D. *Jerome, His Life, Writings, and Controversies*. New York: Harper & Row, 1976.

Liddell Hart, B. H. *A Greater than Napoleon: Scipio Africanus*. Boston: Little, Brown, 1927.

MacMullen, Ramsay. *Constantine*. New York: Dial Press, 1969; New York: Harper & Row, Torchbooks, 1971†.

Marsh, F. B. *The Reign of Tiberius*. Oxford: Oxford University Press, 1931; New York: Barnes & Noble, 1959.

Momigliano, A. *Claudius, the Emperor and His Achievements*, 2d edition. Translated by W. D. Hogarth. New York: Barnes & Noble, 1961.

Perowne, Stewart. *Hadrian*. London: Hodder & Stoughton, 1960; New York: Norton, 1962.

Scullard, Howard H. *Scipio Africanus: Soldier and Politician*. Ithaca: Cornell University Press, 1970.

Seager, Robin. *Tiberius*. Berkeley: University of California Press, 1972.

Smith, John Holland. *Constantine the Great*. London: Hamilton, 1971; New York: Scribner's, 1971†.

Smith, Richard E. *Cicero the Statesman*. Cambridge: Cambridge University Press, 1966.

Shackleton-Bailey, D. R. *Cicero*. New York: Scribner's, 1971.

Stockton, David. *Cicero: A Political Biography*. Oxford: Oxford University Press, 1971†.

Turton, Godfrey. *The Syrian Princesses: The Women Who Ruled Rome, A.D. 193–235*. London: Cassell, 1974.

PHILOSOPHY AND SCIENCE

Africa, Thomas W. *Science and the State in Greece and Rome.* New York: Wiley, 1968.
Arnold, E. Vernon. *Roman Stoicism.* Cambridge: Cambridge University Press, 1911.
Bevan, E. R. *Stoics and Sceptics.* Oxford: Oxford University Press, 1913.
Farrington, Benjamin. *Science and Politics in the Ancient World.* 2d edition. New York: Barnes & Noble, 1966.
Hicks, R. D. *Stoic and Epicurean.* New York: Scribner's, 1910.
Wenley, R. M. *Stoicism and Its Influence.* Boston: Marshall Jones, 1924.

Index

Finley Hooper is professor of history at Wayne State University, where his courses in ancient history are enhanced by a wide-ranging knowledge of art and archeology. He is the author of *Greek Realities: Life and Thought in Ancient Greece,* published originally by Scribner's in 1967 and now reissued by Wayne State University Press as a companion volume to *Roman Realities.*

The book was designed by Richard Kinney. The type face for the text and display is Weiss Roman, based on the original design by Emil Rudolf Weiss about 1923. The text is printed on International Paper Company's Bookmark paper. The hardcover edition is bound in Holliston Mills' Kingston cloth over binder's boards, and the paperback edition is bound in Carolina cover, CIS. Manufactured in the United States of America.